CENGAGE

The *new* Harbrace Guide

Genres for Composing

Fourth Edition

Includes the
MLA 9th Edition
& APA 7th Edition
Updates

Cheryl Glenn

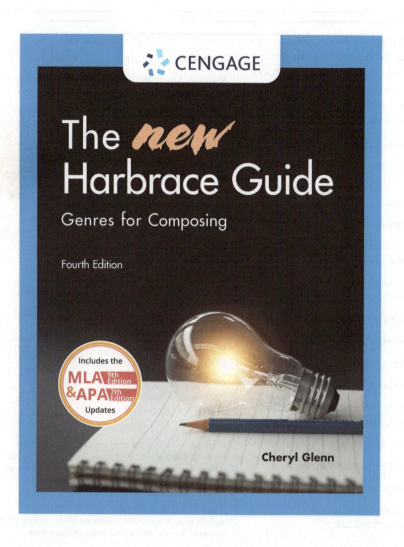

CENGAGE

Australia • Brazil • Canada • Mexico • Singapore • United Kingdom • United States

D0073775

The New Harbrace Guide: Genres for Composing, Fourth Edition with 2021 MLA and 2020 APA Updates Cheryl Glenn

Product Team Manager: Catherine Van Der Laan

Product Manager: Matt Filimonov

Development Editor: Lisa Moore

Senior Content Manager: Rachel Kerns

Product Assistant: Celia Smithmier

Executive Marketing Manager: Kina Lara

Marketing Coordinator: McKenzie Keneavy

Learning Designer: Leslie Taggart

In-House SME: Anne Alexander

Digital Delivery Lead: Matt Altieri

IP Analyst: Ashley Maynard

Senior IP Project Manager: Betsy Hathaway

Production Service: SPi Global

Art Director: Lizz Anderson

Cover Designer: Nadine Ballard

Cover Image: © Lustrator/ ShutterStock.com

Library of Congress Control Number: 2020924561

Student Edition:
ISBN-13: 978-0-357-509074
Loose-Leaf Edition:
ISBN-13: 978-0-357-509081

Cengage
200 Pier 4 Boulevard
Boston, MA 02210
USA

Cengage Learning is a leading provider of customized learning solutions with employees residing in nearly 40 different countries and sales in more than 125 countries around the world. Find your local representative at **www.cengage.com.**

To learn more about Cengage platforms and services, register or access your online learning solution, or purchase materials for your course, visit **www.cengage.com.**

The content in this textbook for which Cengage holds the copyright has been updated according to the latest MLA guidelines for inclusion and diversity. However, note that external content published herein for which Cengage does not own the copyright has not been updated as Cengage does not have permission to edit third-party content from other copyright holders. This content includes excerpts from articles as well as student papers. This is an inconsistency that learners are likely to encounter while reading pieces of literature in which outdated terms were used but were considered proper at the time.

Printed at CLDPC, USA, 04-23

Contents

III

3 Academic Literacies: Reading Rhetorically 34

4 Rhetorical Success in a Digital World 49

Position Arguments 128

14 The Power of Paragraphs 257

15 Rhetorical Strategies for Development 278

16 Style: An Essential Guide to Effective Sentences 295

17 Strategies for Editing Common Problems 322

25 Social Media and the Possibilities of Gender 491

26 Navigating Safety in Public Spaces 507

Preface

Preface for the Instructor

The fourth edition of *The New Harbrace Guide* brings student-friendly support for first year writing, co-req, dual enrollment, and integrated reading-writing courses with its trademark approach to writing in multiple media. As with previous editions, this rhetoric, reader, and research manual, now with a brief handbook, is based on current rhetorical theory, providing step-by-step guidance and sustained attention to the rhetorical situation in a variety of genres.

New chapters include information on powerful paragraphs (Chapter 14), stylish sentences (Chapter 16), and common problems (Chapter 17). Special features of the new edition also focus on analysis and persuasion (Chapter 2), academic literacy and the literacy narrative (Chapter 3), and strong thesis statements (Chapter 13). Its contemporary approach includes 36 fresh new readings on topics from veganism and apolitical food to how young people are changing the climate conversation.

The book is also dedicated to promoting intellectual curiosity, writing confidence, and rhetorical power by helping students transfer the reading and writing skills learned in this course—through a Knowledge Transfer feature for each writing project—to writing in other college courses, the workplace, and the community.

Key Features

The New Harbrace Guide distinguishes itself from other writing guides by its sustained focus on the rhetorical situation and the question, "Why Write?" The rhetorical approach focuses on understanding that the reasons for writing are as integral to the rhetorical situation as are audience and purpose. Identifying opportunities where writing can create a change of heart, mind, or action reinforces the vitality of the writing process, whether in or out of school. Guidance on specific rhetorical techniques for writing effective introductions, bodies, and conclusions is provided to help students shape ideas into language that is best suited for each writing project, with an emphasis in each chapter on analysis, synthesis, and writing persuasively for different media. The key features of *The New Harbrace Guide* include

- **A Rhetorical Approach.** By emphasizing rhetorical techniques that will help students understand how to evaluate a rhetorical situation, identify and respond to an opportunity for change, and address a problem rhetorically, this introduction to rhetoric teaches principles that have empowered readers, speakers, and writers for millennia—techniques that are transferable to other writing tasks, whether in school, the workplace, or the community. Part 1 introduces the rhetorical principles that underlie all writing situations and provides a basic method for using those principles in the digital, print, and multimodal spheres of composing.

- **A Guide to Genres and Persuasion.** The principles outlined in Part 1 are also reinforced for each genre (memoir, profile, investigative report, position argument, proposal, evaluation, critical analysis), with a featured Writing Guide for composing persuasively. Following a demystified step-by-step process, each Writing Guide breaks down composing into manageable tasks that build toward a larger writing project. These Writing Guides for each genre use simple, direct, and incremental advice to help students create forceful, persuasive introductions, bodies, and conclusions for a variety of genres.

- **Integrated Multimodal/Multimedia Coverage.** Today, all writers take into consideration the most effective medium (print, digital, verbal, visual, multimodal) for delivering their message. *The New Harbrace Guide* supports effective, twenty-first-century composing practices in Part 1 with a chapter on rhetorical success in a digital age that builds on the knowledge of rhetoric and media that students bring with them to the classroom—from text messages to Facebook profiles to Internet searches and more—with multimodal examples and guidance for each genre to help them choose when and how to use digital, verbal, visual, and print media for various audiences, purposes, and situations. Sections on Writing in Three Media and Additional Knowledge-Transfer Assignments present a number of multimodal possibilities for each genre.

- **An Emphasis on Revision and Peer Review** continues to offer robust coverage and advice on using peer review in sections on Revision and Peer Review in each genre.

New Features

- **"The Mandalorian," Baby Yoda Memes, and *Star Wars* Controversies.** New examples are included in Chapter 1 to engage students in coverage of the rhetorical situation, reasons for writing, and how rhetoric can be used as an opportunity to create change.

- **A Focus on Analysis from Day 1.** After an introduction to the rhetorical situation that includes Analyzing the Rhetorical Situation activities and a writing assignment (Chapter 1), Chapter 2 enhances this coverage with an emphasis on analyzing rhetorical choices in a context of problem-solving and persuasion, including an emphasis on the classic rhetorical appeals (logos, pathos, ethos) and an assignment on writing a rhetorical analysis.

- **Academic Literacy.** Chapter 3 has been thoroughly revised to marry ample advice on reading for college to academic literacy skills, with several new examples, including Frederick Douglass's learning-to-read-and-write literacy narrative from his *Narrative of the Life of Frederick Douglass, An American Slave.* Chapter 13 also includes a new section on Expectations for Academic Writing that includes Tips for Analyzing Assignments.

- **Thesis Statement.** The section on Crafting a Working Thesis Statement has been considerably expanded and now includes more instruction, numerous examples, and includes Tips for Developing A Working Thesis Statement.

- **The Power of Paragraphs** (Chapter 14). This new chapter to the fourth edition includes twenty-five examples of paragraphs and abundant guidance on topic sentences, transitions, unity and coherence, and creating strong introductions and conclusions.

- **Style: An Essential Guide to Effective Sentences** (Chapter 16). This new chapter to the fourth edition includes the basics of sentence structure for avoiding mismatched sentence parts and creating complete sentences and focuses on the most important attribute of academic style—clarity. Guidance also includes coverage of sentence variety, precision, and inclusive language.

- **Strategies for Editing Common Problems** (Chapter 17). This brief handbook, rhetorically oriented toward editing, supports instructor guidance by helping strengthen student editing skills with coverage of the 15 most common sentence-level problems.

- **Updated APA Style:** American Psychological Association (APA) guidelines in Chapter 23, Acknowledging Sources in APA Style, reflect updates in the 2020 *APA Publication Manual,* 7th edition, which simplifies the APA documentation style in citing diverse print, online, and oral sources.

- **36 New Readings.** New examples for the Genre in Focus feature include: The NASA social media profile (Chapter 6, Profiles); opposing film reviews of the newest *Little Women* remake (Chapter 8, Evaluations), and Roxane Gay's analysis of media coverage and race in "A Tale of Two Profiles" (Chapter 11, Critical Analyses). New annotated examples include: Sandy Banks' "How Coronavirus Turned Supermarket Workers into Heroes" (Chapter 6, Profiles); Michael Rosen's "Why Reading Aloud Is a Vital Bridge to Literacy" (Chapter 9, Proposals); and Pat Mora's poem, "Sonrisas," with a poetry blog analysis by AP student Gabriella Fiorenza and a sample student analysis by Alex Sibo.

- **Four New High-Interest Themes.** Chapter 25, Social Media and the Possibilities of Gender, explores the various ways social media has affected gender (and vice versa). Chapter 26, Navigating Safety in Public Spaces, includes readings on school shootings, pandemic shaming, disability, "hostile" [anti-homeless] architecture, and Michael-Aime Musoni's thoughtful memoir on "Being an 18-Year-Old Black Man a Year after Mike Brown." Chapter 27, Im/Migration, Displacement, Asylum Seeking: A Global Phenomenon, examines repercussions on Asians due to the COVID crisis, the economic impact of immigration, and border communities like El Paso, a longer profile to help students practice sustained reading of longer works. Chapter 28, How Young People Are Changing the Climate Conversation, includes readings on the weird weather that creates droughts, fires, and hurricanes, Greta Thunberg, young evangelicals and young farmers, and a longer piece by Elaine Kamarck, "The Challenging Politics of Climate Change," which includes infographics and notes to help students use sustained reading and academic literacy skills. These themes and selections have been specially selected as models of the genres in this book and to engage and inspire student interest as the articles and topics jumpstart their writing.
- **Learning Objectives.** Each chapter now begins with Learning Objectives to help students focus their efforts and understand how the skills they are being taught are useful beyond the first-year writing courses. These same learning objectives can help instructors assess the effectiveness of student work.

In short, then, *The New Harbrace Guide* guides students through various composition processes and genres that enhance student success across college, the workplace, and the community.

How Does the Book Work?

In this new streamlined edition, you'll find many innovations (large and small) that have helped to create a more user-friendly, portable, and easy-to-access guide (both in print and through an online MindTap version).

- **Colorful Tabs** help students quickly locate the information they need in the book. Each chapter has a tab, color-coded by the part of the book where the chapter is located. These tabs can be seen at the top of the page and when you flip through the book.
- **Color-Coded Writing Guidance** uses purple for advice on creating effective introductions, green for advice on creating coherent bodies of text, and blue for advice on conclusions. This is especially useful in the annotated essay example in each chapter in Part 2 and in the corresponding Writing Guides in each chapter.

- **Writing Guides** in each chapter in Part 2 provide step-by-step guidance for creating effective compositions, broken down by advice on the introduction, body, and conclusion of each genre. To locate this information more easily, a tab runs down the entire page to create an easy-to-use finder's index for the Writing Guides in each chapter.
- **Marginal Glossary Definitions** for rhetorical terms are placed next to the term for easy reference.
- **Marginal Cross-References** to other parts of the book are provided where a refresher—or additional information—on particular topics might come in useful.
- **Thematic Readings Cross-References for Each Genre** direct students to additional examples that can help jumpstart their writing.

What Will You Find Online?

MindTap® English for Glenn's *The New Harbrace Guide: Genres for Composing*, Fourth Edition, engages your students to become better thinkers, communicators, and writers by blending your course materials with content that supports every aspect of the writing process.

Key Features

- **"Check Your Understanding" exercises** after each chapter help students and instructors assess learning by asking students to apply what they have learned to very short scenarios of writing. Problems are auto-graded and report to the gradebook.
- **"Collaborate" activities** can be used in the online and face-to-face classroom. These two different versions provide specific, comprehensive directions for students. Assignment worksheets give students a way to record their ideas, and optional individual reflection questions ask students to summarize what they have learned about the subject, the process of collaboration itself, or themselves.
- **Writing Organizers in Part II** and **Research Organizers in Part IV** are worksheets with open-ended questions that help students stay organized and focused on the most important elements of what they need to do. These Word docs can be downloaded, printed, or filled out onscreen, and then uploaded to the instructor if desired.
- **The "Just in Time Plus" series** includes foundational topics that range from writing an essay, to using commas correctly, to paraphrasing, summarizing, and quoting. Each unit includes instruction, a video, and auto-graded assessment.

- **Focused Support for Key Topics** includes nine topics in argument, evaluating sources, and critical thinking. Each unit includes a reading of instructional text; a video example of a student working with the topic; an auto-graded review activity; an annotated student essay; and two professional readings with discussion questions.
- **A "50 Readings" module features readings on ten current themes**, ranging from Fake News on Social Media and The Value of College to Cultural Appropriation and Gender Identity. Each reading includes auto-graded comprehension and discussion questions.

Instructor Resources

Additional instructor resources for this product are available online. Instructor assets include an Instructor's Manual and Educator's Guide. Sign up or sign in at www.cengage.com to search for and access this product and its online resources.

Preface for the Student

Your writing process is as individual as you are. You may be a writer who especially likes composing the first draft—by hand or keyboard. Maybe you enjoy the tactile sensation of writing with a gel pen on a yellow legal pad or the friction of moving a felt-tipped pen across pulpy paper. Maybe you draft at your computer, entertaining yourself by connecting particular fonts with particular ideas in your draft.

Or maybe you're one of those writers who is relieved when she finishes a draft so that she can use her energy to work with and against that draft. You may like to print out your piece, sit back in a comfortable chair, and read it line by line, penciling in new sentences, crossing out entire sections, fiddling with your word choice, and drawing arrows to reorganize your paragraphs. However you write and revise, you'll want to find a way to enjoy polishing your writing until you're proud to submit it. As internationally known writer Susan Sontag put it:

> **You write in order to read what you've written and see if it's OK and, since of course it never is, to rewrite it—once, twice, as many times as it takes to get it to be something you can bear to reread.**
>
> **—Susan Sontag, "Directions: Write, Read, Rewrite. Repeat Steps 2 and 3 as Needed."**

For writers like Sontag, the enjoyment they get from rereading their revised work is the best part, whether or not they send it on to someone else to read.

What Is a Rhetorical Approach?

Ever since you began thinking of your audience when you asked for something or proposed an idea, you've been taking a rhetorical approach to speaking and writing. And you're bringing your rhetorical knowledge to this course. *The New Harbrace Guide* has been carefully designed so that you can respond strategically, effectively, and yes, rhetorically, to your writing assignments in your first-year composition course, co-req, or AP English course. That said, *The New Harbrace Guide* is designed to help you develop skills you can transfer to other rhetorical situations beyond your class, whether you find yourself writing for another class, for a social or civic setting, or for the workplace.

Part 1: Entering the Conversation

As you get started with *The New Harbrace Guide*, you'll notice that Part 1, Entering the Conversation, introduces you to the rhetorical principles that underlie all writing situations and provides you with a basic method for using those principles. The examples in Part 1 reinforce the skills that every first-year students can reach.

- **Chapter 1, Understanding the Rhetorical Situation,** focuses on understanding writing as an opportunity to create change. This is the most powerful part of answering the age-old question: Why write? Through analyzing strategically your rhetorical context you will understand better when and how your writing can create a change of heart, mind, or action. Activities that prompt Analyzing the Rhetorical Situation also occur in this chapter and throughout the book to reinforce your understanding of the rhetorical situation.
- **Chapter 2, Analyzing Rhetorical Choices,** focuses on persuasive writing. When you understand how writing can change you and your audience, you will be better able to recognize when purposeful writing delivered in any of its forms is the best, most persuasive response to a rhetorical situation. Examples of persuasive writing in a variety of media help make concrete the principles of persuasion (commonly referred to as *ethos, logos,* and *pathos*). These principles are part of the guidance in each of the assignments in this book.
- **Chapter 3, Academic Literacies: Reading Rhetorically,** provides a foundation for reading both critically and rhetorically and for using the skills of synthesis and analysis that are required in college writing and beyond. This new chapter shows how analyzing what you read rhetorically is helpful both in understanding what you read and in creating those broader thinking skills that are embedded in persuasive writing practices. Rhetorical reading also assists you in conducting research in college and in life on those occasions when you bring sources together that must be weighed, reflected on, explained, and often challenged.

- **Chapter 4, Rhetorical Success in a Digital World,** helps you identify and analyze the rhetorical elements of multimedia compositions and recognize when multimedia is part of a fitting response. Today, choosing a medium that effectively reaches the audience you hope to change is part and parcel of being a successful citizen of the world, and this emphasis is reflected in all the assignments included in this book.

Part 2: Writing Projects

Examples, examples, examples. We all learn best when the desire to create a change is married to an example of how to do it. A genre is a type of writing with identifiable characteristics that have emerged over time. The assignments in Part 2, Writing Projects: Rhetorical Situations for Composing, provide eight writing projects anchored in the fluid concept of a genre (such as memoir, position argument, critical analysis), each chosen because it exercises specific skills that should be helpful as part of your toolkit for responding to a broad range of writing situations. The strategies you use to create a memoir (storytelling or the use of poignant personal examples) might find their way into a position argument and vice versa. To say you are writing one genre or another is to identify the primary purpose and social context for your writing and your audience—especially since no single genre limits the rhetorical strategies you can employ in response to a rhetorical opportunity for change.

These chapters break down the writing process into incremental steps that are straightforward and manageable. Each chapter includes

- **Identifying an Opportunity for Change** at the beginning of the chapter with advice on a consideration of the visual, audio, digital, and print options for each genre.
- **Color Coded and Annotated Examples.** Each chapter begins with a short example of the genre (such as a food memoir, a public service announcement, or a film review) in the Genre in Focus section and then a full-length annotated example—often by a student—in the sections on Reading Rhetorically. These annotations help you identify the Key Characteristics of that genre and provide guidance on Using Synthesis and Analysis. The readings are also color-coded to further support well-developed essays, with strategies for introductions in purple, bodies in green, and conclusions in blue. Additional examples can be found in MindTap, the Thematic Reader, and the Writing in Three Media examples in each chapter.
- **Step-by-Step Writing Support** for each of these eight chapters provides tips for research in that genre, helps you develop a topic, and guides you in identifying your rhetorical audience and purpose so that you can make effective rhetorical choices given the advantages and limitations each genre

allows. These chapters also include guidance for revision, your own as well as your peers'. You may find yourself required to evaluate the writing of a fellow student ("peer"), or you might want your peers to advise you on your own work. To that end, you will find a section titled Revision and Peer Review.

- **Writing Guides.** A Writing Guide—color-coded to correspond with the sample essay in each chapter—breaks down into manageable tasks specific guidance on writing persuasively and walks you through writing a strong introduction, a well-supported body, and a meaningful conclusion.
- **Knowledge-Transfer Assignments** will also help you recognize the specific ways your academic assignments prepare you for composing in other contexts (work and community) as well as in different print, visual, audio, and digital media.

Part 3: Processes and Strategies for Composing

Whatever your writing process, Part 3, Processes and Strategies for Composing, provides a number of tips that could save you time and strengthen your writing practice.

Chapter 13, From Tentative Idea to Finished Project, includes examples for getting started if you've hit a writing block as well as for writing a thesis statement, creating a structure for your writing, drafting, revising, and editing.

As you adapt your own habits to writing for college, you will also find abundant advice on the development of paragraphs in Chapter 14, The Power of Paragraphs, and Chapter 15, Rhetorical Strategies for Development, where you'll find examples of additional strategies for developing skills in narrative, description, definition, exemplification, comparison-contrast, classification and division, process analysis, cause-and-effect analysis, and argument. These methods are cross-referenced in the margins of the text when one of these rhetorical strategies is particularly useful for a particular assignment in Part 2.

Your style in writing largely comes down to the way your words and sentences are put together. Just as paragraphs are the building blocks of essays, your sentences define your writing style. Chapter 16, Style: An Essential Guide to Effective Sentences helps you make sure your sentences are complete, varied, and precise. The guidance in this chapter will also help you achieve clarity with your writing. Clear writing is interesting, varied, and understandable—not *dull*. This chapter will help you flavor your writing so that your reader enjoys learning what you have to say.

Chapter 17, Strategies for Editing Common Problems, is a brief guide to help you avoid fifteen of the most common writing problems. While the word *grammar* may make you think of the word *rules,* grammar rules provide you with beneficial advice on how to achieve success as a writer. It might be more useful to think of grammar rules as statements about how language is commonly used, ways you already use language, even if you haven't yet developed the vocabulary for what, exactly, you're doing. At the editing stage, your focus will be on sentence-level problems, language issues, and punctuation. But as you check for missing words and appropriate apostrophes, you might find yourself rewriting a sentence, so do not be surprised if editing reveals the need to add more information or to rethink some of your ideas entirely.

Taken together, the chapters in Part 3 provide additional support to be used as needed as you develop your writing process.

Part 4: A Guide to Research

This research guide opens with thinking rhetorically about research, which presents research as an effective way of responding to certain rhetorical opportunities, rather than as a set of rules and requirements. Not only is there guidance on finding and evaluating sources for their credibility and usefulness for college research, there is also a full chapter on synthesizing sources to help you avoid plagiarism by citing your sources correctly. *The New Harbrace Guide* also includes two separate chapters—with sample papers—on formatting papers in the most up-to-date styles in MLA (Modern Language Association) and APA (American Psychological Association), two of the most common styles used for citing sources. Research can be daunting, so *The New Harbrace Guide* also includes Tricks of the Trade tips from fellow students throughout these chapters.

Part 5: A Thematic Reader

The reader in *The New Harbrace Guide* includes high-interest readings and themes chosen to inspire you with exemplary models of good writing and to jumpstart your own writing process. Each chapter includes five readings on a contemporary topic (from Chapter 24, Food and the (Cultural) Experience of Taste to Chapter 28, How Young People Are Changing the Climate Conversation), and most of the readings are new to this edition. You'll find articles on veganism and apolitical food, social media and the end of gender, safety issues in schools from Parkland journalists, pandemic shaming, border culture for a cheer team in El Paso, and young evangelicals and young farmers on the march against climate change.

A Value Proposition

Of course, textbooks are expensive. What is the "value proposition" that makes *The New Harbrace Guide* worth it? In addition to the specific writing advice, *The New Harbrace Guide* includes a Guide to Research, a Thematic Reader, a brief handbook in Strategies for Editing Common Problems, and unparalleled digital support in MindTap. The added value of MindTap includes the text itself online—with enhanced media support for your learning and writing—as well as additional online readings and an online handbook. For research, you'll find the Gale College Collection in MindTap—a premier tool for researching sources and formatting your research papers.

What Does This Mean for You?

So far, I've been telling you about all the ways that this *Guide* will support your academic writing, the kind of writing that too often intimidates new college students. But you shouldn't feel intimidated; after all, you've been writing almost all your life. When you were a small child, you grabbed crayons, felt-tip markers, or chalk and wrote on whatever surfaces you could find: paper, coloring books, sidewalks, chalk boards, table tops, walls, lampshades. As you think back on your earliest memories of composing, keep in mind the process of composing that you practiced then. You gathered up your materials and set to work. The entire process—from start to finish—was simple, often fun. Like the human animal you are, you were marking your territory—leaving messages for the people who entered your world. Award-winning author Joyce Carol Oates cannot recall a time when she wasn't writing:

> **Before I could write what might be called human words in the English language, I eagerly emulated grown-ups' handwriting in pencil scribbles. My first "novels" ... were tablets of inspired scribbles illustrated by line drawings of chickens, horses and upright cats.**
>
> **—Joyce Carol Oates, "To Invigorate Literary Mind, Start Moving Literary Feet"**

Like the writing you did as a child, let college composing be satisfying, even when it isn't *always* fun, let alone easy. The process might, at times, seem demanding, but the results are often exhilarating, something you're proud of. If that weren't the case, you wouldn't worry about writing well or care what your teacher thought of your writing. Perhaps the best way to make composing a pleasurable activity is to build on what you already do well and enjoy as you write. Use this book as your guide as you fulfill your assignments for this class—it is designed to do that—but also use the book to discover the skills you already have and use them as you prepare to write outside of class.

For writers like you, the enjoyment you get from writing may be learning to develop your thinking into clear words and images, submitting your essays to instructors who respond with proof that they've actually read your words, or transforming your ideas into a multimedia message for your friends. Writing doesn't require any one specific satisfaction but often calls up many overlapping ones. Here's hoping that your college writing launches your thinking, creativity, and intellectual curiosity as you write your way through college and on into the workplace and community.

Acknowledgments

All books demand time, talent, and plenty of hard work. I could not have produced this textbook without the help and support of a number of colleagues, friends, and students. I found myself calling on their expertise at various times throughout the creation of this book. Emily Nicole Smith and Ray Rosas provided me examples of successful student essays, for which I'm grateful, including the essay by Alex Sibo. In addition, both Emily and Ray gave generously of their time and wisdom as teachers, scholars, and writers. Emily did the heavy lifting so far as finding hard-to-find examples of perfect APA and MLA documentation. She also helped me conduct research into multimedia sources and locate new readings as well as contributors for various parts of the book. Mohammed Samy allowed us to reprint an infographic on how a genre comes to be (which he had originally composed for Professor Pavel Zemliansky's composition course at the University of Central Florida). I remain grateful to them all, as well as to those whose work as students comes to us from previous editions: Caledonia Adams, Grace Randolph, and the Viz-a-GoGo web creators from Texas A&M University, whose work appears in Part 1; Anna Seitz, Alicia Williams, and Alexis Walker, who contributed papers to Part 2; Anastasia Simkanin, who allowed us to see her process as well as her paper in Part 3; and for Part 4, Cristian Nuñez and Keith Evans, for tips in Tricks of the Trade, Jacob Thomas, for his summary of "DoubleSpeak," Greg Coles, whose paper appears in the MLA chapter, and Catherine L. Davis, whose paper appears in the APA chapter. I am especially grateful to Malcolm Aime-Musoni, who wrote his essay while still a student himself, as did the student journalists from Marjorie Stoneman Douglas High School, Hannah Kapoor, Elama Ali, and Nadia Murillo. Likely there are others I've missed, but suffice it to say this book would not have been possible without the contribution of students to the book and to my teaching and learning.

At Cengage, Senior Content Manager Rachel Kerns oversaw the progress of the project, relying (as we all have) on the good sense and keen insights of Product Team Manager Catherine Van Der Laan, Product Manager Matt Filamonov, and Learning Designer Leslie Taggart. Executive Marketing Manager Kina Lara has already demonstrated her marketing prowess. For their painstaking production work, I thank the team at SPi Global, especially project manager Praveen Kumar RS. But my biggest thanks goes to my editor extraordinaire, Lisa Colleen Moore, whose intellect and publishing sense have far exceeded my greatest expectations. What a pleasure it's been to spend a second tour with such a terrific intellectual companion in developing this new edition.

And for this fourth edition, I'm grateful for the thoughtfulness of the comments by those who reviewed this book. Their good suggestions helped make this book better.

Gregory J. Underwood, *Pearl River Community College*
Karen Campbell, *Grayson College*
Jody Jones, *Alabama A & M University*
Abigail Crew, *Colorado Mountain College*

Cheryl Glenn
December 2020

Praise for *The New Harbrace Guide: Genres for Composing*

It's the best treatment of rhetoric I've seen in any text in 8 years of teaching.
— Justin Jory, Salt Lake Community College

The "knowledge transfer" sections highlight re-purposing possibilities for projects to be delivered to different audiences with multimodal opportunities. This is an attractive feature.
— Jerry Peterson, Utah Valley University

Quite honestly, the best outline/guide structure I have seen yet in a text.
— Jamie Sadler, Richmond College

I like the student-friendly language and step-by-step guidance.
— Tyler Farrell, Marquette University

User friendly. Current. I like the structure!   — Anna Maheshwari, Schoolcraft College

I really liked the focus on rhetorical situations as opportunities for change. I think that is a great emphasis for helping students understand the importance of writing well for different audiences and purposes.   — Craig Bartholomaus, Metropolitan Community College

The book takes a rhetorical stance to writing, offering students clear advice for how several different genres can be rhetorically persuasive.
— Jeremiah Dyehouse, University of Rhode Island

This book makes critical thinking relevant to students.
— Krysten Anderson, Roane State Community College

GUIDE TO IDENTIFYING THE ELEMENTS OF ANY RHETORICAL SITUATION

As you enter any rhetorical conversation—from friendly texting to college papers to hallway exchanges and business presentations—consider the elements of the rhetorical situation to help you shape a persuasive message.

AJ_Watt/Getty Images

- **Opportunity** Identify the issue, problem, or situation where writing provides an opportunity for change. Identifying an opportunity where writing (or speaking) can make a difference encourages you to enter the rhetorical situation. Ask yourself: What is it that tugs at me? Why do I feel the need to speak, write, take a photo, share an image? What attitude, action, or opinion do I want to change?

- **Purpose** Connect the opportunity for change with your purpose (and then your audience). Ask yourself: What can I accomplish with rhetoric? How do words or visuals allow me to respond to this opportunity?

- **Audience** Knowing that your purpose is to stimulate change in a specific audience, carefully consider the character of that audience: Who are its members? What opinions and values do they hold? And, most important, how might they help you address or resolve the problem?

- **Stance** The success of your message often depends on the attitude you project toward your topic and your intended audience. A respectful tone toward your topic and audience is often the most effective.

- **Genre** Each genre is distinguished by well-established yet flexible features and formatting, so determine what form will best convey your message—an academic essay, an evaluation, a memoir, report, proposal, profile, résumé, letter, or review. The genre you choose should not only fulfill your purpose but also be familiar to your audience.

- **Medium** Your choice of materials and medium—spoken or written (perhaps with additional visual elements)—depends on the elements of the specific rhetorical situation, especially the ability of your audience to access that medium.

1 Understanding the Rhetorical Situation

The prime characteristic of the rhetorical situation is identifying an opportunity for change.

LEARNING OBJECTIVES

- Identify the key components of the rhetorical situation.
- Explain the function of those key elements.
- Assess the suitability of genre and media given your audience and purpose.
- Analyze various rhetorical situations.

≫ RHETORIC SURROUNDS US

Too often, the word *rhetoric* implies empty words, manipulation, deception, or persuasion at any cost. But rhetoric and rhetorical situations are frequently neutral, often positive. They are everywhere—as pervasive as the air we breathe—and play an essential role in our daily lives as we work to get things done efficiently and ethically.

Rhetoric is the purposeful use of language and images. That definition covers a great deal of territory—practically every word and visual element you encounter every day. But it's the word *purposeful* that will guide you through the maze of words and images that saturate your life. When you use words or images to achieve a specific purpose—such as explaining to your instructor why you must miss class—you are speaking, writing, or conveying images rhetorically.

rhetoric
communication to achieve a specific purpose with a specific audience

ACTIVITY: Analyzing the Rhetorical Situation
Your Writing Experience

Take a few minutes to list the kinds of writing you do every day. Include all instances when you write down information (whether on paper, whiteboard, chalkboard, smartphone, tablet, or computer screen). Beside each entry, jot down reasons for, and the potential audience for, that type of writing. Be prepared to share your answers with the rest of the class.

≫ IDENTIFYING A REASON TO WRITE

We speak, write, listen, and watch all day long. Most often we don't enter the rhetorical situation, but when we do it's because we have a reason. After all, when you have an issue, problem, or situation that you want to change, language can help you do it. Maybe you and your friend have argued. You might want to phone to say, "I'm sorry," motivated by a desire to change the situation between you and your friend. Or you might need to ask a question in class, prompting a change in the classroom (usually a change in your own understanding but often also everyone's understanding in the class). It is similar with written language, when used to change understanding, opinions, or behavior. In the business world, for example, your company may want to grow its online business. To do so, it will need to update its website and online marketing plan—through language. In your personal life, you may want to write a letter of condolence, motivated by a desire to comfort someone who is grieving a loss. In college, you will likely be asked to write an essay, report, analysis, or proposal. Situations such as updating a website, writing a letter, or researching a paper for college are opportunities to use language to make a difference. In this book, we call this an opportunity for change.

rhetorical opportunity the issue, problem, or situation that motivates the use of language to stimulate change

Unless you have an authentic reason to do so, you probably will not respond to the **rhetorical opportunity**, that is an opportunity to enter the rhetorical conversation and use language to make a difference. In other words, *something* needs to stimulate or provoke your interest and call for your response. When you take an essay examination for an American history midterm, you might be given the choice of answering one of two questions:

1. The great increase in size and power of the federal government since the Civil War has long been a dominant theme of American history. Trace the growth of the federal government since 1865, paying particular attention to its evolving involvement in world affairs and the domestic economy. Be sure to support your analysis with relevant historical details.

2. Compare and contrast the attempts to create and safeguard African American civil rights in two historical periods: the first Era of Reconstruction (post–Civil War years to the early twentieth century) and the second Era of Reconstruction (1950s to 1970s). Consider government policies, African American strategies, and the responses of White people to those strategies.

If you are lucky, one of these questions will spark your response and engage your intellectual energy. Think of every college writing situation as a rhetorical opportunity for you to use language in order to resolve or address an issue, problem, or situation.

ACTIVITY: Analyzing the Rhetorical Situation
What Is an Opportunity for Change?

Decide whether the issues, problems, or situations listed below are opportunities where writing can help change an attitude, opinion, or action. Be prepared to share the reasoning behind your responses with the rest of the class.

- The Internal Revenue Service is charging you $2,000 in back taxes, asserting that you neglected to declare the income from your summer job.
- Your college library has just sent you an e-mail informing you that you are being fined for several overdue books, all of which you returned a month ago.
- After Thanksgiving dinner is served, your brothers and mother resume their ongoing argument about Black Lives Matter, healthcare, the pandemic, and the economy.
- In the student section at the football stadium, some fans throw empty soda cans, toss beach balls, boo the opposing team, and stand during most of the game. You're quickly losing interest in attending the games.

⟫ DECIDING TO WRITE

The most important feature of any rhetorical opportunity is the **writer** or the author or speaker, who believes that language, spoken, written, or visual, can bring about change. If you witness a car accident, for example, you are an observer; you may decide to volunteer to testify about it and thus engage in the opportunity as a speaker. If you identify an old friend from a newspaper photograph, you may decide to e-mail him. You might hear a song and decide to perform it and post a video of your performance on YouTube. Or you might decide to begin introducing yourself to people participating in an online video game. Whatever the opportunities are and however they are delivered (whether spoken, printed, online, or in some other way), you can decide how or whether you want to act on them.

writer someone who uses language to bring about change in an audience

Every day, you encounter dozens of rhetorical opportunities to make a change by engaging with language. If your good friend applies for and gets the job of her dreams, you have an opportunity to engage with a response. How will she know that you are happy for her unless you send her a congratulatory card, give her a phone call, invite her to a celebratory lunch—or all three? The death of your neighbor creates an opportunity to respond with a letter to the family or a bouquet of flowers and an accompanying condolence note. A friend's illness, an argument with a roommate, a tuition hike, an essay exam, a sales presentation, a job interview—these are all opportunities for change through spoken or written words or with visuals.

© Cengage Learning

Figure 1.1 *When a writer enters a rhetorical situation, she composes a purposeful message for a specific audience and chooses whether to deliver the message verbally, orally, with images, in print, or digitally.*

As the writer or speaker, you engage the opportunity with a **message** that includes content you have shaped in a way that stimulates change (Figure 1.1). What information must you include to teach, please, and change your **audience**, those readers, viewers, or listeners you are trying to influence with your message? Consider the message in the release of posters for the first movie of the final Skywalker trilogy, *Star Wars: The Force Awakens* (Figure 1.2).

The Force Awakens // NOVEMBER 4, 2015

Photo 12 / Alamy Stock Photo

message the main point of information shaped to influence an audience

audience those who receive and interpret the message of a communication

Figure 1.2 Star Wars: The Force Awakens – *Character Posters Revealed.*

See stunning new images of Rey, Leia, Kylo Ren, Han Solo, and Finn!
Star Wars: The Force Awakens is almost here—and now you can get an up-close look at the film's classic and new characters.

The official character posters for Rey, Leia, Kylo Ren, Han Solo, and Finn were revealed today, featuring powerful portraits and a striking design motif. Rey holds her staff defiantly; Leia confidently peers through a data screen; Kylo Ren's lightsaber crackles; a grim Han Solo holds his blaster at the ready; and Finn looks stoic with a blue-bladed Jedi weapon.

Carrie Fisher, Daisy Ridley, and John Boyega each revealed their own posters via Twitter and Instagram.

Star Wars.com. All Star Wars, all the time.

With museum exhibitions, television commercials, trailers, and spoilers, the creators of *Star Wars: The Force Awakens* leveraged the features of various rhetorical situations for the purpose of stimulating worldwide ticket sales for the new trilogy of films in the franchise. Online, the *Star Wars* website featured the latest news (global and national) about the films, as well as updates on the characters and actors. The online community features photographs of its members when they meet face to face, as well as background on the various characters in the saga.

With the new trilogy, the franchise creators wanted not to just tell a riveting story, but to expand its audience domestically and internationally. The films brought back fan favorites but also introduced a female protagonist and a more diverse cast of characters. Online, televised, and print news sources, however, highlighted controversies surrounding the much-anticipated film: CNN asked, "Does the ethnically diverse cast mean the film is 'anti-white'?" The controversy continued with the release of the second film in the trilogy, *The Last Jedi*, as commentators affiliated with ultraconservative political points of view criticized the installment for featuring not only diverse characters but a storyline that many saw as feminist. Actress Kelly Marie Tran, who played the character of Rose Tico (Figure 1.3), the first major female character of color, would end up withdrawing from social media after an onslaught

Photo 12/Alamy Stock Photo

Figure 1.3 *Rose Tico, played by Kelly Marie Tran, in* The Last Jedi.

of online harassment. Her reduced visibility in the third film, *The Rise of Sky-walker,* although explained by the filmmakers, was viewed by many as yielding to the pressure of hostile online trolls. Such tensions illustrate the complexities of managing global entertainment brands in the face of a volatile cultural landscape.

»» ANALYZING THE ELEMENTS OF THE RHETORICAL SITUATION

When you decide to engage a rhetorical opportunity, understanding the elements of the **rhetorical situation** helps you shape the content of your message to enhance your chances of changing your audience's attitude, action, or opinion. Creating change through language is not about overpowering your audience or winning an argument. Rather, creating change involves understanding the rhetorical situation you are entering. Before speaking or writing, taking the time to analyze the elements of your rhetorical situation is a first step in discovering what you might say or write.

rhetorical situation the context that influences effective communication

Opportunity What is happening? What has motivated you to engage in a rhetorical opportunity for change?

Purpose How might your message change your audience in some way? What do you want your language to accomplish? What action do you want to occur because of what you compose?

Audience To whom are you writing (or speaking)? What is your relationship to the person or group of people? After all, you will direct your writing, speaking, or visual display to a specific audience in an attempt to change some opinion, attitude, or action.

Stance How do you view your message and its recipients? Your attitude toward your audience and topic is revealed through your word choice and tone and can be positive, negative, neutral, reasonable, unreasonable, or something else.

Genre Which format should your message follow? The well-established yet flexible features and formatting of each genre—profile, memoir, analysis, biography, proposal, evaluation, and so on—help you frame your message, connect with your audience, and achieve your purpose.

Medium How will the medium of delivery (online, visual, print, oral) enhance or detract from your message? Are you sure that your audience can receive (access) your message through this medium?

ACTIVITY: Analyzing the Rhetorical Situation
Identify the Elements of the Rhetorical Situation

For each of the rhetorical situations in the examples that follow, reflect on the way that the genre, medium of delivery, and stance are considered to help you craft an effective response to the opportunity and the purpose, as well as the audience and the message.

- A friend of a friend, whom you have never met, has invited you to be his Facebook friend.
- You are applying for a scholarship and need three letters of recommendation. You do not know any of your instructors very well.
- As a member of a wedding party, you are expected to make a toast at the reception in front of two hundred guests.

After considering the following rhetorical situations, share your response to the numbered activities with the class.

1. Describe a time when you identified an opportunity to address a problem but either did not respond at all or did not respond well. If you could do it over, how might you respond? How would you take into consideration each element of the rhetorical situation in order to come as close to persuasion as conditions allowed?

2. Describe a problem, issue, or situation that compelled a written or spoken response. Describe the features of the rhetorical situation and how you took them all into consideration in your response.

purpose in rhetoric, the reason for a communication

rhetorical purpose the specific change the writer wants to accomplish through the use of language

rhetorical audience the specific audience most capable of being changed by a message or of bringing about change

≫ THINKING RHETORICALLY ABOUT PURPOSE AND AUDIENCE

Many writers equate **purpose** with their reason for writing: they are fulfilling an assignment, or meeting a deadline; they want a good grade or want to make money. When you are writing with a **rhetorical purpose**, however, you move beyond goals like those to consider how you might influence a specific **rhetorical audience**, those people you hope to influence in some way.

Although you may not have the budget to create a media project on the scale of *Star Wars*, their producers implicitly understand—and expect—that their creations will be appropriated and reused in any number of different ways in the culture at large. With the launch of their digital streaming channel, Disney+, the creators of their tentpole series *The Mandalorian* were rewarded when one of the main characters, "Baby Yoda," became a viral sensation. Possessed of preternatural cuteness, Baby Yoda has become a favorite subject for fan posts, GIFs, videos, and memes, a true mark of success in terms of reaching a rhetorical audience. In one such fan-created video (which has had over 18 million views at the time of writing) the singer even croons, "You're more than a meme to me" (Figure 1.4). The humor of the line is a direct consequence of the author's understanding of who the core audience for the video will be: fans who love Baby Yoda memes.

As you direct your message to your rhetorical audience, you will need to keep in mind the nature of your audience (their power, status, values, interests) and their character (sympathetic or unsympathetic, opposed to or in favor of your message). These people are capable of being influenced by your message and bringing about change, either by their own actions or their influence on others. How you approach your rhetorical audience affects the success of your message. Your writing conveys an attitude toward your topic and audience, your **stance**. Try to shape your stance in terms of content, tone, examples, appropriateness,

stance the attitude your writing conveys toward your topic, purpose, and audience

Figure 1.4 *Baby Yoda from the Disney+ Star Wars spinoff,* The Mandalorean, *inspired* A Baby Yoda Song - A Star Wars Rap *by ChewieCatt.*

and timeliness to enhance its chances of influencing your audience. Consider whether you are talking to your instructor, one of your parents, your physician, or a friend—and how in each case you would respectfully and truthfully represent your beliefs and values if your audience held beliefs and values that differed from yours. Try to keep in mind the kind of information you would need to deliver—as well as how and when to deliver it.

»» THINKING RHETORICALLY ABOUT GENRE AND MEDIA

As you know by now, narrowing your purpose is important because each rhetorical opportunity for change requires its own audience, genre, and medium of delivery. Fortunately, genre and medium are fairly easy to identify.

Considering Genre

genre a category of writing that has a particular format and features, such as memoir or argument

A **genre** is a type of writing categorized by a well-established format with familiar features. Writers deliberately choose a single genre or a purposeful combination of genres in order to reach a specific audience. For instance, the genre of memoir usually follows a chronological narration (sometimes peppered with flash forwards or flashbacks), features distinctive characters who contribute to dialogue in unique ways, and presents a well-described setting—all of which are rich in sensory details. You would never mistake a memoir for a lab report. And you would not want to submit a memoir instead of a résumé to a potential employer. But, because the features of any genre are flexible and adaptable, you might employ many of the same features as those in a traditional memoir in a job application letter—such as describing the significant points in your life that led you to a particular career. Or you might include your personal experience as evidence in an argument. And you might find yourself considering a memoir as a historical document in your research. Some familiar genres include the position argument, profile, evaluation, and proposal. The more you learn about the qualities of each of these genres, the easier it will be to determine which genre is most effective for your message and when it would be effective to blend genres to best address your rhetorical situation.

medium method of communication: oral, visual, verbal, digital, or print

Considering Medium of Delivery

media (plural of medium) *mass media* is a term used for media like radio, television, and various online forums that reach a broad audience

You choose a particular **medium** (method of communication)—or a combination of spoken, visual, written (digital or print) **media**—for delivering your message because it most effectively reaches your rhetorical audience. How you deliver your message can be just as important as the content of that message, whether you are speaking, building a website, or text messaging. A person without a powerful computer may prefer print documents; a techno-wizard may abhor paper and prefer to receive everything digitally.

Because we enjoy so many ways of communicating—visually, verbally, digitally—we rarely stop to consider why we have chosen a particular medium for delivery. Thinking rhetorically, however, you will consider which medium you should use to deliver your purposeful message in order to reach your rhetorical audience: a letter, an e-mail, a phone message, a greeting card, an oral presentation with PowerPoint, or a YouTube video. Naming the medium is not as important as analyzing the reasons for the writer's decision, however. What are the advantages to this choice of medium? Are there limitations, or disadvantages, in this choice? Should you deliver your message orally (face to face or over the phone), in writing (using a letter or note, an e-mail or instant message, or a web page), or via film, video, still images, or other visuals? Where might you most successfully deliver that message: in class, at church, at the coffee shop, at a town meeting? For instance, if you are interviewing for a job, would you prefer to present yourself on paper, in person, over Skype, or in a phone call?

In the last few years, students have begun to use multimedia to address rhetorical opportunities in a number of inventive ways. *TXTmob, coup de texte, going mobile, text brigades,* and *swarms* are some of the terms used all over the world for the ways political mobilizations are conducted, allowing group leaders to control, minute by minute, the appearance and movements of demonstrators. The demonstrators themselves—the TXTmobbers and text brigaders—analyze the multimedia messages in order to read the situation, decide what to do, and stay synchronized. Thanks to such untraditional media outlets as Twitter and YouTube, the rest of the world became aware of Iraqi protests over the internet and satellite channel shutdowns ordered by the Commander-in-Chief of the Armed Forces, Major General Abdul Karim Khalaf in 2019 (Figure 1.5).

Not all situations that call for multimedia responses or analysis involve wide-scale political movements. Not everyone will be able to stream videos or download podcasts. While some people might be browsing from a smartphone or a powerful notebook, others might be using a computer lacking the capacity to handle large video or audio downloads.

Sajjad Harsh/ShutterStock.com

Figure 1.5 *Najaf, Iraq - January 10, 2020, Iraqis demonstrate against the internet shutdowns imposed by the government.*

Figure 1.6 *The "I'm Not A Plastic Bag" tote was designed by Hindmarch in collaboration with Antidote and the global social change movement We Are What We Do (now known as Shift).*

Mario Tama/Getty Images

Still others may not always have access to broadband connections. Knowing that people could be easily reached with the use of everyday items, designer Anya Hindmarch sent messages on tote bags as an expression of creative vision as well as a political statement (Figure 1.6).

In other words, accessibility is always a rhetorical issue for you and your audience: the medium of delivery you select affects how much of, and what parts of, your message an audience ultimately sees, hears, and appreciates. Thus, your delivery choices determine not only who constitutes your audience but also how your audience experiences your message.

 ASSIGNMENT: IDENTIFYING REASONS TO WRITE

Whether you are reading an essay, listening to a speech, or looking at a visual, you will understand the message better if you begin by determining the rhetorical opportunity that calls for specific words or visuals. Very often, the responses you are reading or viewing call for even further responses. Whether your response is spoken, written, or composed visually, its power lies in your understanding of the rhetorical opportunity. Reading for rhetorical opportunity helps you develop your skills in analyzing the way the elements of the rhetorical situation work together to influence change.

Life as We Know It

MICHAEL BÉRUBÉ

© Steve Tressler, 2006

English professor Michael Bérubé writes widely about academic matters: curriculum, teaching loads, classroom management, tenure, and cultural studies. But with the birth of his second son, James (Jamie), Bérubé ventured into another kind of writing aimed at a wider audience. The following piece is from the introduction to Life as We Know It: A Father, a Family, and an Exceptional Child, *a chronicle of his family's experiences with Jamie, who has Down syndrome.*

My little Jamie loves lists: foods, colors, animals, numbers, letters, states, classmates, parts of the body, days of the week, modes of transportation, characters who live on Sesame Street, and the names of the people who love him. Early last summer, I hoped his love of lists—and his ability to catalogue things *into* lists—would stand him in good stead during what would undoubtedly be a difficult "vacation" for anyone, let alone a three-year-old child with Down syndrome: a three-hour drive to Chicago, a rush-hour flight to LaGuardia, a cab to Grand Central, a train to Connecticut—and *then* smaller trips to New York, Boston, and Old Orchard Beach, Maine. Even accomplishing the first of these mission objectives—arriving safely at O'Hare—required a precision and teamwork I do not always associate with my family. I dropped off Janet and nine-year-old Nick at the terminal with the baggage, then took Jamie to long-term parking with me while they checked in, and then entertained Jamie all the way back to the terminal, via bus and shuttle train. We sang about the driver on the bus, and we counted all the escalator steps and train stops, and when we finally got to our plane, I told Jamie, *Look, there's Mommy and Nick at the gate! They're yelling that we're going to lose our seats! They want to know why it took us forty-five minutes to park the car!*

All went well from that point on, though, and in the end, I suppose you could say Jamie got as much out of his vacation as might any toddler being whisked up and down New England. He's a seasoned traveler, and he thrives on shorelines, family gatherings, and New Haven pizza. And he's good with faces and names.

Then again, as we learned toward the end of our brief stay in Maine, he doesn't care much for amusement parks. Not that Nick did either, at three. But apparently one of the attractions of Old Orchard Beach, for my wife and her siblings, was the small beachfront arcade and amusement park in town, which they associated with their own childhoods. It was an endearing strip, with a roller coaster just the right size for Nick—exciting, mildly scary, but with no loop-the-loops, rings of fire, or oppressive G forces. We strolled among bumper cars, cotton candy, games of chance and skill, and a striking number of French-Canadian tourists: perhaps the first time our two little boys had ever seen more than one Bérubé family in one place. James, however, wanted nothing to do with any of the rides, and though he loves to pretend-drive and has been on bumper cars before, he squalled so industriously before the ride began as to induce the bumper cars operator to let him out of the car and refund his two tickets.

Jamie finally settled in next to a train ride designed for children five and under or thereabouts, which, for two tickets, took its passengers around an oval layout and over a bridge four times. I found out quickly enough that Jamie didn't want to *ride* the ride; he merely wanted to stand at its perimeter, grasping the partition with both hands and counting the cars—one, two, three, four, five, six—as they went by. Sometimes, when the train traversed the bridge, James would punctuate it with tiny jumps, saying, "Up! Up! Up!" But for the most part, he was content to hang onto the metal bars of the partition, grinning and counting—and, when the train came to a stop, pulling my sleeve and saying, "More, again."

This went on for about half an hour, well past the point at which I could convincingly share Jamie's enthusiasm for tracking the train's progress. As it went on my spirits began to sink in a way I do not recall having felt before. Occasionally it will occur to Janet or to me that Jamie will always be "disabled," that his adult and adolescent years will undoubtedly be more difficult emotionally—for him and for us—than his early childhood, that we will never *not* worry about his future, his quality of life, whether we're doing enough for him. But usually these moments occur in the relative comfort of abstraction, when Janet and I are lying in bed at night and wondering what will become of us all. When I'm *with* Jamie, by contrast, I'm almost always fully occupied by taking care of his present needs rather than by worrying about his future. When he asks to hear the Beatles because he loves their cover of Little Richard's "Long Tall Sally," I just play the song, sing along, and watch him dance with delight; I do not concern myself with extraneous questions such as whether he'll ever distinguish early Beatles from late Beatles, Paul's songs from John's, originals from covers. These questions are now central to Nick's enjoyment of the Beatles, but that's Nick for you. Jamie is entirely *sui generis*, and as long as I'm with him I can't think of him as anything but Jamie.

I have tried. Almost as a form of emotional exercise, I have tried, on occasion, to step back and see him as others might see him, as an instance of a category, one item on the long list of human subgroups. *This is a child with Down syndrome,* I say to myself. *This is a child with a developmental disability.* It never works: Jamie remains Jamie to me. I have even tried to imagine him as he would have been seen in other eras, other places: *This is a retarded child.* And even: *This is a Mongoloid child.* This makes for unbearable cognitive dissonance. I can imagine that people might think such things, but I cannot imagine how they might think them in a way that prevents them from seeing Jamie *as* Jamie. I try to recall how I saw such children when I was a child, but here I guiltily draw a blank: I don't remember seeing them at all, which very likely means that I never quite saw them *as* children. Instead I remember a famous passage from Ludwig Wittgenstein's *Philosophical Investigations:* "'Seeing-as' is not part of perception. And for this reason it is *like* seeing, and then again *not* like." Reading Wittgenstein, I often think, is something like listening to a brilliant and cantankerous uncle with an annoying fondness for koans [riddles]. But on this one, I know exactly what he means.

ACTIVITY: Analyzing the Rhetorical Situation
"Life as We Know it"

1. What rhetorical opportunity called for the writing of this essay? State that opportunity in one sentence.

2. Who composed this message? What information does the writer supply about his identity?

3. What does this essay say? Compile the details that describe the writer's feelings about his son; then write one sentence that conveys Bérubé's main message.

4. Why does the essay say that? Drawing on your previous answer, identify three or four passages from the text where Bérubé supports his main message.

5. How does the essay respond to that opportunity? What change in attitude, opinion, or action does the author wish to influence in his audience?

2 Analyzing Rhetorical Choices

Rhetoric is the art of observing in any given situation the available means of persuasion.

LEARNING OBJECTIVES

- Explain how a fitting response to a rhetorical situation helps shape a message that solves a problem.
- Identify the issue, claim, and common ground of an argument.
- Analyze how the available means of persuasion (ethos, logos, and pathos) shape rhetorical choices and affect the audience.
- Explain how the resources and constraints of a rhetorical situation affect your rhetorical choices.
- Apply rhetorical choices that do not seek to "shout down" an argument so much as to create a new understanding.
- Articulate the expectations of the rhetorical analysis assignment.

≫ THINKING RHETORICALLY ABOUT PERSUASION

The Greek philosopher Aristotle, who coined an authoritative definition of *rhetoric* over 2,500 years ago, tells us, "Rhetoric is the art of observing in any given situation the available means of persuasion." Let's take this definition apart and examine its constituent elements. "Rhetoric is the art [or mental ability] of observing. . . ." Notice that Aristotle does not call for you to overpower your audience (your readers or listeners) with words or images, nor does he push you to win an argument. Instead, he encourages you to observe what kind of rhetorical situation you are entering. Chapter 1 stressed the importance of identifying the elements of a rhetorical situation (opportunity, purpose, audience, stance, genre, and medium of delivery): Who is your audience? What is your relationship to that person or group of people? What is the occasion? What do you want your language to accomplish (that is, what is your purpose)? By answering these questions, you are establishing the elements of the "given situation."

Now that you can identify these elements, you can evaluate the wide range of possible responses you can offer. Of course, each rhetorical situation is different, and you will need to consider that you can come only as close to persuasion as the rhetorical situation allows. Still, with experience and knowledge, you will take note of the tools that comprise "the available means of persuasion" to make more informed, strategic decisions. Rhetorical consciousness (and success) comes with recognizing the vast array of options at your disposal, including those already in existence and those you can create, and leveraging all the "available means" to achieve your purpose.

»» A PROBLEM-SOLVING APPROACH

The opportunity for change arises from a **problem** that can be addressed or even resolved by you and your audience. The writer (or speaker) enters the rhetorical situation in order to shape a message that can address a problem. It is up to you to observe what measure of change is possible in each case and to choose a response that will be most persuasive in achieving that change—be it an attitude, action, or opinion—in your intended audience. The writer identifies that problem as an opportunity to make change through the use of language, whether visual, written, or spoken. The response is dictated by the situation, by the specific opportunity for change.

problem in rhetoric, a question for discussion, exploration, and possible solution

Some responses to a problem will address the problem better than others. To be persuasive you need to choose a response that suits the problem. In other words, a **problem-solving approach** invites a response that *fits* the rhetorical situation. For instance, if you were bothered by your friend's weekend alcohol consumption, you would probably want to find an appropriate time and place to talk with her about it in a calm, respectful manner. You may want to focus on the dangers to her own well-being and physical safety, or you might discuss the pros and cons of drinking for college students. This situation invites such a **fitting response**—not a subpoena, lawsuit, call to her parents, or visit from a physician (at least not yet).

problem-solving approach in rhetoric, an examination of a question on an issue or situation directed at a specific audience

When you successfully use language to address a problem, you deliver a fitting response using the available means of persuasion, the medium you use to send your message, and the rhetorical appeals to your audience. Depending on the problem, responses in different media may reach and satisfy the rhetorical audience. Dictated by the situation, a fitting response to a problem

fitting response a communication whose tone, content, and delivery are carefully constructed to connect to the interests of a specific audience

- addresses the opportunity for change;
- is appropriate in content, tone, and timing;

- is delivered in an appropriate medium; and thus
- reaches, satisfies, and maybe even changes the actions, opinions, or attitudes of the intended audience.

>>> MAKING CLAIMS

After you have identified a problem (from your friend's weekend alcohol consumption or bad food at a restaurant to something larger like poor-quality public schooling or homelessness in your town), it is up to you to determine which measure of change can be accomplished at this point given the interests and values of your audience. Your purpose may be to convince your audience that a situation needs a solution or to call your audience to action to resolve the problem. You may want to help your audience make a decision. Or you may want your audience to explore an issue further. Your proposed change becomes your purpose, which you will shape into a **claim** (or assertion) that identifies the problem and proposes your solution. Your claim—usually expressed as a single, clearly focused, specifically worded **thesis statement**—invites the audience to understand your position and anchors your response. (For more on thesis statements, see CHAPTER 13, CRAFTING A WORKING THESIS STATEMENT.)

The kind of claim you make will also be guided by your rhetorical situation, however. If you are composing a memoir, for example, the change you are proposing is likely one of self-realization. Your claim in a proposal will be a call to action. A literary analysis will include the main point of your interpretation of the work of a particular author. A

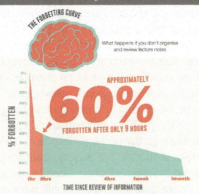

Produced by urbanest student

Through a combination of words, images, and statistics, this infographic on note taking uses the web to deliver its message that note taking will solve the problem of forgetting important information in class lectures.

claim an assertion that identifies a problem and proposes a solution

thesis statement a clearly worded statement of your claim that guides the structure of a paper, presentation, or multimedia text

pages 239–241

Persuasion

position argument is likely to focus on new evidence that the audience has not yet considered on a particular issue. Whether you are writing an evaluation or a profile, your thesis statement should include enough of the unexpected to arouse interest in the main point you are making about the problem you have identified. You may not have a clear thesis statement in mind when you begin writing. What you think about an issue is likely to evolve while you are writing and researching your topic. This is as it should be. Just as your audience will learn something from your response, so you will likely discover new ways of looking at a topic as you translate your purpose into a compelling message.

»» USING THE AVAILABLE MEANS OF PERSUASION

Earlier in this chapter, you learned that Aristotle defined *rhetoric* as "the art of observing in any given situation the available means of persuasion." Given that the prime characteristic of any rhetorical situation is its opportunity for change, the most significant part of any claim is that you can make a case for the change you have proposed using the available means of persuasion. The **available means of persuasion** include the place where you create a message (via your laptop or other electronic device, in person, over the telephone, by postal service), the physical means you use to deliver your message (in person, digitally, visually, in print), and the rhetorical elements you use in your presentation to appeal to your audience. Basically, you will want to establish your authority (or credibility) on the issue at hand, provide evidence that supports your claim, and make an authentic emotional connection with your audience. Altogether, authority, evidence, and connection are the available means of persuasion in any message, whether it is delivered verbally, visually, in print, or digitally. (See also CHAPTER 15, ARGUMENT.)

> **available means of persuasion** include the methods of communication (visual, verbal, digital, print) as well as rhetorical appeals of ethos, logos, and pathos (see pp. 23–24)
>
> pages 292–294

The Available Means Are Anchored to the Writer's Place

Every time a writer sends a message, he or she does so from a particular place. Whether that person is writing at a desk, talking on a cell phone, preaching from a pulpit, speaking from a podium, typing on a laptop, or skywriting in a plane, both the message itself and its means of delivery are influenced by that specific place.

The 2014 Nobel Peace Prize awardee Malala Yousafzai began life in rural Pakistan, where she studied at a school run by her father. She loved school—the learning, the friendships, the sports. But when the Taliban government took over, life in the Swat Valley changed drastically and for the worse. By 2007, education and shopping were banned for girls and women, while television watching and

Malala Yousafzai, the Pakistani advocate for girls' education who was shot in the head by the Taliban when she was a teen, opens the Library of Birmingham (England).

music were banned for everyone. Suddenly, women and girls were expected to wear burqas (long, loose garments that cover the entire body and feet).

Despite the bans and the physical danger to her and her family, Malala recognized a rhetorical opportunity, one that invited her words on the problem of repression. She began speaking about education rights as early as 2008, accompanying her father to local civic groups. Soon, she was "discovered" by the BBC. A representative of BBC Urdu (the official language of Pakistan) asked if she would be willing to blog anonymously about her life—about violence and politics—under the Taliban. With her parents' permission, she agreed, writing out her thoughts by hand and passing them off to a BBC reporter who scanned and e-mailed them to the BBC offices. Malala was eleven years old when she began writing a diary for BBC Urdu.

BBC Blog Entries

I AM AFRAID—3 JANUARY 2009

"I had a terrible dream yesterday with military helicopters and the Taliban. I have had such dreams since the launch of the military operation in Swat. I was afraid going to school because the Taliban had issued an edict banning all girls from attending schools. Only 11 students attended the class out of 27. The number decreased because of Taliban's edict.

On my way from school to home I heard a man saying 'I will kill you.' I hastened my pace . . . to my utter relief he was talking on his mobile and must have been threatening someone else over the phone."

INTERRUPTED SLEEP—15 JANUARY 2009

"The night was filled with the noise of artillery fire and I woke up three times. But since there was no school I got up later at 10 a.m. Afterwards, my friend came over and we discussed our homework. Today is the last day before the Taliban's edict comes into effect, and my friend was discussing homework as if nothing out of the ordinary had happened.

"Today, I also read my diary written for the BBC in Urdu. My mother liked my pen name Gul Makai. I also like the name because my real name means 'grief stricken'."

ACTIVITY: Analyzing the Rhetorical Situation
Malala's Blog

1. If the purpose is to raise awareness for girls' education, what, exactly, is the rhetorical opportunity?
2. Who is the rhetorical audience, the specific audience she hopes to change with her words? Who can actually help bring about this change? Who will be affected by such a change?
3. What means were available to Malala from her place in rural Pakistan to get her message to reach her rhetorical audience?
4. How did Malala use her physical place to her advantage in making her case for girls' education in rural Pakistan?

The Available Means Include the Rhetorical Elements of the Message Itself

When writers and speakers purposefully compose messages for their intended audience, they consider how best to appeal to the interests and values of that audience. To do so, writers and speakers turn to three persuasive strategies, which are referred to as the **rhetorical appeals** of ethos, logos, and pathos. The use of these appeals is balanced in most successful messages, for to exaggerate any one of the three is to risk losing the audience and thereby fail to achieve the rhetorical purpose.

rhetorical appeals the strategies established by ancient Greeks as the foundation for persuasion: ethos (the writer's credibility), logos (the good reasons of the argument), and pathos (the emotional connection with the audience)

Ethos

Writers and speakers can leverage the available means in different ways. First of all, when you compose your own message for a specific audience, you will also need to keep in mind exactly how you will come across to your audience, how you can assure them that you have their best interests in mind. Often this includes establishing common ground with the interests of your audience in order to get that audience to listen. **Ethos** is the ethical appeal of the writer's credibility, goodwill, and trustworthiness. Will the audience find the writer believable? Does the speaker or writer establish **common ground**, a belief or value that provides the basis of agreement? By calibrating the tone of your response, you can also control the attitude you project to your intended audience.

ethos the ethical appeal of the writer's credibility, goodwill, and trustworthiness

common ground a belief or value shared by the writer and audience that provides the basis for agreement

Logos

pages 258–260

Logos is an appeal to reason or logic. (See CHAPTER 14, STATING THE MAIN IDEA, for a discussion of deductive and inductive reasoning.) When you shape your message, you will need to provide good reasons that are supported by evidence that connect coherently to your claim. In other words, does the evidence support the claim you are making about a problem or issue? **Evidence** includes testimonials and anecdotes, statistics, facts, and expert opinions. The rhetorical situation guides you in determining what structure and evidence will be most effective. (See also

pages 260–262

CHAPTER 14, DEVELOPING THE MAIN POINT.) As you shape your response, what stories do you tell, what examples do you use, and what facts and figures do you use to establish logos? Statistics and facts might be used more extensively in a position argument than in a profile, where testimonials and anecdotes prove the point. You are likely to use examples to make your point in an evaluation, and possibly relate an extended anecdote (or story) about a particular person or situation in a memoir. A cause-and-consequence structure might be used to support the logic of your position argument. (See CHAPTER 15 for more on using rhetorical strategies for development, such as EXEMPLIFICATION, NARRATION, and CAUSE-AND-EFFECT ANALYSIS.) You will want the logos of your response to support your ethos by making a positive impression with the evidence you deliver and demonstrating that you are both well-informed and fair-minded.

logos an appeal to the audience's reason through the logical construction of the argument

evidence support for your claim that includes testimonials and anecdotes, statistics, facts, and expert opinions

Pathos

pages 270–272

Evidence alone is not always enough, however. Human beings are not always persuaded to believe or act in a certain way based exclusively on facts or only on what can be proved. Using the available means of persuasion also means making an authentic emotional connection with your audience. **Pathos** is the emotional appeal of language and examples that stir the audience's feelings (within a reasonable limit). When you appeal to emotion, you are appealing to your audience's sympathy and empathy, which means you will need a clear understanding of the beliefs and values of your intended audience.

pathos an authentic emotional connection with the audience

Ain't I a Woman?

SOJOURNER TRUTH

As you think through the available means of persuasion, consider the following passage from a speech that former slave Sojourner Truth (born Isabella Baumfree, 1787–1883) delivered at the 1851 Women's Rights Convention in Akron, Ohio. Truth's speech provides a useful textual context for examining the available means of persuasion. Truth used the example of her own hardworking life to establish her authority as a woman just as suited for voting rights as any man. And for

Persuasion

evidence to support her argument, Truth wisely went straight to the Bible, which served not only as the ultimate authority but also as the highest form of evidence for all her listeners, whether they were Northern or Southern, Black or White, male or female, educated or uneducated. Truth's 1851 speech circulated in at least four versions. The famous "ain't I a woman" refrain first appeared in 1878 in Sojourner Truth's Narrative and Book of Life *and is the most well-known version today.*

Well, children, where there is so much racket there must be something out of kilter. I think that 'twixt the Negroes of the South and the women of the North, all talking about rights, the white men will be in a fix pretty soon. But what's all this here talking about?

Sojourner Truth, whose 1851 speech survives as an example of the available means of persuasion skillfully used.

That man over there says that women need to be helped into carriages and lifted over ditches, and to have the best place everywhere. Nobody ever helps me into carriages, or over mud puddles, or gives me any best place! And ain't I a woman? Look at me! Look at my arm! I could have ploughed and planted, and gathered into barns, and no man could head me! And ain't I a woman? I could work as much and eat as much as a man—when I could get it—and bear the lash as well! And ain't I a woman? I have borne thirteen children, and seen them most all sold off to slavery, and when I cried out with my mother's grief, none but Jesus heard me! And ain't I a woman?

Then they talk about this thing in the head; what's this they call it? ["Intellect," somebody whispers.] That's it, honey. What's that got to do with women's rights or Negros' rights? If my cup won't hold but a pint, and yours holds a quart, wouldn't you be mean not to let me have my little half measure-full?

Then that little man in black back there, he says women can't have as much rights as men, 'cause Christ wasn't a woman! Where did your Christ come from? Where did your Christ come from? From God and a woman! Man had nothing to do with Him.

If the first woman God ever made was strong enough to turn the world upside down all alone, these women together ought to be able to turn it back, and get it right side up again! And now they is asking to do it, the men better let them.

Obliged to you for hearing me, and now old Sojourner ain't got nothing more to say.

ACTIVITY: Analyzing the Rhetorical Situation
Rhetorical Appeals

Ethos, logos, and pathos are often distributed among three sections of any piece of powerful writing, with ethos emphasized in the introduction, logos throughout the body, and pathos in the conclusion—appearing separately and in richly overlapping forms. Reread "Ain't I a Woman?" to identify Truth's use of the rhetorical appeals as available means of persuasion.

1. A speaker in Truth's position (Black female, uneducated) had to devote most of her words to establishing her ethos; after all, she needed to be heard and believed as the Black woman she was. In her opening paragraphs, Truth describes the struggle for women's rights as she sees it. How does this description help establish her ethos?

2. How does her first paragraph establish common ground with the White women in her audience? What is their basis of agreement?

3. What is her purpose in demonstrating her goodwill toward her audience, her good sense and knowledge of the subject at hand, and her good character?

4. Like many successful speakers, Truth spends the body of her speech emphasizing logos, the shape of her reasoning, particularly her response to arguments against women's rights. Paraphrase in one sentence the logic of her argument.

5. In the closing sentence of her speech, how does her expression of gratitude for being allowed to speak emphasize pathos?

The Available Means Deliver a Message in a Genre and Medium That Reach the Audience

The genres and media of delivery people choose for their message reflect the specific ways they take advantage of the available means, whether their message takes the form of a video, audio, petition, concert, debate, speech, lecture, phone call, e-mail, and so on. For example, Malala Yousafzai took advantage of the available means of blogging to reach an audience beyond her place in rural Pakistan. Sojourner Truth used the available means of an oral genre, a speech, given the venue of the Women's Rights Convention, to reach her rhetorical audience of educated White Northerners, mostly women. Only these women could help Truth bring about the change that was women's rights. It was important that they realize the importance of women's rights for Black women as well as for White women like themselves. To enhance the oral medium of delivery, Truth emphasized her able body, pulling up her sleeve to show her bare arm and her developed muscle, a daring embodiment of rhetorical prowess for anyone, especially for a woman.

The efforts of the Amethyst Initiative exemplify a similarly fitting response to a serious problem.

Given the nationwide concern about binge drinking and its consequences, college and university administrators, Mothers Against Drunk Driving (MADD), the Center on Alcohol Marketing and Youth (CAMY), and other concerned groups are all working together to combat this national health concern. Statistics such as those on the MADD35 website (Figure 2.1) underscore the dangers that the administrators want to address. In addressing the problem, those

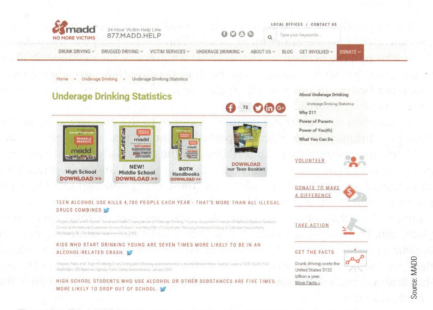

Source: MADD

Figure 2.1 *This MADD35 web page emphasizes the little-known statistics about the dangers of underage drinking.*

administrators have come to rely on yet another genre to reach their rhetorical audience (those they are trying to influence to initiate change): the petition. Representing the Amethyst Initiative (from the ancient Greek *a methustos*, or "not intoxicated"), these administrators hope their petition will spark a sustained, national conversation on underage drinking. The administrators who wrote the Amethyst Initiative's petition realize that college and university presidents and chancellors are those most capable of starting campuswide conversations about policies that can encourage responsible alcohol use, and so they chose this group as their rhetorical audience.

With its long and rich history, the petition, a written request (or demand), usually signed by many people, can work almost like a pledge on the part of the signees. Its key characteristics include

- an explicit statement of the problem,
- essential background information,
- a statement of what should be done to resolve the problem,
- a specific audience who can initiate change (that is, a rhetorical audience),
- a request for signatures or support, and
- strategic delivery of the message, often accompanied by some kind of publicity.

Every petition is a response to a rhetorical opportunity for change that calls for spreading the effort more widely. Those who compose the petition, those who sign the petition, as well as those who receive the petition will likely understand the public nature of the petition because they have encountered that genre before. In other words, the genre itself creates expectations in the writers, signers, and readers.

In addition to comprising a fitting response to the problem at hand, the Amethyst Initiative's statement is posted online to reach an even broader audience: the community at large. Although the writers clearly indicate their principle rhetorical audience in that only college and university presidents and chancellors have been invited to sign (those best positioned to address the problem), others are also enlisted in influencing this audience. "If you are not a president or chancellor, but would like to become part of this larger effort, please sign up here." The sentence ends with a link to the website of a broader organization called Choose Responsibility. By doing this, the petitioners expand their persuasive reach, because in this case, the community at large can influence the rhetorical audience of university chancellors and presidents to sign on to the Amethyst Initiative.

It's Time to Rethink the Drinking Age

THE AMETHYST INITIATIVE

In 1984 Congress passed the National Minimum Drinking Age Act, which imposed a penalty of 10% of a state's federal highway appropriation on any state setting its drinking age lower than 21.

Twenty-four years later, our experience as college and university presidents convinces us that . . .

Twenty-one is not working

A culture of dangerous, clandestine "binge-drinking"—often conducted off-campus—has developed.

Alcohol education that mandates abstinence as the only legal option has not resulted in significant constructive behavioral change among our students.

Adults under 21 are deemed capable of voting, signing contracts, serving on juries and enlisting in the military, but are told they are not mature enough to have a beer.

By choosing to use fake IDs, students make ethical compromises that erode respect for the law.

How many times must we relearn the lessons of Prohibition?

We call upon our elected officials:

To support an informed and dispassionate public debate over the effects of the 21-year-old drinking age.

To consider whether the 10% highway fund "incentive" encourages or inhibits that debate.

To invite new ideas about the best ways to prepare young adults to make responsible decisions about alcohol.

We pledge ourselves and our institutions to playing a vigorous, constructive role as these critical discussions unfold.

Please add my signature to this statement:

Name _____

Signature _____

Institution _____

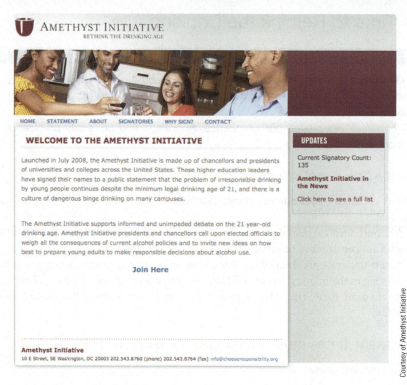

One means available to the Amethyst Initiative for creating a fitting response is this website.

ACTIVITY: Analyzing the Rhetorical Situation
A Fitting Response

For each of the following problems, decide whether you could shape a response that fulfills the three requirements for being fitting: language that suits the problem, is delivered in an appropriate medium, and reaches the intended audience. Be prepared to share your answers with the rest of the class.

1. Consider a problem that you are currently experiencing. Consider, too, who could resolve or help you resolve that problem.

2. Your English instructor has announced that she must use the entire range of grades. Less than 50 percent of your class can receive an A.

3. The person you are dating wants to get engaged. But you do not.

4. Your history instructor has assigned a research paper that is due on the same day as your biology midterm.
5. After taking your LSATs, you receive mailings from more than twenty law schools.
6. In order to obtain a green card (indicating U.S. permanent resident status), your Romanian friend wants to arrange a fraudulent American marriage.

»» RESOURCES AND CONSTRAINTS

Persuasive writers know that no two situations are ever exactly the same. In each situation, you will need to evaluate what **resources (advantages)** you have to effect change and what **constraints (limitations)** you might have to overcome to achieve your purpose. The advantages you have—as well as the limitations you face—are part of any rhetorical situation and affect the rhetorical choices you are able to make to achieve your purpose.

> **resources (advantages)** in rhetoric, the means needed to effect change in an audience

As a writer in an academic setting, you are no doubt aware that many of your rhetorical situations share various constraints. For instance, an academic research assignment usually involves some specifications from an instructor. Following are some common constraints for such writing assignments:

> **constraints (limitations)** the obstacles a writer has to overcome to reach and perhaps persuade an audience

- *Expertise*. As a student, you rely to some degree on documenting what others have said in order to build credibility.
- *Geography*. Although the internet gives researchers unprecedented access to materials not available locally, most students are still somewhat constrained by what is close at hand.
- *Time*. In most cases, your research will be subject to a time limit. Your readers—whether they are instructors, colleagues, or other decision-makers—need to see your research before it goes out of date and before the deadline to make a decision (about what action to take or what grade to assign) has passed.

Just as in the case of Malala Yousafzai and Sojourner Truth, constraints such as these can, however, suggest resources. What primary documents might you have access to in your geographical location? What unique opportunities do you have for reaching your audience that a recognized expert might not have? Given that you are just learning about the topic, might you be more respectful of, and engaged with, the research of others? Might working within an assigned time frame provide motivation? In every rhetorical situation there will be advantages (given your resources) and limitations (given your constraints).

Consider the limitations faced by Malala Yousafzai, Sojourner Truth, and the Amethyst Initiative and how they turned these into advantages through the rhetorical choices they made. For example, Sojourner Truth was the only Black person in attendance at the 1851 conference. Truth had been listening carefully to the speeches, many of which denounced the rights of women. She delivered her speech at a time when White women were rarely permitted to speak in public, especially to an audience that included men. Truth was constrained by being illiterate, Black, and a woman, and she knew her spoken ideas would be met with resistance if not outright objection. Some of her constraints, however, proved to be her richest resources. Truth's use of dialect, for example, authenticated her as a formerly enslaved person who did not have access to formal education. Her not being an educated White "lady" permitted her to ascend the platform and address the audience.

 ASSIGNMENT: WRITING A RHETORICAL ANALYSIS

Choose a selection for rhetorical analysis that meets the following criteria.

- The text responds to an opportunity to make a change through spoken, written, or visual language.
- The text identifies a rhetorical opportunity for change.
- The text is intended for a rhetorical audience.
- The text offers a solution or recommendation for change.

After you have selected a text, read it carefully, keeping in mind that *the ultimate goal of a rhetorical analysis is twofold: (1) to analyze how well the rhetorical elements work together to create a fitting response, and (2) to assess the overall effectiveness of that response.* Then, write answers to the following questions, citing material from the text or visual itself to support each answer:

Are the available means anchored to the writer's place?

1. Who created the text? What credentials or expertise does that person or group have? Why is the creator of the text engaged with this opportunity? Is this an opportunity that can be modified through language? What opinions or biases did the person or group bring to the text?
2. What is the place (physical, social, academic, economic, and so on) from which the creator of the text forms and sends the response? What are the resources of that place? What are its constraints (or limitations)?
3. Who is the audience for the message? What relationship is the creator of the text trying to establish with the audience? What opinions or biases might the audience hold? How might the audience feel about this rhetorical opportunity? And, most important, can this audience modify or help bring about a modification of the rhetorical opportunity? How?

Do the available means include the rhetorical elements of the message itself?

1. Identify the rhetorical elements of the message itself. In other words, where and how does the person or group employ the rhetorical appeals of ethos, pathos, and logos? How are credentials, goodwill, or good sense evoked to establish ethos? How is evidence (examples, statistics, data, and so forth) used to establish logos? And how is an emotional connection created to establish pathos? Keep in mind that the rhetorical appeals can sometimes overlap.

2. What kind of language does the creator of the text use? Is it plain or specialized, slang or formal? How does the choice of language reveal how the person or group views the intended audience?

Do the available means deliver a message in a genre and medium that reaches the audience?

1. Is the intended audience for the text a rhetorical audience? Draw on evidence from the text to support your answer.

2. If the audience is a rhetorical one, what can it do to resolve the problem?

3. Does the response address and fit the rhetorical opportunity? How exactly? If not, how might the response be reshaped so that it does fit?

4. Is the response delivered in an appropriate medium that reaches its intended audience? Why is that medium appropriate? Or how could it be adjusted to be appropriate?

5. Can you think of other responses to similar rhetorical situations? What genre is commonly used? Does the creator of this text use that genre? If not, what is the effect of going against an audience's expectations?

Now that you have carefully read the text and answered all of the questions, you are ready to write your rhetorical analysis. How does your analysis of the use of the available means reveal

1. *How well the rhetorical elements work together to create a fitting response to an opportunity for change?*

2. *How effective the response is?*

As you begin, search your answers for an idea that can serve as your claim or thesis. For example, you might focus on the declared goal—if there is one—of the creator of the text and whether it has been achieved. You might assess how successfully that creator has identified the rhetorical audience, shaped a fitting response, or employed the best available means. Or you might focus on the use of the rhetorical appeals and the overall success of their use. Whether or not you agree with the text is beside the point. Your job is to analyze in an essay how and how well the text's creator has accomplished the purpose for that text.

3

Academic Literacies: Reading Rhetorically

LEARNING OBJECTIVES

- Identify the specific strategies of rhetorical reading.
- Apply those strategies to the development of academic literacies.
- Assess the rhetorical situations in print in terms of complexity.
- Analyze and then synthesize information.
- Enumerate specific ways to improve academic reading practices and develop academic literacies.

Many people consider writing an *active* intellectual activity and reading a *passive* one. But that is not the case. As you know well, reading in college can be, well, hard work. College-level reading demands that you up your game in terms of expanding your vocabulary, building background information, and becoming more familiar with the various genres and situations in each of your courses. Improving your ability to read rhetorically will support you as you develop several academic literacies at once. Each different course that you take seems to call for different vocabulary, context (or background), even reading strategies. For instance, when you enter the field of psychology, you may feel pounded by all the new vocabulary (often technical terms) you need to learn: *anxiety, attachment disorder, cohort, disregulation, egocentric, stimming, threshold*. Of course, turning to a dictionary always helps, but so does figuring out how those terms are used in context, as does checking for a glossary of specific terms you need to know.

College-level reading also demands that you familiarize yourself with different genres, from textbooks, online supplements, and trade (or popular) books to scientific reports, literature reviews (a summary of scholarly articles on a particular topic), and editorials (opinion pieces). Each of these academic genres calls for specific reading strategies, specific literacies. For instance, you will read essay exam questions much more strategically (knowing how best to respond efficiently and effectively) than you might read a literature review (understanding what various experts are contributing to the scholarly conversation), just as you will read a physics problem differently and for different reasons than you will read a historical account.

Just as various genres ask you to take a different role as reader, different rhetorical situations ask you to do the same thing, whether you are reading for specific information, for critical analysis, for visualizing the arc of a narrative, or for problem-solving. You will be asked to read opinions with which you readily agree (on abortion, free speech, right-to-carry laws, climate change, migration, or the president) and those with which you do not. Thus, you will often be expected to read with Democrats and Republicans, with liberals and conservatives, with internationals and Americans, with feminists, neurodiverse and sexually diverse people, with atheists and with religious fundamentalists. In short, college-level reading asks that you be rhetorically nimble, willing and able to participate in the complex multitude of reading situations for a number of different courses.

College-level reading demands that you expand your academic literacies, your writing skills, your critical analysis. Experts in the fields of reading and

When you read rhetorically, you read purposefully, actively analyzing the writer's purpose and choice of genre, the key parts of the text itself, and your own preparation and purpose for reading.

writing call for eight habits of mind that are crucial for college success: curiosity (wanting to know more), openness (willingness to consider other ways of thinking and doing), engagement (involvement in your learning), creativity (generating new ways of doing things), persistence (sticking to it), responsibility (taking ownership for the project and its consequences), flexibility (ability to adapt), and metacognition (your ability to reflect on how you are thinking and why you are thinking in such a way). As Adrienne Rich would advise you, you must "claim your education." And in doing so, you respect your learning curve, learn from mistakes, and become ever nimble rhetorically.

»» READING STRATEGIES

When you read actively, you are using your rhetorical skills, taking into consideration who composed the message, the purpose of the message, and your role as reader (as audience). The best of critical readers follow a **reading process**, a series of steps much like the ones you employ when you write.

reading process series of steps, including previewing, skimming, reading, and annotating

1. **Preview** You begin by previewing the entire text to gauge the time and expertise necessary to read it—and your reason for reading. You might examine the title, the table of contents (or headings), and any follow-up questions. Your goal at this point is to estimate your familiarity with the vocabulary, content, and genre of the reading itself—in other words, what the reading demands of you and what you demand of the reading.

2. **Skim** While you skim, stay alert for the author's major points, pausing to read over any information about the author and examine any visuals that accompany the text. Your goal is to learn what you can about the author of the text (what the author's relationship is to the subject matter), its audience and purpose (where the text originally appeared—and for whom), and the rhetorical context in which it was written (what rhetorical opportunity the author was addressing).

3. **Read** Next, you will read quickly for comprehension, to glean content information while you follow the author's line of reasoning. At this point, your goal is to consider the line of reasoning, the logic (logos) of the message, the major claim, and supporting information. At the same time, you will look up vocabulary, mark places you do not understand, and highlight major points, all the while keeping in mind your reason for reading.

4. **Annotate** Finally, after skimming and reading, you will pass through the text once again, this time reading deliberately and critically for analysis. You will annotate the margins with questions and mark contradictory

information, unsupported reasoning, unacknowledged assumptions, omitted information, and emotional connection or manipulation. You may find yourself wanting to respond to or question the author's important points, as though you were carrying on a conversation. To do so, you can use a pen, sticky notes, or an online annotation tool.

Using different methods of annotation, we all try to mark important passages and indicate our questions and responses.

The Believing and Doubting Game

One strategy to help you think about what you read is to play the **Believing and Doubting Game**, which Peter Elbow proposes in *Writing without Teachers*. When you withhold any kind of judgment as you read, you are playing the "Believing Game." By wanting to believe what the author is saying, you are better able to understand the author's message, ideas, and reasoning. Playing the "Doubting Game," on the other hand, demands that you read critically, asking questions and challenging the author as you read. Elbow advocates a balanced approach—one that uses "believing" as well as "doubting"—in college reading.

Believing and Doubting Game strategy that includes both reading while believing the writer (and in so doing understanding the writer's message better) and reading while doubting the writer (and in so doing finding the gaps and questions that emerge from the selection)

Reading Rhetorically

As you annotate the text, you will ask questions that help you locate and respond to the specific features of the rhetorical situation: the writer's opportunity to propose change; the purpose of, and audience of, the message; the genre shaping the message; and your reason for reading. As you consider the context of the message, you will also think about the writer's place (where the writer is "coming from") and how that place influences the writer's stance toward the topic and you, the audience. Your challenge is to identify the rhetorical elements used to persuade you to believe the message and perhaps act on it (or understand it enough to respond to it), and then evaluate the effectiveness of the delivery of the text in terms of genre and medium.

Reading for the writer's place

Questions about the writer's place provide information about the author that enriches your understanding of the message. You want to know as much as possible about the author so you can consider how social, educational, historical, or cultural influences affected the author's message. What rhetorical opportunity called for the author's use of specific words or visuals? Who is the author writing to? If not readily available, you can usually find out about the author's educational background, personal experiences, and stance (position or attitude) toward the topic by conducting some quick online research.

Reading for rhetorical elements

To understand the author's argument, you will need to identify the author's thesis. What claim is the author making about the topic? Follow your annotations to map your agreements, disagreements, and questions with the author's line of reasoning. Focus on those specific points as you develop your response. You will also attend to the author's use of the available means of persuasion: how the rhetorical appeals of ethos, logos, and pathos have been established (or not), especially how well the author makes an authentic connection with the audience and whether the evidence adequately supports the reasons the author employs to support and develop that claim.

Reading for genre and medium

Because we enjoy so many ways of communicating—visually, verbally, digitally, in print, and vocally—we rarely stop to consider why we are choosing a particular medium. We just use it. As you annotate the text, however, you need to ask questions about the author's success in using the key characteristics of the chosen genre to make a particular point, or the decision to use a particular medium to deliver the author's message. What are the advantages to these choices? Are there disadvantages?

Hone your skills as an active, informed, nimble reader and use these reading strategies—one at a time—to read the following essay rhetorically, considering the elements of the rhetorical situation.

1. First, preview the essay quickly. For example, what does the title tell you about the topic? What knowledge of Frederick Douglass and his life did you bring to the essay? In one sentence, what do you expect to learn from this article?
2. Then, skim the essay. Who is the author, and what is his relationship to the subject matter? Why did the author write the article, and for whom? Write down five key words that indicate the author's major points in the article.

Reading

3. Now, read the essay, marking places you do not understand. Write out the major claim and some supporting information.
4. Finally, annotate the essay as if you were having a conversation with the text, asking questions, checking for contradictory information or unsupported points, and confirming assertions. You can write in the margins or on sticky notes, or if you are reading online, use the "comment" feature.

Learning to Read and Write

FREDERICK DOUGLASS

Frederick Douglass (1818–1895), an escaped slave, was an abolitionist who traveled and lectured internationally on the cruelty of slavery. The publication of his Narrative of the Life of Frederick Douglass, an American Slave *by the Anti-Slavery Office in 1845 made him more vulnerable to capture and return, but friends contacted his owner and bought his freedom in 1846. This excerpt from his first book is considered a literacy narrative, a type of memoir that describes learning to read and write.*

The idea as to how I might learn to write was suggested to me by being in Durgin and Bailey's ship-yard, and frequently seeing the ship carpenters, after hewing, and getting a piece of timber ready for use, write on the timer the name of that part of the ship for which it was intended.

When a piece of timber was intended for the larboard side, it would be marked thus—"L." When a piece was for the starboard side, it would be marked thus—"S." A piece for the larboard side forward, would be marked thus—"L.F." When a piece was for starboard side forward, it would be marked thus—"S.F." For larboard aft, it would be marked thus—"L.A." For starboard aft, it would be marked thus—"S. A." I soon learned the names of these letters, and for what they were intended when placed upon a piece of timber in the ship-yard. I immediately commenced copying them, and in a short time was able to make the four letters named. After that, when I met with any boy who I knew could write, I would tell him I could write as well as he. The next word would be, "I don't believe you. Let me see you try it." I would then make the letters which I had been so fortunate as to learn, and ask him to beat that. In this way I got a good many lessons in writing, which it is quite possible I should never have gotten in any other way. During this time, my copy-book was the board fence, brick wall, and pavement; my pen

Reading

and ink was a lump of chalk. With these, I learned mainly how to write. I then commenced and continued copying the Italics in Webster's Spelling Book, until I could make them all without looking on the book. By this time, my little Master Thomas had gone to school, and learned how to write, and had written over a number of copy-books. These had been brought home, and shown to some of our near neighbors, and then laid aside. My mistress used to go to class meeting at the Wilk Street meeting-house every Monday afternoon, and leave me to take care of the house. When left thus, I used to spend the time in writing in the spaces left in Master Thomas's copy-book, copying what he had written. I continued to do this until I could write a hand very similar to that of Master Thomas.

Thus, after a long, tedious effort for years, I finally succeeded in learning how to write.

ACTIVITY: Analyzing the Rhetorical Situation
Frederick Douglass, Learning to Read and Write

1. To what opportunity is the author responding?
2. Who is the audience for his response? In other words, what was the work's original purpose? What is his main point? What does the author want you to do with the information?
3. Do you find the author a trustworthy authority on this topic? How does he establish his credibility (ethos)? What does the author know about these issues?
4. How does the author employ logic and reason (logos) to structure his essay? What evidence does the author use to support his point? Do you find his reasons convincing? Does he provide sufficient evidence to persuade you? What are the overall strengths and weaknesses of Douglass's essay?
5. Does the author make an authentic emotional connection (pathos) with his audience?
6. How effective is his choice of a mix of genres—memoir, position argument, evaluation, critical analysis—and the use of print to deliver his message? How might he have used other media to effectively deliver his message?

≫ SUMMARY

summary a type of writing that condenses a selection to its main points

Now that you have carefully read the text and answered all of the questions, try to summarize the essay. A **summary** condenses the main points of a piece to represent its message objectively. Summary writing forces you to engage with the text closely, enhances your memory of it, and helps you understand it. When writing a summary, it is crucial that you understand the hierarchy of information in the original text, identifying the thesis statement, the major points, the supporting evidence and details, and the concluding thoughts. When you are reading for information, you are playing the Believing Game. Whether or not you actually agree with the text is beside the point. In your summary, you will show that you have understood the main point of Douglass's essay. Summaries are short—but they are powerful. In college, you will find summaries (sometimes referred to as **abstracts**) at the beginning of research articles, in conference programs, and on book jackets. You will also be required to write them. The following summary is one example of how to condense the Douglass essay into one paragraph, taking care to include information from the introduction, the body, and the conclusion to identify his thesis and supporting evidence to show a full understanding of Douglass's argument.

Reading

> **The idea as to how Douglass might learn to read and write was suggested to him by being in Durgin and Bailey's shipyard, where he watched ship carpenters marking pieces of timber according to which part of the ship each was intended. By observation and practice, he learned to make the letters L, S, F, and A. Douglass would then bet any white boy who knew how to write that he could write as well as the white boy, a contest that led to the white boy teaching Douglass even more letters. The boys practiced on fences, walls, and pavement, using pieces of chalk. Soon, Douglass took his skills indoors, where he practiced with Master Thomas's school books, including his copy-book, where Douglass spent his spare time "writing in the spaces left." After years of such effort, Douglass finally learned how to read and write.**

abstracts brief objective summaries of articles, especially used in writing papers for the social sciences

Douglass uses process analysis, based on his shipyard observations, to support the thesis. He uses description to emphasize his point. And he uses cause-and-effect analysis to demonstrate how his practices led to his learning how to read and write. (See CHAPTER 15, PROCESS ANALYSIS, DESCRIPTION, and CAUSE-AND-EFFECT ANALYSIS for more on rhetorical strategies for development.)

pages 280–281 and 286–291

Now condense the essay into one sentence. The following is a sample of a one-sentence summary of Douglass's essay.

By tapping his natural engagement, creativity, and persistence,

Frederick Douglass was able to learn how to read and write.

» CRITICAL RESPONSE

When you read critically, you show that you know how to play the Doubting Game, questioning, agreeing, and talking back to the text. You may be in full agreement with the author, but you are, nevertheless, nudging and prodding the text in order to reveal the rhetorical situation from which it was composed, sent, and received:

- when, where, and how the rhetorical exchange takes place;
- the writer's credibility;
- the appropriateness of the message in terms of both content and delivery; and
- the connection the writer makes with the audience.

critical response a reaction in writing to a text that explains why you agree or disagree with the text

Whether you are reading or writing, your task in a **critical response** is to summarize the main point of the work and then explain your reaction to it. *Critical* does not mean negative. It does mean prioritizing your comments, establishing patterns in the text, and remaining civil if not positive. In a critical response you need to react to the text—explaining why you agree or disagree (wholly or partly) with a particular point the text is making—but it is more important to support your reaction with strong reasons based on the evidence from the text itself than it is to agree or disagree. Include the title of the work, anchor your response in a thesis statement that shows how or why you think the author got it right (or wrong), and then support that thesis with evidence from the original text itself. A sample thesis for a critical response to the Douglass essay follows.

Example of critical response thesis that disagrees with Douglass

> Frederick Douglass's memories of how he learned to read and write seem romantic and easy, not authentic or replete with problems.

Example of critical response thesis that agrees with Douglass

> Frederick Douglass's *Narrative* provides an inspiring story for teachers, parents, and their school-age children who need examples of authentic, independent learning.

»» ANALYSIS AND SYNTHESIS

Your role as a college-level reader and writer includes understanding, interpreting, contextualizing, questioning, and analyzing the material you read, some of it complex, challenging, even contradictory. Two of the most valuable intellectual skills you can develop are analysis and synthesis, which will sustain you throughout college—and beyond. You conduct **analysis** when you break something down into its constituent parts or elements, critically examining each part so that you understand it, just as you did when you annotated the Douglass essay. You use analytical skills when you determine the main point in a summary and as you respond to a text, both by analyzing the rhetorical situation and by determining how well the writer has used the available means of persuasion. Your analysis will provide a reliable basis of discussion or interpretation. **Synthesis**, you will be happy to know, is a natural outgrowth of analysis. With synthesis, you combine those separate, already analyzed parts or ideas into a coherent whole, creatively producing a new thesis, theory, or understanding. Both of these skills are valuable, with analysis preparing you to conduct synthesis, and synthesis preparing you to research, discuss, converse, and interpret both responsibly and knowledgeably.

analysis a breaking down of a text into its constituent parts accompanied by a critical examination of the ways the text responds to the rhetorical situation

synthesis an examination of how the individual parts of a text or different points of view from different texts fit together and diverge to bring a new perspective to the whole work

Managing the Complexities of Reading

No longer are you learning by rote or by memorization. In the process of reading deeply and widely you very often encounter conflicting information, wildly different viewpoints about an issue. Very often, your reading for class or for a research project requires that you encounter conflicting information. Perhaps two authors disagree, perhaps one study contradicts another, or perhaps your own experience provides evidence counter to another author's thesis. You may also have found flaws in the reasoning or gaps in the evidence. Look closely at these areas of complex tension, because they indicate your growing ability to read critically and to analyze an issue from many dimensions—historically, contextually, socially, politically, personally. Recognizing such complexity as you read also signals your ability to imagine alternative solutions, approaches, and opinions. You have moved beyond the simplistic "right-or-wrong" thinking and are moving into the complex world of more adult problem-solving. Such complex tension can provide a rhetorical opportunity and a purpose for your reading and your writing. It may also find its way into your thesis statement, surely into the body of your argument. One thing is for certain: when your own audience realizes that you have considered multiple viewpoints, including theirs, they are more likely to consider your argument.

Reading to Synthesize Ideas

Twentieth-century rhetorician Kenneth Burke calls our need to engage with others the "unending conversation," urging each of us to "put in our oar":

> Imagine that you enter a parlor. You come late. When you arrive, others have long preceded you, and they are engaged in a heated discussion, a discussion too heated for them to pause and tell you exactly what it is about. . . . You listen for a while, until you decide that you have caught the tenor of the argument; then you put in your oar.

> —Kenneth Burke, *The Philosophy of Literary Form*
> [Put In Your Oar]

Writers are "putting in their oars" when they enter an ongoing "conversation" on a topic. Sometimes you may know a fair amount about the topic that you have been asked to examine, but, chances are, you will encounter new topics in college that you do not know much about yet. In those instances when you are asked to read just one author's contribution to a conversation, it helps to familiarize yourself with what others have said.

The synthesis question

The best synthesis essays often grow out of an author's discomfort with the current positions on the topic. Such discomfort serves as a rhetorical opportunity, a problem for the author to address or resolve. Often, that discomfort is translated into a **synthesis (or critical) question**, one question that directs, focuses, and launches your research. Douglass, for instance, asks how deliberately uneducated slaves could possibly learn how to read and write.

synthesis (or critical) question the question that directs, focuses, and launches your research

> I soon learned the names of these letters, and for what they were intended when placed upon a piece of timber in the ship-yard. I immediately commenced copying them, and in a short time was able to make the four letters named. After that, when I met with any boy who I knew could write, I would tell him that I could write as well as he. The next word would be, "I don't believe you. Let me see you try." I would then make the letters which I had been so fortunate as to learn, and ask him to beat that. In this way I got a good many lessons in writing, which it is quite possible I should never have gotten in any other way.

> —Frederick Douglass, *Narrative of the Life of Frederick Douglass, An American Slave* [Learning to Read and Write]

The synthesis process

Critical analysis and synthesis—as reading and writing strategies as well as intellectual skills—are crucial when you consult various sources. You will need to analyze them (their agreements, disagreements, and contradictions), synthesize their research, and then establish your own stance toward the topic. (See also CHAPTER 21: SYNTHESIZING SOURCES: SUMMARY, PARAPHRASE, AND QUOTATION.) Sometimes, your instructor will provide you with a topic. More often, however, you will be expected to come up with a topic of your own, a topic that interests you enough to spend time researching, thinking, and writing about it. The following representative studies offer a set of complex tensions around the vast research on literacy development. Successful synthesis writing relies on several steps.

1. Identify a problem to address or resolve.
2. Review the articles and books you have read (the scholarly conversation) pertaining to the problem. Critically analyze and summarize the strongest voices in the conversation.
3. Prepare to enter that conversation with your own view.
4. Offer a synthesis question that quickly turns into a thesis statement as a way to contribute to what has already been said about the topic.
5. Combine ideas from the research you have read and your experiences at the same time you forward your thesis.

pages 395–411

Read through the following selections on literacy to get a general idea of who the author is, what the author's relation to the topic is, and what the author's main point is. In the first selection, renowned educator Lisa Delpit describes how teachers can best develop their students'—every student's—repertoire of literacies:

> **Teachers need to support the language that students bring to school, provide them input from an additional code, and give them the opportunity to use the new code in a nonthreatening, real communicative context. Some teachers accomplish this goal by having groups of students create bidialectal dictionaries of their own language form and Standard English. Others have had students become involved with standard forms through various kinds of role-play. For example, memorizing parts for drama productions will allow students to "get the feel" of speaking Standard English while not under the threat of correction. Young students can create puppet shows or role-play cartoon characters. (Many "superheroes" speak almost hypercorrect Standard English!) Playing a role eliminates the possibility**

of implying that the *child's* language is inadequate, and suggests, instead, that different language forms are appropriate in different contexts. Some other teachers in New York City have had their students produce a news show every day for the rest of the school. The students take on the persona of some famous newscaster, keeping in character as they develop and read their news reports. Discussions ensue about whether Walter Cronkite [a renowned, highly trusted news anchor from the 1970s] would have said it that way, again taking the focus off the child's speech.

—Lisa Delpit, *Other People's Children* [Codes]

In his memoir about moving from being accidentally misplaced in the vocational track, back to the college-prep track (where he was woefully behind), then on to college and his professional career, Mike Rose thanks four professors from his small Catholic college for his stunning turn in literacy:

Those four men collectively gave me the best sort of liberal education, the kind longed for in the stream of blue-ribbon reports on the humanities that now cross my desk. I developed the ability to read closely, to persevere in the face of uncertainty and ask questions of what I was reading—not with downcast eyes, but freely, aloud, realizing there is no such thing as an open book. My teachers modeled critical inquiry and linguistic precision and grace, and they provided various cognitive maps for philosophy and history and literature. They encouraged me to make connections and to enter into conversations— present and past—to see what talking a particular kind of talk would enable me to do with a thorny philosophical problem or a difficult literacy text. And it was all alive. It transpired in backyards and on doorsteps and inside offices as well as in the classroom. I could smell their tobacco and see the nicks left by their razors They liked books and ideas, and they liked to talk about them in ways that fostered growth rather than established dominance. They lived their knowledge. And maybe because of that their knowledge grew in me in ways that led back out to the world. I was developing a set of tools with which to shape a life.

—Mike Rose, *Lives on the Boundary* [Reading Closely]

Working at the scholarly intersection of the humanities and literacy studies, scholar Richard A. Lanham argues that developing a range of styles is the best way to develop academic literacies and should be a "central rather than a peripheral part of undergraduate education":

This study of style is the study of a whole range of human behavior, and an essential one if we are to feel ourselves whole. To think about style in this evolutionary way is to envisage it as itself a core curriculum in miniature, providing on a smaller scale the oscillation between serious and rhetorical worlds that we are talking about. To think in this way suggests that, in embryo at least, a dynamic core curriculum *already* exists on campus—in the composition course. . . .

Composition provides both the most expedient and the most logical place to begin the reconstruction of the undergraduate curriculum. . . . The reason we think a training in prose style is so important is that, in its rhythms of writing and revising, it models the oscillation from central to social self. . . . Here exactly lies its "humanizing" function. Good teachers build their patterns into their teaching whatever the curriculum. . . .

The writing course thus forms the perfect introduction to whatever course or courses we assign the function of making the "core" clear, giving the undergraduate students their curricular compass. . . . Above all, it allows, indeed encourages, the fullest scope to both the teacher's way of teaching and the student's way of learning.

—**Richard A. Lanham,** *Literacy and the Survival of Humanism*
[The Study of Style]

Read through the preceding perspectives on literacy once again. What, for instance, is Delpit asking of her audience? What about Rose and Lanham? Reading critically means analyzing the text in order to understand the context in which the author is composing a message. Crucial to that understanding is knowing about the ongoing conversation that the message is entering. After all, few of us can work alone—we converse with others and read others' writing to learn information and to get things done. Either annotate the selections or take notes, answering the following questions.

- What do all the authors have in common?
- What question (or problem) are they each trying to address?
- How is each author's point of view distinctive?
- How do they differ? How do their differences align?
- What resources, expertise, experience, and/or knowledge are these authors leveraging? Or is the lack of any of those features the author's biggest constraint?
- Using your answers from the preceding questions, briefly describe (or synthesize) the various views—and stances—that people have toward literacy, illiteracy, or literacy development. Share your answer with the rest of the class.
- Now describe the (tentative) position you might take in the scholarly conversation about any of these issues. Write it out—and share it.

Depending on your own experience with issues of literacy—as a student, a classmate, a family member, or a consultant or aide—you may think of literacy in ways different from your classmates, and you may think the causes of literacy or illiteracy are many and varied. Despite different attitudes toward literacy (as the previous three excerpts demonstrate), what everyone seems to agree on is that "literacy" (however it is defined) enhances the development of our individual selves as well as our role as social beings.

 ASSIGNMENT

The Synthesis (or Research) Essay

Whether you are reading for a class or for a research project—in literature, history, psychology, or anthropology—you will want to familiarize yourself with what others have said about a topic (the scholarly conversation). (For more on research projects, see PART 4, A GUIDE TO RESEARCH.)

page 350

- Choose two sources on a topic that interests you. What do each of these sources have to say about the topic? Where do they agree—or not?
- Blend (or synthesize) their ideas in order to create a synthesis question, one that responds to the rhetorical opportunity or problem these sources present.
- Create a thesis that shows how these sources are different, what their areas of tension are, and what your position is toward the information in these sources.
- Analyze the rhetorical situation and use of available means of persuasion in these sources.
- Conclude with points of similarity.

4 Rhetorical Success in a Digital World

LEARNING OBJECTIVES

- Analyze how medium affects message and influences audiences.
- Evaluate advantages (resources) and limitations (constraints) related to various multimedia genres.
- Explain your purpose in choosing a particular medium.
- Articulate your message in that digital medium.

You are the generation that has always had access to the World Wide Web for your academic, social, and work needs. Yet, it is just this immersion in an increasingly digital and visual culture that requires you to pay careful attention to the information you might otherwise simply take for granted. In CHAPTER 2, you explored the principles of persuasion. Those same principles can be applied to the use of **multimedia** (images or visuals, text, audio, and video) in compositions. In this chapter, then, you will learn to consider how the constituent elements of a multimedia (also referred to as *multimodal*) composition work separately and together to convey a persuasive message.

pages 18–33

multimedia images or visuals, text, audio, and video used in combinations in a composition

»» THINKING RHETORICALLY ABOUT MULTIMEDIA TEXTS

Multimedia compositions can be as simple as using a flip chart with your speech, and adding tables and graphs to your essay, or as digitally complex as creating websites and PowerPoint presentations that include a range of embedded media. Whether you choose an audio recording with words and music (a podcast), a video (like Snapchat), still images, live conversation (Zoom or Skype, for instance), or a written text (Twitter, a blog, an online application), your medium or combination of media affects your message and your audience. As you know well, when composing is done in digital environments, the boundaries among the different media begin to blur. Nearly all major platforms allow you to add text, as a caption or on top of the image you are sending and receiving. For instance, Instagram, Foursquare, and Snapchat allow you to layer images (you can add filters or accents to your photo: you can add an angel halo to a picture of your baby cousin). Of course, you can respond to messages with text, but Instagram makes it easy to respond with an emoji (sending a heart to a picture of a beautiful bird). Such "layers" are not merely additions; the images/text/sound interact with one another to craft a specific message for your rhetorical audience. The decisions of which media to prioritize are rhetorical too: there is a difference between posting a thumbs up emoji and writing, "I agree! That movie didn't need a sequel." Knowing how and when to mix and blur the lines among media is an important rhetorical skill.

All these digital and print technologies offer opportunities for you to enhance your message as well as adapt it for an audience who might not otherwise have access to it. To organize multimedia elements, such as images or sounds, multimedia designers pay attention to the elements of the rhetorical situation—opportunity, audience, purpose—and apply the same rhetorical principles you use when writing an essay or drafting a speech: principles of design, style, persuasion, and delivery. The best composers, whether working with multimedia or a single form, take their rhetorical situation into consideration as they shape a message:

- Who is the source?
- What is the opportunity for change?
- What is the purpose?
- Who is the intended audience, and what is the author's relationship to the audience?
- Why has the author chosen this genre or medium?
- How effective is the medium of delivery in reaching the rhetorical audience?

ACTIVITY: Analyzing the Rhetorical Situation
Reading a Visual Text for Rhetorical Opportunity

Whether you are reading an essay, listening to a speech, communicating over Zoom, or looking at a visual, you'll understand the message better if you begin by determining the rhetorical opportunity that calls for specific words or visuals. Very often, the responses you are reading or viewing call for even further responses. Whether your response is spoken, written, or composed visually, its power lies in your understanding of the rhetorical opportunity. Consider the Callout Card here and the ways it addresses the problem of electronic harassment (Figure 4.1). This card may well be an effective response to a rhetorical opportunity for change. Obviously, the sender of "David, wrapped in a towel" does not want to receive visuals that are "naughty," maybe even pornographic. Studying this image and text as a rhetorical response helps you analyze it rhetorically and "read" it more thoroughly than you might have otherwise.

1. *Who composed this message?* Consider what you know or can find out about the groups responsible for the message: the Family Violence Prevention Fund, the Office on Violence Against Women, and the Ad Council for the website Thatsnotcool.com.

2. *What is the rhetorical opportunity that called for the creation of this visual?* Using the information you have compiled in response to the previous questions, identify the opportunity that calls for this visual response.

3. *How does the visual respond to the opportunity?* What message does this visual send to viewers? How might this visual work to address the problem of electronic harassment? It might help to keep in mind that Callout Cards can also be shared through e-mail or Facebook.

THATSNOTCOOL.COM

Figure 4.1 *This Callout Card, available at Thatsnotcool. com, is a visual response to a rhetorical opportunity.*

Sponsored and co-created by the Family Violence Prevention Fund, the Office on Violence Against Women, and the Ad council.

»» DESIGNING MULTIMEDIA TEXTS TO PERSUADE

Writers organize words into sentences and paragraphs that establish coherence, develop ideas, and achieve their purpose, just as multimedia designers structure the visual, verbal, and sound elements of their texts to do the same. In addition, multimedia compositions provide resources (images, videos, music, web links, and audio) to strengthen their message. In so doing, multimedia texts use the same rhetorical appeals of ethos, logos, and pathos that were discussed in CHAPTER 2.

pages 23–26

- **Ethos** How you establish your credibility in a multimedia composition includes creating images that have not been "doctored" to create a false impression and using design elements, such as fonts (see the box on Font Styles), that are appropriate for your message. As you know, a polished composition—whether written, spoken, or recorded—is always important in establishing your ethos.
- **Logos** Logos, the logical appeal of your response to a rhetorical situation, lies in the (literal) shape—or arrangement—of the argument of your multimedia text. The arrangement and layout should logically highlight the most important elements. Infographics, such as tables and charts, also condense information visually to support an argument.
- **Pathos** Advertisements are often pathos-driven, but any image or design element that is used to make an emotional connection appeals to pathos, as do colors that draw on your emotion and graphic images. (See, for example, Figure 4.15, an image of the COVID-19 first responders who do not have the personal protective equipment they need.)

fonts styles of print type

serif fonts with foot-like tips on the ends of letters

sans serif fonts with no serifs on the ends of the letters

layout the way words and images are positioned in relation to each other on a page

white space blank areas around text, graphics, or images

Multimedia texts purposefully (and often persuasively) design words in a particular font style and size and use color, layout and arrangement, images, and often sound as a means of capturing a particular mood, delivering a specific message, or provoking a specific action. Review the elements of design that follow and see how these elements work together in the Pink Ribbon website on page 54.

- **Fonts** Styles of print type, called **fonts**, are composition's most basic visual element. **Serif** fonts (with those little foot-like tips, called *serifs*, on the ends of some letter strokes), such as Times New Roman, make reading printed documents easier. **Sans serif** fonts such as Verdana (with no serifs on the ends of the strokes) have become the standard for websites, making online reading easier.

FONT STYLES

Fonts (styles of print type) can enhance or detract from the effectiveness of your message. For example, many advertisements and nearly all websites use clean, professional-looking, and audience-friendly fonts like Verdana, Arial, or Helvetica. Informal and light-hearted documents, on the other hand, might use Comic Sans. Among the serif fonts, mostly used for professional communications, Bookman Old Style is considered the "most trustworthy" of fonts.

Curlz	
Papyrus	
Bookman Old Style	
Arial	
Typewriter	Futura
Baskerville	Comic Sans
Garamond	Helvetica
Mrs. Eaves	Avenir
Walbaum	Neutraface
Archer	Verdana

- **Color** Color should be used for both emphasis and visual balance. Most designers recommend using no more than three main colors in your multimedia document design, although you may use varying intensities or shades of the same color to connect related materials (see Figure 4.2).
- **Arrangement** The organizational pattern of visual, verbal, and sound (if used) elements of your composition creates a hierarchy of information that makes obvious which information is most important and which is less so.
- **Layout** The **layout** helps readers scan and yet absorb large amounts of information quickly, using position, size, and **white space** (blank areas

© MariyaF/Shutterstock.com

Figure 4.2 *Bright, noticeable colors, such as yellow and red, can be used to emphasize a point or idea, even danger or emergency.*

Because we read from left to right and from top to bottom, the top left corner is often the first place we look. The PinkRibbon.org website uses that space for a logo; as a result, the organization's promotional materials are always prominent on the website.

The PinkRibbon.org website uses a subtle gray as a secondary color to balance the thematic pink menu and highlights. Shades of pink and gray project femininity and calmness in the home page.

The image of a perfectly manicured hand, a live flower, and freshly cut grass communicates vitality and connects perfectly with the headline, "Let's live together."

The hierarchy of information is clear in the layout with a prominent focus on the large banner urging readers to "Donate Now."

Although "Donate Now" and "Support Us" appear just under this image and headline, the emphasis on what readers can do for Pink Ribbon quickly balances with what Pink Ribbon can do for readers: "Pink Ribbon is very interested in your opinion" and "Welcome." The "Quick Poll" and "Welcome" sections invite the audience into the site and emphasize the major claim of living together.

Shorter chunks of text, in conjunction with that main image, help the audience focus on the important elements of the site. The additional text is kept in small, contained blocks to make it easy for the audience to scan and absorb large amounts of information quickly.

Figure 4.3 *Pink Ribbon International home page.*

Visual headings highlight major ideas ("Forum," "Blog," "Calendar," and "Shop"), helping the audience scan the webpage.

Most websites use images to break up large blocks of text, just as Pink Ribbon does with the image-heavy attention to the thesis: "Let's live together."

Not only does the website allow easy access to information about breast cancer, but it does so using links to a forum, a blog, and a calendar.

around blocks of text or around graphics or images) to identify the most important information.

- **Images** Whether still or moving, images tell a story. Images can bring in characters, dialogue, plot, setting, and theme. Culturally significant images draw on visual symbols (for example, the eagle as a symbol for freedom).
- **Sound** Sonic elements, too, enhance your message. Consider the solemn, stately soundtrack that complements *Parasite,* the fascinatingly new-yet-familiar score of *The Mandalorian,* the lively musical score that brings to life the upbeat plot of *Frozen* and *Frozen 2,* and the nostalgia-drenched musical displays throughout *Once Upon a Time in Hollywood.*

When organizations like Pink Ribbon International decide to use online multimedia, their web designers and content suppliers choose purposefully from a seemingly infinite assortment of images, texts, and layouts. Pink Ribbon International's home page (see Figure 4.3) balances text and images to help its audience absorb information quickly, using a layout that helps readers immediately identify the most important information. Visual headings aid readers as they quickly scroll through the site. (Remember that most people do not linger over a webpage the way they might over a book page.) The organization also takes care to use inviting, easy-to-read sans serif fonts that have proved to be visually effective and taken seriously on web pages, again demonstrating an awareness of the best way to engage and reach its rhetorical audience. The simplicity of the font allows the sincere message to take precedence. As a fundraising organization, Pink Ribbon International needs to solicit donations—a focus made prominent on its website. A visitor to the site is likely to notice immediately the large banner urging readers to "Donate Now."

ACTIVITY: Analyzing the Rhetorical Situation
Using Design to Create Emotional Connection

As mentioned above, the pinks and grays of the PinkRibbon.org website home page echo the name of the site itself, connect with the feminine, and soften the horrors of cancer. The Santa Fe, New Mexico, website (Figure 4.4) uses brown and blue, no doubt intending to conjure up images of the browns of the surrounding mountains and adobe architecture and the blues of turquoise jewelry and the stunning northern New Mexico skies. Browns convey comfort and dependability, while blues express honesty and loyalty. Such colors connect easily with potential visitors to Santa Fe.

Multimedia

Figure 4.4 *Santa Fe travel website.*

Analyze the Santa Fe travel website. As an in-class writing exercise or a formal assignment, produce a composition that responds to the following questions:

1. To what opportunity for change is the author responding?
2. How is the situation or phenomenon described?
3. How does this situation or phenomenon affect the audience? Who is the audience?
4. What is the author's purpose?
5. Identify the thesis statement or major claim.
6. How does the author establish ethos? Where in the presentation is logos confirmed? How does the author make an authentic emotional connection with the audience (pathos)?
7. How do images support or advance the thesis? What about the colors? And sonic (sound) elements?
8. Is there any kind of conclusion? In other words, what does the author want you to take away from the multimodal document in terms of information, attitude, or action?

»» HOW IMAGES TELL A STORY

Ours is a visually intense environment of photographs, magazines, graphic novels, Facebook (and other social media sites, including dating sites), Pinterest, Etsy, Instagram, TikTok, television, movies, YouTube, and other media. Whether consciously or unconsciously, we respond to visual culture in the same ways we respond to print. We sense the rhetorical appeals of ethos (trustworthiness), logos (logic), and pathos (emotional connection) conveyed by the key features of visual representation: point of view, focal point, characters, setting, color and alignment, and visual references that are culturally significant. Such visuals are often accompanied by sound (voices, music, nature, noise) that enhance or detract from the effectiveness of these rhetorical appeals. Images make use of these key features to tell a story and create a dominant impression, with or without sound. As you analyze images, look at how these key features work together to create an immediate overall effect and ask yourself: What story does the image tell? What am I supposed to take away from it?

Multimedia

- **Point of View** Point of view is the **angle of vision** used to create an image. The image might be seen from eye level, from above (bird's eye view) or below (worm's eye view) (see Figure 4.5). It might be a close-up or a panoramic view from a distance. The point of view creates drama, frames the image, and leads your eye to the central focus of the image.
- **Focal Point** The focus (person, place, product, or activity) is the center of activity or attention in the image.
- **Cropping**—where parts of an image are edited out of the overall image—might be used to help draw the viewer's attention to what is central and create more visual drama. For any image, ask yourself these questions: What holds the central image? What might it signify?
- **Characters** The objects that are represented in an image work together in the same way that characters work together in a novel. The main character is the focal point. Other objects around the focal point bring in harmony or discord. When determining the story, ask yourself these questions: What are the specific parts (background, objects, activity, people) of the visual? How are they arranged? How are these parts pieced together? In other words, how does the author draw the viewer to the focus?
- **Setting** The way objects and people are arranged, the lighting, and a contrast in color or sizes work together to create the setting in the image. The setting can identify the time and place for the image and contribute to the mood created by the image. When analyzing an image, ask yourself these questions: What might be the significance of the background, especially in relationship to any text? What about colors? What mood or feeling do the colors convey? How do the visual elements contrast in terms of color, size, or lighting?
- **Cultural Signs** Cultural signs include symbols and significant cultural references, such as costumes or historical references. Some are obvious, such as the traditional skull-and-crossbones symbol for danger and thumbs up and down for approval and disapproval, while others are implied, such as a happy face that indicates approval. The happy face is just one of hundreds in the ever-expanding catalogue of emojis.
- **Sound** Voices, music, nature, and noise can all be used to enhance the visual presentation, whether they indicate suspense, resolution, joy, disaster, or character.

angle of vision the position of the camera in relation to the image

cropping the process of editing an image to draw the viewer's attention to the focal point

© Lynn Wohlers

Figure 4.5 *Photographer Lynn Wohlers describes point of view as the "creative stance you take when you shoot." This close-up creates drama through an unusual angle on plants emerging from the soil.*

ACTIVITY: Analyzing the Rhetorical Situation
Visuals

We respond to visuals by making judgments about the overall quality, strengths and weaknesses, characters, setting, as well as any measure of dialogue, plot, or theme. Examine the photograph of the wildfires that scourged the Australian forests (see Figure 4.6). Evaluate its effectiveness in telling a story, the power of the visual representation itself, and how well the design elements work together to create a dominant impression. What story is the photograph trying to tell?

1. Who or what holds the central position in the photograph? To what significance?
2. What is the significance of the setting?
3. What are the cultural symbols or references?
4. What might the "plot" of the visual be?
5. How credible is the visual in terms of plot, characters, setting? In what ways are any of these features "doctored"?
6. How well does the photographer establish ethos, logos, and pathos?
7. What is the overall effect of this photograph? What action, attitude, or belief are you being asked to consider, maybe even to change?

Illonajalll/ShutterStock.com

Figure 4.6 *Nearly sixteen million acres burned and one billion wildlife died during the 2019–2020 Australian bush fires.*

⟫ INFOGRAPHICS

Whether yours is a print-only text with a thesis and well-supported and purposefully ordered assertions or a multimodal composition that includes words, images, and sounds that advance and support a claim, the arrangement of information in your composition affects how reasonable your argument appears to your audience (logos). Many documents—print and multimodal— include **infographics**—images, tables, charts, pie charts, and figures that condense statistics, facts, and other information into a persuasive visual representation that helps support your argument. Infographics such as those included here, the 2021 Federal Budget (Figure 4.7) and "Protecting Our Planet" from the National Oceanic and Atmospheric Administration (Figure 4.8), are densely packed with information about a single topic yet clearly arranged, with words and visuals that are large enough to comprehend. Easy to read and easy to understand, infographics present detailed information quickly and clearly.

infographics
images, tables, charts, pie charts, and figures that condense information into a visual presentation

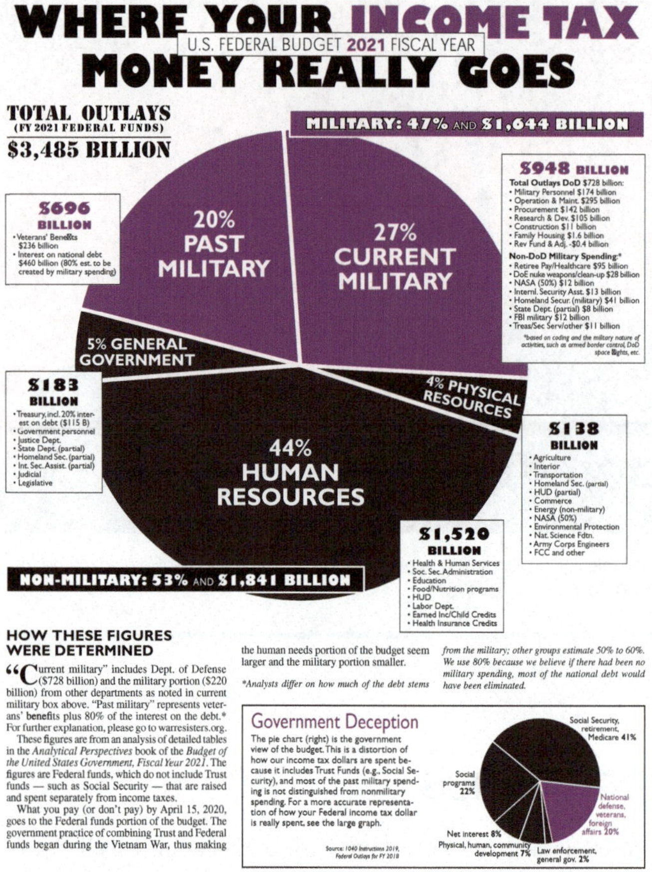

WHERE YOUR INCOME TAX MONEY REALLY GOES

U.S. FEDERAL BUDGET 2021 FISCAL YEAR

TOTAL OUTLAYS
(FY 2021 FEDERAL FUNDS)
$3,485 BILLION

MILITARY: 47% AND $1,644 BILLION

$948 BILLION
Total Outlays DoD $728 billion:
• Military Personnel $174 billion
• Operation & Maint. $295 billion
• Procurement $142 billion
• Research & Dev. $105 billion
• Construction $11 billion
• Family Housing $1.6 billion
• Rev Fund & Adj. -$0.4 billion
Non-DoD Military Spending:*
• Retiree Pay/Healthcare $95 billion
• DoE nuke weapons/clean-up $28 billion
• NASA (50%) $12 billion
• Interntl. Security Asst. $13 billion
• Homeland Secur. (military) $41 billion
• State Dept. (partial) $8 billion
• FBI military $12 billion
• Treas/Sec Serv/other $11 billion
*based on coding and the military nature of activities, such as armed border control, DoD space flights, etc.

$696 BILLION
• Veterans' Benefits $236 billion
• Interest on national debt $460 billion (80% est. to be created by military spending)

20% PAST MILITARY

27% CURRENT MILITARY

5% GENERAL GOVERNMENT

$183 BILLION
• Treasury, incl. 20% interest on debt ($115 B)
• Government personnel
• Justice Dept.
• State Dept. (partial)
• Homeland Sec. (partial)
• Int. Sec. Assist. (partial)
• Judicial
• Legislative

4% PHYSICAL RESOURCES

44% HUMAN RESOURCES

$138 BILLION
• Agriculture
• Interior
• Transportation
• Homeland Sec. (partial)
• HUD (partial)
• Commerce
• Energy (non-military)
• NASA (50%)
• Environmental Protection
• Nat. Science Fdtn.
• Army Corps Engineers
• FCC and other

$1,520 BILLION
• Health & Human Services
• Soc. Sec. Administration
• Education
• Food/Nutrition programs
• HUD
• Labor Dept.
• Earned Inc/Child Credits
• Health Insurance Credits

NON-MILITARY: 53% AND $1,841 BILLION

HOW THESE FIGURES WERE DETERMINED

"Current military" includes Dept. of Defense ($728 billion) and the military portion ($220 billion) from other departments as noted in current military box above. "Past military" represents veterans' **benefits** plus 80% of the interest on the debt.*
For further explanation, please go to warresisters.org.

These figures are from an analysis of detailed tables in the *Analytical Perspectives* book of the *Budget of the United States Government, Fiscal Year 2021*. The figures are Federal funds, which do not include Trust funds — such as Social Security — that are raised and spent separately from income taxes.

What you pay (or don't pay) by April 15, 2020, goes to the Federal funds portion of the budget. The government practice of combining Trust and Federal funds began during the Vietnam War, thus making the human needs portion of the budget seem larger and the military portion smaller.

*Analysts differ on how much of the debt stems from the military; other groups estimate 50% to 60%. We use 80% because we believe if there had been no military spending, most of the national debt would have been eliminated.

Government Deception

The pie chart (right) is the government view of the budget. This is a distortion of how our income tax dollars are spent because it includes Trust Funds (e.g. Social Security), and most of the past military spending is not distinguished from nonmilitary spending. For a more accurate representation of how your Federal income tax dollar is really spent, see the large graph.

Source: 1040 Instructions 2019, Federal Outlays for FY 2018

Social Security, retirement, Medicare 41%
Social programs 22%
National defense, veterans, foreign affairs 20%
Net interest 8%
Physical, human, community development 7%
Law enforcement, general gov. 2%

Figure 4.7 *The U.S. Federal Budget in 2021 is explained in an infographic that includes two simple pie charts.*
Source: The War Resisters League's famous "pie chart" flyer, *Where Your Income Tax Money Really Goes*

≫ CONSIDERING AUDIENCE, PURPOSE, AND ACCESSIBILITY IN MULTIMEDIA COMPOSITIONS

Your design decisions as well as your choice of media (your means of communicating orally, visually, verbally, digitally, or in print) usually depend on the rhetorical situation itself: What media do you know how to use? What media can your audience easily access? What media will most effectively deliver your purposeful message to your audience? If your purpose is to address or resolve the opportunity for change, then you must find ways to ensure that your purposeful message reaches its destination.

When thinking about issues of audience, especially on sites like Facebook, consider the complicated nature of who exactly constitutes your audience in such a public, online forum. Even though the primary audience for your Facebook profile might be your friends, anyone with a Facebook account can become part of your audience unless you have carefully adjusted your privacy settings. Having such a large potential audience is not necessarily bad—unless you are unaware of it. After all, social networking sites can be effective tools for announcing information, stimulating collaborations, and celebrating achievements you think are important.

Accessibility is also a rhetorical issue: the medium of delivery influences what parts of your message an audience ultimately sees and hears. Not everyone will be able to stream videos or download podcasts and audiobooks. Some people might be browsing from a smartphone or a netbook; others might be using an older computer that lacks the memory capacity to deal with large video or audio downloads. Still others (grandparents, perhaps) may have no interest in learning how to do so. People with physical disabilities will face their own challenges with regard to seeing, hearing, or manipulating the keyboards necessary for full access to various media. Therefore, when you begin designing a multimedia composition

accessibility in rhetoric, the extent to which a message is designed to be easy to read by those with disabilities that affect seeing, hearing, and manipulating a particular medium

Multimedia

Figure 4.8 *This infographic from the National Oceanic and Atmospheric Administration quickly provides ten things you can do to protect the earth, all of which support the thesis, "Protecting Our Planet Starts with You."*
Source: From oceanservice.noaa.gov, The National Oceanic and Atmospheric Administration

such as a website, you should consider what information is accessible to which people in what ways. Your delivery choices determine not only who constitutes your audience but also how your audience experiences your composition.

A Rhetorical Approach to Social Networks as a Medium of Delivery

Although you probably do not consciously think of the rhetorical principles of design, style, persuasion, and delivery each time you tweet or update your Facebook, Match.com, or Instagram status, these principles are always at work—otherwise, you would not use the "edit" button when you wanted to make improvements on your social media page.

The success of Instagram, for instance, with its over one billion followers, can be credited to the brilliant implementation of rhetorical principles by so many of its contributors, many of whom add SuperZoom, Boomerang, Rewind, and Stickers to their photo-with-text posts. Instagram is an international phenomenon, with the most popular Instagram account held by Portuguese footballer Cristiano Ronaldo, who has 211 million followers, and the second most popular by American singer Ariana Grande, with 180 million followers. But established famous people are not the only ones with Instagram clout. Around the globe, Instagrammers are building their fame as social influencers who promote fashion, lifestyles, travel, cooking, health and fitness, sports, the arts, music, and, of course, their own personal branding. Internet personalities like magician Zach King attract sponsorship opportunities once their site hits over 500,00 followers, the best way to establish their brand. Financial backing from Coca-Cola, Kellogg's, Tic-Tacs, Nickelodeon, and Chick-fil-A allows King to perfect his digital magic, entertain his viewers, expand his business team, and support himself and his family (with an income of over $200,000 a year). As you examine social influencer King's Instagram page (Figure 4.9), analyze the rhetorical choices he has made through combining various media to form a fitting response to the rhetorical situation.

King leverages the rhetorical advantages of using Instagram to build and further his career. His digital sleight of hand tantalizes followers and sponsors alike; he draws attention to the product (in this case, Chick-fil-A) (Figure 4.10) through the medium of his fantastic digital magic. Instagram accommodates both King's pursuit of wide distribution as well as a familiar and standardized interface. The versatility, accessibility, and interactivity of the Instagram platform are crucial to King's ability to increase his visibility. A secondary rhetorical purpose for his Instagram account is to build community among magicians, illusionists, videographers, and lifestyle gurus, all of whom can communicate with one another on the informal wall accompanying each of his posts.

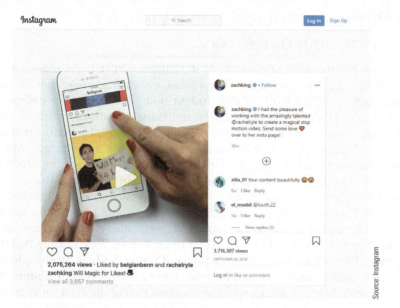

Figure 4.9 *@ZachKing, the magician, interacts directly (via video) with his fans.*

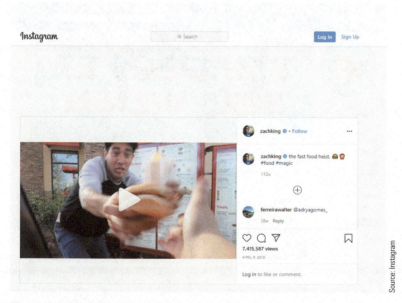

Figure 4.10 *@ZachKing, the magician, turns the Chick-fil-A drive-through screen into actual food.*

A Rhetorical Approach to a Webpage as a Medium of Delivery

For over twenty years now, students in visualization sciences classes at Texas A&M (the Aggies) have held Viz-a-GoGo, a visual art show that introduces multimedia student work to the student body and the larger college town community (Figure 4.11). By giving individual artists and other interested students something to link to (via Twitter, Facebook, LinkedIn, Instagram, Tumblr, Vimeo, or an e-mail message), the website helps target a broader rhetorical audience for the show than just the program alumni, the "Aggie Vizzers" who had long been the sole audience. In fact, once the organizers opened the sophisticated website, news of the visual art show quickly began to reach a wide audience of students, instructors, and community members. This wider audience joined the "Aggie Vizzers," many of whom have careers at Industrial Light & Magic (ILM), DreamWorks, Walt Disney Animation Studios, Pixar, Blue Sky, Electronic Arts, Rhythm & Hues Studios, Reel FX, Sony Pictures Imageworks, and Microsoft. In turn, the program alumni shared the site with their coworkers, who then became part of the even wider audience.

Figure 4.11 *Visitors to the site can preview the artists' work in the gallery.*
Source: Texas A&M University

A Rhetorical Approach to YouTube as a Medium of Delivery

Video provides yet another medium for composing and delivering multimedia compositions.

Actress and activist Calpernia Addams uses YouTube videos to discuss transgender issues that are often ignored by the mainstream media (Figure 4.12). In one of her many videos, she posts her musical rendition of "Bye, Bye, Baby" from *Gentlemen Prefer Blondes,* transgendering the performance of iconic blond bombshell Marilyn Monroe. In her performance, Addams achieves two goals: (1) she lampoons offensive stereotypical transgender labeling (she's a terrific performer), thereby (2) promoting positive images of transgender people. Many of her videos link to websites such as genderlife.com and responses to her critics. Any critical analysis of what Addams says or sings (and what she leaves unspoken), how she chooses to deliver her message, who comprises her audience (and who does not), and the purpose of her message is the best means of assessing the overall success of any of her multimedia compositions.

Good delivery in a video follows many of the principles that apply to effective audio compositions—you should speak clearly into the microphone, pace yourself when delivering a monologue, and practice your performance

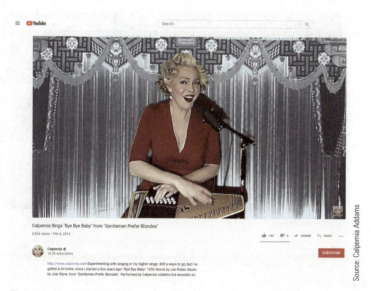

Figure 4.12 *In this image from one of Calpernia Addams's YouTube videos, Calpernia sings "Bye, Bye, Baby."*

ahead of time. However, you must also consider the visual dimensions of video, including what you and other performers wear and what material and visual elements you include in each scene. For instance, in the *Beyond the Trailer* segment in which she reviews director Bong Joon-ho's *Parasite* (available on YouTube), Grace Randolph orchestrates the setting, costuming, and delivery of her review. Wearing a subtle, snake-print blouse, she sits in front of a Manhattan skyline and alongside giant digital slides of the movie while she delivers her monologue-review (Figure 4.13). The slide show features video clips from the movie itself, including stars, Song Kang Ho, Lee Sun Kyn, Cho Yeo Jeong, and Park So Dam, who are negotiating their lives as members of markedly different socioeconomic classes, to which they are loyal. Randolph is casually well-dressed, choosing her attire and props purposefully, establishing her ethos and logos as an up-to-date, well-informed film critic. She has a fairly easy time establishing pathos because *Parasite* itself is a study of the huge social chasm between wealthy and low-income people, making it easy for viewers to sympathize with the struggles of the underclass at the same time that they appreciate the naïve kindnesses and privileged ignorance of the very rich. The combination of the visual elements, her fact-filled monologue, and her richly detailed and contextualized review confirms her status as an expert reviewer.

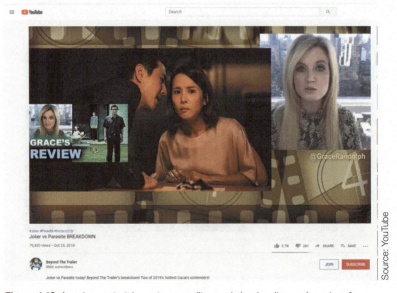

Source: YouTube

Figure 4.13 *American entertainment personality, comic book writer, and creator of YouTube channels* Beyond the Trailer, Movie Math, *and* Think About the Ink *Grace Randolph hosts a review of* Parasite *on YouTube*

Delivery does not just apply to your performance on film, however. You also need to consider how you will distribute (or deliver) the video to your audience. YouTube and other sites that host streaming video have made distribution easier. However, because of the public nature of such sites, you may want to choose a different distribution method, such as e-mail, in order to more carefully control who is in your audience.

A Rhetorical Approach to Oral Presentations as a Medium of Delivery

When Demosthenes, a renowned ancient Greek orator, was asked to name the three most important features of rhetoric, his response was "Delivery, delivery, delivery." His concerns included the properties of the speaker's voice, diction, and gestures as well as the style of his sentences and the quality of his argument. Like all ancients, Demosthenes was also concerned with the speaker's appearance. His were multimodal concerns even then.

Location

Ultimately, the success of an oral presentation depends on your strategic employment of the available means. You will want to establish the rhetorical appeals of credibility, reasonableness, and connection (ethos, logos, and pathos) in the content of your presentation, but your oral presentation will also be affected by the resources and constraints (limitations) of the physical location itself. If you are speaking in front of a classroom, you will reach all of your classmates if you speak clearly and look up from your notes as often as possible. If you are speaking in a lecture hall, however, you may find yourself dependent on a microphone, and you may want to practice with it beforehand. A lecture hall offers a few other challenges as well, not the least of which is the need to ensure that audience members who have hearing or visual impairments can follow your presentation. You may want to make printed handouts available so that individuals with hearing impairments can follow along more easily. And you will want to concentrate on facing your audience so that they can see your facial expressions and even read your lips, all the better to "hear" your words.

If yours is a Zoom or Skype presentation, be sure you appear in a quiet, well-lit area and have elevated your camera to face level (and close). Then take some time to explore the setup options, selecting "Settings" and deciding on the virtual background option and consulting the "Touch up my appearance" option as well. As you speak, look directly into the camera, so that your audience knows you are speaking directly to them. If you choose the "active speaker" option in settings, the person speaking will appear right under your camera, which will make responding to and looking right at them easy and natural.

Presentation Software

When you must make a decision about whether to deliver your information as spoken words only or as spoken words along with other media (visuals, videos, other sonic elements), consider that your oral presentation states your claim, while the visual and sound elements expand and energize that claim. You can decide whether to bring items such as a handout, a flip chart, a transparency, a poster, a film clip, a podcast or an audio stream, or a PowerPoint, Prezi, or other type of digital presentation. Nothing can be more aggravating than a speaker reading a series of bulleted points to the audience while the audience is reading along. Your goal is to get the attention of your audience and impress them. Text-heavy slides will do just the opposite so concentrate on using big bold images and sound elements to emphasize your words. Even as you use big bold images, you can still maintain a consistent design throughout all your slides as well as consistent background color. In fact, some experts go so far as to say that the background colors you use in your slides should complement the colors of the room in which you are presenting! Thus, as you consider the use of visuals and audio, keep in mind that they should complement your words—not mirror them. Some of the most effective digital presentations are cascades of visuals that accompany—and enhance—a speaker's words.

The Rhetorical Arrangement of Presentation Elements

As with any other multimodal composition, the text, images, and sound you decide to include need to reflect your rhetorical situation as well as the topic of your presentation. For instance, you may have identified a problem that you can address by way of research, a public controversy that you want to investigate, or a personal problem that you want to resolve. Perhaps your church has asked you to do a presentation for its drive to help those left unemployed by the pandemic.

- If your purpose is to provide background for the rising numbers of unemployed in your area, then you could provide a range of images such as statistical tables that show the strategies businesses are using to stay afloat, the numbers of people visiting local food banks, the employment and unemployment numbers, or the number of confirmed COVID-19 cases and deaths (Figure 4.14 and Figure 4.15).

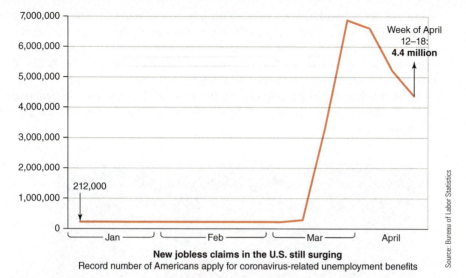

New jobless claims in the U.S. still surging
Record number of Americans apply for coronavirus-related unemployment benefits

Source: Bureau of Labor Statistics

Figure 4.14 *MarketWatch is documenting the rising rate of unemployment in this bar chart, from April 2020.*

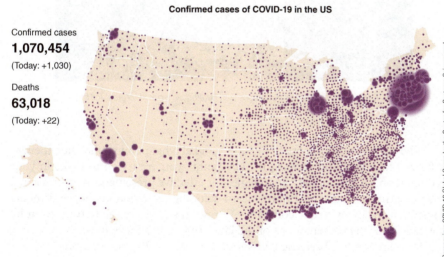

Last updated 1 May 12:25pm EDT Source: Johns Hopkins CSSE *Note: The CSSE states that its numbers rely upon publicly available date from multiple sources.

Sources: Coronavirus COVID-19 Global Cases by the Center for Systems Science and Engineering (CSSE) at Johns Hopkins University; the Red Cross; the Census American Community Survey, the Bureau of Labor and Statistics.

Figure 4.15 *Johns Hopkins has taken public data to create this state-by-state map of Coronavirus cases and deaths, from May 1, 2020.*

- On the other hand, if your presentation is purposefully persuasive rather than informative, your choice of images can greatly influence the overall effectiveness of your work. Photographs showing people standing in long lines at a food bank, COVID-19 patients dying alone, or the faces of first responders, for instance, could heighten the appeal of pathos if your thesis involves finding a solution to the spread of the virus, to restarting the economy gradually, or to subsidizing rents for the unemployed (see Figure 4.16).

Figure 4.16 *In Harlem, New York, nurses and healthcare workers protest for more personal protective equipment.*

The elements you choose to include—and at what point you include them—will need to reflect and support the key points you are trying to make in your presentation. In developing his strategies for effective presentations, professional coach Carmine Gallo (an Emmy award–winning television anchor and media consultant for many major companies) draws his advice directly from what he noticed about the presentations of the late Apple CEO Steve Jobs.

Here are the five basic elements found in every Jobs presentation:

1. **A headline.** Steve Jobs positions every product with a headline that fits well within a 140-character Twitter post. . . . In his 2007 iPhone launch, he wrote, "Apple reinvents the phone" (Figure 4.17).

2. **A villain.** In every classic story, the hero fights the villain. . . . This idea of conquering a shared enemy is a powerful motivator and turns customers into evangelists. For Jobs, all other cell phones were villains, in that they were not smart and were hard to use. Apple's iPhone would prove to be smart and simple.

3. **A simple slide.** Apple products are easy to use because of the elimination of clutter. The same approach applies to the slides in a Steve Jobs presentation. In this presentation, he showed one picture of the iPhone—nothing else on the slide—and called it "gorgeous."

4. **A demo.** Neuroscientists have discovered that the brain gets bored easily. Steve Jobs doesn't give you time to lose interest. [In most of his presentations] he's . . . demonstrating a new product or feature and having fun doing it. . . . So, he pulls out his iPhone and starts playing around with it, demonstrating its functions as an iPod, a computer, and a phone.

5. **A "holy smokes" moment.** Every Steve Jobs presentation has one moment that neuroscientists call an "emotionally charged event." Jobs was so excited about the iPhone that he admitted to his huge audience, "I didn't sleep a wink last night." The emotionally charged moment is the equivalent of a mental sticky note that tells the brain, Remember this! . . . (From *Business Week*, "Uncovering Steve Jobs' Presentation Secrets," October 6, 2009.)

Jim Goldstein/Alamy Stock Photo

Figure 4.17 *Indeed, Apple reinvented the phone, as Jobs demonstrated in this simple slide backdrop for his 2007 launch of the product.*

ACTIVITY: Analyzing the Rhetorical Situation
Planning an Oral Presentation

Not every presentation has a villain in the way Steve Jobs's presentation would. Use these same basic elements to plan a presentation that builds consensus. In your presentation, recast the "villain" as a rhetorical opportunity to achieve a goal.

1. If you decided to make one key change to your presentation, how would that influence the other elements of your presentation? For instance, what if you were to use an audio clip in place of a key image, or what if your thesis were primarily informative rather than persuasive?

2. What rhetorical opportunities or challenges are best resolved by the strategies described? How did the strategies described help you to address engaging your audience and structuring your approach to the topic?

3. In academic presentations, using the idea of a "villain" may seem counterintuitive. But if the purpose is to find something that most everyone in the room can agree on (e.g., Steve Jobs's contention that cell phones could do more but still be easy to use), how might such a strategy help you to build consensus around issues instead of inflaming differences? What kinds of topics or rhetorical situations might suggest dropping the "villain" altogether?

4. If you liked the ideas you came up with in your outline, think about ways in which you might address this topic in a different assignment. How would you do this as an essay?

 ## ASSIGNMENT: ANALYZING IMAGES

Nike's market dominance in the United States does not look like it will fade anytime soon. What with clothing, shoes, and accessory lines for every single sport as well as for men, women, and children, the Nike brand is flourishing, thanks, in no small part, to its legendary logo, the "swoosh." "Just Do It," Nike's long-time challenge, has been translated into languages all around the globe, exerting a significant force on consumers. In the twenty-first century, Nike has swooshed its way beyond that simple challenge as fitness itself has become one of America's most noble goals, to some almost a religion.

ACTIVITY: Analyzing the Rhetorical Situation

Imagine, if you can, the amount of purposeful planning that went into the Nike advertisement in Figure 4.18 and analyze it accordingly, considering the overall rhetorical power of the ad itself. After answering all of the following questions, compose a short essay in which you analyze and synthesize your findings to determine the effectiveness of the Nike advertisement. Consider all the rhetorical elements: opportunity, purpose, audience, and medium of delivery as well as the advantages and limitations of that medium. Consider, too, how this ad employs the rhetorical appeals of ethos, logos, and pathos to persuade viewers to buy Nike products.

1. What holds the central position in this poster? What might it signify?
2. What other features—culturally significant, familiar, and fresh—are in the poster? What might be missing?
3. What might be the significance of the background (especially in relationship with the text itself)?
4. What role does the text play? What might be the significance of the different sizes of text?
5. How do the colors in this advertisement vary? What mood do the colors create?
6. How does the positioning of the runner affect your perception of the ad?

MOVE MORE.
MOVE BETTER.
THE NIKE DRI-FIT KNIT TANK

Image courtesy of The Advertising Archives

Figure 4.18 *Nike advertisement.*

5 Memoirs

LEARNING OBJECTIVES

- Identify rhetorical situations in which a memoir would be an effective choice.
- Explain the purpose of a memoir in terms of its key rhetorical features and principles of development in various media.
- Apply storytelling techniques (personal voice, characters, plot) to creating a memoir.
- Reflect critically on a relatable (can be seemingly insignificant) moment in your life that changed your thinking about something in an unusual and unexpected way.
- Evaluate personal experience as research and develop the ability to incorporate primary sources into your memoir.
- Apply peer review and self-evaluation to revise, edit, and proofread a memoir as a credible and meaningful personal exploration.

Human beings have always been storytellers, whether telling stories about a successful hunt, a dangerous journey, a harrowing childhood, the intervention of a god, even a good meal. We humans have always made connections in the world by telling stories, and now we regularly do so over pizza, in the car, and through e-mail, Facebook, blogs, and Twitter. Even a 280-character tweet can carry a punch:

← **Tweet**

Dr. C, rhetorical agent
@DrCCedillo

Today a student gave me a weird look when I said I scheduled projects so they wouldn't have work over Spring Break. When I asked what was wrong, he said no prof had ever said they should only rest over Spring Break. I think stealing students' chance to recharge really stinks.

12:42 AM · Feb 27, 2020 · Twitter for Android

14 Retweets   **6** Quote Tweets   **198** Likes

In her tweet, Dr. C reflects on her students' memories of school breaks past that were complicated if not ruined by various school projects—and she does so in fewer than 280 characters. This memory offers an opportunity for change—one that is accomplished through words.

Throughout this chapter, you, too, will identify an opportunity for change that can be addressed or resolved with words. As you determine what you want to share in your memoir, consider which medium of delivery will give you the best chance for reaching and engaging your rhetorical audience.

IDENTIFYING AN OPPORTUNITY FOR CHANGE

 Print Memoir written for a community or campus newspaper or a local zine or church

 Audio Memoir recorded for a local radio station, for a podcast, or for your family back home

 Online (Multimodal or Multimedia) Memoir written as a blog entry, a series of tweets, a contribution to a website, or a YouTube video

Memoirs can focus on disasters, of course, like the traumatic pandemic that is COVID-19. But they can also focus on everyday subjects like family, travel, spirituality, and food. Food triggers vivid memories for all of us—some joyous or satisfying, others painful or awkward. For example, a memoir might be about a difficult adolescence as revealed through a traditional holiday meal or it might be about discovering your family eats foods your peers don't, a discovery that leads you to explore living between two cultures in your role as a new immigrant. Food-related memoirs, like other memoirs, present past experiences that resonate with a larger historical, psychological, or social meaning. In her blog *Chocolate & Zucchini,* Clotilde Dusoulier's description of high-quality chocolate suggests that Parisians connect food more with pleasure and fun than with nourishment and sustenance. Her exploration of place and food is a staple of long-running television programs that take viewers around the world by showcasing food cultures. And her memoir also shows how the memory of a particular food often evokes emotions, in this case "chocolate" and "happiness."

memoirs
narratives that reflect on personal experience or series of experiences

> On a Sunday afternoon, after a copious lunch, wait for your next-door neighbor Patricia to knock on your window with a wooden spoon. Agree to come over to their place for coffee. From the special chocolate cabinet in your kitchen (surely you must have one) grab what's left of the excellent dark chocolate with fragments of roasted cocoa beans that your friend Marie-Laure brought you last time she came for dinner. Walk next door in your socks. Leave Maxence and Stéphan to chat about Mac OS-X and guitar tuners in the living room, while you watch Patricia brew coffee on their espresso machine. When asked, opt for the designer coffee cups. Bring the four cups to the table on a metal tray. Take a cup, break a square of the chocolate, sit down, relax. Have a bite of chocolate, then a sip of coffee.

> —Clotilde Dusoulier, "Happiness (A Recipe)"

iStockphoto.com/creativepictures

The rhetorical response of a food memoir can serve to explore our relationships, just as one about music, art, travel, sports, or small children might do.

To determine if a memoir is the most fitting response to your rhetorical opportunity, keep in mind your opportunity for composing, your audience, and your purpose. If, as you are composing, you realize that your message includes characters, dialogue, an event (or two), and a specific setting, you can rely on the memoir for all or part of your message. (See CHAPTER 15, NARRATION, DESCRIPTION, and CAUSE-AND-EFFECT ANALYSIS.) As you reflect on your own experience, you may find yourself writing to entertain, explain, evaluate, or connect with your audience—all elements of the memoir.

pages 279–281 and 286–289

»» READING RHETORICALLY

 ASSIGNMENT

Think back to a meaningful moment in your life, maybe a pivotal event (or sequence of sensory, physical, or emotional events) from your childhood or one from the more recent past. Then, relying on the narrative techniques of fiction, draft a memoir in which you include vivid, sensory-rich descriptions, characters, dialogue, setting(s), and plot (a cause-and-effect narrative structure). Since your memoir is not fiction, you will want to take special care to establish yourself as a trustworthy observer of your own life by including a reasonable analysis and establishing the significance of your experience for you as well as your readers. As you write, vary your descriptions by emphasizing different descriptive and sensory features of the situation: pleasant or unpleasant memories, people, feelings, and other senses that this experience stimulated.

You can read an entertaining, inspirational, or instructional memoir with pleasure and profit if you read rhetorically. You might read chronologically (in order of occurrence) or recursively (moving forward and looping back), a process that includes: (1) previewing the text itself (to determine what the text demands in terms of time, effort, and previous knowledge); (2) reading for content (to note the author's major points, key terms, and phrases); and (3) rereading for understanding (to determine the author's specific purpose, the overall organization, and the specific development of ideas). (See CHAPTER 3, ACADEMIC LITERACIES: READING RHETORICALLY.) When reading a memoir, pay special attention to the feelings the memory has stimulated in the writer, both during the experience itself and now, upon reflection. You will also want to determine how the writer's memoir works to connect with readers.

pages 34–48

Key Features of a Memoir

A memoir focuses on an experience or series of experiences in the writer's life and their significance in shaping the writer's perspective. Sensory details help readers visualize, hear, smell, feel, and even taste key events in a writer's life.

Dialogue reveals the characters, with specific words or phrases helping the reader "hear" the relationship of the characters with the writer and the connections among the characters. Transitions are crucial to keeping the narrative moving forward with clarity and grace. Memoirs share the following characteristics:

- Memoirs focus on a significant or then-insignificant experience or series of experiences in the writer's life. Rather than narrating from birth to adulthood, the way an autobiography does, a memoir focuses on those experiences or events that have proved to be meaningful in shaping who the writer is and their perspective on the world.
- Memoirs contain ample sensory details to help readers visualize, hear, smell, taste, or feel key events, characters, experiences, and objects.
- Memoirs include dialogue or quoted speech that reveals something unique about, or central to, a character or the character's relationship with other people, events, or objects in the story.
- Memoirs include clear transitional phrases to show how events relate to one another in time and how the action of the narrative unfolds. (See CHAPTER 13, COMMON TRANSITIONAL WORDS AND PHRASES.)
- Memoirs provide reflection on, or analysis of, the key narrative events to help readers understand their significance for the writer's development and their perspective on everyday life.

page 242

The student example that follows is annotated to show the characteristics found in most memoirs. As you read the following essay, ask yourself:

- Who is the author? What does the memoir tell you about her?
- What is her relationship to the subject of this essay? Is she angry, happy, remorseful about this experience? Why is it important to her? What is her purpose in writing the essay?
- Which of Seitz's major points and key terms did you notice?
- What specific details, key terms, and dialogue did Seitz use to sustain her purpose?

What storytelling techniques does she use to try to make her memoir come to life? How successful is she?

Herb's Chicken

ANNA SEITZ

The following memoir centers on a turning point in the writer's life. Seitz and her husband dreamed of being sustenance farmers until she witnessed the reality of such sustenance: killing a chicken. Why is the memoir a good choice for Seitz's rhetorical situation?

Last year, my husband Bill and I, fueled by farmers' market fantasies, decided we wanted to keep some backyard chickens. Since we had to wait until spring to order birds, we spent the winter getting our coop, and ourselves, ready. We read stacks of books and magazines on raising chickens, and we decided to ask our friend Herb to teach us to "process" them.

Seitz's memoir uses the narrative form, which includes a setting, characters, dialogue, and a sequence of events.

The significant experience related in this memoir arose from Seitz's "farmers' market fantasy" of raising chickens. [Seitz provides the context for the memoir as well as her opportunity for writing.]

When we pulled into Herb's driveway on the big day, he was already hanging out the back door, gesturing to the cane at the bottom of the steps. He's 87 years old and has been a poultry farmer since he got back from the war. He shuffles slowly, hunched over. He can't hear much of what we say. When he can hear, he usually just rolls his eyes. Bill handed him the cane, and Herb led us to the last of his coops that still has chickens. His farm of 6,000 birds is down to 75. "Well, how many you want?" Herb asks.

Seitz includes many sensory details to help her readers visualize the setting and Herb's character.

"I don't know," said my husband. "Got one that's not layin'?"

The husband offers a detail important to the memoir. The dialogue reveals the characters' relationships to one another as well as to the raising of chickens.

"Get that one there," said Herb. He pointed his finger in the direction of a group of three birds, and my husband, appearing to know which one Herb meant, took a couple of steps toward them. They immediately dispersed.

Herb grabbed a long handle with a hook at the end, resembling the sort of wand I've used to roast weenies over a campfire, and handed it to Bill. He pointed again. "There," he said. Bill grabbed the tool and managed to at least tangle up the bird's feet. Herb snapped up the bird with the efficient movement of someone who has snapped up tens of thousands of birds and handed the bird, upside-down, to me.

I held it carefully by the ankles and got a little shiver. It flapped its wings a few times, but it didn't really try to fight me. It actually looked pretty pitiful hanging there. Herb was already walking back to the house.

"Pull up that bird feeder, Billy," barked Herb, in his thin voice.

My husband had worked digging graves with Herb since he was fifteen, and he was used to taking orders. "Yup," he said. He walked up to a bird feeder on a stake and pulled it up from the ground.

This paragraph works as a transition between the present series of events and the past relationship of the characters.

Herb unhooked a metal cone which he'd been using on the stake as a squirrel deterrent and slid it off the bottom. "For the chicken," he told me as I caught up to them. "I'll open the cellar."

Bill and I waited outside the bulkhead for Herb. He opened it up, still holding the metal cone in his hand. "Come on," he instructed. We made our way down into the dark. The chicken tried to arch its head up, to peck me. I handed it over to Bill.

In the cellar, Herb hooked the cone to a beam. "Give me that," he said to me, gesturing at a dusty bucket on the floor next to me. I pushed it with my foot until it was under the cone.

Seitz describes the chicken-killing process in detail.

"All right!" said my husband brightly. I stiffened. He pushed the chicken head-first into the cone, until her head poked through the opening at the bottom and her feet stuck out the top. The chicken got one wing free, but my husband put a rubber band around her feet and hooked it on the nail that held the cone. She was stuck.

Seitz's dialogue is vivid and purposeful, moving the narrative forward. This series of five short paragraphs includes graphic details and purposeful dialogue.

Herb fished through his pocket for his knife, and my eyelids started to wrinkle. I held my lips tightly closed. "You just need to go through the roof of the mouth and get them right in the brain," said Herb. "It's better than chopping the head off because they don't tense up. Makes it easier to get the feathers off."

"Won't it bite you?" I asked.

"So what if it does?" answered Herb. "Last thing it'll ever do." Herb easily pried the mouth open with his left hand, and with his right, he pushed the knife into its brain and turned it. It was over. I furrowed my brow.

"Then you gotta bleed it," he said. Herb pulled the knife down, and in one quick motion, cut the chicken's throat from the inside. Blood spilled from its open beak into the bucket. My husband watched with interest, offering the same occasional "Yup" or "Uh-huh" that he uses when listening to any good story. I watched with my eyes squinted and my face half turned away.

Herb rinsed the knife in the washbasin and announced, "Gotta get the water. Anna, it's on the stove. Hot but not boiling." I went up to the kitchen and fiddled with the temperature under a big soup pot. It looked about right, I guessed.

By the time I got the water down to the cellar, Herb and Bill had already pulled the chicken out of the cone and tossed the head into the bloody bucket. It looked more like food when I couldn't see the eyes. Herb told my husband to dip the bird in the hot water a few times, and he did, holding it by the rubber-banded legs. When he pulled it out, some of the feathers on its chest started to drop off.

"From under the stairs" begins a strong transitional sentence.

From under the stairs, Herb pulled out a large plastic drum, the sides dotted with rubber fingers. He put the chicken inside and switched it on. After a few minutes, he pulled out a mostly featherless chicken. The feathers stuck to the sides of the drum. "Get that," he said to Bill. While Bill pulled feathers out of the plucker, Herb held the chicken by the feet and pulled off the remaining feathers—mostly large wing and tail feathers, and a few small pin feathers. By now there really wasn't any blood left, and the chicken looked pretty close to what you might get in the store, except skinnier.

Seitz uses specific vocabulary like "plucker" to bring life to her memoir.

Bill brought the chicken and the bucket up to the kitchen, and Herb and I followed. Herb took the bird and dropped it down into the sink with a smack. "Now, you cut out the crop," Herb said. He pointed to something I couldn't see, then cut into the throat and showed us a little sack full of stones and grain. "It's how they chew, I guess," he added. He tugged on it, and it brought with it a large section of the windpipe. "To get the rest of the guts out, you gotta cut in the back."

Herb made an incision and stuck in his hand, making a squishy sound. He pulled out a handful of guts and dropped most of it into the bucket. He cut off one section and held it toward Bill. "You got the wrong bird," he said. The slimy tube was sort of transparent, and through it we could see a string of about eight little eggs of increasing size, beginning with a tiny yolk, and ending with an almost full-sized egg.

"Can you eat'em?" I asked.

"Guess you could," said Herb, throwing the whole mess into the bucket, "but I got eggs." He turned the chicken, lopped off the feet, and tossed them into the bucket. They landed toes up, like a grotesque garnish. "Well, want a plastic bag?"

I accepted the grocery bag and some plastic wrap and wrapped the carcass up while Herb and Bill took the bucket outside. They talked for a while, and then Herb directed Bill up onto a ladder to check a gutter. I stood with my back to the carcass, examining Herb's wife's display of whimsical salt and pepper shakers.

When my husband and I got back in the car, I put the carcass at my feet. "That was great!" said my husband. "Think we can do it on our own?"

I thought through the steps in my mind. "I think I can," I chirped. I thought of the bucket and the toe garnish. "But I'm not eating it."

Seitz reflects on the narrative events, helping her readers understand their significance to her changing perspective.

Using Synthesis and Analysis

When composing a memoir, you will be translating lived events into a narrative, one that triggers your reflection on, or analysis of, those events in a way that helps your readers understand the significance of those events to your development. In these ways, reflection and analysis underpin the body of a memoir. You will want to synthesize the people and events as the whole of one experience and then analyze that experience for its significance and its consequence. Whether you are reading or composing a memoir, pay attention to the ways specific details relate to the significance of a particular experience for your own or a character's self-development.

See also CHAPTER 2, MALALA YOUSAFZAI [I Am Afraid] [Interrupted Sleep] (blog entries)

See also CHAPTER 3, **FREDERICK DOUGLASS,** *Narrative of the Life of Frederick Douglass, An American Slave* [Learning to Read and Write]

See also CHAPTER 24, **EDDIE HUANG,** *Fresh Off the Boat* [Eddie Huang Learns to Eat, American Style]

See also CHAPTER 26, **MICHAEL-AIME MUSONI,** *Being an 18-Year-Old Black Man a Year after Mike Brown*

»» RESPONDING TO THE RHETORICAL SITUATION

Memoirs provide an opportunity to explore or explain a turning point in your life. The need to introduce yourself, explain your old (or new) self, analyze your change of plans or heart, or describe a transformative experience calls for the memoir. But who will read, watch, or listen to your memoir and perhaps be influenced by what you have to say? A fiancé, parent, teacher, hiring committee, friend, or classmate might be a suitable rhetorical audience, one needing your introduction, explanation, analysis, or description. A personal letter, face-to-face meeting, letter of application, YouTube video, podcast, and personal essay are all possible media for delivering a fitting response in the genre of memoir.

| Opportunity | Audience and Purpose | Genre/Memoir | Medium of Delivery |

Understanding the Rhetorical Situation

Memoirs are used to narrate and analyze significant—even sometimes seemingly insignificant—life experiences (sharing chocolate, killing a chicken) that have shaped the writer's perspective. Memoir writing helps us investigate, contemplate on, and understand more deeply the impact of incidents, events, and people in our lives. Each of the following questions provides an opportunity to think about your life experiences in a way that could launch a memoir.

- What is one food-related moment in your life that changed how you thought, acted, or felt? For instance, were you treated surprisingly well in a restaurant you thought was snobbish? Or, identify a key moment when you were first introduced to an unfamiliar kind of food. How did that event affect you?
- Have you ever given in to peer pressure with good—or unfortunate—results?
- When you witnessed (or participated in) racism or sexism, did you intervene, make amends—or not?
- Was there a first impression you or someone else made that changed later?

RESEARCHING THE MEMOIR

Memoir writing seems to be rooted in memory or recall. But the best memoirs often incorporate research, which can include conducting interviews with family and friends; researching contemporary newspaper accounts of weather, current events, dates, addresses; or examining photographs and documents that are stored at home or in an institution of some kind. (Think of rummaging through family photos, looking over childhood keepsakes in the attic, or examining legal documents that are stored in a shoebox.) Research findings like these are analyzed and then synthesized into the interesting details, facts, and anecdotes that help you compose a personalized, and, thereby, effective memoir.

Identifying an Opportunity for Change

What you are searching for is an experience, event, or relationship that has played a vital role—and has helped you understand something about life that you want other people to know. How did this experience change you, your attitude, your actions? How would writing about this experience help you learn more about yourself? How would relating this experience to others change those who read about it or help them understand you better?

1. Make a list of your three most memorable or meaningful experiences. Put a plus or minus in front of each experience, listing detailed reasons for its being positive or negative. Then, sketch out the contributing factors (including people, occasion, dialogue, setting) that led up to each experience and the possible transformative results of each experience.
2. Choose one of the experiences in your list and make sketches or take photos of the location where your experience, event, or relationship occurred, paying particular attention to the sensory details, characters, and dialogue that you still remember as being most intriguing about the experience. Write out two or three different ways that you and others might perceive that same experience.

Relating Rhetorically to Your Audience

The following questions will help you identify your rhetorical audience as well as their relationship to the experience you have decided to write about. Knowing your audience helps you decide whether your purpose is to be informative, entertaining, explanatory, analytical, or argumentative. After you have connected your audience with your purpose, you are in a good position to select effective descriptive details and decide on the most fitting way to deliver your message to that audience.

1. List the names of the persons or groups who might be most receptive—or most resistant—to your story and need to hear about it.
2. Next to the name of each potential audience list the personal, professional, social, or spiritual reasons they would have for acknowledging the significance of your experience.
3. Think about the kinds of responses to your memoir you might reasonably expect from each of these audiences. Consider similar experiences that the audience might have had, their openness to new opinions, or their desire for familiar, confirming experiences.
4. Keeping the interests, experiences, and perspectives of your audience in mind, review your visual and verbal descriptions and the significance of that experience (#2 in the preceding section, "Identifying an Opportunity for Change"). Determine which of those descriptions will most likely engage your audience, maybe connecting your experience with their own. Now is the time to revise those descriptions accordingly, tailoring them to your rhetorical audience.

Planning an Effective Rhetorical Response for Your Purpose

After you identify your opportunity and audience, use the following questions to help you narrow your purpose and shape your response:

1. What purpose do you have in conveying your memoir to this audience?
2. Might your memoir change a specific perception, attitude, opinion, or action of your rhetorical audience? Might they rethink their own experience in terms of yours? Or might they reassess you and your experience?
3. What would be the most effective medium for delivering your memoir to your audience? What medium or media do they have easy access to? As you consider the various options for delivering your memoir (print, electronic, verbal, visual, multimodal), focus in on the one that will best convey the purpose of your message and reach your audience.

Links may change due to availability.

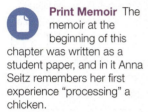

Print Memoir The memoir at the beginning of this chapter was written as a student paper, and in it Anna Seitz remembers her first experience "processing" a chicken.

Audio Memoir This audio memoir about assimilation, food, and cultural identity is an irreverent reflection from "Eddie Huang Learns to Eat, American Style," recorded for *The Dinner Party Download*.

Online Memoir This memoir on YouTube from Gaz Oakley @ avantgardevegan describes "What Made Me Go Vegan Overnight."

Memoirs

✦ WRITING A PERSUASIVE MEMOIR: A Guide

To be persuasive, a memoir should rely on the narrative techniques of fiction (novels and short stories): vivid descriptions, characters, dialogue, and setting as well as a cause-and-consequence structure. Like fiction, memoirs are structured as a chronological sequence of events, sometimes using flashbacks and flash forwards to emphasize specific moments. But memoirs are not fiction, so you will need to establish your personal credibility as an insightful observer of your life experiences (your ethos) as well as the reasonableness (logos) of your feelings so that your story makes an authentic emotional connection (pathos) with the lives and experiences of your readers. (See CHAPTER 2, THE AVAILABLE MEANS INCLUDE THE RHETORICAL ELEMENTS OF THE MESSAGE ITSELF*.)*

pages 23–26

ADVANTAGES AND LIMITATIONS

Advantages

- **Writer:** You have considerable latitude to explore a more personal voice to engage readers, taking a casual, even intimate, tone.

- **Message:** The memoir allows you to build ethos and pathos through personalized anecdotes and vivid experiences, all of which shape the body, the supporting material, of your memoir.

- **Media and Design:** Memoirs can be presented in numerous ways: through audio, video, print, electronic series of print images, or images and text.

Limitations

- **Writer:** Be sure that you are comfortable with a personal voice—and that it is appropriate for your intended audience. Resist breaching your boundaries of personal privacy for the sake of a memoir.

- **Message:** Memoirs rely on personal experiences, knowledge, and observations for logos, the logical appeal. Facts and figures work best when they are rooted in the writer's own experience or in related research.

- **Media and Design:** Reaching and engaging your rhetorical audience are the determining factors for your choice of medium.

Introduction

- **Engage your audience.**
- **Establish your trustworthiness as a narrator (ethos).**

Announce Your Focus As you have learned in this chapter, a memoir focuses on a specific event or series of meaningful events. The introduction hooks readers by dropping them right in the middle of an interesting situation or an especially vivid description of your specific event, experience, or personality. For instance, Anna Seitz writes, "We read stacks of books and magazines on raising chickens, and we decided to ask our friend Herb to teach us to 'process' them."

Ask Yourself . . .
- How does my opening situation or compelling language engage my reader(s)?
- How have I stated or alluded to the main point(s) my memoir will address?
- Will approaching my main topic directly or indirectly be more effective?
- How have I begun to establish my ethos as a writer or character to my audience?

Body

- **Present the main narrative in a distinctive setting.**
- **Provide specific sensory details of sight, sound, taste, feeling, and smell.**
- **Develop characters and dialogue.**
- **Begin to reflect on and analyze what has happened.**

Structure your memoir as a story The body of a memoir presents the narrative, which focuses on a specific sequence of events. Use transitional phrases that help readers see how the events relate to one another in time. These events allow you to illustrate a point or convey the message you want to send by means of vivid language, memorable characters, and dialogue. Seitz's second paragraph fulfills all of these criteria of using transitions ("When we pulled into Herb's driveway on the big day, he was already hanging out the door") and memorable characters ("He shuffles slowly, hunched over. He can't hear much of what we say. When he can hear, he usually just rolls his eyes").

Add vivid description Vivid descriptions and sensory details invite readers to imagine, connect with, and invest themselves in the lives and activities of the major characters, including you. Seitz's description of the processing itself includes "Herb made an incision and stuck in his hand, making a squishy sound. He pulled out a handful of guts and dropped most of it into the bucket."

Create dialogue Equally important, you will want to create dialogue among the characters to reveal their personalities and relationships. Dialogue or quoted speech gives readers deeper insight into the thoughts and emotions of your characters. Herb and Bill discuss the chicken to be processed with "How many do you want?" and "Got one that's not layin'?"

Reflect on your experience You can achieve rhetorical success as you narrate the events in your memoir by stopping the action to provide a few sentences of reflection and analysis. Midway through the chicken processing, Seitz reflects that the bird "looked more like food when I couldn't see the eyes."

Ask yourself . . .
- How do I know that I am relating all the pertinent details of the event?
- As I reconsider my narrative, which details have I purposefully excluded? Which ones might I want to include now?
- Which of my details are especially vivid, especially sensory?
- How have I described the characters in my memoir so that they seem realistic? How do they present contrasting viewpoints that enhance the complexity of the events?
- How exactly do the events and characters I am describing connect to the main point I want to make?

- **Satisfy your audience with an understanding of the significance of the events for you as well as for them.**
- **Reinforce your message.**

Relate the significance of the event to your readers' interests You might conclude your memoir with a scene that captures precisely the mood you want readers to experience or the image you want them to remember. Or you might decide to conclude

(continued)

your memoir with a more traditional paragraph that, like your reflective components, speaks fairly explicitly about the point of the events that you have described. Either way, your readers will respond favorably to your conclusion if it helps them see how the events have significance both for you as the writer and for them as your readers. Seitz's comparative descriptions of Herb's, Bill's, and her own response to the processing make for a humorous, though realistic, account that turns serious when she announces that she will not eat it. Many readers will identify with her response.

Check your message in your conclusion The conclusion of a memoir reinforces the message or the point of your story. The important consideration here is to be sure the events you have narrated, the details you have provided, and the reflection you have composed all work together to deliver a clear, coherent message. Seitz's final sentence, "But I'm not eating it," makes for a perfect conclusion.

Ask yourself . . .
How explicit do I want my language to be?
- How "conclusive" do I want my conclusion to be? Am I really certain about how I feel?
- Might it be more effective to leave some questions unanswered, so that readers can arrive at their own conclusions?

»» REVISION AND PEER REVIEW

After you have drafted your memoir, ask one of your classmates to read it, providing advice on revising and strengthening it. Ask your peer to help you address your rhetorical audience, fulfill your purpose, and deliver it in an appropriate medium.

Questions for a Peer Reviewer

1. What change does the writer hope to make? How do you know?
2. What do you think the writer's thesis or main point is? Where, exactly, did you get your information?
3. Who might be the writer's rhetorical audience?
4. What might be the writer's purpose? How do audience and purpose connect?
5. What suggestions do you have for the writer for enhancing the effectiveness of the introduction?
6. Underline descriptive details that are especially vivid. Which ones describe characters, the setting, emotions?
7. How and where, exactly, do transitions help the reader keep track of the narrative? Identify places that could use transitional words or phrases.
8. Which passage did you most enjoy? Why?

9. What did you learn from the conclusion that you did not already know after reading the introduction and the body? What information does the writer want you to take away from the memoir? Does the writer attempt to change your attitude, action, or opinion? In other words, how does the writer address the opportunity for change?

10. What changes would you make if this were your memoir?

ADDITIONAL ASSIGNMENTS

Knowledge Transfer

Too often we classify the memoir as personal writing, almost private. But memoir writing can be used in contexts other than English courses. Your field notes, application letters, letters to the editor (op-eds), and even lab reports employ many of the same features as the memoir: a sequence of events, characters (from baboons to chemical elements), a setting, synthesis, and analysis.

COLLEGE Literacy Narrative Typically, the academic memoir has focused on learning to read and write in academic English. Compose a two- to three-page memoir in which you chart your literacy development, failures, breakthroughs, and successes. As you include features of narrative, characters, dialogue, and setting, be sure to synthesize and analyze the sequence of events so that your literacy memoir makes a significant point.

COMMUNITY Eulogy Your best friend's father has passed away, and the family is asking that close friends—like you—speak at the funeral. Tapping the genre of the memoir, compose a narrative that captures a significant sequence of events that you shared with this man, making sure to include characters, dialogue, and setting. You will want to include rich descriptive details that capture how this good man lived his life.

WORKPLACE Application Letter Compose a one- to two-page letter of application for a job, scholarship, or academic program. After you establish your credibility as a candidate (ethos), provide a narrative of events, your experience (including other characters), and your accomplishments that strongly position you for the job. Correct formatting helps build credibility in a business letter. Business letters are single spaced, with a skipped space between paragraphs. The most common format includes your address at the top of the letter, flush left, then the date, then the name and address of the person who is responsible for the position. Address your letter formally (Dear Ms. Jones) and follow the salutation with a colon. Paragraphs are flush left with a space

(continued)

between them in most business letters. Include the position you are seeking in the first sentence of your letter.

MULTIMODAL PowerPoint Presentation: Technology Literacy Narrative By now, you are no doubt computer, smartphone, and iPad literate. You can keyboard without thinking, access podcasts, upload YouTube videos, and sustain your active Twitter account. In an essay of two to three pages, compose a technology literacy narrative, one that focuses on your experiences as you have learned to process, produce, maybe even build technologies that allow you to engage with others, take pleasure, and experience deep frustrations. You might explore the positives of mastering technologies, or you might consider what you might be missing by not reading a physical book, sending or receiving letters through the mail, or being off-line, unhooked. Incorporate the features of a traditional memoir as you compose your narrative, but do not limit yourself to a print delivery. Try PowerPoint or PechaKucha.

6 Profiles

LEARNING OBJECTIVES

- Identify rhetorical situations in which readers need to know more about a person (or place or phenomenon).
- Explain the purpose of a profile in terms of its key rhetorical features and principles of development in various media.
- Apply direct quotations, short anecdotes, and revealing details that help readers understand the unique features of a person, place, or phenomenon.
- Reflect critically on the dominant impression you are creating in your profile.
- Evaluate such materials as interviews, observations, diaries, library and online research, scrapbooks, and other stored memorabilia and their relevance to acknowledging, engaging, and citing primary and secondary sources into your profile.
- Apply peer review and self-evaluation to revise, edit, and proofread your profile for a fresh take that supports a reader's particular emotional response and logical connection to the subject of your profile.

We all like to compose profiles, whether we are preparing our parents to meet our romantic partner, describing the Coachella Valley Music and Arts Festival to our friends, or writing a letter of application. Whether it analyzes, informs, entertains, or even provokes, a **profile** may characterize people, places, or events

profile a portrait in words of a person, place, or event

91

by emphasizing their unique features: your partner's musical abilities, the musical performances at Coachella, or the promising alignment of your background with the job description. Profiles of local people, celebrities, vacation destinations, rock concerts, racehorses, and former presidents regularly appear in newspapers and magazines, sometimes in the form of interviews. In this chapter, we will focus on profiles of people.

Profiles are not always wildly positive—or negative. As you work to discover what person most interests you, consider the medium, or the most fitting means of delivery for your profile.

IDENTIFYING AN OPPORTUNITY FOR CHANGE

 Print Profile written for a community, campus, or corporate newspaper or magazine; a flyer, or a performance program

 Audio Profile recorded for a local radio station or as a podcast, perhaps in concert with your subject

 Online Profile composed as a blog entry, class bulletin board, multimedia presentation, or YouTube video (using SlideShare, PechaKucha, or iMovie)

GENRE IN FOCUS The Social Media Profile

According to Statista.com, in 2008, 10 percent of Americans had social media profiles; by 2019, 79 percent (or 247 million people) had posted one. The most popular social networks worldwide include Facebook, YouTube, WhatsApp, WeChat, Instagram, Tik Tok, and QQ. The availability of so many social networks makes access to one (or more) easier and, in some ways, almost essential.

As you all know, some social media profiles are more effective than others, the best ones optimize the relationship between content and presentation. Online expert Julia McCoy offers three basic ways to optimize a social media profile, including (1) unifying all your profile pictures across all platforms, making sure they effectively enhance your personal "brand"; (2) creating an informative profile bio that tells users who you are, what exactly you do, and when you are available; and (3) inserting memorable, relevant keywords in your headlines, photo captions, hashtags, and status updates (Figures 6.1-6.3).

Source: NASA

Figure 6.1 *The image and logo on the page for NASA on Facebook are repeated in various social media platforms to create a consistent profile.*

Source: NASA

Figure 6.2 *NASA on Twitter with the same rocket image and logo, in addition to memorable, relevant keywords like* explore *and* universe *in its "explore the universe and our home planet" message.*

Figure 6.3 *NASA's government web presence includes icons for various social media platforms and an informative profile bio with its vision statement: "to discover and expand knowledge for the benefit of humanity."*

Writers create profiles of people (as well as of organizations and businesses) to help readers (including themselves) gain a deeper understanding of another person (or entity), whether that person is well known or not. Sometimes writers create profiles to analyze the individuals who have shaped history, influenced other people, set a good example, or caused great harm. Well known throughout the world, NASA continues to draw steady attention, for the people who comprise NASA continue to work steadily to explore our solar system and beyond, provide resources for STEM (Science, Technology, Engineering, Math) educators, and monitor natural disasters all over the world. Many STEM students and professionals dream of working at NASA and participating in its many programs and initiatives.

The rhetorical response of a profile can serve to provide insight into a person through several rhetorical strategies of development, from narration, description, and argument to cause-and-effect analysis, process analysis, and

exemplification. (See CHAPTER 15, RHETORICAL STRATEGIES FOR DEVELOPMENT.) Profiles explain, describe, analyze causes and effects or processes. Some profiles
even inspire or entertain.

pages
278–294

 ASSIGNMENT

Among the people you know, whom do you find fascinating? What intrigues you
about them—their approach to life, their accomplishments, their unusual interests
or hobbies? As you consider which individual to profile, think about each person in
more detail: What is your dominant impression? What do you already know about
this person that supports your impression? What seems to contradict or temper
that impression?

In your profile, you will select details that together add up to the dominant
impression of your subject that you have developed and refined through further
investigation, including, possibly, interviews with the subject and about the subject,
as well as online and library research. Gather anecdotes about your subject from
diverse sources, facts that may interest your readers, and any other kinds of information that will allow your readers to become as fascinated by your subject as you are.

≫ READING RHETORICALLY

Profiles demonstrate to readers the dominant impression the subject makes.
In these relatively brief pieces, you want to be able to identify the subject and
examine that person's personality, words, actions, maybe body language, and
influence on others. You should also get a sense of the opportunity to which the
writer may be responding as well as the writer's purpose.

Key Features of a Profile

In a biographical profile, for instance, writers paint a portrait with words to
describe a person in detail and to show how the descriptive pieces fit together to
form the whole person. If you want to share your understanding (or judgment)

with a specific audience, consider writing a profile. Biographical profiles commonly have the following features:

- Profiles have as their subject someone readers will find compelling, interesting, maybe even puzzling.
- Profiles provide descriptive, sensory details to help readers imagine how the subject looks, sounds, acts, maybe even smells!
- Profiles include several direct quotations from the subject or others that help readers understand the person's opinions and perspectives.
- Profiles draw on evidence and insights from a variety of sources, such as personal observations, interviews, and library and online research.
- Profiles present several anecdotes about the subject that show readers the background and experiences that have shaped the subject.
- Profiles lead readers to a particular emotional response to, fresh take on, or logical conclusion about the subject.

In the following profile, *Los Angeles Times* writer Sandy Banks offers a profile of typical grocery store workers—checkers, stockers, and managers—many of whom have risen to the challenge of serving people during the pandemic. Vons employee Raymond Lopez says, "Everybody's nerves are heightened, but we don't have time to sit and panic. We have a job to do." Such words are launching heroic acts across our nation.

As you read through the following essay, consider the following:
- What makes these workers worthy of a profile?
- What makes them likable people you want to know more about?
- How are they ordinary people? First responders?

How Coronavirus Turned Supermarket Workers into Heroes

SANDY BANKS

Our world has been turned upside down by the novel SARS-CoV-2 coronavirus, a pandemic that took hold in Wuhan, China, quickly moved through Thailand, Japan, South Korea, and Europe, before moving to all the other continents, including North America. Healthcare workers continue to be hailed as "first responders," but theirs is not the only profession that has gone beyond the call of duty. This profile, written by Sandy Banks, illustrates the influence and sacrifice of our supermarket workers.

Jay L. Clendenin/Los Angeles Times via Getty Images

Raymond Lopez doesn't carry a stethoscope or wear a gun. He's more at home on a loading dock than in a fire station.

But as a grocery store worker, Lopez is on the front lines of our daily battle against a new enemy: coronavirus pandemic panic. •·····································

Banks makes clear that Raymond Lopez is an interesting figure, someone we want to know more about.

He's been working at Vons since he snagged a summer job as a bagger in Camarillo, 33 years ago.

"Back then, everybody aspired to be a grocery worker," Lopez told me. "It put food on the table, and you could support a family."

Today, supermarkets are playing a ground-zero role in our struggle to adapt to restrictions imposed by COVID-19. And grocery workers are bearing much of the brunt of our anxiety and frustration, as we descend on depleted stores.

Without masks or barriers, employees are working long hours, risking infection and battling exhaustion to do their jobs. They connect us to material essentials, like bread and toilet paper. But they're also part of the social fabric that holds us together in unsettling times. •·····································

The writer provides descriptive details to help us imagine the ordinary yet essential work Lopez does.

That friendly chat with the guy restocking the egg case this morning might be my only social interaction on this shelter-at-home day. And I feel better whenever I see my favorite cashier at her register. There's something reassuring about the familiar in a world where everything has changed.

Markets are about the only place we're still allowed to gather en masse. And their employees—pressed into service in ways they never expected—are our new first responders. They're apt to see us at our worst, and they aim to ease our strain.

We ought to thank them for their service, not blame them because market lines are long or inventory is low.

"We're being asked to do a lot more than we naturally would be," said Lopez, who lives in Pasadena and works in Glendale. •·····································

Throughout the profile, Banks quotes Lopez directly, offering readers an insight into his thinking, his personality.

Beyond the deep cleaning, shelf replenishing and crowd-control tasks, "there are all these new things, like figuring out the protective gear and learning how to interact with someone in the checkout line who is coughing or might be sick," he said.

"It's definitely an atmosphere where everybody's nerves are heightened, but we don't have time to sit and panic. We have a job to do."

Lopez manages the order and delivery process at his Vons. He's the person we expect to keep the shelves stocked, and Lopez and his team are working on overdrive.

"We're all very grateful that customers are patronizing our stores," he said. "But things snowballed incredibly fast . . . It's a whirlwind right now, and I think people are getting really tired.

"We're working six and seven days in row, staying late and coming in early. Because a lot of people are still out there, panic shopping for something."

Stores are limited now in how much they can order from main warehouses, "so we more or less put our puzzle pieces together and try to figure out what we're going to get," he said.

They've taken guff from rude customers, "but we don't fault them," he said. "We have some snappy customers, some unhappy people, but we understand their frustration. They're just trying to manage, like all of us."

Still, I've witnessed scenes that make me marvel at their patience and understand why nerves are fraying. •

Banks draws on her own observations and experiences to enhance the quality and substance of Lopez's profile.

On my Tuesday-morning foray to a local market for "senior shopping hour," an angry woman delayed our entrance while she loudly berated the employee at the door because she wasn't old enough to be admitted. We waited anxiously in line, in rubber gloves and paper masks, until he calmed her down and ushered us into the store.

That's a common scenario, according to John Grant, a former meatpacker who is president of the union that represents grocery employees in Southern California. "We've heard from 2,400 members raising concerns about safety protocols, crowd control, and access for seniors," he said.

"They're dealing with a public that's fearful, apprehensive and frustrated, and it gets hostile," Grant said. "This wasn't what they signed up for, but they realize it's their responsibility. They've cursed how vulnerable they are, and yet they keep going out of their profound dedication to their communities."

I hadn't thought about it much until now, but the supermarket has always been a place that bonded communities together. It's the sort of impromptu gathering spot where I was apt to run into that old soccer-mom buddy, or find myself in line behind the principal I locked horns with when my kid was in middle school. •

The writer leads readers to a fresh emotional response about the value of grocery-store culture and especially of grocery-story workers to provide a sense of stability, familiarity, and warmth.

I was in the grocery store when I found out Kobe Bryant died; the cashier and I were both crying as she checked me out. And all around us, people from every walk of life were grieving in clumps or wandering around shell-shocked until they found someone to hug.

My chat with Lopez, who still loves his job, made me think about how I felt the last time I was stuck in a crowd of fearful shoppers: impatient and desperate to gather what I needed and leave, because everyone seemed to be sneezing or standing too close to me. •

In the conclusion, the writer connects the treatment of the subject with the readers' sensibility and emotions.

I remember rolling my eyes when the cashier stalled our checkout process so she could teach the elderly man in front of me how to use the Apple Pay app.

"My son put this on for me," he announced, as he fumbled with his phone. It took forever to settle up for the $14 of dried lentils and canned tuna he bought.

I could hear the grumbling in the line behind me then: The cashier was inefficient; the old man was wasting our time. But now I think about that scene differently.

I imagine that man wandering aisles alone, confused and searching bare shelves. And I realize that cashier was not blind to the impatience of our line.

She was truly a first responder, attending to a more important but less visible need.

Source: Sandy Banks, "How Coronavirus Turned Supermarket Workers into Heroes," reprinted by permission from the Los Angeles Times, March 25, 2020.

Using Synthesis and Analysis

With purpose linked to audience, you will want to determine who the writer's intended audience might be: who might care about this subject? As you read, the overall impression you are making of the subject depends, in great part, on the writer's stance toward the subject (positive, negative, puzzled, or neutral). And that stance is often revealed by the kinds of research findings the writer includes: interviews, observations, firsthand experience, or library and online research. As you read through the profile, analyze the opening, the way the writer works to hook you into the story. Pay careful attention to the organization of the profile (chronological, emphatic, or rhythmic, with the give-and-take of an interview). And then observe carefully the closing. What words, what impression does the writer leave you with?

See also CHAPTER 1, **MICHAEL BÉRUBÉ,** *Life as We Know It*

See also CHAPTER 24, **RUBY TANDOH,** *Rachel Ama and the Trouble with Apolitical Food*

See also CHAPTER 27, **THE MARSHALL PROJECT,** *Cheer Team Caught Between Two Worlds*

See also CHAPTER 28, **LUCY DIAVOLO,** *Greta Thunberg Wants You — Yes, You — to Join the Climate Strike*

»» RESPONDING TO THE RHETORICAL SITUATION

Profiles are often the best response to a rhetorical opportunity that calls for specific information about a person, place, or event. Although profiles can be used to describe, judge, or reevaluate, most profiles are descriptive and informative. Academic departments, for instance, often feature profiles (also known as personal web pages) of the faculty and staff, along with information on course offerings, scholarships, majors, and minors. Businesses, hospitals, and organizations purposefully design electronic web pages, printed brochures, and portfolios, using descriptive words, specific details, and images to deliver relevant information about their personnel or their services to students, clients, and patients. When an opportunity calls for you to describe someone or something to an interested audience, a profile may be the best genre for you to develop.

Opportunity ▸ Audience and Purpose ▸ Genre/Profile ▸ Medium of Delivery

Understanding the Rhetorical Situation

Whatever opportunity you take to write a profile, you will be shaping it purposefully for a specific audience. In the process, you will be conducting research, summarizing your findings, synthesizing your research into a dominant impression, and then assembling supporting details, examples, facts, figures, and anecdotes. In a profile, you describe the dominant impression your subject makes. What are the traits that convey this impression? What words, behaviors, and appearances bring this impression to life? You may need to conduct informal and formal research—at the library, in person, or on the screen. You also may need to conduct some interviews. (For more on observation and interviews, see FIELDWORK in CHAPTER 19.) Drawing on your research findings, your observations, and your insights, compose a profile that is rich in revealing details of appearance, speech, experience, education, beliefs, or actions. Your glimpse into a person's private life and personal experience might even explain the very visible work or actions that person performs.

pages 375–377

Identifying an Opportunity for Change

To identify a rhetorical opportunity, consider the people who work, study, or perform in your community. Whose voices are shaping the dialogue about pressing campus, community, church, or even national concerns? Whose voices are influencing the attitudes and actions of others? Ministers, for instance, often craft their messages with deft rhetorical style, as do teachers, coaches, civic leaders, and certain family members. These individuals create opportunities for others to develop talents, activism, and abilities, or they work behind the scenes unnoticed. Maybe you want to learn more about these people. Maybe others need to know about them as well. (Many of the following ideas can be translated into a profile of a place, event, or memorial as well.)

1. List three people who have recently impressed you. Have any of your fellow students motivated others to action through their words? Any teachers encouraged students to develop their talents and join conversations or activities on campus? What about entertainers, or writers, or local leaders in your community (maybe an elected official who suspended rent or mortgage payments during the pandemic, or someone who started a food-relief program)? For each person on your list, write a few sentences describing your initial impressions. Explain those impressions by writing down as many details as you can about these people and what drew you to them. Who else might find these individuals impressive?

2. For one or two of the people you listed in response to question #1, locate images—or, if the opportunity presents itself, take photos (with permission)—that capture the individuals' qualities or actions. Then spend several minutes writing about what the visuals convey about the ability of these individuals to inject life, energy, and direction into their words or actions. Who might want to know about these people?

3. Select one person for your profile and compose four or five sentences describing instances and ways that this person has succeeded or failed. Spend several minutes freewriting about the contexts in which this person has influenced and inspired people. Describe what you know about the person's background and analyze how this background might have shaped the person's drive, purpose, or success.

Relating Rhetorically to Your Audience

The following questions will help you identify your rhetorical audience for your profile. Your answers will also help you describe and analyze your subject's effective way with words, action, or even silence.

1. List the names of the persons or groups (students, faculty, administrators, community members, or alumni) likely to be engaged—positively or negatively—by your subject.

2. Next to the name of each potential audience, write reasons that audience could have for appreciating the subject. In other words, what would persuade these audiences that they need to learn about this person's experiences, perspectives, and motivations in greater detail?

3. How could each of these audiences be influenced by a profile of this individual? What emotional responses or logical conclusions could you expect your profile to lead to? Consider the implications of these emotional responses or logical conclusions for each audience and the motivations each audience might have for learning more about the personal experiences, values, and worldview that have affected your subject.

4. With these different audiences' interests and motivations in mind, consider what descriptive details, images, and compelling quotes or audio snippets (if you conduct and record interviews) will enable your readers to feel invested in exploring the life of this person who has helped shape the campus or the local or broader community. A compelling description will help your

audience more clearly visualize the person in action, appreciate how he or she has moved people, and understand how this individual has affected you or the local or broader community. Tailor your best description to connect closely to your audience's needs and interests.

Planning an Effective Rhetorical Response for Your Purpose

Once you have identified a reason to compose a profile, you will want to focus on your audience, the people who want to learn more about your subject, whether that subject is you, another person, an event, or a place. Different audiences require different kinds of texts—delivered through different media. For example, if you are writing a profile about yourself, say in a résumé and cover letter, you will want to deliver those informative materials according to a potential employer's preference: electronically through an online portal or in print via the postal service. If you are writing a profile about an unsung student researcher on campus, you could compose an inspiring feature article for the alumni magazine or create a YouTube video for the Office of Student Life website. Your celebratory profile of a family member—even one capturing family lore—could be the PowerPoint centerpiece of a family reunion. Once you identify your opportunity, locate your audience, and find your purpose, you will determine what kind of text will best respond to the rhetorical situation.

Use the following questions to help you narrow your purpose and shape your response:

1. What facts, details, and images are necessary for creating a vivid picture of your subject and your subject's influence? What research will produce that information?
2. What experiences, activities, actions, and personal qualities make your subject compelling to your audience?
3. What specific information does your audience need to understand your subject's motivation and appreciate that person's significance for the family, school, or community? What research is necessary?
4. What is your rhetorical purpose? Will your audience adopt a new perspective on your subject, take a specific action, or something else?
5. What is the best way to reach this audience? That is, to what kind of text—print, electronic, verbal, visual, video—will this audience most likely respond?

Profiles

Minerva Studio/Alamy Stock Photo

AP Photo/Toby Talbot

Lori Waselchuk/The New York Times/Redux Pictures

Print Profile In the example at the beginning of this chapter, *L.A. Times* writer Banks wrote a profile on supermarket workers, everyday heroes.

Audio Profile Podcaster Phil Stubbs profiles Bill McKibben in "Bill McKibben—Lion of the Climate Movement" for *The Environment Show*, an environmental podcast and blog.

Online Profile The online profile of Beverly Wright of the Deep South Center for Environmental Justice was composed by Faiza Elmasry.

WRITING A PERSUASIVE PROFILE: A Guide

Writing a persuasive profile involves evidence. Profiles persuade by using vivid details, snippets of conversation, short anecdotes, and maybe even images that reveal the subject's character. Most profiles are organized around the rhetorical appeals of ethos, logos, and pathos. The writer must establish the credibility of the subject (ethos), shape the argument with evidence and good reasons (logos), and make an emotional connection (pathos) with the reader. (See CHAPTER 2, THE AVAILABLE MEANS INCLUDE THE RHETORICAL ELEMENTS OF THE MESSAGE ITSELF.) pages 23–26 After capturing your readers' attention in the introduction with a brief image of the subject, you will want to shape the body of your profile with assertions that point to the fuller description of the subject and influence to come.

ADVANTAGES AND LIMITATIONS

Advantages

- **Writer:** Profiles offer the opportunity for you to find out more about someone who (or something that) already impresses you, a subject that does not have to be globally known or significant. Your subject can be close by, even familiar. Researching and composing a profile helps satisfy your curiosity about your subject and often reveals new, refreshing details.

- **Message:** Profiles provide insight into a person, place, or event, using rhetorical strategies of narration, description, exemplification, and argument. You can deliver your profile in an energetic, friendly way, if you choose.

- **Media and Design:** Profiles offer you the pleasure of sharing your impression with others, through conversation, a print essay, or a visual presentation.

Limitations

- **Writer:** Unfortunately, you cannot always meet your subject in person. Most profiles require research, at the library, online, through interviews, and by observation.

- **Message:** Commissioned profiles are often much more formal in tone and frequently demand clear images.

- **Media and Design:** Unless you have been asked by an organization to produce a specific profile, you must make an effort to locate a rhetorical audience, one that could be changed in some way by learning more about your subject.

Introduction

- **Show readers that the subject is someone they need to know more about.**
- **Present the dominant impression made by the subject and highlight key features of the subject's personality, character, or values.**

Highlight features your readers will want to know more about Supply your readers with a compelling incident about, a powerful description of, or convincing results produced by your subject to persuade them to keep reading. Sandy Banks, for example, opens with a description of Lopez, who neither carries a stethoscope nor wears a gun, a man she goes on to describe as a hero for his commitment to serving the public, especially during disasters like those brought on by COVID-19. This information is followed with, "Without masks or barriers, employees working long hours, risking infection and battling exhaustion do their jobs. They connect us to material essentials, like bread and toilet paper. But they're also part of the social fabric that holds us together in unsettling times." Readers have to wonder what more could lie ahead in a tale of everyday grocery-store workers, who "see us at our worst, and . . . aim to ease our strain."

Create goodwill for your subject To entice readers to continue, a profile writer must quickly establish the rhetorical appeal of credible ethos. The same writer goes on to capture the modesty of Lopez, who does not "fault" the "rude customers," who are "just trying to manage, just like us." His humility and kindness help create a sense of goodwill and good sense, all the while alluding to a hard-working grocery man. Thus, this writer supplies a believable, trustworthy account of Lopez and others who are dedicated to their communities.

Connect your subject to your readers' interests and values By establishing a positive ethos, the writer connects Lopez's story of dedication with the appreciation, even admiration of the readers. "Have I thanked my cashier?" "Have I waited patiently in line?" "Have I behaved generously?" "Have I worn a mask?" Thus, the writer establishes common ground with her readers as well as the shared concern of those working hard to supply us with groceries and other necessary items during the pandemic.

Ask yourself . . .
- How can I connect my concerns about my subject with the interests of my audience?
- What incident, descriptive details, and examples might most successfully engage my readers' interest at the same time they reveal my dominant impression of my subject?
- How can I best establish my credibility and my subject's significance?

- **Present a fuller description of the subject, emphasizing the key features of that overall impression.**
- **Include specific details, descriptions, conversations, and anecdotes that help readers visualize the subject in body, words, and actions.**
- **Provide logical appeals in the form of good reasons, backed up with detailed examples that demonstrate the effect of that subject on the lives of people like the readers themselves.**

Establish good reasons for your dominant impression of the subject Writers use the body of a profile to establish logos, the logical appeals of good reasons. These reasons often appeal in the form of multiple supporting examples and details. The assertions and supporting examples make obvious the work, influence, personal qualities, and actions of the subject.

Show how your subject has made a difference Thirty-three years ago, Lopez began working at Vons grocery store: "Back then, everybody aspired to be a grocery worker. It put food on the table, and you could support a family." Today, he describes his gratitude that "customers are patronizing our stores, . . . It's a whirlwind right now, and I think people are getting tired." Including Lopez, who is working "six and seven days in a row, staying late and coming in early," so his customers can put food on the table.

Provide quotations that give the profile credibility Throughout the essay, the writer draws on her own experience of shopping for groceries in a familiar place where she knows the checkers and the stockers, of sharing grief when Kobe Bryant died, of witnessing a checker's patience with a line of frustrated customers. Her direct quotations from Lopez, from the president of the grocery union, from an older man who learned how to use the Apple Pay app, and from the patient cashier all support the dominant impression of calm and order in the face of high stress and confusion. These details also capture the measure of Lopez's significance—and that of grocery workers everywhere—to their communities and to a sense of community at large.

Create a story through vivid description Incorporate narrative to draw readers closer to the subject. The stories of crying for Bryant and of the older man fumbling with Apple Pay provide readers a glimpse into the social significance of the workers we too often take for granted.

Ask yourself . . .
- What assertions am I making about my subject that bring the dominant impression to life?
- What specific examples, details, anecdotes, and results can I supply for each assertion?
- How believable or relatable do these examples seem to be?

- **Capture with one final quote or anecdote the dominant impression of the subject.**
- **Trace the influence of the subject and perhaps predict that person's future influence.**
- **Work to connect the treatment of the subject with the readers' sensibility or emotions.**
- **Bring readers into the present day, if the profile has had a historical scope.**

Capture the essence of your subject in a final quotation The conclusion of a profile often contains one final quote or anecdote that nicely captures the essence of the individual. In the case of supermarket workers, Banks ends with the story of just one: "She was truly a first responder, attending to a more important but less visible need."

Reinforce the connection to your readers By capturing the humility and generosity of the workers—their dedication, patience, even gratitude—the writer reinforces the dominant impression of good people doing good things for the greater good.

Ask yourself . . .
- What impression do I most want to leave with my readers?
- How can I stimulate the readers to consider the lasting effects of my subject(s)?

»» REVISION AND PEER REVIEW

After you have drafted a strong version of your profile, ask one or two of your classmates to read through it. You will respond to your work in a way that helps you revise it into the strongest profile it can be, one that addresses your intended audience, helps you fulfill your purpose, and is delivered in the most appropriate means available to you. In other words, if your profile were your peer's, how would that classmate revise it?

Questions for a Peer Reviewer

1. What is the dominant impression the profile expresses?
2. Who might constitute an interested audience for this profile?
3. What is the writer's purpose in composing for this audience?
4. Why might the writer feel a need to compose this profile?
5. Where in the profile do you find the answers to the first four questions?
6. How and where did the writer "hook" you into the story? How might that hook be strengthened?
7. How and where did the writer establish credibility or ethos? (This might be in several places.)
8. Mark the supporting details and examples the writer provides that bring the subject and subject's influence to life, that shape the logos of the profile.
9. Highlight the experiences and actions that make the subject interesting to you. In what way could the writer help you better understand what influences this subject has or what the effects of this subject might be? Be specific.
10. Where and how does the writer make an emotional connection (establish pathos) with the reader? How might the writer strengthen this rhetorical appeal?
11. What did you learn from the conclusion that you did not already know after reading the introduction and body? What information does the writer want you to take away from the profile? Does the writer attempt to change your attitude, action, or opinion?
12. Which section of the profile did you most enjoy? Why?
13. Which section of the profile was the most difficult for you to follow? Why?

✎ ADDITIONAL ASSIGNMENTS

Knowledge Transfer

The profile need not be limited to people. Places, organizations, and events also merit profiles. When you visit the Smithsonian Institution museums, national parks, or famous landmarks, you can usually obtain a profile in the form of a brochure, which relays the dominant impression you should take away from the place and supplies a multitude of facts and details that breathe life into that place. Businesses and organizations, too, post profiles, often online, as do events, like Burning Man, the Macy's Thanksgiving Day Parade, even your first-year writing course.

COLLEGE Ethnography An ethnography is a profile of individual peoples and cultural customs using personal observation and experience. It is often used in anthropology courses. After, or instead of, conducting an interview, you might arrange to observe the person you interviewed at work, shadowing that person throughout the day and interviewing coworkers. Again, you will want to glean ample background information (education, experience) in order to connect the person's present to the past—and then to the future. You might ask coworkers what impresses them most about the person, what challenges that person has overcome, or what problems continue to vex that person.

COMMUNITY Introduction Compose a profile of your hometown, delivering it in print, in visuals, or electronically (with visuals and audio), and introduce yourself by way of advertising your hometown. You can rely on your own observations and experiences, interviews, and some local research in order to collect enough detailed information that you can create a dominant impression. Be sure also to reveal the places and events that distinguish your hometown.

WORKPLACE Interview If you know someone whose occupation interests you, arrange to conduct an interview with that person, taking with you a list of generative questions that will help you arrive at a dominant impression. Be sure to ask about background, education, experience, daily life on the job, goals, and, if appropriate, domestic life. Come up with a question that might reveal something about the individual's personality: What role has disappointment played in your life? Or, what place would you most like to visit?

MULTIMODAL Video Résumé Although the use of video job applications is not yet widespread, chances are it soon will be, given that Skype interviews have already replaced many face-to-face ones. Compose a profile of yourself, showing how your experience, education, and goals align with specific job criteria. Before recording yourself and your voice, write out a script you want to follow, deciding whether the job calls for you to present yourself as businesslike, formal, casual, or creative. The same goes for your dress. Whether you use iMovie, your smartphone, or a camera to film yourself, you can easily revise what you see and hear.

Profiles

7 Investigative Reports

- Identify an issue, problem, or phenomenon, possibly something controversial, where an investigative report could correct misinformation, explain a process, or analyze the causes behind particular consequences.

- Explain the purpose of an investigative report in terms of its key rhetorical features and principles of development in various media.

- Define an issue such that its importance is clear to your rhetorical audience.

- Apply *who, what, where,* and *why* questions to an issue to create an investigative report.

- Evaluate factual, data-driven, observed, and experiential research and develop the ability to support your report with direct quotations, facts, and data, citing your research appropriately.

- Apply peer review and self-evaluation to revise, edit, and proofread an investigative report to create a fair-minded, data-driven, and logical conclusion.

If you think investigative reports appear only on *Law & Order* or *CSI* (*Crime Scene Investigation*), then you may want to reconsider. Print, online, and televised news provide investigative reports; textbooks report subject-specific information, just as organizations (museums, clubs, initiatives, and government agencies) give you factual information that has been objectively investigated—or researched. The result of fact-finding or data-driven research, a **report** serves to highlight the author's expertise with the purpose of informing or educating an audience.

report a presentation of objective information on a topic

Throughout this chapter, you will work to identify an opportunity to investigate and then report your findings to a specific audience. As you determine what you want to investigate and who could be educated by your report, consider, too, the most fitting means of delivery.

IDENTIFYING AN OPPORTUNITY FOR CHANGE

Print Report written for a community or campus newspaper or as a lab report for your chemistry professor

Video Report filmed for your cultural anthropology course or filmed and uploaded to YouTube for your friends and family

Online Report composed for your online campus newspaper or your personal blog

GENRE IN FOCUS The Explainer Report

In only 0.42 second, Google provides 153,000 hits for the phrase "bad student writing." The American public has long complained about the quality and character of student writing, blaming the influences of television, rock 'n roll, teen apathy, self-absorption, and now digital communication. (See CHAPTER 15, pages 286–289 CAUSE-AND-EFFECT ANALYSIS.) When researchers at Carnegie Mellon University investigated the issue, they outlined several contributing factors:

> **During their high school careers, most of our students were not writing with the frequency we might expect, nor were they doing the types of writing that we will require of them in their college years. In a study at George Washington University (2007), first-year undergraduates reported that the most frequently assigned high school writing tasks required them to offer and support opinions, with a secondary emphasis on summarizing and synthesizing information. Students were rarely required to criticize an argument, define a problem and propose a solution, shape their writing to meet their readers' needs, or revise based on feedback. Furthermore, according to a survey conducted by *The Chronicle of Higher Education* (2006), 61% of high school teachers said their students have never written a paper that was more than five pages. As a result, students have not had enough practice to develop a set of sophisticated writing skills. When students lack skills in these areas, their writing may be unsatisfactory in multiple ways—from poor grammar and syntax to unclear organization to weak reasoning and arguments.**
>
> **—"Why Are Students Coming into College Poorly Prepared to Write?"**

In "Bad Student Writing? Not So Fast!" Laurie Fendrich takes issue with the Carnegie Mellon explanation. In her article, Fendrich compares complaints about the most recent generation of students to those made by ancient Greeks. (See CHAPTER 15, COMPARISON AND CONTRAST.)

pages 285–286

It would be good for the blood pressure of everyone involved in criticizing education—state legislators, education policy professionals, professors, school administrators, parents—to take a deep breath. Put aside the statistics, the studies, the anecdotes, and take a look at the big picture.

Here's what Edith Hamilton had to say about education, in *The Echo of Greece* (1957), one of her many trenchant books on the subject of the ancient Greeks:

> If people feel that things are going from bad to worse and look at the new generation to see if they can be trusted to take charge among such dangers, they invariably conclude that they cannot and that these irresponsible young people have not been trained properly. Then the cry goes up, "What is wrong with our education?" and many answers are always forthcoming.

investigative report an analysis of the "who, what, where, and why" of a topic

Note the droll and ironic, "and many answers are always forthcoming." Perhaps studying people who lived so long ago—people who invented the very idea of education as a route to genuine freedom, and understood freedom to be worthwhile only when coupled with self-control—gave Hamilton one of those calm, stoical uber-minds that comprehends competing pronounce-ments about education never to be more than opinion.

—Laurie Fendrich, "Bad Student Writing? Not So Fast!"

A protester from the Turkish-Arabic Media Association holds a poster of an investigative journalist, who was critical of the Saudi Kingdom. Jamal Khashoggi was murdered on October 2, 2018, at the Saudi consulate in Istanbul.

Chris McGrath/Getty Images

An **investigative report** provides information on the "who, what, where, and why" of a situation or topic. It is a rhetorical response often triggered by a desire to correct misinformation. A report will first need to define the issue being investigated (see CHAPTER 15, DEFINITION.) After establishing the "what," an investigative report might focus on an explanation for the situation or process (see CHAPTER 15, PROCESS ANALYSIS) or an analysis of the causes behind particular consequences, as in the Carnegie Mellon report. Even an objective and fair-minded report of information will have to present evidence that supports your conclusion. (For more on types of evidence, see CHAPTER 2, LOGOS.) If you are interested in an issue about which there is a need for more information, especially a problem that is controversial or one where you have come across information with which you do not agree—such as students are not writing well because they are not well prepared for college writing—an investigative report helps you get information to interested readers.

pages 282–284

pages 289–291

page 24

 ASSIGNMENT

When you want to find out more about why a particular issue is the way it is, you will want to research the topic and then compose an investigative report in order to present the results of research you have conducted about that problem (or one with which you have personal experience). To begin, you need to decide what topic bothers you to the point that you would like to investigate and report on it? What misinformation would you like to correct? What audience is affected by this topic and would be interested in your report?

If you live in a college community, you may be wondering how underage drinking, pandemic parties, physical assault—or even homelessness—affects your community in some way. On or away from campus, you might either have firsthand knowledge of, or want to research consequences of, such issues as divorce, eating disorders, chemical waste, or genetic testing. For your investigative report, gather trustworthy and factual information that enables you to confidently report your findings in a manner that establishes your fair-mindedness, the reasonableness of your argument, and an authentic connection to the concerns of your audience.

»» READING RHETORICALLY

When you read an investigative report, your charge is to read what is there—and identify what has been left out. Because investigative reports are presented as factual and objective, it can be difficult to measure the amount of research the writer undertook. It is up to you to imagine what sources or points of view are not represented. You also want to determine the audience for the report. Who are likely affected by the information? How are they affected? How might they use the information?

Key Features of a Report

An investigative report commonly has the following features:

- Defines an issue, problem, or phenomenon in precise terms.
- Makes clear why the topic under consideration needs to be investigated.
- Provides trustworthy facts and details that help readers understand the effects of this topic and determine who has a stake in the situation.
- Uses direct quotations to convey the perspectives of various groups with a stake in the issue.
- Relies on appropriate organization and design.
- Identifies the conclusion readers should reach.

In the report that follows, Christine Rosen responds to the common student complaint that e-mail is just too slow, taking the opportunity to explain the common perceptions—and misperceptions—about multitasking. As you read through Rosen's report, keep notes on what is really happening in our brains when we try to pay attention to many things at once.

- What experts does Rosen consult? What are their viewpoints on multitasking (its causes, consequences, and complications)?
- How does Rosen establish her credibility?
- Who is her rhetorical audience?
- How is her report a fitting response to the problem, particularly in terms of reaching her rhetorical audience?

The Myth of Multitasking

CHRISTINE ROSEN

Christine Rosen is a senior editor for The New Atlantis: A Journal of Technology & Society, *where she frequently writes about ethics and the cultural impact of technology.*

Kris Connor/Getty Images Entertainment/ Getty Images

In one of the many letters he wrote to his son in the 1740s, Lord Chesterfield offered the following advice: "There is time enough for everything in the course of the day, if you do but one thing at once, but there is not time enough in the year, if you will do two things at a time." To Chesterfield, singular focus was not merely a practical way to structure one's time; it was a mark of intelligence. "This steady and undissipated attention to one object, is a sure mark of a superior genius; as hurry, bustle, and agitation are the never-failing symptoms of a weak and frivolous mind."

Rosen opens with age-old advice about the wisdom of doing one thing at a time. She has identified a rhetorical opportunity for addressing the modern-day practice of multitasking.

In modern times, hurry, bustle, and agitation have become a regular way of life for many people—so much so that we have embraced a word to describe our efforts to respond to the many pressing demands on our time: *multitasking*. Used for decades to describe the parallel processing abilities of computers, multitasking is now shorthand for the human attempt to do simultaneously as many things as possible, as quickly as possible, preferably marshalling the power of as many technologies as possible.

Rosen defines her topic in precise terms: multitasking has become a way of life, or at least an expectation.

In the late 1990s and early 2000s, one sensed a kind of exuberance about the possibilities of multitasking. Advertisements for new electronic gadgets—particularly the first generation of handheld digital devices—celebrated the notion of using technology to accomplish several things at once. The word *multitasking* began appearing in the "skills" sections of résumés, as office workers restyled themselves as high-tech, high-performing team players. "We have always multitasked—inability to walk and chew gum is a time-honored cause for derision—but never so intensely or self-consciously as now," James Gleick wrote in his 1999 book *Faster*. "We are multitasking connoisseurs—experts in crowding, pressing, packing, and overlapping distinct activities in our all-too-finite moments." An article in the *New York Times Magazine* in 2001 asked, "Who can remember life before multitasking? These days we all do it." The article offered advice on "How to Multitask" with suggestions about giving your brain's "multitasking hot spot" an appropriate workout.

Because we cannot remember life before multitasking, Rosen determines that the practice should be investigated.

But more recently, challenges to the ethos of multitasking have begun to emerge. Numerous studies have shown the sometimes-fatal danger of using cell phones and other electronic devices while driving, for example, and several states have now made that particular form of multitasking illegal. In the business world, where concerns about time-management are perennial, warnings about workplace distractions spawned by a multitasking culture are on the rise. In 2005, the BBC reported on a research study, funded by Hewlett-Packard and conducted by the Institute of Psychiatry at the University of London, that found, "Workers distracted by e-mail and phone calls suffer a fall in IQ more than twice that found in marijuana smokers." The psychologist who led the study called this new "infomania" a serious threat to workplace productivity. One of the *Harvard Business Review*'s "Breakthrough Ideas" for 2007 was Linda Stone's notion of "continuous partial attention," which might be understood as

Rosen provides facts and details that complicate the once-easy notion of multitasking. She enumerates the negative effects of multitasking on specific people and provides compelling facts and details.

Throughout her report, Rosen uses direct quotations to convey various perspectives, both positive and negative.

a subspecies of multitasking: using mobile computing power and the Internet, we are "constantly scanning for opportunities and staying on top of contacts, events, and activities in an effort to miss nothing."•

Dr. Edward Hallowell, a Massachusetts-based psychiatrist who specializes in the treatment of attention deficit/hyperactivity disorder and has written a book with the self-explanatory title *CrazyBusy*, has been offering therapies to combat extreme multitasking for years; in his book he calls multitasking a "mythical activity in which people believe they can perform two or more tasks simultaneously."• In a 2005 article, he described a new condition, "Attention Deficit Trait," which he claims is rampant in the business world. ADT is "purely a response to the hyperkinetic environment in which we live," writes Hallowell, and its hallmark symptoms mimic those of ADD. "Never in history has the human brain been asked to track so many data points," Hallowell argues, and this challenge "can be controlled only by creatively engineering one's environment and one's emotional and physical health." Limiting multitasking is essential. Best-selling business advice author Timothy Ferriss also extols the virtues of "single-tasking" in his book, *The 4-Hour Workweek*.

Changing Our Brains

To better understand the multitasking phenomenon, neurologists and psychologists have studied the workings of the brain. In 1999, Jordan Grafman, chief of cognitive neuroscience at the National Institute of Neurological Disorders and Stroke (part of the National Institutes of Health), used functional magnetic resonance imaging (fMRI) scans to determine that when people engage in "task-switching"—that is, multitasking behavior—the flow of blood increases to a region of the frontal cortex called Brodmann area 10. (The flow of blood to particular regions of the brain is taken as a proxy indication of activity in those regions.) "This is presumably the last part of the brain to evolve, the most mysterious and exciting part," Grafman told the *New York Times* in 2001—adding, with a touch of hyperbole, "It's what makes us most human." •

Evidence from careful research helps Rosen establish her ethos and enhances the logos of her overall argument as well as its trustworthiness.

It is also what makes multitasking a poor long-term strategy for learning. . . . In one recent study, Russell Poldrack, a psychology professor at the University of California, Los Angeles, found that "multitasking adversely affects how you learn. Even if you learn while multitasking, that learning is less flexible and more specialized, so you cannot retrieve the information as easily." His research demonstrates that people use different areas of the brain for learning and storing new information when they are distracted: brain scans of people who are distracted or multitasking show activity in the striatum, a region of the brain involved in learning new skills; brain scans of people who are not distracted show activity in the hippocampus, a region involved in storing and recalling information. Discussing his research on National Public Radio recently, Poldrack warned, "We have to be aware that there is a cost to the way that our society is changing, that humans are not built to work this way. We're really built to focus. And when we sort of force ourselves to multitask, we're driving ourselves to perhaps be less efficient in the long run even though it sometimes feels like we're being more efficient."

If, as Poldrack concluded, "multitasking changes the way people learn," what might this mean for today's children and teens, raised with an excess of new entertainment and educational technology, and avidly multitasking at a young age? Poldrack calls this the "million-dollar question." Media multitasking—that is, the simultaneous use of several different media, such as television, the internet, video games, text messages, telephones, and e-mail—is clearly on the rise, as a 2006 report from the Kaiser Family Foundation showed: in 1999, only 16 percent of the time people spent using any of those media was spent on multiple media at once; by 2005, 26 percent of media time was spent multitasking. "I multitask every single second I am online," confessed one study participant. "At this very moment I am watching TV, checking my e-mail every two minutes, reading a newsgroup about who shot JFK, burning some music to a CD, and writing this message."

The Kaiser report noted several factors that increase the likelihood of media multitasking, including "having a computer and being able to see a tele-vision from it." Also, "sensation-seeking" personality types are more likely to multitask, as are those living in "a highly TV-oriented household." The picture that emerges of these pubescent multitasking mavens is of a generation of great technical facility and intelligence but of extreme impatience, unsatisfied with slowness and uncomfortable with silence: "I get bored if it's not all going at once, because everything has gaps—waiting for a website to come up, commercials on TV, etc." one participant said. The report concludes on a very peculiar note, perhaps intended to be optimistic: "In this media-heavy world, it is likely that brains that are more adept at media multitasking will be passed along and these changes will be naturally selected," the report states. "After all, information is power, and if one can process more information all at once, perhaps one can be more powerful." This is techno-social Darwinism.

Other experts aren't so sure. As neurologist Jordan Grafman told *Time* magazine: "Kids that are instant messaging while doing homework, playing games online and watching TV, I predict, aren't going to do well in the long run." "I think this generation of kids is guinea pigs," educational psychologist

Noting potential negative effects on children is a good way for Rosen to establish pathos, to make a strong emotional connection with her readers.

Jane Healy told the *San Francisco Chronicle*; she worries that they might become adults who engage in "very quick but very shallow thinking." Or, as the novelist Walter Kirn suggests in a deft essay in *The Atlantic*, we might be headed for an "Attention-Deficit Recession."

Paying Attention

Rosen moves toward a conclusion by quoting Newton and James, historical figures whose contributions to culture have been monumental. Each of them, like Lord Chesterfield, recommends paying attention to one thing at a time.

When we talk about multitasking, we are really talking about attention: the art of paying attention, the ability to shift our attention, and, more broadly, to exercise judgment about what objects are worthy of our attention. People who have achieved great things often credit for their success a finely honed skill for paying attention. When asked about his particular genius, Isaac Newton responded that if he had made any discoveries, it was "owing more to patient attention than to any other talent."

William James, the great psychologist, wrote at length about the varieties of human attention. In *The Principles of Psychology* (1890), he outlined the differences among "sensorial attention," "intellectual attention," "passive attention," and the like, and noted the "gray chaotic indiscriminateness" of the minds of people who were incapable of paying attention. James compared our stream of thought to a river, and his observations presaged the cognitive "bottlenecks" described later by neurologists: "On the whole easy simple flowing predominates in it, the drift of things is with the pull of gravity, and effortless attention is the rule," he wrote. "But at intervals an obstruction, a set-back, a log-jam occurs, stops the current, creates an eddy, and makes things temporarily move the other way."

Rosen organizes her report appropriately, opening with a problem to be investigated, objectively reporting various viewpoints, providing factual evidence, quoting the experts, and building toward a sensible conclusion.

To James, steady attention was thus the default condition of a mature mind, an ordinary state undone only by perturbation. To readers a century later, that placid portrayal may seem alien—as though depicting a bygone world. Instead, today's multitasking adult may find something more familiar in James's description of the youthful mind: an "extreme mobility of the attention" that "makes the child seem to belong less to himself than to every object which happens to catch his notice." For some people, James noted, this challenge is never overcome; such people only get their work done "in the interstices of their mind-wandering." Like Chesterfield, James believed that the transition from youthful distraction to mature attention was in large part the result of personal mastery and discipline—and so was illustrative of character. "The faculty of voluntarily bringing back a wandering attention, over and over again," he wrote, "is the very root of judgment, character, and will."

Rosen reaches the conclusion that "our collective will to pay attention seems fairly weak," and she has provided factual, objective evidence to support that conclusion.

Today, our collective will to pay attention seems fairly weak. We require advice books to teach us how to avoid distraction. In the not-too-distant future we may even employ new devices to help us overcome the unintended attention deficits created by today's gadgets. As one *New York Times* article recently suggested, "Further research could help create clever technology, like sensors or smart software that workers could instruct with their preferences and priorities to serve as a high tech 'time nanny' to ease the modern multitasker's plight." Perhaps we will all accept as a matter of course a computer governor—like the devices placed on engines so that people can't drive cars beyond a certain speed. Our technological governors might prompt us with reminders to set mental limits when we try to do too much, too quickly, all at once.

Then again, perhaps we will simply adjust and come to accept what James called "acquired inattention." E-mails pouring in, cell phones ringing, televisions blaring, podcasts streaming—all this may become background noise, like the "din of a foundry or factory" that James observed workers could scarcely avoid at first, but which eventually became just another part of their daily routine. For the younger generation of multitaskers, the great electronic din is an expected part of everyday life. And given what neuroscience and anecdotal evidence have shown us, this state of constant intentional self-distraction could well be of profound detriment to individual and cultural well-being. When people do their work only in the "interstices of their mind-wandering," with crumbs of attention rationed out among many competing tasks, their culture may gain in information, but it will surely weaken in wisdom.

> Rosen admits that perhaps it's too late to turn back the clock on multitasking and that modern society may need to resign itself to a tradeoff between information and wisdom.

Source: Christine Rosen, "The Myth of Multitasking." *The New Atlantis*, no. 20, spring 2008, pp. 105–110.

Using Synthesis and Analysis

Take a minute to review Rosen's report. Cluster all the positive statements about multitasking, keeping track of the differences among the responses. Then do the same with all the negative statements. What is the overall opinion of each side of the argument? How do the opinions on each side vary? What opinions may be missing from her report?

Although Rosen offers positive and negative opinions rooted in facts, she concludes with a negative report about multitasking. Can you determine what her opinion might have been as she entered her investigation? Why the topic captured her interest in the first place? What textual evidence supports your belief?

See also CHAPTER 24, **MICHAEL POLLAN,** *Out of the Kitchen, Onto the Couch* [The Collapse of Home Cooking]

See also CHAPTER 26, **FREYA DROHAN,** *Anti-Homeless Architecture*

See also CHAPTER 25, **ASSOCIATED PRESS,** *Federal Study Finds Race and Gender Affect Face-Scanning Technology*

See also CHAPTER 28, **MEERA SUBRAMANIAN,** *Generation Climate: Can Young Evangelicals Change the Climate Debate?*

See also CHAPTER 28, **ELAINE KAMARCK,** *The Challenging Politics of Climate Change*

» RESPONDING TO THE RHETORICAL SITUATION

In every case, reports are responses to rhetorical opportunities, problems, or questions that might be addressed or resolved by research findings. "What can be done about 'bad student writing'?" "How much 'underage drinking' is there on my campus?" "What are the disadvantages and advantages of multitasking?" These are the kinds of issues that often launch the research necessary for composing a knowledgeable, credible report for an audience who wants to know.

Opportunity	Audience and Purpose	Genre/Report	Medium of Delivery

Understanding the Rhetorical Situation

pages 375–377

Whatever topic you choose, your investigation might take the form of personal experience as well as observations, interviews, surveys (see FIELDWORK in CHAPTER 19), or traditional research in the library or online. The quality of your research findings (factual, data-driven, observed, and experienced) will enhance your ethos, help you strengthen the logos of your message, and perhaps bolster your pathos, the emotional connection you make with your audience. (See CHAPTER 2, THE AVAILABLE

pages 23–26

MEANS INCLUDE THE RHETORICAL ELEMENTS OF THE MESSAGE ITSELF.)

 RESEARCHING THE INVESTIGATIVE REPORT

As you research your topic, you will want to be clear about your own stance. Why does the topic interest you in the first place? What specific belief, attitude, or action do you want to investigate—maybe even challenge? Once you have established your attitude toward your topic, you will want to measure the gap between what you already know (or think you know) and do not know about the topic. And you will want to use your library and online research to fill that gap. As you discover how experts (published authors and scholars) weigh in on the topic, you might compare their views with your own as well as with those of people in your circle whom you have interviewed. If you are lucky, you can apply some of your own personal experience to the topic. During your research process, you may discover that your topic is too narrow or too broad and that you need to adjust it accordingly so that it meets the criteria for your assignment. Your goal is to compose an investigative report that interests both you and your audience.

Identifying an Opportunity for Change

Identify an issue that affects your community or you personally. How does it affect the people on your campus or in the surrounding community? Maybe the gym closes too early on weekends, the cafeteria serves only pick-up meals on Sundays, or the library has no writing center. Freewrite for five minutes on your issue. (For exploration strategies in addition to freewriting, see CHAPTER 13, EXPLO- pages 231–236 RATION.) In your investigative report, clearly describe the problem and explain its significance to the lives of certain individuals or groups.

- Describe the problem or issue with as much objective detail as possible.
- What individuals or groups are affected by this issue?
- Who might be interested in, or disagree with, your determinations?
- What are the consequences of the particular issue you are exploring? Where might you begin researching for information to answer your question?
- What groups or individuals might have a stake in the findings of an investigative report on this topic?

Relating Rhetorically to Your Audience

The following questions will help you identify the rhetorical audience for your report. Once you identify an audience who will be interested in, or affected by, your analysis, you will be able to choose the best way to deliver your report.

1. List the names of the persons or groups who are affected by, or have an interest in, your topic. (This step may require some research.)
2. Write out the reasons that your investigative report might be important to each of them.
3. Explore what might motivate each potential audience to learn more about the topic. Emotionally, how might each audience respond to your report? What logical conclusions might the potential audiences reach? What actions or attitudes might they change in response?

4. Keeping in mind the interests and values of your audience, tailor your description so that your audience feels invested in your topic and in the ways it affects them.

Planning an Effective Rhetorical Response for Your Purpose

Once you identify your rhetorical opportunity, audience, and purpose, you need to determine what kind of text will best respond to the rhetorical situation. Use the following questions to help you narrow your purpose and shape your response:

1. What facts and details do you need to provide in order to get your audience to recognize the significance of the topic you are investigating?
2. What are the various (perhaps conflicting) perspectives that you must acknowledge?
3. What is your purpose in reporting this information? Are you asking the audience to adopt a new perspective, or do you want the audience to take a specific action?

What is the best way to reach this audience—and get their response? If it is in print, you can insert pictures, figures, and tables. You can also quote from and cite sources. But if you deliver your report online, you can insert videos and direct links to supporting sources.

LINKS TO REPORTS IN THREE MEDIA   MindTap®

Links may change due to availability.

Print Report In the report at the beginning of this chapter, Christine Rosen uses print journalism to report on multitasking.

Video Report *PBS News Hour* filmed a report on climate change demonstrations.

Online Report Nielson's online report investigates "'Pandemic Pantries': Pressure Supply Chain Amid COVID-19 Fears."

⊘ WRITING A PERSUASIVE INVESTIGATIVE REPORT: A Guide

To be persuasive, an investigative report should present different perspectives in a fair, even-handed way, balancing the ethical appeal of good sense with the logical appeal of trustworthy support and concluding with an emotional connection with the audience (their interests and values) that invites them to change their attitude or actions.

ADVANTAGES AND LIMITATIONS

Advantages

- **Writer:** Investigative reports offer you an opportunity to research a topic that interests you and that affects you and others. Because you already care about the topic, chances are others will as well.

- **Message:** As you clarify your own informed stance with regard to the topic, you can better visualize your audience, modifying your purpose to that specific audience whose attitudes or actions you hope to change.

- **Media and Design:** Because investigative reports appear in nearly every medium (print, sound, visuals, digital), you can choose the medium that your audience can most easily receive and appreciate.

Limitations

- **Writer:** Your stance toward your subject should appear objective and fair-minded, so discover a problem you would like to address and be careful to use neutral language in discussing it.

- **Message:** If you are investigating a topic you care about, chances are you will end up with more factual information and data than you will be able to use. Your task is to select the information that best supports your thesis, purposefully organizing that information.

- **Media and Design:** When the expectations of your rhetorical audience limit you to print or digital delivery, call on the strengths of print (words and visuals) or of digital media (videos, audios, print, and multimedia). Most colleges now have multimedia labs where you can go for assistance—and ideas.

Introduction

- **Establish the topic as interesting by hooking the reader.**
- **Establish your expertise (ethos).**
- **Describe or define the issue.**
- **State the thesis.**

Describe the issue in your introduction The introduction of a report provides readers with a specific description of the topic. In "The Myth of Multitasking," Rosen defines multitasking as

(continued)

"the human attempt to do simultaneously as many things as possible, as quickly as possible, preferably marshalling the power of as many technologies as possible." After setting up the problem, Rosen moves to her thesis: "[M]ore recently, challenges to the ethos of multitasking have begun to emerge."

Ask Yourself . . .

- What specific incident, startling statistic, or personal narrative can I use to hook my readers into my topic?
- Why does my topic matter to me? Why might it matter to others?
- How have I established my credibility, my ethos?

Body

- **Establish the objectivity of your report with evidence (logos).**
- **Provide facts, details, and direct quotations.**
- **Organize the information purposefully.**
- **Trace the effects of the issue on various groups.**

Provide facts, details, and direct quotations to clarify the issue Rosen cites research that challenges the efficiency of multitasking: "Numerous studies have shown the sometimes-fatal danger of using cell phones and other electronic devices while driving." "Workers distracted by e-mail and phone calls suffer a fall in IQ more than twice that found in marijuana smokers." Rosen's use of quotations clarifies the issue, shapes the logic, and enhances the persuasiveness of her report. Graphics or other visuals would augment the credibility of her sources.

Attribute your evidence to credible sources to establish trust Every use of examples, facts, statistics, and other data is an opportunity to build trust between you and your audience. For that reason, Rosen quotes the research of physicists, investigative reporters, professors, psychiatrists, psychologists, and neuroscientists, identifying where each piece of credible evidence comes from.

Describe groups affected by the issue The body of a report fairly and factually characterizes the positions and motivations of the different groups affected by the issue. Rosen describes the negative effects of multitasking on drivers, office workers, school children, teens, and adults.

Arrange information purposefully, either spatially, chronologically, or emphatically Rosen arranges her information emphatically, starting with the power of single-tasking and moving through the various categories of humans who experience the negative effects of multitasking. She closes with a prediction that our overstimulated children will face a future "that may gain in information but . . . will surely weaken in wisdom."

Ask yourself . . .

- How am I presenting a balance of factual evidence?
- Which of my sources is the most—and least—trustworthy?
- How have I identified the individuals and groups most affected by this topic?
- Which of my supports is the most powerful? Where should I place it for the greatest impact?

Conclusion

- **Bring together various perspectives, making an emotional connection.**
- **Make a final attempt to connect with the audience, establishing pathos.**
- **Include a (reasonable) appeal to the audience to adopt a particular attitude or undertake a specific action.**

Bring together various perspectives In her conclusion, Rosen softens her stance to "our collective will to pay attention seems fairly weak," followed by "then again, perhaps we will simply adjust and come to accept what James called 'acquired inattention.'" Nevertheless, she comes down on the negative side of the issue with her last line about gains in information but losses in wisdom.

Connect the issue with the interests of your readers A report often concludes with a final appeal for readers to adopt a specific attitude or take a specific action. Rosen strongly suggests that we dial back "this state of constant intentional self-distraction," using an emotional appeal (pathos) to connect her own concerns about the future with those of her audience.

Ask yourself . . .

- How can I best connect my concerns with the values and interests of my rhetorical audience? What part of my findings will be most convincing to them?
- Have I suggested a plan of action based on my investigation?

>> REVISION AND PEER REVIEW

After you have drafted a strong version of your report, ask one of your classmates to respond to it, helping you revise it into the strongest report it can be. Be sure to identify a rhetorical opportunity, purposefully address your intended audience, consciously arrange your research findings, and deliver it in the most appropriate medium available to you and your audience.

Questions for a Peer Reviewer

1. What reasons does the writer give for investigating this topic?
2. What information does the writer provide that makes you want to continue reading?

3. How does the writer describe the issue, problem, or phenomenon? What suggestions do you have for the writer with regard to the introduction?
4. Who is the intended rhetorical audience? Why do they care about this topic?
5. What is the writer's purpose? Is it obvious from the thesis statement? How can that specific audience help the writer fulfill this purpose?
6. What kinds of factual evidence does the writer provide for support? What are the sources? Who is quoted? How do you know these sources are credible? Whose perspectives are represented? Whose are not? Why? Mark any place where the writer needs stronger evidence or more detail to support a point.
7. What facts and details explain how the issue affects different individuals or groups?
8. Follow the line of argument the writer uses. How is it organized, spatially, chronologically, or emphatically? How does that order enhance the report's overall effectiveness? Which of the assertions might you reorder? Why?
9. How does the writer establish ethos? How could the writer strengthen this appeal?
10. How does the writer make use of pathos? How exactly does the writer connect their cause with the interests of the rhetorical audience?
11. What specific conclusion do you reach about the issue or phenomenon as a result of reading the report?
12. What one thing did the writer do especially well? Look back through your feedback and list the three things that you think are most important for the writer to focus on while revising. What one thing will most improve the report?

 ## ADDITIONAL ASSIGNMENTS

Knowledge Transfer

As you take on more responsibilities, you will find that you are conducting investigative reports—large and small reports that deliver information. Which school to attend, which neighborhood to live in, which car to buy—these kinds of decisions are all made in response to investigative reporting, whether the reporting is done through conversation or delivered in print. Your investigative report is always the result of your fact-finding or data-gathering investigation.

COLLEGE Hospitality Report on Campus Eateries When your Hospitality Management professor asks you to investigate the problem of food waste in the dorms, you can conduct an investigative report, gathering, preserving, and evaluating evidence of food waste. You may want to focus on the practices of just one dorm cafeteria, gathering evidence by conducting library and online research focusing on the amount of food that is wasted each year at your school, interviewing the head of Food Services, observing several pick-up meal lines—and trash lines—in that cafeteria, and interviewing cafeteria workers as well as students. After researching the amount of food waste in this dorm, you might compare your findings with the official, campus-wide findings, and even with national results. Various types of research will all contribute to your results.

COMMUNITY Report on Neighborhood Safety Your Neighborhood Watch Organization has asked you to investigate one facet of neighborhood safety: thefts and break-ins. You will conduct an investigative report, gathering, preserving, and evaluating evidence of those particular crime statistics (from the police department) as well as those unreported crimes that you learn about when you are conducting interviews with your neighbors. Using either a flip chart or a sequence of PowerPoint slides, you will present your findings orally at the next neighborhood gathering, where the group will decide if it wants to invest in hiring a security guard.

WORKPLACE Worker Satisfaction Report You have just been selected as a representative to the committee for improving worker satisfaction at your job. Your charge is to interview fellow employees, research similar companies, and help devise a set of desired recommendations, in collaboration with the other committee members.

MULTIMODAL YouTube Video on a National Controversy For your Contemporary American Politics course, you have decided to analyze a current widely televised national controversy (on immigration, healthcare, sytemic racism, etc.), a controversy on which you have not yet developed an opinion, only curiosity. You want to study the quality and character of the assertions and responses of various spokespeople, the credibility of their sources, the trustworthiness of their answers, and their onscreen deliveries. You plan to do some fact-checking as well. In order to provide pivotal scenes from the controversy as well as links to informational sites, you will submit your investigative report as a YouTube video, one that allows you to deliver your script, insert debate footage, and include your fact-checking findings.

8 Position Arguments

LEARNING OBJECTIVES

- Identify rhetorical situations that prompt you to take a position and make a claim that you can reasonably support as more than an opinion.
- Explain the purpose of a position argument in terms of its key rhetorical features and principles of development in various media.
- Apply evidence or examples that validate your claim in ways that appeal to your rhetorical audience's beliefs, attitudes, experiences, and capabilities.
- Reflect critically on counterarguments you need to address.
- Evaluate the credibility of evidence and examples, including personal anecdotes, statistics, or other details, to bring your supporting reasons to life; cite your research appropriately.
- Apply peer review and self-evaluation to revise, edit, and proofread a position argument for a carefully constructed point of view based on strong reasons and compelling evidence.

Throughout this chapter, you will work to identify an opportunity to compose a position argument. As you determine the position you want to take, keep in mind that composing a position argument will help you understand a controversy and clarify what you actually believe. You will also need to understand the values and beliefs of your rhetorical audience—the audience that might be changed by your argument—as you choose the most fitting means of delivery for reaching that audience.

We take positions and argue them every day: "I must drop this course"; "Our Congress members must find a way to work together"; "Everyone should exercise." A **position argument**, like the antismoking ad that follows, takes a point of view and uses ethical, logical, and emotional appeals to help an audience understand, maybe even accept, that claim. In "Smokers Never Win," the former smoker in the bottom right-hand corner establishes the credibility or ethos of the argument by kicking cigarettes; the game of Hang Man indicates the logos of the argument by indicating the steps to losing; and the filth of the cigarettes themselves, along with the dirty chalkboard, makes an emotional connection with the audience. Such pathos might even inspire some members of the audience to kick the habit themselves. (See also CHAPTER 2, THE AVAILABLE MEANS INCLUDE THE RHETORICAL ELEMENTS OF THE MESSAGE ITSELF and CHAPTER 15, ARGUMENT.)

position argument the assertion of a point of view about an issue supported by reasons and evidence

pages 23–26 and 292–294

Source: NeilMan Communications

IDENTIFYING AN OPPORTUNITY FOR CHANGE

Print Argument
written in essay form (with or without visuals for illustration) for a community or academic publication

Visual Argument
composed as a cartoon or an advertisement for a print or online publication

Online Argument
written as a blog entry, a contribution to a website, even a tweet

GENRE IN FOCUS The Commentary

pages
20–21
and
pages
239-241

Position arguments, which assert their claim in the thesis statement (see CHAPTER 2, MAKING CLAIMS and CHAPTER 14, CRAFTING A WORKING THESIS STATEMENT), often serve as an individual's or a group's means for participating in debates on a range of issues. In the following commentary, for instance, linguist Geoffrey Nunberg, a researcher at Stanford University's Center for the Study of Language and Information and radio commentator for National Public Radio, joins the debate on the political, economic, social, and cultural consequences of language diversity in the United States. In this article, Nunberg examines the reasoning process behind English-only advocates who concern themselves with the symbolic importance of the English language, which Nunberg claims signals for them a commitment to American ideals and values.

Linguistic diversity is more conspicuous than it was a century ago. To be aware of the large numbers of non-English speakers in 1990, it was necessary to live in or near one of their communities, whereas today it is only necessary to flip through a cable television dial, drive past a Spanish-language billboard, or (in many states) apply for a driver's license. As a best guess, there are fewer speakers of foreign languages in America now than there were then, in both absolute and relative numbers. But what matters symbolically [are] the widespread impressions of linguistic diversity, particularly among people who have no actual contact with speakers of languages other than English. . . .

The debate is no longer concerned with the content or effect of particular programs, but the symbolic importance that people have come to attach to these matters. Official English advocates admit as much when they emphasize that their real goal is to "send a message" about the role of English in

David McNew/Staff/Getty Images News/Getty Images

American life. From this point of view, it is immaterial whether the provision of interpreters for workers' compensation hearings or of foreign-language nutrition information actually constitute a "disincentive" to learning English, or whether their discontinuation would work a hardship on recent immigrants. Programs like these merely happen to be high-visibility examples of government's apparent willingness to allow the public use of languages

Position Arguments

other than English for any purpose whatsoever. In fact, one suspects that most Official English advocates are not especially concerned about specific programs per se, since they will be able to achieve their symbolic goals even if bilingual services are protected by judicial intervention or legislative inaction (as has generally been the case where Official English measures have passed). The real objective of the campaign is the "message" that it intends to send.

What actually is the message? . . . . Proponents of Official English claim that they seek merely to recognize a state of affairs that has existed since the founding of the nation. After two hundred years of common-law cohabitation with English, we have simply decided to make an honest woman of her, for the sake of the children. To make the English language "official," however, is not merely to acknowledge it as the language commonly used in commerce, mass communications, and public affairs. Rather, it is to invest English with a symbolic role in national life and to endorse a cultural conception of American identity as the basis for political unity.

Gertrude Käsebier Collection, Division of Work & Industry, National Museum of American History, Smithsonian Institution

Native American students at the Carlisle Indian School in Pennsylvania were not allowed to wear their traditional clothing or use Native American languages. In Impressions of an Indian Childhood *(1921), Zitkala-Ša argues that English-only practices at the Carlisle Indian School led to "ridiculous" and "unjustifiable frights and punishments" from a "cold race whose hearts were frozen hard with prejudice." Thousands of Native American children went to off-reservation English-only boarding schools at the turn of the twentieth century.*

—Geoffrey Nunberg, *The Official English Movement: Reimagining America* [Political Unity]

Issues surrounding language diversity have been part of the country's history since at least the early 1800s, when French-speaking Louisiana was admitted to the Union. Nunberg presents his reasons for opposing Official English not only as a practical matter affecting bilingual education and social services but also as a culturally significant issue. Nunberg also shows his understanding of the issue when he includes the position of those who favor the legislation of a common language as a cultural glue to help unify the country.

ASSIGNMENT

Compose a position argument on a significant problem (or issue) and direct your argument to a specific audience. Whether you are taking a stand on a personal experience, a newsworthy situation, or a lifestyle, educational, or religious belief, provide a vivid description of the issue so that your audience can appreciate the significance of the problem and understand your position (or claim). Your description should reveal the importance of the issue to you as well as its effect on your audience. Your clear position on the issue should appear in your thesis statement. Support your thesis with reasons that are themselves supported by specific details, examples, and anecdotes. As you draft your position argument, be sure to acknowledge and address any concerns or beliefs that oppose your own.

»» READING RHETORICALLY

When reading a position argument, your first challenge is to locate the writer's position. What opportunity is the writer taking to deliver a point of view or position? As you move from there, you will want to trace out the reasons the writer supplies for that position, marking or underlining those reasons as you go. Do the reasons provide the overall organization for the position argument? Are the reasons believable, logical, and feasible? After you have mapped out the reasons the writer provides, circle back and locate the support the writer supplies for each reason. Many writers tap examples, details, personal anecdotes, statistics, tables, and research findings to support their claim. Are these reasons and their support credible and persuasive? Finally, read the conclusion to see what the writer is asking you to do or think. These steps help you analyze the credibility, logic, and emotional connection of the argument (or the lack thereof).

Key Features of a Position Argument

A position argument offers a focused, well-presented claim that is organized by credible, well-supported reasons. Position arguments commonly have the following features:

- Arguments vividly describe a problem or issue.
- Arguments are directed toward an audience with a clear connection to, or an investment in, the problem being addressed as well as a clear understanding of the audience's beliefs and values.
- Arguments include a concise statement of the writer's claim, or position, which appears in a thesis statement.

- Arguments provide background information about the issue and why it matters.
- Arguments provide good reasons in support of the writer's position, and each supporting reason takes into account the audience's beliefs, attitudes, and values.
- Arguments contain specific, convincing evidence—details, examples, direct quotations, statistics, anecdotes, research findings, and testimony—that support each reason.
- Arguments acknowledge counterarguments, positions different from, maybe even in opposition to, the writer's claim. Writers consider, accommodate, even accept, if possible, some or parts of the counterarguments.
- Arguments appeal to readers' values by describing the benefits that will be achieved by responding to the writer's position in the intended way or explaining the negative situation that will result from ignoring it.

The key features of a position argument are illustrated in the following paper written by Alicia Williams on American Sign Language (ASL). She points out that Deaf people have been pressured to lip-read and speak English—not sign it—for years. Williams takes the position that ASL should be considered yet another language in our already language-diverse nation. As you read rhetorically, look for answers to the following questions:

- What is Williams's position on the topic? What is her claim?
- What did you learn about the author? How did she establish herself as trustworthy?
- What is Williams's purpose for including the images that she took herself?
- What good reasons does Williams supply for her position? How are those reasons organized? How effective is her organizational pattern?
- What kinds of evidence does she supply (personal anecdotes, research findings, statistics, examples, and so on)?
- How does she connect her position to the interests and sympathies of her readers? How successful is she?

The Ethos of American Sign Language

ALICIA WILLIAMS

Williams is no stranger to the Deaf community. She has a hearing impairment, and her sister is an interpreter. Educated in "bilingual" schools that approached ASL as a language just like Tagalog, Spanish, or Mandarin Chinese, she has personal experiences that have influenced her strong feelings on this subject. She is a graduate of Penn State University.

The termination of the Bilingual Education Act was followed by the No Child Left Behind Act (2001), thus removing a bilingual approach from the education tracks of non-English native speakers. The loss of bilingual education has caused the political group English First to lobby hard for an English-only education that purports to produce truly American citizens. This, in turn, produces more momentum for the group's side project: making English the official language of the United States of America. Not only does this negate the melting pot of languages in America, but it diminishes the impact of a truly unique language—American Sign Language (ASL). The drive for English-only education treats the manifestations of language through a purely verbal platform, thereby perpetuating long-held prejudices and the common mistaken assumption that ASL is not, in fact, a language.

Only fifty years ago did ASL receive its long overdue recognition as a distinct language, rather than being perceived as a "hindrance to English," a "bastardization of English," or even a "communication disorder." By the end of the nineteenth century, during the rise of formal educational instruction in ASL for the Deaf, an oppositional camp known as Oralists had fervently portrayed signing by the Deaf community as a pathological version of spoken language.[1] A few even preposterously correlated deafness with low intelligence. Ironically, the husband of a Deaf woman, Alexander Graham Bell, who was the inventor of the telephone and hearing aids, was a supporter of the Oralists' philosophy. He endorsed "genetic counseling for the deaf, outlawing intermarriages between deaf persons, suppression of sign language, elimination of residential schools for the deaf, and the prohibition of deaf teachers of the deaf" (Stewart and Akamatsu 242).

Oralism faced counteractions by the numerous, though less famous, people who were working for the needs of the Deaf community as its educators. They understood that ASL is requisite for a deaf person's social, cultural, and lingual needs. The Deaf community managed to keep its educational programs intact without losing ASL, though not without struggle. It was not until a half-century later, in the 1960s, that William Stokoe's linguistic analysis of ASL produced the much-needed equilibrium between the Deaf and hearing communities concerning the legitimacy of ASL. Even so, when most people talk about language, their thinking assumes communication through speaking: most classify as unconventional forms of language outside of a verbal modality. Native signers such as myself understand that our minority language must coexist with a dominant majority language, but the practice of reducing ASL to a type of communication

---

(Left margin annotations:)

Williams identifies a problem and establishes herself as an informed, engaged, and reasonable writer. At the end of this paragraph, she directs her readers to her thesis, a concise statement of her point of view regarding the problem.

Williams provides a historical overview of the problem as well as reasons for her point of view. She includes specific details and a direct quotation as evidence (logos). Williams's superscript indicates that she will supply additional information in an endnote at the conclusion of her essay.

Williams is quoting from page 242 in Stewart and Akamatsu, an essay listed in her Works Cited.

Williams makes an assertion related to her thesis, which is followed by specific narrative details, arranged in chronological order (logos). She ends this paragraph with an emotional connection with her audience (pathos).

disorder or, worse, obliterating it for the spoken English-only movement, ignores the historical presence of Deaf culture in America, as well as the key characteristics ASL shares with the evolution of languages.

ASL was derived from French Sign Language (FSL) in the early nineteenth century. Harlan Lane and François Grosjean, prominent ASL linguists, found supporting evidence for this date from "the establishment of the first American school for the deaf in 1817 at Hartford, Connecticut. . . . Its founders, Thomas Gallaudet and Laurent Clerc, were both educated in the use of FSL prior to 1817" (Stewart and Akamatsu 237). Historically speaking, David Stewart and C. Tane Akamatsu have determined that "approximately 60% of the signs in present-day ASL had their origin in FSL" (237). The modification of a parent language, such as FSL for the birth of ASL, is part of the process spoken language has undergone in its evolution throughout history, producing our contemporary languages. For instance, the English spoken in England during Shakespeare's lifetime is not the same English spoken in America today; nonetheless, they are both of English tradition.

Williams continues to shape her argument with additional specific details and facts (logos).

Another characteristic that ASL has in common with other languages is that it changes from one generation to another. Undoubtedly, spoken languages continue to change. For instance, slang words used now may not be the same when the toddlers of today are in college. ASL also experiences these changes, which is contrary to a common misconception that the signs in ASL are concrete in nature, meaning there are no changes. For example, an obsolete sign for "will/future" is conveyed by holding your right arm bent in a ninety-degree angle with your fingertips parallel to the ground. Then you move your entire forearm upward to a forty-five-degree angle in one swift movement. The modern sign starts with an open palm touching the right jawline, underneath the ear; then the forearm moves forward until the arm is in a ninety-degree position, equivalent to the starting position of the arm in the old form. The evolution of signs is comparable to the changing connotations of various words found in the history of languages.

Williams opens this paragraph with another assertion that supports her thesis (logos), using process analysis with information arranged chronologically for support.

In the process of its shift to physical hand gestures and appropriate facial expressions, ASL does not discard the traditional syntax of language, maintaining its legitimacy as a distinct language. The rich complexity of ASL's syntax conveys itself through designated facial expressions and specific sign constructions, demonstrating that "ASL is governed by the same organizational principles as spoken languages . . . [despite] essential differences based on the fact that ASL is produced in three-dimensional space" (Neidle et al. 30). As every language has a syntactical structure, so does ASL.

Another assertion is supported with a detailed comparison-and-contrast analysis and direct quotations (logos).

Despite its similarities to languages such as English, it is a mistake to think of ASL as a pathology of spoken English. Perpetuating this myth is the misconception that ASL signs are direct translations of English. ASL has rules of its own, which are not identical to those of English syntax. In English, for instance, one says, "Who hates Smitty?" but in ASL, it is signed "Hate Smitty who?" The photos in fig. 1 show another example of how signs in ASL are not a direct translation of English, but also show how differing hand placements denote different pronouns used with the verb *give*.

An assertion is supported with specific examples, including the use of visuals (logos).

Stokoe's work establishing the legitimacy of ASL spurred a movement for a bilingual approach in educating the deaf. The teaching of ASL was a top priority because of the hardship of expecting the Deaf community to acquire English as our native language, which carries a disadvantage by working on a modality inaccessible to us—hearing. In the bilingual approach, after the deaf child has attained a solid working background in ASL, some parents elect to have oral English taught as a second language. The success of English as a second language is largely subject to the individual's capabilities, which are dependent on numerous factors. My parents chose the bilingual approach in my education track at Rufus Putnam Elementary School (for the Deaf). While I maintained my fluency in ASL, I developed an efficacy at speech reading (informally known as lip reading). For instance, when I speak, I am able to convince hearing persons that I am not deaf. In my Deaf community, I always resort to my first language—ASL. All this would not be possible if Oralism or English First were successful in a push for *spoken* English only.

More historical background leads into Williams's personal experience as a Deaf person, thereby establishing logos, ethos, and pathos.

My bilingual background has been met with fierce opposition from hearing people who believe ASL is a crutch language and that it is an antiquated solution for the Deaf community. In other words, they believe the advances of medical technology will enable researchers to develop revolutionary digital hearing aids,

Williams addresses the opposing point of view and refutes it with specific support for her stance, reasonable questions, and good examples. In this paragraph, she augments her ethos, logos, and pathos.

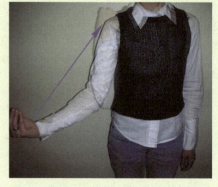

Fig. 1. The photograph on the left shows the signing of "Me give to him or her," and the photograph on the right shows that of "Me give to you." (Photographs by the author.)

while aggressively diagnosing deaf children at younger ages should cause a decreasing need for ASL, which they assume is a diminished form of English. But if ASL meets all other criteria of what linguists consider a language—with the exception of the use of a vocal apparatus—how can it be called a "crutch language"? And hearing aids only amplify whatever remaining hearing a deaf person has, if any at all; they do not compensate for hearing loss. Even if a doctor diagnoses a deaf child at birth, the child's sensorineural hearing loss may be so severe that spoken language will be impractical to acquire, whereas ASL will be a better approach for the child.[2] In rare cases, adults who become deaf later in their lives find comfort in ASL, rather than English. The naturalization associated with the visual-spatial lingual framework of ASL is uniquely characteristic of the Deaf community because it operates to their advantage, bypassing the confines of oral-aural languages. The use of a verbal apparatus in spoken languages is a natural reaction from the body possessing a functional audio-physiological system. Often this is not the case within the Deaf community; hence that is why ASL is deeply embedded in its culture and will remain the staple of its community, regardless of technology's novelty or the hearing community's desire to push for English-only education.

The most primeval function of language is to create a medium for people's desire to outwardly express themselves to others. Whatever form language may take—visual or verbal—it lays the foundation for humanity's collective identity as great storytellers. Through language we have been able to pass on stories of past heroes and enemies, warn future generations of failed philosophies, create new ideals for better living, share our aspirations and fears, even express our wonder at all that remains unknown to us. Language binds us as humans, and its diverse forms are reflected in the embodiments of its heterogeneous natives. ASL is but another paintbrush of language, and yet proof of humanity's palette of mutability.

The final paragraph establishes a strong emotional connection with the audience (pathos).

Notes

Williams supplies both Notes and a Works Cited list at the end of her essay, enhancing her ethos and her logos.

1. I realize the use of the term *Deaf* might seem archaic, but for the purpose of this paper, it is representative of all members who psychologically or linguistically identify themselves as members of the Deaf community through ASL as their common language, regardless of their physiological hearing capacity.

2. There are three basic types of hearing loss: conductive hearing loss, sensorineural hearing loss, and mixed hearing loss, which is any combination of the first two. All three types can make speech hard to acquire.

Works Cited

Neidle, Carol, et al. *The Syntax of American Sign Language: Functional Categories and Hierarchical Structures.* MIT Press, 2000.

Stewart, David A., and C. Tane Akamatsu. "The Coming of Age of American Sign Language." *Anthropology & Education Quarterly,* vol. 19, no. 3, Sept. 1988, pp. 235–52. *JSTOR,* www.jstor.org/stable/3195832.

Using Synthesis and Analysis

When we readily agree with a position or claim, we rarely analyze the argument for its careful reasoning. But when we do not agree or begin to get suspicious, we begin to notice problems of sloppy reasoning, snap judgments, quickly drawn conclusions, missing data, or one-sided opinions. Even the most experienced writers inadvertently make these errors in arguments. Start your analysis by rereading the argument to detect flaws in reasoning. (See the box on Logical Fallacies.) Rereading the article with an eye toward detecting fallacies can also be helpful when analyzing an argument with which you readily agree, perhaps one in this chapter (Nunberg's or Williams's). As you read, note that in most cases, readers are persuaded to change by the writer's or speaker's trustworthiness and by a well-reasoned argument.

LOGICAL FALLACIES

Non sequitur Latin for "it does not follow," the *non sequitur* presents a faulty conclusion about consequences, such as "Helen loves the stars; she will major in astronomy."

Ad hominem Latin for "toward the man himself," an *ad hominem* attack draws attention away from the actual issue under consideration by attacking the character of the person rather than the opinion that person holds.

Appeal to tradition Many people resist change—it unsettles their routines and makes them uncomfortable. Such people often invoke an appeal to tradition; in other words, "That is how it has always been done, so it should continue." This appeal is often used in political campaigns ("Four more years"), by social groups ("We have never invited X or Y to our events; why start?"), and in many other situations ("My family always fills the gas tank before getting on the highway, so you should fill up now.").

Bandwagon The bandwagon argument is "Everyone is doing it, so you should, too." For example, highway patrol officers often hear "Everyone else was speeding, so I was merely keeping up with the traffic."

Begging the question Often referred to as a "circular argument," begging the question involves simply restating the initial claim as though it were already a conclusion or a good reason. "We must test students more in order to improve their test scores." The initial claim needs to be established and argued in order to establish whether low test scores can be blamed on too little testing.

False analogy Effective writers often use analogies to equate two unlike things, explaining one in terms of the other—for example, comparing a generous grandma with an ATM machine or a diamond ring with eternal love. False analogies, however, stretch beyond the valid resemblance to create an invalid comparison. "Vietnam War veterans were greeted by the animosity of an antiwar U.S. populace; Iraqi war veterans will surely return to the same antipathy."

False authority False authority fallacies assume that an expert in one field is credible in another field. Just think of all the professional athletes and celebrities who argue that a particular brand of car, coffee, undershorts, or soft drink is the best one.

False cause Also referred to by the Latin phrase *post hoc, ergo propter hoc*, the fallacy of false cause is the assumption that because A occurs *before* B, A is therefore the *cause* of B. We all know that events that follow each other do not necessarily have a direct causal relationship—although they may have some relationship: "Jim got fired from his job, and his wife divorced him; therefore, his job loss caused his divorce." Jim's job loss might have been the last of several job losses he suffered in the past three years, and his wife, tired of depending on him to hold a job, filed for divorce.

False dilemma Also referred to as the "either/or fallacy," the false dilemma fallacy sets up only two choices in a complex situation, when in fact there are more than two choices. The false dilemma offers the writer's choice as the only good choice, presenting the only other choice as unthinkable. "If we do not spank our children, they will run wild." "If you do not get straight A's, you will not be able to get a job."

Guilt by association An unfair attempt to make someone responsible for the beliefs or actions of others, guilt by association links that person with untrustworthy people or suspicious actions. Social tensions in the United States often stem from this fallacy and are passed on for the same reason: "those people" are bad—whether they are members of a racial, ethnic, or religious group, a particular profession, or a certain family.

Hasty generalization A conclusion based on too little, exceptional, or biased evidence, the hasty generalization results in statements such as "Fred will never get into law school when he did not even pass his poli sci exam." The otherwise very intelligent Fred may have a good reason for failing one exam.

(continued)

Oversimplification Closely related to hasty generalization, oversimplification occurs when a speaker or writer jumps to conclusions by omitting relevant considerations. "Just say 'No'" was the antidrug battle cry of the 1980s, but avoiding drug use can be much more complicated than just saying no. The "virginity pledge" is an oversimplified solution to the problem of unwanted teenage pregnancy, as it ignores the fact that many teenagers need to become educated about human sexuality, safe sex practices, sexually transmitted disease, and aspects of teen social and sexual behavior.

Red herring A false clue or an assertion aimed at diverting attention from the real issue, the red herring is intended to mislead, whether it appears in a mystery novel or in an argument. "We cannot defeat the piracy in Somalia when we are involved in the Israeli-Palestinian conflict." The real issue in the preceding statement (defeating piracy) is blurred by other issues that, while important, are not the primary ones under consideration.

Slippery slope In order to show that an initial claim is unacceptable, increasingly unacceptable events are said to be sure to follow from that initial claim: "Confidential letters of recommendation allow for damning comments." We hear slippery slope arguments every day, in contexts from weight loss ("You are losing too much weight; you will end up anorexic") to entertainment preferences ("You are spending too much time playing video games; you are likely to become antisocial").

See also CHAPTER 2, **SOJOURNER TRUTH,** *Ain't I a Woman?*

See also CHAPTER 3, **LISA DELPIT,** *Other People's Children* [Codes]

See also CHAPTER 24, **MARGARET MEAD,** *The Changing Significance of Food* [Overnourished and Undernourished in America]

See also CHAPTER 25, **RILEY R.L.,** *Selfies Help Trans and Nonbinary People Create Our Own Narrative*

See also CHAPTER 26, **CLAIRE EDWARDS,** *The Experiences of People with Disabilities Show We Need a New Understanding of Urban Safety*

See also CHAPTER 27, **NATASCHA UHLMANN,** *No-More-Deaths Volunteer Scott Warren Was Acquitted. But Humanitarian Aid Should Never Be Considered a Crime*

» RESPONDING TO THE RHETORICAL SITUATION

Every day, you find yourself witnessing the positions others have taken, whether you are discussing films and television with your friends, posting tweets, or watching sports news. Bullying, gun control, marriage rights, standardized testing, and immigration are just a few of the many issues you are likely to encounter. After you have established your position, or claim, determine the most appropriate audience for considering your position. Your goal is to reach that rhetorical audience, the audience that is capable of helping you resolve the issue.

| Opportunity | Audience and Purpose | Genre/Argument | Medium of Delivery |

Understanding the Rhetorical Situation

Many times you will be asked to take a stand—take a position on an issue. A position argument can serve to explore both the stated and underlying reasons why we take positions. Is your opinion one you have inherited from your family or your friends? Have you witnessed firsthand the consequences of your position—or that of people who take a position different from yours? What opportunity does your position respond to? Often, you must conduct research to supply evidence and examples for your reasons. By demonstrating your own good reasons at the same time you acknowledge the values, concerns, and interests of your audience, you establish your ethos, logos, and pathos.

RESEARCHING A POSITION ARGUMENT

A position argument is not just your opinion. It is a carefully constructed point of view based on reasons and evidence. Bring your supporting reasons to life with research through detailed, credible evidence and examples, whether personal anecdotes, statistics, or other details.

Because you want your audience to consider seriously your position, conduct research to see what evidence your opposition uses. Acknowledging the values and beliefs of your audience helps you establish common ground. In doing so, you make clear that you respect and understand you audience—and hope they will try to understand you as you work to persuade them to change their attitudes or actions.

Identifying an Opportunity for Change

Consider the communities you are part of—academic, activist, artistic, athletic, professional, civic, ethnic, national, political, or religious. What practices or attitudes have shaped your experiences within each group? You might, for example, think about what it means for you that you have a new kind of close relationship with your soccer team members (or other sport), one not shared by family members or friends on the sidelines. Or perhaps you are bilingual and want to explore why your ability to communicate in more than one language has been seen as a positive thing in many of your communities but not, strangely, in others. Maybe you are a member of an online community and have witnessed cyberbullying, shaming, and name-calling and want to speak out about it. The point is to reflect on an issue where your unique role within a particular group helps you identify a rhetorical opportunity for change.

1. Make a list of the communities with which you identify most strongly. For each group, list several experiences that have marked your participation in that group. If the experiences were positive, explain why, providing as many details as possible. If the experiences were negative, describe the factors that made them difficult or unpleasant. Also, write down any rules—whether written or unwritten—that influence the ways you or other group members participate in the community.

2. Choose one or two of your communities, and take photos or sketch pictures of group members interacting. Or download a screenshot illustrating a relevant example of the group's interactions, possibly a text or an update posted to Facebook or Twitter (with the group members' permission). Whatever visual you choose should illustrate details or features that make the community compelling to examine.

3. Choose the community you want to write about and compose four or five descriptions of a problem related to that community. Vary the ways you describe the problem. For example, one description might emphasize how some people are marginalized by that community, and another might emphasize the ways in which others in the community respond to the unwritten rules of participation in that community. Another description might focus on the process by which new group members are subtly initiated into the group, and yet another might describe what ideal seems to guide that particular community.

4. You can also move through steps 1–3 by focusing on a community to which you do not belong, for whom you are an outsider.

Relating Rhetorically to Your Audience

The following questions can help you locate your rhetorical audience as well as identify the audience's relationship to the problem you are addressing. After you have established the audience's values as well as the positions other people may hold about the problem, you will be in a better position to describe that problem responsibly and knowledgeably.

1. List the names of the persons or groups who are affected directly or indirectly by the problem you are addressing.
2. Next to the name of each potential audience, write reasons that audience could have for acknowledging the existence of your problem. In other words, what evidence or personal connection would persuade these audiences that something needs to change or that they need to view the situation in a new way?
3. What actions could these audiences reasonably be persuaded to perform? What new perspectives could they be expected to adopt? In other words, consider what each audience would be able to do to resolve this problem.
4. With your audience's interests and capabilities in mind, look again at the descriptions of the problem that you composed in the preceding section. Decide which description will best help your audience feel connected to the situation as you have described it. Be open to revising your best description in order to tailor it to the audience's attitudes, beliefs, experiences, and values.
5. Consider what others have already said and done about the problem, especially if their ideas are counterarguments, ideas markedly different from or maybe even opposed to yours.

Planning an Effective Rhetorical Response for Your Purpose

Different purposes and different audiences require different kinds of texts. For example, a lack of local resources for people who speak languages other than English might prompt you to create a church newsletter that draws attention to the daily challenges these people face and argues for a greater church commitment to alleviating this problem. Parent association debates over an open-carry policy or teachers-with-guns program might lead you to write an Op-Ed to the local newspaper or a letter to the school board to highlight an important feature of the ongoing gun-control debate that they—and their teachers—may be overlooking. As these two examples suggest, once you identify your problem, position (or claim), audience (and their values), and purpose, you need to determine what kind of text will best respond to the rhetorical situation.

Use the following questions to help you narrow your purpose and shape your response:

1. What is the issue that prompts your taking a position, making a claim?
2. What is your explicit claim?
3. What reasons support the argument you want to make? What evidence or examples can you provide to persuade readers that each supporting reason is valid? What else has been said or done about this issue?
4. Which supporting reasons are most likely to resonate with your audience? How might you adapt a reason or two to accommodate the interests of your audience? What beliefs, attitudes, experiences, and capabilities on the part of the audience help guide you as you shape your argument? What are the counterarguments that you need to address?
5. What exactly do you want your audience to do? Feel more confident in its current position? Listen to and consider an overlooked position? Or make a change in attitude or take a specific action to address the problem you are trying to resolve?
6. How best can you reach your audience? That is, what kind of text is this audience most likely to respond to?

LINKS TO ARGUMENTS IN THREE MEDIA   MindTap®

Links may change due to availability.

Courtesy of S. Adair Rispoli

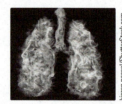

kiszon pascal/ShutterStock.com

Gary Conner/Getty Images

Print Argument
In the essay at the beginning of this chapter, student Alicia Williams uses a position argument on ASL to help her develop and present her thoughts for others—especially policy-makers.

Visual Argument
This visual argument shows smoke-filled lungs in a *Newsweek* article claiming "Vaping May Be Just as Bad as Smoking When It Comes to Lung Disease-Causing Bacteria."

Online Argument
The National Rifle Association's NRA Blog Staff posted "Does Your Child Know What to Do If He or She Finds a Gun?"

WRITING A PERSUASIVE POSITION ARGUMENT: A Guide

*Y*ou are likely familiar with the form and arrangements of position arguments because you come across examples of this genre in your daily life. The author's introduction grabs your attention because it relates a problem to your own values; the body of the position argument outlines the reasoning behind the author's point of view; and the conclusion reinforces the issue's significance at the same time that it connects with you emotionally.

ADVANTAGES AND LIMITATIONS

Advantages

- **Writer:** Position arguments allow you to showcase your credibility and research skills. You can be friendly, open, and knowledgeable.

- **Message:** Position arguments invite you to investigate a troublesome issue, clarify your own understanding, and take a reasonable position that might help alleviate the problem for you and your audience.

- **Media and Design:** Position arguments can be delivered in print, digitally, verbally, and with art and images—or any combination.

Limitations

- **Writer:** Your challenge is to discover the values, interests, and concerns of your audience so that you can work to accommodate them at the same time as you advance your argument.

- **Message:** What you consider to be a problem may not be perceived as one by others—or they may take a position markedly different from your own. The challenge is to establish common ground where you can come together to discuss your differences.

- **Media and Design:** Deciding on which medium and design will reach your rhetorical audience—maybe even please them—can be daunting, until you take the time to analyze your audience.

Introduction

- **Establish your credibility (ethos).**
- **Describe the problem.**
- **Make clear how the problem concerns the audience.**
- **Emphasize why the time to address the problem is now.**
- **State an explicit claim in a thesis statement.**

Establish your credibility One way to establish the reasonableness of your argument is by taking a fair-minded tone and respectful stance toward the issue. It is easy to feel like those who disagree with you are "the enemy," but note how Williams creates common ground

(continued)

with references to the American "melting pot" and draws on the emotions of her audience to sympathize with her position by invoking a fresh surprise in the English First debate—"the impact of a truly unique language—American Sign Language (ASL)."

Identify an immediate problem The introduction of an argumentative essay grabs an audience's attention as it describes the problem in a way that helps readers see how it concerns them as well as explains why the situation needs their attention right now. When you look back over Williams's essay on ASL, you will see that the elimination of bilingual education removed opportunities for Deaf students to be mainstreamed in classes. The introduction leads up to the thesis statement.

Make your claim, or position, in your thesis statement The thesis presents the writer's argument in a single sentence or short string of sentences; supporting reasons might also be presented in the introduction in a cluster of concise sentences following the thesis statement. Williams's thesis statement is concise and explicit: "The drive for English-only education treats the manifestations of language through a purely verbal platform, thereby perpetuating long-held prejudices and the common mistaken assumption that ASL is not, in fact, a language."

Ask yourself . . .
- How is the issue I am exploring actually a problem for others?
- Who are the others who might share my concern?
- What is my position on the issue?
- Have I translated my position into an explicit thesis? Library and online research—as well as interviews, observations, and lab experiments—all help you finalize and support your position (your thesis statement).

- **Outline the major reasons supporting the position.**
- **Connect the reasons to the thesis statement.**
- **Present evidence and examples in the form of facts and figures, direct quotations, brief narratives, statistics, testimony, and so on.**
- **In other words, establish logos by supplying a well-reasoned, well-supported, and well-organized argument.**

Organize your reasons The body of an argumentative essay provides the major reasons supporting the argument. You must decide whether to organize the major reasons chronologically, spatially, or emphatically. Many writers choose the emphatic arrangement, either starting or ending with the most significant reason.

Support your claim with reasons that connect to your readers' values Here you not only present your supporting reasons in a purposeful order but also explain how each reason strengthens your position. The stronger supporting reasons are those that connect to readers' beliefs, values, and attitudes.

Present evidence for your reasons In addition, you use the body of an argumentative essay to present evidence and examples. Writers present facts and figures, direct quotations, and brief narratives to persuade readers that each supporting reason strengthens the larger argument. Any of these supports may be presented through words (written or spoken) or images.

Acknowledge counterarguments The body of an argumentative essay also acknowledges and responds to counterarguments and opposing viewpoints. This helps you address possible gaps in opposing arguments while you strengthen the logic of your own argument. By acknowledging other points of view, you project a more convincing ethical appeal to readers to consider, even accept, alternative perspectives on the issue. Williams acknowledges and refutes the viewpoints that ASL is a "crutch language" and an "antiquated solution."

Body

Ask yourself . . .
- Which of my reasons is the most compelling? Have I organized my reasons in a way that leads to or ends with that compelling reason?
- Which of my reasons is the weakest? How might I strengthen it?
- What is the most compelling evidence I have provided for my reasons?
- How have I acknowledged viewpoints different from my own position?
- How have I assimilated any of those other positions into my own position?

- **Reinforce for an audience the benefits of responding to the writer's argument in the intended way.**
- **Illustrate the negative situation that will result if the writer's argument is ignored.**
- **Work to connect the writer's claim with the interests and values of the audience, establishing pathos.**

Conclusion

Conclude with the benefits of your position for your readers Finally, the conclusion of an argumentative essay reinforces the benefits that will be realized if the audience responds to the writer's argument in the intended way. Or, conversely, the conclusion may illustrate the negative situation that will result if the writer's argument is ignored. The conclusion is your last opportunity to connect with your audience. In her conclusion, Williams uses pathos to appeal to her readers by citing humanity's common desire for self-expression.

Ask yourself . . .
- How have I made clear that this topic matters to more people than just myself?
- How have I asked my audience to do something within their capabilities?
- How have I asked them to do something that will benefit them as well as others?
- Where do I indicate that my position aligns with their interests?

⟫ REVISION AND PEER REVIEW

After you have drafted your argument, ask one of your classmates to read it. You will want your classmate to respond to your work in a way that helps you revise it into the strongest argument it can be, one that addresses your intended audience, helps you fulfill your purpose, and is delivered in the most appropriate means available to you.

Questions for a Peer Reviewer

1. To what opportunity for change is the writer responding?
2. Who might be the rhetorical audience?
3. What might be the writer's purpose?
4. How does the writer establish the importance of the topic? What suggestions do you have for improving the introduction?
5. Note the writer's thesis statement. If you cannot locate a thesis statement, what explicit thesis statement might work for this position argument or claim?
6. Note the assertions the writer makes to support the thesis. Are they presented in chronological, spatial, or emphatic order? How might you reorder some of the assertions for overall effectiveness?
7. If you cannot locate a series of assertions, what assertions could be made to support the thesis statement?
8. Note the supporting reasons that the writer uses to reinforce their assertions. What specific evidence and examples (anecdotes, statistics, research findings, details, etc.) does the writer use for support?
9. How does the writer establish ethos? Logos? Pathos? How could the writer strengthen these appeals? (See questions 6–8.)
10. Where does the writer acknowledge other points of view? Where does the writer accept the validity of another point? Might doing so strengthen the writer's credibility?
11. What did you learn from the conclusion that you did not already know after reading the introduction and the body? What information does the writer want you to take away from the argument? Does the writer attempt to change your attitude, action, or opinion?
12. Which section of the argument did you most enjoy? Why?

✎ ADDITIONAL ASSIGNMENTS

Knowledge Transfer

We use position arguments every time we want to persuade an audience to modify their attitude, action, or belief on issues as large as whom to vote for in a presidential election and as small as where we should call to order pizza.

COLLEGE Social Organization Your college social organization is considering becoming an alcohol-free zone. You have been elected to take a position against (or for) the ban, and your job is to interview your friends; conduct research on the feasibility, advantages, and disadvantages of such a ban; and use personal experience as well as observations to support your position. You and one other person will present your positions at the next organizational meeting.

COMMUNITY Op-Ed People submit opinion pieces to their local news-papers when they feel strongly about a community issue and want local citizens to join them in supporting or protesting that issue. For instance, if your schools are in bad repair and yet the tax levies are voted down year after year, you may want to gather research and shape it into a position argument in favor of a tax levy. Stay alert to local issues so that you can join the discussion, obtain important information, understand the issue, and take a clear position. Then compose an opinion piece for your local newspaper or community magazine.

WORKPLACE Cover Letter Every time you apply for a job, you take a position, arguing that you are the best person for the job. Referring to the job position and your résumé, compose a letter of application arguing that your experience and education align perfectly with the criteria for the position.

MULTIMODAL Short Film on Controversial Topic If a topic such as your school's attendance policy, the price of tuition, charges of college students' binge drinking, or some other social issue bothers you, create a short film on the topic. First, you will want to compose a script and then consider the features of background music, images, video clips, and text that will enhance your script. As you create your film (with a camera, your smartphone, or your computer), practice reading the script while the film is progressing, editing as you go. Be sure to bring in a peer to help you make editing decisions.

9 Proposals

LEARNING OBJECTIVES

- Identify a problem or concern where a proposal would be an effective response to the rhetorical situation.
- Explain the purpose of a proposal in terms of its key rhetorical features and principles of development in various media
- Apply specific details about the costs, feasibility, acceptability, and benefits of the solution proposed for your rhetorical audience.
- Evaluate competing proposals, facts and data, interviews, observations, research studies, and personal experience to support your solution and develop the ability to incorporate sources into your proposal.
- Apply peer review and self-evaluation to revise, edit, and proofread for a clear call to action that aligns with your thesis and is acceptabie to your audience.

Every day, we seek to solve problems. Sometimes, all we need is expert advice and friendly suggestions: "New tires will reduce your gas mileage"; "Take a baby aspirin every morning to prevent a heart attack"; "Why not take your draft to the Writing Center?" Any one of these homely suggestions serves as a **proposal**, a message that calls for improvement, calling an audience to action, using a rhetorical "ought." Of course, proposals are just as often more formal and aimed at a larger audience. Public service announcements (PSAs) addressing social problems—from bullying, gun violence, and littering to food shortages, pandemics, and climate change—work to convince a large group of people to take action (or maybe feel guilty if they do not!).

proposal
message that calls
for improvement
through action

150

IDENTIFYING AN OPPORTUNITY FOR CHANGE

 Print Proposal
written for a community or campus newspaper or sent directly to the rhetorical audience

 Oral Proposal or Short Film
recorded as a short film or video podcast

Online Proposal
posted to an appropriate site and featuring images illustrating the problem and/or solution

This chapter gives you the opportunity to consider problems that you might like to address, even resolve. As you consider a topic that engages your passion, also consider the most fitting means of delivery for your proposal.

GENRE IN FOCUS The Public Service Announcement

In 2010, Philadelphia launched an UnLitter Us campaign through a series of public service announcements. Their purpose was to inspire the cleanup of a big city that had long suffered from a reputation as "filthy, dirty." Once civic leaders identified the opportunity for action, they created purposeful proposal arguments aimed directly at their city's residents, the only people who could resolve the problem.

The poetry that overlays the man's head in the accompanying ad identifies the problem itself: "The city has a heartbeat/with broken glass/plastic wrappers/clogging its arteries." It also targets a specific audience: "The city has a heartbeat/and it's waiting for you/to provide hope/to become change/to become litter free." But the bold blue letters of "UNLITTER US" are what we see first; they serve as the thesis statement, the "ought" of the proposal.

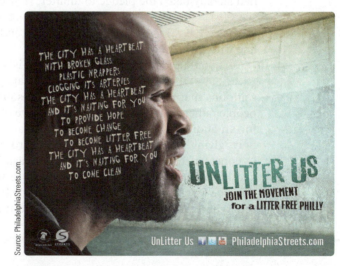

Source: PhiladelphiaStreets.com

This call to "Unlitter Us" uses poetry as part of the public service campaign. Just as the poetry appears to be in the man's head, "UNLITTER US" seems to be coming out of his mouth.

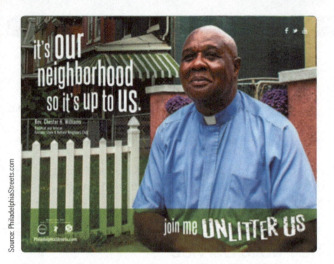

This proposal focuses on specific profiles of "real Philadelphians" who were committed to unlittering the city.

Imagining that Philadelphia's youth would be drawn to the message itself by the delivery of poetry, the civic leaders were disappointed when their poetry-based PSAs did not work, so they took another tack: they used profiles of "real Philadelphians" who were committed to unlittering the city.

The focus on specific neighborhoods and neighborhood leaders who wanted to clean, improve, and, therefore, strengthen their communities was a more successful proposal: it used the rhetorical appeals of ethos, logos, and pathos much more effectively than the previous PSA, especially the pathos that connected the audience emotionally with people in other neighborhoods who had already taken the pledge to unlitter. (For more on ethos, logos, and pathos, pages 23–26 see CHAPTER 2, THE AVAILABLE MEANS INCLUDE THE RHETORICAL ELEMENTS OF THE MESSAGE ITSELF.) Both PSAs are proposals, and both end with a call for action in line with their thesis: "UNLITTER US."

As you, no doubt, realize, a proposal is arranged much like an argument. pages 275–278 (See CHAPTER 15, ARGUMENT.) Audiences are more likely to be persuaded by solutions that make responsible use of resources and that benefit a group of people rather than just a few. After you have identified and defined the problem for an audience who can help resolve that problem, either by showing support, giving permission, or working toward the solution itself, you can begin to consider the acceptability, cost, and feasibility of your proposal. Proposals like Philadelphia's are a common response to this question: how can something be feasibly and acceptably improved? In the case of this PSA campaign, the writers make clear that it costs little to unlitter—all it takes is community involvement.

When you have identified a social, university, or community problem or practice that you would like to address or resolve, you will want to compose a proposal argument. Your job is to describe the problem that you feel should and can be changed in such a way that your audience understands what is at stake, especially for them. You will want to chart out your proposed plan of action, a proposal that should be possible, desirable (by your audience), and financially responsible, keeping in mind that some proposals will cost nothing at all. Your goal is to convince your audience that your proposed solution is the most effective option available to them.

≫ READING RHETORICALLY

Reading a proposal rhetorically means working through the following steps:

1. Identify the problem itself, assessing whether a significant problem actually exists and why it has not been resolved before. Who, exactly, does this problem affect—and to what extent?
2. Evaluate the proposed solution, taking into consideration the amount and quality of research the author has undertaken before advising readers what ought to be done. How feasible and acceptable is the proposal in terms of cost, time, and effectiveness?
3. Weigh the pros and cons of enacting the proposal; after all, the benefits ought to outweigh the costs, with this proposal proving to be better than the alternatives. Assess the reasons the author provides for justifying this proposal.

Key Features of a Proposal

When you want to argue for the best way to improve on a situation, consider composing a proposal. Proposals commonly have the following features:

- There is a clear, identifiable problem that the proposal seeks to resolve.
- This problem is of concern to a significant number of people.
- The proposed solution will resolve the problem in a way these people will find acceptable (without harming or greatly inconveniencing others).

- The proposal contains specific details about the costs, feasibility, acceptability, and benefits of the solution.
- The proposal is directed to an appropriate audience and demonstrates a good understanding of that audience's needs and interests.
- The proposal clearly explains the steps or processes required to enact the solution.

In the following proposal, internationally known literacy specialist at Goldsmiths, University of London, Michael Rosen proposes reading aloud as a solution to the widely touted problems of illiteracy. He argues that young people develop reading and writing skills—not by following the programs of school-controlled literacy but—by being immersed in language, in narrative, in plot lines. Reading aloud is his simple solution. He published his essay in *The Guardian*, a British daily newspaper aimed at middle-class educated readers, who might give his proposal serious consideration, maybe even application at home. As you read through Rosen's proposal, pay careful attention to the features of a proposal.

- What serves as his opportunity to respond?
- What problem does he identify?
- What is his purpose for writing to this rhetorical audience? How are purpose and audience connected in this proposal?
- How feasible, costly, and acceptable might his proposal actually be?

Why Reading Aloud Is a Vital Bridge to Literacy

MICHAEL ROSEN

British professor of children's literature Michael Rosen shares his specialty in his roles as children's author and poet, TV producer, and political columnist. In this proposal, he advises that children should be read to even as teenagers. Rosen believes that reading aloud supports teenagers as they are learning the complex gear changes between speech and prose.

Martin Doyle/FilmMagic/Getty Images

I was very lucky to have been brought up in a household where my older brother and my father read out loud to me as a teenager. It was a form of conversation or entertainment. They were "hey-listen-to-this" moments, taking in Dickens, Hardy, *Catch 22*, *Catcher in the Rye*, the Molesworth books, newspapers, magazines, Konrad Lorenz's science books, Alan Moorehead's accounts of exploration, and any random passage from their studies. Come to think of it, my father didn't stop! In his 70s, when I was in my 40s, my father still read me the stories he wrote about his childhood. His intonation, his pronunciation of Yiddish, our cackling at his jokes live on.

The author identifies a problem for many parents and teachers: instilling a love of reading in young people.

This week, it was suggested that in order to foster a love of reading, parents and teachers should continue reading aloud to children well into their teen years. To get a handle on why doing so is important, we have to take a step back and look at something that is right in front of our noses but not always obvious.

The way we speak is very different from the way we write—especially from the way we write continuous prose. When we speak, we hesitate, we contract phrases (as with "wouldn't've"), we repeat ourselves, we often leave gaps for others to fill in. Or we might just tail off. We use intonation and gesture to indicate or color meaning. We use more pronouns than we do when we write, because we can specify who we are referring to with gesture and tone. We use a lot of "ums" and "errs" and "you knows" to give ourselves time to think or to hold a listener's attention. And we avoid front-loading sentences with phrases and clauses that delay getting to the main point.

The solution to the problem, reading to children aloud, is one that can be easily solved, once teachers and parents understand the process. Such a process is inexpensive, acceptable, and readily beneficial.

Continuous prose flows without hesitation. Sentences close. We can front-load, refer backwards and forwards, organize "points" in an argument. We can avoid repetition, and use syntax and vocabulary for emphasis color. "Who," "which," "that," and "where" clauses get more use in writing than in speech.

The author offers knowledgeable details about the differences between speaking and writing.

I read continuous prose every day but tell me I've got to read 10 pages of something: Can I put it off till tomorrow?

What follows from this is that in order to understand and be able to write continuous prose, we need to spend a good deal of time immersed in it. One way to do this is to hear it read out loud. This gets round that moment of resistance when we see a slab of writing on the page. I read continuous prose every single day of my life but if you tell me that I've got to read 10 pages of something, study it closely in order to extract some information (a common task in schools), I have at the very least the feeling: can I put it off till tomorrow? I've seen my own children thinking up every possible ruse to avoid it, too.

Some books are better (and more fun) for reading out loud than others. One of the reasons we invented continuous prose was to lay out an argument, piling points on top of each other, weighing one view against another, even to invite the reader to look back at something earlier or later in a book. It can be tough going listening to this kind of writing if you don't have the book in front of you. Ideal for reading out loud are things such as short stories, poems, plays, modern novels, journalism, texts of speeches, biography, and narratives connected with scientific discovery, history, geography, and the arts.

Rosen explains the steps required to enact the solution to separation between the written and the oral.

Ideally, any teenager being read to (at home or at school) would have the text in front of them, so that we can stop and talk about things as we go along, referring back to what's just been read. This means we make bridges, from the written to the oral and back again.

Copyright Guardian News & Media Ltd 2020

Using Synthesis and Analysis

Rosen's proposal gives you much to consider: the history and purpose of literacy instruction, who currently owns and controls literacy development (schools!), the advantages of taking back control of literacy, and what a difference doing so would make in the lives of children and their families. As you break down his argument, consider the elements of the rhetorical situation: Who is Rosen? What is the context for his column in *The Guardian*? What does he hope to accomplish? How does knowing who the author is and the context for his proposal affect your interpretation of his argument?

When you analyze to understand, interpret, and contextualize a text, you will also question the material you read. Break down Rosen's arguments for incorporating reading aloud in homes and schools. What is his main point? What evidence does he present for moving away from typical school literacy practices? What does he present as the most troubling effects of those practices? How does he demonstrate the feasibility, acceptability, and benefits of his proposed solution? How does he address any possible arguments against his proposal? What perspectives might be included that are currently missing? Explain the logic of his reasons and whether you agree with this logic.

Given Rosen's arguments and the context for making them, how do you see rhetoric—either written or spoken—helping to resolve the problem? Who will be positively (and negatively) affected by this solution? Who has the capability to resolve or affect the resolution of the problem? Are you persuaded that his proposal presents a viable solution and a reliable basis for discussion, interpretation, or action? Why or why not?

See also CHAPTER 2, **THE AMETHYST INITIATIVE**, *It's Time to Rethink the Drinking Age*

See also CHAPTER 24, **CORBY KUMMER**, *Good-bye, Cryovac* [Local Food, College Food Service, and Scraping Your Own Plate]

See also CHAPTER 25, **PARIS LEES**, *Facebook's Gender Identities Are a Good Start – But Why Stop at 56?*

See also CHAPTER 25, **ANN COFFEY**, *Dating Sites and Social Media Firms Must Do More to Protect Users from "Catfishing"*

See also CHAPTER 27, **ARTURO BAÑUELAS**, *The Advent Posada Is an Act of Resistance*

See also, CHAPTER 28, **NATIONAL YOUNG FARMERS COALITION**, *Young Farmers Call for Climate Action*

»» RESPONDING TO THE RHETORICAL SITUATION

To understand the full complexity of the situation, you will first want to identify the problem and consider whom it affects. Then, you will want to consider who of those people could serve as your rhetorical audience, the people who could actually help you work toward a solution. Your purpose is to invite them to join you in resolving or addressing the problem. Your genre, then, is "proposal." How you deliver your proposal depends on how best you can reach your intended audience: e-mail, letter, PSA, talk, and so on.

Problem ▸ Audience and Purpose ▸ Genre/Proposal ▸ Medium of Delivery

Understanding the Rhetorical Situation

When you identify a problem, you often think about possible solutions. Proposals offer an analysis of the problem and the best of solutions, best in terms of feasibility, cost, and benefits. Your task as a proposal writer is to give the problem a presence in the lives of your audience. Because not everyone will readily accept your proposal, it is important that you recognize other possibilities and weigh their pros and cons as well. You may even want to include some of the best ideas in your own proposal. In the end, you will need to justify why your proposal is the best one, the one most beneficial to your audience and yet not harmful to others.

RESEARCHING A PROPOSAL

Successful proposals (whether informal advice or formal proposals) rely on research, knowledge, and personal experience. As you advocate for your plan, take into consideration similar as well as competing proposals, researched facts and data, and the interests and values of your audience. Library, online, field, and naturalistic research (interviews, observations) as well as experiential knowledge will provide you with the specific facts, figures, and research studies you need to persuade your audience to act on what you propose. But you will also need to research your rhetorical audience in order to make your case, establishing that what you propose is in their best interest. After all, you want to be especially careful to introduce ideas that can be proved to be feasible, acceptable, and financially responsible, rather than reintroducing parts of a proposal they have already rejected. Without the necessary research, your proposal is merely your opinion.

Identifying an Opportunity for Change

You want to identify a problem that merits a solution that you can propose. How does this problem affect you? How does it affect others? How present is it in your life? How would writing about this problem help you begin to conceptualize a solution? How might a solution affect you and others?

1. Identify three problems that you encounter on a daily or weekly basis. How do they make themselves present in your life? Which of them could easily be resolved—if only someone would make a change? If it were resolved, how would you be affected? How would others be affected?

2. In terms of the problem that offered the richest details for development, how might it be resolved? What other possible resolutions can you think of? What is the feasibility of each of the proposed resolutions? What is the cost? What are the benefits?

3. Freewrite for ten minutes, identifying one problem, describing how it manifests itself in your life and how it affects your life and the lives of others. (For more on freewriting and other ways to jump-start your writing, see pages 231–236 CHAPTER 13, EXPLORATION.)

4. Then write for another ten minutes, outlining a proposed solution to that problem. Be sure to include the steps necessary for making your proposal a reality. Who else needs to be involved? What ought they do? How, exactly, will you and they benefit? What are the pros and cons of your proposal?

5. In order to vary your emphasis, describe other proposals that may be in circulation. What are the pros and cons of those proposals? Whom will they benefit? Whom might they harm?

Proposals

Relating Rhetorically to Your Audience

The following questions can help you locate your rhetorical audience as well as identify its relationship to the problem you have identified. Then, you will be able to choose the best way to describe that problem.

1. List the names of the persons or groups who are in the best position to help you make your proposal a reality. This step may require some research and legwork.
2. Next to the name of each potential audience, write reasons that audience could have for acknowledging the very real presence of your problem. In other words, what would persuade these audiences that something needs to change?
3. What actions could these audiences reasonably be persuaded to perform? Consider what each audience would be able to do to address the problem—and what each audience ought to do.
4. With your audience's interests and capabilities in mind, look again at the descriptions of the problem that you composed in the preceding section. Decide which description will best help your audience feel connected to the features of the problem you outlined and invested in improving them. At this point, it may be necessary to revise your best description to tailor it to your audience. Remember to consider whether the most fitting description will include print, images, video, and/or audio.

Planning an Effective Rhetorical Response for Your Purpose

Identifying a problem and getting others to recognize it as a problem are only the first steps in responding to a rhetorical situation. You also need to identify and support a suitable solution to the problem. Your solution should consider the information you gathered about your audience, such as their interests and capabilities, as well as detailed information about the problem itself (its history and its presence) and your proposed solution (its actual benefits, costs, and feasibility). In terms of feasibility, your proposal ought to be an efficient, cost-effective, and widely beneficial way to go about making a positive change.

Use the following questions to help you narrow your purpose and shape your response:

1. How would you efficiently and effectively solve the problem you have identified?
2. What does your proposed solution require of your audience?

3. Are you asking your audience simply to support your solution or to perform a particular action?
4. What is the best way to reach this audience? You might draft a petition, compose a video, or speak to student and community groups. The point is that after you have identified your problem, audience, and purpose, you need to determine how best to deliver your proposal.

LINKS TO PROPOSALS IN THREE MEDIA   MindTap®

Links may change due to availability.

Print Proposal Michael Rosen passionately proposes reading aloud to teenagers to promote literacy.

Oral Proposal or Short Film The National Football League sponsors PSAs on Domestic Violence (this short film aired during Super Bowl XLIX).

Online Proposal Many proposals, like this water conservation PSA, feature images illustrating the problem and/or solution and are posted to an appropriate online site.

⊛ WRITING A PERSUASIVE PROPOSAL: A Guide

To write persuasively, you will need to establish your credibility, or ethos, as you demonstrate your understanding of the situation and the ways it affects your audience. Next, you will establish logos (the logic of your proposal) by creating an information-based argument: the background of the problem, the immediate effects of the problem itself, and the feasibility and acceptability (monetary, practical, and aesthetic) of the solution you are proposing. Finally, you will create pathos when you connect with your audience, showing them how the implementation of your proposal will benefit them—and not at great expense or inconvenience to others.

ADVANTAGES AND LIMITATIONS

Advantages

- **Writer:** You have insight into a troublesome situation, and you have some good ideas about addressing or resolving that problem.

- **Message:** Proposals invite you and others to improve the world you live in, on both a broad, public scale and a smaller, private one.

- **Media and Design:** The possibilities are many, from print and visual to online and multimodal. You can select the medium of delivery that will reach, maybe even please, your audience.

Limitations

- **Writer:** Because you may not be the first person to identify and try to resolve the problem, your audience may not be (immediately) receptive to your proposal (or any proposal, for that matter).

- **Message:** Not everyone will agree that improvements are needed, especially if they are expected to take action. Or they may not agree on your proposed solution.

- **Media and Design:** Like the UnLitter Us campaign at the beginning of this chapter, your first attempt to reach your audience may need to be revised. Often, writers find themselves having to revise and resubmit their proposals.

Introduction

- **Frame the problem** by offering necessary background and by emphasizing the presence of the problem.
- **Establish the problem** as one both the writer and audience share and will want to resolve (establishing credibility as a writer or speaker).
- **State your thesis** by defining the problem and outlining a sensible solution.

Define the problem The introduction emphasizes the presence of the problem and offers credible information on the history of that problem, maybe even its causes or consequences. For example, in his proposal, Rosen first recounts how his father's reading aloud helped him develop his literacy. He refers to himself as "lucky," before moving on to the problem that many parents face: how to foster their children's love of reading.

Present a sensible solution The introduction states Rosen's thesis, which conveys the essence of the proposed sensible solution: "parents and teachers should continue reading aloud to children well into their teen years." For him, the solution is ethical, feasible, and practical.

Ask yourself . . .
- Have I described the context of the problem with enough detail so that my audience understands its urgency?
- Have I demonstrated the ways that the problem not only affects me but them as well?
- Have I proposed a solution that is sensible, feasible, and acceptable—as well as ethical?

- **Support the proposed solution with researched evidence, establishing logos.**
- **Review previous attempts to resolve the problem. You may also be able to establish how this solution has worked elsewhere but do not overpromise benefits.**
- **Discuss the feasibility of the solution: the time, money, and effort required.**
- **Address the acceptability of the solution, including possible objections.**

Use evidence to support the logic of your solution The body of a proposal provides supporting evidence for the suggested solution, particularly in terms of its consequences or results. The researched content of the overall argument helps establish logos. Rosen, for instance, draws on his expertise to explain the differences between the ways we write and speak—and the ways we put sentences together in each medium of delivery. "In order to understand," he writes, "and be able to write continuous prose, we need to spend a good deal of time immersed in it." And, for Rosen, the best immersion is being read to, regardless of age.

Show how the solution is acceptable and feasible in terms of time, money, and human effort Take your readers through the steps necessary to bring the proposal into reality. Careful research is crucial to the success of this section. Rosen demonstrates the ease and simplicity of his proposal: all parents need to do is pick something up and read aloud. Of course, Rosen supposes that *Guardian* readers who enjoy what they are reading and want to share it and that they think print literacy is important to develop.

Provide examples of success Provide examples of other instances in which your proposed solution (or a similar one) has had positive results, not just for a few, but for many. Benefits may include saved time, saved money, happiness, less suffering, and so on. A professor of literacy, Rosen refers to himself as "lucky" to have been "brought up in a household where my older brother and father read out loud to me as a teenager. It was a form of conversation or entertainment."

List the logistical challenges Concede the challenges to your proposal and supply detailed responses to each of the challenges, demonstrating how all or most of them can be overcome. Weigh the benefits with the costs. The biggest challenge Rosen's readers might face is having suitable reading materials at home, but, then, *Guardian* readers are already assumed to have middle-class values that include education and a quest for literacy.

Acknowledge objections and tradeoffs Not everybody will approve of your proposal. Acknowledge those objections and discuss tradeoffs. Rosen does not state objections to his proposal, knowing that his educated readers are well aware of who knows and controls literacy development: the schools. His proposal, that families take back (some) control of literacy activities, does not displace the literacy training within schools but rather enhances it.

Ask yourself . . .
- Have I researched the background of this problem?
- Am I informed about previous proposals for resolving this problem?

- How, exactly, can my audience benefit from my proposal?
- Will anyone be harmed by it?
- Have I researched and addressed the possible objections to my proposal?
- Do I have the necessary information to address each of those objections?
- What further research must I conduct in order to present a well-rounded argument for my proposal?

Conclusion

- **Predict positive outcomes of the solution.**
- **Establish an authentic emotional connection with the audience by linking the solution to their benefit.**

Predict the positive results of your solution Finally, the conclusion of a proposal predicts the positive consequences or improvements that will result from the proposed solution, results that far outweigh any negatives. Rosen shows us how reading aloud enriches a child's literacy development at any age, ending his narrative stating that ideally a teenager who is being read aloud to would have the text in front of them, "so that we can stop and talk about things as we go along, referring back to what's just been read. This means we make bridges, from the written to the oral and back again." What could be better?

Identify the solution with the interests of your readers The conclusion should make clear just how the audience will profit from this proposal, which will benefit many, not just a few. Using pathos, you will connect your proposed solution with the needs and interests of your audience. In this case, Rosen speaks to a readership who is interested in the development of literate, responsible citizens who will contribute to the intellectual, economic, and political development of Britain. All Britons will profit from such an investment in the literacy development of their children.

Ask yourself . . .

- How can I demonstrate that my proposal is the most beneficial to the most people?
- What additional research should I conduct?
- What else do I need to know about the needs and interests of my audience?
- Have I listened carefully to all of their concerns?

>> REVISION AND PEER REVIEW

After you have drafted your proposal, ask one of your classmates to read it. You will want your classmate to respond to your work in a way that helps you revise it into the strongest proposal it can be, one that addresses your intended audience, helps you fulfill your purpose, and is delivered in the most appropriate means available to you.

Questions for a Peer Reviewer

1. What problem has the writer identified? How does the writer frame that problem? How does the problem offer an opportunity to respond?
2. Who is the writer's rhetorical audience? Why might this audience care about the problem?
3. Where does the writer indicate how the problem will affect the audience? What does the writer think the audience ought to do? How does the writer establish ethos?
4. Identify the writer's thesis statement, which should clearly state the proposed solution, perhaps repeating the problem as well. If you cannot locate a thesis statement, what thesis statement might work for this document?
5. What kinds of research has the writer conducted in order to provide support for the proposed solution, in terms of its feasibility, cost, and acceptability?
6. What steps are necessary for realizing this solution?
7. Identify the supporting ideas (presented through narration, cause-and-effect analysis, description, exemplification, process analysis, or definition) that the writer uses to support their assertions.
8. What additional evidence might the writer provide to better support the solution's feasibility? How has the writer established logos?
9. Where does the writer address potential objections to the solution?
10. How does the writer make use of images? Is there any place where a graph or chart could be included, to display costs or otherwise provide readers with a sense of what will be expected of them or the community?
11. What does the solution ask of the audience? Is the requested action explicit or merely implied?
12. How does the writer connect with the audience in terms of aligning the proposed resolution with their needs or expectations (establishing pathos)?
13. What did you learn from the conclusion that you did not already know after reading the introduction and the body? What information does the writer want the audience to know? Does the writer attempt to change readers' attitudes, actions, or opinions?
14. Which section of the proposal did you most enjoy? Why?

ADDITIONAL ASSIGNMENTS

Knowledge Transfer

Often, students collaborate with community service agencies or businesses to fulfill their research or writing assignments, conduct scholarly collaborative projects via social networking sites, and spend their summers as interns, earning professional experience rather than money for next semester's expenses. Proposal writing is useful beyond English classes for all these venues.

COLLEGE Letter to the School Administration You are required to take an upper-division writing course in your major, but you—and many of your classmates—cannot register for that writing course until the last semester of your senior year. You and some of your closest friends compose a joint letter to the dean of your college, asking her to help you resolve this problem: after all, you all need to have that course much earlier in your college careers. You propose a solution that you think she can implement, perhaps by working with the dean of the College of the Liberal Arts (where writing courses are housed). You might consider asking for more sections of this course, hybrid courses, or even priority for majors.

COMMUNITY Letter to the Editor As you consider your entry into college, make a list of the resources (advantages)—and constraints (limitations)—associated with your experiences so far. Describe factors that make them positive or negative. Finally, choose one feature of your *experience* that has been problematic. Write a letter to your campus newspaper (see one example that follows, which appeared in the *Centre Daily Times* [State College, PA]).

There is a recurring problem in . . . State College to be exact. Local drivers continue to pass stopped mass-transit buses in neighborhoods clearly marked with solid double yellow lines. These lines have one purpose: Do not pass in these areas! You . . . are inviting a collision with an oncoming car in the other lane. You are at fault should you kill another driver. Stop it. . . . Obey the traffic laws or buy a bike.

Dan Stoicheff
State College

(continued)

WORKPLACE Memorandum for Reallocation of Resources You have noticed that many people in your office have hotpots and small microwaves in their offices or cubicles, leaving the entire office area messy and sometimes smelly. Many people complain about the situation but cannot think of how best to resolve it. You and a couple of close colleagues have noticed that a janitor's closet is no longer being used as such. Because it already has a sink and electrical outlets, you propose that it be transformed into a kitchenette of sorts, with an electric teakettle, microwave, and small refrigerator. In fact, the three of you will be happy to make the transformation during work hours or with overtime. You agree to write the proposal memo to your supervisor, outlining the problem; the effects of the problem; the feasibility, cost, and acceptability of your proposed solution; and the benefits for all.

MULTIMODAL Public Service Announcement As you review the UNLITTER US campaign used by the city of Philadelphia presented earlier in this chapter, consider ways that your community (campus, city, church, or hometown) could be improved. What is an abiding problem in that community? What have been the attempts to address that problem? Who has tried? What insights can you offer into the problem? How do you propose it be addressed? Who could help you? How would they benefit? Using a multimodal approach (any combination of words, images, video, audio), compose a Public Service Announcement aimed at and easily available to your rhetorical audience.

10 Evaluations

LEARNING OBJECTIVES

- Identify rhetorical situations where an evaluation would be useful for making a decision or understanding a response.
- Explain the purpose of an evaluation in terms of its key rhetorical features and principles of development in various media.
- Reflect critically on why someone or something needs to be evaluated and what criteria will be meaningful to your rhetorical audience for determining your judgment.
- Apply descriptive, relevant details and compelling examples to persuade your audience that the criteria you use in your evaluation support a clear claim articulated in your thesis.
- Evaluate evidence (from books and articles, interviews with experts, conversation, facts, details, or your personal experience) that support your conclusion about how the features of what or who you are evaluating do or do not meet your criteria, and cite appropriately for your evaluation.
- Apply peer review and self-evaluation to revise, edit, and proofread an evaluation so it is reasonable, insightful, and persuasive.

Your familiarity with evaluations has developed over a lifetime of reading them and making your own. You have seen examples of this genre in the form of movie reviews that regularly appear in newspapers, magazines, and conversations; you have also seen product reviews that appear in print and online publications such as *Consumer Reports* and *PC Magazine*. Both kinds of evaluations work to persuade you that particular films, appliances, and electronics are the best, average, or not so hot. By now, you also intuitively know that an **evaluation** (or a review) has two basic components: (1) a judgment meant to persuade, and (2) the criteria used to arrive at that judgment.

As you determine the specific situation, problem, phenomenon, or cultural element (movie, art object, political event, or everyday detail of life) that merits your evaluation and relevant criteria, consider, too, the most effective means of delivering that evaluation to your audience: print, online, orally, visually, or multimodally.

IDENTIFYING AN OPPORTUNITY FOR CHANGE

Print Evaluation
written for a campus newspaper or zine

Oral Evaluation
presented live to your rhetorical audience using a video, digital slide show, or presentation software

Online Evaluation
posted on a film review site, a video game site, an educational site, or other website

evaluation a judgment based on relevant criteria and meant to persuade

GENRE IN FOCUS The Film Review

Consider one of the most common forms of an evaluation: the movie review. A reasonable and insightful movie evaluation establishes the criteria and includes judgments on those criteria, such as the overall quality, strengths and weaknesses, cast, setting, and technical features in the film. In addition, a movie review might include a consideration of the significant cultural references in the film, such as costumes or historical references in the movie's plot line—or, as in the following review of *Little Women*, references to eight previous film adaptations.

In an early positive review of the most recent film iteration of Louisa May Alcott's long-beloved 1868 book, critic Wendy Ide calls it "a rare achievement." She opens with the assertion that "one-hundred-and-fifty-year-old literature never felt so alive" as when she watched Greta Gerwig's version of *Little Women*.

Throughout her enthusiastic review, Ide lays out the criteria she uses to evaluate a truly fine film: the setting, the story itself, the characters and the actors who play them, the dialogue, and the directorial vision. To prove that her assessment is the right one, Ide offers detailed descriptions of the film itself that call up her positive response, that Gerwig's creation is "true to its roots and bracingly current." For her, the setting provides an authentic backdrop for the story line itself, as Gerwig shot the film in Alcott's hometown of Concord, Massachusetts, allowing the "vividly exuberant new England autumn colors" to tint the scenes. Of course, the story features the "enduring phenomenon" of main character Jo March, whose independence, determination to write and be published, and refusal to marry "well" have long established her as a young girl's hero. But it is the "tumultuous" interaction of all the family members that propels the story (and theme of women's fulfillment) forward with the early marriage of Meg, the competition of Amy and Jo, the death of Beth, and the immeasurable velocity of the main character. Together, the sisters "take the dialogue as written by Alcott" and deliver it according to the director's vision: "in a tumbling clutter of ideas and mass hilarity." Marmee, as ever, provides the anchor of home-grown generosity, empathy, and, above all, sacrifice, characteristics that have long earned the March family admiration. These characters and their dialogue are all familiar, but, according to Ide, better, more contemporary than ever before. Finally, Ide discusses Gerwig's directorial vision, which includes "restructuring the timeline into a multilayered playground where the child and adult stories interact . . . subtly foregrounding existing themes of female fulfillment and the economics of creativity." But Ide's review is not thoughtlessly positive. She is disappointed with the musical score, as she makes clear in her review:

Lifestyle pictures / Alamy Stock Photo

Little Women *(2019) is the seventh film adaption of Louisa May Alcott's 1868 novel chronicling the lives of the March sisters—Jo, Meg, Amy, and Beth.*

> **. . . By encouraging a merry chaos of overlapping personalities and performances—restructuring the timeline into a multilayered playground where the child and adult stories interact—and subtly foregrounding existing themes of female fulfillment and the economics of creativity, [Greta] Gerwig creates something that is true to its roots and bracingly current. . . . [T]his is the freshest, most light-footed literary adaptation of the past year.**

. . . [T]he vividly exuberant New England autumn color palette flushes through the childhood scenes. . . . Gerwig acknowledges the commercial pressure to marry off a fictional female character, and argues that the real happy ending is the publishing of Jo's book. . . . Alexandre Desplat's unremarkable mulch of a score—one of the film's few weak points—does little more than provide decorative wallpaper for the bustle of family life. But the design departments, interiors and costumes, excel. Laura Dern's Marmee raises her girls in a magpie stash of bohemian jumble, punctuated with impromptu midnight baking sessions and amateur dramatics. It's a home that radiates warmth. . . . And if that's not the perfect sentiment for holiday viewing, I don't know what is.

—Wendy Ide, "*Little Women* review—the freshest literary adaptation of the year"

Taking a different position, *Stylist* film reviewer Moya Lothian-McLean, offers a negative evaluation of *Little Women* as she weighs various criteria (plot, theme, characters) and comes to the conclusion (and headline) that she may be "the only person in the world who hates *Little Women*."

Little Women. Ugh.

Apparently, this is a "controversial opinion." Indeed, I hadn't expected that despising *Little Women*—which has been turned into a film *again*. . . .

Millions of people the world over have taken the March sisters—pretty, fretting Meg, tomboy Jo, saintly Beth, and spoiled brat Amy—and their devout "Marmee" to heart since the first print run of Louisa May Alcott's *Little Women* in 1868. At the time it was a revelation; an early 20th century text that bucked gender norms. These girls were 3D. . . .

. . . However, the real draw of the March girls were their hopes and dreams. Jo, with her inky fingers and fantasies of writing a bestseller; Meg, who wants to swap managing a household for the life of a normal 16-year-old girl; Beth, who lives for music; and Amy who *likes* art but *loves* compliments . . . —the girls at least had dreams.

"They're real!" crow fans. "They want more than to be bedecked by a white veil one day."

But come the end of the book, the March sisters *are* all bedecked by that treacherous headpiece. Well, all save for boring Beth, who has sadly been whisked away by consumption so that the others can be suitably humbled by her pure little life.

. . . By a mile, Beth is portrayed as the most deserving March girl but god! Is! She! Boring!

. . . The point of all this is: *Little Women* doesn't deserve to be feted in 2019. There are plenty of new stories about women to be told, and lots of them don't punish a girl for wanting to go to a party. It's a tale of its time and it has dated badly. . . .

—Moya Lothian-McLean, "Am I the only person in the world who hates *Little Women*?"

A film review is essentially an argument that often begins with a thesis statement and is intended to persuade others that your evaluation is accurate. (See **CHAPTER 15, ARGUMENT**.) Thus, even though Ide presents a set of evaluation criteria similar to those of Lothian-McLean, the second critic arrives at a different conclusion, a negative evaluation that she supports with specific evidence and compelling examples. Ultimately, both movie critics are trying to persuade their readers that the criteria they use to evaluate the film (and the examples from the film to which they apply the criteria) are the most important ones to consider. Whatever the reviewer argues, it is paramount that he or she supplies specific—and relevant—evidence to support that claim (for example, that a movie is ground-breaking or derivative, suspenseful or confusing). (For more on thesis statements, claims, and evidence, see **CHAPTER 2, MAKING CLAIMS**.)

pages 292–294

pages 20–21

ASSIGNMENT

Whether conscious or unconscious, evaluations are value judgments about whether an object, event, individual, or document meets, exceeds, or does not satisfy the criteria. Every day we evaluate movies, political candidates, academic programs, partners, green designs for new cars or architecture, or issues and objects that affect our daily life. Often you will determine the relevant criteria for your evaluation; at other times, the criteria are already in place (symptoms for a specific illness, for example).

As you consider your evaluation, focus on an object, phenomenon, event, or person that merits your attention as well as the attention of your audience. You may want your audience to understand your topic differently from how they currently understand it. Describe your topic and list detailed criteria (either traditional or fresh) for your evaluation, synthesizing your overall evaluation into a thesis statement. Your goal is to help your readers appreciate the significance of your evaluation by aligning the criteria you have developed with the object of your evaluation and the interests of your audience.

≫ READING RHETORICALLY

You regularly make judgments or choices determined by criteria. When you read rhetorically, you examine an evaluation through the criteria used to make that judgment. You may be examining the evaluation of an event or phenomenon that affects you, an object you need to buy, or a choice you need to make. As you read, place your object—and the criteria—within a social, cultural, and/or financial context, explaining how the object coincides with or diverges from the criteria used as the basis of your evaluation. Read actively and critically for the key features of a strong evaluation. In fact, the better you can analyze someone else's evaluation, the stronger your own evaluations will be.

Key Features of an Evaluation

Evaluations help us make decisions and are particularly useful for understanding the logical and emotional responses that are being shaped in ourselves and others. Whether spoken, visual, or written, evaluations argue either whether something *meets* a specific set of criteria or whether the set criteria *determine* the status of that object under consideration. In addition, to be persuasive, evaluations often draw on a particular emotional response with the use of descriptive, relevant details. Such details help the audience visualize the criteria and match them with the features of the object being evaluated. In short, evaluations commonly share most of the following features:

- Evaluations make clear why a particular object or phenomenon needs to be evaluated.
- Evaluations describe the particular object or phenomenon in a way that the rhetorical audience will understand and value.
- Evaluations ultimately identify the precise category into which the object or phenomenon fits: successful movie, effective detergent, dependable computer, easy-to-use smartphone. Just consider the ways your doctor evaluates your symptoms before determining your illness.
- The criteria on which the object or phenomenon is to be evaluated are presented clearly, persuasively, authoritatively, and often in an order indicating importance. Criteria can be categorized into three groups: *necessary* (crucial but not enough to meet your overall assessment), *sufficient* (meeting all of your minimum standards, including the necessary ones), and *accidental* (unnecessary but an added bonus to the necessary and sufficient criteria).
- Concrete evidence and relevant examples from your personal experience and research illustrate the ways (usually in the form of assertions) the object or phenomenon does or does not meet each evaluative criterion. These fair and balanced assertions support the thesis statement.
- Evaluations articulate a clear argument (usually in the form of a thesis statement) about whether or not the object or phenomenon meets the criteria on which it is being evaluated.
- The evaluator has demonstrated an ethical approach to the process.

You can see how these key features work in the following essay by Penn State-Fayette student Alexis Walker. In it Walker evaluates the effect of a new Dunkin' Donuts on the aesthetics of the downtown area where she lives. As you read, consider the rhetorical situation and the key criteria Walker presents.

- Determine Walker's motive for writing. What does she want to accomplish?
- Identify the criteria used to evaluate Dunkin' Donuts at Easton's Center Circle.
- Examine the language Walker uses to frame her evaluation as fair and balanced. Does her evaluation seem fair to you?
- Decide whether you agree with Walker's evaluation. Why or why not?

Donuts at Easton's Center Circle: Slam Dunk or Cycle of Deterioration?

ALEXIS WALKER

Faced with the problem of a big ugly welcome sign in the shape of a Peace Candle, Alexis Walker was determined to write. She could have devised a PowerPoint presentation for the city council, e-mailed photos of the architectural defacement to the local historical preservation association, or composed a purposeful verbal evaluation of the situation. She chose to do the latter, arguing for a downtown renewal initiative based on bringing in major businesses and sponsoring local events as a way to attract the townsfolk to the city center. She distributed her evaluation to her friends and neighbors.

The way any city looks—its skyline, the buildings, the streets, even the greenery—affects how we experience that city and perceive what that city has to offer us. Whether from the hectic, crowded environment of New York to the calming, empty quality of a farming town, our feelings are influenced by what surrounds us. Therefore, the center of any city or town should, ideally, portray the very best the city has to offer (or, at least, what it hopes to offer). The most obvious are the visual clues, the businesses and events that populate the downtown area and indicate the values and interests of the town and bring people together, even a town as small as our own Easton.

A quick scan around the downtown of my hometown, Easton, on a winter weekday afternoon makes disappointingly clear that this eastern Pennsylvania town leaves much to be desired. Prominently placed at the center of the traffic circle sits a huge Peace Candle. No matter from which direction one enters the circle, the Peace Candle is straight ahead, failing to actualize its intended

Walker defines and describes a typical city center.

The criteria for an inviting city center. Walker opens her evaluation by describing city centers and the specific one she plans to evaluate in a way that all her friends and neighbors can readily understand and value. In a two-sentence thesis statement, Walker asserts why the downtown scene she describes merits evaluation and clearly states her two criteria for how a town can achieve its best.

Walker describes the necessary criteria: an attempt to invite people to the city center must be made, even if it's not enough.

purpose from any and every direction. Grungy, neglected, off-white concrete representing the melted wax drips down the sides of the candle, with light blue cascades of faded color encrusting each corner of the so-called candle holder. An unassuming, dull, stiff flame of orange and red metal sits atop the structure, unable to project any vibrancy. And the entire creation is supported by a series of highly visible black cables emphasizing the candle's behemoth existence. It would be a menacing sight were it not so pitiful. This sad display of candlelight is supposed to signify the fire, energy, and soul of Easton, as though it's a bustling hub of city commerce rather than the old, dull, and mostly rundown commercial space it actually is. Encircling the mammoth centerpiece are darkened windowpanes and boarded up entrances.

The bright white, freshly painted outside of the new Dunkin' Donuts contrasts sharply with the lifeless grey buildings that surround it. The signature orange and pink lettering adorns both sides of this corner edifice, and its large windows showcase the kinds of satisfied patrons the establishment wants to attract (figure 1). All of these attributes (freshness, cleanliness, paying customers), dissimilar to the dreary display downtown Easton usually offers, might suggest that the area is on the rise. Indeed, the revamped Dunkin' Donuts building and the business it brings are nice—but they are not nearly enough.

Dunkin' Donuts is one of a small number of notable exceptions to the lifeless environment of downtown Easton, intermittent exceptions among the otherwise rundown and abandoned properties. Despite its neon green sign, Pearly Baker's restaurant sits inconspicuously in one corner. And Crayola crayons, an Easton institution, makes its colorful (if not gaudy) presence known. A relatively new and clean building complex dominates the city center, advertising all things Crayola and its McDonald's. And a giant crayon box serves as a sign to the Crayola gift shop entrance.

Considering the already successful Crayola complex, what with its built-in McDonald's, it is clear that bigger corporations are present and welcome in our downtown. And with the addition of a new Dunkin' Donuts, a precedent has been set for what types of companies

Figure 1. Historic downtown's Dunkin' Donuts (photograph courtesy of James Kirkhuff).

can succeed within the city circle: any big name company. Crayola, Dunkin' Donuts, and McDonald's all have major name recognition, which is a primary reason they are the most prominent attractions to Easton's center. The chance the center circle once had to become a thriving, eclectic, small-town neighborhood is now impossible. Even if small businesses remain for a while, it is a Dunkin' Donuts or a McDonald's that will draw business from Crayola's downtown existence, not insurance companies, bakeries, boutiques, five-and-dimes, or hair salons. The patronage these major businesses will bring to downtown might create some spillover business for the other establishments, but these primary attractions seem to complement one another the most.

And so the problem remains: the fewer the small businesses, the fewer downtown attractions for Eastonians. There will never be tantalizing postcards of a charming, bustling Easton to sell, only that of an easily imaginable but much less compelling image of a humdrum town with a mediocre strip mall.

• There are bright spots within this dismal image, though. During the summertime, providing good weather, Easton's center circle plays host to a weekly farmers' market. Farmers with stands of products, ranging from fresh farm produce and honey to freshly milled soaps and flowers, can draw a local crowd. This alternative business-offering, transient as it may be, brings people to the downtown city center. And those crowds are outside, socializing, and enacting a lively image of our downtown, livelier than it's been for decades.

Next, she points out a concrete reason why the circle won't succeed: most businesses don't meet the criteria for success. In mentioning the farmers' market, Walker offers one concrete example of how the center circle might meet the second criterion of drawing patrons to the downtown.

Should one take a picture of these two different downtown environments, position them next to each other, and then draw conclusions about what type of place Easton is to live in, the results would obviously be quite different. Whether one picture is more accurate, or whether the real Easton experience is somewhere in between, ultimately is irrelevant. The fact remains that a city projects a certain experience through its surroundings. Is it welcoming, impressive, expansive, busy, or a combination? • Usually a trip to Easton's center circle would not yield a particularly promising impression of what Easton has to offer. Maybe the recent addition of a Dunkin' Donuts will improve downtown's condition. On the other hand, maybe it will cement its deterioration.

Finally, Walker articulates a clear argument that Easton is not meeting the criteria required for a thriving center circle.

Using Synthesis and Analysis

Usually, the alignment (or matching) of each criterion with the problem (an object, phenomenon, event, or person—in this case, the new Dunkin' Donuts downtown) becomes an assertion that supports the thesis statement. Using analysis, determine the criteria used in the evaluation and consider such questions as the following: What is the immediate overall effect of the event, object, or phenomenon? What are its specific parts? How are these parts pieced together? What is the overall effectiveness of these parts? These types of questions lead to detailed evaluations as well as thoughtful analyses of issues or objects that we experience, use, or need every day and that often shape our society. Synthesize the results by determining the author's main point and whether she has delivered a carefully reasoned, ethically derived evaluation.

See also CHAPTER 2, **MIKE ROSE,** *Lives on the Boundary* [Reading Closely]

See also CHAPTER 27, **FRANK SHYONG,** *"It's Just Too Much": Asian Americans Confront Xenophobia, Economic Devastation and the Coronavirus*

See also CHAPTER 28, **AMINA KHAN,** *Fires, Droughts and Hurricanes: What's the Link Between Climate Change and Natural Disasters?*

»» RESPONDING TO THE RHETORICAL SITUATION

Situations that call for clarity, a decision, a plan, or a change are situations that call for an evaluation. Whether you are evaluating the quality of potential living quarters, a set of physical symptoms, a college course, a specific airline, or a movie, an effective evaluation is based on a set of carefully researched criteria that is then delivered to a specific audience (possibly yourself).

In addition to the wide range of opportunities for evaluation are the means of delivering those evaluations: visually, verbally, orally, or by some combination of these media. Your challenge is to choose the medium of delivery that will most easily reach and please your rhetorical audience, the people who could be affected by your evaluation. A personal letter, newspaper opinion piece, PowerPoint presentation, recommendation letter, or YouTube video are all possible media for delivering a fitting response in the genre of evaluation.

Opportunity ‣ Audience and Purpose ‣ Genre/Evaluation ‣ Medium of Delivery

Understanding the Rhetorical Situation

Evaluations are used to review, analyze, and synthesize the features of a problem, object, phenomenon, or other cultural element, whether it is the latest film sensation, the city center, brides' dresses, or a required course. To succeed with any rhetorical exchange, you must start by evaluating the rhetorical situation itself, the context. Your evaluations are rooted in context. In other words, where you are, the specific audience you want to reach, and your purpose are features of the context that help you develop specific criteria for the evaluation as well as assess where the most reliable and expert information comes from.

Evaluations—whether others' or our own—persuade us as we answer questions, resolve problems, and make decisions within specific contexts. For instance, you see your doctor for a professional evaluation (she diagnoses your symptoms of fever, cough, and weakness as pneumonia). You turn to your well-read, movie-going friends for an evaluation of the best movie to see on Friday night. And when you decide to apply to graduate school, you work with a respected faculty member to evaluate, using the criteria that you develop together, which programs are best for you. You seek or make evaluations within a specific context, using specific, often context-specific, criteria.

 RESEARCHING AN EVALUATION

Evaluation writing is rooted in judgment—not the kind of judgments we make on a daily basis, but rather on *informed* judgment. For your judgment to be informed, it must be based on research, whether online searches, traditional library research (professional books and articles), interviews with experts in the field, or conversations. The results of your research will guide you as you establish criteria for your evaluation and match those criteria with specific features your topic has to offer. Furthermore, the results of your research will also enrich your ability to evaluate within a specific context. Those research findings will also assist you in establishing a thoughtful hierarchy of criteria: necessary, sufficient, and accidental. Thus, researching will improve your ability to establish criteria, deepen your understanding of your topic, and enhance your rich descriptive details and facts that comprise an effective evaluation.

Identifying an Opportunity for Change

Rhetorical situations that call for a judgment are those calling for an evaluation. The opportunity for change is the opportunity to replace uncertainty with clarity—for yourself and others. As simple as a weekend outing might be, it calls for a cascade of evaluations: whom to invite, which movie to see, how good the movie was, where to eat afterwards, how good the pizza was. All of these evaluations were initiated by you and your friends, calling for you to establish criteria; match the criteria to your topic (potential invitees, movie, pizza); decide which criteria are necessary, sufficient, and accidental; and direct your persuasive evaluation to one another as well as to other friends who are interested in the movie or the pizza joint.

pages
231–236

To identify an opportunity for change, freewrite for five minutes in response to the following everyday opportunities. (For more on freewriting and other ways to jump-start your writing, see CHAPTER 13, EXPLORATION.)

1. What big purchase did you make before enrolling in college? A smartphone, computer, car, bicycle? What process did you go through before making the purchase? What criteria did you develop for this purchase? Where did you turn (a person, an organization, a professional reviewer) for advice? What did you learn through the process of researching, developing criteria, and purchasing? When have you evaluated something or someone without developing and following through with specific criteria? What were the results? What did you learn about yourself and/or the evaluation process?

2. As you contemplate your major, make a list of criteria that are important to you, keeping in mind that your criteria for a major may or may not align with your criteria for a career. Be prepared to share your reasoning with the rest of the class.

3. Make a list of five problems you have encountered over the past week that affect the work or play of people on your campus. For example, are there any computer labs that make you feel mentally and physically exhausted— or all revved up? Are there any couches or chairs in the common area that seem to be particularly inviting—or just the opposite? Write a few sentences describing the problem and your overall impressions when you first noticed it. Provide as many details as you can to help readers visualize and emotionally respond to the problem (in either a positive or negative way).

Relating Rhetorically to Your Audience

The following questions can help you locate your rhetorical audience as well as identify the relationship they have to what you are writing about. Answering them can help you determine the best medium (or media) for delivering your evaluation.

1. List the names of the persons or groups most likely to be affected by what you have chosen to write about. These are potential audiences for your evaluation.

2. Next to the name of each audience member, list reasons that person might have for considering your topic in more detail. In other words, what would persuade these audiences that what you are writing about needs to be evaluated?

3. Explore how each of these people could reasonably be influenced or persuaded by an evaluation. In other words, what emotional responses or

changes in attitudes, behavior, or beliefs might they have after reading, hearing, or seeing your evaluation? What motivations might they have for analyzing this subject?

4. With your audience's interests and motivations in mind, look again at the descriptions that you composed in the preceding section. Which description(s) will enable your readers to feel engaged in your evaluation and invested in exploring your topic in greater depth? A richer, detailed description not only allows readers to create a vivid mental picture but also helps them understand why and how your subject affects them. At this point, it may be necessary to revise your best description to tailor it to your audience's needs and interests.

Planning an Effective Rhetorical Response for Your Purpose

As you know, focusing your purpose is important, because different purposes require different kinds of texts, delivered through different media. For example, if you are evaluating an image such as a photograph or a painting, you might compose an essay that would appear as part of a museum display or in an exhibition catalog. Your evaluation of a visually uninspiring university web page could be crafted as a letter to the staff in the admissions or alumni relations office. Your evaluation of the dysfunctional design of a computer lab could take the form of a widely distributed e-visual of a redesigned lab or an e-mail message aimed at gaining student support for the proposed changes. After you have identified your opportunity, audience, and purpose, you will want to determine what kind of text will best respond to your rhetorical situation.

Use the following questions to help you narrow your purpose and shape your response:

1. What kinds of researched facts or details and personal experience define the context in which your topic influences or affects people on a daily basis?
2. What kinds of facts or details make your topic particularly compelling? What specific audience do these details attract?
3. Are you asking your rhetorical audience to adopt a new perspective, or do you want the audience to perform a particular action in response to your persuasive evaluation?
4. What is the best way to reach this audience? That is, what kind of text is this audience most likely to respond to?

Links may change due to availability.

Courtesy of James Kirkhuff

Source: YouTube

IMDb

Evaluations

Print Evaluation In the essay at the beginning of this chapter, student Alexis Walker locates a rhetorical opportunity in the changing landscape of her city's downtown.

Oral Evaluation @studyquill evaluates "The 12 best podcasts for students" on YouTube.

Online Evaluation IMDb (Internet Movie Database) provides information online for thousands of movies, including film clips, trailers, cast listings, as well as information on the film director and writer, and reviews. See IMDb.com for the user rating, the metascore from metacritic.com, as well as reviews from critics and IMDb users that evaluate *Little Women* (2019) online.

WRITING A PERSUASIVE EVALUATION: A Guide

Persuasive evaluations are researched, well-reasoned, ethically derived, and connected to the values and interests of a specific audience. In addition, every evaluation should have a thesis statement that is richly supported with specific evidence. In these ways, an effective evaluation establishes your ethos (or credibility), validates the logos (or good reasons) of the overall argument, and authenticates pathos (an authentic emotional connection with your audience). (For more on ethos, logos, and pathos, see CHAPTER 2, THE AVAILABLE MEANS INCLUDE THE RHETORICAL ELEMENTS OF THE MESSAGE ITSELF.)

pages
23–26

ADVANTAGES AND LIMITATIONS

Advantages

- **Writer:** You have considerable latitude in the topic you select (from laundry detergent or pizza to a film or artwork) and the way you place that topic in context.

- **Message:** An evaluation can be casual, negotiated among friends, and rooted in personal experience (emphasizing ethos and pathos) or more research-based and formal (emphasizing ethos and logos).

- **Media and Design:** Evaluations are presented in many ways: as conversation, video, print, or multimodally (as most evaluative advertising is done).

Limitations

- **Writer:** We evaluate so regularly throughout our day that we often skip over the important step of establishing criteria, let alone researching those criteria.

- **Message:** Given the frequency of our casual evaluations, we must take time to consider the interests and values of our intended audience—and our purpose for reaching and engaging them.

- **Media and Design:** Given the many visual, verbal, and multimodal possibilities for delivering an evaluation, the primary consideration must be the audience's access to, and interest in, the medium of delivery.

Introduction

- **Define the subject to be evaluated.**
- **Establish the author's ethos.**
- **Explain why the subject should be evaluated.**
- **Identify the ways in which the subject is to be evaluated.**
- **Explain why readers should care about the evaluation.**
- **Offer a persuasive thesis statement.**

Define what you are evaluating Writers of evaluations use the introduction to define and describe the topic, explain its cultural significance, enumerate the evaluation criteria, and persuade readers that the evaluation has significance for them. These concepts come together in a persuasive thesis statement, such as Walker's claim that "the center of any city or town should, ideally, portray the very best the city has to offer."

Establish your expertise By providing researched details, cultural understanding, and often personal experience, the writer establishes her expertise and knowledge, qualifying her as an ethical evaluator. Walker establishes her credibility when she calls Easton "my hometown." By recognizing the ways the evaluation meets the values and interests of her audience, she confirms her positive ethos.

(continued)

- Why do I care about this topic?
- Who else will care about it?
- Does my detailed description connect with the interests and values of my audience?
- How do the criteria I offer reflect on my ethos?
- How does my thesis statement present a reasonable evaluation?

Body

- **Provide evaluative criteria.**
- **Match those criteria to features of the topic.**
- **Explain the context that gives the topic particular significance.**
- **Establish logos through good reasons and persuasive matches of criteria to detailed examples from the topic.**

Establish your criteria The body of an evaluation provides the criteria for the topic, object, or phenomenon to be evaluated. Following the concepts of sufficient, necessary, and accidental, the criteria will be presented as assertions that support the thesis as Walker does with her assertion that a decline in small businesses downtown will result in less downtown traffic. These criteria make—and shape—the argument at the same time that they establish the logos (the good reasons) of the evaluation.

Use facts, details, even quotations To accompany each criterion, the writer offers researched facts, details from cultural observation or social experience, and even direct quotations in her analysis of how features of the topic being evaluated match (or do not match) the specific evaluative criteria. Such specific facts and details enhance the description of the topic, explain its cultural significance, and strengthen the connection of the topic with the audience. Walker explains the cultural significance of the decline by describing the central position and "sad display" of the peace candle in downtown Easton.

Use sensory details as evidence Details grab and maintain the readers' interest. Sensory details (such as Walker's "neon green sign" and "giant crayon box") help the writer to persuade her readers that the evaluation is based on a careful, complete analysis of all the elements that make up the object or phenomenon.

Explain the context for your evaluation The body of an evaluation often attempts to explain the political, economic, social, or cultural context that gives this object or phenomenon particular significance. For Walker, the addition of a new Dunkin' Donuts as a generic chain store thwarts "the chance the center circle once had to become a thriving, eclectic, small-town neighborhood." This contextual evaluation helps deepen readers' understanding of how the object or phenomenon influences their daily lives.

Body

Ask yourself . . .
- How do I know that my criteria for evaluation are ethical, logical, and informed?
- Which of them are necessary, sufficient, or accidental? Are they important in that same order?
- How do I connect my criteria with the interests and values of my audience?
- Which persuasive details come from my research? Which from my observation and experience?
- What are the contextual details that demonstrate the significance of this topic, this evaluation, to me and to my audience?

Conclusion

- **Synthesize criteria and collected evidence.**
- **Make one final appeal for readers to adopt a specific attitude or opinion.**
- **Confirm pathos.**

Connect the criteria and supporting evidence in your conclusion The conclusion of an evaluation synthesizes the evidence of matches between various criteria and the features of the topic itself in order to make one final appeal for readers to adopt a specific attitude or opinion (for Walker, for example, that the new Dunkin' Donuts contributes to the "deterioration" of downtown Easton).

Confirm pathos Throughout the evaluation, you have worked to connect your persuasive thesis (for Walker, that the city center reflects the "best the city has to offer") in an ethically responsible manner to the interests and values of your audience (which Walker does when she asks if downtown Easton is "welcoming"). The conclusion offers you one last chance to confirm that you have made an authentic emotional connection.

Ask yourself . . .
- How can I reaffirm my thesis statement without repeating it? How might I close with the implications of my argument if it is accepted or rejected?
- How can I make a final appeal to my audience without seeming to be manipulative or desperate?

❯❯ REVISION AND PEER REVIEW

After you have drafted your evaluation, ask one of your classmates to read it. You will want your classmate to respond to your work in a way that helps you revise it into the strongest evaluation it can be, one that addresses your intended audience, helps you fulfill your purpose, and is delivered in the most appropriate means available to your audience.

Questions for a Peer Reviewer

1. Why is this evaluation necessary, even important?
2. Why is the topic important to the writer?
3. How might it be important to the writer's intended audience as well?
4. What might be the writer's purpose? How do audience and purpose come together in this evaluation?
5. What information did you receive from the introduction? How does the writer introduce the particular object or phenomenon she is exploring? How does the writer suggest why it needs to be evaluated? What suggestions do you have for the writer regarding the introduction?
6. Note the writer's thesis statement. If you cannot locate a thesis statement, what thesis statement might work for this evaluation?
7. Note the assertions the writer makes to support the thesis. (These may be in the form of criteria the writer establishes.) Are they presented in chronological spatial, or emphatic order? Does the writer use the order that seems most effective? How could the writer improve the order of these assertions?
8. If you cannot locate a series of assertions, what assertions could be made to support the thesis statement?
9. Note the concrete evidence and examples that the writer uses to show how the subject meets or does not meet the criteria established.
10. How does the writer establish ethos? How could the writer strengthen this appeal?
11. What material does the writer use to establish logos? How might the writer strengthen this appeal (see questions 6–8)?
12. How does the writer make use of pathos?
13. What did you learn from the conclusion that you did not already know after reading the introduction and body? What information does the writer want you to take away from the evaluation? Does the writer attempt to change your attitude, action, or opinion?
14. Which section of the evaluation did you most enjoy? Why?

✏️ ADDITIONAL ASSIGNMENTS

Knowledge Transfer

📑 **COLLEGE Literature Review** *Literature* in this context refers to scholarship on a particular topic. When your instructor asks for your evaluation of a book, research study, or scholarly article, your job is to take a position and argue it. In response to such an assignment, compose a literature review in which you make a claim (advance a thesis) and argue a position about the quality of the work. You will use textual evidence from the work itself, information you have researched, and your own experience to support your assertions.

👥 **COMMUNITY Low-Income Housing Evaluation** You are a member of the township council, and you have all been charged with evaluating bids for the low-income housing project. As you consider the bids, you will need to review the criteria for the low-income housing that you produced a year ago and match those criteria with the information in each bid. The bids may prompt your council to rethink the criteria themselves or the hierarchy of criteria. In evaluating your final selection, be sure to offer a thesis statement, provide assertions of how each criterion is met (or exceeded) by the successful bid, and supply concrete examples and evidence that support each of the assertions.

🗂️ **WORKPLACE Professional Recommendation** When you supervise or collaborate with others, they may ask you to serve as a reference for them. In response to a request for a recommendation, your task is to evaluate your colleague according to the criteria constituting the new position, promotion, fellowship, internship, or graduate school. Compose a recommendation for a colleague in which you match (or do not match) the criteria of the new position with the personal and professional qualities of your colleague.

🖥️ **MULTIMODAL Presentation with Visual Evidence** You have been asked to evaluate the effectiveness of the additional traffic lights (traffic signals) that were installed in your downtown a year ago. In order to define "effectiveness," you will need to conduct research on the status of traffic accidents, speeding, and other traffic violations over the past year as well as on the degree of driver and pedestrian satisfaction with the new lights. Then, you'll need to compare these results with those of preceding years. In order to present the information effectively and efficiently, your evaluation must include charts and graphs. You may even want to include online links to the reports of citizens you have interviewed and videos of current traffic flow improvements or impediments.

11 Critical Analyses

LEARNING OBJECTIVES

- Identify a critical question complex and open-ended enough to prompt a critical analysis that brings a new perspective to the topic.

- Explain the purpose of a critical analysis in terms of its key rhetorical features and principles of development in various media.

- Apply close examination to reveal logical connections between the phenomenon and its causes and/or consequences.

- Reflect critically on alternative perspectives.

- Evaluate the types of data (from the library, field, or experience) that best provide insights and understanding; reframe the question if necessary; and; cite research appropriately.

- Apply peer review and self-evaluation to revise, edit, and proofread a critical analysis to create a clear and logical explanation for the cause or consequences.

---

pages 278–294

critical analysis a careful examination of the causes or consequences of a situation or phenomenon

You analyze critically every day—every time you examine something carefully and closely in order to identify its patterns and relationships. Often times, you hone in on a scholarly article, a legal decision, or a design; other times you establish the causes or consequences of a feature of the world you live in. (See CHAPTER 15, CAUSE-AND-EFFECT ANALYSIS.) Based on careful examination, insights, and understanding (and including library, field, or experiential research), a **critical analysis** breaks something into parts, analyzes each part separately, studying the ways the parts work together, and then synthesizes those findings into a claim or thesis statement. (See CHAPTER 3, ANALYSIS AND SYNTHESIS and CHAPTER 2, MAKING CLAIMS.) Throughout this chapter, you'll work to identify an opportunity to conduct a critical analysis on a topic (or phenomenon) that interests you. You'll also consider the most fitting means of delivering your analysis to your rhetorical audience, using precise language.

pages 43–48

pages 20–21

IDENTIFYING AN OPPORTUNITY FOR CHANGE

 Print Analysis written for a community or campus newspaper

 Oral/Multimedia Analysis presented live to your rhetorical audience

 Online Analysis posted on a blog

GENRE IN FOCUS Media Critique

News of the Boston Marathon bombing in 2013 generated a rallying cry of "Boston Strong" for overcoming the threat of terrorism. The terrorist threat involved a lockdown of the city to discover the culprits, a teenage boy and his brother. In the following piece, Roxane Gay looks at the way race invisibly affects media coverage and how the substance of such news also shapes public opinion.

There is no way to truly know whom we need to protect ourselves from. Dangerous people rarely look the way we expect. We were reminded of this in early 2013 when Dzhokhar ("Jahar") Tsarnaev, who looks like the "boy next door," was identified as one of the two young men suspected in the terrorist bombings near the finish line of the Boston Marathon. Three people were killed and nearly three hundred others injured. This notoriety, I imagine, explains why Tsarnaev was featured on the cover of the August 1, 2013, issue of *Rolling Stone*.

A photograph of suspect Dzhkokhar Tsarnaev is played on a television in a shopping center near the site of the Boston Marathon bombings on April 23, 2013, in Boston, Massachusetts.

Mario Tama/Getty Images

The magazine was accused of exploiting tragedy, glorifying terrorism, and trying to make a martyr or a rock star out of Tsarnaev. But protests aside, the cover is provocative and pointed. It is a stark reminder that we can never truly know where danger lurks. It is also a reminder that we have certain cultural notions about who looks dangerous and who does not. These notions are amply reinforced by the article accompanying the cover, something few people seem to be talking about. The tone of Janet Reitman's reportage and the ongoing conversation about Tsarnaev as a "normal American teenager" are an interesting and troubling contrast to the way we talk about, say, Trayvon Martin, also a "normal American teenager," but not a criminal or terrorist. George Zimmerman killed Martin because Martin fit our cultural idea of what danger looks like. Zimmerman was acquitted for the very same reason.

. . .

A cardboard photo-realistic figure of Trayvon Martin at a crowd gathered to peacefully protest the Trayvon Martin case in Union Square in Manhattan on July 14, 2013.

Lukas Maverick Greyson/Shutterstock.com

When Trayvon Martin was murdered, certain people worked overtime to uncover his failings, even though he was the victim of the crime. Before his death, Martin had recently been suspended from school because drug residue was found in his backpack. There were other such infractions. This became evidence. He was a normal teenager but he was also a black teenager, so he was put on trial and he was indicted. With Tsarnaev, people continued to look for the good. The bounds of compassion for the "tousle-haired" young man know few limits. Trayvon Martin, meanwhile, should have walked home without "looking suspicious." He should have meekly submitted himself to Zimmerman's intentions instead of whatever took place on the fateful night of his murder. He should have been above reproach. As Syreeta McFadden noted, "Only in America can a dead black boy go on trial for his own murder."

Reitman's article is a solid piece of journalism. It reveals complex truths about the life of Dzhokhar Tsarnaev. Imagine, though, if *Rolling Stone* had dedicated more than eleven thousand words and the cover to Trayvon Martin to reveal the complex truth of his life and what he was like in the years and months and hours before his death. How did he

deal with the burden of being the face of danger from the moment he was born? This is a question fewer people seem to be asking.

—Roxane Gay, "A Tale of Two Profiles"

As you consider Gay's critical analyses of the media coverage of these two individuals, consider, too, how much you agree with the influence the media has on public opinion. Reflect on the ways your own campus or community critically examine invisible messages, like those mentioned in Gay's analysis of what and who embodies danger, and the consequences that such unexamined views can have.

 **ASSIGNMENT**

When you ask the question "Why?" you are already engaged in critical analysis. You and people around you are probably questioning the causes or consequences of a situation, phenomenon, object, person, or text. For your critical analysis, identify a situation, phenomenon, object, person, or text you are interested in. Perhaps, like Roxane Gay, you will focus on a feature of the world we live in that troubles you. You will examine your topic closely and carefully until you can determine patterns, details, and relationships within the topic you are analyzing. Whether you are interested in the fallout from pandemics, recent and past, a lost sports season, the occurrence of Type 2 (adult-onset) diabetes, or the ways media shapes public opinion, your goal is to analyze the topic in order to establish the causes or consequences that your audience needs or wants to know about. Often, you will rely on research findings to help support the determinations you have made.

≫ READING RHETORICALLY

Close examination is the key to any critical analysis—whether you are writing or reading one rhetorically. The twofold purpose of critical analysis is for the author to analyze closely a phenomenon in order to establish a clear understanding of that phenomenon and then to explain a synthesis of it (often a cause or consequence) for the audience. As you read for the features of the rhetorical situation—who the writer is, what occasion prompted the composition, who the writer's intended audience is, and what the purpose of the composition is—you can also gauge how well the writer incorporates the key rhetorical features of the genre into the critical analysis. Look for the critical question that prompts the analysis and determine how clear and logical the explanation is of the relationship between the cause or consequences and the phenomenon under analysis.

Key Features of a Critical Analysis

You are probably familiar with the form and arrangement of critical analyses because you read many of them in your daily life: editorials and feature articles, for example, are often in this genre. Whether you are writing or reading, you will notice that critical analyses typically include the following features:

- A critical question prompts the analysis and focuses the thesis.
- Precise description of the phenomenon helps readers understand why it merits analysis and why they should be invested in the analysis.
- Researched evidence, data, and examples sufficiently support that logical connection between the situation or phenomenon and its causes or consequences.
- The causes and/or the consequences connect logically to the situation or phenomenon.
- Alternative perspectives on the situation or phenomenon are acknowledged, analyzed, synthesized, and responded to.
- The author conducts and synthesizes research (from the library, observations, personal experience, or calculation/experiment) in order to enhance the analysis.

These features are illustrated in the following student essay by Anna Seitz, who uses her own experience with online learning for her critical analysis. As you prepare to read Seitz's essay, consider the following questions:

- What does the title tell you?
- What do you imagine the consequences of pursuing and receiving an online degree might be?
- What might she mean by "real-time"?
- What audience will be interested in or affected by the topic of an online degree?

The Real-Time Consequences of an Online Degree

ANNA SEITZ

As she explains in her introduction, wife and mother Anna Seitz wanted to pursue the coursework for her graduate degree from her home computer. She excelled in both her courses and her practicum—questioning the consistency of the teaching and her learning all along the way.

I'm a mother of three small children, and I'm much more interested in spending time with my kids than spending time in a classroom. When I decided to pursue an advanced degree, I opted for an online program. I didn't know exactly what it would be like, but I knew what I wanted out of it—flexibility to complete the program on my own schedule. And while I got that, I also found that my decision had other consequences. ●┈┈┈┈┈┈┈┈┈┈┈┈┈┈┈┈┈┈┈┈┈┈┈┈┈┈┈┈

> Seitz sets up her thesis: that there are both expected and unexpected consequences of working toward a degree online.

The primary consequence of taking online classes was that I did, in fact, have even more flexibility than I'd imagined. ●That was good and bad. I had an impressive selection of electives each term, especially because my advisor gave me almost total freedom to select my courses. The secondary consequence of this freedom is that I won't be graduating with the exact same skills and experiences as everyone else in my class—we all have different specialties and will be competing for different jobs. Also, none of my classes had set meeting or chat times, and I was able to do my readings, write my papers, and participate in discussion forums in fits and spurts (and in pajamas!). ●I read at night and during nap times, in the car, and at the playground. I learned to do most of my research online, and when I had to use local libraries, I simply packed up my gang for the children's story hour. Some of my professors provided the entire term's contents on day one, which helped me plan my work.

> She opens with a positive consequence, one familiar to the millions of students getting degrees online.

> She provides detailed support for her assertion about the first consequence.

The flip side of this particular consequence was that planning my work was a bigger challenge than doing the work. ●Because my days with the children were always unpredictable, I lost a lot of sleep while learning how to pace myself in terms of taking care of my family and keeping up with my school work. There were times when my kids got stuck with a distracted mommy who cut corners on suppers and bedtime stories. I had to keep careful records of tasks and due dates, and I had to create my own deadlines as I learned how to divide big projects into manageable sections. After all, with online courses, the only regular reminders and announcements from the teachers are discussion board reminders (only useful if you log in and read them, of course). I'm nearly finished with the program, and I still haven't settled on an acceptable frequency for checking the class message board. Either I waste time checking constantly and finding nothing, or I go out for a day only to come home and find out that I've missed contributing to some major discussion or development.

> Seitz moves on to a second consequence, which isn't as positive. This paragraph is detailed with incidents from her life, a life familiar to many parents who are working toward a degree (online or off).

Taking responsibility for my own learning at my own pace has always been comfortable for me. I've always been independent, and the idea of doing these classes "all by myself" was very appealing. ●Unfortunately, a secondary consequence of the online environment caught me by surprise. I was soon forced to admit that as much as I wanted to do things myself, my way, my professors

> Seitz claims that independent learning feels natural and easy to her—but admits that her independent nature doesn't always lend itself to online learning.

and my classmates profoundly affected my learning, my grades, and my enjoyment of the classes. I had a few professors who spent as much or more time on my online classes as they would have on a face-to-face class, producing online PowerPoint lectures, enrichment activities, and discussion prompts, and making personal contact with each student. In those classes, I got to know my classmates, worked with others on projects, and learned things that I can still remember years later. The efforts of our professors inspired us to put in our own best efforts, and I would count those experiences to be on par with my best face-to-face classroom experiences.

I also had a few "teachers" who simply selected textbooks that came with lots of extras, such as a publisher's website with quizzes and assignments. In one of those classes, the publisher's website actually did the grading for the quizzes and calculated my class grade. I was really offended and kind of disgusted that my "teacher" would be so lazy. I felt that I wasn't getting what I'd paid for, and I felt neglected. Ultimately, I was embarrassed because I felt that it gave merit to all of the criticisms that I'd heard about online education. In one of those classes, I simply sat down with my textbook and did the entire term's quizzes in one night. I didn't learn a thing. I should have acted like a grown-up and made the best of it, but I just jumped through the hoops and collected my credits. I got an A in that class doing work which would have flunked me out of any face-to-face class, and that made me mad, too.

One of the secondary consequences is that I began to consider my teacher's performance, and to discuss it with my classmates. When I was in college at 18, I was more focused on what I was putting into my classes than what I was getting out of them. I didn't notice what the teachers were or were not doing. In my current program, however, nearly all of the students are busy adults with careers and families who are paying their own way through school so that they can enhance their careers. My classmates and I are only there to improve our skills, and we want to get our money's worth. There are a lot of complaints when we don't. I can think of dozens of examples of students voicing their complaints about the teacher, materials, or assignments as part of the class discussion, and because the communication is public, the teachers nearly always have to make improvements.

Another secondary consequence is that there is surprisingly little privacy in an online class when compared to a face-to-face class, and that was very difficult to get used to. I can't just slink in, sit in the back of the class, keep my head down,

As she provides logical support for her assertions, Seitz also gives readers authentic glimpses into herself, a rhetorical move that emphasizes her credibility.

Seitz carefully differentiates the immediate from the remote consequences of taking an online degree.

and hope the teacher never learns my name. The comments I am required to post each week can be read, and in fact *must be read* by the entire class. Everyone knows what I've read, what I think about it, and how well I express myself. Everyone reads my papers, and I read theirs. For an independent person like me, this was tough to swallow. I didn't like comparing my work to others', even when it compared favorably. I dreaded the times when it compared unfavorably, and when I saw a classmate do particularly good work, I wanted to, too. It was a healthy and productive sort of peer pressure, and I did things I'd never tried to do before, and sometimes even did them well. •

Seitz's relationship with her fellow students helps her successfully establish a sympathetic connection to her readers.

Using Synthesis and Analysis

Whether you are reading or composing a critical analysis, pay careful attention to the ways specific details and evidence connect the constituent parts and promote causes or consequences. In her critical analysis, Seitz examines her own experience in a way that clarifies her conclusions for others.

- How has she broken down her experience?
- What does she say about how the elements of her experience work together?
- What insight and evidence does she use in her analysis?
- How do conflicting opinions illuminate her analysis?
- What conclusion does she draw and why?

When you work through your own analysis and synthesis of Seitz's essay, bring together all the information you have collected such that your analysis and synthesis can serve as the foundation of your critical analysis of the success of her essay, leading you toward a clear understanding of the causes or consequences of the phenomenon itself. Explain whether you have a clearer understanding of online education after reading Seitz's critical analysis.

See also CHAPTER 3, **RICHARD A. LANHAM,** *Literacy and the Survival of Humanism* [The Study of Style]

See also CHAPTER 25, **JOHANNA BLAKLEY,** *Social Media and the End of Gender*

See also CHAPTER 26, **HANNAH KAPOOR, ELAMI ALI, AND NADIA MURILLO,** *Code Red: Can "Hard Corners" and Classroom Drills Protect Students from Shooters?*

See also CHAPTER 26, **AMELIA TAIT,** *Pandemic Shaming: Is It Helping Us Keep Our Distance?*

See also CHAPTER 27, **BRENNAN HOBAN,** *Do Immigrants "Steal" Jobs from American Workers?*

»» RESPONDING TO THE RHETORICAL SITUATION

What rhetorical opportunity invites your engagement? After you identify an opportunity, establish a purpose for your writing as well as an audience. Then, you need to determine what kind of text (or message) you can deliver that will best respond to your rhetorical situation. A critical analysis might be useful for examining issues such as whether new technologies give powerful people and nations a louder voice, leaving poor and powerless people and nations to fend for themselves—or, conversely, whether those who traditionally have not had a political voice can now announce their interests by transmitting their messages publicly. The most successful critical analyses often include research—library, laboratory, data-driven, or experiential research that supports the analysis and the findings. In addition, a critical analysis is best for exploring the causes and/or consequences of a situation or phenomenon.

| Opportunity | Audience and Purpose | Genre/Critical Analysis | Medium of Delivery |

Understanding the Rhetorical Situation

Writers use critical analysis to help readers understand specific cultural, economic, political, and social forces, as well as to explore the consequences that have occurred or might occur as a result of these forces. A critical analysis can help people become more aware of the "how" and "why" in their daily lives. In some cases, a critical analysis can change how people think or act to create the kinds of communities in which they want to live and work.

 RESEARCHING A CRITICAL ANALYSIS

When Sandra Bullock, Jennifer Lawrence, and other stars asked if Hollywood values were gendered, they raised a critical question that prompted critical analysis of Hollywood hiring practices. Through research, interviews, and observations, these women could cite facts, figures, and other documented data (including salaries, number of leading roles, number of directing opportunities) as well as their personal experiences. As they analyzed their data and synthesized their findings, they realized that Hollywood hiring practices are, indeed, gendered, and to the financial and cultural advantage of Hollywood men. Viola Davis has extended the argument to that of the disadvantaged Black woman in Hollywood, regardless of demonstrated talent, her awards, and her box office power. Often, your instincts will lead you toward a critical analysis. But you will want to conduct the kinds of research the Hollywood women conducted to compose an ethically derived, evidence-based conclusion, one based on careful analysis and skillful synthesis.

Identifying an Opportunity for Change

Consider your understanding of and participation in the world in terms of the people with whom you communicate. To begin, freewrite for five minutes in response to each of the following prompts (or use any of the invention techniques presented in CHAPTER 13, PLANNING): pages 231–238

1. Make a list of the communications technologies you use regularly. For each technology, list the kinds of content you create or consume. Providing as many details as possible, describe each type of content and explain whether you found your experiences with that type of content to be positive or negative.

2. Locate two consumer-oriented websites or magazines that analyze something you need to buy: an electronic, an appliance, an insurance plan, for example. Carefully analyze them for their critical question, precise description of the object, rationale for analyzing it, researched evidence, alternative perspectives, and ultimate finding, keeping a record of your analysis. Then present the analysis you find more persuasive along with the reasons for your judgment.

3. Make two columns in which you list the positive and negative features of a course you are taking: difficulty and interest in subject matter; quality and variety of the instruction, assignments, and evaluations; and cultural or social connections or differences. Analyze each of these features, providing specific details and discussing the causes or consequences of each feature and the ways the features work (or do not work) together.

4. Critically analyze your own sleep patterns to determine the causes as well as the consequences of a good night's sleep. You will want to describe and define what a good night's sleep actually is, using examples from your own experience as well as information you have researched. You will analyze each feature of a good night's sleep separately as well as together, synthesizing your insights, experience, and research findings into a short essay.

5. Take five minutes to analyze the differences between your virtual and physical interactions with people who live a distance from you, maybe even across the globe. How and what do you learn through each type of interaction? Be prepared to share your analysis with the rest of the class.

Relating Rhetorically to Your Audience

The following questions can help you locate your rhetorical audience as well as identify the relationship they have to the phenomenon you are analyzing, whether it is a situation, text, event, or something else. Then, you will be able to choose the best way to present your analysis.

1. List names of groups who directly contribute to or who are directly affected by the phenomenon you are analyzing. On another list, write the names of groups who indirectly contribute to or are indirectly affected by the situation or phenomenon. You may need to do some research to compose a list that accounts more fully for all the various groups with a stake in analyzing this situation or phenomenon.
2. Next to the name of each potential audience, write possible reasons that audience could have for wanting a better understanding of the causes or consequences of the phenomenon.
3. What responses could these audiences reasonably be expected to have to your analysis? In other words, what conclusions might they be persuaded to draw, what attitudes might they be likely to adopt, what actions might they be willing to take? After exploring these possible responses, decide which audience you most want or need to reach with your critical analysis.
4. With your audience's interests and capabilities in mind, look again at the descriptions of the types of content that you composed in the preceding section on identifying a rhetorical opportunity. Decide which description might enable these readers to feel connected to the phenomenon you want to analyze—and might help them become invested in understanding its causes or consequences. At this point, you may need to revise, tailoring your best description to your intended audience.

Planning an Effective Rhetorical Response for Your Purpose

As you know, different audiences and different purposes require different kinds of texts, delivered through different media. Your goal is to create a response that reaches and engages your intended audience, addresses your critical question, and follows through the features of an ethical, logical critical analysis.

After all, critical analysis can be used on many objects, events, and phenomena and be targeted to a wide range of audiences, just so long as you accommodate their technological expectations and demands. (See CHAPTER 4, CONSIDERING pages 60–73 AUDIENCE, PURPOSE, AND ACCESSIBILITY IN MULTIMEDIA COMPOSITIONS.) For instance, if you decide to analyze the consequences for international understanding that derive from virtual tourism websites or software such as Google Earth, you might create your own webpage or post an extended comment on the message board of such a site. On the other hand, your analysis of the causes that lead to the emergence of online communities for the world's youth might lead you to create a pamphlet for distribution at local public libraries.

Still, you might be more interested in analyzing the consequences of good coaching and practice by studying an individual sport at your college—gymnastics or track, for example. You might observe and analyze the critical elements that comprise the process of coaching and practice. You may want to photograph key moments, videotape practice, or tape conversations between the coach and the athlete. Your analysis could develop into a newspaper article, conference presentation, inspirational essay, or slim handbook.

As you work to develop a topic for a critical analysis, use the following questions to narrow your purpose, identify an audience, and shape your response:

1. What critical question has led you to this topic?
2. What specific claim do you want to make about the causes or the consequences of the phenomenon you are analyzing? What reasons support this particular claim? What evidence or examples can you provide to convince readers that each reason logically supports your analysis? What research do you need to do?
3. Which supporting reasons for your claim are most likely to resonate with or be convincing to your audience? What are the audience's beliefs, attitudes, or experiences that lead you to this conclusion?
4. What specific response are you hoping to draw from your audience? Do you want to affirm readers' existing beliefs about the phenomenon? Do you want to draw their attention to overlooked information or have them reconsider their views on a particular type of content? Do you want readers to perform different types of activities as a result of your analysis?
5. What might be the best way to present your analysis to your audience? That is, what kind of text is this audience most likely to respond to and easily receive?

Print Analysis In the essay at the beginning of this chapter, student Anna Seitz examines the advantages and limitations of online education.

Oral/Multimedia Analysis In this interview, a young Malawian man named William Kamkwamba explains the causes that led him to build a windmill to harness electricity at his rural home and traces the amazing consequences. A link is also available to "Moving Windmills," a short film.

Online Analysis This online article analyzes the consequences of the YouTube video "Star Wars Kid," which is in the *Guinness Book of World Records* for most video downloads.

⊘ WRITING A PERSUASIVE CRITICAL ANALYSIS: A Guide

*T*o write persuasively, you will need to use language that seems precise and careful to your audience, which means you must understand how familiar your audience already is with the phenomenon and how well they already understand its possible causes and consequences. You will need to use facts, data, and other specific information (perhaps gleaned from your close and careful observations) to establish your claim about the phenomenon and use that explicit factual information to expand and support your claim. You will undoubtedly start with a question of how or with what causes or consequence the phenomenon occurs. You might even use a startling fact in your introduction, to "hook" your readers. In the process of helping your audience understand as well as you do, you will want to clarify which causes and/or consequences are primary and which are secondary, articulating how each cause contributes to or each consequence follows from the phenomenon you are analyzing.

ADVANTAGES AND LIMITATIONS

Advantages

- **Writer:** Critical analyses offer you the opportunity to follow your instincts (or insights) as to the causes and consequences of any situation or phenomenon. You have the opportunity to understand clearly a phenomenon that interests you—and then to educate an audience who is affected by the topic.

- **Message:** Research, insights, close examination, together with breaking the phenomenon down into significant steps or features, all combine to form a message that connects emotionally with the interests of your audience.

- **Media and Design:** The flexibility of critical analyses and the diversity of interested audiences invite you to post your analysis online, compile a print report, or compose an oral delivery. You can use visuals (tables, graphs, photographs), videos (of the process itself), or audio (music, interviews, other sounds) to enhance the delivery and design of your message.

Limitations

- **Writer:** Upon conducting the necessary research, you may discover that your instincts were wrong and that you must pursue another line of inquiry, starting with another close examination of the phenomenon.

- **Message:** Although it is tempting to conduct a critical analysis on the basis of your insights alone, analyses rooted in researched facts and data or in authenticated experience and observation are always more persuasive, at the same time that they enhance the ethos and logos of the message itself.

- **Media and Design:** Because critical analyses can be designed and delivered in so many ways, you will want to consider the expectations of your audience (or your instructor). A critical analysis for an English course, for instance, may call for a different design and medium (print only, perhaps) than for a political science or business course, which may call for graphs, tables, statistics, and visuals.

Introduction

- **Describe the situation or phenomenon.**
- **Establish the rhetorical opportunity for analysis.**
- **State the thesis, a claim about causes or consequences.**
- **Build credibility by providing explicit, researched support for the claim.**

Begin with an example that illustrates why you are analyzing this specific situation or phenomenon The introduction of a critical analysis hooks readers' attention, presenting a detailed example that helps them recognize the rhetorical opportunity and understand why this situation or phenomenon should be analyzed. In "The Real-Time Consequences of an Online

(continued)

Degree," Anna Seitz describes the opportunity for her analysis: "I'm a mother of three small children, and I'm much more interested in spending time with my kids than spending time in a classroom. When I decided to pursue an advanced degree, I opted for an online program."

Introduce your claim with support to explain the causes or consequences of the situation The introduction also presents the writer's thesis, a claim about the causes or the consequences of the situation or phenomenon, with some support so that the readers trust the writer on this topic. Seitz's claim was that an online degree would give her "flexibility to complete the program on my own schedule." And she soon discovered that her "decision had other consequences."

Ask Yourself . . .

- How does my introduction feature a question that merits analysis—and audience interest?
- How clearly have I stated my thesis?
- Will I focus on causes or consequences of this phenomenon?
- What expertise or experience am I offering that helps me establish my ethos?

- **Present and elaborate on causes and/or consequences of the situation or phenomenon.**
- **Articulate how each cause contributes to or each consequence follows from the situation.**
- **Present researched reasons supporting the claim about each cause or consequence.**
- **Acknowledge and respond to alternative viewpoints from experience or research.**

Connect causes to consequences The body of a critical analysis presents and elaborates on the primary (and, depending on the depth of the analysis, the secondary) causes and/or consequences of the situation or phenomenon being analyzed. Seitz writes of the primary consequence of flexibility, enriching that flexibility with the fact that she "had an impressive selection of electives each term, especially because [her] advisor gave [her] almost total freedom to select [her] courses." But she found that such flexibility led to another consequence: "I won't be graduating with the exact same skills and experiences as everyone else in my class—we all have different specialties and will be competing for different jobs."

Make consequences vivid through anecdotes, quotations, and statistics Writers also create strong appeals to logos as they present brief anecdotes, direct quotations, and data and statistics to strengthen each supporting reason and to help readers see more clearly how each cause or consequence is linked to the situation or phenomenon. For Seitz, another consequence of online learning was planning out her work. Seitz writes that "because [her] days with the children were always unpredictable, [she] lost a lot of sleep while learning how to pace [her]self . . . ." At the end of her program, she still has not "settled on an acceptable frequency for checking the class message board. Either [she] waste[s] time checking constantly and finding nothing, or [she goes] out for a day only to come home and [find] that [she has] missed contributing to some major discussion or development.

Bring in alternative viewpoints The body paragraphs of a critical analysis also acknowledge and respond to alternative viewpoints, a rhetorical move that enhances the believability of the writer's analysis by establishing the writer as fair-minded. Although Seitz is mostly positive about the consequences of online learning, particularly in terms of the flexibility it provided her, she also discusses her "worst fears" about online classes. And given Seitz's own independent nature, she was struck by the secondary consequence of having to post her reading analyses, class comments, and written work publicly, as participating in an online public forum was a requirement of the course, a requirement that other students enjoyed.

Ask yourself . . .

- How does my analysis reveal my close, careful examination of the phenomenon?
- What are the sources of my explicit evidence? How do they enhance (or not) the logos of my message?
- What research evidence do I include for each of my supporting assertions?
- Where do I include alternative viewpoints (professional and popular) on the phenomenon?
- Which passages feature the most precise language?

- **Reinforce the positive benefits to readers from analyzing the situation or phenomenon or the negative situation that may result if such analysis is ignored.**
- **Create effective appeals to pathos, making an authentic emotional connection with the audience.**

Emphasize consequences, positive or negative, for the reader Finally, the conclusion of a critical analysis reinforces the positive benefits that readers can reap from analyzing this situation or phenomenon. Or, depending on the topic, the conclusion can illustrate the negative situation that may result if readers ignore the writer's critical analysis. As Seitz recounts the consequences of her online degree program, she admits that when she compared her work with the work of her peers, she was often inspired to do better—even though such comparisons had never been part of her educational experience. In fact, she writes, she found the online experience to result in a "healthy and productive sort of peer pressure" that led her to do things she had "never tried to do before, and sometimes even did them well."

Ask yourself . . .

- What exactly am I encouraging my audience to do?
- Where do I balance the positive and the negative causes or consequences—or does my message require such balance?
- How, exactly, do I make an authentic emotional connection with my audience?

Body

Conclusion

»» REVISION AND PEER REVIEW

After you have drafted a strong version of your critical analysis, ask one of your classmates to read it. You will want your classmate to respond to your work in a way that helps you revise it into the strongest analysis it can be, one that addresses your intended audience, helps you fulfill your purpose, and is delivered in the most appropriate means available to you and your audience.

Questions for a Peer Reviewer

1. To what critical question is the writer responding?
2. What are the strengths and weaknesses of the description of the situation or phenomenon? How might the audience better visualize the situation?
3. How does the writer establish the need to analyze this particular situation or phenomenon? Where does the writer indicate how the situation or phenomenon concerns the audience?
4. Who might be the writer's intended audience? Why might they be interested?
5. Identify the thesis statement of the analysis, in which the writer clearly states a claim about the causes or the consequences of the phenomenon being analyzed. If you cannot locate a thesis statement, what thesis statement might work for this document?
6. Identify the researched facts, data, evidence, and examples the writer provides in support of the claim.
7. Where does the writer address varying perspectives on the causes or consequences of the situation or phenomenon being analyzed?
8. Where does the writer establish an authentic emotional connection (pathos) with the audience?
9. What did you learn from the conclusion that was not already in the document? What does the writer want you to take away from the document in terms of information, attitude, or action?
10. Which section of the document did you most enjoy? Which section was most persuasive? Why?

✎ ADDITIONAL ASSIGNMENTS

Knowledge Transfer

Business, history, sociology, and psychology courses all ask students to conduct critical analyses.

COLLEGE Bilingualism Analysis for Applied Linguistics Your family has been bilingual for three generations now, a phenomenon you take for granted. So when your applied linguistics professor assigns a critical analysis of bilingualism, you decide to analyze the consequences (social, intellectual, political) of being bilingual for yourself and others. Your researched analysis will be about ten pages long.

COMMUNITY Address to City Council As president of your housing association, you are expected to report to the city council with regard to the mailbox vandalism in your neighborhood. You have been allotted ten minutes (four, double-spaced pages of script) during which, using precise language, you will describe the vandalism itself, explain the extent and frequency of the vandalism (including facts and figures on the matter), and provide a logical explanation of what you understand to be the causes of and perhaps the solution to the vandalism.

WORKPLACE Ad Campaign Analysis As part of your advertising internship, you are working with a research team focusing on an ad campaign that will be delivered as a television commercial. Your assignment is to critique it for credibility, logic, and emotional connection with the target audience. In the process, you will gather the preliminary findings from a focus group, combine them with the careful notes you have been jotting down as the ad has been taking shape, and compose a five-page summary on the potential consequences of this ad for the target audience. Your audience is the producer, who is already proud of the almost-final product.

MULTIMODAL News Analysis and Presentation Every week, another tragedy occurs in the United States, if not a shooting of some kind, then a terrible natural disaster or plane crash. Focus on one event in order to analyze the causes or consequences of that event. Watch television reports to see how the coverage of the event differs, taking careful notes and taping important segments, after which you will read online and print commentary about the event. Your purpose is to make an oral presentation to your Communication class, analyzing the event, synthesizing the variables in the coverage, and describing your findings. You will enhance your presentation with video and audio clips.

12 Literary Analyses

LEARNING OBJECTIVES

- Identify rhetorical situations for determining what most interests you in a literary work and responding with a literary analysis.
- Explain the purpose of a literary analysis in terms of its key rhetorical features and principles of development in various media.
- Apply close reading skills for a careful examination of the style and structure of a text.
- Reflect critically on making connections among different elements and evaluating how they work together as a whole.
- Identify appropriate evidence in the form of direct quotations and other references to the text that support your analysis, engaging, integrating, and citing research and source materials.
- Apply peer review and self-evaluation to revise, edit, and proofread a literary analysis that supports your argument for why and how a text should be read a certain way—your way.

literary analysis an argument for reading a text in a certain way

You have been conducting literary analyses for years—ever since you first started talking about the movies your parents took you to and the books they read to you. Some you liked and wanted to experience again; others, not so much. You talked about plot, characters, and setting, taking that ability with you when you entered school and began reading texts more closely. In a **literary analysis**, you make an argument for why and how a text should be read a certain way—your way.

In this chapter, your goal will be to identify rhetorical opportunities for analyzing literary works, fiction, drama, poetry, essays, creative nonfiction, and memoirs. Maybe you belong to a book group, or you have given a favorite novel to a friend with a note saying, "Drop everything and read this book." Or perhaps you have returned from a film adaptation of a favorite novel complaining that one of the characters was miscast. In each of these situations, you were responding to and analyzing a literary work. Such a situation provides a starting point for determining what most interests you. As you work, then, consider the most fitting means of delivery for your literary analysis.

IDENTIFYING AN OPPORTUNITY FOR CHANGE

Print Literary Analysis written for an undergraduate journal or as a review for your campus paper

Oral Literary Analysis recorded as a podcast, to be played for your class

Online Literary Analysis posted on a website such as GoodReads.com or LibraryThing.com, where you are participating in a book club

GENRE IN FOCUS The Poetry Slam

Local book clubs and other such community programs seek to encourage people to carve out time and space to read, discuss, and write about literature of all kinds. Many people regularly read their essays, stories, and poetry to audiences in clubs, bars, coffeehouses, libraries, student unions, and writing centers in communities and on campuses across the nation. A prominent part of the movement to make poetry and other literary forms more accessible has been the Poetry Slam initiative, which features competitive performance poetry. Randomly selected members of the audience judge the different poets on their lyrical skills as well as their stage presence.

Phoenix-based Myrlin Hepworth, a poet, rapper, hip-hop artist, social-justice activist, and educator, earned his way through college by performing slam poetry on the street. Hepworth still often delivers his work at slams, although he has recently turned to hip-hop, performing his poetry to music. A *Phoenix New Times* article by Glenn Burnsilver on the "Phoenix Poet Myrlin Hepworth" quoted Hepworth as saying: "The job of the poet is to speak to the humanity of everyone. My job is to humanize and create avenues for people to reach inside and find out more about themselves. . . . That's what I want to do, absolutely!"

Myrlin Hepworth performs his poetry at Tucson Youth Poetry Slam.

Although some literary critics have attacked the Poetry Slam movement as, in the words of Harold Bloom, "the death of art," many others, such as Hepworth, dispute such a claim. In the *Phoenix New Times* article, Hepworth counters by celebrating the connection between poet and listener: "What I care about is that feeling you get when you see an artist, when there's nowhere else you want to be. There's a vibration, and you're connected. Not because you're supposed to idolize [the artist], but because you trust and feel naturally."★ Susan B. A. Somers-Willett, an award-winning poet and member of three national poetry slam teams, researched the impact of public poetry projects and writes,

> **More and more poets are ferrying the divide between [the academy and slam]. Former and current slam competitors are now studying or teaching in MFA programs; likewise, winners of academic poetry's most prestigious honors—the Yale Younger Poets Series, the National Poetry Series, and the Pulitzer Prize to name a few—have performed on the slam stage to acclaim. Still other slam competitors have taken their poetry to larger mainstream audiences, namely through commercial ventures such as the HBO series *Russell Simmons Presents Def Poetry* or through spoken word albums.**

★From "Phoenix Poet Myrlin Hepworth: 'The Poetics of My Time Are in Hip-Hop,'" Glenn BurnSilver, Phoenix New Times.com. 8 Jan. 2015. Web. 20 Sept. 2015.

The growing history and influence of the poetry slam, especially on a younger generation of writers, suggests that the practice is not just a passing fad. The serious critic must cease treating the slam as a literary novelty or oddity and recognize it for what it is: a movement which combines (and at times exploits) the literary, the performative, and the social potential of verse, and which does so with the audience as its judge and guide.

—Susan B. A. Somers-Willett, "Can Slam Poetry Matter?"

Whether inspired by a poetry slam, a hip-hop or dramatic performance, or a college literature course, the rhetorical opportunity for a literary analysis enables you to make an argument through a **close reading** of the text—a reading that carefully examines a text's style and structure. In a close reading you will examine literary elements individually (see the box on the Elements of Literature, pp. 208–209) and then look at the relationship of those elements in how the text works as a whole. (See CHAPTER 3, ANALYSIS AND SYNTHESIS.) Your literary analysis may focus on one element as key or locate several factors that taken together make a work significant. In the case of the poetry slam, for example, Somers-Willett looks at the way "the literary, the performative, and the social potential of verse" work together to affect an audience. Most often, you will take a position on a question about the meaning, structure, or significance of the text and support your position using text-based evidence, usually quotations. In this way, your literary analysis creates an argument that shows how other readers should interpret the elements of a text and make meaning from them.

pages 43–48

close reading an examination of the key characteristics (including style and structure) of a text

 ASSIGNMENT

Every time you read a piece of literature, you work to establish how that text should be read, because stories do not easily reveal themselves. Whether you are concentrating on the significance of a character, a repeated image, a specific scene, or the underlying theme of the text, you are reading and rereading the text in order to analyze it, to answer interesting questions about it. As you follow your initial reading of the text, work to establish the position you want to take on it, locating textual evidence—gleaned from a close reading—to support your thesis statement as well as the supporting assertions you are making.

You may want to focus on a text you are reading for class now, one you have long enjoyed but puzzled over, or one you recently heard read aloud. List the literary elements of that text—plot, for example, or main character—and consider which of them intrigues you most. Write a short essay in which you analyze the significance of that element to the text, making sure to compose a thesis statement and use details, examples, and evidence to support your assertions.

Literary Analyses

CHAPTER 12 LITERARY ANALYSES **207**

>> READING RHETORICALLY

Whether it is fiction or nonfiction, there is no one specific way to make sense of any literary work. But reading a text actively—recording your reactions in the margins, highlighting passages that confuse you, noting sections that seem to be central to the events or the characters—is a first step toward making an argument about that work and its significance. During the reading process, you will sharpen your ability to read closely, synthesize meaning from the various elements of a text, and, thus, come to a better understanding about each of these individual elements and the ways in which they interact with one another. Moreover, you will be able to use evidence from the text to demonstrate to other readers, including your classmates, why your particular reading of the text is an important one for them to consider. That is, you will be able to convince readers that your interpretation helps improve their understanding of the literary text.

ELEMENTS OF LITERATURE

In a literary analysis, you will likely discuss the work's structure (character, plot, setting) and the writer's style (such as word choice, tone, figurative language).

Characters   The characters in a literary work are the humans or humanlike person-alities (aliens, creatures, robots, animals, and so on) who carry along the action. The main character is called the *protagonist*. In prose literature, you often find extensive descriptions of the characters' physical, mental, or social attributes and appearance. In a play, you learn what a character is thinking by the thoughts he or she shares either with another character in dialogue or as "dramatic soliloquy" (a speech delivered to the audience by an actor alone on the stage).

Point of view   Each literary work is told from a certain point of view by a narrator (the speaker who is telling the story in the text, not to be confused with the actual author): *first-person narration* uses the first-person pronoun *I*; *third person, omniscient*, tells readers about the thoughts, motivations, and attitudes of all characters, referring to them by name or third-person pronouns (*he, she*, etc.); *third person, limited*, follows one character around, revealing just that character's thoughts.

Plot   The plot encompasses what happens in the work: the *exposition* introduces the characters, setting, and background and soon moves to a *conflict* that sets a sequence of significant events in motion, which leads to the climax, the most intense *turning point*, and ends in the *dénouement* (or *falling action*), a resolution of the conflict.

Setting   There is a physical setting as well as a social setting (the morals, manners, and customs of the characters). Setting also involves time (historical time and also the length of time covered by the narrative) and includes atmosphere, or the character's and the reader's emotional response to the situation.

Theme   The theme refers to the message the text delivers about a character, a relationship, an event, or a place. Common themes include person versus person, person versus self, person versus nature or technology, and person versus society.

Figurative language   Writers often use figurative language such as *metaphors* and *similes* to communicate complex ideas and meanings to readers. Using a metaphor, the writer refers to one thing as something else ("Hope is the thing with feathers"). Using a simile, the writer says that an object, idea, or person is *like* something else ("My love is like a red, red rose").

Symbol   A symbol is usually a concrete object that stands for an abstract one. A vivid description of a kitchen table, for example, might be a symbol for the significance of everyday experiences that take place around the table.

Imagery   Imagery refers to words and phrases that appeal to readers' senses, helping them "see" a particular image in their mind's eye. (The poet Pat Mora, for instance, calls on her readers to appreciate the importance of a "doorway/between two rooms.").

Rhythm and rhyme   Poets, in particular, arrange syllables, words, and line breaks to have either a regular rhythm and rhyme, with each line containing a particular pattern of short and long syllables and of corresponding internal or terminal sounds, or a less structured, even patternless rhythm and rhyme.

Key Features of a Literary Analysis

A literary analysis explains and interprets your reactions to a text. Whether you are writing or reading such an analysis, you will find that it has the following features:

- A literary analysis introduces interpretations of the literary work under investigation, often explaining what these perspectives might be missing.
- A literary analysis presents a specific question about the literary work that the writer believes needs to be answered.
- A literary analysis presents a clear argument, or thesis, about the literary work and explains how this thesis addresses some concern that other readers of this work may have ignored or misrepresented.
- To provide evidence supporting its thesis, a literary analysis quotes specific passages from the text.
- A literary analysis explicates, or explains, all quoted passages, directing readers' attention to specific features of the literary work that support the thesis.

In "Gaby's Blog," Gabriela Fiorenza examines Pat Mora's bilingual poem "Sonrisas" ("Smiles"), a post that illustrates some characteristics of a literary analysis: an interpretation, an argument, textual evidence, and explication (or explanation). To produce her brief, effective analysis, Gaby uses familiar literary terminology and analytical moves, such as sounds, structures, setting, characters, vivid descriptions, and textual evidence.

In a longer analysis, Alex Sibo, like Gaby, employs a comparison between the two rooms, the two different kinds of women, the two ethnicities, but Alex takes the analysis further, reading the poem through a post-colonial lens.

As you read Mora's poem, analyze the elements of her rhetorical situation.

- What does the title "Sonrisas" mean?
- Why might Mora have begun her poem with the line, "I live in a doorway/ between two rooms." Who might be her rhetorical audience? What rhetorical opportunity might Mora want to address with this poem?
- How does Mora use comparison and contrast to expand the meaning of her title? How does Alex use comparison and contrast to analyze the title?
- What purpose does Gaby see in poetry? In this poem? How does her judgment align with that of poet Myrlin Hepworth?
- What about Alex's purpose and judgment in comparison to that of Gaby and Hepworth?

Sonrisas

PAT MORA

Pat Mora grew up in El Paso, Texas, and now lives in Santa Fe, New Mexico, where she continues her life's work as an advocate of bilingual literature and literacy. A popular presenter, Mora writes poetry, essays, memoirs, and stories for people of all ages—adults, teens, and children—always celebrating creativity, her own as well as her readers', and always striving for inclusivity and what she calls "book joy." For her efforts, Mora has been awarded two honorary doctorates, numerous literary awards and fellowships, and a Distinguished Alumni Award from the University of Texas at El Paso. This poem is from her collection, Borders.

I live in a doorway
between two rooms. I hear
quiet clicks, cups of black
coffee, *click, click, click*, like facts
    budgets, tenure, curriculum,

from careful women in crisp beige
suits, quick beige smiles
that seldom sneak into their eyes.

I peek
in the other room señoras
in faded dresses stir sweet
milk coffee, laughter whirls
with steam from fresh tamales
    sh, sh, mucho ruido,
they scold one another,
press their lips, trap smiles
in their dark, Mexican eyes.

"Sonrisas" is reprinted with permission from the publishers of "Borders"
by Pat Mora ((c) 1986 Arte Publico Press-University of Houston)

Gaby's Poetry Blog

GABY FIORENZA

Gabriela Fiorenza wrote this literary analysis on the internal structure of Pat Mora's "Sonrisas" and posted it on her poetry blog, along with many other poetry analyses, while a student of AP English.

Courtesy of Gabrielle Fiorenza

Mora sets the poem of "Sonrisas" in "a doorway between two rooms." This interesting place symbolizes to me the door to two different places/worlds to the speaker in the poem.

In her opening, Gaby concentrates on the internal structure of the poem, explaining it in terms of setting and structure: "Mora sets the poem of Sonrisas in "a doorway between two rooms."

In the first room the speaker observes uptight women in "crisp beige suits, quick beige smiles that seldom sneak into their eyes." This observations sharply contrasts to the relaxed view of people in the other room, "laughter whirls with steam from fresh *tamales sh, sh, mucho ruido* (a lot of noise)," this atmosphere seem happier and more comfortable in the eyes of the speaker than the first one. Relaying these observations of both rooms over the noises of coffee being brewed, "I hear quiet clicks, cups of black coffee, *click, click,*" Mora shows an example of the descriptive structure that is the base of her poem. The step by step way the speaker wanders around two rooms, describing the people inside and their movement, is the discursive process of organizing the observations

Gaby quotes from the poem to provide evidence of the two different worlds, contrasting "quick beige smiles" with "laughter."

one by one. • This was interesting to me because it is a very limited point of view for the reader.

I also noticed how there were only two stanzas in the poem. This I thought was interesting because the speaker is meant to be "between two rooms." • The first stanza is the observation of the people in one room and the second stanza, is the speaker observing the people in the other room. The different language used in the second stanza and second room, helps make the two rooms even more separate worlds. Throughout these observations, the speaker seems to be comparing and contrasting both worlds.

Gaby focuses on the effects of the poem's two-part structure: two rooms, two different kinds of women, two ethnicities, American and Mexican.

Gaby concludes her essay by invoking her opening, emphasizing her now-developed idea of the two rooms, two worlds.

Reprinted with permission of Gabrielle Fiorenza

Source: Gabrielle Fiorenza

ALEX SIBO

Courtesy of Alex Sibo

As an undergraduate student, Alex Sibo submitted the following literary analysis of Mora's poem. Like Gaby and the poet herself, Alex was taken by Mora's steady use of comparison and contrast. Alex uses post-colonial theory to emphasize the dominance of U.S. culture over Mexican culture on the border. This essay uses MLA citation style.

Alex Sibo

Professor Bond

English 200

December 4, 2019

Sonrisas Diferentes: A Postcolonial Criticism

The daughter of Mexican immigrants living in Texas, Pat Mora was born into a clash of cultures. Her poem "Sonrisas" allows a window into her own experience living between the "colonizing" American culture and the "colonized" Mexican culture. "Sonrisas" explores the difficulty in living between these cultures, presenting that difficulty in such a way that an Anglo-centric reader can understand. As in most cases of cultural clash, Mora feels a sense of double consciousness, invoking empathy in her readers. Mora demonstrates how she is unable to simply accept one culture and reject the other without feeling discomfort and abandonment. Each metaphor, sound, and adjective used by Mora immerses Anglo-centric readers further into the plight and alienation of the "Other" culture.

The most prominent device used by Mora is the metaphor of the "doorway/between two rooms" (1-2). The speaker exists between two rooms described within the rest of the poem. The first room represents white American culture, while the second room represents Mexican culture. This distinction is made clear with the description

Alex opens by situating Mora biographically and culturally, demonstrating that they have conducted research.

The second sentence in the essay is Alex's thesis statement, though the following sentences in this first paragraph extend the idea of the thesis.

Alex uses strong topic sentences that direct the reader to what each paragraph holds. This first topic sentence offers the metaphor of the doorway, which is revisited throughout the essay.

of the women in the first room as "beige" (5-6), those in the second room as "señoras" (10). By using this metaphor of two doorways, Mora allows for American and Mexican culture to be directly contrasted. For example, Mora contrasts the women's smiles with those of the Americans' perhaps disingenuous ones, "seldom sneak[ing] into their eyes" (8). The Mexican women, on the other hand, "trap smiles/in their . . . eyes" (16-17), genuine smiles.

Using the smile metaphor to contrast these two cultural differences, Mora both identifies and ranks them, indicating that she prefers the warmer, more genuine culture, even though those of the Mexican women are "trapped," indicating their forced colonization into Anglo culture (16). The American women do not genuinely smile, a sharp contrast to the openness of the señoras, whose trapped smiles indicate the strain of their Otherness. Mora also shows us that she prefers the expressiveness of the Other culture, not only by using the sinister verb "sneak" to describe the smiles of the American women but also by describing them as beige like their suits, something disingenuous, to be put on (6-8).

While Mora appreciates the genuine expressiveness of Mexican culture, that does not mean she is able to feel at home by accepting that culture and rejecting American culture; key aspects of the poem would indicate just the opposite. For example, the American women are mentioned first in the poem, the señoras last, which adds to the hierarchy of the colonizer and the colonized. As a poet and student of American universities, Mora has needed to accept more of the dominant culture in order to succeed financially and professionally. To succeed, she had to accept the language, teachings, and ideals of the United States in order to appeal to potential readers or face being left in the margins for those who appreciate Spanish and Mexican culture and ideals, as Mora can only "peek/in the other room" (9-10). She is no longer able to fully re-experience her Mexican culture; thus, she feels a sense of alienation from her family's culture, as well as never being fully assimilated into American culture. With one simple word, "peek," Mora shows readers how perilous it can be for her to walk the multicultural tightrope.

> Alex demonstrates biographical and literary knowledge of Pat Mora.

Mora's use of sounds throughout "Sonrisas" conveys her resentment of the tedium of American culture and her longing for the merriment of Mexican culture. The sounds "*click, click*" emulate the noise of the keyboard and of the Mr. Coffee maker (5). Coupled with the following line, "budgets, tenures, curriculum" (5), the boring, repetitive sounds efficiently sum up Mora's feelings toward American culture. The entire first stanza includes harsh "k" sounds: "quiet clicks, cups" (3), "coffee, *click, click*, like facts" (4), and "careful . . . crisp" (6). These harsh sounds further imitate a typewriter, as well as

> Alex crafts another strong topic sentence, one that introduces the subject of the paragraph and also extends the idea of the thesis statement.

> And again, Alex draws specific examples from the text itself to support this point.

ascribing a clipped and businesslike tone to the stanza, which makes for a purposefully dull sound. In stark contrast, the second stanza creates a delightful audial scene. Mora describes how "laughter whirls" throughout (12), which compared to the "quiet clicks" in the first room (3), gives the reader a sense of how much more fun and engaging the Other culture can be. The second stanza also features many sibilant and soft "s" and "sh" syllables that give the rest of the poem a soft-mellifluous sound: "señoras" (1), "stir sweet" (11), "*sh, sh*" (13), and "press their lips" (16). The use of Spanish in the stanza gives a sense of verisimilitude, drawing a greater connection between the Other culture and the harmony of its sounds. In this fashion, Mora lulls the reader to sleep in the first stanza before waking them up in the second.

By contrasting both cultures through the use of differing adjectives, the Anglo-centric reader can experience the tensions of double consciousness. Coffee is a major difference between and descriptor for the two cultures. The American women drink "cups of black/coffee" (3-4), while the Mexican women drink "sweet/milk coffee" (11-12). The black coffee is bitter, like colonizer culture, while the colonized culture is sweet like their milk coffee. Readers can *taste* the sweet and bitter sides of double consciousness. The attire of the

Alex continues to acknowledge the thesis statement as they acknowledge their limitations as a reader, as an "Anglocentric" one at that.

different groups of women is also notable. The beige women wear "crisp beige/suits" (6-7), while the señoras wear "faded dresses" (11). Quality of attire clearly indicates the differences of social class, indicating that Mora might have felt compelled to accept American culture, while sacrificing the fun and the valuable relationships inherent in her Mexican culture. The Anglo-centric reader is able to see that double consciousness has created a tug-of-war between personal relationships and financial, material success.

Alex has skillfully incorporated sensory elements into this literary analysis, sensations of taste, smell, sounds, and sight. Alex also alludes to Mora's bank of bicultural, bilingual memories.

Without adopting a postcolonial lens, very little of the tensions and conflicts between cultures would be apparent in "Sonrisas." I might not have noted that the women in beige suits were American. The use of Spanish also demands attention. Most important, to develop my argument I had to look outside of the poem itself and use some of Mora's biographical information. I believe there may have been many feminist aspects of the poem that I did not examine because they fell outside of the scope of postcolonialism. The poem, however, would lend itself to an examination of how colonial tensions affect women in multicultural areas.

In the conclusion, Alex circles back to the opening paragraph, the thesis statement, but they do not simply repeat information. Alex takes those initial ideas further, referring to the ways one has to look outside of the poem itself to glean the necessary information (biographical, linguistic, theoretical) that supports the analysis. Alex also refers to outside knowledge (feminism, in this case) that might have helped them further.

Works Cited

Mora, Pat. "Sonrisas." *Borders*. Arte Publico Press, 1986.

Reprinted by permission of Alex Sibo.

Using Synthesis and Analysis

When reading each of the preceding selections, ask: Who might be the rhetorical audience for Mora? Gaby? Alex? How does the purpose of each writer connect with that audience? For example, what is revealed about Mora's purpose and audience by her insertion of Spanish words and phrases in a mostly English poem? Of Gaby's use of such terms as "internal structure," "comparing and contrasting," "stanza," and "the speaker"? Or of Alex's use of "colonizing," "colonized," "Anglo-centric," "double consciousness," and "Other"?

Turning to either Gaby's shorter analysis or Alex's longer analysis—or to both,

- What major points did you notice in the analysis?
- What is the basic thesis for the essay?
- Where and how does the writer make an emotional connection with a rhetorical audience?
- Where does the writer analyze particular passages of the poem? Where does the writer synthesize the analysis?

Synthesis, which is a crucial part of analyzing a text, begins by making connections among different elements and evaluating how they work together as a whole. Examine how Gaby uses these connections to relate to the thesis and to the interests of her readers: "the speaker seems to be comparing and contrasting both worlds."

- How does she extend and support her thesis with specific details from the text?
- In what ways does she work to connect her thesis with the interests of her readers?
- How could she have used outside sources to support her thesis, especially information on the poet herself?
- How does she combine the use of examples from the primary source with outside information to create a unique reading of the work?
- Then turn to Alex's analysis and answer these same questions.

There is no single way to accomplish the many goals of a literary analysis. Approach the work with an analytical frame of mind and synthesize multiple views—your own, those of other sources, and examples from the work itself—to go deeper as you read the text.

» RESPONDING TO THE RHETORICAL SITUATION

People compose literary analyses after reading or experiencing a text or performance. Most often, they make arguments about how readers (including themselves) should interpret the elements of a text, what subtle elements should be noticed, and how to make meaning from those elements. Such situations are opportunities for writers to compose a literary analysis for a rhetorical audience who is ignoring, misreading, or failing to understand (or notice) significant features of a text. They also compose literary analyses in order to discover answers to interesting questions, questions about the text itself, its potential influence on people and their interactions, and the various historical receptions of the text. Their analyses can be delivered orally (in book club discussions), in print or online (in newspapers, zines, and discussion boards), verbally (in podcasts or on the radio), and as YouTube videos or other visual media.

| Opportunity | Audience and Purpose | Genre/Literary Analysis | Medium of Delivery |

Understanding the Rhetorical Situation

Although all imaginative literature can be characterized as fictional, the term **fiction** applies specifically to the prose narratives of novels and short stories. **Poetry**, on the other hand, is primarily characterized by its extensive use of concentrated language, or language that relies on imagery, allusions, figures of speech, symbols, sound and rhythm, and precise word choice, all of which allow poets to make a point in one or two words rather than spelling it out explicitly. However, poetry, like fiction, may have a narrator with a point of view, and some poems have a plot, a setting, and characters. **Drama** shares many of the same elements as fiction (setting, character, plot, and dialogue), but differs in that it is meant to be performed—whether on stage, on film, or on television—with the director and actors imprinting the lines with their own interpretations. And like fiction, non-fiction, and poetry, drama can be read; in this case, you bring your interpretative abilities to what is on the printed page rather than to a performance of the work.

fiction prose stories based on the imagination

poetry a concentrated language relying on sound and image

drama a performance where a director and actors interpret a script

- Which form of literary expression would you be most interested in learning more about or analyzing in more detail?
- What most interests you about this form?
- What about this kind of text or the context in which it would normally be encountered makes it particularly compelling to you?

RESEARCHING A LITERARY ANALYSIS

As you consider your literary analysis, be sure to start by consulting the notes you took in your close reading of the text. Consider your personal responses and insights into specific elements of the text as the first steps toward the best reading of that text. Evidence for your literary analysis begins with the text itself, so dissecting text-based quotations is important in building your case, but evidence can also include facts and statistics (for example, how often a writer uses the word *blue* or has references to a *mirror*). Formal research can help by providing expert opinions from literary scholars that you might use to support your position or to show the complexities surrounding a text or even as a rhetorical opportunity to address a misreading of the text. Whether or not you use them, you will have more information to consider. But you may find that discussing your ideas with your teacher and classmates provides you with even more fruitful research findings; after all, you may discover why a particular reading of the text is important to them. After conducting this formal and informal research, be sure to read and then reread the text itself. When you read it aloud, you will notice details and connections that you would have otherwise missed.

Identifying an Opportunity for Change

To compose an analysis that provides readers with significant insight, choose a feature of the literary work that genuinely interests you. Then, formulate an **interpretive question** that you will answer as the subject of your analysis, with supporting evidence provided throughout your essay. To help you craft your interpretive question, consider keeping a **reading journal** in which you can freewrite in response to the following series of prompts. (For more on freewriting and keeping a journal and other ways to jump-start your writing, see CHAPTER 13, PLANNING A RESPONSE.) Reading these prompts *before* you read the literary text will help you focus your thinking as you read; you can draft responses to the prompts after you have read the text once or twice. Later, your journal freewrites will help you identify and clarify the interpretive question on which you will focus your analysis of the literary work.

interpretive question a question about the meaning, structure, or significance of a text

reading journal a record of personal thoughts, ideas, and questions about a text

pages 239–244

1. Freewrite for ten minutes in response to these questions about the characters in the literary work: Who is the most important character in the piece? What actions or inactions does this character take that most affect the work as a whole? In what ways does the character change—or not—throughout the course of the work? To what effect? How do the other characters in the piece contribute to, react to, or prevent this change?

2. Freewrite for ten minutes on the importance of the setting in the literary work: When and where does this literary work take place? How does "place" help explain the motivations of the characters or the events in the plot? Do you notice anything significant about the setting that affects how you read the piece?
3. Freewrite for ten minutes about the point of view of the literary work: Who is telling the story? What does the narrator (or speaker) know and not know? Is the narrator reliable? Biased or unbiased? How do you know? How does the narrator's (or speaker's) knowledge about events and the other characters shape how you read and understand the piece?
4. Freewrite for ten minutes, recording the sequence of events, or plot, of the literary work: What is the single most important event or moment? Why do you think this moment is so important or crucial? For whom is it crucial?
5. Freewrite for ten minutes about the theme, what the author is trying to say through the literary work: What kind of conflict does the piece make you think about? What are the effects of that conflict on the people and events of the story?

Relating Rhetorically to Your Audience

The following questions can help you establish a rhetorical audience and identify the relationship it has to your overall purpose in composing. Once you have established the connection, you can choose the best way to present and support your answer.

1. List the persons or groups who are talking about the literary work you are analyzing or who have questions about its meaning or importance.
2. Next to each name, write reasons that audience might have for acknowledging, even appreciating, your analysis of the literary work. In other words, what would persuade these people or groups to read and interpret the literary piece in a different way?
3. What responses could these audiences reasonably be persuaded to have to your essay and to the text you are analyzing?
4. With your audience's interests and capabilities in mind, look again at the question and initial answer you composed in the preceding section on identifying an opportunity. Decide how you might engage your audience with your question and interpretation. At this point, you may find it necessary to revise your question so that it speaks more directly to the interests of your audience.

Planning an Effective Rhetorical Response for Your Purpose

Identifying an audience, purpose, and interpretive question is the first step; getting your audience to engage in your work is the second. After these initial steps, you are ready to plan out your analytical essay, keeping in mind what your audience already thinks about the text as you help them expand their under-standing of that text. To be a fitting response, your literary analysis must also address the context within which your audience is likely to consider it. For example, you might consider writing an essay for the "Arts & Entertainment" section of the local newspaper or posting a blog entry on a website devoted to the work you are analyzing. In other words, after you identify your opportunity, audience, and purpose, consider what kind of literary analysis will best respond to the rhetorical situation.

Use the following two questions to help you narrow your purpose and shape your response:

1. Are you asking the audience to simply reread the literary work in a new light or to perform some particular action in response to this new way of interpreting the text?

2. What is the best way to reach this audience? That is, with what kind of text is this audience most likely to engage?

LINKS TO LITERARY ANALYSES IN THREE MEDIA   MindTap®

Links may change due to availability.

© Katrina Outland/Shutterstock.com

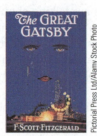

Pictorial Press Ltd/Alamy Stock Photo

Courtesy of J. Keim Swanson

Print Literary Analysis In the literary analysis at the beginning of this chapter, Alex Sibo explores the nature of postcolonialism through an analysis of Pat Mora's poem, "Sonrisas."

Oral Literary Analysis *Slate's* online Audio Book Club provides book reviews and discussions regularly. Among the archives is a podcast for *The Great Gatsby*, in which critics discuss what makes the novel endure, despite its flimsy plot.

Online Literary Analysis J from Kent, Ohio, has posted more than eighty in-depth commentaries for his network of thirty-five friends on GoodReads.com. To view J's analysis of *The Historian*, by Elizabeth Kostova, go to GoodReads.com.

*W*riting a literary analysis will give you an opportunity to sharpen your ability to read, interpret, and formulate ideas about the significance of literary texts. To make an effective argument for your interpretation, your primary focus will be on establishing the opportunity for, and significance of, your interpretive question, providing evidence from the text to support your interpretation and explaining the larger implications of your answer for understanding the text. A careful, close reading enhances the writer's ethos, giving credibility to fresh interpretations. That interpretation (a series of assertions supported with textual evidence) provides the logos. Any authentic emotional connection the writer makes with an already engaged audience can supply pathos. (See CHAPTER 2, THE AVAILABLE MEANS INCLUDE THE RHETORICAL ELEMENTS OF THE MESSAGE ITSELF.)

pages 23–26

ADVANTAGES AND LIMITATIONS

Advantages

- **Writer:** Literary analyses can serve as productive—even fun—discussions among people who are sharing the same literary experience. The writer can take advantage of other readers' desire for a deeper appreciation of the literature and its timelessness, as many literary texts connect to current events and trends.

- **Message:** A literary analysis provides an opportunity to advocate for an interpretation that has personal meaning and larger implications about the significance of a particular work.

- **Media and Design:** Literary analyses can be delivered in endless ways and variations: online, in print, through video or podcasting, or enhanced with music, audio, and images.

Limitations

- **Writer:** Compared to reviews, locating a rhetorical audience for the analysis outside of the traditional classroom may be difficult, especially if delivering the work in a purely print/text medium.

- **Message:** Missing details or connections (or simply getting them wrong) in the literary work distracts from the writer's credibility, the logos of the argument, and any positive emotional connection with the audience.

- **Media and Design:** Although an analysis of a purely written text can sometimes be hard to deliver in an alternate media or in multimedia, many people successfully do just that, thereby broadening their audience.

- Identify the literary work being analyzed.
- Present an interpretive question and argue for its importance.
- Summarize other answers to the question.
- Present the thesis statement (the writer's answer to the interpretive question).

Introduction

Explain the work's significance Your introduction should explain which literary work you are going to analyze and why. Alex, for example, states that they will examine how Pat Mora's poem reveals the double-consciousness of postcolonial reality.

Present your interpretive question The introduction also presents your interpretive question about the literary work as well as your initial attempt to persuade readers that your question is an interesting and important one to answer. Alex's interpretative question asks how postcolonial theory might help us unveil the double-conscious of postcolonial life.

Summarize possible answers to your question You can briefly summarize the different answers that other readers, including your classmates, have posed or might be likely to pose to this question. Alex, for example, offers sensory examples, those of sounds (language, office noises), vision (beige suits, colorful dresses), taste (bitter and sweet coffees), and emotion (differences in smiling faces) to develop their analysis of a bicultural, bilingual poem.

Clarify your main point Keep in mind, too, that you might need to quickly summarize a main point or describe a main element of the text in order to help your readers understand the precise nature of the question that you are asking.

Include the answer you are prepared to support as your thesis The thesis statement advances a particular interpretation of the meaning of the text. Provide your thesis statement— which can be a one- or two-sentence answer to the interpretive question you have posed. You might present this answer in a statement that begins "In this essay, I argue that. . . ."

Ask yourself . . .
- How do I explain the reasons for my interpretation?
- How do I describe the significance of my interpretation?
- Have I shaped an opening that immediately engages my audience?
- Have I identified a rhetorical audience?

Body

- Present supporting reasons for the writer's answer to the interpretive question, usually one reason per paragraph.
- Strengthen the writer's appeal to logos by building toward the most interesting or persuasive reason.
- Include direct quotations from the literary work as evidence and support.
- Address others' interpretations of the text.

Body

Structure your analysis around the reasons for your answer Strengthen the logic of your argument (logos) by arranging your paragraphs in a pattern that moves readers progressively toward the most interesting or most persuasive of your supporting reasons.

Quote the literary work as evidence The body paragraphs provide readers with direct quotations and other supportive evidence from the literary work. Early in their analysis, Alex cites a short passage from the beginning of Mora's "Sonrisas" that launches their analysis: "doorway/between two rooms." This snippet introduces several key moments in the poem that Alex can compare: sounds, sights, and tastes. They organize their analysis accordingly.

Bring in the experts Another way to support your thesis in the body paragraphs is to address other interpretations of the text. By citing other literary critics who share your perspective and those who do not, you have more credibility (ethos). Although Alex does not cite any experts, the essay demonstrates that they have read biographical information that was not included in the poem itself, information that gives some measure of insight into the experiences that might well have led to the subject of Mora's poem. Conversely, you can also support your thesis by conceding or refuting alternative interpretations.

Ask yourself . . .
- How am I using assertions and textual evidence to establish my credibility, my ethos?
- How do those same features help to establish my logos?
- Which of my assertions is the most compelling? Why?
- Where have I addressed the possibility of other possible interpretations, especially those my audience may believe?
- In what ways have I established that my interpretation is the best one?

Conclusion

- **Explain how this analysis deepens readers' understanding.**
- **Point to related questions that could unlock additional meanings of the text.**

Situate your analysis as part of a critical conversation After providing sufficient textual evidence to support your major reasons, conclude your literary analysis by situating it within a larger conversation about the work you are analyzing. In other words, explain to readers how your answer to your interpretive question helps deepen their understanding of the entire work.

Ask yourself . . .
- How have I addressed the possibility of other interpretations?
- How have I tried to connect my interpretation with the interests of my audience?
- How assured do I want to be that mine is the best interpretation?
- What questions have I left with the audience?

›› REVISION AND PEER REVIEW

After you have drafted a strong version of your literary analysis, ask one of your classmates to read it. You will want your classmate to respond to your work in a way that helps you revise it into the strongest analysis it can be, one that addresses your intended audience, helps you fulfill your purpose, and is delivered in the most appropriate means available to you and your audience.

Questions for a Peer Reviewer

1. How does the title of the analysis arouse your interest and guide your reading?
2. To what rhetorical opportunity is the writer responding? Why is it significant?
3. Where does the writer clearly state the interpretive question? How might they help the audience better understand—and care about—that question?
4. How does the writer establish ethos?
5. Who might comprise the writer's intended audience?
6. Identify the thesis statement, in which the writer clearly states their response to the interpretive question. If you cannot locate a thesis statement, what thesis statement might work for this analysis? What does the writer want the audience to do in response?
7. How is the analysis organized? Where does the writer use strong topic sentences? Which ones could be improved—and how?
8. Identify the evidence (in the form of direct quotations and other references to the text) the writer provides in support of and against the claim. In what other ways does the writer strengthen the logos of the writing?
9. How does the writer establish pathos?
10. Where do you agree and disagree with the writer's analysis?
11. What did you learn from the conclusion that you did not already know from reading the analysis? How did the writer give you a better understanding of the literary work overall?
12. Which idea or passage in the analysis is handled most successfully, and which least successfully?
13. What are two questions you have for this writer?

ADDITIONAL ASSIGNMENTS

Knowledge Transfer

Literary analyses are terrific preparation for other kinds of textual analyses, particularly those that demand understanding of the human condition.

COLLEGE History Research Paper on Twentieth-Century America You have been assigned to research the working conditions of twentieth-century Mexican Americans in Texas. For your paper, you enhance your research by reading Julia Alvarez's novel *Return to Sender*, applying the insight from the novel to Emilio Zamora's *The World of the Mexican Worker in Texas.* For your paper, you synthesize these books to describe the bleak conditions of a vulnerable workforce.

COMMUNITY Book Club Discussion Your book club is reading Wally Lamb's 2008 *The Hour I First Believed* to explore mass shootings. You have been asked to provide some background information for the book, so it is a good thing you have access to newspaper and online accounts of the Columbine massacre, the first school shooting to imprint our nation's consciousness. In your book club, you and your fellow readers discuss your understanding of the alleged motivations behind the shootings, using the techniques of literary analysis to comparing Lamb's fictional assessment of the shootings with the nonfiction ones you are reading.

WORKPLACE Case Brief You have been charged with composing a legal brief on a current case, the videotaped killing of an African American citizen. Your deep textual analysis of those previous cases will establish patterns of judicial action that are relevant to the current case. For your brief, you will use the techniques of literary analysis to synthesize previous cases of the same kind, particularly where it comes to the precedents set by those previous cases.

MULTIMODAL Genre Comparison You have been assigned to compose a comparison between a book and its film adaptation. You must understand both deliveries, analyzing their constitutent parts. Then you must synthesize their differences and similarities, using relevant passages from the book as well as links to excerpts from the film posted on YouTube either as part of a multimodal paper that is submitted digitally or as embedded video files in a PowerPoint for a class presentation.

13 From Tentative Idea to Finished Project

LEARNING OBJECTIVES

- Identify suitable topics for exploration and development.
- Articulate your focused ideas.
- Draft a purposeful thesis statement.
- Define your writing process, from exploration, drafting, and the crafting of a thesis statement to the development of ideas and revising.
- Discern genre-specific expectations of organization and appropriate transitions.
- Integrate peer-evaluation comments to develop revising and proofreading skills.
- Determine your academic writing process.

In this chapter, you will move through the three general steps of the writing process: planning, drafting, and revising. These steps are the same whether you are working online or off, whether you are writing at school, work, or home. As you read about each of these steps, you will learn when to consider the components of the rhetorical situation (components that include a problem, an opportunity for change, and a purpose, message, audience, genre, and medium of delivery) and when to set those components aside and just write. Eventually, all writers find a writing process that works for them, whether it is spending a lot of time up front on planning for details and organization or drafting first, giving shape to the writing, and then going back to tease out the main points. Although the writing process can seem private, when we write we actually connect socially—as the following infographic shows—to a larger community of writers who have struggles and successes similar to our own.

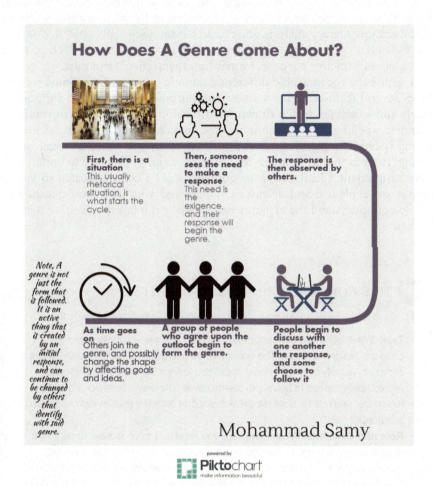

How Does A Genre Come About?

First, there is a situation
This, usually rhetorical situation, is what starts the cycle.

Then, someone sees the need to make a response
This need is the exigence, and their response will begin the genre.

The response is then observed by others.

Note, A genre is not just the form that is followed. It is an active thing that is created by an initial response, and can continue to be changed by others that identify with said genre.

As time goes on
Others join the genre, and possibly change the shape by affecting goals and ideas.

A group of people who agree upon the outlook begin to form the genre.

People begin to discuss with one another the response, and some choose to follow it

Mohammad Samy

powered by
Piktochart
make information beautiful

Mohammad Samy, a first-year student at the University of Central Florida, created this rhetorical infographic for his writing class. Exigence is another way of describing the rhetorical opportunity for change, which is the reason or perceived problem that motivates writing.

»» EXPECTATIONS FOR ACADEMIC WRITING

The writing expected of you as a student will vary according to the assignments you receive within various academic disciplines. You are already familiar with many of the genres of academic writing, such as those that have been explored in this book: memoir, profile, evaluation, argument, proposal, investigative report, critical analysis, literary analysis, and research essay. (See CHAPTER 15, RHETORICAL STRATEGIES FOR DEVELOPMENT for ways to flesh out each genre.) Each of these genres has a distinctive purpose, format (or organization), and tone.

pages
278–294

Despite the recognizable differences among genres, all academic writing shares several features: a thesis statement; purposefully organized supporting details and examples (often drawn from outside sources); and conventional grammar, spelling, punctuation, and mechanics. In other words, academic writing is carefully planned out and seriously delivered—unlike casual, social writing. To meet the expectations for academic writing, you need to understand every assignment. Ideally, your assignments will be communicated to you in writing and explained and discussed in class. Ask your instructor questions if you do not understand the assignment, especially if it has not been written out for you.

 TIPS FOR ANALYZING ASSIGNMENTS

For each assignment, make sure you understand the following requirements.

- **Task.** What task does the assignment ask you to complete? What strong verb does the assignment use? The imperative verb (argue, describe, explain, analyze, compare, classify, narrate) should direct you toward the expected purpose. Are you being asked to solve a problem, research an issue, answer a question, remember and retell a significant event, support a thesis, explain a process, define a concept?
- **Role and audience.** What stance are you expected to or allowed to take with regard to your audience? Are you being asked to assume the role of expert, analyst, explainer, narrator, questioner, arguer? Are you writing from a position of knowledge and power, from that of a learner, or from an opposing point of view?
- **Format.** What are the instructor's expectations with regard to length, manuscript form (electronic or print? verbal or visual? Mixed media or modes?), documentation style, and so on? What manuscript format should you follow (that of a report, an essay, an oral delivery)?

- **Process to be followed.** Are you expected to conduct library or laboratory research? What is the schedule for completion of research, drafts, peer reviews, workshops, revisions, and so forth? Are you expected to submit your rough drafts with the final draft?
- **Criteria for evaluation.** How will the final product be graded? What are the criteria for success? Keep in mind that these same criteria can be applied to workplace writing assignments. They are also helpful criteria for you to use when writing for personal or civic reasons.

›› PLANNING

Experienced writers employ a variety of methods for exploring a topic or inventing things to say about it. The problem you have identified establishes your starting point. (See CHAPTER 2: A PROBLEM-SOLVING APPROACH.) Planning your response helps you identify the opportunity for change your writing can address and focus on a purpose that can effectively influence the audience you can reach with your words.

pages 19–20

Exploration

The most commonly used methods of exploration (also known as *invention strategies*) are listing, freewriting, questioning, and keeping a journal. But experienced writers also regularly use conversation, meditation, reading, and listening as ways to discover good ideas. They realize that good ideas come to them in all sorts of ways, so they keep a pen and a notebook with them all the time, even at night, because ideas often come just as they are falling asleep. They grab the notebook (paper or electronic), scribble down or type their idea, and sleep soundly, no longer worried that they will forget the idea.

As you plan your college writing assignments, you will probably continue to rely on the methods that have worked for you in the past. When you are stuck, however, you may want to try out a new method, if only as a way to jump-start your writing.

Listing

As soon as you have some idea of what you are expected to write about, start a list of possibilities—and keep adding to it. These are the kinds of lists that can spark your thinking and writing.

On the first day of the semester, when her professor reviewed the syllabus for the course Writing and Technology, Stacy Simkanin learned about the requirements for her first formal essay: students were to establish a personal connection with the course theme in a position argument of three to four pages, tapping whichever rhetorical methods of development worked most effectively. They were to submit a proposal for their instructor's approval; generate ideas and examples for developing their position argument; compose a rough draft for peer-evaluation; and revise, edit, and proofread—all in preparation for submitting their final essay. So, during the first week of classes, she started **listing**—jotting down some tentative ideas, knowing that, as time went by, she would keep adding possibilities for her position argument that focused on her personal experience with writing and technology. You can follow Simkanin's example and keep your list going for a few days. Or you can jot down all your ideas at one sitting, a kind of listing often referred to as **brainstorming**. What follows is the list Simkanin made and kept adding to.

listing jotting down tentative ideas to explore a topic

brainstorming listing tentative ideas at one sitting

computers	web searches	downloadable essays
chat rooms	Statistical Universe	forum discussions
visual culture class	plagiarism	electronic requests
photo essays	convenience	internet
quality	online databases	time saver
constantly developing	online course notes	Google
full-length journal	classroom computers	
articles	social networking	

Freewriting

freewriting writing to explore ideas on a topic without concern for spelling, grammar, style, or who will read it

Freewriting means just what it says: it is the writing you do that costs you nothing. You do not have to worry about spelling or grammar; you do not even have to worry about writing complete sentences, because no one is going to grade it. In fact, no one (except you) may ever even read it. It is the kind of writing you do to loosen up your thinking and your fingers; it is the kind of no-pressure writing that can yield an explosion of ideas.

When Simkanin's teacher asked everyone in class to write for five minutes about the connection between technology and their college success (as a way to prime the pump of their thinking), Simkanin wrote the following:

Spanish 3: used chat room discussion.

English 202: used chat room discussion to analyze internet communication as it relates to literacy.

English 202 and Phil 197: used CANVAS's online forums.

Being an English major, I tend to see the biggest advantages of modern technology as those that have most helped my writing. My courses require hours of writing from me each week, and I know that, without access to all the online resources that have been available to me, the amount of time I have to spend working on a paper would probably double. For instance, technology helps me write a research paper before I've even typed the first word, because I can research my topic so much faster by first consulting the online catalogues, instead of going to the library and getting lost in the stacks. If there is material I need that this library doesn't have, I simply have it sent to me through interlibrary loan. Then, when I actually start writing, the process is made easier through referencing certain websites that I can't live without. And once I'm finished writing my paper, I can choose from plenty of webpages designed to show the proper way to cite any resources I've used. Of course, there are also some things that students get from the internet that they'd be better to stay away from, such as downloadable essays and book notes that help you skip out of actually reading a text. With technology being so accessible, so fast, so convenient, so easy to use, so full of information, etc., it can be hard to make sure you don't rely on it too much. For instance, I don't think it's a good idea to always use information from the internet as a replacement for going to the library, because sometimes I've found that the perfect resource for a paper I'm writing is sitting on a shelf in the university library. I think the best way for students to make use of modern advances is to draw on them to help build their own ideas and abilities, and not use them as a means of avoiding any real work.

Notice how Simkanin starts with a list of some courses that used technology. She does not seem to be heading in any one direction. Then suddenly she is off and running about how the use of technology affects her life as an English major.

Questioning

Sometimes when you are in a conversation, someone will ask you a question that takes you by surprise—and forces you to rethink your position or think about the topic in a new way. By using structured **questioning**, you can push yourself to explore your topic more deeply.

questioning structured speculation used to explore a topic in a new way

You are probably already familiar with the **journalists' questions**, which can readily serve your purpose: *Who? What? Where? When? Why? How?* As Simkanin answered these questions, she began to form an opinion about her topic.

journalists' questions Who? What? Where? When? Why? How?

Who is using technology? Teachers, students, librarians—everyone on campus, it seems. But I'm going to talk about how it affects me.

What technology is being used, and what is it being used for? All kinds of technology, from e-mail and web searches to PowerPoint presentations and voice mail, is being used, for instruction, homework, student-to-student communication, student-and-teacher communication, and research. I'm going to concentrate on my use of computer technology, mostly access to the internet.

Where is technology being used? At the library, in the classroom, but most often in my bedroom, where my computer is.

When is technology being used? Usually at night, after I come home from classes and am doing my homework.

Why do students use or not use technology? I use it because it's more convenient than walking over to the library and searching. Not all students have internet access in their apartments; others may not know all the online research techniques that I know.

How are students using it? Some students are using it to advance their education; others are using it to subvert it (like downloading essays and cheating schemes).

Keeping a Journal

Some writing instructors expect you to keep a weekly journal, either in print or online. When you are writing in your journal, you do not need to be concerned with punctuation, grammar, spelling, and other mechanical features. If you write three pages a week for a journal or as part of your online class discussion, you may not be able to lift a ready-to-submit essay directly from your work, but you will have accumulated a pool of ideas from which to draw. Even more important, you will have been practicing getting thoughts into words.

journal a private record of your understandings and reactions to reading, assignments, class discussion, and lectures

In addition to using journal entries as a way to explore your topic, you might also use your **journal** to write out your understandings of and reactions to your reading and writing assignments and class discussions and lectures.

As Simkanin considered her own upcoming assignment, she wrote in her ongoing electronic journal:

I think I tend to take modern advances for granted, but when I look at how much more I use technology as a college student than I did, say, eight years ago as a junior high student, it's amazing to think of how much my studies have become dependent on it. I need computer access for almost everything anymore, from writing papers to updating my Facebook status, to doing research on the web. Not only that, but some of my favorite classes have been those that incorporated some form of technology into the course format. I think this is one of technology's major advantages—turning learning into something new and interactive, which gets students involved. I've had courses that used technology in basic ways, like my Biology class, in which the class lectures were recorded and saved online for students to listen to later. Some of my other courses, though, have used it in lots of interesting ways. In one of my English classes, for instance, we took a day to hold class in a chat room, and we all logged into the room from our computers at home. It was great as part of our discussions about literacy, because experimenting with computer literacy allowed us all to see how people communicate differently when they're not face to face. Of course, some people would argue that kids my age spend way too much time "chatting" and texting and that instant messaging is one of a student's biggest distracters. I guess, like any good thing, technology also carries with it some disadvantages.

The Double-Entry Notebook

Whether you keep your notes in a notebook, on separate note cards or pieces of paper, or on your laptop, you can choose among various ways of recording what you observe and your responses. A **double-entry notebook** is a journal that has two distinct parts: observational details and personal response to those details. The double-entry notebook thus allows you to explore your observations separately from your responses (including biases and preferences) toward what you observe. In addition, it encourages you to push your observations further, with responses to and questions about what you see or think you see. Some writers draw a heavy line down the middle of each page of the notebook, putting "Observations" at the top of the left-hand side of the page and "Response" at the top of the right-hand side. Others lay the notebook flat and use the right-hand page for recording their observations and the left-hand page for

double-entry notebook a journal with two distinct columns pairing observation and personal response

responding to those observations. If you are using a computer, you can format your entries the way Simkanin did:

Observations

My classmates and I rely on technology for our classes and our social lives—and for our personal lives as well. We rarely write anything. We type our to-do lists, our homework assignments, our communications to one another. We don't go anywhere without our phones, not even to the gym. I look at my e-mail messages while I'm walking on the treadmill, and my best friend does her e-mail while she works out on the stairmaster machine. We sleep with our phones nearby, and we always check our messages during meals and during class. We all carry our computers in our backpacks so we can take class notes on our computers.

Response

I just realized that my friends and I take technology for granted, to the point that it's almost invisible to us. We refer to things as "technology" or say that we're having "technological problems" only when we're still figuring out how to use them—not when we're already good at them, like with our cell phones. When I decided to pay closer attention to how we all take notes in class, I realized that many of us sneak away from our notes and answer e-mails, check Facebook, even shop. Yep, I've done most of my Christmas shopping online and during class. When I say that I use technology more now than I did as a junior high student, I have to admit that the notes I took in class back then were probably better than the ones I think I'm taking now.

After trying several methods of exploration (listing, freewriting, keeping a journal, and using a double-entry notebook), Simkanin found that she was starting to repeat herself. She did not yet have a point she wanted to make, let alone a controlling idea for her essay or a thesis. (See Crafting a Working Thesis Statement on page 239.) She needed to try a new tack.

Organization

After you have explored your topic as thoroughly as you can, it is time to begin organizing your essay. Two simple methods can help you get started: clustering and outlining.

Clustering

Clustering is a visual method for connecting ideas that go together. You might start with words and phrases from a list you compiled or brainstormed and link them with arrows, circles, or lines, the way Simkanin did. Notice how Simkanin used different sizes of type to accentuate the connections she wanted to make between technology and learning. (You might want to use color as well to help you make connections.) Interestingly, Simkanin has not yet put herself into her essay's plan.

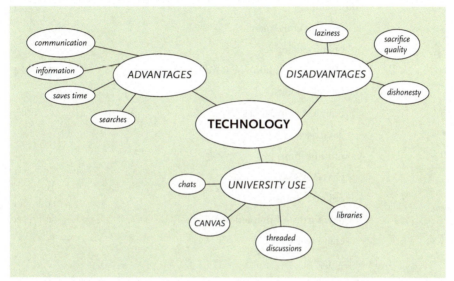

clustering a method using arrows, circles, lines, or other visual cues for connecting ideas

Outlining

An **outline** establishes the limits of your topic at the same time as it lists the main parts. Outlining is a good way to plan, but only if you think of the result as a rough—not formal or final—outline. You will want to allow yourself to add and delete points and move things around so that outlining, like clustering, helps you visualize how things relate to one another. Simkanin's outline shows a close relationship to her clustering, but she has added details and a general title.

Notice that Simkanin started out using Roman numerals for her main sections, but she switched to simply listing subpoints, thereby creating an informal list as her outline, which was easier for Simkranin to put together and work with.

outline a structure that lists the main parts and supporting points of an essay

As she was constructing her outline, Simkanin began thinking about rhetorical strategies for developing her paper that would be best suited to her purpose.

pages 278–294 (See CHAPTER 15, RHETORICAL STRATEGIES FOR DEVELOPMENT.) She also began thinking of what her thesis statement might be.

Technology and Learning

I. Advantages

    Information

        fast and convenient

        online catalogues

        eBay's First Edition or Rare Books page

        Google Books

        online concordances

        databases

    Communication

        CANVAS

        online forums

        new forms of interaction

        chat rooms

II. Disadvantages

    Academic laziness

        ignore traditional forms of research

        quality vs. convenience

        lose the value of a trip to the library

    Dishonesty

        free online book notes

        downloadable essays

        plagiarism

» CRAFTING A WORKING THESIS STATEMENT

After you decide on a topic (or a focus on an assigned topic), ask yourself what you would like to say about it—and why. To bring your topic into focus, consider your individual interests, the opportunity for change, your purpose, the needs of your audience, and the time and space available. Look over your explorations to determine where, exactly, your interests took hold. Often, your interest provides the most fruitful site for sharpening your focus, developing a working thesis, and then drafting an essay.

The most important step to take as you begin to prepare your thesis statement is to identify the main assertion or claim you are making about your topic. (See **CHAPTER 2, MAKING CLAIMS**.) Chapter 2 stressed that your thesis anchored your response and helped the audience understand your position. More specifically, a thesis statement is a central idea stated in the form of an assertion, or claim, that indicates what you believe to be true, interesting, or valuable about your topic. By combining your topic (for example, studying another language) with your point about that topic (it's important because it prepares students to participate in a global economy), you will create a thesis statement, an explicit claim you are making about your topic. Your thesis statement focuses the overarching idea of your entire paper.

pages 20–21

thesis statement an explicit claim about your topic, usually in one sentence, that expresses the overarching idea of your paper (a topic and your stance on that topic)

> Thesis Statement: Students who study another language become better communicators, both in their own language and with others within our global economy.

Many pieces of academic writing have a thesis statement, a declarative sentence that identifies your topic and your stance on that topic. As such, your thesis statement conveys a single idea, clearly focused and specifically stated. If your thesis statement presents two or more related ideas, be sure that it allows for a single direction and focus. For example, the following thesis statement, composed of two sentences, coordinates two ideas, indicating a discussion that will contrast the human brain with those of other animals:

> **There is something unusual about primates in general, and humans in particular. Compared with other animals, they have strikingly large brains relative to their bodies.**
>
> —Tom Standage, *Writing on the Wall: Social Media—The First Two Thousand Years*

If you wish to sharpen a thesis statement by adding information that qualifies or supports it, subordinate such material to the main idea:

In elementary school, I had noticed the mean-spiritedness of some kids, part of it directed at me and my siblings.

—Mary Pipher, "Growing Our Souls"

As you develop your thesis statement, resist using such vague qualifiers as *interesting, important,* and *unusual,* which can signal that the topic lacks focus. For example, in the thesis statement "My education has been very unusual," the word *unusual* conveys very little. It might indicate that the writer's topic is weak and unfocused—or it might be masking a wonderfully wild, interesting idea that would appeal to an audience: "After my parents decided to teach me at home, I pursued educational avenues I didn't know existed." If you feel you need to soften your thesis or claim, then turn to such qualifiers as *frequently, often, generally, rarely,* or *sometimes.* The following examples show how thesis statements can be improved:

VAGUE	It is important to balance work with school.
BETTER	Hardworking students who balance a part-time job with academic success often gain maturity and self-confidence.
VAGUE	The concept of stem-cell research is interesting.
BETTER	If controlled successfully in a laboratory setting, human stem cells could become the basis of transplantation-based therapies.
VAGUE	Student-athletes choose a college for a number of reasons.
BETTER	No matter what their sport or their professional aspirations, student-athletes generally use the same criteria in choosing a college: opportunity to play the sport, geographic location, financial aid, and emotional connection with the school.

Keep in mind, however, that although your thesis statement identifies your topic and your stand on that topic, after you have drafted your thesis statement, you may need to adjust it. By forming a **working thesis**, you can test a possible framework for your response to an opportunity for change. A working thesis lets you test your thesis as you try to support it in the body of your paper. It is just as important to allow your thesis statement to remain tentative in the early

working thesis a statement that tests a possible framework and controlling idea for your paper

stages of writing as it is to allow your essay to remain flexible through the initial drafts, responsive to your ongoing research findings and insights. Rather than sticking with your original thesis, which you might have to struggle to support because it was not well conceived, let your final thesis statement evolve as you think, explore, draft, and revise. Do not be concerned if you change your mind; writers often do. Writing a thesis is just a starting point in the drafting process.

As you draft your paper, remember every thesis must be supported by good reasons, evidence, and details. (For more on evidence, see CHAPTER 2, LOGOS.) page 24 Therefore, as you continue to write and revise, check your thesis statement frequently to make sure that all your supporting material (your assertions, good reasons, examples, and details) remain anchored to that thesis. Your thesis should influence your decisions about which details to keep and which to eliminate as well as guide your search for appropriate additional information to support your assertions. (For more on thesis statements and assertions, see CHAPTER 2, MAKING CLAIMS.) pages 20–21

Although it is often phrased as a single sentence, it does not need to be. Here is Simkanin's first attempt at a thesis statement:

> Thesis Statement: Technology provides many advantages for students and teachers alike, but it also brings with it some disadvantages. In this essay, I'm going to talk about my experiences with technology, the advantages I've experienced and the disadvantages I feel.

Simkanin identified her topic—use of technology by students and teachers—and forecast that she would be talking about both advantages and disadvantages. The following tips might help you develop a thesis statement that is neither too obvious nor too general.

 TIPS FOR DEVELOPING A WORKING THESIS STATEMENT

- Decide which specific feature of the topic interests you most, which feature opens up a rhetorical opportunity that your words might resolve or a change they might bring about.
- Write down your point of view, opinion, or assertion about that feature.
- Draft a thesis statement that includes your topic, features your point of view, and clarifies your coverage of the topic.
- Determine how your thesis relates to your overall purpose and the interests of your rhetorical audience.

»» DRAFTING

After you have explored your topic, you will begin drafting. While some writers find the first draft the toughest part of the process, many others derive great pleasure from the two-step drafting process: drafting and evaluating. The joy of putting words together is exhilarating for many writers; in **drafting** they enjoy the freedom of combining an informal list of points and subpoints with a freewrite to create a working outline as they work to attend to all the elements of the rhetorical situation, including audience, purpose, genre, medium of delivery, and the opportunity for change that motivated you to write in the first place. A first draft is just that—words you will revisit again and again as you adjust your message to take into account all the elements in your rhetorical situation.

Some writers do not write the introduction and conclusion until they have drafted the body of the paper. Others use a loose introduction, body, conclusion structure to organize their draft. Most **introductions** will include the thesis. Simkanin also establishes her credentials for writing about this topic by introducing her experience. In the first draft that follows, she goes on to draft the **body** of her paper, where she links ideas about her topic that explore the implications of her thesis. In a first draft it is most important to get your words onto the page (screen) and explore your topic with broad brushstrokes. Transitional phrases and words can help to connect your ideas. In this part of your composition you point out the logic of the claim in your thesis and bring in supporting evidence, which can be fleshed out more fully when you revise. In your **conclusion**, a final appeal to your audience reveals or reinforces how the topic of your paper affects them or has larger implications. (See CHAPTER 14, THE POWER OF PARAGRAPHS.)

drafting a process that combines an informal structure with a freewrite

introductions openings for papers, often including the thesis and establishing credibility on the topic

body an exploration of a topic that builds a logical structure to support a thesis

conclusion a final appeal to your audience by making clear how the issue you are exploring affects them

pages 257–277

Common Transitional Words and Phrases

above all	for instance	in sum
also	however	on the contrary
as a result	in addition	on the one hand/other hand
at any rate	in contrast	then
at first	in fact	therefore
besides	in other words	thus
for example	instead	

When you are drafting, you will be considering your intended audience as well, particularly in terms of what you are hoping your audience can do to address (or help you address) the opportunity for change that sparked your writing in the first place. The following list may help you as you reconsider audience:

- Who can resolve the opportunity for change (or the problem) that you have identified?
- What exactly might that audience do to address, resolve, or help resolve it?
- What opportunities (if any) are there for you to receive feedback from that audience?

Answers to these questions will help you tie your purpose to your particular audience.

By thinking of her assignment as a rhetorical situation and considering the Tips for Analyzing Assignments on page 230, Simkanin developed a better idea of how to approach her draft. When an instructor does not write out an assignment, you should feel free to ask them to explain it in terms of the rhetorical situation—that is, ask your instructor specific questions about task, purpose, audience (or receiver), context, and constraints.

Here is Simkanin's first draft.

Technology for teaching and learning is especially strong here at State. It provides many advantages for students and teachers alike, but it also brings with it some disadvantages. In this essay, I'm going to talk about my experiences with technology, the advantages I've experienced and the disadvantages I feel. I'll draw upon my experiences in Spanish 3, English 202, Philosophy 197, Biological Sciences, Art History, and my internship.

Technology is rapidly becoming increasingly advanced, and much of it is used to enhance learning and writing. Not only does it increase the amount of information available, but it allows for stronger writing. I can search libraries around the world, use eBay to find rare manuscripts, use interlibrary loan, and file electronic requests for needed items.

Technology also makes the writing process faster, more convenient. I often access online concordances, view library books on my PC, e-mail librarians, and read full-text journal articles online. This technology is also allowing for more ways to develop ideas and new forms of written communication. For instance, I'm now experienced with chat room communication, forum discussions, and photo essays.

But at the same time that technology brings these advantages, it also inhibits learning and writing. I know that when I'm conducting online research I may be missing out on information or lowering the quality of information because I'm limiting my searching to electronic sources. Nowadays, students don't really have to learn to use the library, where often more information can be found than what appears in an online search. I fear that students are placing convenience over quality. I know I do sometimes. The information online isn't always reliable, either. Students don't often take the time to investigate sources.

For these reasons, campus technology may be promoting academic laziness in some students, and dishonesty as well. So much information is available that you can practically write a book report without ever reading the book. And online papers make plagiarism easy. In conclusion. . . .

Simkanin's first draft has begun to address the components of the rhetorical situation: she understands that she needs to talk about her own experiences with technology and describe the technology that she uses. In getting her thoughts down, she is beginning to sketch out an organizational structure that starts with the advantages of this technology and ends with the disadvantages. She has made certain to add that some students take advantage of technology only in a way that cheapens their learning experience. Notice that she has not begun to shape a strong thesis yet, let alone a conclusion. Still, she is ready to begin revising.

»» REVISING

revision a process of rethinking and rewriting parts of your draft

Revision means evaluating and rethinking your writing in terms of the rhetorical situation. Writers use several techniques during revision. Some put the draft aside for twenty-four hours or more in order to return to it with fresh ideas and a more objective viewpoint. Others like to print out the draft and actually cut it into different sections so that they can experiment with organization.

 TIPS FOR REVISION

- Identify the specific feature of your topic that best opens up a rhetorical opportunity—a problem your words might resolve or address.
- Finalize your claim about that specific feature so that your thesis statement includes the topic and your assertion about it.
- Mark the passages in your draft that best match your thesis.

- Adjust unmarked passages or qualify your thesis accordingly, acknowledging any conditions under which your assertion might not hold up.
- Establish how your introduction orients your readers to the purpose of your essay as well as engages them.
- Determine how the specific placement of your thesis statement guides your reader.
- Establish how your conclusion emphasizes significant points in your essay as well as wraps it up in a meaningful, thought-provoking way.

»» PEER EVALUATION

One of the most popular—and most effective—revision techniques is peer evaluation. **Peer evaluation** is a form of collaboration that provides productive advice and a response from a fellow student writer. If the thought of letting a peer (a classmate or friend) read your first draft makes you uncomfortable, if you have tried peer evaluation before and it did not work, or if you are worried that you will not receive good advice, please reconsider. All effective writing is the result of some measure of collaboration, whether between colleagues, editors and writers, publishers and writers, actors and writers, students and teachers, or friends. Just consider for a moment all the writing you read, hear, and see every day—newspapers, magazines, online chat, billboards, commercials, sitcoms, newscasts. A great majority of the words that you experience daily come to you as a result of collaboration and peer evaluation. Every day, experienced writers are showing their first drafts to someone else in order to get another point of view, piece of advice, or evaluation.

Peer evaluation is a valuable step in the writing process that you, too, will want to experience. No matter how good a writer you are, you will benefit from hearing what one or more real readers have to say about your message. They may ask you questions that prompt you to clarify points you want to make, nudge you to provide more examples so that your prose comes alive, or point out attention-getting passages. When you respond to a peer's first draft, you are not only helping that writer but also strengthening your own skills as a reader and writer. As you discover strengths and weaknesses in someone else's writing, you also improve your ability to find them in your own. Most important, the successful writing of a peer will energize your own writing in ways that the successful writing of a professional might not. A peer can show you how attainable good writing can be.

peer evaluation
a form of collaboration that provides writing advice from fellow students

Although it is sometimes helpful to get pointers on things like grammar and word choice, you will usually want a peer reviewer to focus first on how well your draft responds to your rhetorical situation. The following set of ten questions can help guide a peer reviewer:

Peer Evaluation Questions

1. What opportunity for change (or problem) sparked this essay?
2. What is the topic of this essay? What is the main idea the writer wants to convey about this topic?
3. What can you tell about the writer of this essay? What is their relationship to this topic?
4. Who is the audience? What information in the essay reveals the audience to you? What do you imagine are the needs and concerns of this audience? What might this audience do to address, resolve, or help resolve this problem?
5. What seems to be the relationship between the writer and the audience? How is the writer meeting the needs and concerns of this audience? What specific passages demonstrate the writer's use of the rhetorical appeals (ethos, pathos, and logos)?
6. What is the purpose of the writer's message? What is the relationship among the writer, the audience, and the writer's purpose? Do you have any other comments about the purpose?
7. What means is the writer using to deliver this message? How is this means appropriate to the situation?
8. What constraints are on the writer and this message?
9. What idea or passage in the essay is handled most successfully? Least successfully?
10. What are two questions you have for this writer?

These questions can be answered fairly quickly. Although you might be tempted to have your peer reviewer go through them quickly and orally, you will be better served if you ask the peer reviewer to write out their answers, either on a separate piece of paper or directly on your draft. When it is your turn to evaluate a peer's draft, you may well come away from the experience surprised at how much you learned about your own writing. There is no better way to improve your own understanding than to explain something to someone else.

The peer reviewer of Simkanin's paper offered her a good deal of advice, most of which had to do with large-scale revising, as you can see from his responses to questions 6 and 9:

6. I cannot tell for sure what your purpose is in writing this essay. You describe technology, but I'm not sure why. Do you want to explain the opportunities, or do you want to show how bad it can be for students? And I cannot tell who you're writing to—maybe just any reader? Still, I think you have a good start on a strong essay because you know so much neat stuff about all the technology here at school. I didn't know half this stuff.

9. The beginning of your essay is the least successful part. I can't tell by reading it where you're headed with your topic, so I think you're going to want to revise with a stronger purpose in mind. But as I said earlier, the strongest part of your essay is all the specific information you already know about using technology. No wonder you get such good grades. You don't have any conclusion yet. I think if you get a better start on your introduction then you can pull together your overall argument in your conclusion. Maybe talk about how technology is always thought of as being better, an improvement, but that it's not always, not really.

The peer reviewer confirmed what Simkanin already thought: the introduction of the essay, especially the thesis statement, merited more of her attention. Her peer reviewer, though, was unclear about what Simkanin's purpose was. So, as she revised, Simkanin focused down on the connection between her purpose and audience as she created a thesis statement that narrowed her topic and made a comment on that topic.

Therefore, Simkanin drafted her initial, general, ho-hum overview of the advantages and disadvantages of using technology at State (an introduction aimed at and engaging no one in particular) into a vibrant introductory paragraph, opening with a provocative question, aimed at an audience interested in the educational advantages of technology, and featuring a specific thesis statement:

Could today's college student survive without a microwave to heat Easy Mac in her dorm room, a smartphone to check in on Facebook friends, and a laptop streaming movies or music to escape the tedium of another evening spent doing coursework?

The answer is debatable. What's not debatable, however, is that **even though technology of various forms has brought a certain ease to the lives of today's college students, it has also allowed them to embark on serious academic pursuits that would not be possible without technological innovation**.

Processes

≫ EDITING AND PROOFREADING A RESPONSE

Although the peer reviewer focused on Simkanin's approach to the rhetorical situation, other evaluative responses had to do with smaller issues related to **editing**: improving word choice, adding specific details, and structuring sentences more effectively. (See CHAPTER 16, STYLE: AN ESSENTIAL GUIDE TO EFFECTIVE SENTENCES.) Some writers revise, edit, and proofread simultaneously, while others focus their efforts on resolving the big issues (thesis statement, organization, and supporting information) before tackling editing and **proofreading**. (See also CHAPTER 17, STRATEGIES FOR EDITING COMMON PROBLEMS.)

editing improving word choice, adding details, and structuring sentences more effectively

proofreading checking for spelling, typos, grammar, and punctuation errors

pages 295–321 and 322–349

After the peer reviewer finished responding to Simkanin's essay (and she to his), Simkanin took his advice, wrote two more drafts, and edited and proofread her way to her final draft. Like most writers, Simkanin stopped revising because she had run out of time—not because she thought her essay was perfect in every way.

≫ DESIGNING THE FINAL DRAFT

Document design within an academic context often means following the style guidelines of the disciplines, such as those published by the Modern Language Association (MLA) for papers in the humanities or the American Psychological Association (APA) for papers in the social sciences. (See CHAPTER 22, ACKNOWLEDGING SOURCES IN MLA STYLE and CHAPTER 23, ACKNOWLEDGING SOURCES IN APA STYLE.) When you submit your report, essay, or manuscript, then, you respect the formatting, style, and design of that academic discipline. In college, such design concerns usually include a title page or header, margins, line spacing, font style and size, works-cited page, and other formatting issues. Simkanin's final draft appears on the following pages. She formatted her paper according to MLA guidelines.

pages 412–449 and 450–476

Anastasia Simkanin

Professor Glenn

Writing and Technology, English 270

22 October 2015

Technology and the Learning Process: One Student's View

Could today's college student survive without a microwave to
heat Easy Mac in her dorm room, a smartphone to check in on
Facebook friends, and a laptop streaming movies or music to escape
the tedium of another evening spent doing coursework? The answer is
debatable. What's *not* debatable, however, is that even though
technology of various forms has brought a certain ease to the lives of
today's college students, it has also allowed them to embark on
serious academic pursuits that would not be possible without
technological innovation.

The Internet, for instance, offers students a wealth of advanced
search engines and online library databases. Many students find that
such tools open up a world of information, allowing more expedient
research and, in turn, stronger essays. But some people argue that the
ease of computer searching and the availability of almost anything
over the Internet expose students to the dangers of academic laziness
and dishonesty. Which side is right? The incorporation of technology

The thesis statement presents Simkanin's position on the topic.

into the learning process is a complex matter and, like any powerful innovation, brings potential pitfalls as well as advantages. Perhaps the best way to approach both sides of the issue is to draw a clear picture of the pros and the cons, thereby assessing the different ways that technology has revolutionized learning in today's universities. •

One major way that technological advances have facilitated the learning process is by supplying students with a wealth of information that could not be obtained without Internet resources. Online catalogues such as *WorldCat*, for instance, allow users to search libraries anywhere in the world for books, articles, and more in a single step. *Borrow Direct* allows students to simultaneously search all Ivy League university libraries, and the University Library (sponsored by the Committee on Institutional Cooperation) allows the same type of search within Big Ten schools.•Alternatively, students can opt to go to a specific library website, such as the online catalogue of Oxford University libraries, and begin their search there. With such a vast array of resources available, only very rarely is a student unable to find pertinent information. Having located a needed item, a student can file an electronic request through interlibrary loan and have the item delivered to a convenient location or even made available as a PDF download. A student in the United States who needs a rare manuscript held at the University of Cambridge in England can view

Processes

Simkanin forecasts her approach, which involves looking at both pros and cons of the use of technology, and also clarifies her purpose: to assess technology's effect on learning.

This is one of the places where Simkanin responds to the peer reviewer's suggestion by including specific details about using resources.

important pages online. Whereas once students' research was limited to the resources in their own neighborhood, technology now allows them access to information in libraries across the Atlantic.

Not only does the Internet allow users to find information that is hard to obtain because it is held in distant locations, but it also allows them access to information that is hard to obtain for a variety of other reasons. On those rare occasions when students are unable to find a needed item by searching library catalogues, they can look on sites such as eBay's *First Edition* and *Rare Books* and possibly locate a volume that is to be found only in someone's living room.

Besides searching *for* books, searching *through* them has been aided by technology as well. Writing a paper on *Great Expectations* and want to find the exact passage where Pip admits that Biddy is "immeasurably better than Estella"? Web resources such as the *Concordance of Great Books* allow users to type in a word or phrase and instantly see all the occurrences of those words in a book, along with the surrounding text and chapter numbers. *Google Book Search* and *Hathi Trust Digital Library* let users search for keywords and phrases within millions of books without any more effort than it takes to Google their topic. The above quotation, by the way, is found in chapter 17 of the Penguin edition.

This transition sentence links this paragraph to the preceding one.

Processes

Even with all the time it can save a student, the average dot-com
site is not necessarily the top rung of the ladder of searching
expediency. Today's students can easily write stronger, more
persuasive papers by taking advantage of the information that online
databases place at their fingertips. Compare, for instance, the
effectiveness of saying "State University conferred many doctoral
degrees in 2009" with the effectiveness of saying "State University
conferred 513 doctoral degrees in 2009." Including statistics in their
papers can make students' points sharper and more vivid, and
databases such as *Historical Statistics of the United States* allow students
to achieve this result. Other databases, such as *JSTOR* and *MUSE*,
let students sort through full-length journal articles simply by moving
their mouse. With libraries containing thousands of volumes of
journals and periodicals, the amount of time saved through computer
searches is immense. And, of course, consulting a database is a lot
faster than surveying the 6,165 graduate students who were enrolled
at State University in 2009.

Not only is technology improving traditional methods of
research and writing, it is also providing students with new ways to
communicate and develop ideas. State University's *CANVAS* site is
designed to give professors and students online space for managing
their courses. By accessing *CANVAS*, students can click on the link

Simkanin includes
another specific
detail that makes
the essay more
persuasive.

for a course and view daily reminders, weekly assignments, selected lecture notes, and more. A favorite feature of *CANVAS* is its threaded discussion board. Online forums and live (online) office hours allow students and instructors to carry on the one-on-one discussion that is precluded by large class sizes and limited lecture time. In another step toward moving course discussion beyond the classroom setting, some instructors at State University—especially those who teach language classes—have experimented with "holding class" in a chat room. Online chats allow students to carry on multiple conversations at once, which gives them more opportunities to share and develop ideas. The fact that most students enjoy chat room discussion is an added bonus, as the appeal of something new and fun can go a long way in keeping students interested and eager to learn.

Given all the ways that technology is changing life for students, it is not surprising that some of the effects are less welcome than others. One possible pitfall of relying on technology is that, ironically, ignoring more traditional ways of research can sometimes reduce information—or at least information quality. Searching a library's database from home while a stereo plays in the background is more appealing to most students than taking a trip to the stacks, but what many students do not realize is that, though online catalogues are a great place to start, they are often not enough by themselves. Finding the approximate spot where a needed item is located and then looking through items on adjacent shelves or discussing resources with a reference librarian will almost always turn up more results than does an online catalogue search alone. When it comes to finding that approximate location, however, the catalogues are indeed the place to begin. The danger lies in placing convenience over quality. What many students find to be most convenient is conducting a simple online search using an engine like *Google*, but this method has its own set of problems. Anyone can create a page on the Internet: for example, my fourteen-year-old brother could post his middle school paper on how Jane Eyre's inheritance reveals Charlotte Brontë's secret obsession with the power of money. Would such a paper help a college student write a sophomore-level essay? Probably not. Being lured by the convenience of Web searches, students can sometimes forget to investigate the reliability of sources, thus compromising the quality of their work.

Perhaps the most serious dangers of depending too much on technology are the possibilities of academic laziness and dishonesty. There is *so* much information available online that a student can practically write a paper on a book without even opening it. Sites like *SparkNotes* are great when a student is running late for class and needs to quickly find out what happens in a particular chapter of a text or needs to refresh his or her memory of something read earlier, but a student will never get as much out of summary notes as out of reading the book. With free online literature notes replacing $5.99-a-copy *Cliffs Notes*, however, the temptation to skip out on one's assignments is becoming all the more pervasive.

More serious than simply consulting summary notes is another danger: plagiarism. Not only are notes on books available online, but so are entire essays on them. Whole sites are devoted to selling papers to students who are looking to avoid writing an essay themselves, and papers are sometimes available for free. Every college student knows the feeling of sitting at a computer screen late at night, trying to write a paper but having little success because of fatigue. Times like these are when the temptation to abuse technology arises, and a student might simply download someone else's essay, hand it in as her or his own, and get some sleep. While having an abundance of information available is usually a wonderful thing, today's college students need to be wary of letting technology do their work *for* them, rather than just helping them with it.

Because technology affects the learning process in so many ways, it cannot be judged as wholly positive or wholly negative. Perhaps it would not be fair to say either but to agree, instead, that though the value of Web content depends on how one uses it, the dramatic changes that have been brought on by recent advances are amazing. Technology is changing the way students learn and the way they write.

Visual Culture, a 400-level English course at State University, encourages students to "write" essays in new ways, using images instead of words. Many students choose to obtain their images off the Internet or to present their visual essay in the form of a PowerPoint presentation or YouTube video. With "writing an essay" no longer requiring actual *writing*, there's little—if any—room to doubt that education today is being constantly shaped and molded as technology continues to progress. It will be interesting to see what the future brings.

Closing the essay with a focus on a course at her school demonstrates Simkanin's awareness of her audience—her instructor.

Reflect upon the information in this chapter, particularly the passage on Simkanin's writing process, and describe two specific ways in which you could improve your own writing process. Be prepared to share your answer with the rest of the class.

14 The Power of Paragraphs

- Articulate a topic sentence that organizes a paragraph.
- Apply the power of a paragraph (its topic sentence, supporting details, and examples) to support and extend a thesis.
- Assess the unity and coherence of individual paragraphs.
- Determine connections among adjacent sentences and paragraphs for paragraph coherence.
- Evaluate transitions among paragraphs.
- Compose effective introductory and concluding paragraphs.

As you develop your own writing process, you may work from an informal list, a guiding outline, or a strong thesis, and begin drafting by developing individual paragraphs, even if you must figure out where you want those paragraphs to take you. If you are working from an informal list, you enjoy the freedom to pursue new ideas that occur to you as you draft, anticipating that your thesis and organizational place will develop as you write. If you are using a firm outline, you can enjoy the security of starting off with a clear direction, anticipate the number of paragraphs you will need, and feel confident about what you plan to accomplish in each paragraph. In either situation, however, your goal is to develop each paragraph fully and then ask yourself what additional paragraphs (or additional supporting information within any single paragraph) would further support your thesis statement and enhance your overall message in terms of your rhetorical opportunity, intended audience, and purpose. (See CHAPTER 13, OUTLINING, and CRAFTING A WORKING THESIS STATEMENT.)

pages
237–238
and
pages
239–241

Paragraphs are groups of sentences (or a single sentence) that are usually set off by indentation and relate to one idea, which is often found in a topic sentence. Working like the thesis statement of an essay, the **topic sentence** states the main idea of a paragraph. All the other sentences in the paragraph relate to that main idea. Paragraphs have no set length, neither in number of words nor sentences. Sometimes, you will develop longer paragraphs, rich in important detail; other times, you will use a short paragraph to add emphasis or establish transition. Typically, paragraphs range from 50 to 250 words, with paragraphs in books typically longer than those in newspapers and magazines. Whether long or short, individual paragraphs serve as the building blocks of every essay, containing examples and details that support the overall thesis.

Just as you naturally (and repeatedly) revise parts of your essay, think of revising individual paragraphs as an opportunity to articulate exactly what you want to say without anyone interrupting you—or changing the subject. Whether a long paragraph exhausts a single point, introduces competitive ideas, or combines too many points or a short paragraph indicates inadequate development, you will want to revise.

topic sentence
a sentence
that states the
main idea of a
paragraph

≫ STATING THE MAIN IDEA

Effective paragraphs are unified around one main idea, often stated in a topic sentence. Whether a paragraph is long or short, it should focus on one main idea or point. Topic sentences often appear at the start of a paragraph to focus readers on what the paragraph is about. If you want to ensure that your paragraphs are unified and coherent, you might want to place the topic sentence at the beginning of each paragraph. A topic sentence in that location will both remind you of your focus and be obvious to your readers, who will recognize and then follow your main idea immediately.

In the following paragraph about business at Hollywood movie studios in the late 1960s, the topic sentence is at the beginning of the paragraph. The support sentences mention the consequences of the event described in the topic sentence.

Between August 1964 and March 1965, four new movies sold so many tickets and made so much money that, collectively, they pointed toward a dramatic shift in the tastes of American moviegoers and suggested an entirely new way for the studios to do business. Hollywood did not react well. Historically, the only event more disruptive to the industry's ecosystem than an unexpected flop is an unexpected smash, and, caught off guard by the sudden arrival of more revenue than they thought their movies could ever bring in, the major studios resorted to three old habits: imitation, frenzied speculation, and panic.

—Mark Harris, *Pictures at a Revolution* [Old Habits]

When you announce your general topic in a topic sentence and then provide specific support for it, you are using **deductive reasoning**. The topic sentence appears first in the following paragraph, which indicates that the author will offer evidence as to why we are suspicious of rapid cognition.

> I think we are innately suspicious of . . . rapid cognition. We live in a world that assumes that the quality of a decision is directly related to the time and effort that went into making it. When doctors are faced with a difficult diagnosis, they order more tests, and when we are uncertain about what we hear, we ask for a second opinion. And what do we tell our children? Haste makes waste. Look before you leap. Stop and think. Don't judge a book by its cover. We believe that we are always better off gathering as much information as possible and spending as much time as possible in deliberation. We really only trust conscious decision making. But there are moments, particularly in times of stress, when haste does not make waste, when our snap judgments and first impressions can offer a much better means of making sense of the world.

—Malcolm Gladwell, *Blink* [Making Sense of the World]

Although the topic sentence is usually the first sentence in a paragraph, experienced writers often add interest to their writing by varying the placement of their topic sentences within different paragraphs. The topic sentence can be announced at the beginning and reaffirmed at the end of a paragraph, as the closing sentence, or arise as an inference from all the sentences together.

If you want to emphasize the main idea of a paragraph or give its organization some extra support, you can begin and conclude the paragraph with two versions of the same idea. This strategy is particularly useful for long paragraphs because it gives readers whose attention may have wandered a second chance to grasp the main idea. In the following paragraph, both the first sentence and the last convey the idea that the English language has become a global language.

> English is the most widely spoken language in the history of our planet, used in some way by at least one out of every seven human beings around the globe. Half of the world's books are written in English, and the majority of international telephone calls are made in English. English is the language of over sixty percent of the world's radio programs, many of them beamed, ironically, by the Russians, who know that to win friends and influence nations, they're best off using English. More than seventy percent of international mail is

deductive reasoning A form of logical reasoning in which a conclusion is formed after relating a specific fact (minor premise) to a generalization

written and addressed in English, and eighty percent of all computer text is stored in English. English has acquired the largest vocabulary of all the world's languages, perhaps as many as two million words, and has generated one of the noblest bodies of literature in the annals of the human race.

—Richard Lederer, *Crazy English: The Ultimate Joy Ride Through Our Language* [English as a World Language]

Placing the topic sentence at the end of the paragraph works well when you are moving from specific supporting details to a generalization about those ideas—that is, when you are using **inductive reasoning**. Effective writers try to meet the expectations of their readers, which often include the anticipation that the first sentence will be the topic sentence; however, writers and readers alike enjoy an occasional departure from the expected, as the next paragraph by Charlotte Hogg illustrates:

inductive reasoning
The reasoning process that begins with facts or observations and moves to general principles that account for those facts or observations

In 1982 my parents moved from Fargo, North Dakota, to Paxton [Nebraska] after a sudden job loss, simply because they weren't sure where else to go, and my brother and I had to be enrolled in school. My grandma told her son, my dad, "Come home for now." When we got to town, it was as if everyone was waiting. Mom took us to school, where the principal said, "You're Jack's kids? You'll do well, then." Down at Hehnke's grocery store, Henry welcomed us, embraced my dad. To me it wasn't a homecoming, despite how excited I was to be near my grandma and aunt. This wasn't our first move. In the past few years, I had lived in Minnesota and both of the Dakotas—I was tired of moving. Yet here it was different. Everything around me was both familiar and unfamiliar. I carried with me the legacy of four generations of Osborns and Hoggs. In this town I was both insider and outsider.

—Charlotte Hogg, *From the Garden Club: Rural Women Writing Community* [Moving to Nebraska]

As you revise your draft, try underlining the topic sentences of each paragraph. If you cannot easily find a topic sentence in one of your paragraphs, add a sentence stating the main idea of that paragraph. If you find that you open every paragraph with a topic sentence, you might try experimenting with another pattern.

»» DEVELOPING THE MAIN POINT

Topic sentences help unify paragraphs. The addition of relevant details, facts, statistics, evidence, experiences, and examples enhance that unity by supporting and extending the main point. (For more on evidence, see CHAPTER 2, LOGOS.) All

page 24

good writing presents general information or an opinion (in a topic sentence, for instance) that is backed up with such evidence. Organizing your paragraph between a general assertion and detailed support adds rhythm and interest to your writing—plus, such an organization propels your main point forward. (For more on assertions, see CHAPTER 2, MAKING CLAIMS.)

pages 20–21

Using Details

A good paragraph developed with details brings an idea to life. Consider the well-developed paragraph by Brenda Jo Brueggemann:

> **This reminds me of how I learned to drive growing up in western Kansas: my parents and grandparents turned me loose behind the wheel of grandpa's old blue Ford pickup in the big, open cow pasture behind their farm house, gave me some basic instructions on gears, clutches, brakes, accelerator—and then let me go.** It was exhilarating to get the feel of the thing, bumping along over gopher holes with dried cow patties flying behind me, creating a little dust cloud to mark the path I had taken, and not worrying about which way I should turn or go next. And I learned well the basics of the machine and its movement by driving this way. But soon I wanted more: a road to travel, a radio that actually worked, a destination and goal, a more finely tuned knowledge of navigation involving blinkers, lights, different driving conditions, and—most of all—the ability to travel and negotiate with others also on the road.
>
> —**Brenda Jo Brueggemann, "American Sign Language and the Academy"**

Notice how the series of details in Brueggemann's paragraph supports the main idea, or topic sentence. Readers can easily see how one sentence leads into the next, creating a clear picture of the experience being described. (For more on creating a picture, see CHAPTER 15, DESCRIPTION.)

pages 280–281

Using Examples

Like details, examples contribute to paragraph development by making specific what otherwise might seem general and hard to grasp. Details describe a person, place, or thing; examples illustrate an idea with information that can come from different times and places. Both details and examples support the main idea of a paragraph. (For more on examples, see CHAPTER 15, EXEMPLIFICATION.)

pages 281–282

Amy Poehler's paragraph from *Yes, Please* uses several closely related examples (as well as details) to expand the idea of fourth-grade pressure with which she begins.

<u>I was in fourth grade and in trouble.</u> **The students of Wildwood Elementary School in Burlington, Massachusetts, shifted in their uncomfortable metal seats as they waited for me to say my next line. A dog rested in my arms and an entire musical rested on my shoulders. I was playing Dorothy in *The Wizard of Oz*, and it was my turn to speak.** <u>Dorothy is *Hamlet* for girls. Next to Annie in *Annie* and Sandy in *Grease*, it is the dream role of every ten-year-old. *Annie* taught me that orphanages were a blast and being rich is the only thing that matters. *Grease* taught me being in a gang is nonstop fun and you need to dress sexier to have any chance of keeping a guy interested.</u> **But *The Wizard of Oz* was the ultimate.** <u>It dealt with friendship and fear and death and rainbows and sparkly red shoes.</u>

—**Amy Poehler, *Yes Please* [*The Wizard of Oz*]**

Adding Essential Information

Writers are always aware of what they have put on the page—but they seldom spend enough time considering what they may have left out. In order to ensure that you have provided all the details and examples necessary for the effective development of each paragraph, review the following questions:

- How does the supporting information support the topic sentence?
- What information does your audience already have—what details might they be expecting, pleased with, or surprised by?
- What additional information might strengthen your paragraph in terms of successfully connecting with your audience?

Keep in mind that your best supporting ideas will not always surface in your first draft; you will sometimes come up with an important idea only after you have finished that draft, let it cool off, and then looked at it again. You might also share your draft with a peer who is working on the same assignment, asking that person to mark the details they were not surprised to find, those that impressed them, and then to list those that are missing and could enrich your paragraph.

» MAKING PARAGRAPHS UNIFIED AND COHERENT

A successful paragraph is well developed, unified, and coherent. Paragraphs are **unified** when every sentence relates to the main idea and is violated when something unrelated to the rest of the material appears. Paragraphs are **coherent** when the relationships among the sentences are clear and meaningful and the progression from one sentence to the next is easy for readers to follow. Some paragraphs are unified but not coherent, however.

When revising the body of an essay, you will likely discover ways to enhance the unity of each paragraph by ensuring that every sentence within the paragraph relates to the single idea (the topic sentence). Those sentences that do not must be deleted or revised—and then examined for their order to enhance the paragraph's coherence. The order of sentences indicates a logical progression that moves forward the main idea.

unified
a paragraph in which every sentence relates to the main idea

coherent
a paragraph in which each sentence follows another in a way that makes the relationship among the ideas logical and clear

Composing Unified Paragraphs

A paragraph's unity is violated when something unrelated to the rest of the material appears. Consider the obvious violation in the following paragraph.

> The first time I visited Ohio State, I was stunned by the sheer size of it all. Nearly 50,000 students mobbed the main campus: undergrad, grad, dental, law, and medical students, people from all over the world. Hundreds of buildings, even more streets, alleys, dead ends, cubbyholes, and tucked-away coffee shops comprise an academic city, somehow separate from Columbus, Ohio, with which it shares a main street. High Street neatly bisects Columbus from north to south, and the shot through campus is lined with head shops, pizza joints, and chains of restaurants, cell-phone companies, and running-shoe stores. <u>Yet that campus became so very familiar to me.</u> The thousands of Ohio State students live on and off campus, spreading out across both sides of High Street and stretching from North High, right smack in Worthington, to South High, in the Short North neighborhood. They live in dorm rooms, suites, old houses chopped-up into apartments, high-rises, condos, and rented rooms. Yet despite the broad swath of student housing, both on and off campus, despite the fact that students constantly bring the gritty and glassy parts of "Columbus" onto campus and the intellectual facets of campus into the city,

the campus itself continues to feel like its own city, a city of museums, parks, lakes, libraries, galleries, arenas, parking decks, auditoriums, halls, and, of course, classrooms. A separate city. A big city. Little wonder that campus administrators have made "town-gown" relations a top priority.

Easy to delete, the sentence about the campus becoming familiar violates the unity of a paragraph devoted to the description of a city within a city. But if the purpose of the essay had been to demonstrate how the biggest of cities could become smaller with each exploration, then the writer could develop that sentence into a separate paragraph.

As you revise your paragraphs for unity, the following tips may help you.

 TIPS FOR IMPROVING PARAGRAPH UNITY

- **Identify.** Identify the topic sentence for each paragraph. Where is each located? Why is each one located where it is?
- **Relate.** Read each sentence in a paragraph and determine how (and if) it relates directly to or develops the topic sentence.
- **Eliminate.** Any sentence that does not relate to the topic sentence violates the unity of the paragraph—cut it, revise it, or save it to use elsewhere.
- **Clarify.** If a sentence "almost" relates to the topic sentence, either revise it or delete it. As you revise, you might clarify details or add information or a transitional word or phrase to make the relationship clear.
- **Rewrite.** If more than one idea is being conveyed in a single paragraph, either rewrite the topic sentence so that it includes both ideas and establishes a relationship between them or split the single paragraph into two paragraphs, dividing up the information accordingly.

Composing Coherent Paragraphs

In a unified paragraph, every sentence relates to the main idea of the paragraph. A coherent paragraph uses strong transitions and the logical order of the sentences to make the relationship among the ideas clear and forward moving. The following paragraph has unity but lacks coherence.

Lacks Coherence

The land was beautiful, gently rolling hills, an old orchard with fruit-bearing potential, a small clear stream—over eleven acres. But the house itself was another story. It had sat empty for years. Perhaps not empty, though that's what the realtor told us. There were macaroni and cheese boxes, how-to-play the mandolin books and videos, extra countertops, a kitchen sink, single socks looking for their mates, a ten-year-old pan of refried beans, and all sorts of random stuff strewn all through the house. Had the owner stayed there until he gave up on remodeling it? Had homeless people squatted there? Or had it been a hangout for teenagers—until the hole in the roof got too big for comfort? Who had been living there, and what kind of damage had they brought to the house? We looked at the house with an eye toward buying it. The price was right: very low, just what we could afford. And the location and acreage were perfect, too. But the house itself was a wreck. It needed a new roof, but it also needed a kitchen, flooring, drywall, updated plumbing and electricity—and a great big dumpster. We didn't know if we had the energy, let alone the know-how, to fix it up. Plus it wasn't like it was just the two of us we had to think about. We had three children to consider. If we bought it, where would we start working to make it inhabitable?

Although every sentence in this paragraph has to do with the writer's reaction to a house offered for sale, the sentences themselves are not arranged coherently; they are not in any logical order. First, the topic sentence could be moved to the beginning of the paragraph, where it could control the meaningful flow of ideas. Then, the other sentences could be clustered according to subtopic: the land, the condition of the house, and the potential advantages and disadvantages of the purchase.

Revised for Coherence

We looked at the house with an eye toward buying it. The land was beautiful, gently rolling hills, an old orchard with fruit-bearing potential, a small clear stream—over eleven acres. But the house itself was another story. It had sat empty for years. Perhaps not empty, though that's what the realtor told us. There were macaroni and cheese boxes, how-to-play the mandolin books and videos, extra countertops, a kitchen sink, single socks looking for their mates, a ten-year-old pan of refried beans, and all sorts of random stuff strewn all through the house. Had the owner stayed there until he gave up on remodeling it? Had homeless people squatted there? Or had it been a hangout for teenagers—until the hole in the roof got too big for comfort? By now, the house needed a new roof as well as a kitchen, flooring, drywall, updated plumbing and electricity—and a great big dumpster. We didn't know if we had the energy, let alone the know-how, to fix it up. Plus it wasn't like it was just the two of us we had to think about. We had three children to consider. Still, the price was right: very low, just what we could afford. And the location and acreage were perfect, too.

The paragraph is now coherent as well as unified.

Patterns of Organization That Create Unity and Coherence

To achieve coherence as well as unity in your paragraphs, study the following patterns of organization (chronological, spatial, emphatic, and logical), and consider which ones you might use in your own writing.

Chronological Order

When you use **chronological order**, you arrange ideas according to the order in which things happened. This organizational pattern is particularly useful for narration (For more on narration as a rhetorical strategy, see CHAPTER 15, NARRATION.)

pages 279–280

chronological order an arrangement of ideas according to the order in which things happened

> When Aunt Em came there to live she was a pretty wife. The sun and wind had changed her, too. They had taken the sparkle from her eyes and left them a sober gray; they had taken the red from her cheeks and lips, and they were gray also. She was thin and gaunt, and never smiled, now. When Dorothy, who was an orphan, first came to her, Aunt Em had been so startled by the child's laughter that she would scream and press her hand upon her heart whenever Dorothy's merry voice reached her ears; and she still looked at the little girl with wonder that she could find anything to laugh at.
>
> —L. Frank Baum, *The Wonderful Wizard of Oz* [Aunt Em]

Spatial Order

spatial order an orientation that focuses from right to left, near to far, top to bottom

pages 280–281

When you arrange ideas according to **spatial order**, you orient the reader's focus from left to right, near to far, top to bottom, and so on. This organizational pattern is particularly effective in descriptions. (For more on using description as a rhetorical strategy, see CHAPTER 15, DESCRIPTION.) Often the organization is so obvious that the writer can forgo a topic sentence, as in the next paragraph.

> I went to see a prospective student, Steve, up on the North Branch Road. His mother, Tammi, told me to look for the blue trailer with cars in the yard. There were lots of junk cars—rusted, hoods up, and wheels off, a Toyota truck filled with bags of trash. The yard was littered with transmission parts, hubcaps, empty soda bottles, Tonka trucks, deflated soccer balls, retired chain saws and piles of seasoned firewood hidden in the overgrowth of jewelweed. A pen held an assortment of bedraggled, rain-soaked chickens and a belligerent, menacing turkey. A small garden of red and yellow snapdragons marked the way to the door.
>
> —Tal Birdsey, *A Room for Learning: The Making of a School in Vermont* [Junk Cars]

Emphatic Order

When you use **emphatic order**, you arrange information in order of importance, usually from least to most important. Emphatic order is especially useful in expository and persuasive writing, both of which involve helping readers understand logical relationships (such as what caused something to happen or what kinds of priorities should be established). (See CHAPTER 15 for more on CAUSE-AND-EFFECT ANALYSIS.) The information in the next paragraph leads up to the writer's conclusion—that the temporary housing she shared with her toddler was truly awful.

pages 286–289

> My mom had flown in with her husband, William, all the way from London, or France, or wherever they were living at the time. The day after Mia's party, they came over—violating the homeless shelter's "no visitors" rule—to help me move to the transitional apartment. I shook my head a little at their outfits—William in his skinny black jeans, black sweater, and black boots; Mom in a black-and-white-striped dress that hugged her round hips too tight, black leggings, and low-top Converse shoes. They looked ready for sipping espresso, not moving. I hadn't let anyone see where we'd been living, so the intrusion of their British accents and Euro outfits made the cabin, our home, feel even dirtier.
>
> —Stephanie Land, *Maid* [Parent Intrusion]

emphatic order an arrangement of information in order of importance, usually from least to most important

Logical Order

Sometimes the movement within a paragraph follows a **logical order**, from specific to general or from general to specific. A paragraph may begin with a series of details and conclude with a summarizing statement, as illustrated in the following paragraph on our criminal justice system by Bryan Stevenson.

logical order an orientation that moves from specific to general or from general to specific

> Delaware County Circuit Judge Howard Reed found that Trina had no intent to kill. But under Pennsylvania law, the judge could not take the absence of intent into account during sentencing. He could not consider Trina's age, mental illness, poverty, the abuse she had suffered, or the tragic circumstances surrounding the fire. Pennsylvania sentencing law was inflexible: For those convicted of second-degree murder, mandatory life imprisonment without the possibility of parole was the only sentence. Judge Reed expressed serious misgivings about the sentence he was forced to impose. "This is the saddest case I've ever seen," he wrote. For a tragic crime committed at fourteen, Trina was condemned to die in prison.
>
> —Bryan Stevenson, *Mercy* [Inflexible Sentencing]

On the other hand, the paragraph may begin with a general statement or idea. That idea is then supported by particular details, as in the following paragraph by Craig Rood on America's gun culture.

> America's gun culture today is sustained by the gun industry and gun-advocacy groups. But gun owners also sustain it: approximately 30 percent of Americans own at least one gun, and estimates suggest that these Americans own between two hundred and three hundred million guns. The gun culture is also sustained by products (hunting gear, targets, movies, books, magazines, video games, toys, etc.), as well as institutions (e.g., the military), events (e.g., gun shows), places (e.g., shooting ranges), education (e.g., hunter safety courses and more informal modes of instruction), relationships (e.g., family and friends), and so on. Gun culture covers a variety of practices—harmless ones, such as collecting guns or shooting clay pigeons, and harmful ones, such as shooting people—and thus includes moments of joy as well as moments of horror. Above all, though, gun culture is animated by stories—whether accurate or not—about who "we" are individually and as Americans.
>
> —Craig Rood, *After Gun Violence* [Harmless and Harmful Gun Culture]

Using Transitions

Even if its sentences are arranged in a seemingly clear sequence, a single paragraph may lack internal coherence, and a series of paragraphs may lack overall coherence if transitions are abrupt or nonexistent. When revising, you can improve coherence by using pronouns, repetition, or conjunctions and transitional words or phrases. (See CHAPTER 13, COMMON TRANSITIONAL WORDS AND PHRASES.)

page 242

Pronouns

In Constance Holden's paragraph on identical twins, the writer enumerates the similarities of identical twins raised separately. She mentions their names only once, but uses the pronouns both, *their*, and *they* to keep the references to the twins always clear. (For more on pronouns and clarity, see CHAPTER 17, VAGUE PRONOUN REFERENCE.)

pages 333–335

> Jim Springer and Jim Lewis were adopted as infants into working-class Ohio families. **Both** liked math and did not like spelling in school. **Both** had law enforcement training and worked part-time as deputy sheriffs. **Both** vacationed in Florida, **both** drove Chevrolets. Much has been made of the fact that **their** lives are marked by a trail of similar names. **Both** married and divorced

women named Linda and had second marriages with women named Betty. **They** named **their** sons James Allan and James Alan, respectively. **Both** like mechanical drawing and carpentry. **They** have almost identical drinking and smoking patterns. **Both** chew their fingernails down to the nubs.

—Constance Holden, "Identical Twins Reared Apart"

Repetition

In Oliver Sacks's paragraph on blind musicians, the repeated use of the adjective *blind* helps bring on his point.

The image of the **blind** musician or the blind poet has an almost mythical resonance, as if the gods have given the gifts of music or poetry in compensation for the sense they have taken away. **Blind** musicians and bards have played a special role in many cultures, as wandering minstrels, court performers, religious cantors. For centuries, there was a tradition of blind church organists in Europe. There are many **blind** musicians, especially (though not exclusively) in the world of gospel, blues, and jazz—Stevie Wonder, Ray Charles, Art Tatum, José Feliciano, Rahsaan Roland Kirk, and Doc Watson are only a few. Many such artists, indeed, have "**Blind**" added to their names almost as an honorific: **Blind** Lemon Jefferson, the **Blind** Boys of Alabama, **Blind** Willie McTell, **Blind** Willie Johnson.

—Oliver Sacks, *Musicophilia* [Blind Musicians]

Physician Oliver Sacks also uses parallelism (another kind of repetition) in his sentences with series. Parallelism is a key tool for writing coherent sentences and paragraphs. (For more on parallelism and repetitions, see CHAPTER 16, USING PARALLELISM FOR CLARITY AND EMPHASIS and REPEATING IMPORTANT WORDS, and CHAPTER 17, PARALLELISM.)

pages 310–311 and page 309 and pages 337–339

Conjunctions

Conjunctions and other transitional words or phrases indicate the logical relationship between ideas. In the following sentences, in which two clauses are linked by different conjunctions, notice the subtle changes in the relationship between the two ideas:

➤ The athlete stretched, **and** he studied her carefully.
➤ The athlete raced **while** he filmed her with his iPhone.
➤ The athlete frowned **because** he was making her nervous.
➤ The athlete shouted out, **so** he walked away.
➤ The athlete won the next race; **later**, he was glad he had left the track.

» GUIDING READERS WITH THE INTRODUCTION AND THE CONCLUSION

Your introduction and conclusion orient your readers to the purpose of your essay as a whole. In fact, readers intentionally read these two sections for guidance and clarification.

An Effective Introduction

Experienced writers know that the opening paragraph is their best chance to arouse the reader's interest with provocative information; identify rhetorical opportunity, topic, purpose, and writer as worthy of consideration; and set the overall tone. Introductions have no set length; they can be as brief as a couple of sentences or as long as two or more paragraphs, sometimes even longer.

Although introductions always appear first, they are often drafted and revised after other parts of an essay. Just like the thesis statements they often include, introductions evolve during the drafting and revising stages, as the material is shaped, focused, and developed toward fulfilling the writer's overall purpose. Most writers experiment with several different introductions to determine which one is most effective. Most important, an effective introduction makes the intended audience want to read on.

In the following paragraph, Robert Stepto introduces his memoir with a story about the family's piano.

> **Here now in its Connecticut home, the black piano nestles in a corner of the dining room, which I like to call the music corner. On the surrounding walls are musical images: Della Robbia's Florentine dancing youths, Vincent Smith's print, "Riding on a Blue Note: Round Midnight." Atop the piano, besides the mail order catalogs which get dumped there, and the trays of cassettes which should be better housed closer to the audio equipment, are piles of music from three generations of family, music that just stuck to the piano like filings to a black magnet, and traveled with it into the present.**
>
> **—Robert Stepto, _Blue as the Lake_ [The Piano]**

Stepto's homely introduction to his life, his home, immediately grabs readers' attention with his plain-spoken description of the piano as heirloom, artistic inspiration, and mail dump!

You can awaken the interest of your audience by writing introductions in a number of ways.

Opening with an Unusual Fact or Statistic

Americans aren't just reading fewer books, but are reading less and less of everything, in any medium. That's the doleful conclusion of "To Read or Not to Read," a report released last week by the National Endowment for the Arts.

—Jennifer Howard, "Americans Are Closing the Book on Reading, Study Finds"

Opening with an Intriguing Statement

I belong to a Clan of One-Breasted Women. My mother, my grandmothers, and six aunts have all had mastectomies. Seven are dead. The two who survive have just completed rounds of chemotherapy and radiation.

—Terry Tempest Williams, "The Clan of One-Breasted Women" [My Mother, Grandmother, Aunts]

Opening with an Anecdote or Example

I chuckled in amusement . . . as President Obama regaled the audience with his humor in what has to be one of the most enjoyable roles for the commander-in-chief: standup comedian at the annual dinner for the White House Correspondents Association. Obama's pace and timing were a lot better than those of the professional comics charged with bringing down the house that night. . . . Obama . . . was smooth and effortless, confident that his zingers would find their mark. His swag quotient was also pretty high that night. He let it be known that his musical prowess consisted of more than a melodically accurate one-off rendition of a line from Al Green's R&B classic "Let's Stay Together," which he had delivered at an Apollo Theater fundraiser three months earlier. Obama's version of the soul legend's tune went viral in Black communities as a sign of the president's effortless embrace of Black Culture despite the criticism that he keeps Blackness at bay. . . . At the Correspondents' dinner, Obama showed his appreciation for Hip Hop and proved his Rap bona fides, and not just by citing the easy or apparent fare. To truly strut his stuff, he'd have to display an aficionado's grasp of Rap Culture's rage and appeal and flash a little insider savvy.

—Michael Eric Dyson, "Orator in Chief"

Opening with a Question

A vast question loomed over all of my learning with the youth of South Vista [California]: what is the purpose of schooling in a pluralist society? The history of schooling in the United States, a country home to epic linguistic, racial, and cultural diversity, has traditionally defined this purpose rather clearly. The purpose of schooling has been to transition or mainstream the ways of knowing and being of those whose cultures and languages fall outside the dominant stream into White, DAE [dominant American English], middle-class norms. Yet volumes of research and theorizing in the past three decades have profoundly challenged these narrow assimilatory goals. This work has critiqued both the unsatisfactory academic results for young people of color and the perpetuation of racial and cultural bias through assimilatory models of education.

—Django Paris, *Language across Difference* [Purpose of School]

Opening with an Appropriate Quotation

"My wife and I like the kind of trouble you've been stirring, Miss Williams," he said, with a smile and a challenge. He had an avuncular, wizardy twinkle, very Albus Dumbledore. It made me feel feisty and smart, like Hermione Granger. They liked my kind of trouble. But let this be a lesson: When a woman of my great dignity and years loses her sanity and starts imagining she's one of Harry Potter's magical little friends, you can be sure that the cosmic gyroscope is wobbling off its center. . . .

—Patricia J. Williams, *Open House: Of Family, Friends, Food, Piano Lessons, and the Search for a Room of My Own* [My Kind of Trouble]

Opening with General Information or Background About the Topic

Scientists have long touted the benefits of the Mediterranean diet for heart health. But now researchers are finding more and more evidence that the diet can keep you healthy in other ways, too, including lowering the risk of certain cancers and easing the pain and stiffness of arthritis.

—Melissa Gotthardt, "The Miracle Diet"

Opening with a Thesis Statement

An unhappy childhood can be the making of a writer, providing the compulsion to tell stories and the themes to put in them. By his own admission, that's the case with Richard Matheson. In an introduction to his *Collected Stories*, he noted that his mother was an orphan before she was ten. In her early teens, she emigrated from Norway to the United States, where, "insecure and frightened, thrust into an alien environment," as Matheson put it, she married a fellow immigrant and taught her children to distrust the outside world. Soon she took to religion while her husband took to drink. Three years after Matheson was born in 1926, his parents separated. Subsequently, his mother and his older sister raised him in an atmosphere of repression and suspicion.

—David Morrell, *Stars in My Eyes: My Love Affair with Books, Movies, and Music* [The Making of a Writer]

However you open your essay, use your introduction to specify your topic, engage your readers' attention, initiate an appropriate tone aligned with your purpose, and establish your credibility.

An Effective Conclusion

Just as a good introduction tantalizes readers, a good conclusion satisfies them. It helps readers recognize the important points of your essay and the significance of those points while, at the same time, wrapping up the essay in a meaningful, thought-provoking way. As you draft and revise, you may want to keep a list of ideas for your conclusion. Some suggestions for writing effective conclusions follow, beginning with the reliable method of simply restating the thesis and main points. This kind of conclusion can be effective for a long essay that includes several important points that you want the reader to recall.

Rephrasing the Thesis and Summarizing the Main Points

The Endangered Species Act should not take into account economic considerations. Economics doesn't know how to value a species or a forest. Its logic drives people to exploit resources to the point of extinction. The Endangered Species Act tells us that extinction is morally unacceptable. It was enacted by a Congress and president in a wise mood, to express a higher value than a bottom line.

—Donella Meadows, "Not Seeing the Forest for the Dollar Bills"

Calling Attention to Larger Issues

While a [maple syrup] boil can have you hanging around the evaporator for twelve hours at a time and doing something to adjust the fire or draw off syrup every twenty or thirty minutes, you're generally just hanging out.

There's no time to grade papers, and not even much time to read. But it's perfect for talking, for dreaming, and for listening to Caleb lift the occasional swirling fiddle tune up into the stream. As when I worked with Matthew putting up the roof, this has proved a great time with both boys. At Middlebury College I can count on extended conversations with students in my office. But our own colleague's children, not surprisingly, rarely want to settle down for a long talk with Rita and me in the living room. At the sugarhouse, though, we can all have a never-ending sequence of five-minute conversations—about family members near and far, about movies or books, about the sounds and animals and boulders and brooks of the surrounding woods. These bursts of talk add up. They are the real sugaring off from the seasons that have brought us here.

—John Elder, *The Frog Run: Words & Wildness in the Vermont Woods* [Sugaring]

Calling for a Change in Action or Attitude

Although [Anna Julia] Cooper published *A Voice* in 1892, its political implications remain relevant to twenty-first-century scholars and activists. As our society grows increasingly multicultural, and the borders between colors and countries grow evermore porous, the strategies for organizing communities of resistance must necessarily follow suit. Academics and activists engaged in efforts to transform inequitable social relations benefit from thinking not only about what separates but also what unites humanity.

—Kathy L. Glass, "Tending to the Roots"

Concluding with a Vivid Image

The more I wrote about [my jealousy] and the more I thought of the [AIDS] movie, the angrier I got at how often this writer friend mentioned her money to me, because that summer Sam and I had almost none, and she knew this. I kept writing about my childhood, about how often I had longed for what other girls had and for what other families seemed to be about. I taped Hillel's line to the wall by my desk: "I get up. I walk. I fall down. Meanwhile, I keep dancing." The way I dance is by writing. So I wrote about trying to pay closer attention to the world, about taking things less seriously, moving more slowly, stepping outside more often. Eventually what I was writing got funnier and compassion broke through, for me and also for my writer friend. And at this point I told her, as kindly as possible, that I needed a sabbatical from our friendship. Life really is so short. And finally I felt that my jealousy and I were strangely beautiful, like the men in the AIDS movie, doing the dance of the transformed self, dancing like an old long-legged bird.

—Anne Lamott, "Jealousy"

Connecting the Introduction and the Conclusion

Throughout his book-length study, Howard Rheingold provides an insightful examination of the ways that new media are shaping our lives at the same time that we are shaping their use, all the while stressing the importance of keeping alert to the powers and limits of any new technology. In *Net Smart*, he opens with the influence of media—and then, in his conclusion, he emphasizes that influence.

Introduction

> The future of digital culture—yours, mine, and ours—depends on how well we learn to use the media that have infiltrated, amplified, distracted, enriched, and complicated our lives. How you employ a search engine, stream video from your phonecam, or update your Facebook status matters to you and everyone, because the ways people use new media in the first years of an emerging communication regime can influence the way those media end up being used and misused for decades to come. Instead of confining my exploration to whether or not Google is making us stupid, Facebook is commoditizing our privacy, or Twitter is chopping our attention into microslices (all good questions), I've been asking myself and others how to use social media intelligently, humanely, and above all mindfully. This book is about what I've learned.
>
> —Howard Rheingold, *Net Smart: How to Thrive Online*

Whatever technique you choose for your conclusion, provide readers with a sense of closure. Bear in mind that they may be wondering, "So what? Why have you told me all this?" Your conclusion gives you an opportunity to address that concern. If there is any chance that readers may not understand your purpose, use your conclusion to clarify why you think they needed to read what they have just read. Rheingold does not leave his readers with any doubt about what his thesis might be: we are being influenced by various media, just as that media is influenced by us.

Conclusion

As laptop-carrying, smart-phone-using members of the digitally connected infosphere, we need to start by learning a new discipline: the literacy of attention. As citizens and cocreators of the cultures that shape us, we need participatory media skills. As collaborators in the collective intelligence that faces massive problems from global warming to water-sharing conflicts, we need to learn literacies of cooperation, mass collaboration, and collective action. As dwellers in the network society, we must understand and master the nature along with use of social networks, technical and human—and grasp the way both mediated and face-to-face social practices can increase or drain social capital. And in a world where nobody can trust the authority of any text they find online, the ability to quickly evaluate the validity or bogosity of information is no longer an intellectual nicety. Critical thinking about media practices has become an essential, learnable mental skill.

—Howard Rheingold, *Net Smart: How to Thrive Online*

≫ REVISING PARAGRAPHS PURPOSEFULLY

When revising an essay, you must consider the effectiveness of the individual paragraphs at the same time as you consider how well those paragraphs work together to achieve the overall purpose, which your thesis statement declares. Some writers like to revise at the paragraph level before addressing larger concerns; other writers cannot work on individual paragraphs until they have grappled with larger issues related to the rhetorical situation (the opportunity, overall purpose, rhetorical audience, and context) or have finalized their thesis statement. The following checklist can guide you in revising your paragraphs.

- Identify the clear (or clearly implied) topic sentence.
- Explain how all the ideas in the paragraph relate to the topic sentence. How does each sentence link to previous and later ones? Are the sentences arranged in chronological, spatial, emphatic, or logical order, or are they arranged in some other pattern?
- What transitions are effective?

- What evidence do you have that the paragraph is adequately developed? What idea or detail might be missing?
- How does the paragraph itself link to the preceding and following ones?

(See CHAPTER 13, TIPS FOR REVISION.)

pages 244–245

Because there is no predetermined order to the writing process, you can do whatever works best for you each time you revise. Be guided by the principles and strategies discussed in this chapter but trust also in your own good sense. As you work to develop your paragraphs into a full essay, you can rely on the various rhetorical strategies for development that are explained fully in the following chapter.

The Power of Paragraphs

15 Rhetorical Strategies for Development

- Identify the rhetorical strategies for development and describe how they relate to one another.
- Explain how and why rhetorical strategies are often combined.
- Determine which rhetorical strategies (or combination of strategies) are most effective for specific genres.
- Evaluate the advantages and limitations of a rhetorical strategy (or a combination of strategies) to fulfill an assignment or compose in a specific genre.
- Assess how different organizational methods and rhetorical strategies can be applied to print, oral, multimedia, and multimodal assignments.

Narration, description, exemplification, definition, classification and division, comparison and contrast, cause-and-effect analysis, process analysis, argument—these rhetorical methods of development are strategies employed to explore, expand, and organize ideas. As you develop paragraphs, essays, and other compositions in various genres across media, understanding the advantages and limitations of each of these strategies can help you make more effective rhetorical choices. They are also the way we make sense of the world, no matter what media or genre we are using. Regardless of culture, nationality, gender, age, and ability, we all turn to these strategies to find what we want to say and to situate it in a context. We also employ these strategies as templates for interpreting what someone else is communicating to us. Each of these strategies can stand alone, but more often they complement one another.

When we use the method of *comparison*, for instance, we often need to *define* what exactly we are comparing.

»» NARRATION

One of the rhetorical strategies you already know well is **narration**, which tells a story that has **characters** (people in the story), **dialogue** (direct speech by the characters), a **setting** (the time and place), description (selected sensory and sensibility details about the characters, dialogue, and setting—see also Description, discussed on pages 280-281),

Strategies

Figure 15.1 *Trip through the bottom of Canyon de Chelly.*

and **plot** (the sequence of events). Narrations help us make sense of the world for ourselves and for others—whether we are retelling a fairy tale or family legend or recounting the final minutes of the Super Bowl or our canyon-bottom tour of Canyon de Chelly (Figure 15.1).

Narration can frame an entire story ("Robin Hood" or meeting your new roommate), or it can provide an example (why you can depend on your brother) or support an argument (those final plays proved the Patriots to be the better team). Usually narrations are verbal—we want to tell "what happened." Verbal narration, which appears in both print and spoken media (including newspapers, movies, television and radio), tells us, for example, about the Minneapolis protests after the killing of George Floyd, the latest COVID-19 vaccine developments, the president's exchanges with the World Health Organization, the ongoing debate about whether fans should be in the stadium, obituaries, and the local school board meeting. Such verbal narrations might consist of one particular sequence of events or include a series of separate incidents that shape an overall narrative.

Were you to compose a narration about the photograph of the jeep and floodwater at Canyon de Chelly, what might it be? Would your narration account for your entire vacation, beginning when you left home, or might you concentrate only on the canyon-bottom tour? In addition to tapping all the elements of a narration (characters, dialogue, setting, description, and plot), would you also use an **anecdote** (a brief, illustrative story that propels the narrative)? From what **point of view** would you tell the story? (For more on point of view, see

narration a detailed account of events as in a story

characters people in the story

dialogue direct speech by the characters in a narration

setting the time and place of a narration

plot the sequence of events in a narration

anecdote a brief story that illustrates a point

point of view the perspective of the narrator in telling a story

CHAPTER 12, ELEMENTS OF LITERATURE.) Would you use your own point of view, that of the Navajo guide, your parents' perspective, or that of your sibling? And what might be the **climax** of your narration, the turning point toward a resolution? Would you recount your narration in chronological order, or might you use **flashback** to account for past events or **flash forward** to account for future events? Purposefully interruptive, these techniques add interest to a story, providing glimpses of other times that illuminate the present as it is being recounted in an otherwise straightforward, chronological organization.

Whether used to supply information, explain, provide an example, set a mood, or argue a point, narration easily reaches most audiences and often serves as a fitting response to opportunities for change. Given its versatility, narration can serve as the basis for a good deal of your academic, personal, and work-related writing.

Strategies

climax turning point in a narration

flashback narrative technique that accounts for past events

flash forward narrative technique that accounts for future events

description a verbal accounting of physical and mental experiences

sensory details what we see, hear, smell, touch, or taste

sensibility details having to do with intellectual, emotional, or physical states

≫ DESCRIPTION

Specific details converge in **description**, a verbal accounting of what we have experienced physically and mentally. Thus, our descriptions always carry with them **sensory details** having to do with our physical sensations (what we see, hear, smell, touch, or taste) or **sensibility details** having to do with our intellectual, emotional, or physical states (alertness, gullibility, grief, fear, loathing, exuberance, clumsiness, relaxation, agitation, and so on).

José Antonio Burciaga's description (and extended definition) of the *tortilla* (Figure 15.2) relies heavily on sensory details:

© Vulpix/Big Stock Photo

Figure 15.2 *The homely, versatile, delicious tortilla.*

For Mexicans over the centuries, the *tortilla* has served as the spoon and fork, the plate and the napkin. . . . When I was growing up in El Paso, . . . I used to visit a *tortilla* factory in an ancient adobe building near the open *mercado* in Ciudad Juárez. As I approached, I could hear the rhythmic slapping of the *masa* as the skilled vendors outside the factory formed it into balls and patted them into perfectly round corn cakes between the palms of their hands. The wonderful aroma and the speed with which the women counted so many dozens of *tortillas* out of warm wicker baskets still linger in my mind. Watching them at work convinced me that the most handsome and *deliciosas tortillas* are handmade. Although machines are faster, they can never

adequately replace generation-to-generation experience. There's no place in the factory assembly line for the tender slaps that give each *tortilla* character. The best thing that can be said about mass-producing *tortillas* is that it makes it possible for many people to enjoy them.

—José Antonio Burciaga, *I Remember Masa* [Handmade vs. Mass-Produced Tortillas]

The sensory details that infuse Burciaga's description of the *tortilla* make it entertaining and memorable. Because description relies on details, it defines what is being described in specific ways.

»» EXEMPLIFICATION

The rhetorical strategy of **exemplification** involves making a generalization and using an example or series of examples in support of that generalization. If you want to clarify why Veronica is the best salesclerk in your favorite sporting goods store, you can provide a series of examples that define *best salesclerk:* Veronica is herself a competitive athlete; she has positive energy and is knowledgeable about all the equipment, from running shoes and jackets to cycles and kayaks. She lets customers know when items will be going on sale, and, best of all, she never pushes a sale. She realizes by now that if customers really want it, they will come back for it when they have the money. Or if you want to add interest to a generalization about your terrific Santa Fe vacation, you might talk about the clear blue skies, warm days, and cool nights; you could include anecdotes about the bargain rate you found online for your hotel room, running into Keanu Reeves at the Folk Art Museum, attending the Santa Domingo Pueblo feast day, and joining a Friday night art gallery walk and meeting artists; you could describe shopping on the plaza, where you found turquoise jewelry, Acoma Pueblo pottery, and Hopi-made Christmas presents. You could also include tantalizing, sensory descriptions of the delicious regional food—Frito pie, chocolate-covered chile creams, *carne adovada*, and *natillas*. All these examples not only add interest to the generalization that you had a "terrific vacation" but also help define exactly what you mean by that phrase.

exemplification the use of examples

In the passage that follows, Pulitzer Prize winner William Styron defines *suicidal* through his examples of suicidal thoughts.

He asked me if I was suicidal, and I reluctantly told him yes. I did not particularize—since there seemed no need to—did not tell him that in truth many of the artifacts of my house had become potential devices for my own destruction: the attic rafters (and an outside maple or two) a means to hang myself, the garage a place to inhale carbon monoxide, the bathtub a vessel to receive the flow from my opened arteries. The kitchen knives in their drawers had but one purpose for me. Death by heart attack seemed particularly inviting, absolving me as it would of active responsibility, and I had toyed with the idea of self-induced pneumonia—a long, frigid, shirt-sleeved hike through the rainy woods. Nor had I overlooked an ostensible accident . . . by walking in front of a truck on the highway nearby. These thoughts may seem outlandishly macabre—a strained joke—but they are genuine.

—William Styron, *Darkness Visible* [Suicidal Thoughts]

Styron admits to his physician that he is, indeed, depressed to the point of being suicidal, but he reserves the persuasive examples of his mental state for readers of his memoir.

»» DEFINITION

If you were to define the animal in the photograph (Figure 15.3), you might classify it as a "mammal" and then distinguish this mammal from others similar to it, describing its features and perhaps coming up with a definitive name for it. Thus, **definition** makes use of other strategies such as classification and division, exemplification, and description.

> **definition** a classification that distinguishes, describes, and names something

Whenever we are introduced to something new—a new word, academic subject, sport, activity, or language—we need to develop a new vocabulary. Whether we are learning the vocabulary of cooking (*chop, slice, mince, stir, fold, whip, fry*), golf (*ace, birdie, bogey, chip, drive, duff*), or human evolution (*prosimians, hominoids, paleoanthropology, australopithecines*), we are expanding our world with new concepts and ideas. Definition is essential to our learning and our understanding.

No matter what we are learning or learning about, we use definition. And whether or not we are conscious of it, we always employ the three steps of definition:

GUDKOV ANDREY/Shutterstock.com

Figure 15.3 *A primate and her baby.*

1. We name the specific concept, action, person, or thing; in other words, we provide a term for it.
2. Then, we classify that term, or place it in a more general category. (See Classification and Division, pages 284-285.)
3. Finally, we differentiate the specific term from all the other concepts, actions, persons, or things in that general category, often using examples. (See Exemplification, page 281.)

For instance, if you are studying human evolution, you will no doubt need to learn what distinguishes primates from other mammals.

Term	Class	Differentiation
Primates are	mammals	that have "a lack of strong specialization in structure; prehensile hands and feet, usually with opposable thumbs and great toes; flattened nails instead of claws on the digits; acute vision with some degree of binocular vision; relatively large brain exhibiting a degree of cortical folding; and prolonged postnatal dependency. No primate exhibits all these features, and indeed the diversity of primate forms has produced disagreement as to their proper classification." —Encyclopedia Britannica

The preceding is a **formal** (or **sentence**) **definition**, the kind you will find in a reference book. But it is not the only kind of definition. An **extended definition**, such as this one from primate.org, provides additional differentiating information:

> **Primates are the mammals that are humankind's closest biological relatives. We share 98.4% of [our] DNA with chimpanzees. Apes, monkeys, and prosimians such as lorises, bush babies, and lemurs make up the 234 species of the family tree. About 90% of the primates live in tropical forests. They play an integral role in the ecology of their habitat. They help the forest by being pollinators, seed predators, and seed dispersers.**

A **historical definition**, like this one from chimpanzoo.org/history of primates, provides a longitudinal (over a period of time) overview of what the term has described over time, offering additional concepts and terms:

> **65 mya** (million years ago): Paleocene epoch begins. . . . The earliest primates evolve. These primates were small insectivores who were most likely terrestrial. During this epoch, primates began to include food items such as seeds, fruits, nuts, and leaves in their diet.

> **53.5 mya:** Eocene epoch begins. Primates diversify and some become arboreal. Primates have developed prehensile hands and feet with opposable thumbs and toes and their claws have evolved into nails. Arboreal primates evolve relatively longer lower limbs for vertical clinging and leaping. Their eye sockets are oriented more frontally resulting in stereoscopic vision. Primates of this epoch belong to the prosimian family.

formal (or sentence) definition a dictionary or encyclopedia reference that classifies, describes, and names something

extended definition a classification that provides extended information to describe, distinguish, and name something

historical definition an overview over a period of time of how a concept or term has been used

Strategies

One of the best things about learning a new subject is that the initial vocabulary introduces more vocabulary, so the learning never ends.

Sometimes, you will need to write a **negative definition** to clarify for your readers not only what a term means but also what it does not mean. In conversation, you might say, "When I talk about success, I'm not talking about making money." For you, success might instead involve having personal integrity, experiencing fulfillment in interpersonal relationships, and taking on exciting professional challenges. Even primates can be defined negatively, as W. E. Le Gros Clark wrote in *The Antecedents of Man*: "The Primates as a whole have preserved rather a generalized anatomy and . . . are to be mainly distinguished . . . by a negative feature—their lack of specialization."

Finally, you may come across or come up with a **stipulative definition**, which limits—or stipulates—the range of a term's meaning or application, thereby announcing to the reader exactly how the writer is using the term in the specific rhetorical situation. For instance, if you find yourself writing about *success*, you might define your meaning for your readers like this: "In this paper, *success* will be defined in terms of how quickly college graduates obtain employment in their chosen fields." Or if you are writing about *primates*, you might stipulate that you are concentrating on a twenty-first-century conception of them. As you can see, definition provides the foundation for learning, understanding, and communicating. and throughout this chapter, classification and division, exemplification, and description all work in service of definition.

negative definition a classification that distinguishes a concept or term by showing what it is not

stipulative definition a classification that is specific to a particular context

⟫ CLASSIFICATION AND DIVISION

classification and division the act of creating categories that distinguish information, objects, or other concepts

Like definition, **classification and division** first places something in a general category and then distinguishes it from other things within that category. Department stores, hospitals, telephone books, libraries, grocery stores, and bookstores are all classified and divided in order to enhance accessibility to their information or contents. When you go into a hospital, for instance, you look at the directory by the entrance to find out how the areas in the building are classified (reception area, visitor information center, emergency room, outpatient clinic, waiting room, obstetrics, patient rooms, gift shop, and cafeteria). Then, when you make your way to one of those areas (patient rooms, for instance), you look to see how that general area has been divided up (into floors and individual rooms on those floors). In important ways, the classification of hospital areas and the further division and distinction of those same areas define those locations. The hospital room you want to find is defined by belonging to the category of *patient rooms* and then differentiated from (or divided from) other patient rooms by being on the fifth floor, at the end of the hallway, to the left. Just as with definition, then, when you use classification and division, you provide a term and then place that term in its general category of origin.

≫ COMPARISON AND CONTRAST

We use **comparison and contrast**, a two-part method of rhetorical development, from the moment we wake up (often comparing the advantages of getting up without enough rest with those of staying in bed) until we go to bed at night (comparing the option of getting rest with that of staying up and working). We use comparison to consider how two or more things are alike, and we use contrast to show how related things are different. This rhetorical strategy, which helps us clarify issues, can be used to explain, make a decision, shape an argument, open a discussion, or craft an entertaining narrative.

When you do decide to get up, you might want to choose a cereal to have for breakfast, knowing that you have Lucky Charms and Cheerios on your shelf (Figure 15.4). Because both of these share the characteristics of cold breakfast cereals, you have a **basis for comparison**. In order to decide which you want

Strategies

comparison and contrast a description of similarities and differences

basis for comparison shared characteristics that are used to understand objects, people, and ideas

© Steven Lunetta Photography, 2007

Figure 15.4 Grocery aisle of cereals.

to eat, you will intuitively set up **points of comparison** to clarify the ways in which the two are the same (both are cereals, served cold, eaten for breakfast) as well as the ways in which they are different (in terms of taste, nutrition, ingredients). You may already know the answers to the questions of which cereal tastes better, which one is better for you, and which one will sustain you until lunch. But you may not be familiar with the information that supports those answers, information that appears on the cereal boxes themselves.

The nutritional information panels on the boxes indicate that both cold cereals have been approved by the American Heart Association because both are low in saturated fats and cholesterol, with 0 grams of saturated fat and 0 milligrams of cholesterol. Both are also pretty low in sodium (200 milligrams and 210 milligrams), carbohydrates (25 grams and 22 grams), and protein (2 grams and 3 grams). But neither of the cereals comes close to fulfilling recommended daily allowances (RDAs) of carbohydrates and protein, as the charts on the boxes show. What about the recommended daily requirements (RDRs) for vitamins and minerals? The nutrition charts show that these cereals provide the same amounts of vitamins A, C, D, B_6, and B_{12}. In terms of other nutrients—calcium, thiamin, riboflavin, niacin, folic acid, and zinc—they are also the same. Cheerios, however, offers more iron (nearly half the RDR), phosphorus, magnesium, and copper. But will those differences affect your choice?

points of comparison areas that show how two things are the same and how they are different

What distinctive contrast will be the deciding factor? The amount of sugar? Lucky Charms has 13 grams, whereas Cheerios has only 1 gram. The extra sugar might make Lucky Charms taste better, which may tip the scale. If you want enough energy to sustain you until lunch, however, you might choose Cheerios, so that you do not start your day with a sugar high and then crash midmorning.

The information you can glean from the side of a cereal box helps you understand the ingredients of the cereal and make an informed choice. If you wanted to discuss the choice of cereal with children and argue for the "right" choice, you could use much of that information. Whether you could ultimately persuade them to choose Cheerios over Lucky Charms is, of course, another story. You would, however, be informing them through the method of comparison and contrast.

cause-and-effect analysis an explanation for how some things have occurred or a prediction that certain events will lead to specific effects

»» CAUSE-AND-EFFECT ANALYSIS

Whenever you find yourself concentrating on either causes or effects, explaining why certain events have occurred or predicting that particular events or situations will lead to specific effects, you are conducting a **cause-and-effect analysis** (sometimes referred to as a *cause-and-consequence analysis*). The opportunity for change in these situations comes with your ability to use words to address your questions, to explore why some things happen, or to predict the effects of an event or situation. Cause-and-effect analysis can be used to explain (your opinion on why Ohio State is going to the Rose Bowl), to entertain (your description of what happens when the family gathers for Thanksgiving), to speculate (your thoughts on the causes of autism), or to argue a point (your stance on the effects of pollution).

We spend a good deal of time considering the causes of situations. For instance, when one of your bookshelves collapses, you check to see if the shelf braces are screwed into studs, if the books are too heavy, or if you need additional supporting braces. If you have a fender bender on the way to school, you think about what led to the accident. Some of the reasons may be outside your control: low visibility, an icy road, a poorly marked road, missing taillights on the car in front of you. Other causes may reside in you: your tailgating, speeding, or inattention (due to eating, putting a CD in, or talking or texting on your cell phone).

We spend just as much time—maybe even more—evaluating the effects of situations and events. You are enrolled in college and already considering the effects of having a college degree, most of them positive (you will have to pay for your coursework and work hard, but you are likely to be well employed when you are finished). If you are considering marriage, you are analyzing the positive and not-so-positive effects of that decision (you will live with the love of your life, but you will have to relocate to Sacramento, where you may not be able to transfer all your credits). If you follow current events, you know that the effects of the controversial wars in Iraq and Afghanistan include the deaths of nearly 7,000 Americans, well over 100,000 Iraqis, approximately 20,000 Afghanis (estimates vary widely), and a good deal of public discontent.

Before-and-after photographs, such as those in Figure 15.5 and Figure 15.6 often lead us to wonder what happened and what caused the change. The first of this pair of photographs shows a beautiful old church surrounded by big trees. It is Trinity Episcopal Church in Pass Christian, Mississippi, which was built in 1849. Set among live oaks and lush lawns, Trinity served as a landmark for over a century. In the second photo, some—but not all—of the big trees are still standing, but there is no church, just the stairs and pathway leading up to the church. This second photograph was taken on August 18, 1969, the day after Hurricane Camille smashed into the Mississippi Gulf Coast, with wind speeds in excess of two hundred miles per hour and water levels twenty-four feet above normal high tide, making it the strongest storm in U.S. history. The effects of Camille, by the time it had dissipated on August 22, included 256 deaths and $1.4 billion in damages, the equivalent of nearly $10,134 billion in 2020. Even though chances are slim that anyone in your class will have heard of, let alone remember, Hurricane Camille, you understand its effects. Developing your ability to examine

Image courtesy of NOAA

Figure 15.5 *Before Hurricane Camille.*

Image courtesy of NOAA

Figure 15.6 *Same location, after Hurricane Camille.*

situations or events for their causes or effects, and teasing out a relevant analysis, will help you better understand your world.

»» PROCESS ANALYSIS

Whenever you develop your ideas in order to explain how something is done, you are engaging in **process analysis**. Process analysis involves dividing up an entire process into a series of ordered steps so that your audience can understand the relationship among those steps and maybe even replicate them. To that end, process analysis always includes a series of separate, chronological steps that provide details about a process and often reads like a narration. Many process analyses take the form of a list, with distinct and often numbered steps, as in recipes, instruction manuals (for tasks from using a small appliance to assembling a toy), and installation guides (for everything from showerheads and garbage disposals to computer software). Whether the purpose of the process analysis is to inform (how volcanoes erupt, how leukemia is treated), entertain (how to gain weight on vacation, how a ten-year-old boy makes hot chocolate), or argue a point (the best way to quit a job, learn to write, develop as a reader), the analysis itself responds to a problem: someone needs to know how to do something or wants to learn how something is done.

process analysis breaking down into a series of steps how something occurs

Television programs and YouTube videos present processes we can duplicate or appreciate: we can watch the Food Network to learn about Rachel Ray's plan for an easy-to-prepare Thanksgiving dinner (one that includes deep-fried turkey and double-chocolate gooey cake) or be entertained by *Say Yes to the Dress*, a not-always-flattering analysis of the process brides-to-be move through in their search for the perfect wedding dress. We can view YouTube videos to learn how to compose an iron-clad will or *How to Draw Comics the Marvel Way*, although these analyses might not provide enough training for us to duplicate the processes they describe. Whether processes are conveyed orally, in writing, or visually, whether we are taking directions from our mom, reading a car-repair manual, or watching *30 Minute Meals*, we are using process analysis.

directive process analysis a series of steps used to teach an audience how to duplicate the occurrence of something

Process analyses come in two basic forms. **Directive process analysis** is used to teach the audience how to do something, how to duplicate the process. **Informative process analysis**, on the other hand, is used to explain a process so that the audience can understand, enjoy, or be persuaded. Either kind of process analysis can constitute an entire message or be one part of a larger message (within a novel, proposal, report, or essay, for example).

informative process analysis a series of steps used to explain how something occurs or has occurred

If you have ever taken an airplane trip, you are familiar with directive process analyses. Both the passenger safety card in the pocket of the seat in front of you

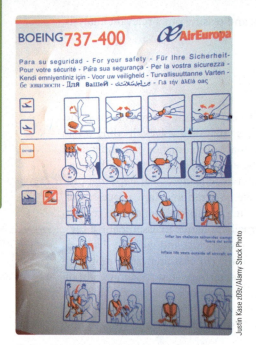

BOEING 737-400   AirEuropa

Para su seguridad - For your safety - Für Ihre Sicherheit-
Pour votre sécurité - Pàra sua segurança - Per la vostra sicurezza -
Kendi emniyentiniz için - Voor uw veiligheid - Turvallisuuttanne Varten -
Бе зопасности - Для Вашей - العربية - Гiá τήν áλεíα oας

Justin Kase z09z/Alamy Stock Photo

Figure 15.7 *A passenger safety card that outlines the necessary steps to take on take-off, landing, and in case of turbulence or an emergency.*

(Figure 15.7) and the oral instructions from the flight attendant serve as perfect examples. As you follow along with the card, the attendant recites and enacts the step-by-step directions for various safety procedures during takeoffs, landings, and emergencies: how to buckle and unbuckle your seat belt, how to put an oxygen mask on yourself and help a child do so, how to locate and inflate the life preserver, and so on. Many passengers can understand the language in which the flight attendant is giving the instructions, but, for those who cannot, the visuals on the card provide the details necessary for full understanding. Whether the passengers take in the information aurally, visually, or both aurally and visually, the directive process analysis allows them to duplicate the steps described.

The following example of the second type of process analysis, informative process analysis, comes from a suspense novel. The author uses process analysis to address the problem emerging in the opening paragraph.

Detective Matt Chacon knew that unlike the TV cop shows—where actors sit in front of a computer monitor and instantaneously pull up a digital fingerprint record that matches a perp or a victim—trying to ID someone using prints in the real world can be mind-numbing work. There are thousands of prints that have never been entered into the computer data banks, and thousands more on file that, because of poor quality, are virtually unusable for comparison purposes. On top of that, figure in the small cop shops who haven't got the money, manpower, and equipment to transfer print records to computers, and the unknown number of print records that were left in closed felony cases and sit forgotten in basement archives at police departments all over the country, and you've got a data-bank system that is woefully inadequate and incomplete. Finally, while each fingerprint is unique, the difference between prints can be so slight that a very careful analysis must be made to confirm a perfect match. Even then, different experts can debate the results endlessly, since it isn't an exact science.

Chacon had started his career in law enforcement as a crime scene technician with a specialty in fingerprint and tool-mark identification, so of course Lieutenant Molina had sent him off to the state police headquarters to work the state and federal data banks to see if he could get a match.

He'd been at it all night long and his coffee was starting to taste like sludge, his eyes were itchy, and his butt was numb. Using an automated identification system, Chacon had digitally stored the victim's prints in the computer and then started scanning for a match against those already on file.

The computer system could identify possible matches quickly, but then it became a process of carefully analyzing each one and scoring them according to a detailed classification system. So far, Chacon had examined six dozen sets of prints that looked like possible equivalents and had struck out. But there was another baker's dozen to review.

He clicked on the next record, adjusted the monitor to enhance the resolution of the smudged prints, and began scoring them in sequence. Whoever had printed the subject had done a piss-poor job. He glanced at the agency identifier. It was a Department of Corrections submission.

Chacon finished the sequence and used a split screen to compare his scoring to the victim's print. It showed a match. He rechecked the scoring and verified his findings.

—Michael McGarrity, *Everyone Dies* [Fingerprints]

As it informs and entertains, this process analysis argues a point—that fingerprint matching is a complicated and often time-consuming procedure, not the quick fix depicted by popular media. Process analysis provides the overall structure of the passage—a thesis statement, chronological organization, and purposeful point of view. In addition, the passage uses several other rhetorical strategies for development: comparison and contrast, narration, description, exemplification, and cause-and-effect analysis.

In our culture, directions are no longer given and received only through print or face-to-face interaction. Instead of reading a cookbook, we might turn on the Food Network; instead of hiring a plumber, we might visit homedepot. com. So whether you decide to convey a process analysis in English or another language, over the telephone, Zoom, or by e-mail, in laborious detail or in shorthand, or with or without an accompanying visual depends on your audience's native language, access to various means of communication, and understanding of the subject matter. With process analysis, as with other rhetorical methods, it is important to consider the physical means of delivering and receiving information.

»» ARGUMENT

The words *argument* and *persuasion* are often used interchangeably, despite the technical distinctions between the two terms. **Argument** refers to the verbal or visual delivery of a point of view and the use of logical reasoning to help an audience understand that point of view as true or valid. **Persuasion**, on the other hand, refers to the use of emotions as well as logical reasoning to move the audience a step or two beyond the understanding that accompanies successful argument. The goal of persuasion is to change the mind, point of view, or actions of the audience. Because any visual or verbal argument can easily include emotional appeals as well as logical reasoning and because any argument holds the potential for changing the collective mind or actions of an audience, the broader term *argument* will be used throughout this chapter and this book. (For more on logical reasoning, including logical fallacies, see CHAPTER 8, POSITION ARGUMENTS; for more on deductive and inductive reasoning, see CHAPTER 14, STATING THE MAIN IDEA.)

We employ and respond to arguments all day long, as we work to understand and explain to others the world around or within us. Sometimes, our arguments focus on defending our opinions or questioning the opinions of others—opinions about whether Charlie Sheen should have returned to *Two and a Half Men*, where to get the best pizza, which music venue offers the best nightlife, or whether a vegan diet is truly healthful. Sometimes, argument involves exploring and clarifying our own opinions, so we weigh all sides of an issue and various possible consequences of our final opinion. Often, we employ that kind of analytical argument when we are considering some of life's big issues: surgery, divorce, marriage, a new job, racism, sexism, and so on.

Other times, argument is invitational, in that it invites the audience to understand your position (even if they are not convinced to change their minds or action) and to explain their position to you (even if you are not convinced to change your mind or action). Invitational argument works especially well when the speaker and the audience need to work together to solve a problem (what to do about remote schooling, the spread of the coronavirus, or unemployment), construct a position that represents diverse interests (for or against universal health coverage, the professionalization of college athletics, or affirmative action), or implement a policy that requires broad support (on establishing a draft system or allowing gay marriage).

When we analyze an argument—our own or one someone else is presenting to us—we can consider several elements: an identifiable issue, a claim, common ground, and rhetorical appeals. (For more on making claims, establishing common ground, and using the rhetorical appeals of ethos, logos, and pathos, see CHAPTER 2, ANALYZING RHETORICAL CHOICES.)

Strategies

pages 128–149
pages 258-260

argument the presentation of a point of view and logical reasoning in an effort to persuade an audience that something is true or valid

persuasion the use of emotions as well as logic to move an audience to change their minds or take action

pages 18–33

An **identifiable issue** is the topic under discussion, one that we choose from a multitude of issues we confront daily, from limited service at the university health center to poverty, homelessness, poor-quality schooling, and so on. We do not always take the time to address any one of those problems in any productive way, perhaps because we cannot pinpoint the specific issue within that problem that we want to argue for or against. In other words, we cannot identify an opportunity for change that can be addressed with words.

Suppose you were experiencing both bad service and bad food at a restaurant. That experience might not be a very big deal unless you became violently ill and you thought it was from the salmon, which did not taste quite right. Now you have identified a specific issue you can argue as you express your opinion that either the storage of the fresh seafood or the sanitary conditions of that restaurant are in need of improvement. Or suppose you have identified one specific issue that contributes to the poor test scores of your neighborhood school: most children do not eat breakfast before they come to school.

identifiable issue specific issue related to a problem that can be argued for or against

After you have identified an issue (that hungry school children test poorly), you can make a claim about it, an arguable position you take regarding that issue. Your claim could be that the school should launch a free breakfast program for students. The need for free school breakfasts would be the position you would take in your argument to parents, teachers, administrators, and the school board (Figure 15.8). As you think through the various claims that could be made about the issue (parents should feed their children themselves; parents should provide better after-school support; children need to work harder; teachers need to concentrate on the basics, and so on), you will want to make sure that your claim is one that can be argued and responded to. Citing research can be one of the most persuasive kinds of support, as the U.S. Department of Agriculture demonstrates in a flyer it produced:

> **There are many benefits of breakfast for children. Breakfast provides children with the energy and essential nutrients they need to concentrate on school work and learn. Studies show that breakfast**

Courtesy of the author

Figure 15.8 *A photo of a happy well-nourished child eating a good breakfast before school supports the claim that eating breakfast is important for students.*

provides as much as 25 percent of the recommended daily allowance for key nutrients, such as calcium, protein, vitamins A and B6, magnesium, iron and zinc.

Research shows that children who eat breakfast have higher achievement scores, lower rates of absence and tardiness, and increased concentration in the classroom. . . .

Another important benefit of breakfast for children is that establishing the healthy habit of eating breakfast early in life could stave off many adulthood health problems associated with poor diet, such as diabetes and obesity.

Among all the possible views of school breakfast programs, yours—that school breakfast programs contribute to academic performance—will ground your thesis statement. (See also CHAPTER 13, CRAFTING A WORKING THESIS STATEMENT.)

pages 239-241

In addition to supplying support for your claim, you will also need to establish common ground: the goal, belief, value, or assumption that you share with your audience. In this case, you might say that "academic performance needs to improve," and you could be reasonably certain that your audience would agree. After you have established common ground, you have assured your audience that, despite any misunderstandings or disagreements, you both actually share a good deal, which provides a starting point from which you can speak or write.

You will also employ the rhetorical appeals of ethos, logos, and pathos to make connections with your audience. (See CHAPTER 2, USING THE AVAILABLE MEANS OF PERSUASION.) By establishing common ground and speaking to a nationwide problem involving children and their school performance, you have emphasized *ethos*. By citing research to support your assertion that eating breakfast improves students' health, behavior, and academic performance, you are employing *logos*. And by listing ten reasons children should eat breakfast, starting with the obvious one that no child should go hungry, you are employing *pathos*.

pages 21-31

Argument is a common part of everyday life, whether we are negotiating to change an airline ticket, discussing why Mike D'Antoni left the Houston Rockets, or explaining why we do not want our roommate borrowing our clothes. In some ways, then, everything is an argument. Every time you transfer meaning or understanding from yourself to another person, you have made a successful argument. And every time you have understood what someone else is saying to you, you have responded to a successful argument. No matter what kind they are—visual or verbal, angry or informative, personal or bureaucratic—arguments work to fulfill one of three rhetorical purposes: to express or defend a position, to question or argue against an established belief or course of action, or to invite or persuade an audience to change an opinion or action.

16 Style: An Essential Guide to Effective Sentences

LEARNING OBJECTIVES

- Identify essential sentence parts that create complete sentences.
- Develop unified sentences by avoiding mismatches in sentence parts.
- Develop unified sentences by including necessary words and details.
- Integrate variety and emphasis in sentences.
- Assess accurate word choices for precise sentences.

When you think of the word *style* you probably think of words like *trendy, urban, emo, or bohemian.* Style is considered a kind of added flavor. In writing, it is the same, and your style largely comes down to the way your words and sentences are put together. Just as paragraphs are the building blocks of essays, sentences are the constituent elements of paragraphs. Your sentences define your writing style. Whether you are writing for an academic, professional, or personal audience, you will want to pay careful attention to your sentences, making sure they are complete, varied, and precise. But your goal in academic writing is not to be urban, dashing, or trendy. The most important attribute of academic style is that your sentences are clear—which is not to say *dull*. Dull writing in any rhetorical situation is monotone, using the same words and the same sentence structure over and over. You will want to flavor your writing so that your reader enjoys learning what you have to say.

This chapter provides guidance on how to keep words like *unclear, awkward,* or *wordy* away from your work. Avoiding mismatched sentence parts and creating complete sentences will bring unity and coherence to your sentences in the same way that making meaningful connections among sentences creates unity and coherence in your paragraphs. By making deliberate rhetorical choices as you craft your sentences, you are demonstrating recognition of your rhetorical audience and an awareness of your rhetorical situation, while providing a better chance of achieving your rhetorical purpose.

≫ SENTENCE ESSENTIALS

So, back to basics! At the most essential level, each sentence consists of two parts:

Subject + Predicate

subject the who or what that carries out the action, experiences something, or is described

The **subject** is who or what does something, experiences something, or is described.

The **predicate** expresses what the subject does, experiences, or is. The predicate contains the verb.

➤ The landlord + renovated the apartment.

predicate the part of a sentence that expresses what a subject is, does, or experiences

The subject (*landlord*) performs an action; the predicate (*renovated*) expresses the action.

➤ They + had sounded reasonable.

The subject (*they*) is described; the predicate (*had sounded*) gives information about the subject.

Subject + Predicate + Complement

complement a word or words used to make the meaning of a sentence clear

Complements are parts of the predicate that make the sentence complete. For example, the sentence *The chair of the committee presented* is incomplete without the complement *his plans*. A complement is generally a noun, pronoun, or noun phrase.

➤ The committee chair introduced **Sylvia Holbrook**. [noun]
➤ The committee chair introduced **her**. [pronoun]
➤ The committee chair introduced **the new but well-known member**. [noun phrase]

Independent and Dependent Clauses

independent clause a group of words consisting of a subject + predicate that expresses the main idea of a sentence

A group of words that contains a subject and a predicate and functions as a complete sentence is known as an **independent clause**, sometimes referred to as the *main clause*. An independent clause can stand alone as a complete sentence. Other clauses can be added to form a longer, more detailed sentence.

➤ The athlete grew up in Argentina.

A **dependent clause** also has a subject and a predicate; however, it cannot stand alone: it is dependent on an independent clause. The word that introduces the dependent clause (*who*, in the following example) reveals that it is dependent on the main idea of the sentence (the independent clause) and cannot stand alone.

➤ The athlete **who placed first** grew up in Argentina.

You can identify the form of a sentence by noting the number of clauses it has. There are four basic sentence forms: simple, compound, complex, and compound-complex. These four basic sentence forms are templates for a variety of sentence structures that can comprise a more effective style.

SENTENCE FORMS

1. A *simple sentence* is equivalent to one independent clause; thus, it must have a subject and a predicate.

       s   p

   • **The lawyer presented her final argument.**
   [one independent clause]

2. A *compound sentence* consists of at least two independent clauses but no dependent clauses. The independent clauses of a compound sentence are most commonly linked by a coordinating conjunction (*and, but, or, yet, so, nor,* or *for*).

   • **The Democrats proposed a new budget, but the Republicans opposed it.**
   [two independent clauses connected by a comma and a coordinating conjunction]

3. A *complex sentence* consists of one independent clause and at least one dependent clause.

   • **Because he was known for architectural ornamentation, his own plain house was a complete shock.**
   [a dependent clause followed by a comma and the independent clause that begins with *his own plain house*]

4. The combination of a compound sentence and a complex sentence is called a *compound-complex sentence*. A compound-complex sentence consists of at least two independent clauses and at least one dependent clause.

   • **Conflict is essential to good storytelling, so fiction writers often create a character who faces a major challenge.**
   [two independent clauses followed by a dependent clause that starts with *who*]

dependent clause a group of words that includes a subject and a predicate and enhances the main idea of the sentence but cannot stand alone without that main idea

What all these sentence forms have in common are that they are complete, including the essential sentence parts (subject + predicate). When the sentence is missing either a subject or a predicate, or is a dependent clause, it is called a **sentence fragment**. (See CHAPTER 17, SENTENCE FRAGMENTS.) When independent clauses aren't connected properly, **run-on sentences**, sometimes referred to as *fused* or *spliced* sentences, are the result. (See CHAPTER 17, COMMA SPLICES AND FUSED (RUN-ON) SENTENCES.)

pages 323–326

pages 326–329

⟫ SENTENCE UNITY

In our spoken language and casual writing, not all sentence parts and words are always necessary. In academic and professional writing, however, sentences must meet minimum standards of sentence unity such that sentences include every sentence part and word necessary to make the meaning of that sentence clear. Consistent, clear, and complete sentences serve as the foundation of academic and professional writing. The following sections illustrate how to correct any mismatches in sentence parts that could confuse your reader. But in addition to properly matched sentence parts, comparisons and intensifiers (words such as *so*, *such*, and *too*) must also be included for your sentences to be unified. In addition, well-chosen details (of time, location, or cause) also bump a complete sentence up a notch or two, adding effectiveness, credibility, and clarity to your writing.

sentence fragment a piece of a sentence that is missing a subject and/ or a verb or is a dependent clause

run-on sentence two sentences or independent clauses run together without punctuation

Mismatches in Subjects and Verbs

On the most basic level, you want your subjects and verbs (predicates) to match, to agree. Because subjects can be more than one word long (*assignment* versus *tough assignment* versus *tough assignment due tomorrow*), choosing the correct verb to form the predicate can sometimes be a challenge. The following examples represent such a tricky situation. In the first example, the subject is *neither smoke alarms nor a fire extinguisher*, and in the second example the subject is *neither a fire extinguisher nor smoke alarms*:

➤ Neither smoke alarms nor a fire extinguisher **was** installed properly. [The noun closer to the verb is singular, so the verb itself is singular.]

➤ Neither a fire extinguisher nor smoke alarms **were** installed properly. [The noun closer to verb is plural, so the verb itself is plural.]

The following chart gives additional examples of various types of subjects and an explanation of why the verb should be singular or plural such that it agrees with the subject to create a unified sentence. (See also CHAPTER 17, SUBJECT-VERB AGREEMENT and CONSISTENT VERB TENSE.)

pages 329–330 and 330–331

SUBJECT-VERB AGREEMENT EXAMPLES AND EXPLANATION

A verb agrees in person and number with the noun that is the subject. The noun in the subject will affect the form the verb takes, singular or plural. These examples represent a few tricky situations in making sure subjects and verbs agree. The verb is in color in the examples.

- *Garages and basements are sometimes used as workshops.*
  [The plural subject consists of two nouns connected by *and*; therefore, the verb is plural.]
- *The designer and owner is responsible for employee safety.*
  [Because the designer and owner are the same person, the subject is singular; therefore, the verb is singular.]
- *There is a workbench at the center of any good shop.*
  [The subject appears after the verb because *there* is an expletive, see p. 320; the subject is *a workbench*, singular subject, singular verb.]
- *There are shelves for small tools.*
  [The subject appears after the verb because there is an expletive, see p. 320; the subject is *shelves*, plural subject, plural verb.]
- *The whole family uses the shop.*
  [Here the family is unified as one: It uses the shop.]
- *The family disagree on the use of the shop.*
  [Here the individual family members are involved: they disagree on the use of the shop.]

Mismatches in Sentence Logic

In addition to matching subjects and verbs, it is important for sentence parts to be related logically. Otherwise there is a gap between what the writer intends and what the reader understands. (For more on sentence logic, see also CHAPTER 17, DANGLING MODIFIERS.) page 337

1. Mismatch between subject and verb

When the subject of a sentence is described as being or doing the logically impossible, the sentence has **faulty predication**. A sentence's subject and verb must create a meaningful idea.

> **faulty predication** a sentence error in which the predicate does not logically belong with the given subject

MISMATCH	The absence of detail screams out at the reader. [An absence cannot scream.]
REVISION	The reader immediately notices the absence of detail.

2. Mismatch between a verb and its complement

A verb and its complement should fit meaningfully together. Mismatches between a verb and its complement can obscure meaning.

MISMATCH	Only a few students used the incorrect use of *there*. [To "use an incorrect use" is not logical.]
REVISION	Only a few students used *there* correctly.

Mismatches in Definitions and Reasons

Just as you will work to avoid mismatches between subjects and verbs, you will want to avoid such mismatches in other parts of your sentences. For instance, when you are relating the separate parts of definitions and reasons, you will want to avoid mismatches, especially when using the following constructions: *is when*, *is where*, and *the reason … is because*.

1. Mismatch of definition

When you write a sentence that states a formal definition, the term you are defining should be followed by a noun or a noun phrase, not an adverbial clause. Avoid using *is when* or *is where*.

➤ *Ecology* is ^the ~~when you~~ study ^of the relationships among living organisms and between living organisms and their environment.

➤ *Exploitative competition* is ^the context between ~~where~~ two or more organisms ^vying ~~vie~~ for a limited resource such as food.

2. Mismatch of *reason* with *is because*

You can see why *reason* and *is because* are a mismatch by looking at the meaning of *because*: "for the reason that." Saying "the reason is for the reason that" is redundant. Be sure to revise any sentence containing the construction *the reason is … because*.

➤ The ~~reason the~~ old train station was closed **is** because it had fallen into disrepair.

Incomplete Comparisons

A comparison has two parts: someone or something is compared to someone or something else. As you revise your writing, make sure that your audience knows who or what is being compared.

➤ Printers today are quite different ^from those sold in the early 1990s .

➤ His first novel was better ^*than the one just published*.

After you are sure that your comparisons are complete, check to see that they are also logical.

➤ Her test scores are higher than ^*those of* the other students.

In the original sentence, scores were being compared to students.

Incomplete Intensifiers

In speech, *so, such,* and *too* (which intensify meaning) are used to mean "very," "unusually," or "extremely."

➤ That movie was **so** funny.

In academic and professional writing, however, *so, such,* and *too* require a completing phrase or clause.

➤ That movie was **so** funny *that I watched it twice.*
➤ Julian has **such** a hearty laugh that *it makes everyone else laugh with him.*
➤ Child custody is just **too** complex an issue *to cover in one class discussion.*

Necessary but Missing Details

Well-chosen details (of time, location, or cause) add credibility to your writing.

MISSING IMPORTANT DETAIL

➤ An astrophysicist from the Harvard-Smithsonian Center has predicted a galactic storm.

WITH DETAIL ADDED

➤ An astrophysicist from the Harvard-Smithsonian Center has predicted **that** a galactic storm **will occur within the next ten million years**.

The added detail about time clarifies the sentence and helps readers accept the information. Every word and every detail you use should contribute to your central thought, as in the following description of brain activity:

> A given mental task may involve a complicated web of circuits, which inter-act in varying degrees with others throughout the brain—not like the parts in a machine, but like the instruments in a symphony orchestra combining their tenor, volume, and resonance to create a particular musical effect.
>
> —**James Shreeve, "Beyond the Brain"**

Necessary but Missing Words

Writing that is incomplete has words left out, often in a way that is conversational:

➤ We discussed a couple ^of issues at the meeting.

A careful writing style will make it easier for readers to follow your message and understand your rhetorical purpose, so take care to include all necessary small words.

➤ Graduation will take place in ^the Bryce Jordan Center.

≫ VARIETY

Variety in your sentences helps you get and keep your reader's attention, maybe even admiration. The preceding sections illustrated the mismatches, disagreements, and incompletions that you should avoid to help you achieve unity and clarity in your sentences. Sentence variety will help you achieve reader interest. To make your writing lively and distinctive, include a variety of sentence types and lengths. Notice how the sentences in the following paragraph vary in length, form (simple, compound, and compound complex, p. 297), and function (statements, questions, and commands). The variety of sentences makes this paragraph about pleasure pleasurable to read.

Start with the taste. Imagine a moment when the sensation of honey or sugar on the tongue was an astonishment, a kind of intoxication. The closest I've ever come to recovering such a sense of sweetness was secondhand, though it left a powerful impression on me even so. I'm thinking of my son's first experience with sugar: the icing on the cake at his first birthday. I have only the testimony of Isaac's face to go by (that, and his fierceness to repeat the experience), but it was plain that his first encounter with sugar had intoxicated him—was in fact an ecstasy, in the literal sense of the word. That is, he was beside himself with the pleasure of it, no longer here with me in space and time in quite the same way he had been just a moment before. Between bites Isaac gazed up at me in amazement (he was on my lap, and I was delivering the ambrosial forkfuls to his gaping mouth) as if to exclaim, "Your world contains this? From this day forward I shall dedicate my life to it." (Which he basically has done.) And I remember thinking, this is no minor desire, and then wondered: Could it be that sweetness is the prototype of *all* desire?

—Michael Pollan, *The Botany of Desire* [Sweetness]

Varying Sentence Length and Form

To avoid the choppiness of a series of short sentences, combine some of them into longer sentences.

SHORT

> ➤ Americans typically eat popcorn at movie theaters.
> ➤ They also eat it at sporting events.

COMBINED

> ➤ Americans typically eat popcorn at movie theaters and sporting events.

SHORT

> ➤ Researchers have found thousand-year-old popcorn kernels.
> ➤ These kernels still pop.

COMBINED

> ➤ Researchers have found thousand-year-old popcorn kernels that still pop.

SHORT

> ➤ Popcorn was in demand during the Great Depression.
> ➤ Low-income families could afford it.

COMBINED

> ➤ Because low-income families could afford it, popcorn was in demand during the Great Depression.

It is also possible to combine sentences by condensing one of them into a phrase.

SHORT

> ➤ Some colonial families ate popcorn for breakfast.
> ➤ They ate it with sugar and cream.

COMBINED

> ➤ Some colonial families ate popcorn with sugar and cream for breakfast.

SHORT

> ➤ The world's largest popcorn ball measured twelve feet in diameter.
> ➤ It took two thousand pounds of popcorn to create.

COMBINED

> ➤ Measuring twelve feet in diameter, the world's largest popcorn ball took two thousand pounds of popcorn to create.

Varying Sentence Openings

Most writers begin more than half of their sentences with a subject, making this pattern common and predictable. Experiment with the following alternatives for starting your sentences.

1. **Beginning with an adverb**

   ➤ **Immediately**, the police officer got out of the car and asked for my driver's license.

2. **Beginning with a phrase**

   ➤ **In the arena**, fans stood with their hands over their hearts and sang the National Anthem.

   ➤ **A town of historic interest**, Santa Fe also has many art galleries and restaurants.

   ➤ **Tapping the power of being seen**, the Oscar nominees appeared on late-night television, morning news programs, and in glossy magazines.

3. **Beginning with a transitional word**

page 242 and pages 268–269

   In each of the following examples, the transitional word shows the relationship between the ideas in the pair of sentences. (See CHAPTER 13, COMMON TRANSITIONAL WORDS AND PHRASES and CHAPTER 14, USING TRANSITIONS.)

   ➤ Many restaurants close within a few years of opening. **But** others, which offer good food at reasonable prices, become well established.

   ➤ Difficulty in finding a place to park keeps some people from going out to lunch downtown. **However**, that problem may be alleviated with the construction of a new underground parking garage.

4. **Beginning with a word that usually comes after the verb**

   ➤ I was an abysmal football player. **Soccer**, though, I could play well.

   ➤ **Vital** to any success I had were my mother's early lessons.

Using Questions, Exclamations, and Commands

You can vary your sentences with an occasional question, exclamation, or command.

1. **Raising a question for variety**

   It can be uncomfortable for a boy to watch the frenzied, uninhibited enthusiasm of girl fans screaming for their idols, whether it's Sinatra, the Beatles,

or Michael Jackson. That is partly jealousy too—who wouldn't want to be the one who inspires girls to make that kind of noise? But it's also partly because we envy that enthusiasm.

—Rob Sheffield, *Talking to Girls about Duran Duran* [Enthusiasm]

You can either answer the question you pose or let readers answer it for themselves, in which case it is called a **rhetorical question**.

 RHETORICAL QUESTIONS

The rhetorical question is not a true question because an answer is not expected. Instead, it is used to imply an opinion. However, a positive rhetorical question can correspond to a negative assertion, and vice versa.

RHETORICAL QUESTIONS

➤ Should we allow our rights to be taken away?

➤ Isn't it time to make a difference?

EQUIVALENT STATEMENTS

➤ We should not let our rights be taken away.

➤ It's time to make a difference.

Because they are more emphatic than declarative sentences, rhetorical questions focus the reader's attention on major points, serving as a topic sentence or thesis statement.

rhetorical question a question that does not require an answer but is instead used to state an opinion and direct readers to major points.

2. Adding an exclamatory sentence for variety

But at other moments, the classroom is so lifeless or painful or confused—and I so powerless to do anything about it—that my claim to be a teacher seems a transparent sham. Then the enemy is everywhere: in those students from some alien planet, in the subject I thought I knew, and in the personal pathology that keeps me earning my living this way. What a fool I was to imagine that I had mastered this occult art—harder to divine than tea leaves and impossible for mortals to do even passably well!

—Parker Palmer, *The Courage to Teach* [Occult Art of Teaching]

The introduction of an exclamatory sentence can break up a regular pattern of declarative sentences.

3. Including a command for variety

Now I stare and stare at people shamelessly. <u>Stare.</u> It's the way to educate your eye.

—Walker Evans, *Unclassified* [Stare]

In this case, a one-word command, *Stare*, provides variety.

Establishing variety with coordination and subordination

Using **coordination** (elements of equal rank) and **subordination** (an element of lower rank) enhances the connections among your ideas and adds variety to your sentences. (See also CHAPTER 17, CREATING PARALLELISM WITH COORDINATING CONJUNCTIONS and CREATING PARALLELISM WITH LINKING WORDS.)

Coordinate grammatical elements that have the same form:

➤ a **stunning** and **satisfying** conclusion
➤ **in the attic** or **in the basement**
➤ **The company was losing money**, yet **the employees suspected nothing**.

To indicate the relationship, choose an appropriate **coordinating conjunction** (*and, but, or, yet, so, nor,* or *for*) or **correlative conjunction** (pairs of words that link other words, phrases, or clauses, such as *both/and; either/or; neither/nor; not only/but also; whether/or*).

By using coordination, you can avoid unnecessary repetition.

➤ The hike to the top of Angels Landing has countless switchbacks. ~~It also has~~ *and* ⋀ long drop-offs.

A semicolon can also be used to link coordinate independent clauses, adding variety to your sentence:

➤ Hikers follow the path; climbers scale the cliff wall.

Because a subordinate grammatical structure cannot stand alone, it is dependent on the main (independent) clause (like the two parts of this sentence). The most common subordinate structure is the dependent clause, which frequently opens with one of the following frequently used **subordinating conjunctions**:

Cause: *because*
Concession: *although, even though*
Condition: *if, unless*
Effect: *so that*
Sequence: *before, after*
Time: *when*

---

coordination the use of grammatically equivalent constructions to link or balance ideas

page 338

subordination the connection of a grammatical structure to another, usually a dependent clause to an independent clause: Even though customers were satisfied with the product, the company wanted to improve it

coordinating conjunction words used to connect other words, phrases, clauses, or sentences connect of equal grammatical rank (words, such as, *and, but, or, nor, for, so,* and *yet*)

correlative conjunction two-part connecting words such as *either/or* and *not only/but also*

subordinating conjunctions words that specify the relationship between a dependent clause and an independent clause

By using subordinating conjunctions, you can combine short sentences and indicate how they are related.

➤ *Even though we*
   ∧ **We** spent all day Saturday studying ⸌,⸍I still managed to hear Kofi Annan at Schwab Auditorium that evening.

If the subjects of the two clauses are the same, the dependent clause can often be shortened to a phrase.

➤ After *eating* ∧ **we ate** our breakfast, we headed back to the construction site.

The **relative pronouns**, *who, whom, which, that,* or *whose,* can also introduce a subordinate or dependent clause, helping you embed details into a more concise sentence.

➤ The Roman temple has a portico **that** opens to the morning sun.
➤ Steven Spielberg produced and directed a film about Abraham Lincoln, **which** quickly won many awards.

Effective subordination requires choosing subordinating conjunctions carefully. In the following sentence, the use of *as* is distracting because it can mean either "because" or "while."

➤ *Because*
   ∧ **As** time was running out, I randomly filled in the remaining circles on the exam sheet.

As you revise your writing, make sure that you have not overused any single sentence pattern, whether the subject + verb + complement of a simple sentence or the subordination or coordination of complex and compound sentences.

relative pronouns words (*who, whom, that, which,* or *whose*) that are used to introduce a clause and that have an antecedent in the main clause

»» EMPHASIS

In any rhetorical situation, some ideas are more important than others. Those are the ideas you want to emphasize by using word placement, punctuation, periodic and cumulative sentences, and order.

Placing Words and Using Punctuation

Words placed at the beginning or the end of a sentence receive emphasis, so take advantage of this tendency by starting or finishing a sentence with the most important information—usually an idea that is new to the reader. If the emphasis is at the beginning, the idea often extends the idea of the previous sentence; if it is at the end, it often connects with the idea in the sentence that follows.

> **By 1857, miners had extracted 760 tons of gold from these hills—and left behind more than ten times as much mercury, as well as devastated forests, slopes and streams.**
>
> **—Rebecca Solnit, *Storming the Gates of Paradise: Landscapes for Politics* [Miners]**

Words (especially nouns) and phrases that come before commas receive stress. In the following passage, the emphasis on *day, astronomy, mathematics, optics,* and *Kepler's Laws* is due, in part, to comma placement.

> **One of the most brilliant and influential scientists of his day, [Johannes] Kepler made numerous contributions to astronomy, mathematics, and optics, including his famous discovery of what are now called Kepler's Laws, describing the motions of the planets round the sun.**
>
> **—Kenneth Libbrecht, *The Snowflake: Winter's Secret Beauty* [Kepler]**

Placing the Main Idea

cumulative sentence a sentence that presents the main idea first, followed by supplementary details and ideas that expand on the main idea.

In a **cumulative sentence**, the main idea in the sentence comes first, followed by supporting ideas and supplementary details that expand on that main idea. A cumulative sentence is a good way to add variety to your sentences.

> **The day was hot for June, a pale sun burning in a cloudless sky, wilting the last of the irises, the rhododendron blossoms drooping.**
>
> **—Adam Haslett, "Devotion"**

periodic sentence a sentence that presents details and ideas first to lead up to the main idea

In a **periodic sentence**, however, the main idea comes last, just before the period, as though the writer is warming up to the main point. This kind of sentence, too, adds sophistication and variety to your writing style.

> **Because the scar resulting from the burn is typically much larger than the original lesion, allowing for less intricacy, the designs tend to be much simpler than those used in tattoos.**
>
> **—Nina Jablonski, *Skin: A Natural History* [Scars vs. Tatoos]**

Both of these types of sentences can be effective. But because cumulative sentences are more common, the infrequently encountered periodic sentence tends to provide greater emphasis at the same time that it enhances your writing style.

Ordering Ideas from Least to Most Important

Just as you arrange paragraphs in emphatic order, you can also arrange the ideas in sentences in emphatic order. By arranging your ideas from least important to most important, you build up suspense, work toward a climax. If the most important idea appears first, a sentence may seem to trail off. If that idea appears in the middle of the sentence, readers may not recognize its significance. If, however, the most important idea appears at the end of the sentence, it will not only receive emphasis but also provide a springboard to the next sentence. In the following example, the writer emphasizes a doctor's desire to help the disadvantaged and then implies that this desire has been realized through work with young Haitian doctors:

> **While he was in medical school, the soon-to-be doctor discovered his calling: to diagnose infectious diseases, to find ways of curing people with these diseases, and to bring the lifesaving knowledge of modern medicine to the disadvantaged. Most recently, he has been working with a small group of young doctors in Haiti.**

Repeating Important Words

Effective writers avoid unnecessary repetition but often use deliberate repetition to emphasize key words or ideas.

> **We forget all too soon the things we thought we could never forget. We forget the loves and betrayals alike, forget what we whispered and what we screamed, forget who we are.**
>
> **—Joan Didion, "On Keeping a Notebook"**

In this case, the emphatic repetition of *forget* reinforces the author's point—that we do not remember many things that once seemed impossible to forget.

Inverting Word Order

Most sentences begin with a subject and end with a predicate. When you move words out of their normal order, you draw attention to them.

➤ *At the back of the crowded room* sat **a newspaper reporter**.

[COMPARE: **A newspaper reporter** sat *at the back of the crowded room.*]

Using an Occasional Short Sentence

In a paragraph of mostly long sentences, try using a short sentence for emphasis. To optimize the effect, lead up to the short sentence with an especially long sentence.

> **After buying the groceries, cleaning the vegetables, marinating the beef, baking a cake, hanging the decorations, and setting the table, I showered and got myself ready to have a good time with my invited guests. Then the phone rang.**

A short sentence can pack a punch, but too many short sentences in a row create a choppy overall effect.

Using Parallelism for Clarity and Emphasis

When you join two or more ideas, whether each is encapsulated in a word or expressed in an entire sentence, the linked ideas need to be parallel in form. Parallel structures allow you to pair ideas and create connections in sentences. **Parallelism** is the repetition of words or grammatically equivalent forms (that is, all noun forms, all verb forms, and so forth) to clarify meaning and to emphasize ideas. By repeating words and phrases and by aligning grammatical forms, you can create parallel structures that are clear and succinct, and that highlight the ideas you wish to emphasize.

parallelism
repeated patterns of words or grammatically equivalent forms

➤ My embarrassment stemmed not **from** the money lost but ∧ *from* shame.

➤ She wanted her audience **to remember** the protest song and ∧ *to understand* ~~be understanding of~~ its origin.

➤ The team vowed **that** they would support each other, **that** they would play their best, and ∧ *that* they would win the tournament.

The following example includes the repetition of grammatical forms, in this case the *-ing* form of two different verbs.

➤ Many Detroit homeowners are selling their houses or ∧ *remodeling* **~~should remodel~~** to enhance value.

You can also create parallelism by using *and*, *but*, or *or*, as in the following sentence.

➤ Mortgage rates ∧ *rise* **~~are rising,~~** and building codes change, but the real estate market remains strong.

Repeating a pattern is also considered aesthetically pleasing, just like the repeated patterns in waves, leaves, or textiles. The following three sentences, all including parallelism, come from a public speech by civil rights activist and political leader Jesse Jackson:

> ➤ **Today's students** can put *dope in their veins* or *hope in their brains*. If **they** can *conceive it* and *believe it*, **they** can *achieve it*. **They** must know it is not *their aptitude* but *their attitude* that will determine *their altitude*.

To create parallelism, Jackson repeats words (*they*), uses rhymes (*dope/hope, veins/brains, conceive/believe/achieve*), and employs similar grammatical forms plus similar-sounding words (*their aptitude, their attitude, their altitude*). However, if you overuse parallel patterns, they will lose their impact. (See also, CHAPTER 17, PARALLELISM.)

pages 337–339

THINKING RHETORICALLY

Parallelism

Parallel elements make your writing easy and pleasurable to read. But consider breaking from the parallel pattern to emphasize a point. For example, to describe a friend, you could start with two adjectives and then switch to a noun phrase.

- **My friend Alison is kind, modest, and the smartest mathematician in the state**.

》》 PRECISION

Using the right words at the right time can make the difference between having your ideas taken seriously or seeing them brushed aside. The right words make your writing easy and pleasurable to read; they achieve a clear style that your audience understands and the occasion requires. Sentences that are ornate—including flowery or fancy language—may not be understood by a broad audience.

ORNATE	The majority believes that achievement derives primarily from the diligent pursuit of allocated tasks.
CLEAR	Most people believe that success results from hard work.

Accurate words convey precise meanings. The right words make your sentences easy and pleasurable to read as well as appropriate for the occasion.

Avoiding Slang, Conversational, Regional, and Technical Language in Academic Writing

You may find yourself writing for an audience that you know will welcome slang and colloquial expressions or for a specialized audience who will immediately understand technical jargon. Otherwise, the following advice can help you determine which words to use and which to avoid. A good dictionary will also help you. Words labeled *dialect, slang, colloquial, nonstandard,* or *unconventional* are generally inappropriate for academic and professional writing. If a word has no label, you can safely assume that it can be used in writing for school or work.

Slang

Slang covers a wide range of words or expressions that are considered casual or fashionable by people in a particular age group, locality, or profession. Although such expressions are used in conversation or in writing intended to mimic conversation, terms such as *totally, on fleek, turnt up,* and *bae* are usually out of place in academic or professional writing.

Conversational (or colloquial) words

Words labeled *colloquial* in a dictionary are fine for casual conversation and for written dialogues or personal essays on a light topic. Such words are sometimes used for special effect in academic writing, but you should usually replace them with more appropriate words. For example, conversational words such as *dumb* and *kid around* could be replaced by *illogical* and *tease.*

Regionalisms

Regionalisms—such as *redd up* for *tidy up, fixing to* for *preparing to,* and *sweeper* for *vacuum cleaner*—can make essay writing lively and distinctive, but they are often considered too informal for most academic and professional writing.

Technical words or jargon

When writing for a diverse audience, an effective writer will not refer to the need for bifocals as presbyopia. However, technical language is appropriate when the audience can understand it (as when one physician writes to another about tachycardia) or when the audience (heart patients, for example) would benefit by learning the terms in question. As computer use has grown, technical terms such as application (app) and cloud computing have become commonly used and widely understood.

Choosing Precise Nouns

After drafting is the best time to consider the precision of your nouns. Choose nouns that express precisely what you want your readers to sense or understand. Many writers forget to include tangible details conveyed through concrete terms. A **concrete noun** refers to someone or something perceivable by the senses: *guitar, vocalist*. An **abstract noun**, on the other hand, refers to a concept, like *entertainment* or *freedom*.

To test whether your nouns are specific and concrete, ask yourself questions about what you want to say: Exactly who? Exactly what? Exactly when? Exactly where? Exactly how? In the following example, notice what a difference Louise Erdrich's specific and concrete nouns and details make in expressing and developing an idea

> **VAGUE**   She has kept no reminders of performing in her youth.
>
> **CONCRETE**   She has kept no sequined costume, no photographs, no fliers or posters from that part of her youth. —Louise Erdrich, "The Leap"

concrete noun nouns that refer to something perceivable by the senses

abstract noun nouns that refer to a concept

THINKING RHETORICALLY

Nouns

Some rhetorical situations call for the use of abstract terms. Your art history paper may require the use of abstractions like *impressionism* and *cubism* that you will want to balance out with tangible details conveyed through concrete nouns, which would enable your readers to see in their minds the colors and brushstrokes of Claude Monet, Pablo Picasso, or any of a number of other painters.

Choosing Verbs

You will also want to determine the best verbs for your sentences, whether they are **action verbs** that convey activity or change, such as *eat, happen, write,* and *study,* or **linking verbs**, such as *be, seem,* and *become* (states of being) or *look, taste, smell, feel,* and *sound* (perceptions). As you revise for accuracy, keep in mind that writers too often depend on linking verbs of being, usually a form of the verb "to be" (*am, is, are, was, were*).

You will also want to determine whether to use an active verb or a passive verb (also called *active* and *passive voice*). The **active voice** emphasizes the person or thing performing the action indicated by the verb.

action verbs verbs that convey action

linking verbs verbs that convey states of being and perceptions

active voice emphasizes the person performing the action

➤ A group of students **planned** the graduation ceremony.

➤ The board **discussed** tuition increases.

Passive voice is used when you want to stress the recipient of the action or when the identity of the actor is unimportant or unknown.

➤ The graduation ceremony **was being planned** by a group of students.

➤ Tuition increases **were discussed** at the board meeting.

Writers of scientific prose often use the passive voice to highlight the experiment rather than the experimenter, as in this excerpt from a student lab report:

➤ First, the slides **were placed** on a compound microscope under low power, a 40Å~ magnification level. The end of the root tip **was located**; then the cells immediately behind the root cap **were examined**.

Using Fresh Expressions

passive voice emphasizes the recipient of the action

Fresh images also add precision to your sentences, helping your readers "see" what you mean, what you are talking about. For instance, Susan Gubar wanted to explain how her mind was working as she listened to various arguments:

> While others, judging by their ardent notetaking, found enlightenment, or, at least, points for debate, I precariously moved along a spider web of speculation.
>
> —Susan Gubar, *Rooms of Our Own* [Speculation]

Spider web of speculation is a fresh phrase that expresses the patterned, if precarious, mental state the author experienced.

clichés an expression that has lost its power to interest readers because of overuse

Often, what were once fresh expressions or examples of vivid language have become so common that they have become **clichés**: *white as snow*, *sick as a dog*, and *strong as an ox* are just a few examples. If you find yourself resorting to clichés in your sentences, revise your prose by using language that does not call forth an image or comparison, try to invent a new expression, or tweak the original expression to make it fresh.

CLICHÉ: *at the drop of a hat*

LITERAL SYNONYM: *immediately*

NEW EXPRESSION: *at the click of the Send button*

Original expression with a slight change:

> We know by now that whenever politics and art collide, art loses—at least, in these United States, where anything cultural can become politicized at the drop of a grievance.
>
> —Peter Schjeldahl, "Those Nasty Brits"

Revising Mixed Metaphors

When you use language that evokes images, make sure that the images are meaningfully related. Replace **mixed metaphors**—combinations of images that evoke conflicting images—with images that make sense together.

➤ As he climbed the corporate ladder, he ~~sank into a sea of~~ debt.
incurred a large

The odd image of a man hanging onto a ladder as it disappears into the water can easily be revised with the removal of one conflicting image.

Revising Mixed Constructions

A sentence that begins with one kind of grammatical pattern and shifts to another is a **mixed construction.**

➤ ~~By practicing~~ a new language daily will help you become proficient.
Practicing

mixed metaphor a construction that includes parts of two or more unrelated metaphors: Her fiery personality dampened our hopes of a compromise

mixed construction a confusing sentence that is the result of an unintentional shift from one grammatical pattern to another

[*Practicing a new language* replaces *By practicing a new language*. *Practicing a new language* can serve as a subject of the sentence.]

Her scholarship award
➤ ^~~Although she won a scholarship~~ does not give her the right to skip classes.

[*Although she won a scholarship* cannot serve as the subject. The revision makes the *Her scholarship award* the subject.]

You can revise a mixed construction by changing the subject or using the beginning of the current sentence as a modifier and adding a new subject after it.

➤ Although she won a scholarship, **she** does not have the right to skip classes.

[The dependent clause, *Although she won a scholarship*, now modifies the independent clause, *she does not have the right to skip classes*.]

Choosing Inclusive Words

By choosing words that are inclusive rather than exclusive, you overtly invite readers into your writing. Prejudiced or derogatory language has no place in any academic or professional sentence; using it undermines your authority and credibility. It is best to use language that will engage, not alienate, your readers. **Inclusive language** includes language that shows equal respect for people of all genders, sexualities, races, ethnicities, cultures, geographical regions, religions, ages, and abilities.

inclusive language writing that shows equal respect for all people, all genders, by using nonsexist and nonracist language

If a writing assignment asks you to refer to people's gender, sexual orientation, race, ethnicity, culture, geographical region, religion, age, or ability, use respectful language by using the terms the people you are writing about prefer.

Race or ethnicity

Nonracist language is inclusive language, as it is rarely necessary to identify anyone's race or ethnicity in any academic or professional sentence. However, you may need to use appropriate racial or cultural-ethnic terms if you are writing a demographic report, an argument against existing racial inequities, or a historical account of a particular event involving ethnic groups or individuals. Determining which terms a particular group prefers can be difficult because preferences sometimes vary within a group and change over time. One conventional way to refer to Americans of a specific descent is to include an adjective before the word American: African American, Asian American, European American, Latin American, Mexican American, Native American.

Age

Although *senior citizen* and *the elderly* have been used to refer to people who have reached the age of retirement, *older adult* has emerged as the preferred term.

Ability

In references to ability, illness, or physical condition, it is best to refer to people with whatever term they prefer to use. While some people prefer to use person-first language, such as *people with disabilities*, others consider identity-first language to be preferable, such as *disabled people*. You can find out which expressions are preferred by noting whether they are used in the articles and books (or by the people) you consult.

Geographical areas

Certain geographical terms need to be used with special care. Though most frequently used to refer to people from the United States, the term *American* may also refer to people from Canada, Mexico, Central America, or South America. If your audience may be confused by this term, use *people from the United States* or *U.S. citizens* instead. The term *Arab* often refers to people who speak *Arabic*. If you cannot use specific terms such as *Iraqi* or *Saudi Arabian*, be sure you know that a country's people speak Arabic and not another language. Iranians, for example, are not Arabs because they speak Farsi. *British*, rather than *English*, is the preferred term for referring to people from the island of Great Britain or from the United Kingdom (England, Scotland, Wales, and Northern Ireland).

Religion

Reference to a person's religion should be made only if it is relevant. If you must mention religious affiliation, use only those terms considered respectful. Because religions have both conservative and liberal followers, be careful not to make generalizations about political stances.

Gender identity and sexual orientation

Effective writers show equal respect for all people. For example, people of all genders can be *firefighters* and *police officers*—words that have become gender neutral alternatives to *firemen* and *policemen*. In addition, effective writers avoid using *man* to refer to people in general because they know the word excludes many other people, most importantly, women. Use the following tips to ensure that each of your sentences is respectful and inclusive.

If your rhetorical situation calls for identifying sexual orientation or gender identity, choose terms used by the people you are discussing. For instance, *LGBTQ+* includes terms preferred by people of a range of sexual orientations and gender identities: lesbian, gay, bisexual, transgender, queer, intersex, asexual/agender, pansexual.

Achievements [OR Human achievements]

➤ ∧ **Man's ~~achievements~~** in science are impressive.

 TIPS FOR USING INCLUSIVE LANGUAGE

When reviewing drafts, check for and revise the following types of noninclusive language.

Generic *he/his*: A senator should listen to *his* constituents.

➤ A senator should listen to **their** constituents. [use of *their* as a singular pronoun]
➤ Senators should listen to **their** constituents. [use of plural forms]
➤ **By listening to their** constituents, **senators obtain important information on the consequences of their votes and decisions.** [elimination *of his* by revising the sentence]

Occupational stereotype: Glenda James, a *female* engineer at Howard Aviation, won the best-employee award.

➤ Howard Aviation engineer Glenda James won the best-employee award. [removal of the unnecessary gender reference]

Terms such as *man* and *mankind* or those with *-ess* or *-man* endings: Labor laws benefit the common *man*. *Mankind* benefits from philanthropy. The *stewardess* brought me some orange juice.

➤ Labor laws benefit **working people**. [replacement of the stereotypical term with a gender-neutral term]
➤ The **flight attendant** brought me some orange juice. [use of a gender neutral term]

Stereotypical gender roles: I was told that the university offers free tuition to *faculty wives*. The minister pronounced them *man and wife*.

➤ I was told that the university offers free tuition to faculty **spouses**. [replacement of the stereotypical term with a gender-neutral term]
➤ The minister pronounced them **husband** and wife. [use of a term equivalent to wife]
➤ The minister pronounced them **husband and husband**.

Inconsistent use of titles: *Mr. Holmes and his wife, Mary,* took a long trip to China.

➤ **Mr. and Mrs. [or Ms.]** Holmes took a long trip to China. [consistent use of titles]
➤ **Peter and Mary** Holmes took a long trip to China. [removal of titles]
➤ **Peter Holmes and Mary Wolfe** took a long trip to China. [use of full names]

Unstated gender assumption: Have *your mother* make your costume for the school pageant.

REVISION

➤ Have **<u>your parents</u>** provide you with a costume for the school pageant. [replacement of the stereotypical words with gender-neutral ones]

Explicit racial marker, even in positive sentences: My *Black* friend is a chess champ. *Jewish* lawyers are always the best. An *Indian American* student always wins the Scripps National Spelling Bee.

REVISION

➤ **<u>My friend Ron</u>** is a world-class chess player.
➤ The **<u>most successful</u>** lawyers are the best lawyers.
➤ **<u>Really smart</u>** students always win the Scripps National Spelling Bee.

⟫ CONCISENESS

Using words that are precise and sentences that are concise can also help you achieve a clear style. If you want readers to take your writing seriously, you must show them respect by not using obscure words when common words will do and by not using more words than necessary.

Eliminating Wordiness

As you edit a draft, look for ways to rewrite sentences in fewer words, without risking the loss of important details. One exact word often says as much as several inexact ones.

spoke in a low and hard-to-hear voice	**mumbled**
a person who gives expert advice	**consultant**

➤ Some unscrupulous brokers are _∧ *cheating* ~~taking money and savings from~~ older adults _∧ *out of their pensions.* ~~who need that money because they planned to use it as a retirement pension~~.

REPLACEMENTS FOR WORDY EXPRESSIONS

instead of	use
at this moment (point) in time now,	today
due to the fact that	because
in view of the fact that	because
for the purpose of	for
it is clear (obvious) that	clearly (obviously)
there is no question that	unquestionably, certainly
without a doubt	undoubtedly
beyond the shadow of a doubt	certainly, surely
it is my opinion that	I think (believe) that
in this day and age	today
in the final analysis	finally

In addition, watch for vague words such as *area, aspect, factor, feature, kind, situation, thing,* and *type.* These words may signal wordiness.

Using *there are* and *it is*

expletive a word signaling a structural change in a sentence, usually used so that new or important information is given at the end of the sentence

There or *it* may function as an **expletive**—a word that signals that the subject of the sentence will follow the verb, usually a form of *be.* Writers use expletives to emphasize words that would not be emphasized in the typical subject-verb order. Notice the difference in rhythm between the following sentences:

➤ Two children were playing in the yard. [typical order]
➤ There were two children playing in the yard. [use of expletive]

However, expletives are easily overused. If you find that you have drafted several sentences that begin with expletives, revise a few of them.

➤ *Hundreds* ~~There were hundreds~~ of fans *were* crowding onto the field.

➤ *Joining the crowd* It was frightening ~~to join the crowd.~~

Eliminating *who, which, that*

Who, which, or *that* can frequently be deleted without affecting the meaning of a sentence. If one of these pronouns is followed by a form of the verb *be* (*am, is, are, was,* or *were*), you can often omit the pronoun and sometimes the verb as well.

➤ The change ~~that~~ the young senator proposed yesterday angered most legislators.

➤ The Endangered Species Act, ~~which was~~ passed in 1973, protects the habitat of endangered plants and animals.

When deleting a relative pronoun, you might have to make other changes to a sentence as well.

➤ Nations ~~that provide~~ _{providing} protection for endangered species often create preserves and forbid hunting of these species.

CHECKLIST FOR REVISING SENTENCES FOR STYLE

The following checklist will guide you as you revise individual sentences for clarity and effectiveness.

✓ Are your sentences complete, including both a subject and a predicate?

✓ Do sentence parts match? Does each verb agree with its subject?

✓ Have you varied the length of your sentences? If your sentences are the same length (whether long or short), revise them for variation.

✓ How many of your sentences use subordination? Coordination? If you overuse any one sentence structure, revise for variation.

✓ Which sentences might be strengthened with parallel structure? Check that lists and series are in parallel form.

✓ Which general words can you make more specific and precise? Which words can be used to eliminate wordiness?

✓ Have you consciously chosen between active and passive verbs?

✓ Are your word choices appropriate for your audience, purpose, and context? Is your language too informal? Have technical or unfamiliar words been defined? Have you used inclusive language?

17 Strategies for Editing Common Problems

LEARNING OBJECTIVES

- Recognize and revise fragments, comma splices, and run-on or fused sentences.
- Assess subject-verb agreement in number and person.
- Provide clear pronoun references that agree with their antecedents.
- Place modifiers such that they clearly modify the subject of the sentence.
- Link parallel forms by repeating words or grammatical structures, or by using correlative conjunctions.
- Spell words correctly that sound alike, especially contractions.
- Evaluate words for appropriate and accurate use to avoid commonly misused and confused words.

pages 228–256
pages 257–277
pages 278–294
pages 295–321

In CHAPTER 13, FROM TENTATIVE IDEA TO FINISHED PROJECT, you moved through the general stages of the writing process. CHAPTER 14, THE POWER OF PARAGRAPHS, and CHAPTER 15, RHETORICAL STRATEGIES FOR DEVELOPMENT, allowed you to dig deeper into drafting and revision. Then in CHAPTER 16, STYLE: AN ESSENTIAL GUIDE TO EFFECTIVE SENTENCES, you focused on editing sentences for clarity and style. The revision process requires you to move back and forth between large-scale revision (often called *global revision*) and small-scale revision (often called *sentence-level editing*)—between making sure that you have provided enough information for your readers to understand your message and ensuring that the information is presented in a way that is easy for them to read. Now that you have a final draft, you are ready to proofread your work.

At this stage your focus will be on grammar, punctuation, and mechanics (language issues, such as spelling and misused words). While the word *grammar* may make you think of the word *rules*, in academic writing your writing is expected to follow the conventions of standard, or academic, English. So, think of grammar rules as providing you with beneficial advice on how to achieve success as a writer. It might be more useful to think of grammar rules as statements about how language is commonly used. Don't get distracted by these concerns when you are first generating your ideas and need creative leeway to develop your work, but when you are planning your writing project, schedule time for a final polish. This chapter provides strategies for avoiding the fifteen most common problems writers encounter as they proofread their work. Avoiding these common problems will help you establish credibility as a writer and keep your reader focused on your message.

DIRECTORY OF COMMON PROBLEMS

1. Sentence Fragments
2. Comma Splices and Fused (Run-On) Sentences
3. Subject-Verb Agreement
4. Consistent Verb Tense
5. Pronoun Agreement
6. Vague Pronoun Reference
7. Misplaced or Dangling Modifiers
8. Parallelism
9. Missing Comma Joining Clauses with Coordinating Conjunctions
10. Missing Comma After an Introductory Element
11. Missing Comma Setting Off Nonessential Elements
12. Unnecessary Commas
13. Unnecessary or Missing Apostrophe (including It's/Its)
14. Spelling
15. Wrong Word

≫ 1. SENTENCE FRAGMENTS

Every complete sentence has a subject (with a noun or pronoun core) and a predicate (with a verb core): *Everyone laughed.* (See CHAPTER 16, STYLE: AN ESSENTIAL GUIDE TO EFFECTIVE SENTENCES.) In academic and professional writing, pages 295–321 complete sentences are expected. A sentence fragment is (1) missing a subject or a verb, (2) missing both, or (3) a dependent clause. Most fragments can be attached to adjacent sentences.

MISSING SUBJECT   Derived from a word meaning "nervous sleep." *," hypnotism* ~~Hypnotism~~ actually refers to a type of focused attention.

MISSING VERB   Alternative medical treatment may include hypnosis. *—the* ~~The~~ placement of a patient into a sleeplike state.

NO SUBJECT OR VERB   *Contrary to popular belief, the* ~~The~~ hypnotic state differs from sleep. ~~Contrary to popular belief.~~

DEPENDENT CLAUSE   Most people can be hypnotized easily. *, although* ~~Although~~ the depth of the trance for each person varies.

Identifying Fragments

If you have trouble recognizing fragments in your own writing, try one or more of these methods:

- **Read each paragraph backwards, sentence by sentence**. When you read your sentences out of order, you may more readily note the incompleteness of a fragment.
- **Locate the essential parts of each sentence: the main verb, then the subject.** Make sure that the sentence does not begin with a relative pronoun or a subordinating conjunction.
- **Put any sentence you think might be a fragment into this frame sentence**: They do not understand the idea that _____. Only a full sentence will make sense in this frame sentence.
- **Rewrite any sentence you think might be a fragment as a question that can be answered with *yes* or *no*.** Only complete sentences can be rewritten this way.

Editing Fragments with Missing Subjects and/or Verbs

A phrase is a group of words that is missing a subject and/or verb. When punctuated as a sentence (that is, with a period or other end punctuation), it becomes a fragment. To edit a phrase fragment, you can often attach it to a nearby sentence or recast the fragment as a complete sentence.

FRAGMENT	Humans painted themselves for a variety of purposes. **To attract a mate, to hide themselves from game or predators, or to signal aggression.**
REVISION	Humans used color for a variety of purposes. **For example, they painted themselves to attract a mate, to hide themselves from game or predators, or to signal aggression.**

Editing Fragments That Are Dependent Clauses

A dependent clause is a group of words with both a subject and a predicate (see CHAPTER 16, STYLE: AN ESSENTIAL GUIDE TO EFFECTIVE SENTENCES) that begins with a subordinating conjunction (words like *because, unless, when* that establish a relationship between an independent and dependent clause), a relative pronoun (*who, whom, which, that, whose*), or other words that designate a relationship. (See CHAPTER 16, ESTABLISHING VARIETY WITH COORDINATION AND SUBORDINATION.) Such words indicate a clause that cannot stand alone as a sentence.

pages 295–321

pages 306–307

➤ The iceberg was no surprise. *because* ~~Because~~ **the *Titanic's* wireless operators had received reports of ice in the area.**

➤ More than two thousand people were aboard the *Titanic.* *, which* ~~Which~~ **was the largest ocean liner in 1912**.

Such words indicate a clause that cannot stand alone as a sentence.

You can also recast the fragment as a complete sentence by removing the subordinating conjunction or relative pronoun and supplying any missing elements.

➤ The iceberg was no surprise. The *Titanic's* wireless operators had received reports of ice in the area.

Fragments

When used judiciously, fragments—like short sentences—emphasize ideas or add surprise. However, fragments are generally permitted only when the rhetorical situation allows the use of a casual tone.

<u>May. When the earth's Northern Hemisphere awakens from winter's sleep and all of nature bristles with the energies of new life.</u> **My work has kept me indoors for months now. I'm not sure I'll ever get used to it.**

—**Ken Carey,** *Flat Rock Journal: A Day in the Ozark Mountains* **[May]**

»» 2. COMMA SPLICES AND FUSED (RUN-ON) SENTENCES

pages 295–321

comma splice two sentences that are punctuated as one sentence when they should be punctuated as two sentences (or two independent clauses).

A **comma splice** refers to the incorrect use of a comma between two independent clauses. (See CHAPTER 16, STYLE: AN ESSENTIAL GUIDE TO EFFECTIVE SENTENCES.)

> Most stockholders favored the merger, ∧ the management did not.
>   *but*

A **fused sentence**, also referred to as a s*pliced* or *run-on sentence*, consists of two independent clauses run together without any punctuation at all.

fused sentence two sentences or independent clauses run together without punctuation

> The first section of the proposal was approved ∧ the budget will have to be resubmitted.
>   *; however,*

To edit a comma splice or a fused sentence, include appropriate punctuation and any necessary connecting words.

Identifying Comma Splices and Fused Sentences

You can find comma splices and fused sentences by remembering that they commonly occur in certain contexts.

- **With transitional words and phrases such as** *however, therefore,* **and** *for example*

COMMA SPLICE	The director is unable to meet you this week,*; however,* next week she has time on Tuesday.

- **When an explanation or an example is given in the second sentence**

FUSED SENTENCE	The cultural center has a new collection of Navajo weavings ∧ *. Many* ~~many~~ of them were donated by a retired anthropologist.

- **When a positive clause follows a negative clause, or vice versa**

COMMA SPLICE	A World Cup victory is not just an everyday sporting event, ~~It~~ ∧ *. It* is a national celebration.

Editing Comma Splices and Fused Sentences

If you find comma splices or fused sentences in your writing, use one of the following methods to edit them.

Link Independent Clauses with a Comma and a Coordinating Conjunction

By linking an independent clause with a coordinating (*and, but, or, nor, for, so,* or *yet*), you signal the relationship between them.

FUSED SENTENCE	The diplomats will end their discussion on Friday ∧ *, and* they will submit their final decision on Monday.

COMMA SPLICE	Some diplomats applauded the treaty, ∧ *but* others opposed it vehemently.

Link Independent Clauses with a Semicolon or Colon, or Separate them with a Period.

Link independent clauses with a semicolon to indicate an addition or contrast. Link with a colon to indicate an explanation. Separate them with a period to indicate each clause is a distinct sentence.

COMMA SPLICE	Our division's reports are posted on our webpage, _∧ *;* hard copies are available by request.
COMMA SPLICE	Our division's reports are posted on our webpage, _∧ *. Hard* ~~hard~~ copies are available by request.
FUSED SENTENCE	Our mission statement is simple _∧ we aim to provide good athletic gear at affordable prices.

Recast an Independent Clause as a Dependent Clause or as a Phrase

A dependent clause includes a subordinating conjunction such as *although* or *because*, which indicates how the dependent and independent clauses are related (in a cause-and-effect relationship, for example). A prepositional phrase includes a preposition such as *in, on,* or *because of that* may also signal a relationship directly.

COMMA SPLICE	*Because the* _∧ ~~The~~ wind had blown down power lines, the whole city was without electricity for several hours.
COMMA SPLICE	*Because of the downed power lines* _∧ ~~The wind had blown down power lines~~, the whole city was without electricity for several hours.

Integrate One Clause into the Other, Retaining the Important Details

When you integrate clauses, you will generally retain the important details but omit or change some words.

FUSED SENTENCE	*the points except assessment procedures.* The proposal covers all _∧ **~~but one point it does not describe how the project will be assessed~~**.

Use Transitional Words or Phrases to Link Independent Clauses

Another way to revise fused sentences and comma splices is to use transitional words and phrases such as *however, on the contrary,* and *in the meantime.*

FUSED SENTENCE	*. After all,* Sexual harassment is not an issue for just women $\wedge$ men can be sexually harassed too.
COMMA SPLICE	The word *status* refers to relative position within a *; however,* group, $\wedge$ it is often used to indicate only positions of prestige.

≫≫ 3. SUBJECT-VERB AGREEMENT

In academic and professional writing, the verb agrees with the subject in number (singular or plural, as in *I* or *we*) and in person (first [*I*], second [*you*], and third [*he, she, it, they*]). In other words, the form of the verb (*run* or *runs*) should agree with the subject. Usually, the third-person, singular subject (*he, she, they, it*) adds an *-s* to the base form to differentiate *I run, you run*, and *they run* from *he runs*. The tricks are to locate the subject and verb, regardless of where they appear in the sentence. Locating the subject helps you choose the correct verb form. (See also CHAPTER 16, MISMATCHES IN SUBJECTS AND VERBS.)

pages 298–299

Words between the Subject and the Verb

Always strike agreement between the number of the subject and the form of the verb even when phrases such as the following separate them.

along with	*in addition to*	*not to mention*
as well as	*including*	*together with*

Subjects Joined by *and*

A **compound subject** that refers to a single person or thing takes a singular verb.

compound subject two nouns joined by *and*

➤ The **founder** and **president** of the art association **was** elected to the board of the museum.

Subjects Joined by *or* or *nor*

When **singular subjects** are linked by *or, either . . . or*, or *neither . . . nor*, the verb is singular as well.

singular subjects two nouns linked by *either/or*, or *neither/nor*

➤ The **provost** or the **dean** usually **presides** at the meeting.

If the linked subjects differ in number, the verb agrees with the subject closer to the verb.

➤ Neither the basket nor the **apples were** expensive. [plural]

➤ Neither the apples nor the **basket was** expensive. [singular]

Inverted Order

In most sentences, the subject precedes the verb, but the subject and the verb are sometimes inverted for emphasis.

➤ The hardest hit by the winter storms **were** the large **cities** of the Northeast.

When *there* begins a sentence, the subject and verb are always inverted; the verb still agrees with the subject, which follows it.

➤ There **are** several **cities** in need of federal aid.

Subjects and Forms of the Verb "to be" (*am, are, is, was, were, will be*)

When a sentence has a singular subject linked to a plural noun by a form "to be," the verb agrees with the subject.

➤ Her primary **concern is** rising healthcare costs.

➤ **Croissants are** the bakery's specialty

》》 4. CONSISTENT VERB TENSE

Every verb tense reflects *time frame*, which refers to whether the tense is *present* (*is*), *past* (*was*), or *future* (*will be*). Verb tenses are also labeled as *simple progressive*, *perfect*, or *perfect progressive*. The simplified chart that follows gives you an overview of how these labels apply to the tense of *walk*.

	VERB TENSES		
	PRESENT	**PAST**	**FUTURE**
SIMPLE	I/you/we/they **walk**	**walked**	**will walk**
PROGRESSIVE	I **am walking**	**was walking**	**will be walking**

PERFECT	I **have walked**	**had walked**	**will have walked**
PERFECT PROGRESSIVE	I **have been walking**	**had been walking**	**will be walking**

Consistency in the time frame of verbs ensures that sentences reporting a sequence of events link together logically. By using verb tenses consistently, you help your readers understand when the actions or events you are describing took place. In the following paragraph, notice that the time frame remains in the past.

past perfect

➤ At that point, Kubrick **had finished** *Dr. Strangelove.* Working

simple past

independently, he **started** his science-fiction *2001: A Space Odyssey*

past progressive

unaware that he **was working** in a new genre.

If you do need to shift to another time frame, you can use a time marker.

now   then   today   yesterday

in two years   during the 1920s

after you finish   before we left

simple present   *time marker*

➤ The Minnesota State Fair **attracts** thousands of visitors. **Last year**, atten-

simple past

dance on Labor Day weekend **exceeded** 650,000.

You may be able to change time frames without including time markers when you wish (1) to explain or support a general statement with information about the past, (2) to compare and contrast two different time periods, or (3) to comment on a topic.

➤ Thomas Jefferson, author of the Declaration of Independence, **is** considered one of our country's most brilliant citizens. His achievements **were** many, as **were** his interests. [The second sentence provides evidence from the past to support the claim in the first sentence.]

Before you turn in your final draft, check your verb tenses to ensure that they are logical and consistent. Edit any that are not.

⟫ 5. PRONOUN AGREEMENT

A pronoun and its **antecedent** (the word or word group to which it refers) agree in number (both are singular or both are plural).

➤ The **supervisor** said **he** would help.

[Both antecedent and pronoun are singular.]

➤ **The supervisor** said **they** would help.

[*They* is also a third-person singular pronoun.]

➤ My **colleagues** said **they** would help.

[Both antecedent and pronoun are plural.]

(For more on *they* as a chosen pronoun, see CHAPTER 25, SOCIAL MEDIA AND THE POSSIBILITIES OF GENDER.)

antecedent a word or group of words referred to by a pronoun

Indefinite Pronouns

Indefinite pronouns (such as *everyone, someone,* or *anybody*) take singular verbs.

➤ **Everyone has** [not have] the right to an opinion.

Writers can use *they* as a third-person singular pronoun. The singular *they* is a gender-neutral alternative to *he or she.*

➤ **Everyone** has the combination to **their** private locker.

The same sentence can also be rewritten with a plural subject and plural verb or with an article.

➤ **Students** have combinations to **their** private lockers.

[plural antecedent and plural possessive pronoun]

➤ **Everyone** has the combination to **a** private locker.

[article]

Two Antecedents Joined by *or* or *nor*

If a singular and a plural antecedent are joined by *or* or *nor*, place the plural antecedent second and use a plural pronoun.

➤ Either the senator **or** her **assistants** will explain how **they** devised the plan for tax reform.

➤ Neither the president **nor** the **senators** stated that **they** would support the proposal.

Collective Nouns

When an antecedent is a **collective noun** such as *team*, *faculty*, or *committee*, determine whether you intend the noun to be understood as singular or plural. Then, make sure that the pronoun agrees in number with the noun.

➤ The choir decided that ⌄ **they** would tour during the winter. [Because the choir decided as a group, choir should be considered singular.]

it

➤ The committee disagree on methods, but ⌄ **it** agree on basic aims. [Because the committee members are behaving as individuals, committee is regarded as plural.]

they

collective noun A noun that refers to a group

⟫ 6. VAGUE PRONOUN REFERENCE

When you use pronouns effectively, you add clarity and coherence to your writing. Most pronouns (*it*, *he*, *she*, *they*, and many others) replace antecedents—nouns or noun phrases that have already been mentioned. The meaning of each pronoun in a sentence should be immediately obvious.

In the following sentence, the pronoun *he* clearly refers to the antecedent, *Jack*.

➤ **Jack** has collected shells since **he** was eight years old.

Ambiguous Pronoun Reference

Edit sentences in which a pronoun can refer to either of two antecedents.

➤ Anna told her sister ~~that she had~~ to call home.

Remote Pronoun Reference

To help readers understand your meaning, place each relative pronoun (*who*, *whom*, *which*, *that*, or *whose*) as close to its antecedent as possible.

that was originally published in 1945

➤ The **poem** ∧ has been published in a new book ∧' ~~**that** was originally written in 1945.~~

[A poem, not a book, was first published in 1945.]

Notice, however, that a relative pronoun does not always have to follow its antecedent directly. In the following example, there is no risk of misunderstanding.

➤ We slowly began to notice *changes* in our lives **that** we had never expected.

Broad Pronoun Reference

Pronouns such as *it, this, that,* and *which* sometimes refer to the sense of a whole clause, sentence, or paragraph.

➤ Large corporations may seem stronger than individuals, but **that** is not true.

[*That* refers to the sense of the whole first clause.]

In academic situations, edit sentences that do not have specific antecedents.

➤ When class attendance is compulsory, some students feel that education

perception

is being forced on them. This ∧ is unwarranted.

[In the original sentence, *this* had no clear antecedent.]

Implied Reference

Express an idea explicitly rather than merely implying it.

Teaching music

➤ My father is a music teacher. ∧ **It** is a profession that requires much patience.

[In the original sentence, *it* had no expressed antecedent.]

Provide clear antecedents when referring to the work or possessions of others. The following sentence requires editing because *she* can refer to someone other than *Jen Norton,* who could be an editor instead of an author.

her   *Jen Norton*

➤ In ∧ ~~**Jen Norton's**~~ new book, ∧ **she** argues for election reform.

The Use of *it* without an Antecedent

It does not have a specific antecedent. Instead, *it* is used to postpone, and thus give emphasis to, the subject of a sentence. If a sentence that begins with *it* is wordy or awkward, replace *it* with the postponed subject.

➤ ∧ ~~It was no use trying to repair the~~ ∧ ~~car.~~

Trying to repair the car   *was useless.*

THINKING RHETORICALLY

Pronouns

Because pronouns must have context to make their referents clear, be sure that you provide your readers with enough information to understand who or what each pronoun represents. Vague uses of *it, they, this,* and *that* can make your writing hard to follow. Notice the difficulty of identifying what *this* is in the following sentence:

- **The study found that students succeed when they have clear directions, consistent and focused feedback, and access to help. <u>This</u> has led to the development of a tutoring center at our university.**

This could refer to the study, the information provided by the study, or perhaps just to the finding that students need access to help. If you find that you have used a vague pronoun, add enough text to make the referent easily identifiable:

- <u>**The finding that successful students have access to help**</u> **has led to the development of a tutoring center at our university.**

»» 7. MISPLACED OR DANGLING MODIFIERS

A **modifier** is a word or word group that describes, limits, or qualifies another. Effective placement of modifiers will improve the clarity and coherence of your sentences.

modifier a word or word group that describes, limits, or qualifies another

Misplaced Modifiers

A **misplaced modifier** obscures the meaning of a sentence.

Placing Modifiers Near the Words they Modify

Readers expect phrases and clauses to modify the nearest grammatical element.

➤ *The* ~~Crouched and ugly, the~~ young boy gasped at the ∧ phantom moving *crouched and ugly* across the stage.

[The repositioned modifiers *crouched* and *ugly* describe the phantom, not the boy.]

Using Limiting Modifiers

Place the limiting modifiers *almost, even, hardly, just,* and *only* before the words or word groups they modify. Altering placement can alter meaning.

➤ The committee can **only** nominate two members for the position.

[The committee cannot appoint the two members to the position.]

➤ The committee can nominate **only** two members for the position.

[The committee cannot nominate more than two members.]

➤ **Only** the committee can nominate two members for the position.

[No person or group other than the committee can nominate members.]

Editing Squinting Modifiers

A **squinting modifier** can be interpreted as modifying either what precedes it or what follows it. To avoid such lack of clarity, you can reposition the modifier, add punctuation, or edit the entire sentence.

SQUINTING	Even though Erikson lists some advantages **overall** his vision of a successful business is faulty.
REVISED	Even though Erikson lists some **overall** advantages, his vision of a successful business is faulty. [modifier repositioned; punctuation added]
REVISED	Erikson lists some advantages; **however, overall,** his vision of a successful business is faulty. [sentence revised]

Dangling Modifiers

Dangling modifiers do not clearly modify anything in the rest of the sentence. If a sentence begins or ends with a modifier, be sure that what follows or precedes it—namely, the subject of the sentence—is actually being modified.

➤ Lying on the beach, *we found that* time became irrelevant. [Time cannot lie on a beach.]

➤ Adequate lighting is a necessity *for anyone* when studying. [Lighting cannot study.]

»» 8. PARALLELISM

Linked ideas need to be parallel in form—that is, they must be formed with all nouns, all adjectives, all prepositional phrases, and so on. Create parallelism by repeating words, linking parallel forms with correlative conjunctions, or making sure pairs of linking words, phrases, or clauses are accompanied by parallel elements. (See also, **CHAPTER 16, USING PARELLELISM FOR CLARITY AND EMPHASIS**.)

dangling modifiers words or phrases that do not clearly modify another word or word group

pages 310–311

Creating Parallelism through Repeated Words

Recognizing parallel grammatical forms is easiest when you look for the repetition of certain words. The repetition of a preposition, the word *to*, or the introductory word of a clause is a good way to edit for parallelism.

PREPOSITION   My break-up was caused **by** my leaving my hometown and also **by** my eagerness to meet new people.

TO   Her students work **to** learn about academic writing and **to** transfer that knowledge to their other courses, their work place, and their personal lives.

INTRODUCTORY WORD OR PHRASE   The team members vowed **that they would** support each other, **that they would** play their best, and **that they would** win the tournament.

Creating Parallelism with Coordinating Conjunctions

To recognize parallelism in sentences that do not include repeated words, look for a coordinating conjunction: *and, but, or, yet, so, nor, or, for.* The words, phrases, or clauses that such a conjunction joins are parallel if they have similar grammatical forms.

WORDS	The young actor was *shy* **yet** *determined*.
PHRASES	Her goals include *publicizing* student and faculty research, *increasing* the funding for that research, **and** *providing* adequate research facilities.
CLAUSES	Our instructor explained *what the project had entailed* **and** *how the researcher had used the results*.

Creating Parallelism with Linking Words

As you edit, make sure pairs of linking words, phrases, or clauses—including *both . . . and, either . . . or, neither . . . nor, not only . . . but also,* and *whether . . . or*—link parallel elements. Notice how words or phrases following each of the paired linking words are parallel.

➤ The new teacher is **both** *determined* **and** *dedicated*.

➤ **Whether** *at home* **or** *at school*, he is always busy.

Be especially careful when using not only . . . but also.

➤ His team practices not only
  Not only practicing at 6 a.m. during the week, **but his team also** scrimmages on Sunday afternoons.

[*Not only* and *but also* are edited so that each is followed by a prepositional phrase, **at** *6 a.m.* and **on** *Sunday afternoons*.]

  OR

➤ does his team practice
  Not only practicing at 6 a.m. during the week, but it his team also scrimmages on Sunday afternoons.

[*Not only* and *but also* are edited so that each is accompanied by a clause, *does his team practice* and *it also scrimmages*.]

Creating Parallelism in Lists, Headings, and Outlines

Each item in a list or formal outline should be parallel to emphasize consistency and connectedness. Headings in any document should be in parallel form whenever possible.

➤ In his speech, the president charged his generation with lofty goals: (1) **reigniting** economic growth, (2) **restoring** the American dream, and (3) ∧ *putting* ~~to make~~ government ∧ *to* work for average citizens.

»» 9. MISSING COMMA JOINING CLAUSES WITH COORDINATING CONJUNCTIONS

A common belief is that commas signal a pause; however, not every pause calls for a comma. Pauses are not a reliable guide for comma placement. Better guidance for using commas comes from some basic principles for comma usage. Use a comma before a coordinating conjunction (*and, but, for, nor, or, so,* or *yet*) to join independent clauses.

➤ George H. W. Bush served as president from 1989 to 1993**, and** his son George W. Bush served from 2001 to 2009.

But when clauses are short, commas may be omitted.

➤ His grandson ran for president but his son did not.

THINKING RHETORICALLY

Commas and Conjunctions in a Series

How do the following sentences differ?

- **We discussed them all: life, liberty, and the pursuit of happiness.**
- **We discussed them all: life and liberty and the pursuit of happiness.**
- **We discussed them all: life, liberty, the pursuit of happiness**.

The first sentence follows conventional guidelines; that is, a comma and a conjunction precede the last element in the series. The less conventional second and third sentences do more than convey information. Having two conjunctions and no commas, the second sentence slows down the pace of the reading, causing stress to be placed on each of the three elements in the series. In contrast, the third sentence, with commas but no conjunctions, speeds up the reading, as if to suggest that the rights listed do not need to be stressed because they are so familiar. To get a sense of how your sentences will be read and understood, try reading them aloud to yourself.

»» 10. MISSING COMMA AFTER AN INTRODUCTORY ELEMENT

Without a comma after an introductory sentence element, a sentence can be hard to read. Consider, for instance, how such a comma helps clarify the following sentences.

UNCLEAR	When they want to cook people must plan.
CLEAR	When they want to cook, people must plan. [without the comma, the sentence might be misread as "to cook people"]
UNCLEAR	After all the students had become ill.
CLEAR	After all, the students had become ill. [without the comma, the sentence might be misread to indicate "all the students had become ill"]

The commas in these sentences help the reader locate the subject of the sentence, which clarifies the meaning of the sentences.

A comma may be omitted after a short introduction as long as the sentence is still clear.

➤ In 2020 the enrollment at the university increased.

Even if your sentence is perfectly clear without a comma, using a comma will never be wrong.

>> 11. MISSING COMMA SETTING OFF NONESSENTIAL ELEMENTS

All nonessential words, phrases, and clauses should be set off by commas because the information they convey is unnecessary for identifying who or what is being described or discussed. On the other hand, no commas are used when the information is necessary, when the information answers the question *Which?*

ESSENTIAL WORD	The mountaineer **Walter Harper** was the first to summit Denali. [Which mountaineer? Walter Harper—no commas are needed]
NONESSENTIAL WORD	The first mountaineer to summit Denali, **Walter Harper,** was an Alaska Native. [Which first mountaineer? does not make sense—commas are needed]
ESSENTIAL PHRASE	The mountain **towering above us** brought to mind our abandoned plan for climbing it. [Which mountain? The one towering above us—no commas are needed]
NONESSENTIAL PHRASE	Denali, **towering above us**, brought to mind our abandoned plan for climbing it. [Which Denali? does not make sense—commas are needed]

>> 12. UNNECESSARY COMMAS

Although commas can play many roles in your writing, overusing them can confuse your meaning. No commas are necessary between the following elements.

SUBJECT AND VERB	**Rain** at frequent intervals, **produces** mosquitoes.
TWO VERBS THAT AGREE WITH ONE SUBJECT	**I read** the comments carefully, and then **started** my revision.
REPORTING VERB AND *THAT*	The author **noted, that** the results of the study were not conclusive.

CONJUNCTION AND SUBJECT	We worked very hard on her campaign for state representative, **but** the **incumbent** was too strong to defeat in the northern districts.
SUCH AS OR *LIKE* AND THE EXAMPLE THAT FOLLOWS	Many university applicants take **entrance** exams **such as** the ACT or the SAT.
ESSENTIAL ELEMENT AND THE REST OF THE SENTENCE	Everyone **who has a mortgage** is required to have fire insurance.
MONTH OR HOLIDAY AND YEAR	The class reunion is tentatively planned for **June, 2022**. The last time she saw them was on **Thanksgiving Day, 2015**.
EXCLAMATION POINT OR QUESTION MARK AND CLOSING QUOTATION MARKS	"Dave, stop. Stop, will you? Stop, Dave. Will you stop?" implores the supercomputer HAL in *2001: A Space Odyssey*.

⟫ 13. UNNECESSARY OR MISSING APOSTROPHE (INCLUDING *IT'S/ITS*)

Apostrophes indicate ownership (*my neighbor's television*), relationships (*my neighbor's children*), or production or creation (*my neighbor's recipe*). They are also used in contractions (*can't, don't*) and in those plural forms (*x's* and *y's*) that would be confusing without them.

Possessive Nouns

possessive case a grammatical construction that indicates ownership and other similar relationships

An apostrophe, often followed by an *s*, signals the **possessive case** of nouns, which are used to express a variety of meanings.

OWNERSHIP	**Fumi's** computer, the **photographer's** camera
ORIGIN	**Einstein's** ideas, the **student's** decision
HUMAN RELATIONSHIPS	**Linda's** sister, the **employee's** supervisor

POSSESSION OF PHYSICAL OR PSYCHOLOGICAL TRAITS	**Mona Lisa's** smile, the **team's** spirit
ASSOCIATION BETWEEN ABSTRACTIONS AND ATTRIBUTES	**democracy's** success, **tyranny's** influence
IDENTIFICATION OF DOCUMENTS	**driver's** license, **bachelor's** degree, **master's** degree
IDENTIFICATION OF THINGS OR DAYS NAMED AFTER PEOPLE	**St. John's** Cathedral, **St. Valentine's** Day
SPECIFICATION OF AMOUNTS	**a day's wages**, **my two cents' worth**

Possessive Pronouns (*your, their, whose, its*)

Although possessive nouns are written with apostrophes (***Linda's*** *sister, the* ***dean's*** *office)*, possessive pronouns are not. Possessive pronouns include *my, mine, our, ours, your, yours, his, her, hers, its, their, theirs,* and *whose* are not written with apostrophes.

➤ The committee concluded **its** discussion.

In Contractions, Numbers, and Colloquial Language *(you're, they're, who's, it's)* (see p. 345), you will learn more about distinguishing possessive pronouns from contractions.

Plural Nouns

Add only an apostrophe to indicate the possessive case of plural nouns that end in *s*.

➤ the boys**'** game   the babies**'** toys   the Joneses**'** house

Plural nouns that do not end in *s* need both an apostrophe and an *s*.

➤ men**'**s lives   women**'**s health   children**'**s projects

These plurals are generally formed by adding *s* only (no apostrophe):

➤ 1990s   fours and fives   YWCAs   two *ands*   the three *Rs*   PhDs

Lowercase letters are made plural by adding both an apostrophe and an *s*: *p*'s and *q*'s. The Modern Language Association recommends the use of apostrophes for the plurals of uppercase letters (four *A's*) in addition to those of lowercase letters (the *x*'s and *y*'s in an equation). Note that letters used as letters (my *ABC*s), rather than as grades or abbreviations, are italicized.

Unlike Mother's Day or Valentine's Day, according to the *U.S. Government Publishing Office Style Manual,* two holidays are spelled without an apostrophe: Veterans Day and Presidents Day.

 TIPS FOR APOSTROPHES AND PLURAL NOUNS

An apostrophe is not needed to make a noun plural. To make most nouns plural, add *s* or *es*. Add an apostrophe only to signal ownership and other similar relationships.

protesters
- The ∧ **protesters'** swarmed the conference center.
- The **protesters'** meeting was on Wednesday.

To form the plural of a family name, use *s* or *es*, not an apostrophe.

Moores
The ∧ **Moore's** participated in the study.

[COMPARE: The **Moores'** participation in the study was crucial.]

Moores
The ∧ **Moore's** live in the yellow house on the corner.

[COMPARE: The **Moores'** house is the yellow house on the corner.]

Nouns That Show Collaboration or Joint Ownership

An apostrophe and an *s* follow the second of two singular nouns. Just an apostrophe follows the second of two plural nouns that already ends in *s*.

➤ the carpenter and the **plumber's** decision [They made the decision collaboratively.]

➤ the Becks and the **Lopezes'** cabin [They own one cabin jointly.]

To show separate ownership or individual contributions, each plural noun is followed by an apostrophe; each singular noun is followed by *'s*.

➤ the **Becks'** and the **Lopezes'** cars [Each family owns a car.]

➤ the **carpenter's** and the **plumber's** proposals [They each made a proposal.]

Names of Products and Geographical Locations

Follow an organization's preference for its name or the name of a product and local conventions for that of a geographical location.

Consumers Union	Actors' Equity	Taster's Choice
Devil's Island	Devils Tower	Lands' End

Contractions, Numbers, and Colloquial Language (*you're, they're, who's, it's*)

Earlier, this section discussed how possessive pronouns (*your, their, whose, its*) (see p. 343) do not take an apostrophe. Possessive pronouns are commonly confused with similar contractions, however, where an apostrophe stands in for the missing letters.

they're [they are]	*who's* [who is]	*it's* [it is]	*you're* [you are]
class of '14 [class of 2014]	*y'all* [you all]	*singin'* [singing]	

 TIPS FOR *ITS* VS. *IT'S*, *THEIR* VS. *THEY'RE*, *WHOSE* VS. *WHO'S*, *YOUR* VS. *YOU'RE*

Be careful not to confuse possessive pronouns (such as *its, their, whose, your*) with contractions (*it's, they're, who's, you're*). Whenever you write a contraction, you should be able to substitute the complete words for it without changing the meaning.

POSSESSIVE PRONOUN CONTRACTION

➤ **Its** motor is small. **It's** [It is] a small motor.
➤ **Their** home is in town. **They're** [They are] going home.
➤ **Whose** turn is it? **Who's** [Who is] representing us?
➤ **Your** resume is impressive. **You're** [You are] sure to get the job.

≫ 14. SPELLING

When you first draft a paper, you might not pay close attention to spelling words correctly. If you are focusing on generating and organizing your ideas at this point and relying on your spell checker, you leave yourself open to spelling errors in your final draft. Handy as they are, spell checkers are not foolproof: they cannot distinguish homophones, capitalize proper nouns, detect whether you intended to type *read* or *red*, and so on. Before submitting your final draft, you will want to make time to read carefully for spelling errors so that you can submit the kind of writing your teacher, employer, or supervisor expects to read: polished.

Spelling and Punctuation

In addition to the problem of wrong words and capitalization, spelling errors include many words in English that are not spelled the way they are pronounced or heard. Some words are typically misspelled because they include unpronounced letters:

➤ condem**n**, forei**g**n, lab**or**atory, mus**c**le, solem**n**

Here are a few that include letters that are often not heard in rapid speech:

➤ can**d**idate, diff**e**rent, gover**n**ment, sep**a**rate, lib**r**ary, Feb**r**uary

You can teach yourself the correct spellings of words by pronouncing each letter mentally so that you "hear" even silent letters.

> ⊘ **TIPS FOR FREQUENTLY MISSPELLED WORDS:** *and, have, than*
>
> The words *and, have,* and *than* are often not stressed in speech and are thus frequently misspelled.
>
>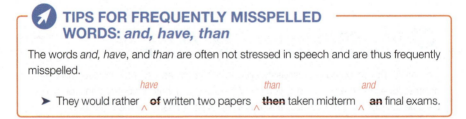

Spell Checker

The spell checker is a wonderful invention, but only when you use it with care. A spell checker will usually flag misspellings of common words and obvious typographical errors (such as *tge* for *the*). However, a spell checker generally will not detect specialized vocabulary or foreign words not in its dictionary, proper nouns that require capitalization, typographical errors that are still correctly spelled words (such as *was* for *saw*), and misuses of commonly confused words (discussed in the next section).

TIPS FOR USING A SPELL CHECKER

The following strategies can help you use a spell checker effectively. A spell checker makes proofreading easier, though you must use it with care.

- **Proofread your work carefully.** Even if you are using a spell checker, spell checkers will not catch all typos, such as *form* instead of *from*.
- **Double-check words you frequently misspell.** If you often misspell homophones (such as *there/their*, *who's/whose*, and *it's/its*), check for these words after using the spell checker.
- **Do not automatically accept changes the spell checker suggests**. Use a dictionary to look up unfamiliar words that are highlighted by the spell checker. Evaluate the alternative words or spellings the spell checker provides because some of them may change the meaning of your sentence.
- **Add correctly spelled words not in the dictionary to the spell checkers dictionary.** If a spell checker regularly flags a word that is not in its dictionary but is spelled correctly, add that word to its dictionary by clicking on the Add button. From that point on, the spell checker will accept the word.
- **Reject any offers the spell checker makes to correct all instances of a particular error.**

»» 15. WRONG WORD

As you write, you're juggling many concerns from establishing a thesis and including pertinent support to choosing how to deliver your message and ensuring its clarity and correctness. Foundational to each of these concerns is the issue of precision. Choosing the right word is key to maintaining precision in your writing. This section should help you avoid using the wrong word for words that are commonly confused and misused. (See also CHAPTER 16, PRECISION).

pages 311–319

Homophones and Homonyms

One of the most common writing errors is choosing the wrong word from those that sound alike. Some words that have different meanings sound exactly alike *(break/brake)*; others sound alike in certain dialects *(marry/merry)*. Pairs of words such as *forth* and *fourth* or *sole* and *soul* are **homophones**. words that sound alike

homophones
words that sound alike but have different meanings

but have different meanings and spellings. Closely related to homophones are **homonyms**, words such as *pen, address, book, band,* and *bright* that sound alike and are spelled alike but have different meanings. The context of your sentence will provide the correct definition of the homonym for your reader.

Two-Word Sequences

Also troublesome are two-word sequences that can be written as compound words or as separate words. The following are examples:

➤ **Everyday** life was grueling. She attended class **every day**.

➤ They do not fight **anymore**. They could not find **any more** evidence.

Other examples are *awhile/a while, sometime/some time,* and *everyone/every one* (also discussed earlier in this chapter under Indefinite Pronouns, p. 332). *A lot* and *all right* are still spelled as two words. *Alot* is always considered incorrect; *alright* is also considered incorrect except in some newspapers and magazines.

homonyms
words that are spelled alike and sound alike but have different meanings

Nouns Ending in *–nce* or *–nts*

Singular nouns ending in *-nce* and plural nouns ending in *-nts* are also easily confused.

Assistance is available.	I have two **assistants.**
His **patience** wore thin.	Some **patients** waited for hours.

Possessive Pronouns and Contractions

Be sure to include an apostrophe in contractions but not in possessive pronouns.

POSSESSIVES	*its, your, their, theirs, whose*
CONTRACTIONS	*it's (it is), you're (you are), they're (they are), there's (there is), who's (who is)*

Also keep in mind that *it's/its* and *their/there/they're* also sound alike, but the problem resides not in the homophone but in the missing or extra apostrophe that changes the intended meaning. These were discussed more fully earlier under Possessive Pronouns (*its, your, their, whose*) (p. 343); Contractions, Numbers, and Colloquial Language (*it's, you're, they're, who's*) (p. 345); and the *Its* vs. *It's, Their* vs. *They're, Whose* vs. *Who's, Your* vs. *You're* box (p. 345).

The Glossary of Usage

Commonly confused words such as *accept/except, affect/effect, cite/site/sight, than/ then, to/too/two,* and *your/you're* are often on lists of the worst-of-the-worst "word crimes." Using these words incorrectly can particularly affect your credibility as a writer. Pay special attention to these and the words in the box on Commonly Confused or Misused Words as you edit your work to avoid using the wrong word.

Commonly Confused or Misused Words

accept/except	disinterested/uninterested	principle/principal
advice/advise		
affect/effect	farther/further	than/then
aloud/allowed		their/there/they're
are/our	here/hear	to/too/two
bear/bare	it's/its	weather/whether
brake/break		which/witch
buy/by	lay/lie	
	lose/loose	you're/your
capital/capitol		
cite/sight/site	one/won	
complement/compliment		

If you are unsure about the difference in meaning between any two words that sound alike, consult the GLOSSARY OF USAGE for help with the most commonly confused or misused words. Organized like a dictionary, it provides not only common meanings for the words but also example sentences demonstrating usage.

pages 587-597

18 Thinking Rhetorically about Research

LEARNING OBJECTIVES

- Summarize the reasons researchers use citation practices.
- Identify types of research that will best suit their audience and purpose.
- Explain how research can be inspired by a question.
- Evaluating a source by gauging your purpose and audience as well as the credibility and quality of a source.
- Assess productive counterarguments.
- Articulate questions that guide your initial research.

Clues to Compulsive Collecting

Separating Useless Junk from Objects of Value

An intriguing new study may help researchers understand why some people are compelled to hoard useless objects. Steven W. Anderson, a neurologist, and his colleagues at the University of Iowa examined 63 people with brain damage from stroke, surgery, or encephalitis. Before their brains were damaged, none had problems with hoarding, but afterward, nine began filling their houses with such things as old newspapers, broken appliances, or boxes of junk mail, despite the intervention of family members.

These compulsive collectors had all suffered damage to the prefrontal cortex, a brain region involved in decision-making, information processing, and behavioral organization. The people whose collecting behavior remained normal also had brain damage, but it was instead distributed throughout the right and left hemispheres of the brain.

Anderson posits that the urge to collect derives from the need to store supplies such as food—a drive so basic it originates in the subcortical and limbic portions of the brain. Humans need the prefrontal cortex, he says, to determine what "supplies" are worth hoarding. His study was presented at the annual conference of the Society for Neuroscience.

—Richard A. Lovett

Why do some people collect useless objects like old newspapers, broken appliances, and junk mail?

WR Publishing/Alamy Stock Photo

1. In "Clues to Compulsive Collecting," Richard Lovett describes research first presented by Steven Anderson and his colleagues at a neuroscience conference. After reading this article, write a paragraph or two in which you discuss the article in terms of Lovett's and the original researchers' rhetorical situations. How are they similar? How are they different?

2. In answering question 1, you likely noted significant differences in the rhetorical situations of the article writer and the original researchers, even though their subject matter was the same. In order to prepare for the research you may have to do for college classes, describe a rhetorical situation you might encounter in one of your classes. Explain how research would help you prepare a fitting response.

»» CONSIDERING THE RHETORICAL SITUATION

Like any other kind of writing you do, your research report needs to address the rhetorical situation. There are many different kinds of research, just as there are many different ways to present research findings. Shaping a fitting response means considering the following kinds of questions:

- *Is your researched response appropriate to the problem?* The focus, and thus the kind of research called for (library, internet, naturalistic, laboratory, or some combination of these), depends on the nature of the problem. Engineers studying the question of how to prevent future natural disasters from causing the kind of damage wrought in Jackson, Mississippi, by the 2020 unprecedented rains and flooding would need to be sure their research focused on environmental and geographical conditions specific to that area. Research on the success of levees built along the Danube in Europe might not be applicable. The researchers would also likely need to combine many different kinds of research in order to determine the best method of prevention.

- *Is your researched response delivered in a medium that will reach its intended audience?* Writers presenting research findings want to be sure their work finds its way into the right hands. Engineers researching the issue of how best to rebuild the levees along the deltaic Mississippi River could certainly summarize their findings in a letter to the editor of the Jackson *Clarion-Ledger.* However, if they wanted approval from a government agency for future work, they would likely need to present the research in a document addressed directly to that agency, such as a written application for funding or a proposal in the form of a multimedia presentation.

- *Will your researched response successfully satisfy the rhetorical audience?* Research papers in different academic disciplines have different types of content and formats. In consideration of your audience, it is important that you take care to notice the research methods used in the discipline and deliver writing that is presented and documented according to the accepted style of the discipline. (For information on the documentation style recommended by the Modern Language Association (MLA), see pages 412–449 CHAPTER 22, ACKNOWLEDGING SOURCES IN MLA STYLE. For information on the documentation style recommended by the American Psychological pages 450–476 Association (APA), see CHAPTER 23, ACKNOWLEDGING SOURCES IN APA STYLE.

pages 31–32
- Of course, each rhetorical situation is different. In CHAPTER 2, RESOURCES AND CONSTRAINTS, you learned how the means available to you for responding are shaped by both the *constraints* (limitations) and the *resources* (advantages) of the rhetorical situation. Every time you begin research, you will face a new set of constraints and resources. To participate effectively in an ongoing conversation, you will need to identify specific resources to help you manage your particular set of constraints.

In reviewing the brief *Psychology Today* article that opened this chapter, you saw how one writer, Richard Lovett, worked with specific constraints and resources. You may have identified the primary elements of the rhetorical situation, such as the need to deliver complex and specialized information from the field of neurology to readers of a popular magazine. To address this constraint, Lovett made allowances for his readers' perhaps limited knowledge of how the brain works by defining unfamiliar terms (*prefrontal cortex,* for example). You may also have noted some of the resources available to Lovett in writing for this kind of publication. The image that accompanies his text allows readers to absorb the topic at a glance, while the pull-quote (the quotation in large type in the middle of the article) makes the scientists' research question explicit.

» IDENTIFYING THE RESEARCH QUESTION

As you know from reading Chapter 1, the starting point for any writing project is determining your rhetorical opportunity for change. For research assignments, that opportunity for change also includes what has prompted you to look for more information. After you are sure of your opportunity, you can craft a question to guide your research.

To make the most of your time, choose a specific question early in your research process. Having such a question helps you avoid collecting more sources than you can possibly use or finding sources that are only tangentially related. Choosing a general topic—say, social welfare—will waste time if you neglect to narrow the topic into a question, such as one of the following: What is the history of homelessness in the United States? What social welfare programs currently assist people without permanent housing? How do public spaces accommodate or repudiate people without permanent housing? What role does public architecture play in the accommodation or repudiation of people without permanent housing?

Good questions often arise when you try to relate what you are studying in a course to your own experience. For instance, you may start wondering about the conditions or remedies for homelessness when, after reading about this topic in a sociology class, you notice the number of times government officials speak disparagingly or compassionately about people without permanent housing in their state or city. (See CHAPTER 26 FREYA DROHAN, "ANTI-HOMELESS ARCHITECTURE.") These pages 512–515 observations may prompt you to look for more information on the topic. Each observation, however, may give rise to a different question. You will choose the question that interests you the most and that will best help you fulfill the assignment.

To generate research questions, you may find it helpful to return to Chapter 13, where you read about journalists' questions (Who? What? Where? When? Why? How?). (See CHAPTER 13, QUESTIONING.) Here are some more pages 233–234 specific kinds of questions that commonly require research:

QUESTIONS ABOUT CAUSES

What reasons does my college give for not offering athletic scholarships?

What causes power outages in large areas of the country?

QUESTIONS ABOUT CONSEQUENCES

What are the consequences of taking antidepressants for a long period of time?

How might the atmosphere in a school change if a dress code were established?

QUESTIONS ABOUT PROCESSES

How can music lovers prevent corporations from controlling the development of music?

How does my hometown draw boundaries for school districts?

QUESTIONS ABOUT DEFINITIONS OR CATEGORIES

How do you know if you are addicted to something?

What kind of test is "the test of time"?

QUESTIONS ABOUT VALUES

Should the Makah tribe be allowed to hunt gray whales?

Would the construction of wind farms be detrimental to the environment?

 TRICKS OF THE TRADE

If the assignment does not specify a topic and you are not sure what you want to write about, you may need some prompting. Consider these questions.

- Can you remember an experience that you did not understand fully or that made you feel uncertain? What was it that you did not understand? What were you unsure of?
- What have you observed lately (on television, in the newspaper, online) that piqued your curiosity? What were you curious about?
- What local or national problem that you have recently heard or read about would you like to help solve?
- Is there anything you find unusual that you would like to explore? Lifestyles? Political views? Religious views?

As you consider which question will most appropriately guide your research, you may find it helpful to discuss your ideas with other people. Research and writing both require a great deal of time and effort, and you will find the tasks more pleasant—and maybe even easier—if you are sincerely interested in your question. Moreover, enthusiasm about your work will motivate you to do the best you can. Indifference breeds mediocrity. By talking with other people, you may find out that the question you have chosen is a good one. Or, you may discover that you need to narrow the question or change it in some other way. You may even realize that the question you initially chose really does not interest you very much. To get a conversation about your ideas started, have someone you know ask you some of the following questions.

- What are good reasons for you to answer this question? What is the answer's significance for you? How will answering the question help you? How is the question related to your rhetorical opportunity?
- Will the answer to your question require serious research? (A genuine research question does not have a simple or obvious answer.)
- What types of research might help you answer your question? (You may already have some ideas; for more on library, online, and field research, see **CHAPTER 19, IDENTIFYING SOURCES**.) Will you be able to carry out these types pages 363–382 of research in the amount of time you have been given?

 TRICKS OF THE TRADE

Save yourself time and frustration by asking your instructor to help you develop your vague idea into a strong research question. After all, yours is the kind of issue best resolved during office hours.

»» LOCATING AN AUDIENCE

Knowing that your purpose is to stimulate change in a specific audience, your response to the opportunity for change needs to reach and satisfy the rhetorical audience. In order to meet the expectations of your readers, you must know something about them. First, you must find out who your audience is. If you are writing in response to a course assignment, your instructor may define your audience for you (usually, it is the instructor and your classmates). However, sometimes your instructor may ask you to imagine a different audience so that you have experience writing for a wider range of people. For example, your instructor might ask you to write a letter to the editor of your local paper. In this case, your audience still comprises your instructor and classmates, but it also includes the editor of the newspaper as well as all the newspaper's readers.

As your writing career progresses, the number of audiences you write for will increase. You may be able to easily name your audience—college students, science teachers, mechanical engineers, pediatricians, or the general public—but to make sure that you satisfy any audience you choose to address, you need to go beyond labels. When you do research, you must take into account what types of sources your audience will expect you to use and which sources they will find engaging, convincing, or entertaining.

Keep in mind that when you write for an audience, you are joining an ongoing conversation. To enter that conversation, you need to pay attention to what is being said and who the participants are. You can begin by reading the sources used by the conversation participants. By reading what they read, you will learn what information is familiar to them and what information may need to be explained in detail.

The webpage for the Pucker Gallery, seen below, as well as the following brief article from *Bostonia,* Boston University's alumni magazine, contains information about the artist Joseph Ablow. The audience for each is different, however. In

Pucker Gallery

HOME
EXHIBITIONS
ARTISTS
DIRECTOR'S CHOICE
SHOP AT THE GALLERY
PUBLICATIONS
ABOUT US

JOSEPH ABLOW

Represented by Pucker Gallery since 1979

BORN: 1928 in Salem, Massachusetts
RESIDES: Brookline, Massachusetts

Most Recent Exhibition:
Together 10 February 2007 - 20 March 2007

Joe Ablow was born in Salem, Massachusetts and has lived, worked and taught in the Boston area his entire life. After studying painting at the School of the Museum of Fine Arts, Boston, receiving his Bachelors from Bennington College and his Masters from Harvard University, Ablow continued his instruction in painting with names such as Oskar Kokoschka and Ben Shahn. In addition to his own exhibitions, Ablow has been a professor at Boston University for thirty-five years and written countless academic articles on Art in the Twentieth Century.

Joseph Ablow
The Usual Suspects
Oil on Canvas
19 x 42"
JA210

Joseph Ablow
A Gathering,
2006
Watercolor
w/gouache on
paper
7 x 11"
JA201

Joseph Ablow
Grey Forms,
2006
Watercolor w/
white over
Graphite
15 x 11 7/8"
JA213

Joseph Ablow
*In the
Balance*, 2001
Oil on canvas
34 x 36"
JA194

The Pucker Gallery Web page for Joseph Ablow.

the *Bostonia* article, the abbreviation *CFA* is not explained, because the intended audience, alumni of Boston University, will know that it refers to the College of Fine Arts. If you were writing an article for an alumni magazine, you too would be able to use abbreviations and acronyms familiar to those who attended that college or university. However, if your audience were broader, such abbreviations and acronyms would have to be explained the first time you used them. The same criterion can be used to make decisions about content. If you were researching one of Joseph Ablow's still life paintings, you would find that sources on Ablow's work do not define *still life*. The authors of these sources assume that their readers are familiar with the term. However, if you were writing for readers who knew next to nothing about painting, you would provide a definition for the term.

Ablow's Objets d'Art

Large Still Life Frieze, oil on canvas, 32" × 66", 1986.

In a lecture this fall at Amherst College, Joseph Ablow described a major change in his artistic direction in the late 1950s. He had been working on large, classically inspired themes for a decade and "something did not feel right."

"My subjects no longer held much meaning for me," said Ablow, a CFA professor emeritus of art, "and I began to realize that painting and inventing from memory had left me visually parched. It was obvious to me that I had to start over."

The reevaluation pulled him back to the studio, where, he says, "simply as exercises, I returned to the subject of still life," something he had avoided since art school. "But it was not long before the motley collection of objects I had assembled began quietly to organize themselves into configurations that suggested unexpected pictorial possibilities to me.

"I soon discovered that these objects may be quiet, but that did not mean that they remained still. What was to have been a subject that suggested ways of studying the look of things within a manageable and concentrated situation became an increasingly involved world that could be surprisingly disquieting and provocative. I may have been the one responsible for arranging my cups and bowls on the tabletops, but that did not ensure that I was in control of them.

"The ginger jars and the compote dishes were real, particular, and palpable and yet had no inherent significance. Their interest or importance would be revealed only in the context of a painting."

Born in 1928, Ablow studied with Oskar Kokoschka, Ben Shahn, and Karl Zerbe. He earned degrees from Bennington and Harvard and taught at Boston University from 1963 until 1995. He is currently a visiting artist at Amherst College, which hosted the exhibition of his paintings that is coming to BU.

Still lifes painted over some thirty-five years highlight Joseph Ablow: A Retrospective, from *January 13 through March 5 at the Sherman Gallery, 775 Commonwealth Avenue.*

Readers of an academic research paper expect the author to be knowledgeable. You can demonstrate your knowledge through the types of sources you use and the ways you handle them. Because you are not likely to have established credibility as an expert on the topic you are researching, you will need to establish a thoughtful tone in your exploration of your topic and depend on the credibility of the sources you use. After you have done enough research to understand your audience, you will be better able to select sources that will give you credibility. For example, to persuade your readers of the value of a vegetarian diet, you could choose among sources written by nutritionists, ethicists, religious leaders, and animal rights proponents. Your decision would be based on which kinds of sources your audience would find most credible.

 TRICKS OF THE TRADE

To determine which sources your audience will find authoritative, study any bibliographies that you encounter in your research. If a source is mentioned on several bibliographic lists, the source is likely considered authoritative.

Readers of an academic research paper also expect the author to be critical. They want to be assured that an author can tell whether the source information is accurate or deceptive, whether its logic is strong or weak, and whether its conclusions are justifiable. Your readers may accept your use of a "questionable" source as long as you demonstrate its significance to your project. (See

pages 383–394 CHAPTER 20, EVALUATING SOURCES.)

» ESTABLISHING YOUR PURPOSE

In Chapter 1, you saw how your rhetorical audience and your rhetorical purpose are interconnected. They cannot be separated. In general, your rhetorical purpose is motivated by an opportunity for change—an opportunity to have an impact on your audience. More specifically, your aim may be to entertain them, to inform them, to explain something to them, or to influence them to do something. Research can help you achieve any of these purposes. For example, if you are writing a research paper on the roots of humor for a psychology class, your primary purpose is to inform. You may want to analyze a few jokes in order to show how their construction can incite laughter, but you will need research to support your claim. Your audience will be more inclined to believe you if you show them, say, experimental results indicating that people routinely find certain incidents funny.

Writers of research papers commonly define their rhetorical purposes in the following ways:

- *To inform an audience.* The researcher reports current thinking on a specific topic, including opposing views but not siding with any particular one.

  Example: To inform the audience of current guidelines for developing a city park

- *To analyze and synthesize information and then offer tentative solutions to a problem.* The researcher analyzes and synthesizes information on a topic (for example, an argument, a text, an event, a technique, or a statistic), looking for points of agreement and disagreement and for gaps in coverage. Part of the research process consists of finding out what other researchers have already written about the subject. After presenting the analysis and synthesis, the researcher offers possible ways to address the problem.

  Example: To analyze and synthesize various national healthcare proposals

- *To persuade an audience or to issue an invitation to an audience.* The researcher states a position and backs it up with data, statistics, texts illustrating a point, or supporting arguments found through research. The researcher's purpose is to persuade or invite readers to take the same position.

  Example: To persuade (or invite) people to vote for a congressional candidate

Often, these purposes coexist in the same piece of writing. A researcher presenting results from an original experiment or study, for instance, must often achieve all of these purposes. In the introduction to a lab report, the researcher might describe previous work done in the area and identify a research niche—an area needing research. The researcher then explains how their current study will help fill the gap in existing research. The body of the text is informative, describing the materials used, explaining the procedures followed, and presenting the results. In the conclusion, the researcher may choose, given the results of the experiment or study, to persuade the audience to take some action (for example, give up smoking, eat fewer carbohydrates, or fund future research).

The sources you find through research can help you achieve your purpose. If your purpose is to inform, you can use the work of established scholars to enhance your credibility. If your purpose is to analyze and synthesize information, sources you find can provide not only data for you to work with but also a backdrop against which to highlight your own originality or your special research niche. If your purpose is to persuade, you can use sources to support your claims and to counter opposing arguments.

» USING A RESEARCH LOG

Without a clear plan and a method for monitoring your progress, it is easy to lose track of your ideas and goals. Research logs come in different forms, but whatever their form—electronic or printed, detailed or brief—they help researchers stay focused. Researchers make decisions about what to include in their logs by anticipating the kind of information that will be most important in helping them answer their research question and document their results. Rereading your initial entry every so often may help you stay focused.

1. In the introductory entry in your research log, identify your research question and your reasons for choosing it. You might include some preliminary, tentative answers to your question if you have any, given what you already know.

2. In your research log, create an entry that describes your prospective readers and explains what you need to keep in mind to ensure that you are addressing them. Let us say you are interested in finding out about the possibilities of commuting by bicycle in your town. If you are aware that your audience knows nothing about bike commuting, you may want to provide an explanation (or process analysis) of how bike commuters get to and from work safely and comfortably. (See CHAPTER 15, PROCESS ANALYSIS.) You might even include a photograph of the kind of bike made for commuting—one with fenders to keep work clothes clean and panniers to hold cargo. However, if you are writing for an audience

pages 289–291

that has already been introduced to this type of transportation, a detailed description is unnecessary.

3. Your introductory entry should also establish how you hope your research will stimulate change in your audience. What is your purpose in presenting your research to others: to inform, to analyze, or to persuade? Discuss why you are asking the question in the first place, what the benefits of answering the question will be, and what types of research are likely to be helpful.

iStockPhoto.com/RyanJLane

A bike commuter.

⬈ RESEARCHING CALENDAR TOOLS

Strategies for planning a research paper are not that different from the general strategies you learned in Chapter 13: listing, keeping a journal, freewriting, questioning, clustering, and outlining. To keep your research moving ahead, take advantage of tools such as calendars. Use the features and tasks on Google Calendar to relate to the ways you work.

For the results of research to be valuable, the process must be taken seriously. Researchers who chase down facts to attach to opinions they already have are doing only superficial research. These researchers are not interested in finding information that may cause them to question their beliefs or that may make their thinking more complicated. Genuine research, on the other hand, involves crafting a good research question and pursuing an answer to it, both of which require patience and care.

19 Identifying Sources

LEARNING OBJECTIVES

- Articulate preliminary research questions that direct an investigation.
- Develop a single question from the preliminary research questions.
- Identify various print, online, and field sources for addressing your question.
- Evaluate the relative strengths of primary and secondary sources.
- Assess sources usefulness for supporting your argument and establishing common ground.
- Apply various tricks of the trade for conducting research.
- Prepare a working bibliography.

Pop Cultures

Refrescos in Spanish, mashroob ghazi in Arabic, kele in Chinese: the world has many words, and an unslakable thirst, for carbonated soft drinks. Since 1997 per capita consumption has nearly doubled in eastern Europe. In 2008 Coca-Cola tallied soda sales in some 200 countries. Even the global recession, says industry monitor Zenith International, has merely caused manufacturers to lean on promotional offers and try cheap social-networking ads.

Consumption of carbonates*
12-ounce servings per person, 2008

U.S.	529
Mexico	501
Malta	425
Czech Republic	413
Chile	391
Norway	381
Australia	377
Iceland	333
Canada	311
Belgium	300

*INCLUDES REGULAR AND LOW-CALORIE SODAS

© 2020 Cengage Learning
NGM Art/National Geographic Stock

Felix Choo/Alamy Stock Photo

But some are sour on all this sweetness. U.S. obesity expert David Ludwig calls aggressive marketing in emerging nations—where people tend to eat more and move less as they prosper—"deeply irresponsible. That's the time of greatest risk for heart disease, diabetes, and obesity."

As that thinking catches on, places—including New York and Romania—are mulling levies on sugared drinks. Others argue that taxing a single product isn't the fix: promoting healthy lifestyles and zero-calorie drinks is. Fizz for thought?

—Jeremy Berlin

1. What good reasons support Jeremy Berlin (and the editors at *National Geographic*) in the decision to use a photograph and a list of statistics within the article "Pop Cultures"? What research question guided their research? What kinds of research might he and his editors have conducted to address that question? In other words, what might they have read or observed, whom might they have questioned, and so on? If you wanted to check their facts, what would you do?

2. Think about a research paper you might write. What preliminary research questions do you have? What kind of research will you need to conduct in order to address those questions? Where will you find relevant sources? Given more time and more resources, what additional kinds of research might you do?

Although the library will probably play an important role in your research, it often will not be the only location in which you conduct research. During the research process, you might find yourself at home using the internet, in your instructor's office getting suggestions for new sources, or even at the student union taking notes on what you observe about some feature of student behavior. All along the process, you will want to use a research log. (See CHAPTER 18, USING A RESEARCH LOG.)

pages 360–362

Identifying potentially productive sources and keeping notes in a research log is a productive way to stay focused, home in on a single research question, identify a rhetorical audience, and establish a clear purpose. As you identify usable sources for your research project, consider the following questions:

- How might this source help address my research question?
- How credible will my audience find this source?
- With what information do I agree or disagree?
- How does this source relate to, agree, or disagree with, what other sources say?
- What do I not understand fully?
- What do I need to know more about?
- Toward what other credible sources does this source direct me?

» SOURCES FOR RESEARCH

In order to make effective decisions, you need to know what kinds of research you will be able to do at the library, on the internet, and in the field. **Primary sources** are original documents, firsthand accounts, field research like interviews or observations, or original research data, which are used as the basis for **secondary sources.** Primary sources include literary works, performances, experiments, historical documents, field research (interviews, for instance), laboratory findings, discovered artifacts, and eyewitness accounts—things or events the researcher examines firsthand. Secondary sources, on the other hand, interpret, analyze, or collect those accounts or data. An analysis of that eyewitness account that brings in evidence that counters, supports, or reinterprets the original account is a secondary source. Some research questions can only be answered by fieldwork, research carried out in a real-world or naturalistic environment. Most research, however, will target three main categories of information: books and periodicals (magazines and journals), online sources, and audiovisual sources. All of these sources can be *scholarly* (professional, scientific, and academic) or *popular* (for a general audience).

primary sources firsthand accounts or original data

secondary sources sources that interpret or collect firsthand accounts or original data

Books

The easiest way to find books on a particular topic is to consult your library's online catalog. After you are logged on, navigate your way to the webpage with search boxes similar to the one that is on this page. An author search or title search is useful when you already have a particular author or title in mind. When a research area is new to you, you can find many sources by doing either a keyword

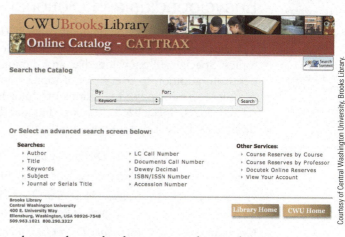

Courtesy of Central Washington University, Brooks Library.

search or a subject search. For a keyword search, choose a word or a phrase that you think is likely to be found in titles or notes in the catalog's records. For a subject search, you may be able to find sources by entering words that are familiar to you. However, if your search does not yield promising results, ask a reference librarian (either in person or online) for a subject heading guide or note the subject categories that accompany the search results for sources you have already found. Three types of books are often consulted in the research process: scholarly, popular (sometimes referred to as *trade*), and reference books.

- **Scholarly books** are written by scholars for other scholars in order to advance knowledge of a certain subject. Most include original research as well as analysis and interpretation. Before being published, these books are reviewed by experts in the field (in a process referred to as *peer review*).
- **Popular or trade books** may also be written by scholars and scientists, though they may be authored by journalists, or freelance writers, as well. But the audience and purpose of trade books differ from those of scholarly books. Rather than addressing other scholars, authors of trade books write to inform the general audience, often about the primary research that has been done by others; therefore, trade books are usually secondary sources.
- **Reference books** such as encyclopedias and dictionaries provide factual information. Reference books often contain short articles written and reviewed by experts in the field. The audience for these secondary sources includes both veteran scholars and those new to a field of study.

scholarly books for a scholarly audience, original research by scholars that includes analysis and interpretation.

popular or trade books for a general audience, books include information, often about the primary research that has been done by others.

reference books provide factual information, often including short articles written and reviewed by experts in the field.

Encyclopedias and Dictionaries

General encyclopedias and dictionaries such as the *Encyclopaedia Britannica* and the *American Heritage Dictionary* provide basic information on many topics. Specialized encyclopedias and dictionaries cover topics in greater depth. In addition to overviews of topics, they also include definitions of technical terminology, discussions of major issues, and bibliographies of related works. Specialized encyclopedias and dictionaries exist for all major disciplines. Here is just a small sampling:

Art	*Grove Dictionary of Art, Encyclopedia of Visual Art*
Biology	*Concise Encyclopedia of Biology*
Chemistry	*Concise Macmillan Encyclopedia of Chemistry, Encyclopedia of Inorganic Chemistry*
Computers	*Encyclopedia of Computer Science and Technology*
Economics	*Fortune Encyclopedia of Economics*
Education	*Encyclopedia of Higher Education, Encyclopedia of Educational Research*

Environment	*Encyclopedia of the Environment*
History	*Dictionary of American History, New Cambridge Modern History*
Literature	*Encyclopedia of World Literature in the 20th Century*
Music	*New Grove Dictionary of Music and Musicians*
Philosophy	*Routledge Encyclopedia of Philosophy, Encyclopedia of Applied Ethics*
Psychology	*Encyclopedia of Psychology, Encyclopedia of Human Behavior*
Religion	*Encyclopedia of Religion*
Social sciences	*International Encyclopedia of the Social Sciences*
Women's studies	*Women's Studies Encyclopedia, Encyclopedia of Women and Gender*

For other specialized encyclopedias, contact a reference librarian or consult *Kister's Best Encyclopedias.*

You may need to do an advanced online search, which allows you to specify a language, a location in the library, a type of book (or a type of material other than a book), and the organization of the results (by publisher, by date of publication, for instance). A keyword search page will provide recommendations for entering specific words. (See the screenshot of an advanced keyword search page from a library online catalog that appears on page 369.)

By using a word or part of a word followed by asterisks, you can find all sources that have that word or word part, even when suffixes have been added. For example, if you entered *environment**, the search would return not only sources with *environment* in the title but also sources whose titles included *environments, environmental,* or *environmentalist.* This shortening technique is called *truncation.* You can enter multiple words by using an operator such as *and* or *or.* You can exclude words by using *and not.* When you enter multiple words, you can require that they be close to each other by using *near;* if you want to specify their proximity, you can use *within,* followed by a number indicating the greatest number of words that may separate them.

After you locate a source, write down or print out its call number. The call number corresponds to a specific location in the library's shelving system, usually based on the classification system of the Library of Congress. Keys to the shelving system are usually posted on the walls of the library, but staff members will also be able to help you find sources. Some libraries invite you to reserve the source online and then pick it up at the main circulation desk. Others allow you to check them out yourself at small stations throughout the library.

In addition to using your library's online catalog, you can access books themselves online, downloading them as PDFs or in other formats for use on a hand-held device such as a Kindle or an iPad. Millions of ebooks are available online as well. In addition, *Google Books* features free, searchable online books. Over two million free books are listed on the University of Pennsylvania's Online Books Page (onlinebooks.library.upenn.edu). And *Project Gutenberg* offers nearly 40,000 free ebooks.

 TRICKS OF THE TRADE

Searching Google Books (books.google.com) or using Amazon.com's "Look Inside!" feature can give you more information about books not available locally. Both sites allow you to search for keywords inside certain virtual texts. If the search locates the keywords, you can then preview the relevant pages of the text to determine if you want to purchase the book or order it from an interlibrary loan service. If the book is in the public domain, you may be able to access the entire text through Google Books.

periodicals
publications such as magazines and newspapers that are published over a specific period of time (daily, weekly, or monthly)

scholarly journals
publications for a specialized audience that contain original research on academic topics

magazines
periodical publications for the general public, sometimes focused on a particular subject

newspapers
regional, local, or national news publications that also include letters to the editor and editorial opinion pieces

Periodicals

Periodicals include scholarly journals, magazines, and newspapers. Because these materials are published regularly and more frequently than books, the information they contain is more recent.

- **Scholarly journals**, like scholarly books, contain original research (they are primary sources) and address a narrow, specialized audience. Many scholarly journals have the word *journal* in their names: examples are *Journal of Business Communication* and *Consulting Psychology Journal*.
- **Magazines** and **newspapers** can provide both primary and secondary sources that are usually written by staff writers for the general public. Magazines can be dedicated to a particular topic and carry a combination of news, investigative reporting, researched essays, and opinion pieces. Newspapers—national (such as *The New York Times* and *The Washington Post*), regional, or local—include news coverage, which is intended to be objective, and may also feature ongoing investigative reports, articles, letters, and editorials of interest to researchers.

Your library's online catalog lists the titles of periodicals (journals, magazines, and newspapers); however, it does not provide the titles of individual articles within these periodicals. Although many researchers head straight to an internet search engine or web browser (Google, Bing, Yahoo!, Internet Explorer, Google Scholar, and JURN), type in the name of the desired article, and locate a copy, many others end up frustrated by such a broad search. You may find that the best strategy for finding reliable articles on your topic is to use an electronic database, available through your library portal. A database (such as ERIC, JSTOR, or PsycINFO) is similar to an online catalog in that it allows you to search for sources by author, title, subject, keyword, and other features. For maps, images, and art consult *Google Maps*, *Bing Images*, and the *Google Art Project*. For news, try *Yahoo! News*. Because so much information is available, databases focus on specific subject areas.

You can access your library's databases from a computer in the library or, if you have a password, via an internet link from a computer located elsewhere. Libraries subscribe to various vendors for these services, but the following are some of the most common databases:

OCLC FirstSearch or EBSCOhost: Contain articles and other types of records (for example, electronic books and DVDs) on a wide range of subjects.

ProQuest: Provides access to major newspapers such as *The New York Times* and *The Wall Street Journal* and to consumer and scholarly periodicals in areas including business, humanities, literature, and science.

LexisNexis: Includes articles on business, legal, and medical topics and on current events.

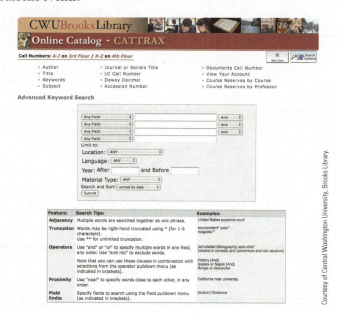

Courtesy of Central Washington University, Brooks Library.

To find sources through a database, you can use some of the same strategies you use for navigating an online catalog. However, search pages often differ, so there is no substitute for hands-on experimentation. Your library may use a general database, such as OCLC FirstSearch or EBSCOhost. The first box on the EBSCOhost search page asks you to specify a subject area. Just underneath that box is a drop-down menu that lets you choose among several databases, including ERIC (Educational Resources Information Center), MLA (Modern Language Association), and PsycINFO (American Psychological Association's database of psychological literature). If you are searching for an older resource that is not included in databases, you may want to consult *The Readers' Guide to Periodical Literature, Magazine Index,* or the *National Newspaper Index*, which list articles by topics.

After you choose the specific database you would like to search, you click on the question-mark icon to the right of the search entry box to get directions for searching by keyword, author, title, source, year, or a combination of these attributes. In the Refine Search menu, you can click on a checkbox to limit a search to full texts only. In this case, your search will bring back only sources that include the complete text of an article, which can be downloaded and printed. Otherwise, the database search generally yields the source's bibliographic information and an abstract, which is a short summary of an article's content. (For more on

pages 40–41

summaries and abstracts, see CHAPTER 3, SUMMARY.) To find the full text, you note the basic source information—author, title, and publication data—and then look up that book or periodical in the library's online catalog, as described earlier.

 TRICKS OF THE TRADE

Although most researchers use databases to find current articles, databases contain other types of information. LexisNexis, for example, provides the following kinds of reference material:

- Biographical information on politicians and other public figures
- Facts and statistics about countries and states
- Polls and surveys conducted by the Roper Center for Public Opinion Research
- Quotations on a range of topics
- A world almanac

Finally, some periodicals are available online. HighWire is a service that lists many scientific and medical journals that offer free articles or issues; you can find this list by going to highwire.stanford.edu/lists/freeart.dtl. The Global Development Network lists journals from a wide range of academic disciplines on its website (gdnet.org). Online articles are not always free, however. Many are stored behind a paywall. Be sure to check for subscription services that are available through your library's website before paying for an archived article on a newspaper's home page. You might save yourself a good deal of money!

Online Sources

Books, journals, magazine articles, and newspaper articles can all be found online. But when you read documents on websites, created specifically for access by computer, you need to determine who is responsible for the site, why the site was established, and who the target audience is. To find answers to these questions, you can first check the domain name, which is at the end of the main part of the internet address. This name will give you clues about the site. An internet address with the domain name **.com** (for commerce) tells you that the website is associated with a profit-making business. The domain name **.edu** indicates that a site is connected to a U.S. educational institution. Websites maintained by the branches or agencies of the U.S. government have the domain name **.gov**. Nonprofit organizations such as Habitat for Humanity and National Public Radio have **.org** as their domain name.

You can find **government documents** by using library databases such as LexisNexis Academic. In addition, the following websites are helpful for

.com the domain name used on the internet for commercial, for-profit entities

.edu the domain name used on the internet for a U.S. educational institution

.gov the domain name used on the internet for U.S. governmental branches or agencies

.org the domain name used on the internet for nonprofit organizations

government documents any information printed/published by the local, state, or national government searching through government reports, records, laws, maps, census information, and legislative voting records:

U.S. Government	USA.gov
FedWorld Information Network	fedworld.gov
Government Publishing Office	gpoaccess.gov
U.S. Courts	uscourts.gov

You can also find out about the nature of a website by clicking on navigational buttons such as About Us or Vision. Here is an excerpt from a page entitled "About NPR" on the National Public Radio website:

What is NPR?

NPR is an internationally acclaimed producer and distributor of noncommercial news, talk, and entertainment programming. A privately supported, not-for-profit, membership organization, NPR serves more than 770 independently operated, noncommercial public radio stations. Each member station serves local listeners with a distinctive combination of national and local programming.

 TRICKS OF THE TRADE

To stay abreast of new developments on a particular topic, create a Google Alert, which will provide e-mail updates of the latest relevant Google results from news websites and blogs based on your topic.

Metasearch engines are also available. *Meta* means "transcending" or "more comprehensive." Metasearch engines check numerous search engines, including those listed on page 375. Try these for starters:

Dogpile	dogpile.com
Mamma	mamma.com
MetaCrawler	metacrawler.com
WebCrawler	webcrawler.com
ZOO Newsletter	zoo.com

Social media Websites and apps that allow users to create and share content, including articles, photographs, and videos, and to network socially.

Social media sources, such as Facebook, Instagram, Twitter, and other online forums are places where people with mutual interests share sources and articles, whether those interests have to do with the Covid-19 pandemic, basketball playoffs, climate change, or hometown news and history. News stories, such as earthquakes, plane crashes, new Apple products, and celebrity deaths, often break on Twitter, for example. (See CHAPTER 4, RHETORICAL SUCCESS IN A DIGITAL WORLD.)

pages 49–73

Finally, be aware that sometimes when you click on a link, you end up at a totally different website. You can keep track of your location by looking at the internet address, or URL, at the top of your screen. URLs generally include the following information: server name, domain name, directory and perhaps subdirectory, file name, and file type.

Be sure to check the server and domain names whenever you are unsure of your location. (For more on evaluating websites, see CHAPTER 20, EVALUATING SOURCES.)

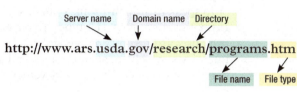

pages 383–394

 TRICKS OF THE TRADE

Before taking notes, jot down essential documentation for your source, in case you need to return to it or cite it. If you expect to have only a few sources, you may want to include complete information on the author, title, and publication data with your notes. If you will be consulting a number of sources, create an entry in your working bibliography, such as the author's name and the page numbers. (See Preparing a Working Bibliography, pages 381–382.)

Audiovisual Sources

The most common audiovisual (multimodal) sources are documentaries, lectures, and interviews, many of which are available on YouTube. In fact, you can search YouTube for topics, people, and places. In addition to multimodal sources, you can search for still images online by using a search engine such as Google Images, Bing Images, Google Art Project, or Google Maps. Most academic libraries have **special collections** that you might also find useful, such as art collections, including drawings and paintings; audio and video collections, including records, audiotapes, CDs, videotapes, and DVDs; and computer resources, usually consisting of programs that combine text, audio, and video. Pursue such sources only when you can use them purposefully, enriching (not merely decorating) your research.

special collections library resources on particular topics, people, and places, often including audiovisual and primary sources

- **Documentary films and television programs** are much like trade books and magazines. They are created for a popular audience, with the purpose of providing factual information, usually of a political, social, or historical nature.
- **Lectures** generally take place live at universities and in public auditoriums or are recorded as podcasts or for distribution through iTunes U or university websites. University-sponsored lectures are usually more technical or scholarly than those delivered in a public auditorium. Lecturers can be expected to deliver more objective information on their topic of expertise or to speak their high-profile opinions.
- **Interviews** are a special type of conversation in which a reporter elicits responses from someone recognized for their status or accomplishments. Interviews, which are aired for a general audience, aim to provide information about the interviewee's achievements or about their views on a specific issue.
- **Images** can be located by navigating through your library's special collections website or by asking a reference librarian for help. The websites of specific libraries, museums, and government agencies (such as the Library of Congress, the Smithsonian Institution, and the U.S. Census Bureau) often have databases of images.

interviews a special type of conversation in which a reporter elicits responses from someone recognized for their status or accomplishments

The last step in using images or audiovisual materials is to give credit to their creators and, if necessary, acquire permission to use them. If you are not publishing your paper in print or online, fair-use laws governing reproduction for educational purposes might allow you to use the image without permission. If you are uploading your paper to a website or publishing it in any other way, determine whether the image is copyrighted; if so, you will have to contact its creator for permission to use it and then include a credit line underneath the image, after the caption.

 TRICKS OF THE TRADE

Images such as photographs, drawings, and charts also count as sources meant to be viewed. Although images are not often accessed on their own in the same ways that books, periodicals, or documentaries are, they may constitute an important part of your research, whether or not your final project is meant to be multimedia. For example, you may use photographs to enhance written descriptions or maps and data-rich charts to support claims.

Additional Advice for Finding Sources Online

Identifying Sources

Most researchers search the internet first in an attempt to locate text, image, video, and audio sources relevant to their projects. But search engines cover only the portion of the internet that allows free access. Access to the rest requires a subscription, which your school may already have. Thus, vast amounts of good materials are only available through your school's library and subscriptions. If you do decide to use the internet, remember that no one search engine covers all of it, and surprisingly little overlap occurs when different search engines are used to find information on the same topic. Thus, using more than one search engine and searching for both free and subscriber-only materials will enrich your search. The following are commonly used search engines:

Ask.com	ask.com
Bing	bing.com
Google	google.com
Yahoo!	yahoo.com

When using a search engine for research, you will probably want to check the Help links to learn about advanced search options. Using these options will allow you to weed out results that are not of interest to you. Advanced searches are performed in much the same way with search engines as they are with online catalogs and databases. You can specify words or phrases, how close words should be to each other, which words should be excluded, and whether the search should return longer versions of truncated words.

» FIELDWORK

Research in the field helps you develop an understanding of a local situation, an understanding that usually cannot be easily reached through traditional library, online, or laboratory research. Therefore, **fieldwork** usually takes place in a real-world environment. Observation, interviews, and questionnaires are the most common kinds of field research.

Observation

Observation—watching closely what is happening and trying to figure out why—plays a central role in a **naturalistic study**, which is based on observation in a real-world environment. The researcher is right there on the scene,

fieldwork real-world research that commonly includes observation, interviews, and questionnaires

observation watching closely what is happening and trying to figure out why

naturalistic study observation based on direct access to the person or phenomenon being researched

conducting the research, with direct access to the person or phenomenon. In his study of the intellectual processes necessary for conducting ordinary kinds of work, Mike Rose describes how observation works in the field:

> **When at a job site or in a classroom, I observed people at work, writing notes on their activity and, when permissible, taking photographs of the task at hand. Once I got a sense of the rhythms of the work—its moments of less intense focus and its pauses—I would begin asking questions about what people were doing and why, trying to gain an understanding of their behavior and the thinking that directed it. As they got more familiar with me and I with them and their work, I was able to ask increasingly specific questions, probing the reasons for using one implement rather than another, for a particular positioning of the body, for the benefits of this procedure over that one. I wondered aloud how they knew what to do, given the materials and constraints of the present task, what they had in mind to do next, how they knew something was wrong. . . . Over time, the exchanges became more conversational, and frequently people on their own began explaining what they were doing and what their thinking was for doing it, a kind of modified think-aloud procedure, long used in studies of problem solving.**

> **—Mike Rose, *The Mind at Work* ["On Observation"]**

Notice how Rose talks about the material conditions of his observation: he watches, takes notes, sometimes takes photographs, and asks increasingly sophisticated questions as he begins to understand the procedures more and more. Each activity occurs in coordination with the others. Rose is a non-participant observer in that he does not work alongside those he is watching. Depending on the research project, researchers might practice participant observation, which entails learning by observing as well as doing, participating in the situations they are observing.

Interviews

All successful questioning involves *background research*—in other words, doing your homework before you choose an interview subject, deciding how you will record the interview, and composing a list of suitable questions. The burden on the researcher is to plan ahead, deciding whether you will tape, video, or take notes during the interview; testing out any equipment you need; learning enough about the person or phenomenon to ask informed, generative questions. Good interview questions will help guide your research. Your **interview questions** should serve your research in two ways. First, they should put your subjects at ease so that they willingly talk, amplify their answers, and provide rich examples (remember to be polite throughout the process, from the initial request to the

interview questions
questions designed to put your subject at ease and purposefully progress from one subject to another

final thank you note). Second, your interview questions should progress purposefully from one subject to another. Interview questions that can be answered with *yes* or *no* will not yield much information unless they are followed with a related question. For example, if you follow a question like "Do you like your job?" with a journalist's question ("Why?" "When?" or "How?"), you give your interviewee a chance to elaborate. Effective interviews usually contain a blend of open, or broad, questions and focused, or narrow, questions followed by fact checking and corroboration by other sources. Here are a few examples:

OPEN QUESTIONS

What are your opinions on _____?
How have people, research, and experience shaped your views on _____?
How did you come to believe _____?

FOCUSED QUESTIONS

How long have you worked as a _____?
When did you start _____?
How has your work evolved over the years?
How does your work affect others?
What does _____ mean?
Why did you _____?

» GILLIAN PETRIE, INTERVIEW OF JAN FRESE

The following selections are written transcripts of an interview conducted by Gillian Petrie, a student who decided to interview a long-time nurse, Jan Frese, about the changes she had seen in the profession during her thirty-eight years on the job. Gillian's first question is open-ended and aimed at making her interviewee comfortable.

GILLIAN: Would you like to tell me, how did you get into nursing in the first place, Jan?

JAN: I was a little late getting into nursing, because I was married and I had four children and . . . things were not going well at home and I was going to get a divorce. Well now, how am I going to take care of my children? So, . . . a friend of mine told me about this LPN [Licensed Practical Nurse] school and, um, it was only a year, it only took a year to be a licensed practical nurse, and I thought that—that sounds like a good idea. . . . I ended up doing pretty much everything the RNs did but still getting the LPN pay. . . . [So] I, um, thought I'll go back to school and be an RN . . .; and . . ., do pretty much what I was doing before, but at least I'll get paid for it!

As the interview progresses, Gillian steers her subject to the topic of changes that she has seen over the years in patients' perception of nurses. Gillian now mixes prepared questions with follow-up prompts that encourage her subject to expand on her responses.

JAN: When I worked, um, as an LPN, in fact, we had to wear white dresses, white socks, white shoes, *and a cap*. You *absolutely had* to wear a cap. And, um, people respected you. They—they knew you were a nurse. . . . They could tell the difference between, er, um, a nurse's aide [laughs], because you dressed differently. . . . They'd say, Well, this is a nurse, she *knows* what she's doing.

GILLIAN: As opposed to . . . ?

JAN: As opposed to now. Well, working in Intensive Care I wear scrubs, which looks like pajamas. You can wear, well—I hate to tell you what I wear on my feet! I've gotten lax in my old age [laughs]. Sloppy old shoes. . . .

GILLIAN: So you think the change in dress has, um—we've sacrificed a little . . .

JAN: I think it has *something* to do with it.

GILLIAN: . . . professional authority?

JAN: When I go into a patient's room, *they* don't know *who* I am. I could be the housekeeper, 'cos they have to wear scrubs too. I could be the housekeeper; I could be dietary, bringing them their tray. They don't know *what* I am and I just, um, . . . I *long* for the old days when I really *looked* like a nurse [laughs]! Because now I—I—I look like somebody who just got out of bed [laughs]!

Toward the end of the interview, Gillian asks if Jan sees any differences in how well people take care of themselves. This question leads into a discussion of nurses' roles as educators. Notice that in the following passage and elsewhere, Gillian summarizes or rephrases what her subject has said to demonstrate that she understands correctly what she has heard in the interview ("So you feel that now it is a continuous process . . . . ").

GILLIAN: An important part of the RN, um, *job* is supposed to be *educating* people. . . .

JAN: Well, I did that, when I was first graduated from RN . . . I had a flip chart . . . and the *people*—they—they *looked* at me with *respect*. Like, *Wow! She* knows what she's *talking* about. . . .

GILLIAN: Do you find it more difficult to educate people now?

JAN: You don't sit down with the *flip* chart like I used to, and educate the whole *family* sittin' there in *front* of you. You just, um, . . . *talk* to 'em when they come out of—of surgery, you just *tell* 'em what's gonna happen. You know, "You've got this breathing tube and when you're a little more awake and your blood gases are good and the tube will come out and then you'll be able to talk. You can't talk now because of the tube." And you just *talk* to 'em. You know, but it isn't like sittin' down, givin' a lesson. But you *teach* all the *time*.

GILLIAN: Mm huh. So you feel that *now* it is a continuous process. . . .

JAN: It *is*!

GILLIAN: . . . rather than a sit down, formalized. . . .

JAN: Well, that's, you know—it *was* kinda fun [laughs], sitting down and—and being "the teacher." But now it's just like a continuous process; you're right.

Questionnaires

Whereas an interview elicits information from one person whose name you know, questionnaires provide information from a number of anonymous people. To be effective, questionnaires need to be short and focused; otherwise, people may not be willing to take the time to fill them out. This sharp focus on your research helps guarantee that the results can be integrated into your paper.

The questions on questionnaires take a variety of forms:

- Questions that require a simple yes-or-no answer

  Do you commute to work in a car? (Circle one.)

     Yes   No

- Multiple-choice questions

  How many people do you commute with? (Circle one.)

    0 1 2 3 4

- Questions with answers on a checklist

  How long does it take you to commute to work? (Check one.)

    ___ 0–30 minutes   ___ 30–60 minutes

    ___ 60–90 minutes   ___ 90–120 minutes

- Questions with a ranking scale

  If the car you drive or ride in is not working, which of the following types of transportation do you rely on? (Rank the choices from 1 for most frequently used to 4 for least frequently used.)

  ___ bus   ___ shuttle van   ___ subway   ___ taxi

- Open questions

  What feature of commuting do you find most irritating?

The types of questions you decide to use will depend on the purpose of your project. The first four types of questions are the easiest for respondents to answer and the least complicated for you to process. Open questions should be asked only when other types of questions cannot elicit the information you want.

Be sure to introduce your questionnaire by stating its purpose, explaining how the results will be used, and assuring participants that their answers will be kept confidential. Send out twice as many questionnaires as you think you need because the response rate for such mailings is generally low. To protect participants' privacy, colleges and universities have **institutional review boards (IRBs)** that review questionnaires to make certain you are following the board's guidelines.

institutional review boards (IRBs) committees set up to protect participants' privacy in field research

Additional Advice on Field Research

When you review the results of a questionnaire or your notes from your observation or an interview, ask yourself questions about what you discovered.

- What information surprised you? Why?
- How does that reaction affect your study?
- What do you now understand better than you did? Which particular results illuminated your understanding?
- What exactly would you like to know more about?

These reflective questions will guide you in determining what else needs to be done, such as to make further observations, go to the library, or conduct another type of field research. The questions will also help with your analysis as you begin the final step of synthesizing or writing up your research. (See also CHAPTER 3, ANALYSIS AND SYNTHESIS.)

pages 43–48

>> PREPARING A WORKING BIBLIOGRAPHY

Whenever you plan to consult a number of sources in a research project, it is a good idea to keep a record of the core elements of your sources. This source information will comprise your **bibliography**—a list of the sources you have used in your research project. To save yourself work later as you prepare the bibliography for your paper, you may want to dedicate a section of your research log to a **working bibliography**—a preliminary record of the sources you find as you conduct your research. The working bibliography serves as a draft for your final list of references or works cited. (See CHAPTER 22, MLA GUIDELINES FOR DOCUMENTING WORKS CITED, and CHAPTER 23, APA GUIDELINES FOR DOCUMENTING REFERENCES.)

pages 416–437 pages 454–468

The following sample templates indicate what source information you should record for books, articles, and websites if you are using MLA style. Even though your citation may not require each piece of information, it will all be useful, should you need to relocate a source.

bibliography a list of sources used in a research project, including author, title, and other publication data

working bibliography a preliminary record of source information such as author, title, page numbers, and publication data

Core Elements of MLA Style

Author(s): _____

Title of Source (e.g., book, article, online posting, etc.):

_____

Title of Container (a *container* is, for example, the anthology where an essay appears; a magazine where an article appears; or a website where a posting appears):

_____

Contributors (*contributors* include, for example, the general editor for a source that appears in an edited collection or a translator for a particular source): _____

Version (include when the source has been published in various versions: for example, The King James Version of the Bible; or the second edition of a textbook): _____

Number (include the number if the source is part of a numbered series, such as a season and episode in a television series [season 4, episode 3] or the volume and number of an issue from a scholarly journal [vol. 217, no. 3]):

_____

Publisher (*note:* magazines, journals, and newspapers do not include the publisher's name):

_____

Publication Date (if you are accessing articles online rather than in print, use the date attached to the online publication rather than the date of the print publication):

_____

Location (cite page numbers for the location in a book, for example; the location of an online work is commonly indicated by its URL (web address) or DOI (Digital Object Identifier), if the publication supplies a DOI):

_____

Sample Works-Cited Entry in MLA Style

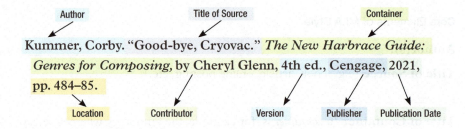

Kummer, Corby. "Good-bye, Cryovac." *The New Harbrace Guide: Genres for Composing,* by Cheryl Glenn, 4th ed., Cengage, 2021, pp. 484–85.

Author / Title of Source / Container / Location / Contributor / Version / Publisher / Publication Date

---

ACTIVITY: Using a Working Bibliography in Your Writing

Find three sources related to your research question and list them in your working bibliography with all relevant information.

---

20 Evaluating Sources

LEARNING OBJECTIVES

- Identify useful, appropriate, relevant sources.
- Evaluate those sources on their currency, coverage, and reliability.
- Assess the reasoning and stance of the author.
- Analyze how identified sources support your argument or help establish credible common ground with your rhetorical audience.
- Prepare an annotated bibliography.

The following is an excerpt from an interview conducted by Sharifa Rhodes-Pitts with Debra Dickerson, author of *The End of Blackness: Returning the Souls of Black Folks to Their Rightful Owners.*

RHODES-PITTS: You've spoken about how *The End of Blackness* grew out of your frustration with the way racial politics get played out in what you call "black liberal" sectors. Can you elaborate a bit on what you mean?

DICKERSON: Part of what brought about the book in the first place was a lifetime spent having to bite my tongue because of the way black liberals wage the battle on race. It doesn't need to be a battle. It ought to be a dialogue—it ought to be a family discussion. Instead you're either with them or you're against them. If you don't think exactly like them you're the enemy or you're insane.

I think that comes from a couple of things. The moral urgency that there once was—when people were being lynched or were sitting in the back of the bus or being defrauded of their citizenship—is no more. But even though it's 2004 and we don't confront the same problems, people go at it as if it's still 1950 and nothing has changed. A lot of people read about what Fannie Lou Hamer and Martin Luther King went through and slip into an us-against-the-world kind of mode and pretend that things are more dire than they are. There's a temptation to want to feel like you're waging a crusade and the forces of evil are arrayed against you. But I think there's a real sloppiness of thought there.

1. What is your immediate response to the quality of information in this interview? How expert is it? How reliable? How reasonable? What are its strengths and weaknesses?
2. In one paragraph, summarize the interview excerpt as objectively as you can.
3. Because summarizing is a kind of evaluation (you are evaluating as objectively as you can), respond in writing to the following questions with regard to your one-paragraph summary:
   a. How did you decide which of the source's ideas to put into your own words?
   b. How did you indicate the source of any direct quotes you included?
   c. How did you respond to the ideas and opinions expressed in the interview?
   d. How did you credit and cite the source?
4. Now, expand on your responses to these four questions, using parts of your summary paragraph to exemplify each response. What does this new combination of summary and response reveal about the interview itself and your response to the interview?

Readers of academic research papers expect the authors to be critical—not mean-spirited but perceptive, analytical, and objective. They want to know whether facts are accurate or erroneous, whether logic is apt or weak, whether plans are comprehensive or ill conceived, and whether conclusions are valid or invalid. Thus, researchers evaluate their sources in terms of how they can responsibly serve their research project—including how their analysis sets up their own research focus. They try to show that previous research or the current conversation on the topic offers a rhetorical opportunity for their own work. For instance, Dickerson remarks that she wrote her book because she had spent a lifetime "having to bite [her] tongue because of the way black liberals wage the battle on race." Thus, the current conversation offered her an opportunity to transform the "battle" into a "dialogue," a "family discussion."

»» RESPONDING TO YOUR SOURCES

Your research log is a good place to record your initial responses. (See CHAPTER 18, USING A RESEARCH LOG.) You can craft more detailed responses to your sources during the process of writing your paper. For example, in the following entry from his log (page 387), Greg Coles noticed a difference between people's attitudes about spoken slang and written slang, and this distinction eventually inspired the thesis of his final draft. (See CHAPTER 22, SAMPLE MLA RESEARCH PAPER.) When you are writing in your log, then, remember that composing your entries carefully may save you time when you write your paper. Notice that Coles wrote down an idea for further research. Like most students, Coles has many obligations besides writing this research paper, so he makes a note about follow-up research he intends to do.

pages 360–362

pages 437–449

 TRICKS OF THE TRADE

Some researchers use different-colored sticky notes, highlighting, underlining, and marginal annotations to indicate different sources. Others keep a computer file of their notes so they can search through that document rather than return to a stack of already read articles.

Reading with Your Audience and Purpose in Mind

Keeping careful, purposeful notes as you read sources can save you from needless scrambling the night before your paper is due. Not only will you have your citations handy, but the notes themselves will prove useful as you work to support your thesis and confirming reasons. You will also want to use those notes that best align with your purpose and audience. In this chapter, you will learn strategies for evaluating and responding to your sources.

MY PURPOSE AND RESEARCH QUESTION

I've been thinking I'd like to learn more about slang words. Some of my writing teachers have told me that I should never use slang when I write because it's sloppy, but a lot of my favorite books have slang in them. Also, my friends and I use slang all the time when we're talking to each other, and even my teachers occasionally speak with slang too. Why is it that talking and writing should have such different rules about slang? I wonder if some words that start out as slang eventually end up as official words in the dictionary. Also, I know there are communities (like my teachers) that discourage slang, but are there any groups that actively promote slang? These are issues I want to research more.

I think my main purpose will be to explain to other college students why they hear such mixed messages about whether slang is an effective or ineffective form of communication. Depending on what I find out, maybe I will also be trying to persuade my audience that they should be more permissive of slang, or more cautious of it. I might start by asking *What motivates people to use slang?*

Using a Research Log to Evaluate Sources

Researchers make decisions about what to include in their logs by anticipating what kind of information will be most important in helping them answer their research question and document their results. Generally, entries in a research log relate to one of the following activities:

- Establishing the rhetorical opportunity, purpose, and research question
- Identifying the sources
- Summarizing and taking notes
- Analyzing and responding to notes

Now that you have taken notes on the kinds of sources that might be useful to you, you will have a log of which sources you have consulted and be able to evaluate how those sources fit into your research. Your research log also serves as a testing ground for information and thoughts you may include in your paper.

Responding to Your Notes

Most of your entries, regardless of your note-taking system, will consist of detailed notes summarizing and analyzing (or evaluating) the research you are conducting. Often these notes will be based on your reading, but they may also cover observations, interviews, and other types of research. You may have included your responses to what you have recorded from the sources, including whether you agree or disagree, what you question, why you find some item of information particularly interesting, and what connections you draw between one source and another.

In evaluating your sources, your responses should be purposeful. When you find a source with which you agree or disagree, copy down or paraphrase excerpts you wish to emphasize or dispute (see **CHAPTER 21, PARAPHRASING** pages 406–408 **SOURCES**). You will want also to note *why* you agree or disagree, so that you can more easily reconstruct your initial response later when you are composing your essay. Taking the time to carefully record your responses to sources will allow you to make a smooth transition from taking notes to composing your essay.

It is crucial to have a system for clarifying which ideas come from the source and which are your own—especially when you are recording source notes and your responses to those notes in the same place. Even professional authors have damaged their research—and their credibility—by assuming that they would remember which ideas came from their sources and which were their own responses to those sources. Guard against this danger by writing your responses in a different-color ink or using a different font, enclosing your responses in brackets, or using some other technique to make the distinction. You might want to use a double-entry notebook. (See **CHAPTER 13, THE DOUBLE-** pages 235–236 **ENTRY NOTEBOOK**.)

In the following excerpt from his research log, Greg Coles includes bibliographic information about a news article he is considering using as a source, his summary of the article, and his analysis of or response to it. The red text is Coles's response to an analysis of his summary.

Robson, David. "The Secret 'Anti-Languages' You're Not Supposed to Know." *BBC Future*, 12 Feb. 2016, www.bbc.com/future/story/20160211-the-secret-anti-languages-youre-not-supposed-to-know.

Sometimes slang is invented specifically to keep certain people from understanding it. Since the fifteenth century, the English language has given birth to a number of "anti-languages," code languages invented by groups of thieves or other social outcasts for communicating with one another without revealing their schemes to other listeners. In order to avoid detection, these slang creators invent a lot of words for a single concept—a practice of "over-lexicalization." In Elizabethan England, for instance, the anti-language use by thieves had over twenty words for "thief." Anti-languages are developed in prisons as well as in resisting criminal activity. For example, a group of villagers in Mali, Africa, developed an anti-language to fool enslavers. Most anti-languages have disappeared over time, but some invented words have become part of Standardized English. "Butch," for example, was invented as part of an anti-language used by the gay community in Britain during the early twentieth century, when homosexuality was illegal. After the anti-homosexuality laws were revoked, "butch" became a more common word.

University of Macau scholar Martin Montgomery (cited here) thinks the internet "will only encourage the creation of slang that share some of the qualities of anti-languages." "You just need to look at the rich online vocabulary that has emerged to describe prostitution." **Maybe he has a negative attitude toward slang, since having more words for sex work isn't necessarily a good thing, but he uses the word "rich," which sounds positive. It's clear that the author of his report considers both slang and anti-languages to be good things.** The report ends with "Our language may be at its richest and most powerful when it is driven underground." **Each of these writers like slang for different reasons. I'm most excited about slang when it helps people, like the Mali villagers. But I guess if slang is making new words for us, then that could be exciting too.**

 TRICKS OF THE TRADE

Instead of keeping a research log, some researchers use the time-tested method of writing information on note cards. Most of these researchers use four-by-six-inch cards, recording one note per card. If a note is particularly long, they staple a second card to it. Keeping separate cards allows a researcher to test different arrangements of information during the drafting stage. If you decide to use note cards, be sure to indicate the source of each note at the bottom of the card so that you will have the information you need to cite or document the source in your paper. (See **CHAPTER 19, PREPARING A WORKING BIBLIOGRAPHY**, for a list of source information to write down.)

pages 381–382

›› QUESTIONING SOURCES

When you read sources critically, you are considering the rhetorical situation from the perspective of a reader, in other words, reading rhetorically. Because you are also thinking about how the sources might be used in your own writing, you are involved in a second rhetorical situation as a writer. Rarely will the rhetorical situation that led to the creation of the source you are consulting be the same as the rhetorical situation you confront in writing for an assignment.

Questions that can help you evaluate your sources fall into five categories: currency, coverage, reliability, reasoning, and author stance. In the following sections, you will learn more about these categories and read brief sample notes that illustrate them.

Currency

Depending on the nature of your research, the currency of sources or of the data they present may be important to consider. Using up-to-date sources is crucial when you are writing about current events or issues that have arisen recently. However, if you are doing historical research, you may want to use primary sources from the period you are focusing on. Those sources are considered appropriately current.

QUESTIONS ABOUT CURRENCY

- Do your sources and the data presented in them need to be up to date? If so, are they?
- If you are doing historical research, are your sources from the relevant period?
- Since you began your project, have events occurred that you should take into account? Do you need to find new sources?

Coverage

Coverage refers to the comprehensiveness of research. The more comprehensive a study is, the more convincing are its findings. Similarly, the more examples a writer provides, the more compelling are the writer's conclusions. Claims that are based on only one instance are likely to be criticized for being merely anecdotal.

QUESTIONS ABOUT COVERAGE

- How many examples is the claim based on?
- Is this number of examples convincing, or are more examples needed?
- Are the conclusions based on a sufficient amount of data?

> Johnson concludes that middle-school students are expected to complete an inordinate amount of homework given their age, but he bases his conclusion on research conducted in only three schools (90). To be more convincing, Johnson would need to conduct research in more schools, preferably located in different parts of the country.

Reliability

Research, especially research based on experiments or surveys, must be reliable. Experimental results are reliable if they can be replicated in other studies—that is, if other researchers who perform the same experiment or survey get the same results. Any claims based on results supported by only one experiment are extremely tentative.

Reliability also refers to the accuracy of data reported as factual. Researchers are expected to report their findings honestly, not distorting them to support their own beliefs and not claiming ideas of others as their own. Researchers must resist the temptation to exclude information that might weaken their conclusions.

Sometimes, evaluating the publisher can provide a gauge of the reliability of the material. As a rule, reliable source material is published by reputable companies, institutions, and organizations. If you are using a book, check to see whether it was published by a university press or a trade (commercial) press. Books published by university presses are normally reviewed by experts before publication to ensure the accuracy of facts. Books published by trade presses may or may not have received the same scrutiny, so you will have to depend on the reputation of the author and/or post-publication reviews to determine reliability. If you are using an article, remember that articles published in journals, like books published by academic presses, have been reviewed in draft form by two or three experts. Journal articles also include extensive bibliographies so that readers can examine the sources used in the research. Magazine articles, in contrast, seldom undergo expert review and rarely include documentation of sources.

If you decide to use an online source, be sure to consider the nature of its sponsor. Is it a college or university (usually identified by the suffix *.edu*), a government agency (*.gov*), a nonprofit organization (*.org*), a network site (*.net*), or a commercial business (*.com*)? There is no easy way to ascertain the reliability of online sources. If you are unsure about an online source, try to find out as much as you can about it. First click on links that tell you about the mission of the site sponsor and then perform an online search of the sponsor's name to see what other researchers have written about the company, institution, or organization. (For more on online sources, see CHAPTER 19, ONLINE SOURCES, AUDIOVISUAL SOURCES, and ADDITIONAL ADVICE FOR FINDING SOURCES ONLINE.)

pages 429–433 and page 375

QUESTIONS ABOUT RELIABILITY

- Could the experiment or survey that yielded these data be replicated?
- Are the facts reported indeed facts? Or are they theories, opinions, or educated guesses?

- Is the coverage balanced and the information relevant?
- Are the sources used acknowledged properly?
- Are there any disputes regarding the data? If so, are these disputes discussed sufficiently?
- Was the material published by a reputable company, institution, or organization?

Online Sources and Reliability

Although it was once the case (and not so long ago) that most sources accessed online were less reliable than those found in print, the difference is becoming less pronounced. Reputable scholarly journals—journals whose content has been reviewed by experts (peer-reviewed)—are found online, and personal web log entries (blogs) are being collected and published in books—even Twitter postings are being archived by the Library of Congress. It is generally still the case, however, that you will locate the scholarly journals you need at your library or through your library's subscription service (such as LexisNexis). Likewise, standards for print publication are still higher than those for the internet—after all, anyone can put up a website on any topic whatsoever, whereas most print materials have met a minimum set of standards.

Soundness of Reasoning

When writing is logical, the reasoning is sound. Lapses in logic may be the result of using evidence that does not directly support a claim, appealing primarily (or exclusively) to the reader's emotions, or encouraging belief in false authority. Faulty logic often appears with logical fallacies. These fallacies occur often enough that each one has its own name. Some of the most common fallacies are listed below; after each is a question for you to ask yourself as you consider an author's reasoning. (See also **CHAPTER 8, LOGICAL FALLACIES**.)

pages 138–140

QUESTIONS ABOUT REASONING

- *Ad hominem* (Latin for "toward the man himself"). Has the author criticized or attacked the author of another source based solely on their character, not taking into account the reasoning or evidence provided in the source?
- *Appeal to tradition.* Does the author support or encourage some action merely by referring to what has traditionally been done?
- *Bandwagon.* Does the author claim that an action is appropriate because many other people do it?

- *False authority.* When reporting the opinions of experts in one field, does the author incorrectly assume that they have expertise in other fields?
- *False cause* (sometimes referred to as *post hoc, ergo propter hoc,* a Latin phrase that translates as "after this, so because of this"). When reporting two events, does the author incorrectly believe (or suggest) that the first event caused the second event?
- *False dilemma* (also called the *either/or fallacy*). Does the author provide only two options when more than two exist?
- *Hasty generalization.* Are the author's conclusions based on too little evidence?
- *Oversimplification.* Does the author provide unreasonably simple solutions?
- *Slippery slope.* Does the author predict an unreasonable sequence of events?

Stance of the Author

All authors have beliefs and values that influence their work. As you read a work as part of your research, it is your job to decide whether the author is expressing strong views because of deep commitment, a desire to deceive, or both. As long as authors represent information truthfully and respectfully, they are acting ethically. If they twist facts or otherwise intentionally misrepresent ideas or ignore critiques, they are being dishonest.

QUESTIONS ABOUT THE STANCE OF THE AUTHOR

- Has the author adequately conveyed information, or has the author oversimplified information or ignored relevant information?
- Has the author been faithful to source material, or has the author distorted information and quoted out of context?
- Has the author adequately supported claims, or has the author used unsupported generalizations?

»» PREPARING AN ANNOTATED BIBLIOGRAPHY

annotated bibliography list of sources that includes commentary on each source

An **annotated bibliography** is a list of works cited, or sometimes works consulted, that includes summative, often critical commentary with each entry. Your response to a source will be based on your evaluation of it. By preparing an annotated bibliography, you demonstrate that you have read and understood your sources, summarized useful information, and considered how to incorporate those sources into your paper. Whether required or not, an annotated bibliography helps you keep track of sources, understand the larger conversation about your topic, and prepare to contribute to that conversation. To prepare entries that will help you solidify your knowledge of sources and your plans for using them, follow these guidelines:

- Begin each entry with complete bibliographic information. See CHAPTER 22, MLA GUIDELINES FOR DOCUMENTING WORKS CITED or CHAPTER 23, APA GUIDELINES FOR DOCUMENTING REFERENCES if your instructor requires you to use one of these styles.
- Below the bibliographic information, write two or three sentences that summarize or describe the source.
- After summarizing the source, write two or three sentences that evaluate the strengths and limitations of the source.
- Then explain its usefulness in terms of your specific research project.

pages 416–437 and pages 454–468

Greg Coles included the following source in his annotated bibliography, summarizing it and analyzing its value as a source for his paper:

Bennett, Jessica. "OMG! The Hyperbole of Internet-Speak." *The New York Times*, 28 Nov. 2015, www.nytimes.com/2015/11/29/fashion/death-by-internet- hyperbole-literally-dying-over-this-column.html.

According to Jessica Bennett, one of the features of internet slang that is currently on the rise is the use of hyperbole—that is, overstatement—to say unremarkable things. She gives examples of phrases like "Omg literally dying" and "I literally can't even," phrases which seem to imply high emotional intensity but are often texted or posted online by straight-faced young people with little thought. While Bennett argues that the rise of slang hyperbole is relatively recent, she also points out that some of the language trends she identifies have been at work for decades. Citing the work of a linguist named Tyler Schnoebelen, she proposes that one explanation for internet hyperbole is the demands of social media, where people try to make themselves as interesting as possible (and therefore as dramatic as possible) in order to get more "likes."

This source might be useful for two reasons. First, it gives an extensive list of examples of the slang hyperbole that is popular in online social media right now. Second, it explains how the unique demands of social media have created the need for this kind of slang. I've already found other sources that talk about internet slang, but this is the only source that shows even reputable news sources like CNN using slang hyperbole. This evidence will help me argue that the boundaries between "good slang" and "bad slang" are not as easy to determine as many people believe. If I use this source in my paper, I may also need to read Tyler Schnoebelen's work in linguistics, because he can help me make the argument that this slang has arisen to meet a particular kind of need.

Annotations can be much shorter, too.

Bennett, Jessica. "OMG! The Hyperbole of Internet-Speak." *The New York Times*, 28 Nov. 2015, www.nytimes.com/2015/11/29/fashion/death-by-internet- hyperbole-literally-dying-over-this-column.html.

Hyperbole (overstatement) is a feature of internet slang. "Omg literally dying" implies high emotions but is texted or posted with little thought. Slang hyperbole is both recent and established. Citing linguist Tyler Schnoebelen, she proposes that hyperbole is a response to social media, where people try to be as interesting (and dramatic) as possible to get more "likes."

Bennett offers an extensive list of examples of online slang hyperbole and explains how social media demands such slang. Other sources also talk about such slang, but this one shows even reputable news sources like CNN using slang hyperbole, which helps me argue that the differences between "good" and "bad" slang are not clear. I may read Schnoebelen's work for my argument that hyperbolic slang meets a specific need.

ACTIVITY: Creating an Annotated Bibliography

pages 381–382

If you have already constructed a working bibliography (see **CHAPTER 19, PREPARING A WORKING BIBLIOGRAPHY**), add annotations for the sources you think will be most useful. Be sure to include both a summary of the source and an explanation of how the source will be useful to you.

21

Synthesizing Sources: Summary, Paraphrase, and Quotation

LEARNING OBJECTIVES

- Incorporate source materials responsibly, ethically, and correctly.
- Analyze and apply ways to avoid plagiarism.
- Incorporate an introductory or parenthetical phrase set off by commas.
- Understand how to incorporate subordinating and coordinating conjunctions.
- Recognize and avoid citation errors.
- Quote, paraphrase, and summarize conscientiously.

1. The coffee cups pictured on the next page may have been familiar to you, but you may not have thought of them as demonstrating the use of sources. How does Starbucks credit the sources of the quotations? What information is given? What does that information tell you? What information about the sources is left out?

2. Even if you have not seen quotations on coffee cups, you have likely seen them elsewhere; they appear on everything from teabags to tee shirts, bumper stickers to baseball caps. If you wanted to place a quotation on something you own, what item and what quotation would you choose? What source information, if any, would you provide to accompany it?

The Way I See It #248

Imagine a world in which every single person on the planet is given free access to the sum of all human knowledge. Wikis give us a place where anyone who is kind, thoughtful and intelligent can come and join us in building a better and more rational world.

-- Jimmy Wales
Founder of Wikipedia and Wikia.com.

This is the author's opinion, not necessarily that of Starbucks. To read more or respond, go to www.starbucks.com/wayiseeit.

The Way I See It #261

All the darkness of the world cannot extinguish the light of a small candle.

-- Reza Deghati
Photographer, humanitarian and National Geographic Fellow.

This is the author's opinion, not necessarily that of Starbucks. To read more or respond, go to www.starbucks.com/wayiseeit.

The Way I See It #220

Evolution as described by Charles Darwin is a scientific theory, abundantly reconfirmed, explaining physical phenomena by physical causes. Intelligent Design is a faith-based initiative in rhetorical argument. Should we teach I.D. in America's public schools? Yes, let's do – not as science, but alongside other spiritual beliefs, such as Islam, Zoroastrianism and the Hindu idea that Earth rests on Chukwa, the giant turtle.

-- David Quammen
Author. His books include The Song of the Dodo *and* The Reluctant Mr. Darwin.

This is the author's opinion, not necessarily that of Starbucks. To read more or respond, go to www.starbucks.com/wayiseeit.

© Steven Lunetta Photography, 2007

»» AVOIDING PLAGIARISM

plagiarism the use of others' words and ideas without adequate acknowledgment

Writers who do not provide adequate acknowledgment of the sources they have used have committed **plagiarism**, the unethical and illegal use of others' words and ideas. By acknowledging your sources, you also give your readers the information they need to find those sources in case they would like to consult them on their own. Such acknowledgment should occur in the body of your paper (in-text citations) and in the bibliography at the end of your paper (documentation). The Modern Language Association (MLA) and the American Psychological Association (APA) provide guidelines for both formatting papers and acknowledging sources. (See

pages 412–449 or pages 450–475

CHAPTER 22, ACKNOWLEDGING SOURCES IN MLA STYLE or CHAPTER 23, ACKNOWLEDGING SOURCES IN APA STYLE.) In this chapter, you will learn to summarize, paraphrase, and quote from sources. Each of these techniques for recording information can help you achieve your purpose and satisfy your audience.

Which Sources to Cite

If the information you use is considered common knowledge, you do not have to include an in-text citation. Common knowledge is information that most educated people know and many reference books report. For example, you would not have to include an in-text citation if you mentioned that China, Italy, and Spain have been devastated by COVID-19. However, if you quoted or paraphrased what various world leaders have said about economic and vaccine-related responses to the virus, you would need to include such citations.

You should include citations for all facts that are not common knowledge, as well as for statistics (whether from a text, table, graph, or chart), visuals, research findings, and quotations and paraphrases of statements made by other people. Be sure that when you acknowledge sources you include the following:

- The name(s) of the author(s) or, if unknown, the title of the text
- Page number(s)
- A bibliographic entry that corresponds to the in-text citation
- Quotation marks around material quoted exactly

Common Citation Errors

To avoid being accused of plagiarism, be on the lookout for the following errors:

- No author (or title) mentioned
- No page numbers listed
- No quotation marks used
- Paraphrase worded too similarly to the source
- Inaccurate paraphrase
- Images used with no indication of the source
- No bibliographic entry corresponding to the in-text citation

To incorporate sources effectively, you will summarize, paraphrase, or quote and document your sources.

›› SUMMARIZING SOURCES

Researchers regularly use summaries in their writing to indicate that they have done their homework—that is, that they are familiar with other work done on a topic. In summarizing their sources, researchers restate the information they have read as concisely and objectively as they can, thereby demonstrating their understanding of it and establishing their credibility. Researchers may have additional reasons for using summaries. For instance, they may use the information to support their own view, to deepen an explanation, or to contest other information they have found. In academic research papers, summaries appear most frequently as introductory material. (See also CHAPTER 3, SUMMARY.)

Using Function Statements

Depending on your purpose, you may decide to summarize an entire source or just part of it. Summarizing an entire source can help you understand it. To compose such a summary, you may find it useful to first write a function statement for each paragraph. A **function statement** goes beyond restating the content of the paragraph; it captures the intention of the author. For example, an author may introduce a topic, provide background information, present alternative views, refute other writers' positions, or draw conclusions based on evidence provided. It is important to include **attributive tags**—words that attribute information to a source—when using function statements. Words like *believes, describes,* or *emphasizes* or phrases like *according to* or *from the author's perspective* help make the source clear.

Jacob Thomas chose the following article by William Lutz as a possible source for a research paper addressing the question, "How do the media use language to deceive the public?" Note the annotations for each paragraph are the function statements that restate the content of each paragraph.

function statement a description of the content of the text and the intention of the author

attributive tags words that attribute information to a source

Doubts about Doublespeak

WILLIAM LUTZ

Lutz begins his article on doublespeak by providing some examples: a "unique retail biosphere" is really a farmers' market; "synthetic glass" is really plastic.

During the past year, we learned that we can shop at a "unique retail biosphere" instead of a farmers' market, where we can buy items made of "synthetic glass" instead of plastic, or purchase a "high-velocity, multipurpose air circulator," or electric fan. A "wastewater conveyance facility" may "exceed the odor threshold" from time to time due to the presence of "regulated human nutrients," but that is not to be confused with a sewage plant that stinks up the neighborhood with sewage sludge. Nor should we confuse a "resource development park" with a dump. Thus does doublespeak continue to spread.

● Doublespeak is language which pretends to communicate but doesn't. It is language which makes the bad seem good, the negative seem positive, the unpleasant seem attractive, or at least tolerable. It is language which avoids, shifts or denies responsibility; language which is at variance with its real or purported meaning. It is language which conceals or prevents thought.

Lutz defines doublespeak as devious language—"language which pretends to communicate but doesn't" (22).

● Doublespeak is all around us. We are asked to check our packages at the desk "for our convenience" when it's not for our convenience at all but for someone else's convenience. We see advertisements for "preowned," "experienced" or "previously distinguished" cars, not used cars, and for "genuine imitation leather," "virgin vinyl" or "real counterfeit diamonds." Television offers not reruns but "encore telecasts." There are no slums or ghettos, just the "inner city" or "substandard housing" where the "disadvantaged" or "economically nonaffluent" live and where there might be a problem with "substance abuse." Nonprofit organizations don't make a profit, they have "negative deficits" or experience "revenue excesses." With doublespeak it's not dying but "terminal living" or "negative patient care outcome."

Lutz describes the wide use of doublespeak. It is used in all media.

● There are four kinds of doublespeak. The first kind is the euphemism, a word or phrase designed to avoid a harsh or distasteful reality. Used to mislead or deceive, the euphemism becomes doublespeak. In 1984 the U.S. State Department's annual reports on the status of human rights around the world ceased using the word "killing." Instead the State Department used the phrase "unlawful or arbitrary deprivation of life," thus avoiding the embarrassing situation of government-sanctioned killing in countries supported by the United States.

Lutz defines the first of four types of doublespeak— euphemism, which is a word or phrase that sugarcoats a harsher meaning. He provides an example from the U.S. State Department.

● A second kind of doublespeak is jargon, the specialized language of a trade, profession or similar group, such as doctors, lawyers, plumbers or car mechanics. Legitimately used, jargon allows members of a group to communicate with each other clearly, efficiently and quickly. Lawyers and tax accountants speak to each other of an "involuntary conversion" of property, a legal term that means the loss or destruction of property through theft, accident or condemnation. But when lawyers or tax accountants use unfamiliar terms to speak to others, then the jargon becomes doublespeak.

Lutz identifies jargon as the second type of doublespeak. It is the specialized language used by trades or professions such as car mechanics or doctors. But Lutz believes the use of jargon is legitimate when it enables efficient communication among group members. Jargon is considered doublespeak when in-group members use it to communicate with nonmembers who cannot understand it.

• In 1978 a commercial 727 crashed on takeoff, killing three passengers, injuring 21 others and destroying the airplane. The insured value of the airplane was greater than its book value, so the airline made a profit of $1.7 million, creating two problems: the airline didn't want to talk about one of its airplanes crashing, yet it had to account for that $1.7 million profit in its annual report to its stockholders. The airline solved both problems by inserting a footnote in its annual report which explained that the $1.7 million was due to "the involuntary conversion of a 727."

• A third kind of doublespeak is gobbledygook or bureaucratese. Such doublespeak is simply a matter of overwhelming the audience with words—the more the better. Alan Greenspan [former Chairman of the Federal Reserve Board for the United States], a polished practitioner of bureaucratese, once testified before a Senate committee that "it is a tricky problem to find the particular calibration in timing that would be appropriate to stem the acceleration in risk premiums created by falling incomes without prematurely aborting the decline in the inflation-generated risk premiums."

• The fourth kind of doublespeak is inflated language, which is designed to make the ordinary seem extraordinary, to make everyday things seem impressive, to give an air of importance to people or situations, to make the simple seem complex. Thus do car mechanics become "automotive internists," elevator operators become "members of the vertical transportation corps," grocery store checkout clerks become "career associate scanning professionals," and smelling something becomes "organoleptic analysis."

• Doublespeak is not the product of careless language or sloppy thinking. Quite the opposite. Doublespeak is language carefully designed and constructed to appear to communicate when in fact it doesn't. It is language designed not to lead but mislead. Thus, it's not a tax increase but "revenue enhancement" or "tax-base broadening." So how can you complain about higher taxes? Those aren't useless, billion dollar pork barrel projects; they're really "congressional projects of national significance," so don't complain about wasteful government spending. That isn't the Mafia in Atlantic City; those are just "members of a career-offender cartel," so don't worry about the influence of organized crime in the city.

• New doublespeak is created every day. The Environmental Protection Agency once called acid rain "poorly buffered precipitation," then dropped that term in favor of "atmospheric deposition of anthropogenically-derived acidic substances," but recently decided that acid rain should be called "wet deposition." The Pentagon, which has in the past given us such classic doublespeak as "hexiform rotatable surface compression unit" for steel nut, just published a pamphlet warning soldiers that exposure to nerve gas will lead to "immediate permanent incapacitation." That's almost as good as the Pentagon's official term "servicing the target," meaning to kill the enemy. Meanwhile, the Department of Energy wants to establish a "monitored retrievable storage site," a place once known as a dump for spent nuclear fuel.

•Bad economic times give rise to lots of new doublespeak designed to avoid some very unpleasant economic realities. As the "contained depression" continues, so does the corporate policy of making up even more new terms to avoid the simple, and easily understandable, term "layoff." So it is that corporations "reposition," "restructure," "reshape" or "realign" the company and "reduce duplication" through "release of resources" that involves a "permanent downsizing" or a "payroll adjustment" that results in a number of employees being "involuntarily terminated."

Lutz attributes increases in the use of doublespeak to a bad economy. Doublespeak serves to gloss over the hardships people experience.

•Other countries regularly contribute to doublespeak. In Japan, where baldness is called "hair disadvantaged," the economy is undergoing a "severe adjustment process," while in Canada there is an "involuntary downward development" of the work force. For some government agencies in Canada, wastepaper baskets have become "user friendly, space effective, flexible, deskside sortation units." Politicians in Canada may engage in "reality augmentation," but they never lie. As part of their new freedom, the people of Moscow can visit "intimacy salons," or sex shops as they're known in other countries. When dealing with the bureaucracy in Russia, people know that they should show officials "normal gratitude," or give them a bribe.

Lutz notes that doublespeak is also used in other countries.

•The worst doublespeak is the doublespeak of death. It is the language, wrote George Orwell in 1945, that is "largely the defense of the indefensible designed to make lies sound truthful and murder respectable, and to give an appearance of solidity to pure wind." In the doublespeak of death, Orwell continued, "defenseless villages are bombarded from the air, the inhabitants driven out into the countryside, the cattle machine-gunned, the huts set on fire with incendiary bullets. This is called pacification. Millions of peasants are robbed of their farms and sent trudging along the roads with no more than they can carry. This is called transfer of population or rectification of frontiers." Today, in a country once called Yugoslavia, this is called "ethnic cleansing."

Lutz singles out the doublespeak surrounding the topic of death as the worst type of doublespeak.

• It's easy to laugh off doublespeak. After all, we all know what's going on, so what's the harm? But we don't always know what's going on, and when that happens, doublespeak accomplishes its ends. It alters our perception of reality. It deprives us of the tools we need to develop, advance and preserve our society, our culture, our civilization. It breeds suspicion, cynicism, distrust and, ultimately, hostility. It delivers us into the hands of those who do not have our interests at heart. As Samuel Johnson noted in 18th-century England, even the devils in hell do not lie to one another, since the society of hell could not subsist without the truth, any more than any other society.

William Lutz, "Doubts about Doublespeak." From State Government News (July 1993).

Clustering and Ordering Information in a Summary

After you have written a function statement for each paragraph of an essay, you may find that statements cluster together. For example, the statements Jacob Thomas wrote for paragraphs 4 through 8 of William Lutz's article all deal with the different categories of doublespeak. If an essay includes subheadings, you can use them to understand how the original author grouped ideas. By finding clusters of ideas, you take a major step toward condensing information. Instead of using a sentence or two to summarize each paragraph, you can use a sentence or two to summarize three paragraphs. For example, Jacob might have condensed his function statements for paragraphs 4 through 8 into one sentence: "Lutz claims that euphemism, jargon, gobbledygook (or bureaucratese), and inflated language are four types of doublespeak."

Summaries often present the main points in the same order as in the original source, usually with the thesis statement of the original source first, followed by supporting information. Even if the thesis statement appears at the end of the original source, you should still state it at the beginning of your summary. If there is no explicit thesis statement in the original source, you should state at the beginning of your summary the thesis (or main idea) that you have inferred from reading that source. Including a thesis statement, which captures the essence of the original source, in the first or second sentence of a summary provides a reference point for other information reported in the summary. The introductory sentences of a summary should also include the source author's name and the title of the source.

After you finish your summary, ask yourself the following questions to ensure that it is effective:

- Have I included the author's name and the title of the source?
- Have I mentioned the thesis (or main idea) of the original source?
- Have I used attributive tags to show that I am referring to someone else's ideas?
- Have I remained objective, not evaluating or judging the material I am summarizing?
- Have I remained faithful to the source by accurately representing the material?

Direct quotations can be used in summaries, but they should be used sparingly—if at all. Guidelines for quotations are discussed in more detail later in this chapter. All quotations and references to source material require accurate citation and documentation. (For accurate in-text citation and documentation formats, see **CHAPTER 22, ACKNOWLEDGING SOURCES IN MLA STYLE** or **CHAPTER 23, ACKNOWLEDGING SOURCES IN APA STYLE.**)

pages 412–449
or
pages 450–475

Sample Student Summary

Jacob Thomas followed the MLA citation and documentation guidelines when writing the following summary. Notice that Jacob chose to include only those details he found most important. The notes he took on paragraphs 3, 6, 9, 11, and 13 were not included.

Thomas 1

Jacob Thomas

Professor Brown

English 101, Section 13

22 January 2016

Summary of "Doubts about Doublespeak"

In "Doubts about Doublespeak," William Lutz describes the deviousness of doublespeak, which he defines as "language which pretends to communicate but doesn't" (22). It is language meant to deceive. "Unique retail biosphere" for *farmers' market* and "revenue enhancement" for *taxes* are just a few of the examples Lutz provides. Such use of deceptive language is widespread. According to Lutz, it can be found around the world and is created anew on a daily basis. Lutz defines four types of doublespeak. Euphemisms are words or phrases that sugarcoat harsher meanings. The U.S. State Department's use of "unlawful or arbitrary deprivation of life" for *killing* is an example (22). Jargon is the second type of doublespeak Lutz discusses. It is the specialized language used by trades or professions such as car mechanics or doctors. Although Lutz believes the use of jargon is legitimate when it enables efficient communication among group members, he considers it doublespeak when in-group members use it to communicate with nonmembers who cannot understand it. Lutz distinguishes the third type of doublespeak, gobbledygook (or bureaucratese), by the large number of words used, which, he says, serve to overwhelm those in an audience. The final type of doublespeak, according to Lutz, is inflated language, which is the use of overelaborate terms to describe something quite ordinary. Lutz concludes his article by establishing the harmfulness of doublespeak. He believes that doublespeak can alter how we perceive the world and thus leave us without "the tools we need to develop, advance and preserve our society, our culture, our civilization" (24).

Thomas 3

Work Cited

Lutz, William. "Doubts about Doublespeak." *State Government News,*
    July 1993, pp. 22–24.

Short Summary

Depending on its purpose, summaries can also be short.

Short Summary of "Doubts about Doublespeak"

In "Doubts about Doublespeak," William Lutz describes
doublespeak as language that pretends to but doesn't
communicate (22). It is commonplace, world-wide, harmful, and
meant to deceive, such as when "revenue enhancement" is used
instead of "taxes." The four types of doublespeak include
euphemisms, jargon, gobbledygook (or bureaucratese), and
inflated language. Doublespeak can alter how we perceive the
world and thus hinder our ability to advance our society, our
culture, our civilization (24).

Work Cited

Lutz, William. "Doubts about Doublespeak." *State Government News,*
    July 1993, pp. 22–24.

Partial Summaries

Jacob Thomas summarized an entire article. Depending on his purpose and the expectations of his audience, he might have chosen to write a partial summary instead. Partial summaries of varying size are frequently found in research papers. A one-sentence summary may be appropriate when a researcher wants to focus on a specific piece of information. If Jacob had been interested in noting what various writers have said about abuses of language, he could have represented William Lutz's ideas as follows:

> In "Doubts about Doublespeak," William Lutz describes abuses of language and explains why they are harmful.

Partial summaries of the same source may vary depending on the researcher's purpose. The following partial summary of Lutz's article focuses on its reference to George Orwell's work, rather than on the uses of doublespeak.

SAMPLE PARTIAL SUMMARY

Authors frequently cite the work of George Orwell when discussing the abuses of language. In "Doubts about Doublespeak," William Lutz describes different types of doublespeak—language used to deceive—and explains why they are harmful. He references a passage from Orwell's "Politics and the English Language" in order to emphasize his own belief that the doublespeak surrounding the topic of death is the worst form of language abuse. Lutz uses Orwell's example of "pacification," a doublespeak term that encompasses the bombardment of defenseless villages, drives inhabitants into the countryside, kills cattle, and sets huts afire. Orwell calls out the "transfer of population" as the means to rob villagers of their homes, farms, cattle, and any belongings they cannot carry.

»» PARAPHRASING SOURCES

paraphrase a restatement of someone else's ideas in your own words

A **paraphrase** is like a summary in that it is a restatement of someone else's ideas, but a paraphrase differs from a summary in coverage. A summary condenses information to a greater extent than a paraphrase does. When you paraphrase, you translate the original source into your own words; thus, your paraphrase will be approximately the same length as the original. Researchers usually paraphrase material when they want to clarify it or integrate its content smoothly into their own work.

A paraphrase, then, should be written in your own words and should cite the original author. A restatement of an author's ideas that maintains the original sentence structure but substitutes a few synonyms is not an adequate paraphrase. In fact, such a restatement is plagiarism—even when the author's name is cited. Your paraphrase should contain different words and a new word order; however, the content of the original source should not be altered. In short, a paraphrase must be accurate. Any intentional misrepresentation of another person's work is unethical.

Below are some examples of problematic and successful paraphrases. The source citations in the examples are formatted according to MLA guidelines.

Source
Wardhaugh, Ronald. *How Conversation Works*. Basil Blackwell, 1985.

Original
Conversation, like daily living, requires you to exhibit a considerable trust in others.

PROBLEMATIC PARAPHRASE

Conversation, like everyday life, requires you to show your trust in others (Wardhaugh 5).

SUCCESSFUL PARAPHRASE

Ronald Wardhaugh compares conversation to everyday life because it requires people to trust one another (5).

Original

Without routine ways of doing things and in the absence of norms of behaviour, life would be too difficult, too uncertain for most of us. The routines, patterns, rituals, stereotypes even of everyday existence provide us with many of the means for coping with that existence, for reducing uncertainty and anxiety, and for providing us with the appearance of stability and continuity in the outside world. They let us get on with the actual business of living. However, many are beneath our conscious awareness; what, therefore, is of particular interest is bringing to awareness just those aspects of our lives that make living endurable (and even enjoyable) just because they are so commonly taken for granted.

PROBLEMATIC PARAPHRASE

Without habitual ways of acting and without behavioral norms, life would be too uncertain for us and thus too difficult. Our routines and rituals of everyday life provide us with many of the ways for coping with our lives, for decreasing the amount of uncertainty and anxiety we feel, and for giving us a sense of stability and continuity. They let us live our lives. But many are beneath our awareness, so what is of interest is bringing to consciousness just those parts of our lives that make life livable (and even fun) just because we generally take them for granted (Wardhaugh 21–22).

SUCCESSFUL PARAPHRASE

Ronald Wardhaugh believes that without routines and other types of conventional behavior we would find life hard because it would be too unstable and unpredictable. Our habitual ways of going about our everyday lives enable us to cope with the lack of certainty we would experience otherwise. Many of our daily routines and rituals, however, are not in our conscious awareness. Wardhaugh maintains that becoming aware of the ways we make life seem certain and continuous can be quite interesting (21–22).

Attributive tags are used with paraphrases just as they are with function statements. Notice how they help the writer vary sentence structure.

>> QUOTING SOURCES

Whenever you find a quotation that you would like to use in your paper, you should think about your reasons for including it. Quotations should be used only sparingly; therefore, make sure that when you quote a source, you do so because the language in the quotation is striking and not easily paraphrased. A pithy quotation in just the right place can help you emphasize a point you have mentioned or, alternatively, set up a point of view you wish to refute. If you overuse quotations, though, readers may decide that laziness prevented you from making sufficient effort to express your own thoughts.

 TRICKS OF THE TRADE

After completing a developed draft of your paper, identify all the direct and indirect quotations used and critically analyze their effectiveness. Try to remember that a paraphrase will work *better* than a quote if all the quote's information is useful but couched in difficult or inexpressive language, and a summary will be preferable if the quote is taking too long to arrive at its crucial point. Only if the exact wording of the quote is what makes it so valuable should it be kept.

Using Attributive Tags with Direct Quotations

The direct quotations in your paper should be exact replicas of the originals. This means replicating not only the words but also punctuation and capitalization. Full sentences require quotation marks and usually commas to set them off from attributive tags. Such a tag can be placed at the beginning, middle, or end of your own sentence.

ATTRIBUTIVE TAG AT THE BEGINNING OF A SENTENCE

André Aciman reminisces, "Life begins somewhere with the scent of lavender" (1).

ATTRIBUTIVE TAG IN THE MIDDLE OF A SENTENCE

"Life," according to André Aciman, "begins somewhere with the scent of lavender" (1).

ATTRIBUTIVE TAG AT THE END OF A SENTENCE

"Life begins somewhere with the scent of lavender," writes André Aciman (1).

Using Attributive Tags with Indirect Quotations

The use of tags and function statements often leads to an **indirect quotation** that will paraphrase, not quote, the words of others. Quotation marks are not used with indirect quotations.

➤ From the author's perspective, online slang is a response to the demands of social media.

➤ Canadian Prime Minister Justin Trudeau believes that a key ingredient of the country's economic recovery must be child care.

Including Question Marks or Exclamation Points

If you choose to quote a sentence that ends with a question mark or an exclamation point, the punctuation should be maintained; no comma is necessary.

➤ "Why are New Yorkers always bumping into Charlie Ravioli and grabbing lunch, instead of sitting down with him and exchanging intimacies, as friends should, as people do in Paris and Rome?" asks Adam Gopnik (106).

➤ "Incompatibility is unacceptable in mathematics! It must be resolved!" claims William Byers (29).

Quoting Memorable Words or Phrases

You may want to quote just a memorable word or phrase. Only the word or phrase you are quoting appears within quotation marks.

> Part of what Ken Wilber calls "boomeritis" is attributable to excessive emotional preoccupation with the self (27).

Modifying Quotations with Square Brackets or Ellipsis Points

In order to make a quotation fit your sentence, you may need to modify the capitalization of a word. To indicate such a modification, use square brackets:

> Pollan believes that "[t]hough animals are still very much 'things' in the eyes of American law, change is in the air" (191).

You can also use square brackets to insert words needed for clarification:

> Ben Metcalf reports, "She [Sacajawea] seems to have dug up a good deal of the topsoil along the route in an effort to find edible roots with which to impress Lewis and Clark . . ." (164).

For partial quotations, as in the example above, use ellipsis points to indicate that some of the original sentence was omitted.

Using Block Quotations

If you want to quote an extremely long sentence or more than one sentence, you may need to use a block quotation. MLA guidelines call for a block quotation to be set off by being indented one-half inch from the left margin. You should use a block quotation only if the quoted material would take up more than four lines if formatted as part of the regular text of your paper. No quotation marks are used around a block quotation, but double (not single) quotation marks are used within the block quotation, when needed. Notice that the block quotation ends with a period, followed by the page numbers in parentheses.

> Francis Spufford describes his experience reading *The Hobbit* as a young child:
>
> By the time I reached *The Hobbit*'s last page, though, writing had softened, and lost the outlines of the printed alphabet, and become a transparent liquid, first viscous and sluggish, like a jelly of meaning, then ever thinner and more mobile, flowing faster and faster, until it reached me at the speed of thinking and I could not entirely distinguish the suggestions it was making from my own thoughts. (279)

APA guidelines call for using a block format when quoting forty or more words. The page number for the in-text citation follows *p.* for "page." (For an example of a block quotation in APA style, see CHAPTER 23, SAMPLE APA RESEARCH PAPER.)

pages 468–476

22 Acknowledging Sources in MLA Style

LEARNING OBJECTIVES

- Apply MLA style to acknowledge, cite, and document sources.
- Recognize occasions in which documentation is necessary.
- Engage sources.

If you are following the style recommended by the Modern Language Association (MLA), you will acknowledge your sources within the text of your paper by referring just to authors and page numbers (a process known as *In-Text Citation*) and include a Works Cited page at the end of your paper. The Works Cited page is sometimes called a *Bibliography*. However, a bibliography is for all works consulted; a Works Cited page only includes those sources you have cited in your paper.

»» MLA GUIDELINES FOR IN-TEXT CITATIONS

By providing in-text citations and a works-cited list at the end of your paper, you offer your readers the opportunity to consult the sources you used. The name of the author is used in the text when citing sources. If the author's name is unknown, you use the title of the source in the in-text citation.

You will likely consult a variety of sources for any research paper. The following examples are representative of the types of in-text citations you might use.

DIRECTORY OF IN-TEXT CITATIONS ACCORDING TO MLA GUIDELINES

1.   Work by one to two authors

Although the state of New York publishes a booklet of driving rules, **Katha Pollit** has found no books on "the art of driving" **(217)**.

No books exist on "the art of driving" **(Pollit 217)**.

Other researchers, such as **Steven Reiss and James Wiltz,** rely on tools like surveys to explain why we watch reality television **(734-36)**.

Survey results can help us understand why we watch reality television **(Reiss and Wiltz 734-36)**.

The authors' last names can be placed in the text or within parentheses with the page number. The parenthetical citation should appear as close as possible to the information documented—usually at the end of the sentence or after any quotation marks. When citing a range of page numbers of three digits, do not repeat the hundreds' digit for the higher number: 201-97.

2.   Work by three or more authors

When citing parenthetically a source by three or more authors, provide just the first author's last name followed by the abbreviation *et al.* (Latin for "and others"): (Stafford et al. 67). The abbreviation *et al.* should not be underlined or italicized in citations.

3. Work by an unknown author

The Tehuelche people left their handprints on the walls of a cave, now called Cave of the Hands (**"Hands of Time" 124**).

If the author is unknown, use the title of the work in place of the author's name. If the title is long, shorten it, beginning with the first word used in the corresponding works-cited entry ("Wandering" for "Wandering with Cameras in the Himalayas"). If you use the title in the text, however, you do not have to place it in the parenthetical reference.

4. An entire work

Using literary examples, **Alain de Botton** explores the reasons people decide to travel.

Notice that no page numbers are necessary when an entire work is cited.

5. A multivolume work

President Truman asked that all soldiers be treated equally **(Merrill 11: 741).**

When you cite from more than one volume of a multivolume work, include the volume number and page number(s). The volume and page numbers are separated by a colon.

6. Two or more works by the same author(s)

Online shopping has breached our privacy: "The growth of market psychology to 'cluster' consumers by region, gender, race, education, and age, as well as the use of computer technology, means that our movements and individual tastes are always being tracked as unerringly as though by a bloodhound" **(Williams, *Open* 57).**

Patricia Williams argues that peace without justice constitutes an illusion **(*Intellectual* 91).**

To distinguish one work from another, include a title. If the title is long (such as ***On Intellectual Activism***), shorten it, beginning with the first word used in the corresponding works-cited entry. Notice that the first entry includes the author's last name, the first word of the book title, and the page number. A comma separates the author's last name from the book title.

7. When the author's name is not given

The financial market collapse of 2008 was predicted by four so-called outsiders (**Lewis, *Big Short*, 1-25**).

When the author's name is not given in the sentence, provide the author's name, the title of the work, and the page number in the parenthetical citation.

8. Two or more works by different authors with the same last name

If the military were to use solely conventional weapons, the draft would likely be reinstated **(E. Scarry 241).**

To distinguish one author from another, use their initials. If the initials are the same, spell out their first names.

9. Work by a corporate or government author

While fifty years ago we wanted to improve the national diet to eliminate dietary diseases like pellagra or rickets, today our dietary concerns focus on chronic life-threatening conditions like heart disease and diabetes (**American Heart Association xiv**).

When the corporation or government agency is listed as the author in the works-cited entry, provide the name of the corporate or government author and a page reference. Sometimes the works-cited entry may include a work by a government or corporate publication first by its title and the government agency or corporation after the title as the publisher. If the work-cited entry begins with a title, treat the in-text citation as you would for an unknown author and cite the title in the in-text citation. (See Item 4, Book by a corporate author, under Books in the Directory of Works-Cited Entries later in the chapter, on page 422.)

10. Indirect source

According to **Sir George Dasent,** a reader "must be satisfied with the soup that is set before him, and not desire to see the bones of the ox out of which it has been boiled" (**qtd. in Shippey 289**).

Use the abbreviation *qtd.* to indicate that you found the quotation in another source.

11. Work in an anthology or book collection

"Good cooking," claims **Jane Kramer,** "is much easier to master than good writing" (**153**).

Either in the text or within parentheses with the page number, use the name of the author of the particular section (chapter, essay, or article) you are citing, not the editor of the entire book, unless they are the same.

12. Poem

The final sentence in **Philip Levine's** "Homecoming" is framed by conditional clauses: "If we're quiet /. . . if the place had a spirit" (**38-43**).

Instead of page numbers, provide line numbers, preceded by *line(s)* for the first citation; use numbers only for subsequent citations.

13. Drama

After some hesitation, the messenger tells Macbeth what he saw: "As I did stand my watch upon the hill / I looked toward Birnam and anon methought / The wood began to move" (**5.5.35-37**).

Instead of page numbers, indicate act, scene, and line numbers.

14. Bible

The image of seeds covering the sidewalk reminded her of the parable in which a seed falls on stony ground **(Matt. 13.18-23)**.

Identify the book of the Bible (using the conventional abbreviation) and, instead of page numbers, provide chapter and verse(s).

15. Two or more works in one parenthetical citation

Usage issues are discussed in both academic and popular periodicals **(Bex and Watts 5; Lippi-Green 53).**

Use a semicolon to separate citations.

16. Material from the internet

Alston describes three types of rubrics that teachers can use to evaluate student writing **(pars. 2-15).**

McGowan finds one possible cause of tensions between science and religion in "our cultural terror of curiosity."

If an online publication numbers pages, paragraphs, or screens, provide those numbers in the citation. Precede paragraph numbers with *par.* or *pars.* and screen numbers with *screen* or *screens*. If the source does not number pages, paragraphs, or screens, refer to the entire work in your text by citing the author.

❯❯ MLA GUIDELINES FOR DOCUMENTING WORKS CITED

To provide readers with the information they need to find all the sources you have used in your paper, you must prepare a bibliography. According to MLA guidelines, your bibliography should be entitled *Works Cited* (not in italics). It should contain an entry for every source you cite in your text, and, conversely, every bibliographic entry you list should have a corresponding in-text citation. Double-space the entire works-cited list and alphabetize your works-cited list according to the author's last name. The first line of each entry begins flush with the left margin, and subsequent lines are indented one-half inch.

The guidelines in the *MLA Handbook*, 9th edition, have been simplified to focus on nine core elements for your works-cited entries, whatever the medium— print or online. You can find a worksheet to help you record these core elements

pages 381–382 for your sources in CHAPTER 19, PREPARING A WORKING BIBLIOGRAPHY, but note that all the core elements are not included for each source in your list. Provide only those elements that apply to the source you are citing.

The core elements include the (1) author(s), (2) title of source, (3) **container**—the source within which an article or posting is found, such as a newspaper or a website, (4) contributors—such as a translator or an editor, when there is one, (5) version—such as the King James Version of the Bible or the fifth edition of a textbook, (6) number—for example, the volume and/or issue number in a series, (7) publisher, (8) date of publication, and (9) location—page numbers and/or the source's URL (preferably a stable or permalink URL address, if available) or DOI (Digital Object Identifier). A DOI is a unique code of numbers and letters assigned to many scholarly articles (https://doi.org/10.1023/A:1015789513985) and is a permanent link so it will not change after it is assigned.

When citing a work, begin with the author, followed by a period, and then the title of the source (e.g., book, article, or online posting), also followed by a period.

1. **Author(s).** Alphabetize your works-cited list by author's last name. Use a comma to separate the last name from the first, and place a period at the end of this unit of information (Welty, Eudora.). Other configurations for author entries, and how to alphabetize them, are included later in this chapter.

2. **Title of Source.** The title of a stand-alone work such as a book is italicized (*The World Is Flat*). If there is a subtitle, use a colon to separate the subtitle from the title and italicize every part of the title and subtitle, including any colon (*Visual Explanations: Images and Quantities, Evidence and Narrative*). If the source is part of a larger whole, such as an article, include the title in quotation marks: "Sounding Cajun: The Rhetorical Use of Dialect in Speech and Writing."

All the elements that follow the title of the source are separated by commas. Provide the appropriate information in the following order. Few source listings will include all nine core elements.

3. **Container,** After the title of the source, include the title of the container in which the source appears (a magazine where an article appears, for example, or a social-networking site where a posting appears). Italicize the full container name—including *A*, *An*, and *The*—for magazines (*The Quarterly*), journals (*Cultural Critique*), and newspapers (*The New York Times*). Also italicize websites (*Google Books*), social-networking sites (*Twitter*), and databases (*ProQuest*). See Online Sources for more on how to include websites, posts on online networks, and databases.

4. **Contributors,** When there are contributors, spell out the relationship of the contributor to the main source (*edited by, translated by*). You will not always have contributors in your works-cited entry.

container
the term used in MLA style for the source within which an article or posting is found

The author's name is followed by a period.

The title of the source is followed by a period.

A comma follows the name of the container.

A comma follows the names of other contributors.

5. **Version,** You will also not always have a version for your works-cited entry, but if you are citing a particular edition of a book, you will indicate what version you are citing (for example, *3rd ed.* or *Unabridged version*) to indicate the version of the source you are citing.

A comma follows the version.

6. **Number,** All journal entries must contain volume and issue numbers, except those journals with issue numbers only. MLA now requires you to abbreviate "volume": *vol.* The issue "number" is abbreviated *no.* Include a period after *vol.* and *no.* and separate with a comma (*vol. 10, no. 3*). A number is also included for a numbered series, such as a season and episode in a television series (*season 4, episode 3*) or a book that is part of a series or is a volume in a multivolume work. As with versions, you will not always have a relevant number for your works-cited entry.

A comma follows the number.

7. **Publisher,** Use a publisher's full name (*Random House* or *Alfred A. Knopf*), not the parent organization (Random House Penguin Group), and use the abbreviation *UP* for University Press (*Yale UP* for Yale University Press). Do not include business information in the name of the publisher (*Company, Co., Corporation, Corp., Inc.,* or *Ltd.*).

A comma follows the publisher.

Note: Magazines, journals, and newspapers do not include the publisher's name. Websites do not include the publisher's name when it is the same as the name of the website.

Do not include the city where the publisher is located unless it helps clarify who the publisher is. For example, the city where a local newspaper is published might be included in brackets if that city is not included in the name of the newspaper (*The Weekly Gazette* [Colorado Springs]).

8. **Date of Publication,** The publication date that you provide depends on the type of publication you are citing. The copyright date is included for a book (found on the title page or the page following the title page, called the *copyright page*). For an article in a monthly magazine, include the publication month and year (*Dec. 2015*). Abbreviate the names of all months except May, June, and July. For a weekly or daily publication, indicate the day, the month, and the year (*17 Mar. 2016*). If you are accessing an article, include the date posted online, even if it is different from the date in the print publication.

A comma follows the date of publication.

9. **Location.** If you are citing a selection within a book or an article within a magazine or online source, you will need to provide the location of your source. MLA now requires that the page numbers be preceded by *p.* or *pp.* or that the online location be included. An online location is indicated with a URL (internet address—use stable or permalink addresses when they have been assigned) or a DOI (Digital Object Identifier). Note, when including page numbers, larger page numbers should include ranges with two digits, pp. 52-55, pp. 102-09 (include the "0"). Include more digits when needed for clarity, pp. 395-401, pp. 1608-774.

A period concludes the works-cited entry.

CORE ELEMENTS

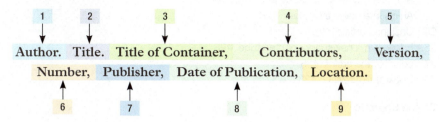

For more details on various types of sources, use the following directory to find relevant sections. For an example of a works-cited list, see the paper at the end of this chapter. If you would like to use a checklist to help ensure that you have followed MLA guidelines, see page 437.

(continued)

Books

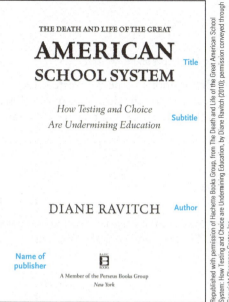

Title page of The Death and Life of the Great American School System.

Copyright page of The Death and Life of the Great American School System.

SAMPLE WORKS-CITED ENTRY FOR A BOOK

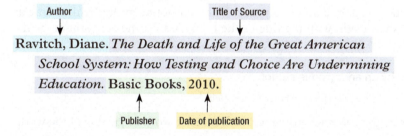

Author

Title of Source

Ravitch, Diane. *The Death and Life of the Great American School System: How Testing and Choice Are Undermining Education.* Basic Books, 2010.

Publisher   Date of publication

Most of the information you need for a works-cited entry can be found on a book's title page. If you cannot find the date of publication on the title page, turn to the copyright page. Works-cited entries for books generally include four core elements.

Author.

Title of Source.

Publisher,

Date of Publication.

1. Book by one author

You, Xiaoye. *Writing in the Devil's Tongue: A History of English Composition in China.* Southern Illinois UP, 2009.

2. Book by two authors

Gies, Joseph, and Frances Gies. *Life in a Medieval City.* Harper and Row, 1981.

When two authors are listed, only the first author's name is inverted. List the authors' names in the order in which they appear on the title page, not in alphabetical order. Include full names for all of the authors, even if they have the same last name.

3. Book by three or more authors

Belenky, Mary, et al. *Women's Ways of Knowing: The Development of Self, Voice, and Mind.* Basic Books, 1986.

For three or more authors, provide the first author's name inverted, followed by the abbreviation *et al.* (not italicized). The first author is the first name as it appears on the title page.

4. Book by a corporate author

American Heart Association. *The New American Heart Association Cookbook.* 6th ed., Clarkson Potter, 2001.

Omit any article (*a, an,* or *the*) that begins the name of a corporate author, and alphabetize the entry in the works-cited list according to the first major word of the corporate author's name. If the corporate author is the same as the publisher, begin with the title of the book and list the corporation as the publisher.

5. Book by an anonymous author

Primary Colors: A Novel of Politics. Warner Books, 1996.

Alphabetize the entry according to the first major word in the title of the work.

6. Book with an author and an editor

Dickens, Charles. *Pickwick Papers.* Edited by Malcolm Andrews, Tuttle, 1997.

Begin the entry with the author's name. Place the editor's name after the title of the book, preceded by *Edited by.*

7. Book with an editor instead of an author

Baxter, Leslie A., and Dawn O. Braithwaite, editors. *Engaging Theories in Interpersonal Communication: Multiple Perspectives.* SAGE, 2008.

Begin the entry with the name(s) of the editor(s), followed by *editors*.

8. Second or subsequent edition

Cameron, Rondo, and Larry Neal. *A Concise Economic History of the World: From Paleolithic Times to the Present.* 4th ed., Oxford UP, 2003.

After the title, include the version of the source. If the source you are citing is a second or subsequent edition, place the number of the edition in its ordinal form, followed by *ed.* for "edition." Note that the letters *th* following the number appear in regular type, not as a superscript.

9. Introduction, preface, foreword, or afterword to a book

Peri, Yoram. Afterword. *The Rabin Memoirs*, by Yitzhak Rabin. U of California P, 1996, pp. 422-32.

Begin the entry with the name of the author of the introduction, preface, foreword, or afterword, followed by the name of the part being cited (e.g., *Afterword*). If the part being cited has a title, include the title in quotation marks between the author's name and the name of the part being cited. Provide the title of the book (see Container, earlier in this chapter), followed by a comma and *by* with the name of the author of the book (see Contributors, earlier in this chapter). Complete the entry with the page number(s) of the part being cited after the publication information.

10. Anthology or book collection

Ramazani, Jahan, et al., editors. *The Norton Anthology of Modern and Contemporary Poetry.* 3rd ed., W. W. Norton, 2003.

The entry begins with the anthology's editor(s), with the first (or only) editor's name inverted, followed by a comma and *editor* or *editors*.

11. Single work from an anthology or book collection

Muños, Gabriel Trujillo. "Once Upon a Time on the Border." *How I Learned English*, edited by Tom Miller, National Geographic Society, 2007, pp. 141-48.

Begin the entry with the name of the author of the work you are citing, not the name of the anthology's editor. The title of the work appears in quotation marks between the author's name and the title of the anthology. The editor's name is preceded by *edited by* (not in italics). After the publisher and date of publication, conclude with the numbers of the pages on which the work appears.

12. Two or more works from the same anthology or book collection

Miller, Tom, editor. *How I Learned English*. National Geographic Society, 2007.

Montero, Mayra. "How I Learned English . . . or Did I?" Miller, pp. 221-25.

Padilla, Ignacio. "El Dobbing and My English." Miller, pp. 237-41.

When citing more than one work from the same anthology, include an entry for the entire anthology as well as entries for the individual works. In entries for individual works, list the names of the author(s) and the editor(s) and the title of the work, but not the title of the anthology. Then specify the page or range of pages on which the work appears.

13. Two or more works by the same author

Rodriguez, Richard. *Brown: The Last Discovery of America*. Penguin Books, 2002.

---. *Hunger of Memory: The Education of Richard Rodriguez*. Bantam Books, 1982.

If you have used more than one work by the same author (or team of authors), alphabetize the entries according to title. For the first entry, provide the author's name; for any subsequent entries, substitute three hyphens (---) or three em dashes (———).

14. Two or more works by the same first author

Bailey, Guy, and Natalie Maynor. "The Divergence Controversy." *American Speech*, vol. 64, no. 1, 1989, pp. 12-39.

Bailey, Guy, and Jan Tillery. "Southern American English." *American Language Review*, vol. 4, no. 4, 2000, pp. 27-29.

If two or more entries have the same first author, alphabetize the entries according to the second author's last name.

15. Book with a title within the title

Koon, Helene Wickham. *Twentieth Century Interpretations of* Death of a Salesman: *A Collection of Critical Essays*. Prentice Hall, 1983.

When an italicized title includes the title of another work that would normally be italicized, do not italicize the embedded title. If the embedded title normally requires quotation marks, it should be italicized as well as enclosed in quotation marks.

16. Translated book

Rilke, Rainer Maria. *Duino Elegies*. Translated by David Young, W. W. Norton, 1978.

The translator's name appears after the book title, preceded by *Translated by* (not in italics). However, if the material cited in your paper refers primarily to the translator's comments rather than to the translated text, the entry should appear as follows:

Young, David, translator. *Duino Elegies*. By Rainer Maria Rilke, W. W. Norton, 1978.

17. Multivolume work

Sewall, Richard B. *The Life of Emily Dickinson*. Farrar, Straus, and Giroux, 1974. 2 vols.

Sewall, Richard B. *The Life of Emily Dickinson*. Vol. 1, Farrar, Straus, and Giroux, 1974. 2 vols.

If you cite material from a multivolume work, include the total number of volumes (e.g., *2 vols.*) after the period that follows the date of publication. Provide the specific volume number (e.g., *vol. 1*) after the title if you cite material from only one volume.

18. Book in a series

Restle, David, and Dietmar Zaefferer, editors. *Sounds and Systems*. De Gruyter, 2002. Trends in Linguistics 141.

Provide the name of the series and the series number.

19. Encyclopedia entry

"Heckelphone." *The Encyclopedia Americana*, 2001.

Begin with the title of the entry, unless an author's name is provided. Provide the edition number (if any) and the year of publication after the title of the encyclopedia. Conclude with the medium of publication. Other publication information is unnecessary for familiar reference books.

20. Dictionary entry

"Foolscap." Definition 3. *Merriam-Webster's Collegiate Dictionary*, 11th ed., 2003.

A dictionary entry is documented similarly to an encyclopedia entry. If the definition is one of several listed for the word, provide the definition number or letter, preceded by *Definition*.

Articles

Article in a Journal

You can generally find the name of the journal, the volume and issue numbers, and the year of publication on the cover of the journal. Sometimes this information is also included in the journal's page headers or footers. MLA does not make a distinction between journals that are numbered continuously (for example, vol. 1 ends on page 208, and vol. 2 starts on page 209) and those numbered separately (that is, each volume starts on page 1). To find the title of the article, the author's name, and the page numbers, you will need to locate the article within the journal. See Online Sources, page 429, for information on citing articles from online sources.

Article in a Magazine

To find the name of the magazine and the date of publication, look on the cover of the magazine. Sometimes this information is also included in the magazine's page headers or footers. To find the title of the article, the author's name, and the page numbers, you will have to look at the article itself. If the article is not printed on consecutive pages, as often happens in magazines, give the number of the first page, followed by a plus sign.

ARTICLE IN A JOURNAL

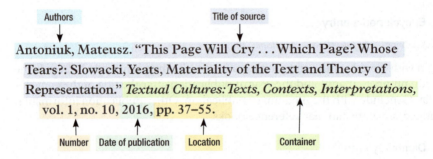

ARTICLE IN A MAGAZINE

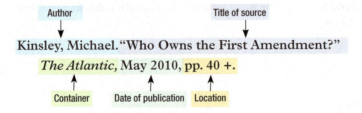

Works-cited entries for articles generally include the following core elements.

Author.
Title of Source.
Container,
Number,
Date of Publication,
Location.

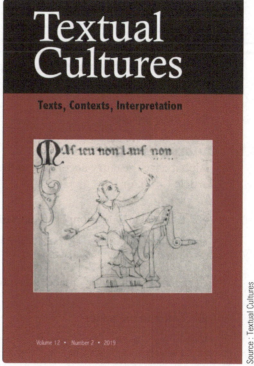

21. Article in a journal

Burt, Susan Meredith. "Solicitudes in American English." *International Journal of Applied Linguistics,* vol. 13, no. 1, 2003, pp. 78-95.

Place the title of the article in quotation marks after the author's name, separated by periods. The container (the name of the journal) follows, in italics. Provide the volume and issue numbers, the year of publication, and the range of pages. The elements that follow the title (container, number, date of publication, and location) are separated by commas.

22. Article in a monthly magazine

Moran, Thomas E. "Just for Kicks Soccer Program." *Exceptional Parent,* Feb. 2004, pp. 36-37.

Include the publication month and year. Abbreviate the names of all months except May, June, and July.

23. Article in a weekly magazine or newspaper

Gonzalez, Jennifer. "Community-College Professor, Visiting Yale, Explores the Ethics of Treating Animals." *The Chronicle of Higher Education,* 23 Apr. 2010, p. A4.

Provide the day, month, and year of publication after the title of the publication.

24. Article in a daily newspaper

Lewin, Tamara. "Teenage Insults, Scrawled on Web, Not on Walls." *The New York Times*, 6 May 2010, pp. A1+.

Provide the day, month, and year of publication. If the article does not appear on consecutive pages, add a plus sign after the first page number.

25. Unsigned article

"Beware the Herd." *Newsweek*, 8 Mar. 2004, p. 61.

Alphabetize the entry according to the first major word in the title, ignoring any article (*a, an,* or *the*).

26. Editorial in a newspaper or magazine

Marcus, Ruth. "In Arizona, Election Reform's Surprising Consequences." *The Washington Post*, 5 May 2010, p. A21. Editorial.

At the end of the entry, place the word *Editorial,* followed by a period.

27. Letter to the editor

Willens, Peggy A. "Re: Government Criticizes BP for Response to Oil Spill." *The New York Times*, 1 May 2010, p. A30.

Following the author's name, add the title of the letter in quotation marks if there is one. If there is no title, insert *Letter* (no italics), followed by a period. Conclude with the name of the periodical, the date of publication, and the page number.

28. Book or film review

Morgenstern, Joe. "See Spot Sing and Dance: Dog Cartoon 'Teacher's Pet' Has Enough Bite for Adults." Review of *Teacher's Pet*, directed by Timothy Björklund. *The Wall Street Journal*, 16 Jan. 2004, pp. W1+.

Place the reviewer's name first, followed by the title of the review (if any) in quotation marks. Next, provide the title of the work reviewed, preceded by *Review of,* and then mention contributors important to the review with an indication of their contribution: *directed by* precedes a director's name; *performance by* precedes an actor's name.

Online Sources

When citing online sources, use the list of core elements to guide you just as you would for print. There are a few variations that are specific to online sources. The location for an online source is indicated with a web address—the DOI (Digital Object Identifier) or a stable permalink of the URL, where possible. In addition, online sources frequently have more than one container—for instance, an article might be found in a journal (container 1), which is accessed as part of an online collection (container 2) within a database (container 3). When there is a second and occasionally third container, the names of the second and third containers are placed at the end of the entry and followed by the web address.

Author.

Treat authors as you would for print, with the exception that internet handles and pseudonyms are acceptable author names for online sources. The author's name is followed by a period.

Title of Source.

Titles are punctuated as they are in print. When there is no title for a tweet, use the full post included in quotation marks as a title. When citing an e-mail message, use the subject line as the title and enclose the subject line in quotation marks. The title is followed by a period.

Container (Container 1),

Italicize online container names, just as you would for print. Journals, magazines, and newspapers, as well as online collections of works and websites where articles are posted, are all containers. Standardize the name of a website if the punctuation is unusual.

Online sources commonly have more than one container. Often a second and sometimes third container simply hosts the first container—rather than contributes to the content of the source (see Container 2, p. 430). Include the name of the host site (in italics) to help others locate the source. It is placed at the end of the entry, prior to the web address. Host sites include YouTube for videos or ProQuest for online subscription services.

Publisher,

The publisher who sponsors a website is usually at the bottom of the home page (for example, the Oxford English Dictionary's website www.oed.com is published by Oxford University Press). Look at the "About" page to find the publisher who sponsors a website if it is not otherwise clear. A publisher contributes to the content of the site. *Blogspot*, for example, might host a blog but it is not the publisher (see Container 2). The publisher's name is not included when the name of the website would simply be repeated as that of the publisher.

Date of Publication,

Include the date of publication that is posted online when you have accessed your source online, even if the print date of publication is different. If the source includes a time stamp (10:00 a.m.), add the time after the date (day, month, year) and separate the date and time with a comma. If the work was published in a different medium, such as a book, before being published online, use the date that provides the most insight into the source. If the date of publication is the last entry before Container 2, conclude with a period as you would with print.

Location (page numbers or web address).

Sometimes page numbers from the print source are available as part of the database that has been accessed. Include them, and follow with a period if this is the last entry before Container 2. If there is no second container, add a comma and the web address.

Container (Container 2),

When the first container is located within a second or third container, include all the container names. Subsequent containers include databases of works (African Journals Online [AJOL]), social media networks (Twitter), or online library subscriptions (JSTOR); these come after the date of publication (and page numbers, when page numbers are available) and are italicized.

Additional information for the second or third container, such as contributors, version, number, publisher, and date of publication, is included when it is available, separated by commas.

Location (web address).

Conclude with a web location. MLA prefers a stable or permalink for the URL or a DOI, which is also a permanent link, if either of these is available. Check with your instructor to make sure your instructor does not require different or additional information.

It is important to include information that helps others locate your source online and to avoid extraneous information that might be confusing. MLA no longer requires the date of access or medium. Only include the date of access if the URL is likely to be removed or updated.

Online sources vary significantly; thus, as you prepare your works-cited list, you will need to follow the models shown here closely.

ARTICLE FROM AN ONLINE JOURNAL

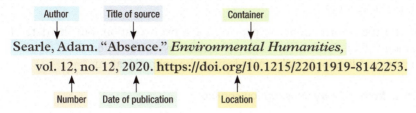

Author   Title of source   Container

Searle, Adam. "Absence." *Environmental Humanities,*
    vol. 12, no. 12, 2020. https://doi.org/10.1215/22011919-8142253.

Number   Date of publication   Location

29. Online book

Austen, Jane. *Emma.* 1815. *Project Guten-berg*, 21 Jan. 2010, www.gutenberg.org/ebooks/158.

Begin with the information you always provide for an entry for a book (author and title). In this instance, the original publication date is included after the title to provide additional insight into the source. The name of the website (italicized) that houses the book, the date of publication, and the web address conclude the entry. Note that MLA guidelines require concluding each entry with a period, even if the web address does not end in a period.

30. Article in an online publication

Dayen, David. "Snapshot of a Broken System: How a Profitable Company Justifies Laying Off 1400 Workers and Moves Their Jobs to Mexico." *Salon*, 22 Mar. 2016, 2:51 p.m., https://www.salon.com/2016/03/22/snapshot_of_a_broken_system_how_a_profitable_company_justifies_laying_off_1400_people_moved_their_jobs_to_mexico/

Absence

ADAM SEARLE
Department of Geography, University of Cambridge, UK

Engaging the surrealist landscapes of René Magritte is an equivocal endeavor. *Les Charmes du Paysage* (The Charms of Landscape; fig. 1) is an invitation into the plurality of absence. Through an explicit presentation of the absence of landscape, however that may be understood, we find ourselves in the presence of our own conjuring. The trace left by Magritte speaks to us in a manifold manner, an exemplification of absence's ontological power. It is a divergent opportunity found through the circumstantial constellation of what is not that indulges a (re)thinking of what has been and what may be. In an epoch characterized by its losses—mass extinction, environmental degradation, Indigenous livelihoods—I propose taking seriously the affective force of absence to accommodate a politics more attuned to the ethical affordances they bring about. This attentiveness to that which we do not or cannot completely know poses a methodological interjection which, at its heart, speaks to the fragility of the earth itself and all of its inhabitants.

Absence is not synonymous with loss. It speaks to much more: what is not anymore and what is not yet, what may never be and what never has been. By speaking to and being spoken to, these ghosts of disjunct pasts and futures help construct an ethics for the present. The environmental humanities may engage this provocation on geologic and evolutionary timescales, facilitating ways of understanding and translating the world that acknowledge the presence of absence. Absences are the disjunctures of geographies and histories, profoundly marked by the traces they leave, as one can only begin to speak in terms of an absence through presumption, reconstruction, or fantasy. And as argued by Jacques Derrida in *Specters of Marx*, these disjunctures are the very possibilities of *an* other ontology.[1]

Absences are not immaterial. Hauntings materialize through their inseparability from pre-existing material conditions,[2] their anachrony realized through the forging of

1. Derrida, *Specters of Marx*.
2. Barad, "No Small Matter."

Environmental Humanities 12:1 (May 2020)
DOI 10.1215/22011919-8142253 © 2020 Adam Searle
This is an open access article distributed under the terms of a Creative Commons license (CC BY-NC-ND 3.0).

MLA

Begin with the information you provide for an entry for a print article. Use the date that is posted on the site you have accessed, including the time stamp when available. Conclude with the location.

31. Article in a print publication accessed online

Cloud, John. "The YouTube Gurus." *Time*, 16 Dec. 2006, content.time.com/time/magazine/article/0,9171,1570795,00.

Begin with the information you provide for a print citation, but the date of publication will be the date it was posted online (even if it differs from the date on the print publication), and conclude with the online location.

32. Article from a library subscription service

Fenn, Donna. "Generation Why Not." *Inc.*, 2014, pp. 46-54. *ABI/INFORM Complete, ProQuest,* ezacess.libraries.psu.edu/login?url=http://search.proquest.com.ezaccess.libraries.psu.edu/docview/1544412697?accountid=13158.

Provide the usual information for the article. A period precedes the listing of subsequent containers. The second container for this article is the *ABI/INFORM Complete* collection that includes all issues of *Inc.* The collection is housed in the ProQuest library subscription service. The web location within ProQuest follows. If there are no subsequent containers, include a comma after the date of publication (or the page numbers, if page numbers are available) and conclude with the web address.

33. Website

Amon Carter Museum of American Art. 2016, www.amoncartermuseum.org.

Provide the title of the site (italicized), followed by a period. Include the version number (if provided), the name of the publisher if different from the name of the website, and the date of publication or latest update. Conclude with the online location.

34. Article posted on a website

"Blowing Smoke: Chemical Companies Say, 'Trust Us,' but Environmental and Workplace Safety Violations Belie Their Rhetoric." *Center for Effective Government,* 22 Oct. 2015, www.foreffectivegov.org/files/regs/blowing-smoke.pdf.

Place the title of the article you are citing in quotation marks before the title of the website. If the name of the website is the same as that of the publisher, only list the website. If the section has an author, list the author's name (inverted) first.

35. Television program accessed online

"AKA Ladies Night." *Jessica Jones*, season 1, episode 1, Marvel Television, 2 Nov. 2015. *Netflix*, www
.netflix.com/watch/ 80002312?trackId=200256157&tctx=0%2C0%2C23e03981-3acf-
4974-97f3-83ac3c876383-69793497.

Begin with the title of the episode in quotation marks, followed by a period.
Include the title of the program in italics, the season number, and the episode
number, followed by the organization that was most responsible for the production or relevant for your research (e.g., the production company or the network
where the series aired) and the date the episode aired or the year(s) the series
was originally broadcast, followed by the online provider in italics and the web
address. See also Items 39 and 40 for Film and Television series.

36. Video posted online

"Jim Holt: 'Why Does the Universe Exist?'" *YouTube*, uploaded by TED, 2 Sept. 2014, www
.youtube.com/watch?v=zOrUUQJd81M.

Provide the title of the video. Then include the container (in italics), who
uploaded the video, the date the video was posted online, and the online location.

37. Twitter post

Janis Krums [@jkrums]. "There's a plane in the Hudson. I'm on the ferry going to pick up the
people. Crazy." *Twitter*, 15 Jan. 2009, 12:36 p.m., twitter.com/jkrums/statuses/1121915133.

38. E-mail message

Kivett, George. Email to Theodore Ellis. 28 Jan. 2010.

Give the name of the author of the message, a description of the communication (including the recipient's name), and the date the message was sent.

Other Sources

Film, television, radio, and music

39. Film

Bus Stop. Directed by Joshua Logan, performance by Marilyn Monroe, Twentieth Century Fox,
1956.

Monroe, Marilyn, performer. *Bus Stop*. Directed by Joshua Logan, Twentieth Century Fox, 1956.

Films are created by directors, screenwriters, actors, and many others. If your focus is the film, begin with the title of the film in italics, and then list contributors (e.g., *directed by, performance by*). If your focus is a contributor to the film, begin with the name of the contributor (last name first), a comma, and a description of the contribution (e.g, *director, performer*), followed by the film title, contributors, the organization that was most responsible for the production, and the year of release.

40. Television series

Downton Abbey. Created by Julian Fellowes, MASTERPIECE, 2010-2015.

Robbins, Anna Mary Scott, costume designer. *Downton Abbey*. Seasons 5-6, MASTERPIECE, 2014-2015.

Television series, like films, have many contributors. If your focus is the series, begin with the title in italics, and then list key contributors with an indication of their contribution. Unlike film, a television series credits an individual as *created by*. Add the organization that was most responsible for the production or relevant for your research (e.g., the production company or the network where the series aired) and the year(s) the series was originally broadcast.

As with film, highlight the contribution of a particular individual by starting with the individual's name (last name first), followed by a comma and an indication of the nature of the contribution (*performer, director, screenplay writer*).

41. Radio program or television episode

"Back Where It All Began." *A Prairie Home Companion*, narrated by Garrison Keillor, episode 1453, National Public Radio, 2014.

"Confessions." *Breaking Bad*, created by Vince Gilligan, performance by Bryan Cranston, season 5, episode 11, AMC, 2013.

Cranston, Bryan, performer. *Breaking Bad*. AMC, 2008-13.

As with a film or television series, if your focus is the contribution of a specific individual, place the individual's name and the contribution before the title. Otherwise, begin with the title of the segment (in quotation marks), the title of the program (in italics), the season and episode numbers, and contributors when they are important to the focus of your research (such as the name of an author, performer, director, or narrator). Conclude with the year of the broadcast. If your focus includes the historical context of the episode, you may want to include the exact date that it was aired. For *Breaking Bad*, for example, "Confessions" aired on 5 Aug. 2013.

42. Sound recording

The White Stripes. "Seven Nation Army." *Elephant,* V2 records, 2003.

Begin with the name of the performer, composer, or conductor, depending on which you prefer to emphasize. When referring to an individual song, provide its name in quotation marks after the name of the performer, composer, or conductor. Then provide the title of the album, the manufacturer's name, and the date of the recording. Note that the above entry should be alphabetized as though it begins with *w,* not *t.*

Live performances

43. Play performance

Roulette. By Paul Weitz, directed by Tripp Cullmann, 9 Feb. 2004, John Houseman Theater, New York.

Begin with the title of the play (italicized) followed by a period. Indicate the key contributors and their contribution, such as *by, directed by, performance by,* and the date of the performance, followed by a comma. Then list the location of the performance (the theater and the city). Do not include the city if it is in the name of the venue.

44. Lecture or presentation

Joseph, Peniel. "The 1960's, Black History, and the Role of the NC A&T Four." Gibbs Lecture, 5 Apr. 2010, General Classroom Building, North Carolina A&T State University, Greensboro.

Ryken, Leland. Class lecture, English 216, 4 Feb. 2010, Breyer 103, Wheaton College, Illinois.

Provide the name of the speaker, followed by a period. Then list the title of the lecture (if any) in quotation marks. If the lecture or presentation is untitled, provide a description after the name of the speaker. The sponsoring organization (if applicable) follows, and the date of the lecture or presentation. The location follows, including the city. The city need not be included if it is part of the name of the location.

Images

45. Work of art

Lange, Dorothea. *Migrant Mother.* 1936, Prints and Photographs Division, Library of Congress, Washington.

Provide the artist's name and the title of the work (italicized). The date the work was created follows, then the name and location of the institution that houses the work. If the work of art has no title, briefly describe its subject.

46. Graphic novel, comic book, comic strip, or cartoon

Martin, George R.R. *The Hedge Knight II: The Sworn Sword.* Pencils and inks by Mike S. Miller, Jet City Comix, 2014.

Cheney, Tom. "Back Page by Tom Cheney." *The New Yorker,* 12 Jan. 2004, p. 88.

A graphic novel or comic book will begin with the author, then the title (in italics). Contributors can be included following the title, along with a description of their contribution. Comic books are often published as part of a larger series. Include the title of the comic book (in italics), followed by a period. Then include the name of the series (in italics), when there is one, the issue number (*no. 12*), the publisher, and the date of publication. For a cartoon or comic strip, begin with the name of the artist. Follow with the title of the cartoon or comic strip in quotation marks. Include the name of the publication in italics where the cartoon or comic strip appeared, followed by the date of publication and the page number.

47. Advertisement

McCormick Pure Vanilla Extract. *Cooking Light,* Mar. 2004, p. 177.

Identify the item being advertised before the usual publication information.

48. Map or chart

Scottsdale and Vicinity. Rand, 2000.

Treat the map or chart as you would an anonymous book before including the usual publication information.

Print

49. Pamphlet or bulletin

Ten Ways to Be a Better Dad. National Fatherhood Institute, 2000.

An entry for a pamphlet is similar to one for a book. List the author's name first, if an author is identified.

50. Government publication

United States, Department of Agriculture, Center for Nutrition Policy and Promotion. *Stay Fit on Campus: 10 Tips for College Students to Stay Active.* Government Publishing Office, 2013, purl. fdlp.gov/GPO/gpo65065.

If no author is provided, list the name of the government (e.g., *United States, Montana,* or *New York City*), followed by a comma and the name of the agency issuing the publication, then any part of the agency that is specifically responsible for the publication. The title of the publication follows. Conclude with the usual publication data. If you have accessed the publication online, add the web location after the date of publication.

CHECKING OVER A WORKS-CITED LIST

✓ Is the title, *Works Cited* (not italicized), centered one inch from the top of the page? Is the first letter of each noun, adjective, adverb, and verb capitalized?

✓ Is the entire list double-spaced?

✓ Are initial lines of entries flush with the left margin and subsequent lines indented one-half inch?

✓ Is there a works-cited entry for each in-text citation? Is there an in-text citation for each works-cited entry?

✓ Are the entries alphabetized according to the first author's last name? If the author of an entry is unknown, is the entry alphabetized according to title (ignoring any initial *a, an,* or *the*)?

✓ Are book and periodical titles italicized? Are databases, library subscription sites, social media networks, and websites italicized?

✓ Are quotation marks used to indicate article titles?

›› SAMPLE MLA RESEARCH PAPER

The MLA recommends omitting a title page (unless your instructor requires one) and instead providing the identification on the first page of the paper. One inch from the top, on the left-hand side of the page, list your name, the name of the instructor, the name of the course, and the date—all double-spaced. Below these lines, center the title of the paper, which is in plain type (no italics, underlining, or boldface). On the right-hand side of each page, one-half inch from the top, use your last name and the page number as a header. Double-space the text throughout the paper, and use one-inch margins on the sides and bottom. Indent every paragraph (including the first one) one-half inch.

Greg Coles

Dr. Cheryl Glenn

ENGL 101

21 April 2019

Slang Rebels

What is slang? Although the word "slang" is used often, research
by Bethany K. Dumas and Jonathan Lighter suggests that people
have very different opinions about which words and phrases should
be classified as slang (10). Robert L. Moore calls slang a
"notoriously slippery concept" (61). Summarizing several definitions
of slang, he states, "These definitions all have one trait in common:
they define slang in terms of an extensive list of traits" (62). Among
these traits are the idea that slang is usually spoken instead of written
(Hummon 77) and the idea that slang is a response to or rebellion
against social norms (Green 103; Moore 61). By combining these
two ideas, I argue in this essay that slang is a rebellion against the
literate mindset—that is, against the way that writing tries to make
us think. Part of the reason slang so easily takes hold of language
(Mattiello 7) is that it fulfills our desire to develop language in
conversation with human beings instead of following the rules of
correctness and incorrectness that usually define written
communication.

Most of today's readers would probably consider words like "gleek" (to squirt water between the teeth), "gurgitator" (a competitive eater), and "paleoconservative" (a very conservative person with outdated beliefs) to be "made-up" words. However, writes Mark Peters, "if 'a real word' is one with multiple citations by different authors over a substantial period of time, then they're all real as rain" (110). Though these words do not appear in most dictionaries, they fulfill the requirements of "official words." Perhaps in fifty years they will be so much a part of our language that scientists and anthropologists will use them in formal papers.

It is the nature of language to be constantly changing, observes Jean Aitchison (18). This effect is particularly noticeable in the area of slang. Slang words come quickly in and out of usage (Aitchison 21). Yet although slang itself might be called "ephemeral" (Mattiello 9) and "short-lived" (Stenström), its effects on language can be permanent. Most slang disappears with time, but some slang terms transition into general usage and become part of the "established" language (Aitchison 19). Keith R. Herrmann provides a number of examples of now-established English words which began as military slang. Three such examples are the words "boycott" (see fig. 1), "lynch," and "shrapnel," all of which were originally the last names of military officers (319).

Each paragraph begins with an indent of one-half inch (or five spaces).

The author uses strong topic sentences that help shape the logos of his argument.

The author includes a reference within the paper to the figure and labels the reference Fig. 1.

Because it is clear from the text that Herrmann is the source of this quotation, this citation only needs to include a page number.

Though these words are no longer considered slang by most people and are not classified as such by dictionaries (*Shorter Oxford*; *American Heritage*), they all came into being as slang terms. By the same logic, it is possible that "gleek," "gurgitator," and "paleoconservative" could lose their labels as slang and become a part of Standard English, no matter how strange or phony they

Fig. 1. While the term "boycott" was originally a slang term named after Captain C. C. Boycott, the term is now common and represented in dictionaries as part of standardized English usage.

may sound to people today. In a recent *New York Times* essay, Kory Stamper uses the flexibility of language to defend the validity of slang, writing,

English is fluid and enduring: not a mountain, but an ocean. A word may drift down through time from one current of English (say, the language of World War II soldiers) to

When a work has no author, use a shortened form of the work's title in your citation.

The block quotation is introduced with a transitional sentence that describes the content of the quotation.

Throughout his essay, the author demonstrates the library research he has conducted, research that enhances not only his ethos but also the logos of the argument.

another (the slang of computer programmers). Slang words are quicksilver flashes of cool in the great stream. (Stamper)

There are two arguments most commonly used to condemn slang, and both rely on a literate, writing-based mindset. The first is that slang is uneducated and improper. Dumas and Lighter, summarizing the broad spectrum of views on slang, quote scholars who call slang an "'epidemic disease' of language, 'the advertisement of mental poverty,' 'at once a sign and a cause of mental atrophy'" (6-7). Those who use slang are called "coarse," "ignorant," or "less educated" (6, 9). By attacking the education of slang users, these scholars reveal their own bias in favor of literacy instead of spoken language. Education has long been defined in terms of reading and writing (Bellous 9). The very idea of scholarship, after all, implies the existence of writing. In cultures that do not write their language, there is no such thing as study (Ong 8-9). To be "educated" means something entirely different for literate people than it does in cultures that use only spoken words. Education in a non-writing culture involves the passing down of wisdom from one generation to the next through apprenticed, experiential learning, listening, repetition, and assimilation. It has nothing to do with internalizing linguistic rules—and without these rules, there is no reason to look down on slang as "rule-breaking."

MLA

A long quotation includes the last name of the author and the page number unless the source has been accessed from the internet and has no page number. Note that in a block quotation, the final period appears at the end of the quotation itself—not after the parenthetical citation.

The author introduces two arguments against the use of slang.

The second argument against slang states that slang is inferior to "standard" language. John C. Hodges calls slang "the sluggard's way of avoiding the search for the exact, meaningful word" (qtd. in Dumas and Lighter 5). Novelist Tom Robbins writes, "Slang … devalues experience by standardizing and fuzzing it" (qtd. in Leahy 305). Both of these statements regard slang words as too vague to communicate well. Though they may give a general impression of what is meant, they do not speak precisely. If a thing is called "awesome," for instance, we know only that the speaker thinks it good. If it is called "delicious," we know that it *tastes* good. Formal language demands accuracy. Slang fails to meet the same standards.

Besides being vague, slang can also be ambiguous. "A major general trend among young people at the current time," writes Aitchison, "is the use of 'bad' words to mean 'good, excellent'" (21). Among the words she lists which may mean "good" are "wicked," "bad," "deadly," "filthy," and "savage." Because these words, in a slang context, mean the opposite of their dictionary definitions, they could easily lead to ambiguous communication. "Your shirt is filthy" might mean the shirt is great, or it might mean the wearer should consider a change of clothes. "This cake is deadly" could be a compliment for the cook or a caution for the people about to eat it. The easiest way to avoid this kind of confusion is to use only

This citation shows that your source is quoting from another source. If you can find the original quotation, however, it is always best to do so.

This strong topic sentence also serves as a transition between subtopics.

MLA

dictionary definitions. Slang, its detractors say, is too ambiguous to be useful in communication.

These complaints, once again, only make sense within the context of written literacy. In writing, the statement "This cake is deadly" is definitely ambiguous. In speech, however, its meaning could be made clear by the use of non-verbal cues. Accompanied by a smile from the speaker, the statement means that the cake is excellent; a look of horror on the speaker's face or a dead body nearby would suggest a more literal interpretation of the speaker's words. In spoken language, the meanings of words are communicated by context, "which is not, as in a dictionary, simply other words, but includes also gestures, vocal inflections, facial expression, and the entire human existential setting in which the real, spoken word always occurs" (Ong 47). A similar answer may be given in response to complaints of slang's vagueness. A physical context of extreme beauty would make the precise meaning of "awesome" clear.

Even in cases where context or nonverbal clues do not clarify ambiguity, spoken language can resolve this ambiguity by leaving room for listeners to ask clarifying questions whenever necessary. If the new arrival at the party still has not figured out whether the "deadly" cake is delicious or poisonous, she need only ask. Spoken language leaves room for creative or ambiguous speech, because

MLA

Throughout his essay, the author skillfully makes assertions that he substantiates with research.

Again, the author uses a topic sentence as a transitional sentence.

words that are spoken do not always need to be understood on the first try. Writing, on other hand, doesn't leave space for question-asking. Walter Ong, reporting Plato's objections to the development of writing, observes that "a written text is basically unresponsive. If you ask a person to explain his or her statement, you can get an explanation; if you ask a text, you get back nothing except the same, often stupid, words which called for your question in the first place" (78). Writing doesn't get a second chance to be understood.

The need for complete clarity in writing may help explain why people tend to oppose the use of slang in writing more than in speech. Leslie N. Carraway, as she cautions against the use of slang in scientific writing, does not argue that slang is altogether unhelpful, just that it is "more appropriate to familiar conversation than to formal speech or science writing" (387). Anna Leahy's objections to slang, specifically regarding its vagueness and inaccuracy, are also set specifically within the written context (305). On the other hand, slang's defenders typically treat it within the context of speech. Elisa Mattiello calls slang "the state-of-the-art vocabulary which people use in familiar relaxed conversations … in which educated formal registers would be situationally inappropriate and unconventional language is instead privileged" (35-36). From her perspective, slang and formal language are each appropriate in some contexts and inappropriate in others. For slang, she believes, the appropriate context is spoken conversation. Joseph P. Mazer and Stephen K. Hunt, who study slang in teacher-student communication, also praise slang as a useful tool for spoken communication while ignoring it in writing. •┄┄┄┄┄┄┄┐

Instead of citing a specific page from this source, the writer has summarized the entire argument of the source.

If slang were defended only in terms of speech and condemned only in terms of writing, there would be no need for disagreement. Thus, some of the current disagreement regarding slang could be avoided by specifying what form of slang is under discussion. If phrases like "Slang is good" and "Slang is bad" are modified to state that "Spoken slang is appropriate" and "Written slang is inappropriate," people who have previously disagreed may find unexpected common ground. Conflict still arises, though, when people who typically think about language in terms of writing try to make the rules of literacy apply to spoken language, or when people who primarily view language as a speaking tool try to carry the freedom of their speech into writing.

One of the typically recognized functions of slang is to "oppose established authority" (Moore 61). This function raises the question of precisely which established authority is being opposed. Slang cannot be used as a weapon in opposition to just any authority. It does not, for the most part, oppose governmental authority, because most governments have not legislated the use of slang. Nor could slang be used to oppose an authority which approved of slang. Slang, in itself, is not oppositional. It can oppose an authority only if that authority disapproves of slang. Since slang views language in terms of speech and violates the "rules" of writing, slang opposes authorities who try to enforce a rule-based mindset of written literacy. Most often, these authorities are parental and academic.

The author works to identify with the interests of his peers (his audience), establishing pathos, an authentic emotional connection with the audience.

Because slang is most often associated with adolescents and young adults (Moore 63), who are already stereotyped as rebellious apart from their linguistic preferences, it is easy to assume that slang is just one more weapon in the arsenal of youths intent on rebellion. However, this is not necessarily the case. Certainly people of this age have a tendency to rebel against authority, and it seems equally certain that slang is a part of this rebellion. Still, a distinction should be made between slang as a part of rebellion and slang as "mere" rebellion with no other rationale. Just because slang fights authority does not mean that it exists for the sole purpose of fighting authority. It is possible that adolescents and young adults who use slang are reacting, at least in part, against the literate mindset being forced onto them. Statements like "Why does it matter how I say it as long as you know what I'm saying?" reveal an innate understanding of language as a spoken, conversational tool defined by social interaction.

•Walt Whitman calls slang "an attempt of common humanity to escape from bald literalism, and express itself illimitably" (573). It is no coincidence that the words "literalism" and "literacy" are so similar in sound: both are derived from the Latin *lit(t)era*, meaning "letter" (*Shorter Oxford*). Slang is an escape from the limits of written letters and the rules that come with them. It is, as William C. Gore writes, "a sign of life in language," a sign that "the structure of language is not liable to stiffen so as to become an inadequate means for the communication of new ideas" (197). In the conflict between spoken language and written language, slang terms are the fighting words of our spoken inheritance.

MLA

The author concludes with an appeal to pathos, invoking our "common humanity."

Works Cited •

Aitchison, Jean. "Whassup? Slang and Swearing Among School • Children." *Education Review*, vol. 19, no. 2, 2006, pp. 18-24.

The American Heritage Dictionary of the English Language. 4th ed., 2000.

Bellous, Joyce. "Spiritual and Ethical Orality in Children: Educating an Oral Self." *International Journal of Children's Spirituality*, vol. 5, no. 1, 2000, pp. 9-26.

The works-cited list begins on a new page, with the heading centered.

Every entry on the list begins flush with the left margin and has subsequent lines indented one-half inch (a hanging indent). Entries are listed in alphabetical order.

Carraway, Leslie N. "Improve Scientific Writing and Avoid

Perishing." *American Midland Naturalist,* vol. 155, no. 2, 2006,

pp. 383-94.

Dumas, Bethany K., and Jonathan Lighter. "Is *Slang* a Word for

Linguists?" *American Speech,* vol. 53, no. 1, 1978, pp. 5-17.

Gore, William C. "Notes on Slang." *Modern Language Notes,* vol. 11,

no. 7, 1896, pp. 193-98.

Green, Jonathon. "Slang by Dates." *Critical Quarterly,* vol. 48, no. 1,

2006, pp. 99-104.

Herrmann, Keith R. "The War of Words." *War, Literature & the Arts:*

An International Journal of the Humanities, vol. 18, no. 1/2, 2006,

pp. 319-23.

Hummon, David M. "College Slang Revisited: Language, Culture,

and Undergraduate Life." *The Journal of Higher Education,* vol.

65, no. 1, 1994, pp. 75-98.

Leahy, Anna. "Grammar Matters: A Creative Writer's Argument."

Pedagogy, vol. 5, no. 2, 2005, pp. 304-08.

Mattiello, Elisa. "The Pervasiveness of Slang in Standard and Non-

Standard English." *Mots Palabras Words,* 2005, pp. 7-41, www

.ledonline.it/mpw/allegati/mpw0506Mattiello.pdf.

Mazer, Joseph P., and Stephen K. Hunt. "'Cool' Communication in

the Classroom: A Preliminary Examination of Student

This entry docu-
ments an article
from a professional
journal.

Perceptions of Instructor Use of Positive Slang." *Qualitative Research Reports in Communication*, vol. 9, no. 1, 2008, pp. 20-28.

McGregor, Erik. "The Right to Boycott." Pacific Press / LightRocket, 9 June 2016. *Getty Images*, www.gettyimages.com/ photos/539161558.

Moore, Robert L. "We're Cool, Mom and Dad Are Swell: Basic Slang and Generational Shifts in Values." *American Speech*, vol. 79, no. 1, 2004, pp. 59-86.

Ong, Walter J. *Orality and Literacy*. Routledge, 2002.

Peters, Mark. *Bull Shit*. Three Rivers Press, 2015.

Shorter Oxford English Dictionary. 5th ed., 2002.

Stamper, Kory. "Slang for the Ages." *The New York Times*, 3 Oct. 2014, www.nytimes.com/2014/10/04/opinion/slang-for-the-ages.html.

Stenström, Anna-Brita. "From Slang to Slanguage: A Description Based on Teenage Talk." *I Love English Language*, aggslanguage .wordpress.com/slang-to-slanguage. Accessed 27 Nov. 2015.

Whitman, Walt. "Slang in America." The Collected Writings of Walt *Whitman: Prose Works 1892*, edited by Floyd Stovall, vol. 2, New York UP, 1964, pp. 572-76.

MLA

"The Right to Boycott" is the title of the photo, but if it were untitled, the description "Photograph" would be used instead.

This entry is for a source taken from a blog. The access date is included because the article posted on this website did not include a date.

23 Acknowledging Sources in APA Style

LEARNING OBJECTIVES

- Assess occasions in which documentation is necessary.
- Determine which disciplines require APA style for documentation.
- Apply APA style to acknowledge, cite, and document sources.

The American Psychological Association (APA) style guide is used by most researchers in the social sciences (anthropology, economics, geography, history, political science, psychology, sociology, and social studies), who regularly acknowledge sources within the text of the paper by referring to the author(s) of the text and the year of its publication (a process known as *In-Text Citation*) and also include a References page at the end. In contrast to a bibliography, which includes all works consulted, a References page only contains those sources cited in the paper.

APA style also includes guidelines for bias-free language. By using language free of bias, writers help ensure that their treatment of groups and individuals is fair. Avoid use of any language that demeans or discriminates, and strive to use accurate, inclusive language at all times. To do this, describe people and groups with an appropriate level of specificity and be sensitive to labels. For details, see apastyle.apa.org/style-grammar-guidelines/bias-free-language.

» APA GUIDELINES FOR IN-TEXT CITATIONS

In addition to the author(s) of the text you consulted and the year of its publication, the APA guidelines require that you specify the page number(s) for any quotations you include; the abbreviation *p.* (for "page") or *pp.* (for "pages") should precede the number(s). For electronic sources that do not include page numbers, specify the paragraph number and precede it with the abbreviation *para.* or the symbol ¶. When no author's name is listed, provide a shortened version of the title of the source. If your readers want to find more information about your source, they will look for the author's name or the title of the material in the References page at the end of your paper.

You will likely consult a variety of sources for your research paper. The following examples are representative of the types of in-text citations you might use.

1.   Work by one or two authors

Wachal **(2002)** discusses dictionary labels for words considered taboo.

Dictionary labels for taboo words include *offensive* and *derogatory* **(Wachal, 2002).**

Lance and Pulliam (2002) believe that an introductory linguistics text should have "persuasive power" **(p. 223).**

On learning of dialect bias, some students expressed outrage, often making "a 180-degree turnaround" from their original attitudes toward a standard language **(Lance & Pulliam, 2002, p. 223).**

Authors' names may be placed either in the text, followed by the date of publication in parentheses, or in parentheses along with the date. When you mention an author in the text, place the date of publication directly after the author's name. If you include a quotation, provide the page number(s) at the end of the quotation, after the quotation marks but before the period. When citing a work by two authors, use the word *and* between their names; when citing two authors in parentheses, use an ampersand (&) between their names. Always use a comma to separate the last author's name from the date.

2. Work by three or more authors

Johnstone et al. (2002) describe the speech of Pittsburgh, Pennsylvania, as *Pittsburghese*.

The speech of Pittsburgh, Pennsylvania, is called *Pittsburghese* **(Johnstone et al., 2002).**

When citing a source by three or more authors, use just the first author's last name along with the abbreviation *et al.* (Latin for "and others"). The abbreviation *et al.* should not be italicized in citations.

3. Work by an unknown author

A recent survey indicated increased willingness of college students to vote in national elections **("Ending Apathy," 2004).**

The documents leaked to the press could damage the governor's reputation **(Anonymous, 2010).**

When no author is mentioned, use a shortened version of the title instead. Capitalize all major words in the title; use italics for titles that are italicized in the References list and quotation marks for titles that are not. If the word *Anonymous* (not in italics) is used in the source to designate the author, use that word in place of the author's name.

4. Two or more works by the same author

Smith (2001, 2003, 2005) has consistently argued in support of language immersion.

Bayard (1995a, 1995b) discusses the acquisition of English in New Zealand.

In most cases, the year of publication will distinguish the works. However, if the works were published in the same year, distinguish them with lowercase letters, assigned based on the order of the titles in the References.

5. Two or more works by different authors with the same last name

J. P. Hill and Giles (2001) and **G. S. Hill and Kellner (2002)** confirmed these findings.

When two or more authors have the same last name, always include first initials with that last name.

6. Work by a group

Style refers to publishing guidelines that encourage the clear and coherent presentation of written text **(American Psychological Association [APA], 2020).**

Spell out the name of the group when you first mention it. If the group has a widely recognizable abbreviation, place that abbreviation in square brackets after the first mention. You can then use the abbreviation in subsequent citations: (APA, 2020).

7. Work by a government author

Taxpayers encounter significant problems with two different taxes: the sole proprietor tax and the alternative minimum tax **(Internal Revenue Service [IRS], 2010).**

Spell out the name of the government entity when you first mention it. If the entity has a widely recognizable abbreviation, place that abbreviation in square brackets after the first mention. You can then use the abbreviation in subsequent citations: (IRS, 2010).

8. Indirect source

According to Ronald Butters, the word *go* is frequently used by speakers born after 1955 to introduce a quotation **(as cited in Cukor-Avila, 2002).**

Use *as cited in* (not in italics) to indicate that you found the information in another source.

9. Two or more works in one parenthetical citation

A speaker may use the word *like* to focus the listener's attention **(Eriksson, 1995; Ferrar & Bell, 1995).**

When you include two or more works within the same parentheses, order them alphabetically. Arrange two or more works by the same author by year of publication, mentioning the author's name only once: (Kamil, 2002, 2004).

10. Personal communication

Revisions will be made to the agreement this month **(K. M. Liebenow, personal communication, February 11, 2010).**

Letters, e-mail messages, and interviews are all considered personal communications, which you should cite in the text of a paper. Because personal communications do not represent recoverable data, you should not include entries for them in the references list.

»» APA GUIDELINES FOR DOCUMENTING REFERENCES

To provide readers with the information they need to find the sources you have used in your paper, you must prepare a list of all these sources. According to APA guidelines, this list should be titled *References* (not italicized). It should contain all the information your readers need to retrieve the sources if they wish to consult them on their own. Except for personal communications, each source you cite in your text should appear in the References list.

Alphabetize your references according to the author's (or the first author's) last name. If the author is unknown, alphabetize according to title (ignoring any initial article—*a, an,* or *the*). When you have more than one source by the same author(s), order them according to the year of publication, with the earliest first.

Frazer, B. (2000).

Frazer, B. (2004).

If two or more works by the same author(s) have the same year of publication, the entries are ordered alphabetically according to the works' titles, and lowercase letters are added to the date to distinguish the entries.

Fairclough, N. (1992a). The appropriacy of "appropriateness."

Fairclough, N. (1992b). *Critical language awareness.*

Fairclough, N. (1992c). *Discourse and social change.*

When an author you have cited is also the first of two or more authors of another entry, list the source with a single author first.

Allen, J. P. (1982).

Allen, J. P., & Turner, E. J. (1988).

When two or more entries have the same first author, alphabetize the list according to the names of subsequent authors.

Fallows, M. R., & Andrews, R. J. (1999).

Fallows, M. R., & Laver, J. T. (2002).

Double-space all of your entries, leaving the first line flush with the left margin and indenting subsequent lines one-half inch. (Your word processor may refer to the indented line as a *hanging indent.*)

For more details on various types of sources, use the following directory to find relevant sections. For an example of a References list, see the paper at the end of this chapter. If you would like to use a checklist to help ensure that you have followed APA guidelines, see page 467.

(Continued)

APA

Books

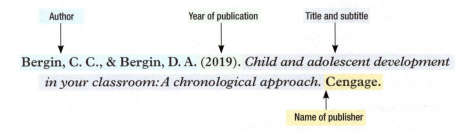

Author   Year of publication   Title and subtitle

Bergin, C. C., & Bergin, D. A. (2019). *Child and adolescent development in your classroom: A chronological approach.* Cengage.

Name of publisher

You can find most of the information you need to write a reference entry on a book's title page. If you cannot find the date of publication on the title page, turn to the copyright page. Reference entries for books generally include four units of information: author, year of publication, title, and publisher.

Author

The author's last name appears first, followed by the first and (if given) second initial. Use a comma to separate the last name from the initial(s), and place a period at the end of this unit of information. If there is more than one author, invert all the authors' names, following the pattern described for a single author. Separate the names with commas, adding an ampersand (&) before the name of the last author.

Hooker, R.   Montgomery, M., & Morgan, E.   McCrum, D., Kurath, H., & Middleton, S.

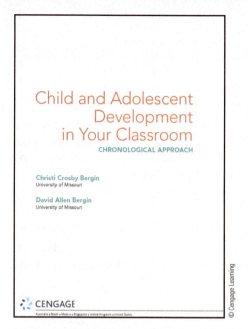

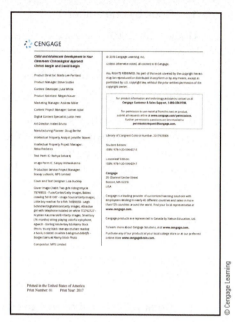

© Cengage Learning

© Cengage Learning

Title page of Child and Adolescent Development in Your Classroom.

Copyright page of Child and Adolescent Development in Your Classroom.

Year of publication

Place the year of publication in parentheses after the author's name. Mark the end of this unit of information with a period.

Title

Include the title and, if there is one, the subtitle of the book. Capitalize *only* the first word of the title and the subtitle, plus any proper nouns. Use a colon to separate the subtitle from the title. Italicize the title and subtitle.

Social cognition: Key readings.

Publisher

Give the publisher's name as it appears on the title page, retaining words such as *Press* or *Books,* but omitting *Ltd. or Inc.*

1. Book by one author

Gladwell, M. (2008). *Outliers: The story of success.* Little, Brown and Company.

2. Book by two or more authors

Alberts, B., Lewis, J., & Johnson, A. (2002). *Molecular biology of the cell.* Taylor & Francis.

For up to 20 authors, provide the names of all authors, inverted, with a comma and ampersand before the final author's name. If there are more than 20 authors, provide the names of the first 19 authors, inverted, followed by an ellipsis (no ampersand) and the name of the final author.

3. Book with editor(s)

Good, T. L., & Warshauer, L. B. (Eds.). (2002). *In our own voice: Graduate students teach writing.* Allyn & Bacon.

Include the abbreviation *Ed.* or *Eds.* in parentheses after the name(s) of the editor(s).

4. Book with an author and an editor

Lewis, C. S. (2003). *A year with C. S. Lewis: Daily readings from his classic works* (P. S. Klein, Ed.). Zondervan.

Place the editor's name and the abbreviation *Ed.* in parentheses after the title of the book.

5. Book by a corporate or other group author

Modern Language Association of America. (1978). *International bibliography of books and articles on the modern languages and literatures, 1976.*

Alphabetize by the first major word in the group author's name. If the author and the publisher are the same, do not repeat the name as the publisher.

6. Book by an anonymous author

Anonymous. (1996). *Primary colors: A novel of politics.* Warner Books.

Use *Anonymous* only if the author is given as *Anonymous*, as in the example. Otherwise, list the title of the book in place of an author, and alphabetize the entry by the first major word of the title.

APA

7. Second or subsequent edition

Cember, H. (1996). *Introduction to health physics* (3rd ed.). McGraw-Hill.

Maples, W. (2002). *Opportunities in aerospace careers* (Rev. ed.). McGraw-Hill.

Provide the edition number in parentheses after the title of the book. If the revision is not numbered, place *Rev. ed.* for "Revised edition" in parentheses after the title.

8. Translated book

de Beauvoir, S. (1987). *The woman destroyed* (P. O'Brien, Trans.). Pantheon Books. (Original work published 1969)

Insert the name(s) of the translator(s) in parentheses after the title, and conclude with the original publication date. Note the absence of a period at the end of the entry. In the text, provide both publication dates as follows: (de Beauvoir, 1969/1987).

9. Republished book

Freire, P. (1982). *Pedagogy of the oppressed* (2nd ed.). Penguin Books. (Original work published 1972)

Conclude the entry with the original publication date. Note the absence of a period at the end of the entry. In the text provide both dates: (Freire, 1972/1982).

10. Multivolume work

Doyle, A. C. (2003). *The complete Sherlock Holmes* (Vols. 1–2). Barnes & Noble.

Maugham, S. W. (1977–1978). *Collected short stories* (Vols. 1–4). Penguin Books.

Include the number of volumes after the title of the work. If the volumes were published over a period of time, provide the date range after the author's name.

11. Government report

Executive Office of the President. (2003). *Economic report of the President, 2003* (GPO Publication No. 040-000-0760-1). Government Printing Office.

Provide the publication number in parentheses after the name of the report. If the report is available from the Government Publishing Office (GPO), formerly named the Government Printing Office, that entity is the publisher. If the report is not available from the GPO, use the parent agency as the publisher.

12. Selection from an edited book

Muños, G. T. (2007). Once upon a time on the border. In T. Miller (Ed.), *How I learned English* (pp. 141–148). National Geographic Society.

The title of the selection is not italicized. The editor's name appears before the title of the book. Provide the page or range of pages on which the selection appears.

13. Selection from a reference book

Layering. (2003). In W. Lidwell, K. Holden, & J. Butler (Eds.), *Universal principles of design* (pp. 122–123). Rockport Publishers.

Provide the page number or range of pages after the title of the book. If the selection has an author, give that author's name first.

Bruce, F. F. (1991). Hermeneutics. In *New Bible dictionary* (p. 476). Tyndale.

Articles in Print

ARTICLE IN A JOURNAL

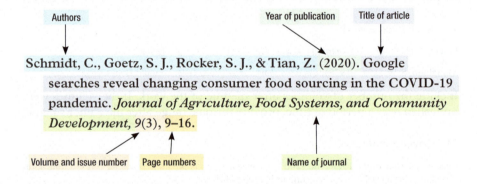

Authors / Year of publication / Title of article

Schmidt, C., Goetz, S. J., Rocker, S. J., & Tian, Z. (2020). Google searches reveal changing consumer food sourcing in the COVID-19 pandemic. *Journal of Agriculture, Food Systems, and Community Development, 9*(3), 9–16.

Volume and issue number / Page numbers / Name of journal

You can generally find the name of the journal, the volume and issue numbers, and the year of publication on the cover of the journal. Sometimes this information is also included in the journal's page headers or footers. To find the title of the article, the author's name, and the page numbers, you'll have to locate the article within the journal.

APA

ARTICLE IN A MAGAZINE

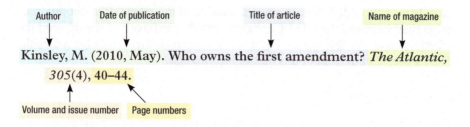

Author | Date of publication | Title of article | Name of magazine

Kinsley, M. (2010, May). Who owns the first amendment? *The Atlantic,*
305(4), 40–44.

Volume and issue number | Page numbers

To find the name of the magazine, the volume and issue numbers, and the date of publication, look on the cover of the magazine. Sometimes this information is also included in the magazine's page headers or footers. For the title of the article, the author's name, and the page numbers, look at the article itself. Reference entries for articles generally include four units of information: author, date of publication, title of article, and publication data.

Author

The author's last name appears first, followed by the first and (if given) the second initial. Use a comma to separate the last name from the initial(s), and place a period at the end of this unit of information. For articles with more than one author, see the information given for book entries earlier in this chapter.

Date of publication

For journals, place just the year of publication in parentheses after the author's name. For magazines, also specify the month and the day (if given). Mark the end of this unit of information with a period.

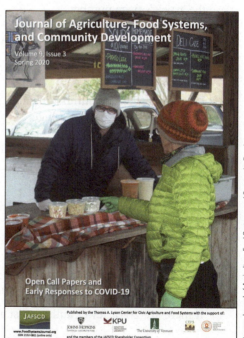

Cover of an academic journal showing the year of publication, volume and issue numbers, and title of the journal.

Source: Journal of Agriculture, Food Systems, and Community Development

APA

Title of article

Include the title and, if there is one, the subtitle of the article. (Do not put quotation marks around the title.) Capitalize only the first word of the title and the subtitle, plus any proper nouns. Use a colon to separate the subtitle from the title. Place a period at the end of this unit of information.

Publication data

The publication data that you provide depends on the type of periodical in which the article appeared. However, for all entries, include the title of the periodical (italicized), the volume number (also italicized), and the page numbers of the article. If you are using a magazine or a journal that has issue numbers, include the issue number as well. Place the issue number (not italicized) in parentheses following the volume number. After the issue number, place a comma and then the article's page numbers.

14. Article in a journal without issue numbers

McCarthy, M., & Carter, R. (2001). Size isn't everything: Spoken English, corpus, and the classroom. *TESOL Quarterly, 35,* 337–340.

Provide the volume number in italics after the title of the journal. Conclude with the page number or page range.

15. Article in a journal with issue numbers

Smiles, T. (2008). Connecting literacy and learning through collaborative action research. *Voices from the Middle, 15*(4), 32–39.

Provide the issue number (placed in parentheses) directly after the volume number (italicized).

16. Article with three to 20 authors

Biber, D., Conrad, S., & Reppen, R. (1996). Corpus-based investigations of language use. *Annual Review of Applied Linguistics, 16,* 115–136.

If there are 20 or fewer authors, list all the authors' names.

17. Article with more than 20 authors

Hodgins, S., Tengström, A., Eriksson, A., Österman, R., Kronstrand, R., Eaves, D., Hart, S., Webster, C., Ross, D., Levin, A., Levander, A., Tuninger, E., Müller-Isberner, R., Freese, R., Tiihonen, J.,

Kotilainen, I., Repo-Tiihonen, E., Väänänen, K., Eronen, M., . . . Vartiainen, H. (2007). A multisite study of community treatment programs for mentally ill offenders with major mental disorders: Design, measures, and the forensic sample. *Criminal Justice and Behavior, 34*(2), 211–228.

Provide the names of the first 19 authors, inverted, followed by an ellipsis and the name of the final author.

18. Article in a monthly or weekly magazine

Gross, D. (2010, May 3). The days the Earth stood still. *Newsweek,* 46–48.

Warne, K. (2004, March). Harp seals. *National Geographic, 205,* 50–67.

Provide the month and year of publication for monthly magazines or the day, month, and year for weekly magazines. Names of months are not abbreviated. Include the volume number (italicized), if any, issue number (not italicized), and the page number or page range (not italicized) after the name of the magazine.

19. Anonymous article

Ohio police hunt for highway sniper suspect. (2004, March 16). *The New York Times,* A4.

Begin the entry with the title of the article, followed by the date of publication.

20. Article in a newspaper

Lewin, T. (2010, May 6). Teenage insults, scrawled on Web, not on walls. *The New York Times,* A1, A18.

If the article appears on discontinuous pages, provide all of the page numbers, separated by commas: A8, A10–11, A13.

21. Letter to the editor

Richard, J. (2004, March 8). Diabetic children: Every day a challenge [Letter to the editor]. *The Wall Street Journal,* A17.

Include the description *Letter to the editor* in square brackets after the title of the letter.

22. Editorial in a newspaper

Marcus, R. (2010, May 5). In Arizona, election reform's surprising consequences [Editorial]. *The Washington Post,* A21.

Include the description *Editorial* in square brackets after the title.

23. Book review

Kakutani, M. (2004, February 13). All aflutter, existentially [Review of the book *Dot in the universe,* by L. Ellmann]. *The New York Times,* E31.

In square brackets after the title of the review, indicate that the work cited is a review, provide a description of the medium of the work (e.g., book, film, or play), and include the title of the work along with the author or other creator.

Sources Produced for Access by Computer

JOURNAL ARTICLE FROM A DATABASE

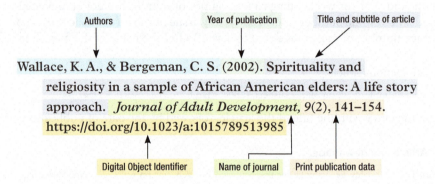

You can usually find much of the information you will need for your reference entry on the first page of the article. Each entry generally includes five units of information: author, year of publication, title and subtitle of the article, print publication data, and digital object identifier (DOI).

Author

The author's last name appears first, followed by the first and (if given) the second initial. Use a comma to separate the last name from the initials, and place a period at the end of this unit of information. For articles with more than one author, see the information given for book entries earlier in this chapter.

Date of publication

For journals, place just the year of publication in parentheses after the author's name. Mark the end of this unit of information with a period.

Title of article

Include the title and, if there is one, the subtitle of the article. Capitalize only the first word of the title and subtitle, plus any proper nouns. Use a colon to separate the subtitle from the main title. Place a period at the end of this unit of information.

Print publication data

The publication data that you provide depends on the type of periodical in which the article appeared. See the information on publication data for periodicals earlier in this chapter.

Digital Object Identifier

Rather than provide a URL for the database or article, include the digital object identifier (DOI), if available. A DOI is assigned to most scholarly articles found online and has the great advantage of being stable. You will usually find the DOI on the first page of the article, near the copyright notice. In cases in which a DOI is unavailable, provide the URL for the article. Do not place a period at the end of this unit of information.

Electronic sources vary significantly; therefore, as you prepare your list of references, follow the models below closely. On occasion, you may not be able to find all the information presented in a particular model. In such cases, provide as much of the information as you can.

24. Article from a database or an online journal

Moore, A. C., Akhter, S., & Aboud, F. E. (2008). Evaluating an improved quality preschool program in rural Bangladesh. *International Journal of Educational Development, 28*(2), 118–131. https://doi.org/10.1016/j.ijedudev.2007.05.003

After the print publication data, include the DOI, if available.

Gordon-Roth, J. (2019). Tracing Reid's "brave officer" back to Berkeley—and beyond. *Berkeley Studies, 28,* 3–22. https://berkeleystudies.philosophy.fsu.edu/sites/g/files/upcbnu886/files/BS%2028%20Gordon-Roth%20%28Revised%29.pdf

If no DOI is assigned, end the citation with the URL of the article.

25. Article in an online newspaper

Connelly, J. (2010, May 2). Lessons from the Gulf oil spill. *Seattle Post-Intelligencer.* https://www.seattlepi.com/local/connelly/article/Lessons-from-the-Gulf-oil-spill-891985.php

APA

Provide the full date of the article after the author's name. Conclude with the URL of the article.

26. Message posted to a newsgroup, forum, or discussion group

Skrecky, D. (2003, May 24). *Free radical theory of aging falsified* [Newsgroup message]. http://extropians.weidai.com/extropians/0305/8738.html

Bradstreet, J. (2010, May 6). *The over diagnosis of ADHD and why* [Electronic mailing list message]. OpEd News. https://www.opednews.com/populum/page.php?f=The-Over-Diagnosis-Of-ADHD-by-John-Bradstreet-100506-469.html

If the author's name is unavailable, the author's screen name may be used. A brief description of the source (such as *Online forum post*) should be provided in square brackets after the subject line of the message.

27. Document from a website

Robinson, J. (2013). *Grass-fed basics.* http://www.eatwild.com/Grass-Fed%20Basics.pdf

Slow Food USA. (2013, August 28). *Slow food on campus takes on food and climate change.* https://slowfoodusa.org/slow-food-on-campus-takes-on-food-and-climate-change/

If no author is given, use the name of the organization hosting the website as the author of the document. Provide the date, the name of the document, and the URL for the specific page where the document can be found.

28. E-mail message

Personal communications such as e-mail messages, letters, telephone conversations, and personal interviews do not appear in the References list, but should be cited in the text as follows: (S. L. Johnson, personal communication, September 3, 2009).

29. Podcast

DiMeo, N. (Host). (2010, March 12). The sisters Fox (No. 27) [Audio podcast episode]. In *The memory palace.* https://thememorypalace.us/2010/03/episode-27-the-sisters-fox/

Other Sources

30. Motion picture

Edwards, B. (Director). (1963). *The pink panther* [Film]. United Artists.

Begin with the name of the director. Include the description *Film* in square brackets after the title. Conclude with the name of the movie studio.

31. Television program

Belkin, A., Shiva, A., Blum, J., Gold, J., & Wiseman, S. (Executive Producers). (2019). *No one saw a thing* [TV series]. Blumhouse Television.

Begin with the name of the executive producer. Italicize the title of the program, and follow the title with the description *TV series* in square brackets. Conclude with the name of the production company.

32. Music recording

Porter, C. (1999). Easy to love [Song recorded by H. Connick, Jr.]. On *Come by me*. Columbia. (Original work published 1936)

White, J. (2010). Seven nation army [Song recorded by The White Stripes]. On *Under great white northern lights*. Warner Bros. Records. (Original work published 2003)

Start with the name of the songwriter and the year the version of the song was published. If someone other than the songwriter recorded the song, add *Song recorded by* and the singer's name in square brackets after the song title. Otherwise, add *Song* in square brackets after the title. If the song is on an album, add *On* followed by the album title in italics. Conclude the entry with the label that released the song. If the publication date of the recording is later than the publication date of the original song, include *Original work published* and the year the song was originally published in parentheses.

33. Interview

Brock, A. C. (2006). Rediscovering the history of psychology: Interview with Kurt Danziger. *History of Psychology, 9*(1), 1–16.

For a published interview, follow the format for an entry for an article. If you conducted the interview yourself, cite the name of the person you interviewed in the body of your paper and include in parentheses the words *personal communication,* followed by a comma and the interview date. Do not include an entry for a personal interview in the list of references.

CHECKING OVER A REFERENCES LIST

✓ Is the title, *References* (boldfaced, not italicized), centered one inch from the top of the page? Is the first letter capitalized?

✓ Is the entire list double-spaced?

(continued)

✓ Are initial lines flush with the left margin and subsequent lines indented one-half inch?

✓ Is there an entry in the References list for each in-text citation (except for personal communications)? Is there an in-text citation for each entry in the References list?

✓ Are the entries alphabetized according to the first author's last name? If the author of an entry is unknown, is the entry alphabetized according to title (ignoring any initial *a*, *an*, or *the*)?

✓ If the list contains two or more entries by the same author, are the entries arranged according to year of publication (earliest one first)?

✓ Are book and periodical titles italicized?

✓ Is capitalization used for only the first words of book and article titles and subtitles and any proper nouns they contain?

»» SAMPLE APA RESEARCH PAPER

The APA provides the following general guidelines for formatting a research paper. The title page is page 1 of your paper. If your instructor requires you to use a running head, on this and all other pages of your paper, in the upper left-hand corner, place a shortened version of your title (no more than fifty characters), all in capital letters. In the upper right-hand corner of this and all the following pages, put the page number. This running head, if used, and the page number should appear one-half inch from the top of the page and one inch from the side(s). Center the full title in the upper third of the title page, using boldface and both uppercase and lowercase letters. Double-space twice, and then, unless your instructor specifies otherwise, center and double-space the following information: your name your department and school, the course number and name, the instructor's name, and the assignment due date.

If your instructor requires one, include an abstract—a short summary of your research—as the second page of your paper. The abstract should be no longer than 250 words. The word *Abstract* (boldfaced, not italicized) should be centered at the top of the page.

The first page of text is page 2 or 3 of the paper (depending on whether you have included an abstract). The full title of the paper, in boldface and with uppercase and lowercase letters, should be centered one inch from the top of the page. Double-space between the title and the first line of text. Use a one-inch margin on all sides of your paper (left, right, top, and bottom). Do not justify the text; that is, leave the right margin uneven. Indent paragraphs and block quotations one-half inch. Double-space your entire paper, including block quotations.

Perceptions of Peers' Drinking Behavior •

Catherine L. Davis

Department of Health Sciences, Central Washington University•

HED 117: Drugs and Health

Dr. Maya Anderson

May 4, 2020

·····The page header can have a running head (no more than 50 characters) on the left and has a page number on the right. It should appear one-half inch from the top of the page and one inch from the left and right edges.

·····The title is in uppercase and lowercase letters and is boldfaced and centered.

·····Depending on what the instructor requires, information given below the title may include the department and school, the course name and number, the instructor's name, and the due date.

Abstract •

•This study is an examination of how students' perceptions of their peers' drinking behavior are related to alcohol consumption and alcohol-related problems on campus. Four hundred nine randomly selected college students were interviewed using a modified version of the Core Survey (Presley, Meilman, & Lyeria, 1995) to assess alcohol consumption and its related problems.

·····The abstract, if required, appears on a separate page, with the heading boldfaced and centered. An abstract generally contains 150–250 words.

·····Use one-inch margins on both sides of the paper.

Perceptions of Peers' Drinking Behavior

Studies typically report the dangers associated with college students' use of alcohol (Beck et al., 2008). Nonetheless, drinking is still highly prevalent on American campuses. Johnston et al. (1998) found that 87% of the college students surveyed reported drinking during their lifetime. Most of the students are 21 or 22 years old and report frequent episodes of heavy drinking (i.e., binge drinking).

Heavy episodic drinking is particularly problematic. Johnston et al. (1998) found that 41% of college students engage in heavy episodic drinking, which they defined as having at least five or more drinks in a row at least once in the 2 weeks prior to being surveyed. Heavy episodic drinking is related to impaired academic performance, interpersonal problems, unsafe sexual activity, and sexual assault and other criminal violations (Moore et al., 1994). The magnitude of such problems has led Neighbors et al. (2007) to conclude that binge drinking is a widespread problem among college students.

Massad and Rauhe (1997) report that college students engage in heavy episodic drinking in response to social pressure or physical discomfort. Almost half of college students in a survey stated their

APA

reason for drinking was to get drunk (Jessor et al., 2006). Recent research suggests that students' misperceptions of their peers' drinking behavior contribute to increased alcohol consumption (Perkins, 2002).

College students commonly perceive their social peers as drinking more often and in greater quantities than they actually do (Neighbors et al., 2007). When these students see their peers as heavy drinkers, they are more likely to engage in heavy drinking (Neighbors et al., 2007; Perkins & Wechsler, 1996). The goal of this study was to determine whether students' perceptions of their peers' use of alcohol are related to alcohol consumption and alcohol-related problems on campus.

Method

Participants

For the purposes of this study, a randomly selected sample ($N = 409$) of undergraduate students from a university in the Pacific Northwest was drawn. The mean age of participants, 55.8% of whom were female, was 24 years; 54.5% of participants were White, 19% were Hispanic, 14.8% were Asian/Pacific Islander, 5% were African American, 0.5% were American Indian, and 6.3% indicated "Other" as their ethnicity.

APA

Two or more sources in the same parenthetical citation are separated by semicolons and listed alphabetically.

The thesis statement forecasts the content of the paper.

In this section, the writer explains her research methods, including descriptions of her research subjects and the research model she followed.

Instrument

The study used a modified version of the short form of the Core Survey (Presley et al., 1995). The Core Survey measures alcohol and other drug (AOD) use as well as related problems experienced by college students. For the purposes of this study, the Core was modified from a self-administered format to an interview format.

Procedure

Interviews were conducted by telephone. Each interview took an average of 16 minutes to complete. The refusal rate for this survey was 12%, and those refusing to participate were replaced randomly.

Alcohol use was defined as the number of days (during the past 30 days) that respondents drank alcohol. *Heavy episodic drinking* was defined as five or more drinks in a single sitting, with a drink consisting of one beer, one glass of wine, one shot of hard liquor, or one mixed drink (Presley et al., 1995). Respondents indicated the number of occasions in the past 2 weeks that they engaged in heavy episodic drinking. *Alcohol-related problems* were defined as the number of times in the past 30 days respondents experienced any of 20 specific incidents.

To determine alcohol-related problems, the interviewer asked students how many times they (a) had a hangover, (b) damaged property, (c) got into a physical fight, (d) got into a verbal fight, (e) got

The writer defines her terms.

The writer supplies specific examples of alcohol-related problems.

APA

nauseous or vomited, (f) drove a vehicle while under the influence,
(g) were criticized by someone they knew, (h) had memory loss, or
(i) did something they later regretted. To determine their perceptions
of their peers' drinking, students were asked to respond on a 7-point
ordinal scale that ranged from 0 = never to 6 = almost daily.

[The data analysis and statistical report of results have been omitted.]

Discussion

The relationship found here concerning the normative
perception of alcohol use is somewhat consistent with past research
(Baer & Carney, 1993; Perkins, 2002) that suggested drinking norms
are related to alcohol use. Readers should note, however, that
respondents' perceptions of the drinking norm were consistent with
the actual norm for 30-day use. This indicates that students are fairly
accurate in assessing their peers' drinking frequencies. Unfortunately,
the current study did not include a perception question for heavy
episodic drinking, making it unclear whether respondents accurately
perceive their peers' drinking quantity. Conceptually, misperceptions
of drinking quantity might be better predictors of heavy episodic
drinking. That is, students might falsely believe that their peers drink
heavily when they drink. Such a misperception would be compounded
by the fact that most students accurately estimate frequency of their

The writer analyzes her findings and then synthesizes them for discussion.

peers' drinking. The combination of an accurate perception of frequency coupled with an inaccurate perception of quantity might result in an overall perception of most students being heavy, frequent drinkers. As expected, this study also revealed a positive and moderately strong pathway from alcohol use, both heavy episodic drinking and 30-day drinking, to alcohol-related problems.

The author draws reasonable conclusions.

This study represents an effort to add to the literature concerning college students' alcohol consumption and its related problems. The results of the study suggest that students' perceptions of their peers' drinking habits are important predictors of drinking or drinking-related problems. Future studies along similar lines might help prevention specialists better design media campaigns related to drinking norms and high-risk behaviors.

Alphabetize the entries according to the author's (or first author's) last name. If two or more entries have the same first author, the second author's last name determines the order of the entries.

Indent second and subsequent lines of each entry one-half inch or five spaces. All entries are double-spaced.

References

Baer, J. S., & Carney, M. M. (1993). Biases in the perceptions of the consequences of alcohol use among college students. *Journal of Studies on Alcohol, 54,* 54–60.

Beck, K. H., Arria, A. M., Caldeira, K. M., Vincent, K. B., O'Grady, K. E., & Wish, E. D. (2008). Social context of drinking and alcohol problems among college students. *American Journal of Health Behavior, 32*(4), 420–430.

Jessor, R., Costa, F. M., Krueger, P. M., & Turbin, M. S. (2006). A developmental study of heavy episodic drinking among college students: The role of psychosocial and behavioral protective and risk factors. *Journal of Studies on Alcohol, 67,* 86–94.

Johnston, L. D., O'Malley, P. M., & Bachman, J. G. (1998). *National survey results on drug use from the Monitoring the Future Study, 1975–1997: Vol. II: College students and young adults* (NIH Publication No. 98-4346). U.S. Department of Health and Human Services, National Institutes of Health.

Massad, S. J., & Rauhe, B. J. (1997). Alcohol consumption patterns in college students: A comparison by various socioeconomic indicators. *Journal for the International Council of Health, Physical Education, Recreation, Sport, and Dance, 23*(4), 60–64.

•Moore, L., Smith, C., & Catford, J. (1994). Binge drinking: Prevalence, patterns and policy. *Health Education Research, 9,* 497–505. https://doi.org/10.1093/her/9.4.497

Neighbors, C., Lee, C. M., Lewis, M. A., Fossos, N., & Larimer, M. E. (2007). Are social norms the best predictor of outcomes among heavy-drinking college students? *Journal of Studies on Alcohol and Drugs, 68,* 556–565.

When citing an article accessed online, always include a DOI if possible. If no DOI is available, include a publicly accessibly URL. (For articles accessed via databases requiring login information, do not include a URL unless requested to do so by your instructor.)

Perkins, H. W. (2002). Social norms and the prevention of alcohol misuse in collegiate contexts. *Journal of American Studies on Alcohol, 14,* 164–172.

Perkins, H. W., & Wechsler, H. (1996). Variation in perceived college drinking norms and its impact on alcohol abuse: A nationwide study. *Journal of Drug Issues, 26,* 961–974.

Presley, C. A., Meilman, P. W., & Lyeria, R. (1995). Development of the Core Alcohol and Drug Survey: Initial findings and future directions. *Journal of American College Health, 42,* 248–255.

Entries with a single author come before entries with that author and one or more coauthors.

APA

24 Food and the (Cultural) Experience of Taste

LEARNING OBJECTIVES

- Consider the cultural significance of food.
- Identify memorable personal experiences with food.
- Implement food experiences to develop various genres.

If you are like most college students, you have participated in lively conversations about food options on and around campus—often new foods that you never tasted before you went to college. You may be one of those who goes through the cafeteria pick-up line or cooks with a roommmate, thinking only about how much better a home-cooked meal would be, remembering with pleasure authentic food from your cultural-ethnic background or geographical area. Yet, years after graduation, many former students long for memorable foods from their college days. When Chowhound. com readers were asked to post stories about their college dining experiences, many contributors to the online discussion wrote about their memories of unique

Hero Images/Corbis

Food can be a fertile topic for writing. In recent years, reminiscing about the best memories of food in college has begun to include the many food trucks that now appear on or near college campuses.

delicacies. "Lidi B" of Penn State University opined, "Oh, to have a grilled sticky from the Ye Olde College Diner à la mode with Penn State Creamery ice cream . . . that would just about be heaven. . . ." On a discussion forum for Roadfood's website, "Mosca" reminisced similarly about a food truck just off Cornell's campus: "After 30 years I can still taste the (great) heartburn from the Ithaca hot truck, which was the source of my personal 'freshman 15.'" That hot truck is just one of numerous food trucks serving college campuses today or in the past, such as the Chinese Kitchen at Harvard, the grease trucks at Rutgers, Chuck's at the University of Miami, and Dia de Los TaKos at the University of New Mexico.

pages 76–77

This chapter focuses on the experience of food. Fitting responses come in many forms, including food memoirs (see CHAPTER 5, GENRE IN FOCUS: THE FOOD MEMOIR), position arguments, investigative reports, proposals, and profiles, as seen in the following selections in this chapter. Your instructor might call on you to consider one of the following opportunities for writing.

1. Chef Eddie Huang manages to jar readers who are accustomed to traditional American food: tuna fish sandwiches and macaroni and cheese. Both these dishes have long been staples of American school lunches and home meals but were startling new tastes for young Eddie. Identify an instance when you tasted something for the first time and your reaction to that experience. Determine the rhetorical audience for your memoir (that is, some person or group in a position to appreciate it), describe the incident, and emphasize the temporary or lasting effects of that first taste. Present your memoir in specific detail, being sure to include a setting, a simple narrative, and characters (including the food). Any dialogue could be internal or with others.

pages 74–90 (See CHAPTER 5, MEMOIRS.)

2. In "Out of the Kitchen, Onto the Couch," Michael Pollan investigates a major food trend along with its disturbing consequences in industrialized nations: few people actually cook (even those who watch Food TV). In an investigative report, analyze a positive or negative food culture trend on your campus, in your community, or at home. Consider Ruby Tandoh's profile of YouTube star Rachel Ama, who promotes veganism. Both Pollan and Tandoh look at the implications of food trends. In your investigative report on food trends, be sure to provide concrete evidence and details to support

pages 110–127 your analysis. (See CHAPTER 7, INVESTIGATIVE REPORTS.)

3. In "Good-bye, Cryovac," Corby Kummer analyze the joys—and luxury—of eating good, high-quality food, whether it is supplied locally or is the result of commerce. Have you recently had a satisfying dining experience that you would like your friends and classmates to enjoy as well? Whether it was a simple snack or a farm-to-table meal, whether it was prepared at home or at

a restaurant, whether the food was organic or not, what specific features of your eating experience made it so good? Write an evaluation of that dining experience. (See CHAPTER 10, EVALUATIONS.) Be sure to specify the criteria on which your analysis is based and provide rich, detailed examples that show how the food itself, any relevant history of the food, the company, the service, and/or the atmosphere contributed to the overall dining experience.

pages
167–185

The Changing Significance of Food [Overnourished and Undernourished in America]

MARGARET MEAD

Margaret Mead (1901–1978) was an American anthropologist and is best known for her study of adolescence in Coming of Age in Samoa *(1928), a work that influenced the 1960s sexual revolution. Mead also researched the culture of food in the United States, arguing that changes in the American diet could best be understood within the context of cultural shifts. Given the current debates over American diets, eating habits, and agricultural practices, Mead's writing now seems prophetic.*

Waring Abbott/Getty Images

In a country pronounced only twenty years before to be one-third ill-fed, we suddenly began to have pronouncements from nutritional specialists that the major nutritional disease of the American people was overnutrition. If this had simply meant overeating, the old puritan ethics might have been more easily invoked, but it was overnutrition that was at stake. And this in a country where our ideas of nutrition had been dominated by a dichotomy which distinguished food that was "good for you, but not good" from food that was "good, but not good for you." This split in man's needs, into our cultural conception of the need for nourishment and the search for pleasure, originally symbolized [by] the rewards for eating spinach or finishing what was on one's plate if one wanted to have dessert, lay back of the movement to produce commercially,

non-nourishing foods. Beverages and snacks came in particularly for this demand, as it was the addition of between-meal eating to the three square, nutritionally adequate meals a day that was responsible for much of the trouble.

We began manufacturing, on a terrifying scale, foods and beverages that were guaranteed not to nourish. The resources and the ingenuity of industry were diverted from the preparation of foods necessary for life and growth to foods non-expensive to prepare, expensive to buy. And every label reassuring the buyer that the product was not nourishing increased our sense that the trouble with Americans was that they were too well nourished. The diseases of affluence, represented by new forms of death in middle-age, had appeared before we had … conquered the diseases of poverty—the ill-fed pregnant women and lactating women,

Food and Culture

sometimes resulting in irreversible damage to the ill-weaned children, the school children so poorly fed that they could not learn.

. . .

What we do about food is . . . crucial, both for the quality of the next generation, our own American children, and children everywhere, and also for the quality of our responsible action in every field. It is ultimately concerned with the whole problem of the pollution and exhaustion of our environment, with the danger that man may make this planet uninhabitable within a short century or so. If food is grown in strict relationship to the needs of those who will eat it, if every effort is made to reduce the costs of transportation, to improve storage, to conserve the land, and there, where it is needed, by recycling wastes and water, we will go a long way toward solving many of our environmental problems also. . . .

Divorced from its primary function of feeding people, treated simply as a commercial commodity, food loses this primary significance. . . . Only by treating food, unitarily, as a substance necessary to feed people, subject first to the needs of people and only second to the needs of commercial prosperity—whether they be the needs of private enterprise or of a developing socialist country short of foreign capital—can we hope to meet the ethical demands that our present situation makes on us.

> The diseases of affluence appeared before we had conquered the diseases of poverty.

Source: "The Wider Food Situation," Food Habits Research: Problems of the Credits 1960s, National Research Council's Committee for the Study of Food Habits Update.

ACTIVITY: Analyzing the Rhetorical Situation

1. What is "overnutrition"? How does Mead argue that it came to be a problem?
2. What specific evidence does Mead provide for her assertion that biological traits as well as social traits lead to the diseases of affluence?
3. Who is the audience for her argument? How are they affected by it?
4. What is her purpose, given that audience? Provide textual evidence for your answer.
5. What rhetorical opportunity does Mead address? What is her thesis statement? What supporting assertions does she make about the roots of this problem? What evidence does she provide to support her assertions about the sources of the problem?
6. How does Mead establish the rhetorical appeals of ethos, logos, and pathos? Provide textual evidence to support your answer. Which of the rhetorical appeals does she rely on most? Be prepared to share your answer with the rest of the class.

Out of the Kitchen, Onto the Couch [The Collapse of Home Cooking]

Stephen Lovekin/Getty Images

MICHAEL POLLAN

Michael Pollan, a professor of journalism at the University of California, Berkeley, is also a regular contributor to The New York Times, *where he writes about topics at the intersection of nature and culture, including food production, cooking, and gardening. He has also written several books on these issues, including* Cooked, Food Rules, In Defense of Food, *and* The Omnivore's Dilemma. *A longer version of this essay was published by* The New York Times *on July 29, 2009.*

It's generally assumed that the entrance of women into the work force is responsible for the collapse of home cooking, but that turns out to be only part of the story. Yes, women with jobs outside the home spend less time cooking—but so do women without jobs. The amount of time spent on food preparation in America has fallen at the same precipitous rate among women who don't work outside the home as it has among women who do: in both cases, a decline of about 40 percent since 1965. (Though for married women who don't have jobs, the amount of time spent cooking remains greater: 58 minutes a day, as compared with 36 for married women who do have jobs.) In general, spending on restaurants or takeout food rises with income. Women with jobs have more money to pay corporations to do their cooking, yet all American women now allow corporations to cook for them when they can.

. . .

The fact is that *not* cooking may well be deleterious to our health . . .

. . . A 2003 study by a group of Harvard economists led by David Cutler found that the rise of food preparation outside the home could explain most of the increase in obesity in America. Mass production has driven down the cost of many foods, not only in terms of price but also in the amount of time required to obtain them. The French fry did not become the most popular "vegetable" in America until industry relieved us of the considerable effort needed to prepare French fries ourselves. Similarly, the mass production of cream-filled cakes, fried chicken wings and taquitos, exotically flavored chips or cheesy puffs of refined flour, has transformed all these hard-to-make-at-home foods into the sort of everyday fare you can pick up at the gas station on a whim and for less than a dollar. The fact that we no longer have to plan or even wait to enjoy these items, as we would if we were making them ourselves, makes us that much more likely to indulge impulsively.

. . .

Cutler and his colleagues also surveyed cooking patterns across several cultures and found that obesity rates are inversely correlated with the amount of time spent on food preparation. The more time a nation devotes

Food and Culture

to food preparation at home, the lower its rate of obesity. In fact, the amount of time spent cooking predicts obesity rates more reliably than female participation in the labor force or income. Other research supports the idea that cooking is a better predictor of a healthful diet than social class: a 1992 study in *The*

The more time a nation devotes to food preparation at home, the lower its rate of obesity.

Journal of the American Dietetic Association found that poor women who routinely cooked were more likely to eat a more healthful diet than well-to-do women who did not. . . .

So cooking matters—a lot. The question is, Can we ever put the genie back into the bottle? . . . Let us hope so.

ACTIVITY: Analyzing the Rhetorical Situation

1. Pollan opens his piece with a comparison between women in the workplace and women who work in their homes. How does this opening challenge cultural stereotypes? How does this comparison strengthen Pollan's broader argument about American eating habits?

2. What rhetorical opportunity created the need for Pollan to write this essay? Does he specifically name it, or is it simply implied?

3. To whom is Pollan writing? How can you tell?

4. What values does Pollan assume his audience will hold? How does he appeal to these values? What other values could he have used to argue for the importance of home cooking if he had been writing to a different audience?

5. Does reading Pollan's essay persuade you that you should spend more time preparing your own food? If so, what did he say to persuade you? If not, what more would he have needed to say? What more would you need to know?

Fresh Off the Boat [Eddie Huang Learns to Eat, American Style]

EDDIE HUANG

Chef Eddie Huang and his brother, Evan, own the NYC Baohaus restaurant, which has been lauded for redefining such Taiwanese staples as the traditional Gua-Bao (pork bun). This selection is taken from his edgy Fresh Off the Boat: A Memoir, *which was the inspiration for the ABC television series.*

Mike Coppola/Getty Images for Busboys and Poets

I walked up to Jeff's room . . . ; I couldn't believe my eyes. Everywhere you walked: toys, games, huge television, stuffed animals. It was like living in a Toys 'R' Us. I remember thinking to myself that if I died, I wanted to come back a white man. . . . I felt like some wild gremlin child living in Chinese hell after going to their house. By that point, I was ready to convert. . . . But then dinner happened.

All of us sat down. I had never eaten at a white person's house, but I just figured they ate pizza, hot dogs, or something like that. After a few minutes, Jeff's mom came out of the kitchen with two bowls. One bowl was filled with goopy orange stuff. For a second, I thought they might be little boiled intestines in an orange sauce, which I could get down with, but on closer inspection they were unlike any intestines I'd ever seen. The other bowl was gray and filled with a fibrous material mixed with bits of celery. I thought to myself, these white people like really mushy food. She also gave us each two pieces of bread, the same plain wonder bread I saw at school.

Jeff started wiping the gray stuff on the bread. I didn't want to come off like an idiot so I did the same thing. I put the other slice on top, lifted up, and went to take a bite. . . . Jeff and his brothers couldn't get enough but I was scared. I took a deep breath, clutched my orange juice, and forced myself to take a

bite. Right on cue, gag reflex, boom went the orange juice.

I couldn't hide it anymore. I had to ask. "What is that, man?"

"You've never had tuna fish sandwiches?"

"No, never. Where do you get it?"

"At the grocery store, you want to see the can?"

"Ok, but what's the orange stuff?"

"Macaroni and cheese."

"What's macaroni?"

"It's pasta."

I didn't know what pasta was, but was really starting to feel like a dumb-*ss so I didn't ask. The sh*t was so nasty. We never ate cheese and it stunk like feet. A lot of Chinese people are lactose intolerant, so it's just not something we eat normally. We drink soy milk instead of cow's milk and stir-fry our noodles instead of covering them with cheese. I suddenly realized that converting to white wouldn't be easy, but still, that toilet paper was like silk. I tried to force myself to eat the macaroni and cheese but literally barfed it through my nose. Jeff and his brothers couldn't believe it. I realized no matter how many toys they had, I couldn't cross over. I'd much rather eat Chinese food and split the one good dinosaur with my brother. Macaroni is to Chinamen as water is to gremlins . . . and Asian is to American. It just didn't fit.

ACTIVITY: Analyzing the Rhetorical Situation

1. In his memoir, Eddie Huang evaluates American food culture. In what ways, if any, does he agree with Pollan or Mead?
2. As a relatively new voice contributing to the on-going conversation about food, how does he establish his credibility to speak on this issue?

3. What audience do you think is most likely to be persuaded by Huang's memoir? How does the author appeal specifically to this audience? What can the author's choice of publication venue and selection of evidence tell us about his intended audience?

4. How would you describe Huang's tone in this piece? Why might he have chosen to write using this tone, rather than being more formal or relaxed, harsher or friendlier, funnier or more serious?

5. Imagine that you are a reader who was thoroughly persuaded by Huang's piece. In what ways has he changed your stance? If so, what new insights did he offer that challenged your previous view?

Good-bye, Cryovac [Local Foods, College Food Service, and Scraping Your Own Plate]

CORBY KUMMER

Corby Kummer is a professional food writer and senior editor of The Atlantic. *As a graduate of Yale University, Kummer writes about the Sustainable Food Project beginning at his alma mater. A longer version of this essay was published in* The Atlantic *in October 2004.*

Stephen Voss/Redux

I recently washed up after a supper consisting of four kinds of vegetables from the farmers' market—all four of them vegetables I usually buy at the local right-minded supermarket. As I considered the vivid, distinctive flavor of every bite, I thought, What is that stuff I've been eating the rest of the year?

One of the twelve residential colleges at Yale University is trying to give students that kind of summertime epiphany at every meal, by serving dishes made from produce raised as close to New Haven as possible. In just two years the Yale Sustainable Food Project has launched two ambitious initiatives to bridge the distance from farm to table: the complete revamping of menus in Berkeley College's dining hall to respect seasonality and simplicity, and the conversion of an overgrown lot near campus to an Edenic organic garden. The garden does not supply the dining hall—it couldn't. Rather, it serves as a kind of Greenwich Mean Time, suggesting what is best to serve, and when, by illustrating what grows in the southern New England climate in any given week. The goal of the project is to sell students on the superior flavor of food raised locally in environmentally responsible (but not always organic) ways, so that they will seek it the rest of their lives.

A few dishes I tasted last summer during a pre-term recipe-testing marathon in Berkeley's kitchen convinced me that this goal is within reach for any college meals program willing to make an initial outlay for staff training and an ongoing investment in fewer but better ingredients. I would be happy to eat pasta with parsnips once a week, for example, the candy-sweet roots sharpened by fresh parsley and Parmesan. In fact, I demanded the recipe. Any restaurant would be pleased to serve fresh asparagus roasted with a subtle seasoning of balsamic vinegar and olive oil alongside, say, filet of beef. Even the chicken breasts, coated with black pepper, grilled, and served with a shallot, garlic, and white-wine sauce, tasted like chicken.

Not long ago a college would never have thought to mention food in a brochure or on a school tour—except, perhaps, in a deprecating aside. Now food is a competitive marketing tool, and by the second or third stop on the college circuit parents and students practically expect to be shown the organic salad bar and told about the vegan options and the menus resulting directly from student surveys. Yale has gone these colleges what I consider to be a giant step further, showing students what they should want and making them want it.

As caring about food has become interwoven with caring about the environment, enjoying good food has lost some of the elitist, hedonistic taint that long barred gourmets from the ranks of the politically correct. The challenge, as with any political movement, is to bring about practical institutional change that incorporates ideals.

> Not long ago a college would never have thought to mention food in a brochure or on a school tour.

It's a very big challenge with college food, almost all of which is provided by enormous catering companies like Sodexho, Chartwells, and Aramark, the company that has run Yale's dining services since 1998. These companies have long offered vegetarian, organic, and vegan choices. But none of those options—not even, sadly, going organic—necessarily supports local farmers and local economies, or shows students how much better food tastes when it's made from scratch with what's fresh. Vegetarian, organic, and vegan foods can all be processed, overseasoned, and generally gunked up, and in the hands of institutional food-service providers they usually are. . . .

Whatever the argument for spending more money on food . . . , the practical successes at Yale should encourage other schools to consider similar changes. [Associate Director of the Yale Sustainable Food Project Josh] Viertel gives the example of granola, a simple seduction tool. At the beginning of this year the Food Project's formula of organic oats, almonds, and raisins, a local honey, and New England maple syrup was so popular that Commons had to take over making it for every college. And the project's recipe is actually cheaper than buying pre-made granola in bulk. Viertel recently began a composting program; the first step is asking students to scrape their own plates, which shows close up the waste involved when they take, say, just one bite of cheese lasagna. Other schools ought to take that same step, even if they stop there. . . .

ACTIVITY: Analyzing the Rhetorical Situation

1. What rhetorical opportunities prompted Kummer's piece on the Sustainable Food Project at Yale University? In what ways is he helping to develop the conversation about the culture of food in the United States?
2. How would you describe Kummer's attitude toward the Sustainable Food Project? Why does he hold this position?
3. What change does Kummer hope to bring about through his writing? Who is the audience with the power to make this change?
4. Kummer's essay includes a narrative element in which he tells the story of his own experience sampling the new food at Yale. Why do you think he includes this story? How effectively does it reach (and move) his audience? How effective might it have been if someone else, not a professional food critic, had written it?
5. What concerns do you think have kept other colleges from making the kinds of dining changes that Yale has made? How does Kummer address, or fail to address, these concerns in his proposal?

Rachel Ama and the Trouble with Apolitical Food

RUBY TANDOH

Great British Bake Off contestant Ruby Tandoh is a food writer and critic of what she calls a "toxic and elitist" food culture. In this piece she profiles Rachel Ama's food activism and her Caribbean inspired vegan dishes.

WENN Rights Ltd/Alamy Stock Photo

The rising vegan YouTube star treads carefully around the tangled politics of race and veganism. For her, making accessible plant-based recipes is a form of activism.

Vegan food is not a fad. Rachel Ama is keen to stress this to me as we stand in the kitchen of her north London home, watching over a pot of simmering pasta sauce. "I want that narrative to go away," the vegan cooking YouTuber shares, breaking jackfruit into soft, fat flakes and stirring it into the tomato sauce for her vegan "juna" (jackfruit "tuna") pasta.

"Because in cultures all around the world people are not necessarily saying 'this is vegan,' they're just eating vegetables and getting on with it."

And Rachel is right. Within Caribbean cooking, for example, a community of plant-based cooks has held fast, creating a legacy that stretches across generations. Traditionally, there's the vegetarianism and veganism of those in the Rastafari movement following an ital diet [a Rastafarian diet promoting spiritual energy through vegetarianism]. A new generation of health-conscious Jamaican vegans is also shaking things up in the country's big cities. And here in the UK, young people are working to build on that heritage, staking out a place in the largely white and middle-class vegan landscape with plant-based incarnations of the flavors their parents and grandparents used to cook.

Take Peckham Institution Deserted Cactus, where chef Esme Carr serves everything from fried plantain to stuffed dumplings, okra fritters and callaloo. Or influencers Craig and Shaun McAnuff, who followed up their popular *Original Flava* cookbook with *Vegan Flava* earlier this year, remixing their family favorites for today's changing tastes. And then there is Rachel Ama, whose YouTube channel, showcasing vegan cooking inspired by her Caribbean roots, has amassed over a quarter of a million followers.

Tumbling from YouTube into the offices of a management company, it looks like Rachel is set to be one of the movement's most bankable figures. Last month she released her first cookbook, *Rachel Ama's Vegan Eats.*

Rachel was born and grew up in the very house where she's now cooking for me, in close contact with a large extended family whose roots stretch from the Caribbean to Sierra Leone and Wales. She beams when she talks about her family, pointing out old sepia-toned family photos in the hallway and talking fondly about her mum (who she still lives with), her filmmaker older brother, and family barbecues with her dad's Caribbean side of the family.

"My grandma Pat was from St Lucia," she tells me. "She was a home cook but also she cooked in schools and nursing homes and hospitals. My parents wanted her to open her own Caribbean restaurant. It didn't happen, but that was one of their plans."

Rachel grew up around the smell of Grandma Pat's cooking, from fish fritters to plantain and bacon. These flavors imprinted themselves on her palate, even though she didn't realise at the time how important these culinary legacies would eventually become. "I never cooked with her, which is annoying because I've become a cook now. But she was incredible." When Rachel became a vegan, she had to be creative to lend new life to these culinary memories, trying new techniques and improvising with plant-based alternatives to meat and fish.

"Caribbean cooking for me is my favourite cooking, and I wanted to share that kind of food because I felt like it wasn't being shared and it should be," she says.

Recipes in Rachel's book draw from her St Lucian roots, from an ackee scramble, in which the fruit's creamy, sunny yellow flesh stands in for eggs, to jackfruit fritters (a fish-free reimagining of Grandma Pat's signature dish). There are moments of wellness faddishness, however. Although Rachel is careful to preface health chat with reminders that it's just her experience, she slips at times into language bordering on Goop-style silliness. "The first thing I noticed after going vegan," she shares in one video, "is I just felt so much lighter! It's almost like you're floating a little bit higher than you were before. I'm telling you guys, it's true."

But still, it's exciting to see a vegan cookbook freed from the tyranny of staid whiteness: the photography shows the busy shelves of Brixton's Afro-Caribbean grocery shops, flashes of colorful batik cloth, and brown

> "Because in cultures all around the world people are not necessarily saying 'this is vegan,' they're just eating vegetables and getting on with it."

hands making great food. "When I first went vegan I would look on YouTube for inspiration, but I didn't find anyone I could relate to," she writes in the introduction. The fact that she now, as a black woman with locs, graces the cover of a mainstream vegan cookbook is something beautiful in itself.

There's a need for more visibility of black vegans. Kaila Stone is a student and London born-and-bred. Her family are Jamaican, many of them following an ital diet. "That was my earliest introduction to veganism as a child, before I really understood it," she tells me. "But I understood enough to recognize how the diet was linked to spirituality and community." When she became vegan as a young teenager, however, the experience was isolating. Although Kaila knew her blackness and her veganism sat in harmony, white vegans thought otherwise. "They couldn't comprehend a black person existing without eating chicken. Those were real conversations I had with people, and I ended up internalizing a lot of those reactions."

For people of color in majority-white spaces, it's rare that we are allowed space just to be.

For people of color in majority-white spaces, it's rare that we are to be allowed space just to be—to cook, eat, share knowledge, make whatever tastes good, for no reason other than it's what we're hungry for in that moment. So, it's refreshing that Rachel Ama is, in many ways, just herself. This is the Rachel Ama who, in her YouTube videos, chats and cooks while dancing to Caribbean songs and old school hip-hop. It is the Rachel Ama who cooked me a (very tasty) vegan tuna pasta when I came round for lunch, just because it's what she always used to eat at uni. And her book is not titled or subtitled with *Caribbean* or *St Lucian*—there are no claims here to being the spokesperson for an entire diverse food culture. Called simply *Rachel Ama's Vegan Eats*, it is exactly what it says it is: a vegan cookbook that crystallizes around one person's food-filled life.

But this self-reflexivity, a kind of culinary selfie, has its limitations. I ask where Rachel finds communities of other black vegans. "Instagram," she says firmly, at first, but then she falters. "I feel like you find each other and you reach out to each other . . . Um." She doesn't offer names. I mention Bryant Terry, the award-winning African-American vegan food writer who, like Rachel, sometimes offers song suggestions alongside his recipes, but Rachel hasn't heard of him. She treads nervously around matters of race, not once in our conversation about the tangled politics of veganism saying the words *black* or *white*.

Rachel is loyal to her YouTube followers, for whom she tells me she wrote the book. "I say when [followers] meet me, 'Come give me a hug, because I know I'm on the other side but we're friends, man.'" And there are friends in the food world, like musician and chef Denai Moore, of vegan Jamaican food business Dee's Table. "Whenever she does something, I put it straight up on my social media like, go check out Dee's stuff!" But beyond these small circles, the sense of community seems to unravel. At points, it feels like being trapped on an Escher staircase, where a tiny circle of writers, vloggers, and creatives hype each other up, and up, and up, in a closed loop of so-called influence.

Betty Vandy is a vegan chef (and cookbook enthusiast) with roots in Sierra Leone, like Rachel. Originally from Liverpool, she travels the length of the country with her

≡ ▶ YouTube   Search   🔍

What I Eat In A Day Vegan & behind the scenes with Munchies

72,194 views • Feb 3, 2019   👍 4K 👎 31   ➤ SHARE   ≡₊ SAVE   ...

Rachel Ama
494K subscribers   SUBSCRIBE

Rachel Ama's vegan YouTube series is filmed in the same house in London where she grew up and where she lives with her mother today.

vegan "African Creole soul" food business Bettylicious Cooks. For Betty, representation alone isn't enough—it's important that black vegans dismantle the white vegan mainframe rather than simply inserting themselves into it. To be vegan and black is, for many, a political position, inseparable from conversations about race and power. "You may look like me, but what really are you representing?" Betty asks. "Who are you standing up for?"

Of course, Rachel shouldn't have to do the heavy lifting of talking about race, gender, pain, and politics every time she shares a recipe. Too often, the pernicious expectation of people of color in food is that we should only talk about food insofar as it relates to identity, race, or belonging. Until we ask this emotional labor of white cooks and writers, the food world cannot ask black women to wade deep into their trauma just to earn a seat at the table.

But the question of solidarity is a pertinent one because, as Rachel reminded me, veganism isn't a fad. It doesn't belong to one time, fashion, country, or person—it spreads its roots wide. Rachel is just one small, vital part of a dynamic black vegan community. She is already feeding parts of that community, with her fritters and plantain and juna pasta. That community can nourish her, too.

Where Rachel chooses to focus her energy, for now, is in making vegan food accessible to her followers, on YouTube and through her book, in ways that bring some Caribbean flavor to the mix. She knows it's not easy for everybody.

Ruby Tandoh, "Rachel Ama and the Trouble with Apolitical Food", July 16, 2019. VICE UK Ltd.

"Everyone's living different lives, has access to different kinds of fruits and vegetables, and only has X amount of time to spend in the kitchen," she explains. But small changes can make a big difference. "That's my activism: to give people vegan options to make that they can enjoy."

ACTIVITY: Analyzing the Rhetorical Situation

1. What is Ruby Tandoh's attitude toward veganism? What stance does she take toward so-called alternative food movements? Toward the subject of her profile, Rachel Ama? What kind of future do these women think the world should be striving for in terms of what we humans eat? What reasons does Ama provide?

2. How does YouTube provide a rhetorical opportunity for Tandhoh's response? How effective would Tandoh or Ama have been without YouTube?

3. What audience has Tandoh envisioned for this piece? How do her topic choice, her tone, and her use of evidence implicate this audience?

4. Ama refers repeatedly to her family and her cultural roots in this essay. What is the effect of this repetition? How does Ama want us to think about the past?

5. Imagine you are an advocate of veganism. What features of Tandoh's essay do you find most persuasive? What counterarguments might you propose?

≫ COMMUNITY CONNECTIONS

1. How do Michael Pollan's reflections and descriptions coincide with or diverge from your experiences with cooking and with food? Take about ten minutes to write your response.

2. Now do the same for the pieces by Mead and Tandoh: how do their analyses coincide with or diverge from your experiences or observations about the culture of food?

3. For what reasons do you agree (or not) with Kummer's proposal that "whatever the argument for spending more money on food . . . , the practical successes of Yale should encourage other schools to consider similar [farm-to-table] changes"? Draw on your experiences at home, in the community, or in college to support your answer.

4. Now that you have considered various arguments made about humans and their relationships with food, how would you describe the culture of food on your campus, in your community, or in your family? What food options or eating habits seem most significant to you? What economic, political, social, cultural, or biological forces have shaped the culture of food?

25 Social Media and the Possibilities of Gender

LEARNING OBJECTIVES

- Describe the invisibility and visibility of social media in your daily life.
- Articulate the ways you and others project your gender online.
- Analyze your gendered online experiences for composing in a specific genre.

Radha Design/Shutterstock.com

What's your pronoun? Generation Z, those born between 1995 and 2010, and Generation Alpha, which follows, are famous for rejecting a gender identity framework that is either male or female, straight or gay—what's now referred to as the "gender binary." Generation Alpha now leads the way in questioning such identifiers as biological sex (the sex assigned to you at birth) as too narrowly reflecting stereotypical constraints of gender roles. For these reasons, colleges and universities all across the country are asking students and faculty alike to announce their pronoun. On the first day of class, many instructors and students introduce themselves by announcing their hometowns, their majors, and then their pronouns. Many others list their pronouns on their syllabi, their office door, or under their e-mail signatures:

Nat Gennaro, Ph.D.
English and Women's, Gender, and Sexuality Studies
pronouns: they/them

Robert Schwartz
Math tutor
he/him/his

Students correct their teachers and vice versa when one of them is addressed by the "wrong" pronoun: "Actually, I am referred to as *they*." Over a third of those in Gen Z indicate they know someone who is nonbinary, according to a survey conducted by *The Daily Beast*. Someone you know may prefer to be referred to as *they*, and you yourself may have already announced your pronoun.

The contemporary conversation about pronouns broadens the issue of inclusivity to incorporate people of all genders: masculine, feminine, nonbinary, gender nonconforming, transgender, cisgender, and any other identification within an ever-widening band of gender fluidity. These days, the plural pronouns *they* and *them* are accepted usage, whether they refer to one person or more.

Given that Gen Z and beyond are avid social-media users, it is likely no coincidence that the pronoun conversation has been taken up on social-media platforms like Facebook. Ninety-eight percent of college students use social media (more than six hours a week), with 80 percent having profiles on such sites as Facebook and Twitter. Many of them also make connections on what they consider to be "cooler" platforms: Instagram, Snapchat, YouTube, Flickr, Reddit, Pinterest, Yelp, LinkedIn, and Myspace. As social-media user Jackson states, "I exist primarily on the Internet, you know? That's pretty much my hometown."*

*Susan C. Herring and Sanja Kapidzig. "Teens, Gender, and Self-Presentation in Social Media." *International Encyclopedia of Social and Behavior Sciences*, edited by James D. Wright, 2nd ed., vol. 24, Elsevier, 2015, pp. 146–52.

In the face of the COVID-19 pandemic, the New Albany City Hall issued this supportive online banner, which uses the plural "their" to refer to the singular "everyone."

Such interactions at the intersection of social media and gender have generated myriad possibilities for gender and identity. Each piece of writing in this chapter is a response to the question of how social media have expanded—or controlled—our notions of sexual orientation and gender identity. Johanna Blakley examines the possibilities for marketing and entertainment when gender identity is not associated with stereotypes. Paris Lees interrogates the still-limited options for declaring one's gender identity. Ann Coffey proposes governmental procedures for monitoring and verifying online-dating profiles and preventing "sweetheart scams." Riley R.L. takes the position that putting selfies on social media sites helps people (including those who are trans and nonbinary) create positive narratives that reflect established, aspirational, developing, or curious personal identities. And Associated Press (AP) writers report on the effects of race, gender, and age on facial-recognition technology. Each of these pieces *defines* some of the characteristics of gender fluidity, *clarifies* how social media helps restrict and support the concept, and *illustrates* a conception of the gender possibilities with examples. As you read these selections, think about ways you would define your use of social media to establish your identity, focusing on your personality, experience, problems and possibilities, education, and social practices and values.

Your instructor may ask you to translate your observations into writing with one of the following assignments.

pages 91–109

1. Choose a public figure who interests you, one who either upholds expectations of traditional gender binaries or one who tests or transcends such binaries (Jason Strathan, Rachel McAdams, Caitlyn Jenner, Miley Cyrus). Paris Lees's essay in this chapter may provide you a way to begin, as might Riley R.L.'s. (See CHAPTER 6, PROFILES.) Although the essays in this chapter may give you a place to start researching, you will also need to do additional library and web research in order to become an expert on your chosen subject of analysis.

2. Each of the essays in this chapter offers an answer to the question "In what ways do gender identity and social media affect each other?" Although the authors do not necessarily disagree with one another, each takes a different approach, resulting in five very different visions of what the connection between social media and gender identity actually means. Putting what you have read (especially the essays by Johanna Blakley and the AP writers) in conversation with your own observations and experiences as a social-media user with a gender identity, write a three-page position argument that takes a stance and uses the rhetorical appeals to help an audience understand,

pages 128–149

maybe even accept, your claim. (See CHAPTER 8, POSITION ARGUMENTS.) Of course, as you write, you will want to keep in mind traditional expectations for gender as well as ever-growing social acceptance for gender fluidity.

3. Work with another student in your class to make a list of all the (perhaps new) terms one of these authors uses to clarify their arguments. Using your list, write a brief critical analysis of these terms for the rest of your classmates that breaks the argument down into parts (the terms), analyzes each term separately, and studies the ways the terms work together. Then synthesize

pages 186–203

your findings into a claim or thesis statement. (See CHAPTER 11, CRITICAL ANALYSES.)

Social Media and the End of Gender

JOHANNA BLAKLEY

Popular culture expert Johanna Blakley specializes in digital technology, entertainment, and the media habits of liberals and conservatives. At present, she serves as Managing Director and Director of Research of the Norman Lear Center, located at the University of Southern California's Annenberg School for Communication and Journalism. In the following critical analysis, she builds on her investigative research to present the effects of social media on traditional gender identities. For the full version, see her TedTalk 2010.

[A]t the Norman Lear Center at USC . . . we've done a lot of research over the last seven, eight years on demographics and how they affect media and entertainment in this country and abroad. . . . [W]ith online networking tools, it's much easier for us to escape some of our demographic boxes. We're able to connect with people quite freely and to redefine ourselves online. And we can lie about our age online, too, pretty easily. We can also connect with people based on our very specific interests. We don't need a media company to help do this for us.

[T]he traditional media companies, of course, are paying very close attention to these online communities. . . . So when you look online at the way people aggregate, they don't aggregate around age, gender and income. They aggregate around the things they love, the things that they like, and if you think about it, shared interests and values are a far more powerful aggregator of human beings than demographic categories.

. . .

Now there's something else that we've discovered about social media that's actually quite surprising. It turns out that women are really driving the social media revolution. If you look at the statistics—these are worldwide statistics—in every single age category, women actually outnumber men in their use of social networking technologies. And then if you look at the amount of time that they spend on these sites, they truly dominate the social media

space, which is a space that's having a huge impact on old media. The question is: what sort of impact is this going to have on our culture, and what's it going to mean for women?

. . .

I think women are actually going to be—ironically enough—responsible for driving a stake through the heart of cheesy genre categories like the "chick flick" and all these other genre categories that presume that certain demographic groups like certain things.

. . .

The future entertainment media that we're going to see is going to be very data-driven, and it's going to be based on the information that we ascertain from taste communities online, where women are really driving the action.

So you may be asking, well why is it important that I know what entertains people? Why should I know this? . . . [O]ur research has shown over and over again that entertainment and play have a huge impact on people's lives—for instance, on their political beliefs and on their health. And so, if you have any interest in understanding the world, looking at how people amuse themselves is a really good way to start.

[I]magine a media atmosphere that isn't dominated by lame stereotypes about gender and other demographic characteristics. Can you even imagine what that looks like? I can't wait to find out what it looks like.

ACTIVITY: Analyzing the Rhetorical Situation

1. Early in her critical analysis, Blakley asserts that "women are really driving the social media revolution" and "dominate the social media space." She goes on to ask what sort of impact women's dominance might have on our culture. Based on these assertions, what information did you expect as you continued to read on?

2. What is Blakley's attitude toward demographics? What evidence does she use to defend her attitude? How does her critical analysis present evidence of her investigative research?

3. How would you describe Blakley's credibility (ethos) as a writer? How does she give you a sense of what kind of person and researcher she is?

4. Who do you think is Blakley's primary audience? What textual evidence helps with your determination?

5. How might you respond to this essay as a member of a younger generation? Are you persuaded? Pleased? Offended? How might your response be different if you were from your parents' generation?

Facebook's Gender Identities Are a Good Start—but Why Stop at 56?

PARIS LEES

English journalist and transgender rights activist, Paris Lees is the first transgender person to become a regular columnist for Vogue. *Lees published the following proposal, which upends any necessity of demographic gender profiling, in* The Guardian, *a mainstream left British daily newspaper.*

WENN Rights Ltd / Alamy Stock Photo

I won't be fiddling with my settings, though I might if I could choose "northern ladette," "loose woman," or "bad girl."

This is a progressive move from Facebook, but wouldn't it be better to leave a blank box for people to dream up their own identities?

"What's your flava—tell me, what's your flava?" I am, of course, invoking the great early 21st-century poet and philosopher, Craig David, to help me find out something I'm dying to know. Just what, exactly, is your gender identity? If you answered "erm, what do you mean?" or "duh, I'm a man/woman" then I'm afraid to say you've become rather passé. Ask a transgender person or a feminist this question and they will know exactly what you mean and will also have a very definite (if not always clear) answer for you.

Most people never really stop to question the identity carved out for them from birth, but for those who do, there's a smorgasbord of options to choose from. Woman. Trans woman. Trans man. Genderqueer. Androgyne. Intersex. Bigender. Gender nonconformist. The list is endless and I suspect most people will never have heard of the various nuanced terms coming their way. Does the word *cis* mean anything to you? It means anyone who isn't transgender; it is to *trans* what *straight* is to *gay*. You'll probably have to get used to it. Sorry. We're trying to change the world.

Changing your gender identity has officially become a thing—Facebook says so. Following years of complaints from transgender people, the world's largest social networking site now recognises 56 gender identities in the US. The plan is to extend this worldwide, all in the name of furthering the rights of all its users.

Overall this is a progressive move and will delight a community that seldom has much to rejoice over. It will also annoy *Daily Mail* readers too, no doubt, and for that we should be thankful. It screams of "political correctness gone mad" and I look forward to right-wing commentators telling us how absurd it is and how affronted they are by something that really isn't a concern for anyone other than those it concerns.

But before we all break into "I'd Like to Teach the World to Sing," let me play chief party pooper. I doubt Facebook did this as an act of pure progressiveness to cater to its transgender users and I can't help wondering what the commercial imperative is. What money is there to be made by sorting people into ever more specific boxes?

Advertisers will be wetting themselves—particularly anyone selling wigs, chest binders, or any of the other specialized products aimed at those of us who seek to change our gender. It's the monetization of minorities.

But—as many of my Facebook friends have pointed out—wouldn't it be better to leave a blank box for people to dream up their own gender identities? Why choose from 56? There are as many possible gender identities as there are people, so why not let people come up with their own categories, or even better, why have a gender box at all?

*Copyright Guardian News & Media Ltd 2020

We take it for granted that we are so frequently asked to declare our gender. We do it with race too, but not so much. When was the last time you filled in a form that didn't ask you about your gender? Every time we circle a Mr, Mrs or Ms, what are we really saying? In some cases it makes sense to sort people based upon their physical anatomy. People aged 25 and over with vaginas need smear tests, so it's useful for doctors to know who has one. But outside of purely medical contexts or situations where people insist on being addressed with some sort of gendered title, what's the point? Do we truly need that information on passports?

I remember when I first came across the term *trans woman*. Up until then I'd assumed I was one of those transsexuals you read about in the paper. Not a woman or a man, really—something in between. It sounds cheesy in retrospect, but I remember feeling truly energised by my discovery. *Trans woman*. Like *black woman*. Or *disabled woman*. Or *French woman*. I realised I could still be a woman while acknowledging the transgender part of my identity. I wasn't an imposter after all, just part of the wide diversity that makes up womankind.

I suspect that the changes will make most difference to people who identify as neither male [n]or female—"outside the gender binary" if you want to be really fancy. I doubt I'll fiddle around with my gender settings on Facebook. I've done enough of that in real life, thank you very much. If I had the option to list myself as *gutsy northern ladette, loose woman,* or *bad girl*, I might change my mind, but until then I'm not fussed.*

> There are as many possible gender as there are people . . . .

ACTIVITY: Analyzing the Rhetorical Situation

1. To what rhetorical opportunity is Lees responding? What circumstances created Lees's need to write?

2. Why might Lees have decided that an op-ed in *The Guardian* was the appropriate medium to deliver her proposal? What bearing do the limitations and advantages of this venue have on the effectiveness of her proposal?

3. What reasons does she give for resisting demographics, checking boxes? How do these reasons support her proposal? How persuasive are these reasons to you?

4. Who is Lees's rhetorical audience, given the publication venue, the subject, the details, and the vocabulary? Describe her writing style and connect it to the expectations of her rhetorical audience. If she has more than one audience, who constitutes them?

5. What rhetorical strategies does Lees use to persuade her audience. Which of the strategies do you think is most effective? Which one seems least effective?

Dating Sites and Social Media Firms Must Do More to Protect Users from "Catfishing"

ANN COFFEY

Former member of Parliament, Ann Coffey, is an activist for issues including children's rights, domestic violence, online safety, and mental health services. Coffey published her proposal for monitoring online identities in THE BLOG, *which appeared in American online news aggregator HuffPost.*

Allstar Picture Library Ltd / Alamy Stock Photo

Many dating sites are riddled with fake profiles and the numbers of people being deceived online has soared.

Online dating in Britain is a massive phenomenon with one in three under 40-year-olds now using dating sites and Apps to find a partner. However, many of the dating websites are riddled with fake profiles and the numbers of people being deceived online has soared.

Half of users say they have come across a false profile, according to figures quoted in the Government's Internet Safety Strategy green paper. I am campaigning for a new law to make it illegal to create a false identity online and pretend to be someone else to form a romantic relationship—known as *catfishing*. Dating websites and social media companies should also be doing more to protect people from "catfish."

One way to force companies to clean up their act would be to introduce a new name and shame league table of dating websites to expose those stuffed with fake profiles.

A star-rated league table of how safe websites are and how likely you are to be duped would expose in bright lights those who are not doing enough to protect their users. The public should not have to continuously contend with the prospect that the person they are in communication with is not who they say they are.

I first became interested in catfishing after being approached by a constituent, Matthew Peacock, a Stockport male model who had his identity stolen online for four years by a catfish who used his pictures on dating websites to lure women.

Mr. Peacock's family has been put under tremendous strain and his wife has been contacted on many occasions to be wrongly told that her husband was cheating on her, asking women for illicit photographs, videos and arranging meetings.

> A star-rated league table of how safe websites are and how likely you are to be duped would expose in bright lights those who are not doing enough to protect their users.

Photographs of Mr. Peacock's nephews and nieces have also been used by the catfish who claimed they were his children in an attempt to attract single mothers by appearing as a "caring dad."

After publicising Mr. Peacock's case in the Commons, I was approached by several other victims of catfishing who had all been traumatised by the experience.

They all told me that they wanted websites to do more to protect people by responding more quickly to complaints and introducing better ID verification procedures. They also wanted catfishing to be made illegal to deter the persistent catfish who keeps reinventing him or herself in a different guise.

Based on conversations with these victims, I have compiled a detailed submission to the Government's consultation on the Internet Safety Strategy which says that dating and social media websites should be forced to introduce more robust ways of checking the identity of people using their sites. This should include scanning passports, driving licenses and using photo recognition software to protect people from being deceived.

The voluntary code of practice proposed by the government does not go far enough and there needs to be a statutory Digital Mediation/Monitoring Complaints Board, which could enforce proper standards and take action. It would be this new monitoring board that would produce the league table of websites.

I have also suggested that websites who do not use verification processes or who allow anonymity should not be allowed to upload photographs because that makes it easier for catfish to create a false profile.

Internet companies are also very coy about how much they spend on keeping users safe. This should be more transparent. Experts tell me that the amount of money spent by the big internet companies on using developing technology to dispute abusive relationships online is "minimal" compared to the money they spend in other areas. The figures are shrouded in secrecy and are not in the public domain.

The House of Commons library has confirmed that information on spending in this area is scarce. The BBC ran a news item on dating website safety earlier this year, which said that safety features of such sites were often not divulged to "maintain competitive advantage."

I would urge the big internet companies to be more transparent about what proportion of their budget they spend on protecting users and developing techniques to verify the ID and age of website users.

Websites have to take more responsibility and put their money where their mouth is and develop more robust ways of checking the identity of people who use their sites.

In addition, making catfishing illegal would be a massive deterrent. If people knew pretending to be someone else was an offense then they would be put off.[*]

[*]Reprinted by permission of Ann Coffey.

ACTIVITY: Analyzing the Rhetorical Situation

1. Identify an obvious thesis statement for Coffey's proposal. If you cannot identify one, then write out a sentence that summarizes her stance on the topic.
2. How can you determine the rhetorical audience for this piece? How might the rhetorical audience help the author address or resolve the problem?
3. How does the perceived credibility (or lack thereof) of a member of Parliament affect the way you read this proposal? How is Coffey's credibility (ethos) established in the proposal itself?
4. How does Coffey employ the other two rhetorical appeals? In terms of establishing persuasive reasoning (logos), how do the quality of her research and her examples affect her proposal? What passages enhance or detract from the emotional appeal (pathos)?
5. How does the concept of "online deception" extend, complicate, or enrich the arguments in the previous essays, essays about demographics, gender fluidity, and the power of social media? In other words, how do all the essays in this section constitute a larger rhetorical situation?

Selfies Help Trans and Nonbinary People Create Our Own Narrative

RILEY R.L.

Beauty writer Riley R.L. identifies as nonbinary and writes on cosmetics, identity, and queer narratives, often contributing to Teen Vogue, Allure, *and magazines that focus on beauty. This position argument appeared in* Allure. *The essay was published July 16, 2019.*

For many trans and nonbinary people, the act of taking selfies can be healing.

A few weeks ago I took the first selfie I felt good about in a while. Getting there felt like a complicated ritual: My hair had just been cut and bleached, I'd shaved, put makeup and my favorite outfit on, and I stood in front of a window during golden hour. It struck me in that moment, looking at the photo of myself, how far I'd come, both in accepting the way I look in selfies and understanding why I'd hated them for so long.

BROADLYGENDERPHOTOS·VICE.COM

Gender Spectrum Collection

Like many young people, I always struggled with the way I looked in pictures. Some days it was a minor discomfort, but other days, seeing a photo of myself—or even just knowing someone had taken a photo of me—could throw me into a tailspin of anxiety and depression after I'd been completely unbothered seconds before.

For years I thought I was dealing with garden-variety insecurity. But like many others, I was on a long path to realizing that what I was facing wasn't just about my appearance; it was also about a dissonance between the person I knew myself to be and the person I saw reflected in a picture.

"I had given myself a kind of tunnel vision that allowed me to not look at or think about my body too directly or frequently," Robin Ford, a trans woman, explains when I ask about her experience with selfies. "Pictures

were an endeavor that essentially forced me to reckon with my body and how I looked." My own experience was much like Ford's; photos forced me to confront the reality of my body in ways that I wasn't always comfortable with, or capable of. But later, when I came to understand myself as nonbinary—not identifying entirely as male or female—I was finally able to look at my selfies and see myself on the screen instead of a stranger.

Understanding and acknowledging my identity allowed me to be honest about my insecurities and anxieties around gender presentation, which allowed me to anticipate where potential issues might pop up. Taking selfies stopped feeling like an impossible task because I gained the ability to single out the things that might make me uncomfortable. My hair, makeup, and the lighting around me all make a huge difference in how good I feel about expressing my identity in a photo. If I'm not happy with one of those things, I probably won't be happy with how the photo turns out, and making small changes to those things can have a big impact.

Kaitlin Rose Williams, who identifies as nonbinary, tells me that taking control of their gender presentation drastically changed how they perceived their selfies: "I was having a whole ordeal last year where every picture I saw of myself, whether I took it or someone else took it, I wanted to throw up. And I think that had a lot to do with my hair before I cut it. I felt like I didn't look like me. Now when I take pictures or look in a mirror, I feel more like me."

Being able to crop, filter, and edit selfies how we see fit is another way we can take control of our presentation and ease dysphoria. While some criticize the way Instagram and other social media platforms let users filter and curate feeds and aesthetics, doing so lets us express ourselves on our own terms, build confidence, and share some of that confidence with others.

Kimberly Vered Shashoua, a therapist who specializes in counseling for trans teens and their families, explains that selfies can be an immensely helpful tool for trans and nonbinary people at any stage of self-discovery or transition. "When you're feeling dysphoric, it can help to have others tell you that, actually, you're a babe," she says. "[It's] a very quick way of getting affirmation. 'Do I look bad?' 'No, you look great.' Boom, done. This is especially potent in terms of gender. Sharing selfies allows others to affirm your expression of gender and sexuality."

Though taking selfies is personal, they are meant to be a form of social expression, and sharing them can allow us to make connections in our community. By participating in popular hashtags like #LGBTQofTwitter, #girlslikeus, and #nonbinarylookslike, trans and nonbinary people can find and support one another in their process of finding self-love and acceptance. It's a simple, accessible way to create solidarity and resist the forces in our everyday lives that try to erase our identities. Proudly posting a selfie sends a message that we have a right to exist and be seen, and that we get to take control of our own narratives. "Sharing a selfie feels like an act of personal assertion: I am trans, this is my presentation, you will see me the way I wish to be seen," Foster Rudy,

Proudly posting a selfie sends a message that we have the right to exist.

a nonbinary author currently documenting their transition, tells me. "Posting my own face every day seemed kind of vain and self-centered at first, but now I feel that I'm claiming a little bit of space for myself."

That kind of confidence is infectious and can help others find the strength to stand proudly in their identity. Seeing someone else live out their truth without fear shows us what's possible for ourselves. For Ford, these kinds of posts were where she found the courage to start her transition. "I can remember the first handful of women I followed on twitter whose selfies made me feel like I could [transition] too," she tells me. "Seeing other people have the courage to love themselves loudly and publicly online gave me the courage to start all of this."

While being out and proud online can have an immeasurably positive impact, it can also come with drawbacks. In a photo, we're left with just our bodies and our style to communicate who we are, which can be a vulnerable feeling, especially for those who don't pass as the gender they identify with. In her experience working with trans clients, Shashoua has found that trans people face complex pressures around gender presentation online, and many of those pressures spring from offline struggles. "On one hand, trans bodies are beautiful, whether or not they 'pass.' People have unique beauty that deserves to shine and be appreciated," she says. "On the other hand, we live in a world where trans women are being killed for merely existing. Feeling like you need to look a certain way may not be coming from vanity as much as self-preservation."

However, for some trans and nonbinary people, the concern isn't about passing as cisgender, but wanting to be seen the way they see themselves—as someone whose gender identity exists outside the labels of male and female. Carlito Espudo described to me how they faced online harassment when they first began to take on a more masculine presentation as an expression of their nonbinary identity. "I would get antagonistic [anonymous messages] in my inbox, like 'You're not nonbinary,' 'You're a f**g girl,' 'There's literally nothing trans about you,' and 'Stop trying to be edgy, you're a girl and an ugly b**.'"

This points to an issue that Shashoua brings up when I ask for her professional perspective on what other challenges might surround sharing selfies in a public forum, where anyone has access to say exactly what they think about you and your identity. "There is a huge amount of identity policing within and around the LGBT community. Queer communities find pressure to conform to standards set by their own groups—'to be queer, trans, lesbian, etcetera enough' . . . This is all bull****, of course," she says. She links this pressure to the community's past of engaging on respectability politics, as well as more

recent examples like the rise in the term *transtrender* as a way to invalidate trans people who don't present in the "right" ways. Ultimately, Shashoua says, "No one should feel like their identity is in a display case for others to rate and judge."

But while transphobia is ever-present on social media, everyone I interviewed expressed that the benefits of sharing selfies online far outweigh the risks. Sean Woodall, who is transfeminine, found that in spite of any transphobia they've encountered as a result of posting selfies, it's been an undeniably grounding practice throughout their transition. "I've taken thousands in the 16 months I've been transitioning," they say. "It just feels like a celebration of a self that I was denied for the first 24 years of my life."

Everyone's timeline of learning how to accept and celebrate themselves is different, and self-love is an ongoing battle. Some days are easier than others, and we can't always predict what challenges might crop up. But no matter how we feel about the way we look, and no matter where we are in our process of self-discovery or transition, our appearance is just one small piece of our identity. As Shashoua notes, "It doesn't make us a better person, a better partner, or a better friend."

Even two years into accepting myself as nonbinary, I still struggle occasionally with the version of myself my camera captures, and I still freeze sometimes when my friends or family pull out a phone to take a photo. But even if I'm not always in the right mindset to see it, I know that there is a community of people like me ready and willing to help me see the best version of myself.*

> For some trans and nonbinary people, the concern isn't about passing as cisgender, but wanting to be seen the way they see themselves.

*Riley R.L, Allure (c) Conde Nast

ACTIVITY: Analyzing the Rhetorical Situation

1. Identify an obvious thesis statement for Riley R. L.'s position argument. If you cannot identify one, then write out a sentence that summarizes the author's position.
2. Riley R.L. reveals information about transitioning and nongender conformity that could make some readers uncomfortable, even resistant. What information do they include to accommodate such readers as they establish ethos, logos, and, especially, pathos. Provide passages from the text to support your answers.
3. What might Riley R.L.'s purpose be in writing this essay? First establish their rhetorical audience. Then link their purpose with their audience. In what ways do they work to change their readers' minds (attitudes or actions)? In what ways was your mind changed by what you read?
4. Riley R.L. writes that there was a "dissonance between the person I knew myself to be and the person I saw reflected in the picture." Which rhetorical methods do they use to develop their argument? Provide examples of each method used. Which other genres do they tap? In what passages?
5. One of the challenges of writing such a personal piece is that it can be hard to transition smoothly from one idea to the next. How does Riley R.L. handle the challenge of transition? Would you say that the piece reads smoothly? Explain your answer with textual evidence.

Federal Study Finds Race and Gender Affect Face-Scanning Technology

ASSOCIATED PRESS

Associated Press staff writers conducted research to produce the following investigative report on the ways race, gender, and age affect face-scanning technology that produce biased results. This article on facial recognition scanning was published in December 2019.

A study by a U.S. agency has found that facial recognition technology often performs unevenly based on a person's race, gender or age.

This is the first time the National Institute of Standards and Technology has investigated demographic differences in how face-scanning algorithms are able to identify people.

Lawmakers and privacy advocates have raised concerns about biased results in the commercial face recognition software increasingly used by law enforcement, airports and a variety of businesses.

But the nuanced report published Thursday is unlikely to resolve differences of opinion between critics and defenders of facial recognition. It cautions against "incomplete" previous research alleging biased facial recognition that has alarmed lawmakers but confirms similar trends showing higher error rates for women, the youngest and oldest people, and for certain racial groups.

"There is a wide range of performance and there's certainly work to be done," said Craig Watson, manager of the National Institute of Standards and Technology research group that studies biometric technology. "The main message is don't try to generalize the results across all the technology. Know your use case, the algorithm that's being used."

The agency, which is a part of the Commerce Department, tested the algorithms of nearly 100 companies on millions of mugshots, visa application photos and other government-held images. Microsoft was among the major tech companies that voluntarily submitted its technology for review. Amazon, which markets face-scanning software to police, did not.*

*Copyrighted 2019. Associated Press. 2159234:0720PF

ACTIVITY: Analyzing the Rhetorical Situation

1. To what opportunity are these writers responding? What passages provide you this information? Who constitutes the rhetorical audience for their response? How might this audience help address or resolve the problem? How do you know? What are the constraints and resources of this rhetorical situation?

2. In which passages do the AP writers employ the rhetorical appeals? For instance, what resources did the AP writers tap in order to produce their investigative report? How persuasive is the information they produced in terms of logos? How do these sources enhance or detract from the ethos of these writers? What information works to connect with you emotionally (pathos)? In other words, why should you as a reader care about the results of their investigation?

3. What is the author's thesis statement? If you cannot locate a specific sentence, write out their stance toward the subject?

4. What is your immediate response to this report? What information invites you to consider the issue? What information has little effect on you or your opinion?

5. What is your experience with facial-recognition software, maybe on your smart phone, in your online activities, at the airport, or somewhere else? How does your experience align or differ from the findings of this report?

»» COMMUNITY CONNECTIONS

1. Write for ten minutes in response to one of the essays you have just read. How do your experiences with social media coincide with, or diverge from, those of the authors? What is your response to one of their arguments?

2. Map out the pronouns of yourself, your classmates, your friends, and your instructors (in terms of frequency and urgency). How often are you prompted to remember their pronouns? How important is the issue of pronouns? Support your answer with experience, evidence, and details.

3. In what ways do all the essays in this section constitute a larger rhetorical situation? What are the elements of the situation? How can you enter that conversation, extending, complicating, or disrupting the arguments, rhetorical appeals, and evidence of these essays?

26 Navigating Safety in Public Spaces

LEARNING OBJECTIVES

- Define public space.
- Assess the capacity of various spaces to accommodate the public.
- Analyze inclusionary and exclusionary public spaces.
- Synthesize various viewpoints about the use of public space.

You have always inhabited public space. Whether you have been waiting six feet apart in a long line at the coffee shop, walking or protesting on city streets, visiting a museum or memorial site, or meeting friends in your campus's student union, you have known how to use the space, sometimes choosing to do so according to the rules for that space, sometimes not, whether those rules include wearing masks, not walking alone at night, or taking care not to appear threatening to other public-space users. By now, you are well accustomed to using and avoiding public spaces of all kinds.

The phrase "public space" implies that it has been designed for the public—for all people. Urban city streets, for instance, are designed for automobile traffic, with designated traffic lanes and signals, pedestrian crossings, and parking spots. Yet, on a regular basis, bicycle messengers dart between parked and moving cars, pedestrians jaywalk, and people walk through slow traffic to sell car washes, bouquets, and spices. Others might have trouble moving their wheelchair on and off the curbs; walking fast enough to make it across the street with the traffic light; or just walking down a public street.

This chapter features responses from five writers who use genres such as the investigative report, position argument, evaluation, and critical analysis to address an issue surrounding the use of public space all over the world, from accessibility and inclusion to experiences of violence, social power, and fear in public spaces. pages 173–175 (See also, Alexis Walker's evaluation of downtown development in CHAPTER 10, "DONUTS AT EASTON'S CENTER CIRCLE: SLAM DUNK OR CYCLE OF DETERIORATION?") As these readings illustrate, public spaces by their very nature affect more than their designers, planners, or dominant users. What such spaces allow or prevent and whom they benefit or harm are issues that call for conversation among members of the public. As you explore this topic, your instructor might call on you to consider one of the following opportunities for writing.

1. Identify a public space that is familiar to you and explain its uses, taking into consideration the purpose of its design and how other uses for that space have emerged. Refer to Claire Edwards's "The Experiences of People with Disabilities Show We Need a New Understanding of Urban Safety" to spark your consideration. In a proposal of three to four pages, describe a familiar public space in terms of the uses it was planned for, those that have emerged, and a way (or ways) to improve upon its uses. (See CHAPTER 9, PROPOSALS.)
pages 150–166

2. Evaluate a public space—on campus or in your community. Explain why it should be evaluated—especially for your rhetorical audience. Provide criteria for your evaluation (function, identity, accessibility, and so on) and evaluate the public space accordingly. As you write, consider your audience (who may or may not share your ideas about criteria), your purpose (which should be relevant for your audience), and the advantages and limitations of using an evaluation to explore your subject. Consider the use of images in Freya Drohan's "Anti-Homeless Architecture" as a way to enhance your essay with images that will strengthen your thesis and support your reasons. (See CHAPTER 10, EVALUATIONS.)
pages 167–185

3. Evaluate a public space in terms of how that space brings people together, keeps them apart, or otherwise controls how they interact. Along with this critical analysis, determine whether some groups of people are encouraged to, or discouraged from, interacting in this space. Consider Amelia Tait's "Pandemic Shaming: Is It Helping Us Keep Our Distance?" as you conduct your own three- to four-page evaluation. Evaluate a social media in terms of both its planned and emergent uses. Who is included or invited to participate in this public online space? Who is excluded or discouraged? Who decides? (See CHAPTER 10, EVALUATIONS.)
pages 167–185

4. For over four-hundred years, Black Americans have had to reckon with public space, where they would be openly welcomed, accepted, merely

tolerated, or even threatened. Consider "Being an 18-Year-Old Black Man a Year after Mike Brown" by Malcolm-Aime Musoni as you inhabit a public space for a while (perhaps repeatedly). Keep a detailed record of who uses the public space freely, with care, or with trepidation and the reasons for your assessments. Compose a three- to four-page investigative report, providing examples and details that support your thesis. (See CHAPTER 7, INVESTIGATIVE REPORTS.) pages 110–127

The Experiences of People with Disabilities Show We Need a New Understanding of Urban Safety

CLAIRE EDWARDS

Courtesy of Claire Edwards

Claire Edwards is the Director of the Institute for Social Science in the 21st Century (ISS21) and has worked for the Disability Rights Commission in the United Kingdom. She is Principal Investigator of the SAFE(R)SPACE project, and her research in Ireland on the experience of people with disabilities in urban areas might lead to improved urban safety for all residents. This position argument, published in February 2020 in The Conversation, *explores the powers and limits of public space for people with disabilities. Despite an ongoing effort to incorporate Universal Design into public planning, the designs too often fall short of their intended mark, especially when social relations are taken into account.*

Creating safe and secure urban spaces is a core concern for city managers, urban planners, and policy workers. Safety is a slippery concept to pin down, not least because it is a subjective experience. It incorporates our perceptions of places and memories, but also norms in society about who is expected to use spaces in the city, and who is considered to be out of place.

The experiences of people with disabilities offer important insights into the complexities of urban safety, because of the varied encounters with space that impairment can bring. Their experiences show that safety is a fluid concept. Places city planners may consider safe can actually make some people feel unsafe, and what is safe for one person might not be for another.

Over the past two years, we have been carrying out research to understand how people with disabilities in Ireland—including people with visual, hearing, and mobility impairments—experience urban safety and the impact it has on their everyday use of different spaces. We have found that issues of inclusion and the idea of who "belongs" in particular spaces are important and should be considered alongside more traditional approaches to urban safety.

Reducing Crime by Design

City planners have often been criticized for prioritizing "situational responses" to urban safety. These focus on a technical understanding of urban safety as a problem to be solved. Greater police visibility, more lighting and CCTV, and the idea that we can design out crime from our cities are all examples of situational responses.

While these initiatives may have a place, they often focus on the public realm at the expense of the smaller spaces of people's lives. They also do not reflect how safety, or a lack of safety, is understood by different groups of city dwellers. There is no neat match between what crime statistics might say about the safety of an area, and how people actually feel fear and safety in that area.

Our study, conducted across three cities in Ireland, revealed that feelings about fear and safety very much shape disabled people's experience of their urban environment. In some cases, they can prevent them from using different spaces. People identified a range of spaces and places in the city that felt unsafe. These included public spaces such as transport hubs, bars and nightclubs, shopping centers, and deserted spaces.

The presence of people they didn't know or trust, crowds, and the inaccessibility of the built environment could make people feel vulnerable in these spaces. In some cases, the absence of people contributed to feelings of insecurity. Others described feeling more unsafe in their homes. This was due to isolation, poor housing design and location and, in some cases, domestic violence.

> There is no neat match between crime statistics and how people actually feel fear in that area.

Changing Perceptions

What is key here is how people interpreted spaces in terms of fear and safety. Spaces were not fixed as safe or unsafe. One person's unsafe space could be another's refuge. Neither can we say that people with disabilities are a group who feel inherently unsafe. The people we spoke to described fear and safety as a result of a range of different factors coming together at specific times and places.

One man with a visual impairment, for example, described feeling fear in spaces which others might consider to be safe. He recalled an incident when, crossing the road in an urban space in the middle of the day, his concentration was distracted by a group of young people who repeatedly teased and shouted out to him that he shouldn't cross when he stepped out using a white cane.

Many people had developed strategies and routines to ensure they felt safe in different spaces. This included using learned transport routes, going out at certain times of day, and only visiting places that they felt were welcoming. These places included restaurants and specific shops where staff knew them or made an effort to accommodate their needs. Other people only went out accompanied by someone or used specific technologies when out and about. This included mobile phones, but also—in cases where people had been subject to hostility—the wearing of bodycams as a deterrent.

Thinking about safety in urban planning and policy is more complex than situational responses give credit for. Providing a wheelchair ramp into a building, or better lighting, may indeed assist in creating more welcoming, safer cities. But it is equally important that urban safety strategies respond to issues of inclusion and justice, by addressing the attitudes which can exclude disabled people from the spaces of their local communities.

The work of Scotland-based charity I Am Me on disability hate crime is an example of this. It works to challenge discriminatory attitudes toward disability in schools, while also encouraging service providers and businesses in local communities to sign up to be safe spaces in case a person with a disability feels under threat when out and about.

Urban safety is as much about changing social relations as it is about technical fixes. Disabled people's experiences show us that it is only by challenging assumptions about who has a right to inhabit urban space that we can create more inclusive, just, and safer societies.

ACTIVITY: Analyzing the Rhetorical Situation

1. For many of us, public space does not seem like a very interesting or controversial thing. For Edwards, though, the way we use public space reflects a society's values, conflicts, and distribution of power. What specific evidence does Edwards give to support this perspective?

2. Edwards teaches her readers about access for the physically disabled at the same time she complicates that issue by introducing the issue of safety. How does the addition of "safety" to the access equation enhance or not the case she is making?

3. Edwards investigates the use of social power in public space, about the ways it empowers some while discouraging and sometimes intimidating others. How do her examples of the dangers for disabled people enhance her thesis? How might she have made a stronger access argument without the addition of the safety element?

4. To whom is Edwards writing? How does her primary purpose line up with that audience? How does she invite her readers to adopt her point of view? What specific passages support your answer?

5. All of these authors discuss the limitations of public space in serving the public. How do these accounts align and differ? What facets of the rhetorical situation account for these similarities and differences?

Anti-Homeless Architecture

Courtesy of Freya Drohan

FREYA DROHAN

Fashion writer Freya Drohan turned her attention to city style after Bored Panda *posted a thread that went viral on how hostile architectural design is used to prevent people without permanent housing from sleeping in public spaces. This investigative report on the* Bored Panda *thread was published in the* Daily Mail, *September 16, 2019. Nearly 600,000 (or two percent of) Americans are without permanent housing. Because they lack fixed, regular, and adequate night-time residences, they seek out temporary lodgings in public spaces, none of which have been designed for their accommodations. In fact, some public spaces have been purposefully designed or refitted to make resting or sleeping impossible for people without permanent housing.*

Shocking online thread sees people calling out cities that have installed "anti-homeless architecture"— from sharp spikes to bench bars—to stop people from sleeping in public places.

- "Hostile architecture" refers to structures purposefully installed to make life harder for homeless people.
- Examples include bars in the middle of benches and spikes laid into the ground.
- The designs have been slammed as "cruel," "depraved," and "unsympathetic."
- Hostile architecture has always existed, but the term first circulated in the United States during the 1980s.
- It was recently revealed that 53 percent of American cities legally prohibit homeless people from sitting and lying down.

Design features intended to deter homeless people have been slammed in a thread detailing the most cruel examples of "hostile architecture." The origin of the term is unknown, but cities throughout the world show examples of the purposefully obstructive design features. However, some—like sloping benches or "artwork" in wide doorways—are subtle enough that members of the public never really pause to think of their intent. The thread called out the most prevalent examples of anti-homeless architecture, causing outrage and forcing people to take notice of inhumane and insidious design practices. Several images show benches with bars in the middle of the seating area—a normal sight in many urban areas.

A Canadian Twitter user shared an image of a park bench painted in LGBTQ-friendly rainbow colors that had multiple dividing bars in the middle. Social media users were angered at how the bench could promote inclusivity to one community while discriminating against people who were seeking a place to sleep. Another image showed a bench in Volgodonsk, Russia that appeared to be chained up overnight to prevent anyone resting on it.

"That is exceptionally mean," someone wrote.

Numerous images showed dangerous-looking spikes in open spaces and underneath bridges. A social media user shared images of a bank in Mumbai, India, which had sharp iron spikes surrounding its exterior; a move to discourage people from seeking shelter there.

Safety in Public Spaces

Michael Vi/Shutterstock.com

Armrests in the middle of benches stop people from sleeping, resting, or lying down on the benches in public transportation passenger shelters.

"Is this for real? Sickening," a commenter denounced.

"This is the most heartless and cruel thing I have ever seen! Shame on you," said another.

A picture was circulated of the area underneath an overpass where tracks of spikes had been laid down to prevent anyone trying to set up camp.

"The brutalist architecture, the anti-homeless aggressiveness . . . it is freaking awful. . . . what the hell does it matter if they sleep under the overpass? Leave them be," slammed a response.

Lest people remain unaware, someone pointed out that spheres or any other shapes inset into concrete might look less intimidating—but the intent is still the same.

"Spikes or balls, it doesn't matter, it's all equally cruel," commented a user—as someone shared an image of what looked like neon green cacti in a doorway.

However, many pointed out at least the spheres or other shapes were not "as dangerous" as metal spikes.

Topic Magazine estimates that the prevalence of hostile architecture began to rise in the 1980s and 1990s in America. "Architects began to use urban design to combat behaviors (like sitting, standing, waiting, or sleeping in public) and hostile architecture became a familiar sight."

"The changes they made to the urban environment were small but ingenious. A nubbin on a handrail could, for instance, send a skateboarder flying, or a warm subway grate would get covered with spikes, turning a potential winter comfort for a homeless person into a form of medieval torture," the outlet reports.

The magazine writes that in a busy metropolis like New York, the details are subtle but substantial. For example, in certain subway stations, there are no benches anymore, having been replaced with "leaning areas." In public

Spikes run along a low wall to deter people from sitting or staying overnight.

parks, almost all benches now have dividing rails making it near-impossible for someone to stretch out to sleep. In the 1990s in downtown Los Angeles, "bum-proof benches" were installed on Skid Row, an area which has the largest homeless population in the United States. Said barrel-shaped benches at bus stops made sitting for any extended period of time highly uncomfortable—let alone sleeping.

A 2019 report from the National Law Center on Homelessness and Poverty studied 187 American cities in a bid to assess the

Close up of skateboard prevention device installed on wood covered surface to prevent surface damage.

number of areas that "criminalize the life-sustaining behaviors of homeless people." The research found that 57 percent of the cities imposed a law prohibiting camping in public. Some 65 percent of cities also prohibit loitering in public places. Of the cities studied, 27 percent prohibit sleeping in particular public places, such as in public parks, while a shocking 53 percent of cities prevent homeless people from sitting or lying down.

ACTIVITY: Analyzing the Rhetorical Situation

1. In her online investigative report on the *Bored Panda* thread, Drohan states that anti-homeless sentiment has become integral to Western contemporary culture. Either locate or compose her thesis. How do the different examples she offers support such a thesis?

2. To what specific rhetorical opportunity is Drohan responding? How is responding with an investigative report (rather than a position argument, for instance) a good rhetorical choice for her?

3. How would you describe Drohan's tone in this essay? Why might she have chosen to adopt this tone to write about an issue like this one?

4. Who appears to be the primary audience for this essay? What clues lead you to that conclusion? How has Drohan shaped her purpose and her report to appeal to this audience?

5. Drohan provides visual evidence for her stance that much public architecture is "hostile." Which passages tilt toward her position? Which passages could be considered neutral, even objective? What is the overall effect on readers of having both subjective and objective passages as well as visuals in an investigative report?

Code Red: Can "Hard Corners" and Classroom Drills Protect Students from Shooters?

HANNAH KAPOOR, ELAMI ALI, AND NADIA MURILLO

This story was reported by student journalists Hannah Kapoor, Elama Ali, and Nadia Murillo of the Eagle Eye, *the award-winning student newspaper of Marjory Stoneman*

Hannah Kapoor

Elama Ali

Nadia Murillo

Douglas High School in Parkland, Florida, where a recently expelled student opened fire February 14, 2018. Seventeen were killed in the shooting and seventeen injured in the Valentine's Day Massacre. This critical analysis was published in partnership with The Guardian US. *Over two decades ago, the Columbine (Colorado) High School shooting became the touchstone for those that have followed, sparking fierce ongoing debates over gun control and school safety. In the past ten years alone, over 180 school shootings have taken place, resulting in over 360 victims. In the following essay, the coauthors critically analyze the ways school architecture and space is being redesigned in ways that anticipate such routine deadly violence.*

One year after the shooting that killed 17, some Parkland students and teachers say efforts to make their school safer won't be enough.

Once a month, students at Marjory Stoneman Douglas high school (MSD) in Parkland, Florida must relive the most frightening day of their lives.

A "code red" drill is called over the intercom. Teachers stop teaching immediately, shut off the lights, and cover their classroom windows.

Students are directed to remain silent and huddle in a designated "hard corner"—an area of the classroom that has been deemed safe because it would be out of the line of site of a shooter in the hallway. In recent weeks, red icons have been painted onto classrooms walls at MSD to indicate a hard corner. The hard corners also feature special "bleeding control kits" affixed to the walls containing materials to stop the blood flow from gunshot wounds.

While school administrators take steps to reduce the stress of these code red drills, including notifying students in advance so they can stay home if they find them too traumatizing, the drills inevitably bring back raw memories of the horrors that students and staff at

MSD experienced one year ago today, when a 19-year-old gunman entered the school with an AR-15 assault rifle and killed 14 students and three teachers, and injured 17 others.

The recommendations to increase code red drills at MSD and identify hard corners in classrooms were part of a major report released last month by the MSD public safety commission, a taskforce created by Florida lawmakers after the shooting. The commission was asked to analyze the shooting at MSD and other incidents of violence in the state to make recommendations to prevent future tragedies.

But the report has faced criticism from some students and teachers in Parkland for its focus on "hardening" schools as potential targets for mass shooters—and its failure to meaningfully address gun laws as a way to improve school safety. While student activists from Parkland kicked off a national movement to change gun laws in America over the last year, gun control receives little attention as a safety solution in the 400-plus-page report.

"Honestly, just having these kinds of drills aren't necessarily going to help," says Faith

Kimmet, a senior at MSD. "You want to teach people what to do in these situations—that's important—but we also need to be doing things to make sure these shootings don't happen at all."

Other recommendations in the report include arming some teachers, adding bulletproof windows to schools and improving mental health services for troubled students. Representatives for the commission did not immediately respond to inquiries for this article.

The commission report found that the lack of code red training and designated hard corners in MSD classrooms contributed to the casualties. According to the report, the shooter "only shot people within his line of sight, and he never entered any classroom. Some students were shot and killed in classrooms with obstructed and inaccessible hard corners as they remained in [the shooter's] line of sight from outside the classroom."

The painted red icons that now designate hard corners at MSD began appearing in classrooms after the holidays, but some students and teachers say the new safe spaces do not make them feel any more secure.

"I don't think hard corners are effective," said Ivy Schamis, a history of the Holocaust teacher at MSD who lost two students during the shooting last year. "If the students were all in what the school deemed as the 'hard corner' they wouldn't have been safe."

The students in her classroom were killed when the shooter shot through a glass window in a classroom door. "While I was crouching on the floor with my students, shaking from bullets flying through the classroom, I was watching. I was waiting for

Parkland kicked off a national movement to change gun laws in America.

a hand to come in [though the broken window] and unlock [the door] . . . he could have easily come in. Thank god he didn't," Schamis said.

Class size is another factor that some say makes hard corners an impractical solution. Many public schools across the county, including MSD, are overpopulated. That means hard corners are only effective for the fastest students who get there first.

"It's great to say that I have a space marked for 25 kids. But if you have 42 kids in your room, you have children that are not going to fit in that space. So then how safe does that space actually become?" asked MSD statistics teacher Kimberly Krawczyk. "I think the numbers become lower for casualties and injuries if there had been room to get everyone in properly into their corners and out of sight."

Some students, however, are grateful for the hard corners and say they can save lives.

"[Hard corners] are the reason why my class was safe during the shooting," says junior Sarah Soares, who was in one of the few MSD classrooms that had a designated hard corner at the time of the shooting last year. "We knew where to go. Some of the classes . . . were harder to hide in and there was no safety aid kit. The kids who were then shot, bled a lot and couldn't have really been helped."

But many in the MSD, Parkland, and Coral Springs community believe school safety is an illusion when someone who is determined to kill has easy access to a gun.[*]

[*]Copyright Guardian News & Media Ltd 2020

ACTIVITY: Analyzing the Rhetorical Situation

1. Hannah Kapoor, Elama Ali, and Nadia Murillo provide a critical analysis of public school architecture that includes "hard corners" and of public school routines that now include "active-shooter drills." According to these writers, what are the emerging uses and practices of buildings designed for public education?

2. What problem do these writers address? How do they align that problem and their purpose with a rhetorical audience? Provide textual evidence for your answer.

3. What rhetorical methods of development do these authors use to develop and support their overall analysis? Again, provide textual evidence.

4. Are the writers attempting to address or resolve the problem they have identified? How do you know? What specific passages help you determine your answer? Assess the overall success of their critical analysis according to their use of the rhetorical appeals and their conception of a fitting response.

Pandemic Shaming: Is It Helping Us Keep Our Distance?

AMELIA TAIT

Courtesy of Amelia Tait

Forbes magazine listed London-based Amelia Tait as one of 30 under 30 to watch in Europe. Amelia Tait's primary focus is digital culture, and her work contributed to increased regulation for child rights on YouTube. This critical analysis, published in The Guardian on April 5, 2020, analyzes public criticism directed at people who do not wear a mask, do not social distance, and meet in large groups during the COVID-19 pandemic. Given how they inhabit public space, students, church-goers, runners, bicyclists, and vendors are all targets of such criticism.

Everyone from dog walkers to flower sellers have been singled out but online humiliation may not shift behavior.

Scholarships have been threatened. LinkedIn and Facebook profiles have been removed. Death threats have been sent in their hundreds, if not thousands. And governments have been spurred into action. Since mid-March, when the government first recommended self-isolation measures as a way to tackle the spread of the world-altering respiratory disease Covid-19, a public shaming frenzy has spread across social media. Thousands of people are blaming, naming, and shaming others for their improper pandemic practices; those targeted include drunk spring breakers, coughing commuters, flower markets, Stereophonics fans, and romcom screenwriter Richard Curtis's daughter.

When it comes to the crime of not taking a global pandemic seriously, perhaps online shaming is the perfect punishment. After all, if you go to a packed public place or hoard paracetamol, you're endangering other people's lives. Yet is pointing the finger actually a productive way to change others' behavior? Are we simply spreading discord at an already distressing time? At worst, are we blaming individuals for the inconsistent and confused measures implemented by the government?

The term "covidiot" was first uploaded to the online slang decoder Urban Dictionary on March 16 and was defined as: "Someone who ignores the warnings regarding public health or safety." On Twitter, #covidiot skyrocketed on the evening of March 22; overnight, nearly 3,000 tweets used it to call out poor practices. That same day, Hilda—a 49-year-old who runs the Facebook and Twitter accounts for Columbia Road flower market in east London—received an influx of notifications.

> The worst was someone saying, "I hope you and your family stay healthy and alive but sadly I doubt all of them will."

"I'm still feeling slightly traumatized by it," says Hilda, whose name has been changed on her request, after a BBC journalist tweeted a picture of the market, which appeared heavily crowded despite social distancing rules. The picture was "liked" nearly 4,000 times, with commenters bemoaning the "stupidity" of those in attendance. Hilda began to receive angry comments, tweets, e-mails, and phone calls complaining that the market should be shut down. To make matters worse, the social media accounts she runs are for market shopkeepers, and she had no control over whether the market as a whole opened (that decision lay with the local council).

"The worst thing I had to open and read was someone saying, 'I hope you and your family stay healthy and alive but sadly I doubt all of them will,'" Hilda says. "They were very vitriolic. . . . The world feels really dark and horrible." A day later, after newspapers splashed pictures from Columbia Road and other markets, the health secretary, Matt Hancock, branded those who visited crowded places "very selfish"—that evening, new lockdown measures were put in place by the government. Yet Hilda argues that, at the time, people hadn't broken any rules. "The government advice was if you're healthy, go outside and exercise . . . that's what people were doing."

Hilda is far from the only person to be "pandemic-shamed." On March 16, activist Scarlett Curtis uploaded an Instagram video of herself washing her hands for nearly 30 seconds, and commenters complained she used an improper technique. "Please can we not shame anyone during this hard time," she countered. "Now is the time for community not judgment."

Perhaps the most egregious shaming came on March 18, when CBS News tweeted a video of American spring breakers partying in Miami. In the video, drunk students flagrantly disregard social distancing recommendations, one declaring: "If I get corona, I get corona." The video was subtitled with the full names of every student interviewed.

The clip was "liked" more than 96,000 times and was flooded with comments berating the students' appearances and intelligence. People began tweeting the students' names and linking to their social media profiles, writing: "I have a feeling the following people will have a hard time finding a job upon graduation" (288 likes) and "Hospitals take note of these names. Do not give these selfish dumbfucks beds and/or respirators"

(84 likes). Some went further and contacted the students' schools, with one tweeter asking for a student's scholarship to be rescinded (the same student later deleted their Facebook page).

The anger behind these messages is understandable—mass-gatherings endanger people's lives by facilitating the spread of the virus. And just three days earlier, internet shaming arguably had a productive outcome. After a Tennessee man received a barrage of angry comments for stockpiling 17,700 bottles of hand sanitizer to sell for inflated prices, he expressed remorse and donated his stock to a local church.

Shaming has also been used effectively to improve employees' lives during the pandemic: after Waterstones' chief executive, James Daunt, announced its stores would be staying open, an online backlash prompted him to reverse the decision within a day. The same happened to Sports Direct, while Wetherspoon's was shamed online and off (with branches graffitied) after its chairman, Tim Martin, claimed that he couldn't afford to pay staff. A tweet calling Martin a "twat" gained more than 30,000 likes, and the pay decision was reversed after he met with hospitality experts.

Yet pandemic shaming can also have dire consequences. On March 18, the Polish press reported that a professor infected with coronavirus, Wojciech Rokita, died after being flooded with hateful online comments. Rumors had spread—both online and in local media—that 54-year-old Rokita had not complied with his quarantine and had visited a car showroom after being diagnosed with coronavirus. On March 19, a lawyer representing Rokita's family claimed the professor had not violated his quarantine, and had taken his own

life as a result of the "wave of hate" he faced online.

The story of the remorseful Tennessee hoarder is also less uplifting on second glance. The *New York Times* reported that the man received hate mail and death threats, with one stranger banging on his door late at night. "Your behavior is probably going to end up with someone killing you and your wife and your children," read one e-mail. The man has also lost his livelihood—he is now banned from selling on eBay and Amazon, previously his sole form of income.

> It is hardly surprising that online shaming can have tragic consequences.

It is hardly surprising that online shaming can have tragic consequences, but when it comes to coronavirus, you could argue that shamers endanger one person in order to save many more. Yet do the shamed actually change their minds as a result of hateful comments? Is shaming actually productive?

"What they were saying was absolutely outrageous," says Laura, a 17-year-old who received online hate after attending a Stereophonics gig in Manchester on March 13 (her name has been changed on her request). Laura emphasizes that when she attended the concert, mass gatherings hadn't been banned by the government (although some artists had cancelled their gigs). "I had people telling me I was going to kill people, someone private messaged me saying, 'I hope you feel great about yourself when you're the one who's killed your whole family,'" she says.

"They didn't change my mind, they didn't make me regret that I went," Laura goes on. She received the comments on a tweet she posted after the gig, and therefore notes: "What they were saying was irrelevant because what had happened had already been and gone, so they couldn't have stopped me from going."

Three days earlier, 24-year-old Jardin May from Texas received a flood of comments after tweeting, "Coronavirus is everywhere. BOOK THAT FLIGHT. Take that trip. You probably won't die from it, but even if you do . . . You wanna die with the Eiffel Tower in the background . . . ."

May says some commenters educated her about coronavirus—those who were calm and polite taught her that she shouldn't be concerned about herself, but rather the elderly and vulnerable people she might infect. "A lot of the stuff I know about coronavirus I didn't learn till the calmer people in the comments were like, 'Hey, just be careful,'" May says. "But Twitter took it and ran with it."

A fortnight later, May is still receiving notifications from the tweet, and she is continually being branded "fucking stupid and selfish," a "bitch," "murderer," and a "moron." "They were extremely aggressive, they were like, 'Oh I hope your family dies'; 'I hope you get sick and you die from it,'" May says of the initial messages she received. "I did feel like a lot of people were wasting their breath, because if you're doing angry tweeting and cursing and threats, I'm not gonna read it."

The venom generated hasn't prevented the state from adopting online shaming during the coronavirus crisis. While individuals use it to police behavior, now the actual police are using it to denounce members of the public. On March 27, Derbyshire police released drone footage which labeled anonymous dog walkers and exercisers on the Peaks as indulging in outlawed "not essential" travel. The former justice secretary, David Gauke, described the shaming as "badly misjudged."

And last Sunday (March 29) after tweeting a photo of his physically distanced birthday visit to his father Neil, Labour MP Stephen Kinnock was criticized by the South Wales police Twitter account—"A lovely thing to do, however this is not essential travel." When Kinnock replied pointing out he had been delivering "necessary supplies," the force thanked him for the "clarification." The Twittersphere was divided over whether this was a good use of police time.

Dr. June Tangney, a psychology professor at George Mason University, and author of *Shame and Guilt*, doubts shaming will prevent poor pandemic behavior. "By shaming people, we're actually encouraging the opposite," she says. "When people feel shamed, they tend to get very defensive, they tend to blame other people, they're disinclined to take responsibility, and they're not any more likely to change their behavior."

So why are we really shaming others during a pandemic? Dr. Lydia Woodyatt is a social sciences professor at Flinders University whose research has shown that schadenfreude [taking pleasure in another's unhappiness] motivates online shaming. "The same things that drive hostility and collective action offline can drive shaming behavior online: anger, identification with others in the cause, schadenfreude, belief that our actions together will make a difference," she explains. She points to recent research by PhD students at her university which found that when an online leader emphasizes the nobility of the "goal" of their shaming, people are more likely to shame.

You'd struggle to find a more noble goal than saving lives, so it makes sense that there's been an increase in shaming in recent weeks. Yet Woodyatt also points to a simpler explanation—with social isolation increasingly common, more and more people are online for longer stretches of time, and this is an issue that encompasses the entire world. "The sense of loss of control can mean that people try and take control of what they feel they can control," she adds.

Schadenfreude and a bit of boredom might explain the reaction to a tweet posted by nightclub owner Fraser Carruthers on March 16. Responding to Boris Johnson's recommendation that the public stop visiting pubs, Carruthers tweeted: "I am a nightclub owner in Kensington and Chelsea. You can't tell the nation to avoid 'pubs and clubs' and not officially 'close us' so that we can claim our insurance." When online sleuths discovered that he had previously tweeted "Anyone but Corbyn" [Britain's Labour Party leader who lost to Conservative Boris Johnson], they mocked the 37-year-old as deserving of his fate.

"It was a mind-blowing response," says Carruthers, who says he had "hundreds and hundreds" of messages for "three days non-stop." He was particularly alarmed by commenters who wished he and his family would end up on the street. "It really makes you think there are some horrible people in this world." Carruthers believes the response was so strong because of the "stigma" of Kensington and Chelsea but notes he didn't actually vote Conservative in the 2019 election—he voted for the Animal Welfare party.

Of course, in the middle of a global pandemic, nightclub owners aren't the people we should feel sorriest for. Yet the vitriol Carruthers received demonstrates that online shaming isn't always altruistic. Dr. Aaron Balick,

> Shame is one of our most primitive feelings. . . . If it happens on a grand scale it can be psychologically traumatic.

a psychotherapist from London and author of *The Psychodynamics of Social Networking*, argues that online shamers are "hardly doing it for the safety of society. They're doing it because they get to be right and someone else gets to be wrong."

Balick says pandemic shaming may be caused by fear, as "people tend to regress when they're frightened." Yet like Tangney, he believes shaming is counterproductive and potentially dangerous. "Shame is one of our most primitive feelings. It does hurt, very, very deeply, and if it happens on a grand scale, like on Twitter, it can be psychologically traumatic," he says.

Arguably, the repercussions of online shaming aren't as severe as they were five years ago, when journalist Jon Ronson wrote his book *So You've Been Publicly Shamed*, chronicling the trauma, job losses, and damaged lives of the internet-shamed. Nowadays, trending topics move so quickly that it is difficult for one individual to capture the entire internet's attention for long. Even actor Vanessa Hudgens, who employed her best vocal fry to say, "Like yeah, people are going to die, which is terrible . . . but inevitable?" on Instagram on March 16, got away relatively unscathed. Though Hudgens was flooded with hate and forced to issue an apology, model Chrissy Teigen came to her defense and gained 75,000 likes for tweeting that when people make misjudged comments, "u don't have [to] ruin their lives."

And indeed, if we now know the consequences of online shaming, we should also know the consequences of what we post online. May, the tweeter who encouraged people to book cheap flights, says she doesn't think the backlash was unfair because she was aware that "this is the internet" and "it's open for everyone to leave their opinion."

It is also possible that while shaming doesn't change the behavior of the shamed, it can adjust cultural norms. An anonymous 27-year-old says that seeing others hectored online changed his own habits. "In general it just made me take it way more seriously," he says, explaining that he had initially still planned to go on holiday and had a "cavalier" attitude to the dangers. "Online hectoring [of others] did force me to see that behavior as selfish and individualistic . . . perhaps more than straight up relaying that information in a calm and dispassionate way would have done."

Yet overall, the experts do not believe in the power of public shame. "By increasing hostility in an otherwise volatile environment we are just promoting the norm of hostility and aggression as a means of coping," Woodyatt says. "I think we should all agree that is not a good idea. Humans can communicate social norms in calm and non-aggressive ways. We are all in this together."

Jon Ronson, too, is not a fan of pandemic shaming (though he notes that we can and should criticize public figures who are putting people in danger). "As we're forced to isolate," he says, "we need to be able to connect with other people. It can make the difference between being happy and stoical and being depressed. The very best thing Twitter could be right now is a nice place for people to visit and find connection."*

*Copyright Guardian News & Media Ltd 2020

ACTIVITY: Analyzing the Rhetorical Situation

1. What good reasons might Amelia Tait have for delivering her critical analysis in print rather than in her usual YouTube medium? What can print do that other digital media might not be able to? What are the constraints of the print medium?
2. Consider Tait's rhetorical situation in terms of the problem she wants to address or resolve, her rhetorical audience, and the complex context she is entering. What are some of the specific complexities of that context, especially in terms of the problem and her audience?
3. What is Tait's thesis? What values lie at the root of Tait's argument? How do her values align or differ from those of her rhetorical audience? How does she negotiate such differences?
4. What public spaces does Tait consider? Within each of those public spaces, how does Tait account for shaming? What is the overall effect of these accounts in terms of supporting her argument?
5. How would you describe the tone of her essay? How do the various examples fit with or contrast with that tone?
6. How does Tait's critical analysis resonate with your own life, at home, at school, and in various public spaces? What behavioral changes is Tait advocating—and what measure of success has she had persuading you?

Being an 18-Year-Old Black Man a Year after Mike Brown

MALCOLM-AIME MUSONI

Entertainment Weekly writer Malcolm-Aime Musoni describes himself as a free-lance writer, social-media editor, and a social strategist. Now living in Los Angeles, where he writes prolifically for a number of news outlets, the Iowa native first attained national recognition when the following excerpt from his memoir appeared in Huffington Post *on August 15, 2015. In this critical analysis, Musoni responds to the death of 18-year-old African American Michael Brown, who was shot and killed by a white police officer in Ferguson, Missouri, in 2014. Inhabiting public space and even private space (think George Floyd, Breonna Taylor, Rayshard Brooks, Amadou Diallo, and too many others) can be a death sentence for America's Black people.*

I made my way down the gravel road out of the cemetery as I had done plenty of times before but to the left of me I saw something that I hadn't seen in all the times I had gone to visit my mom at the cemetery since February; a police car. The cop car had just pulled up and was parked facing my way. It was a hot day and I had been running without my shirt on. I put my shirt on, crossed the street, took my phone out of my pocket and when I was far enough away I turned around to make sure the police car wasn't following me. Never before had I ever felt such a wave of anxiety hit me like that due to being in the presence of the police. Long gone are the childlike days when I viewed the police as heroes or the pre-teen days when it seemed like it was the cool thing to flip a policeman off with our middle fingers if they were driving behind us. Those days are gone. I didn't do anything wrong, I didn't commit a crime, I was just minding my own business and going to visit my mom. But the notion that I could mind my own business and not be persecuted in the streets from a policeman was stripped away from me on August 9th 2014 when Mike Brown was unlawfully gunned down by the police.

I was 17 when Mike Brown was killed but now I'm 18; the same age as he was and never have I ever been more aware of the racism going on in this country. I'm aware of what can happen to me; in the blink of an eye my name can follow a hashtag and have supporters drumming up support for real justice to take place in my honor. It's a scary thing to know that people view you as the enemy and have such hatred for you just because of your skin color and can get away with killing you just because of systematic oppression and racism. Once you realize that, your view of the world changes. When Mike Brown was killed I was immediately scared for my brother. He's the same build as Mike and all I could think of was someone trying to kill him. Whenever we would go to stores I would always try to shush my brother if he was being loud because I didn't want to draw a scene and cause problems. A year later I'm scared for myself. Now I don't think that just because I'm 3 years younger, taller and skinnier that I have no chance of being gunned down. That's not a reality that lays in my future. My previous naive reality isn't the reality anymore. They're not gonna look at me and say "Hey just because you don't sag your pants you're a good Black" and then go and kill my brother because he sags his pants. It's not going to happen. The articles of clothing that we wear don't define us to them and that's something that took time to realize and understand.

When I hit 8th grade I felt this conflict between myself and my white classmates due to what I would wear and how I talked. There was this constant "You talk so white," "You're the whitest black kid I know." I would sit and try to ask myself and figure out what did that mean. Their comments turned into "Oh I can say the N word Malcolm doesn't care, he's the whitest black kid I know." But the reality was I did care and I did voice my opinion on them saying the N word but that wasn't listened to. You top that conflict with the internal struggle I dealt with of feeling like I was less of a beauty or a person for being a dark-skinned black person rather than a light-skinned black person and that can manifest into self hate. For a year after that I started to sag my pants and dress a little bit differently. It lasted for a year because my mom and dad weren't putting up with that and because I realized that dressing like that wasn't me. It wasn't who I was. And then Trayvon Martin happened. And a conversation started to take place about black men wearing hoodies. I lived and still live in a neighborhood where we are the only black family living in it. If I was walking through the neighborhood in the rain with a hoodie I didn't think they would gun me down. I didn't think that

> **I'm just dangerously trying to exist without my existence being threatened in my own home, my neighborhood, my city, my state.**

was a reality for anyone. But fast forward a couple years later and the cloth of innocence has been violently ripped from my face and I'm just dangerously trying to exist without my existence being threatened in my own home, my neighborhood, my city, my state, and the country my parents decided to call their new home 20 some years ago. It's the struggle of a lifetime that we are having to endure. Nothing is safe anymore.

I see Sandra Bland and I see my 22-year-old sister. It's such a twisted reality that it took that happening to really let it sink in that my sister too could be gunned down as well. It took that for me to know and feel the same fear I feel for my brother for my sister as well. Her taillight needs to be fixed and that's all it takes for a policeman to pull her over and a routine stop turning wrong. She's never been in contact with the police so I'm not sure how she would react. But her reaction doesn't even matter because no matter how you treat the police or how much you know your rights it's not going to change anything. And that's something that I fear when I get my car. I have to hope that my music isn't too loud that it bothers someone at a gas station or I have to hope that a routine stop is just a routine stop that I can be able to leave and not end up in a jail cell. It's all this fear and baggage that comes with the new responsibilities of being an adult. Not just being an adult but a black man entering adulthood. I live in a smallish town of 48 thousand in Iowa and everyone is always saying "Oh that will never happen to us, we live in a good small town." But the town isn't the problem it's the people in the town and the systems that are put in place to let people get away with abusing their power and using their power as a tool to explore their own personal racism. That's really what it comes down to, it's not the victims.

As time goes on I'm more and more increasingly aware of my own digital imprint operating under the moniker "fijiwatergod" and what that can mean for me. Just being a teen on social media has ramifications beyond my existence. They can take my tweets and say that I was someone who "had no respect for the law" as a reason to justify what could happen to me. They can take my old tweets from when I was an 11th grader seriously battling depression and say that I killed myself. They can take my pictures of me throwing up the peace sign and say that I was a thug and throwing up a gang sign. They can find marijuana in my system from months prior and say that I was a druggie who was out of his mind and instigated the altercation with the police. Will the media label me as a thug and not an angel and try to humanize my killer? Will the media launch a smear campaign against me? Will it take my own killing to get my white friends to use the Black Lives Matter hashtag instead of the All Lives Matter hashtag? Will my dad be forced to go on TV and say he forgives them? Will there be marches in my honor? Will the mayor of my town encourage peace before the verdict announcing that the policeman will get off unlawfully killing me is read? Will the cop camera and body camera be on or will that not even matter due to the systems put in place that hold police at an unfair advantage? Will I be the topic of an incredulous Don Lemon panel with Marc Lamont Hill being the voice of reason? Will they find a twisted way to bring my mom's recent death into this and vilify me? These are the questions and thoughts that plague me as an 18 year old black man.

What will they do?

ACTIVITY: Analyzing the Rhetorical Situation

1. How has the death of Michael Brown affected Musoni? For what reasons might Musoni have written this piece even if Brown had not been killed?

2. In what ways does Musoni establish his ethos as a trustworthy communicator? How does he establish logos, the good reasons for his analysis? And how does he make authentic emotional connections with his readers (pathos)? Provide textual evidence for your answers.

3. Who comprises Musoni's rhetorical audience? Are there primary and secondary audiences? What passages help you determine your response?

4. What might the audience(s) do to address or resolve the problem that Musoni is responding to? What actions or attitudes does Musoni hope to change on the part of his audience(s)?

5. Given the continued killings of Black people by white police officers since Brown's death, Black Lives Matter protests have also continued. What resources and constraints must these protesters manage?

»» COMMUNITY CONNECTIONS

1. Analyze a public space where you feel completely comfortable: a coffee shop, a campus bar, a grocery store, a museum, a government building, for instance. What are the criteria for your own comfort and ease there? Are there any criteria that the space does not meet in your case? In a three- to four-page essay, describe the place you are analyzing and the reason the analysis is important for you and your audience. State a thesis about the space and then articulate the causes or consequences of your comfort in the space. Be sure to consider the needs and expectations of people who are not comfortable in that same space as you consider alternative viewpoints.

2. Write for ten minutes about the causes or the consequences of being in a specific public space where you do not feel comfortable, following the instructions of the previous prompt (#1), making sure to identify the criteria that make others feel very comfortable there. You might consider a gym, a street at night, a club, a restaurant alone, a classroom. Be prepared to share your response with the rest of the class.

3. Given your experience and observations, consider how social media influence the ways people inhabit online public space. In a brief investigative report, define the problem you are addressing, explaining its significance to you and your audience. Be sure to state a thesis, developing it with good reasons that you support with specific examples, details, anecdotes, or data. Your report will include various perspectives, examples, and effects of people inhabiting online public space. Be prepared to share your findings.

4. Write for ten minutes about your response to Edwards's position argument or Drohan's investigative report. How does either set of arguments about the use of public space coincide with or diverge from your experiences in a town or city you know well?

27

Im/Migration, Displacement, Asylum Seeking: A Global Phenomenon

LEARNING OBJECTIVES

- Examine immigration as a global phenomenon.
- Evaluate the pros and cons of immigration.
- Integrate positive, negative, and new understandings with regard to the phenomenon.
- Apply knowledge of immigration, displacement, and asylum seeking to various genres.

The most traveled im/migration routes in 2020

The sustained media attention on Donald Trump's negative stance against immigration has highlighted the problems of migration everywhere. His 2017 "Buy American and Hire American" Executive Order, his 2018 "zero-tolerance" immigration policy, and his constant push for a border wall are all attempts to reduce the immigration of undocumented, refugee, and low-skilled foreign labor to the United States. These initiatives have also resulted in the separation of over 5,000 children from their parents at the U.S.-Mexican border. Such focus diverts attention from the thousands of highly skilled workers and students who migrate annually and contribute to the American workforce as medical professionals, researchers, business leaders, and entrepreneurs. Less skilled migrants constitute about one-third of workers in such industries as farming, fishing, forestry, caregiving, cleaning, and maintenance—often jobs that others do not want. All of these U.S. workers pay taxes and contribute to Social Security and Medicare funds, benefiting the entire nation. But such movement is far from national. Im/migration is a global phenomenon.

Never have so many humans been involved in migration, displacement, and asylum seeking—well over 270 million in all. Migration is now a top-tier political issue interconnected with human rights, economic development, and geopolitics all over the world. Hundreds of millions of people are displaced, either within their own country or in another country. Adults and children leave their homes and countries for a range of compelling and tragic reasons: war, economic crisis, persecution, conflict, and weather-related disaster.

The United States has been the main country of destination for international migrants since 1970, especially for those seeking economic security, stability, and safety after a war, economic crisis, or natural disaster. Some believe that limiting immigration will help restore our nation's economy and prevent crime. Then again, governments outside the United States (in Eastern, Central, and Southern Asia; Latin America; and the Caribbean) have in place policies for attracting immigrants, particularly highly skilled workers. Since one out of every seven international migrants is below the age of twenty, many countries allow migration for the purpose of family reunification, at least under certain conditions. Many countries also have generous policies that accommodate international students. Unfortunately, immigration is often linked with human trafficking, illegal migration, drugs and criminal activity, and forced and exploited labor—all of which complicate governmental policies on immigration. As you know well, people (and nations) shape different responses to the same rhetorical opportunity for change: some of the following responses are part of the national conversation about immigration in the United States.

The responses to migration in this chapter include a profile by the Marshall Project, (see CHAPTER 6, PROFILES), a critical analysis by Brennan Hoban (see CHAPTER 11, CRITICAL ANALYSES), a position argument by Natascha

pages 91–109
pages 186–203

pages
128–149
and
pages
167–185
and
pages
150–166

Uhlmann (see CHAPTER 8, POSITION ARGUMENTS), an evaluation by Frank Shyong (see CHAPTER 10, EVALUATIONS), and a proposal by Arturo J. Bañuelas (see CHAPTER 9, PROPOSALS). Many writers sympathize with migrants on religious or human-rights grounds, as can be seen in Natascha Uhlmann's "No-More-Deaths Volunteer Scott Warren Was Acquitted. But Humanitarian Aid Should Never Be Considered a Crime" and Arturo Bañuelas's "The Advent Posada Is an Act of Resistance," while others, like Frank Shyong in "'It's Just Too Much': Asian Americans Confront Xenophobia, Economic Devastation and the Coronavirus," speak for people that are being ostracized for immigrating to the United States. Still others examine the financial consequences of immigration, as Brennan Hoban does in "Do Immigrants 'Steal' Jobs from American Workers?" Whether immigration policies and practices contribute to ethnic, racial, or national tensions or remain ineffective and toothless, you can decide as you read the essays in this chapter and conduct further research for your own essays. What do you think?

After you have read the essays in this chapter, your instructor might call on you to develop your own ideas through one of the following prompts.

1. The Marshall Project illuminates the movement of students who cross the Mexican-American border to attend high school, while our national media focus on the parent–child separations that have been occurring across that same border. With problems connected with border crossings as your focus, choose a visual or print text by a person or a group with a vested interest in the effect of such crossings. The text can be from this chapter or you can turn to an image or text you find online or in print. In a critical analysis, pages 186–203 assess whether the response is a fitting and successful one. (See CHAPTER 11, CRITICAL ANALYSES.) To achieve that goal, consider these questions:

   • How is the intended audience for the text a rhetorical audience, someone who is affected by the issue and has a vested interest in it? Draw on evidence from the text to support your answer.

   • What can the rhetorical audience do to resolve the problem?

   • Does the response address and fit the rhetorical opportunity for change? How exactly? If not, how might the response be reshaped so that it does fit?

   • How is the response delivered in an appropriate medium that reaches its intended audience? Describe why the medium is appropriate. If it is not, explain how it could be adjusted so that it would be appropriate.

   • Can you think of other responses to similar rhetorical situations? What genre is commonly used to respond to such situations? Does the creator of this text use that genre? If not, what is the effect of going against an audience's expectations?

Using your responses, craft a formal critical analysis of your chosen text. Begin by choosing a thesis in which you analyze what makes the text rhetorically effective or ineffective. Then, organize your most interesting observations into several major points, using specific examples from the text to elaborate each individual point. Be sure to choose an audience for your critical analysis and write with that audience in mind.

2. Like Father Arturo José Bañuelas, take a stand (positive, negative, or exploratory) on undocumented immigration into the United States in the form of a position argument. (See **CHAPTER 8, POSITION ARGUMENTS**.) After reading the essays in this chapter, conduct online and library research, tap into your own experiences and observations, and draft a thesis statement that reflects your position toward such immigration, perhaps focusing on criminal activity, human trafficking, or asylum seeking. Develop your thesis with richly supported reasons and make an authentic, purposeful connection with your audience. Adopt a thoughtful, respectful tone and bring in opposing viewpoints to build your credibility on the subject. Your print essay should be at least five pages long so you can be sure to acknowledge a wide range of opinions about the movement. You may include images and links to sound and videos if you think doing so will enhance your essay.

pages
128–149

The Cheer Team Caught Between Two Worlds

THE MARSHALL PROJECT

The Marshall Project is a nonprofit online news organization that combines long investigative articles with short Web-oriented pieces. The organization often collaborates with other media outlets, and this in-depth profile of the Bowie Cheer Team in El Paso, Texas, was a joint project with National Geographic.

For Texas high schoolers who cross the Mexican-American border every school day, border-crossings are more about the logistics of getting an education than the politics of a border wall. In the following profile, The Marshall project focuses on the lives of individual students and their practical struggles and personal rewards.

Ashley Esquivel's alarm goes off at 5:45 a.m. in Juárez, Mexico. It's a Friday in November, and she's heading to high school in Texas, which means football. She pulls on blue sweats branded with the frowning bear mascot of her high school, stuffs her cheerleading skirt into her backpack and gets in the car. Her dad drops her at the U.S. border on his way to work.

Although the days are still warm, dawn in the desert hovers around 30 degrees. A yellow mist settles across a motionless line of cars that seems to stretch from the horizon to the border checkpoint. Vendors hawk newspapers and burritos to commuters bound for El Paso, who can wait three or four hours to cross the bridge each morning. A stream of children with backpacks, earbuds in, hands shoved in pockets, weave between traffic and funnel onto a pedestrian walkway.

Every day, Ashley makes this crossing to get to high school. An estimated 40,000 children cross the U.S. border each day for school, not just into Texas, but also California, New Mexico, and Arizona. Most of these cross-border students, known as transfronterizos, attend elementary and high school. Even as the United States plans to add 450 miles of border wall this year, life between Mexico and the United States remains fluid. On average, more than 35,000 passenger vehicles make this northbound journey into El Paso each day, along with nearly 20,000 pedestrians. Annually, more than $80 billion in international trade moves across this part of the border and into Texas. Ashley is just one student amid the daily back and forth of people crossing between the United States and Mexico to shop, work, visit family, and get an education.

Perhaps no other two cities represent the overlap of nations like El Paso and Juárez. By population, it's the second-largest urban area on the U.S.-Mexico border, after San Diego and Tijuana, but it's arguably the most tightly connected part of the 2,000-mile boundary. From a bird's eye view, the two meld together seamlessly. El Paso, with its quiet suburbs, and Juárez, with its lively plazas, have a combined population of 2.5 million people, many of whom lead lives that straddle both sides. At ground level, though, an increasingly militarized border divides them.

The Rio Grande, which marks the boundary between the United States and Mexico, is only a stream here, but it's reinforced with an 18-foot metal wall and multilane freeway. This

This map shows that El Paso and Juárez are right next to each other at the U.S.-Mexico border.

combination is passable via four traffic-clogged bridges. One runs right from the vendor-filled sidewalks of Juárez into El Paso's main shopping street. Another practically empties into Bowie (pronounced Boo-ey) High School. Known to locals as La Bowie, this historic school has deep roots in the debate over immigration.

In the past year, students say, a series of migrant caravans from Central America have clogged the already congested crossing points, leading to wait times reminiscent of the months after Sept. 11, 2001, when crossings slowed to a trickle. For seven of the 21 members of the Bowie cheer team who cross the border from Juárez to El Paso every day, this is just a logistical adjustment. They live in Juárez, but as holders of U.S. passports or long-term visas are able to get an education in Texas. This diploma,

iStockPhoto.com/DenisTangneyJr

Sister Cities. Downtown El Paso seamlessly blends into Juárez. The Sierra Juárez mountain range in northern Mexico is visible from El Paso.

their parents hope, will be the stepping stone to a good college, a well-paying job, the American dream. So, they set their alarms a little earlier and spend chilly mornings in line to enter the country.

At the base of the bridge, Ashley links up with her friend Melanie Vidal, who's already in her cheerleading skirt despite the chill, and the two speed through a chain-link-enclosed path. Ten minutes later they're deposited at the end of a long line snaking out of the Customs and Border Protection building—a half hour wait, at least. Some days it takes five minutes and others it takes three hours.

Ashley, who is 17, was born in El Paso, but her brother, who is 16, was born in Juárez. With her American passport, she goes to school here, while he remains across the border. Ashley,

who's quiet and serious, would rather study in Juárez, where she thinks the academics are more rigorous. (Her little brother is studying the same topics as she is and he's a junior.) But her parents wanted her to learn English, and Bowie is where her friends are. She shrugs off questions about the border wall. There are more pressing things to think about: that night's football game and, later, whether she wants to become official with the boy she's dating. For politicians, journalists and much of the country, this border is the epicenter of a crisis. For Ashley, it's a morning commute.

Inside, immigration officers scan their papers, and they put their backpacks through an X-ray machine. Then they're in America. Ashley pops her American passport card into the back of her phone case, and the two walk across lanes of Mexico-bound traffic, a small park, and into the Bowie cafeteria. The sun is bright now, and Bowie is so close to the border that the wall is visible from the back of the school, where students tend to gardens and study in overflow classrooms. In the hallways, Spanish is the lingua franca. English is a second language for nearly two-thirds of Bowie students. Later that Friday afternoon, the school will celebrate Día de los Muertos and then play the last home game of football season.

The border wall along Highway 85 in El Paso.

Ashley and Melanie grab trays and join their friend Jasmine, who's sitting at a table by the doors with her computer and a heap of books. She lived in El Paso for a year with a legal guardian but missed her family too much. So, now, Jasmine wakes up at 4:30 a.m., takes two buses from her parents' house in Juárez and gets to the border bridge by 7 a.m. After school she does softball, student council, National Honor Society, and a handful of other extracurriculars. If she has an away game, she returns home around 1 a.m. "That's why I look like this," she says, gesturing to her sweatshirt and the curls falling out of her ponytail. On her screen is an early acceptance application for the University of Texas at Austin, where she hopes to study environmental engineering.

Due in part to the recession of the mid-2000s and an uptick in immigration enforcement, the number of U.S.-born minors living in Mexico doubled between 2000 and 2015. Today, an estimated half a million reside south of the border.

Ashley, Melanie, Jasmine, and many other students who cross each day were born in the United States to Mexican parents, raised in Mexico, and then sent to El Paso for high school. According to a 2017 study, 81 percent of cross-border students were born in the United States. Some have mothers who were living in America at the time, others came just to give birth, some were undocumented. In El Paso, their children learn English, receive an education, and see the prospect of well-paying jobs. They visit Juárez regularly, to visit family, get affordable medical care, and also have some fun: from throwing blow-out quinceñera parties to club hopping on their 18th birthday. "The problems our kids have are truly different than anywhere else," says Joel Rodriguez, a social studies teacher at Bowie. He's in the courtyard, directing the set-up of a Día de los Muertos celebration. On the steps of the sunken amphitheater, altars honor the dead with candles, snacks and drinks, and photographs of family members, pets, celebrities—as well as victims of a massacre that killed nearly 22 people at a Walmart in El Paso three months earlier. The school food truck serves pan de muerto, a sweet bread, and hot chocolate. A mariachi band fiddles with instruments, and the dance team dons colorful costumes paired with striking skeletal face paint.

When Rodriguez was growing up in El Paso, as the undocumented son of agricultural workers, the border wall was little more than a fence with holes in it. Some of those holes were directly behind Bowie and a nearby middle school. Rodriguez remembers that sometimes a chase would cut through their classrooms if the door was left open. "That's your uncle!" students would joke to each other as an immigrant raced through. "That's your other uncle!" they'd yell when an immigration officer followed in hot pursuit. That was life on the border—everyone was connected to both sides.

To catch people sneaking into the country, Border Patrol agents would patrol Bowie and interrogate anyone they deemed suspicious. As a freshman in 1992, Rodriguez watched

his classmates get stopped and questioned in the school's hallways. Later that year, something happened that became a turning point in immigration enforcement: Bowie students sued the federal government for violating their civil rights—and *won*. Immigration officers were no longer allowed to question anyone about their citizenship status unless they had reason, the judge wrote, "involving more than the mere appearance of the individual being of Hispanic descent."

Today, the wall still sits directly behind the school, but students seem more focused on their ever-unfolding teenage drama than political turmoil. The border is an inconvenience—one that makes them late for school or prompts sleepovers with family or friends in El Paso on game nights—and, perhaps most importantly, a cause of their sleep deprivation. "Sometimes I'm too tired to wake up at 4 a.m. to cross at five," says 15-year-old cheerleader Megan Mejía, who usually stays with her sister in El Paso after a late night. "Sometimes I'm so tired at practice."

One morning, as Megan raced from the border bridge to cheer practice, already five minutes late, she reflected on whether she'd rather go to school in Juárez. "No," she said, her glasses sliding down her nose as she jogged toward the gym. "Juárez is too much drama."

The school doesn't collect data on how many students cross each day—to enroll, they are supposed to live in the district. Some use a relative's address, rent an apartment or post-office box, or pay tuition. Rodriguez says that half his

Source: YouTube

A Bear TV YouTube video of the Día de los Muertos *(Day of the Dead) celebration in the amphitheater at Bowie High School includes this Bowie dance team member in striking skeleton makeup.*

students are "walkers" who cross the border every morning. Some of them come early so they don't get stuck in the rush hour line. He gestures to the cafeteria: "We have kids who get here at 6 a.m. and sleep on those tables." Despite that, he says, his walkers have the best attendance and some of the highest scores in math and sciences. At graduation, they're often alone—their parents can't cross.

It wasn't always like this. Antonia Morales is one of the last residents of Barrio Duranguito, El Paso's oldest neighborhood, which has been largely emptied for a development project. When Morales moved from Juárez in the 1940s or '50s—she can't remember exactly—crossing was easy. She and her husband would go to dinner in Juárez, where the restaurants were full of visitors from around the world and American soldiers on leave from Fort Bliss in Texas. On New Year's Eve they'd dance, drink, and, on the bridge back to El Paso, crack cascarones—hollow eggs filled with confetti—over immigration officers' heads.

> "The border was so beautiful when I was young," she said. "There wasn't the racism we see now."

Over the years, it's become harder to navigate life on both sides of the border. A rise in undocumented immigrants coming to the United States in the 1980s and '90s, peaking in 2000, politicized the border. At the start of the 21st century, around 4,000 agents patrolled the border, but the attacks of Sept. 11, 2001 changed everything. Heightened security led to hours-long lines into Texas. A few years later, when cartel violence made Juárez one of the most dangerous cities in Mexico, it increased again. Today, more than 21,000 agents work on the southern border, although the number of people both turned back at the border and apprehended while crossing illegally had been declining over the past.

Morales is 91 now and hasn't been back to Juárez since the violence started in 2008. "The border was so beautiful when I was young," she said. "There wasn't the racism we see now. Everyone was accepting. The longer I live the more I see things I don't like."

El Paso is nearly 80 percent Hispanic, and political posturing from Washington D.C. hits home. The immigration debate is an everyday reality: Residents volunteer at migrant shelters and share the road with white U.S. Customs and Border Protection SUVs. In his 2019 State of the Union

Source: YouTube

BearTV YouTube video shows Bowie cheerleaders at a Homecoming Assembly. Seven of the 21 cheer members cross the border from Juárez to El Paso every day.

address, President Donald Trump called El Paso "one of our nation's most dangerous cities" before the border wall was installed and said the wall's presence had saved lives. This claim was refuted by the city's mayor and local leaders on both sides of the aisle.

The emotions stirred by the immigration debate crystallized in El Paso after August's Walmart shooting. The attacker, who drove nearly 10 hours from his home outside Dallas, is believed to have written an anti-immigrant manifesto and targeted a store frequented by Hispanic shoppers.

Over the years, it's been harder to navigate life on both sides of the border.

In the 1800s, small settlements began to grow along the Rio Grande. In 1846, El Paso, which had belonged to Mexico, was seized by Texas. Then, two years later, the United States and Mexico were officially divided along the Rio Grande. There were few restrictions on cross-border movement until 1917. That year,

the U.S. Immigration Act was passed to slow refugees fleeing the Mexican revolution. A few years later, the first Border Patrol was formed.

Despite the increasingly fortified physical division, the cities are still so interwoven that shops take both U.S. Dollars and Mexican Pesos, and businesses move between the two countries. "The understanding of how tied together we are crosses political lines," says Leyva. "Our economic survival depends on working together."

At the football game on Friday night, the 21 cheerleaders chant and dance energetically even as Bowie gets badly beaten by a rival team. In Texas, cheerleading is practically a higher calling, and other teams are packed with girls who started training as toddlers. Most squads have coaches for stunts and tumbling, but there's no money for that at Bowie. When they go to competitions, the disadvantage is stark; no one can remember the last time the Bowie cheerleaders won. But they have a new coach, and his goal is to find a sponsor for tumbling classes and make sure every member can do a cartwheel by the school year's end.

Ana Castañeda—homecoming queen, student council vice president, co-captain of the cheer team and former border-crosser—watches from near the top of the stands. After a couple of rough days at school, she's sitting this game out and thinking about what she wants to do after Bowie.

For a long time, her dream was to become a Border Patrol agent. She'd seen her parents

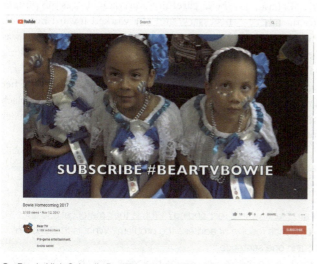

Source: YouTube

On Bowie High School's BearTV channel, these little girls are shown with Day of the Dead make-up and already in training for the "higher calling" of cheer as they attend a Bowie Homecoming.

struggle with the border bureau-cracy as Mexican citizens and wished she could make their lives easier. She changed her mind last year after hearing about the widespread detention of children. Plan B was to make YouTube videos, but that would make her mom mad, so she's moved on to Plan C—dentistry.

For part of elementary and all of middle school, Ana commuted from Juárez to El Paso. Every morning at 5 a.m., her mother drove her to the bridge. Ana Maria Torres wanted her daughters to have a better life than she'd had growing up in Mexico. "At least I did something well that my kids were born here," she said, sitting in her living room a few days before the game. Before they moved to El Paso, her older daughter, Elsa, would drive the other siblings over the bridge, drop them at school and then take herself to Bowie High. Elsa didn't tell anyone she lived in Juárez. She graduated from high school without doing a single extracurricular activity and with few friends.

Ana was luckier—after the peak of cartel violence in Juárez, when the family almost

In this video, posted on Bowie's Bear TV channel on YouTube, Bowie Cheerleaders lead a chant at a Bowie High School Homecoming Assembly. Cheerleaders who cross the border consider the border a logistical problem that can makes them late for practice rather than a political struggle.

never ventured outside, they moved back to El Paso, where she had been born. The illusion she'd carefully maintained was no longer necessary, and she worked toward her goal: homecoming queen of Bowie High. She was crowned in the queen's crystal tiara and long blue cape in early October.

"Most girls didn't know," Ana says of her days as a border crosser. She flicks her long black hair over a shoulder and shoves her hands in her jacket. "They thought I had a perfect life.'"

'Nina Strochlic

ACTIVITY: Analyzing the Rhetorical Situation

1. To what opportunity are these writers responding? Who is their rhetorical audience, and how might that audience resolve or address the problem? What is the thesis of this profile? Write it out in one sentence.

2. How do the writers for the Marshall Project use the rhetorical appeals to make their argument? How do they establish their ethos? The shape of their argument, their logos? And how do they make an emotional connect with their readers, their pathos?

3. Some migrants come into the United States illegally. How do the Marshall Project writers distinguish among the border crossers (citizens, legal migrants, undocumented migrants, and asylum seekers)? What role do "legal" and "illegal" status play (or not play) in this essay?

4. Moving from the United States into Mexico and Central America, these writers tap a broad geographical area for their supporting examples and details. What advantages does such a broad scope give them in composing the profiles that constitute their profile? Describe any related limitations in their ability to effectively make their case. Provide textual evidence for your answers.

5. What core values lie at the root of this essay? Do the writers seem to expect that their readers will share these values? Do you think they are right? If so, which arguments persuade you? Which ones do not?

Do Immigrants "Steal" Jobs from American Workers?

BRENNAN HOBAN

Former Communications Manager at Washington D.C.'s Brooking Institution, Brennan Hoban is now a Communication Specialist with a practice in both the Public and Social Sectors. She is a frequent commentator on social, economic, and political issues. In "Do Immigrants 'Steal' Jobs from American Workers?," Hoban offers a critical analysis of the situation.

Throughout his campaign and into his presidency, President Trump has promised to implement new immigration policies that will help improve the U.S. economy and job market.

A motivating factor behind Trump's proposed policies—including the construction of a new U.S.-Mexico border wall, more border patrol agents, and stricter deportation policies—is his belief that immigrants are stealing job opportunities from American workers. As he said in July 2015, "They're taking our jobs. They're taking our manufacturing jobs. They're taking our money. They're killing us."

But is that really the case? In new research, Brookings experts explore how immigration affects the economy, and what Trump's proposed policies could mean for the future of the U.S. workforce.

Trump's Proposed Policies Aim to Decrease Immigration

In one of his first proactive attempts to decrease the number of immigrants illegally entering the United States and the nation's workforce, Trump has vowed to increase the number of U.S. Border Patrol Agents to an unprecedented 26,370.

Trump has also proposed building a wall along the U.S.-Mexico border in order to prevent immigration into the United States. This border wall has been a priority for President Trump since his campaign. At a recent campaign rally in Arizona, Trump threatened to shut down the government if Congress does not allocate funding to building a border wall.

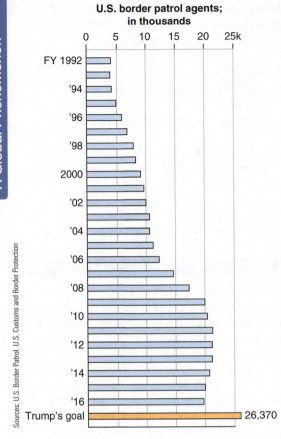

U.S. border patrol agents; in thousands

| | 0 | 5 | 10 | 15 | 20 | 25k |

FY 1992
'94
'96
'98
2000
'02
'04
'06
'08
'10
'12
'14
'16
Trump's goal — 26,370

Sources: U.S. Border Patrol. U.S. Customs and Border Protection

Immigrants Often Fill the Jobs Americans Don't Want

However, some argue that the work of these agents to protect against "job-stealing" immigrants may be in vain. As Brookings Senior Fellow Vanda Felbab-Brown explains in her new Brookings Essay, "The Wall," immigrants may not actually be "stealing" as many U.S. jobs as Trump thinks. As she put it, "the impact of immigrant labor on the wages of native-born workers is low …. However, undocumented workers often work the unpleasant, back-breaking jobs that native-born workers are not willing to do."

Felbab-Brown explains that many of the jobs occupied by undocumented workers in the United States are physically demanding jobs that Americans do not want, such as gutting fish or work on farm fields. She argues, "fixing immigration is not about mass deportations of people but about creating a legal visa system for jobs Americans do not want. And it is about providing better education opportunities, skills-development and retooling, and safety nets for American workers. And to date, Trump hasn't offered serious policy proposals on many—if any—of these areas."

Prioritizing only Highly-Skilled Immigrants Isn't Necessary

But what about *legal* immigrants and high-skilled workers? Brookings Senior Fellow William Frey takes issue with a proposal from President Trump to cut quotas for legal immigration in half and to prioritize the entrance of those with high skills. He argues that "these [proposals] fly in the face of census statistics that show that current immigration levels are increasingly vital to the growth of much of

America, and that recent arrivals are more highly skilled than ever before."

As for prioritizing immigrants with high skill levels, Frey points out that recent immigrants are already more highly educated than those of the past. In fact, he explains that "college graduates are more prevalent among recent immigrant adults than among all adults in 90 of the 100 largest metropolitan areas."

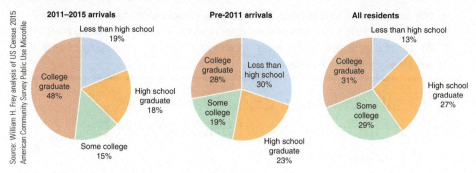

Source: William H. Frey analysis of US Census 2015 American Community Survey Public Use Microfile

2011–2015 arrivals

Less than high school
19%

College graduate
48%

High school graduate
18%

Some college
15%

Pre-2011 arrivals

College graduate
28%

Less than high school
30%

Some college
19%

High school graduate
23%

All residents

Less than high school
13%

College graduate
31%

High school graduate
27%

Some college
29%

Education attainment of US adults (age 25 and above), 2015

Immigration Is Tied to Positive Economic Growth and Innovation

Frey also explains that immigration is especially important for areas that are experiencing a decline in domestic migration and that U.S. immigration levels are currently fueling most community demographic gains. These gains are especially important as the nation's population gets older and fertility remains low.

Brookings Senior Fellow Dany Bahar also examined the positive link between immigration and economic growth. Bahar explains that while immigrants represent about 15 percent of the general U.S. workforce, they account for around a quarter of entrepreneurs and a quarter of investors in the United States and that over one third of new firms have at least one immigrant entrepreneur in its initial leadership team.

Moreover, Bahar explains that the impact of immigration on the wages of native-born workers is very small. "If anything," he concludes, "negative impacts occur for the most part on wages of prior immigrants with similar set of skills."

As Bahar mentions, "by cutting on immigration, the country will miss an opportunity for new inventions and ventures that could generate the jobs that the president is so committed to bring back. Thus, if the current administration wants to create jobs and 'make America great again,' it should consider enlisting more migrants."

Brennan Hoban, "Do Immigrants Steal Jobs from American Workers," Brookings Now, August 24, 2017. Reprinted by permission of Brookings Institution.

ACTIVITY: Analyzing the Rhetorical Situation

1. What is the central argument that Hoban makes in her critical analysis? What evidence does she use to make her case?
2. To what rhetorical opportunity is Hoban responding? How does understanding her context change the way you understand her writing?
3. In what ways does Hoban's essay offer a fitting response to her rhetorical opportunity? What textual evidence can you provide for your answer?

4. Why does Hoban spend so much time discussing the educational level of contemporary migrants? How do her examples and dates advance or detract from her argument?

5. What are the most persuasive features of this piece? Where does the argument seem less likely to persuade its audience?

No-More-Deaths Volunteer Scott Warren Was Acquitted but Humanitarian Aid Should Never Be Considered a Crime

NATASCHA UHLMANN

Natascha Elena Uhlmann is a writer and immigrant rights activist from Sonora, Mexico. Her writing has appeared in Teen Vogue *and* Truthout. *She is also the editor of President Andrés Manuel López Obrador's book,* A New Hope for Mexico: Saying No to Corruption, Violence, and Trump's Wall. *In the following op-ed essay, Uhlmann takes a position that the humanitarian volunteer should have never been prosecuted for trying to save human lives.*

This week, a federal jury in Arizona acquitted human rights activist Scott Warren on charges of harboring undocumented migrants. Warren faced up to 20 years in prison for providing food, water, and shelter to two men from Central America who were traveling through the Sonoran desert. It's a victory for activists across the country in a case that has come to define the stakes of humanitarian aid.

Warren was arrested by Border Patrol agents last year at an outpost maintained by No More Deaths, a faith-based humanitarian nonprofit organization providing basic necessities to migrants passing through the blazing desert that stretches across the Southwestern United States. That morning the organization released a report accusing U.S. Border Patrol of interfering with their aid efforts. Over a 46-month period, No More Deaths members tracked their humanitarian aid drop sites and found that Border Patrol agents vandalized

Between 1998 and 2018, more than 7,000 people have died crossing the U.S.-Mexico border.

water left for migrants 415 times, or twice a week on average. They released footage of Border Patrol agents appearing to kick over water jugs and laughing, which quickly went viral, garnering millions of views within days. Border Patrol officials denied charges of retaliation: "We're protecting immigration laws in the area, and there was a situation in which we needed to do the arrest because there were some illegal individuals in that area," Carlos Diaz, a spokesman for U.S. Customs and Border Protection, told *The Washington Post.* The No More Deaths report painted a damning picture of the agency, indicating a pattern of cruelty against undocumented migrants. As one migrant said in the report, "I needed water, some of the other people in the group needed water, but we found them [jugs of water] destroyed. [I felt] helplessness, rage. They [the U.S. Border Patrol] must hate us. It's their work to capture us, but we are humans. And they don't treat us like humans. It's hate is what it is. They break the bottles out of hate."

For many, Warren's case has become a touchstone at the intersection of human rights and religious freedom. The question of whether humanitarian aid can be criminalized has far-reaching implications for activists across the country. The Trump administration has moved swiftly to prosecute aid workers and immigrant rights activists. It seems they want to send the message that standing up for the vulnerable has consequences. Warren's acquittal represents a victory for activists across the country, but the fight isn't over. In 2017, then attorney general Jeff Sessions declared new enforcement priorities for U.S. prosecutors. Among them, he stated, prosecutors *must* consider prosecution for anyone found transporting or "harboring" migrants. The implications are chilling: Aid workers who come across undocumented migrants in desperate need of shelter or medical assistance could face charges for helping them get emergency care. By conflating aid work with human trafficking, the administration dramatically raises the risks of humanitarian aid work.

Between 1998 and 2018, more than 7,000 people have died crossing the U.S.-Mexico border, according to data from the U.S. Border Patrol. The desert terrain is hostile, with scorching daytime temperatures, long, empty stretches without water, and the ever-present threat of being picked up by Border Patrol agents prepped to detain and deport. As members of No More Deaths have argued, it's physically impossible to carry enough water to survive a few days in the desert. This is what makes their work so crucial—and literally a matter of life and death.

Last year, I spoke to Justine Orlovsky-Schnitzler, a member of No More Deaths. The border has become an even deadlier place, she told me, thanks to policies the U.S. government

has set in place to make the journey harder. But the blame can't be placed solely at the feet of Republicans: President Bill Clinton implemented a policy known as "prevention through deterrence" that has had far-reaching impacts on undocumented migrants traveling through the desert. "In the mid 1990s, urban areas were walled off, checkpoints were added strategically along major roads and routes, and there was a sharp increase in agents patrolling the border," Orlovsky-Schnitzler said. "Where deaths along the border were previously incredibly low, numbers quickly multiplied. The goal of prevention through deterrence was to push those crossing without papers into the most dangerous parts of the desert to avoid detection. The U.S. government knew people would die and argued that this would deter other crossers." The cruelty is not an unintended side effect of the policy—it's built right into the plan. According to the report by No More Deaths, Border Patrol's metrics for the program's success in the 1990s included "fee increases by smugglers," "possible increases in complaints," and "more violence at attempted entries."

The policy has been devastating. Migrants making the journey are pushed deeper into the hostile desert, facing blistering days and freezing nights. Dehydration is a leading killer, but migrants face a host of other threats too: Cartels have sprung up along the borderlands, lying in wait for telltale signs of a vulnerable migrant. They're easy prey for extortion, rape, and robbery.

As No More Deaths sees it, this policy will lead to needless human suffering. As long as the root causes of migration are unaddressed, they argue, people will continue risking their lives in search of safety, no matter how perilous the journey. And as long as people make the journey, No More Deaths will be there, fighting alongside them.[*]

[*]Natascha Uhlmann, Teen Vogue (c) Conde Nast

ACTIVITY: Analyzing the Rhetorical Situation

1. How did the arrest of Scott Warren affect Uhlmann? For what reasons might she have written this piece even if Warren had not been charged with a crime?

2. What attempts does Uhlmann make to establish herself as a trustworthy communicator? In what ways does she work to develop a relationship with her readers?

3. Who is Uhlmann's audience for this piece? What strategies does she use to appeal specifically to this audience, whether they agree or not agree with her?

4. How does Uhlmann try to establish an emotional connection with her audience, establishing pathos? What ready connections do you see between her topic and how successful she is in making this connection?

5. How does Uhlmann want her readers' actions or thoughts to change after reading her writing? How specially does she try to inspire these changes?

"It's Just Too Much": Asian Americans Confront Xenophobia, Economic Devastation, and the Coronavirus

FRANK SHYONG

Frank Shyong is a columnist for the Los Angeles Times. *He grew up south of Nashville, Tennessee, and moved to Los Angeles in 2006 to study economics at UCLA. He joined* The Times *in 2012 and writes about Chinese immigration and the Asian American community. This column—an evaluation—appeared on March 23, 2020, as shelter in place orders began to be put into effect.*

It's been a long week for all of us, so forgive me if I don't have the energy to participate in a debate about whether President Trump calling the virus "Chinese" is racist.

Of course it is. And it's something we've all seen before, when Vincent Chin was murdered in 1982 during a recession that politicians blamed on Japan; when Muslim Americans were targeted after 9/11; when the AIDS crisis was blamed on gay men; when Japanese Americans were sent to incarceration camps during World War II. When this country faces an existential threat, fear looks for a target.

I'm weary of this debate because the harm to Asian Americans is already done, and what

a pundit says will never change that. Nor will yelling at Trump do any good—he has repeatedly shown throughout his presidency that he values his ego over the safety of the American people. What we need to be talking about is how to protect people and neighborhoods from more economic and physical harm. This epidemic threatens and affects all of us in ways we are all still trying to understand, but what's increasingly clear is that the most permanent, drastic effects will be on the most vulnerable among us.

Asian American communities whose support systems have already been eroded by gentrification are fighting to protect their most vulnerable residents. And for months, they've been suffering an economic slowdown fueled by misplaced xenophobic fear.

On Monday, I called community leaders in Chinatown. Many Asian enclaves, like Chinatown, house large, low-income senior populations who are language-isolated— people who are most vulnerable to COVID-19 but least equipped to weather it.

In Chinatown, which houses more than 2,000 seniors in various living facilities, a longtime activist, King Cheung, says volunteers with the Chinatown Community for Equitable Development are trying to organize shopping runs for seniors. Many of them lack internet access and speak dialects for which official information has not been translated, so volunteers have been knocking on doors and trying to get the word out.

Don Toy, another community leader, has been setting up lunch orders for the residents of Cathay Manor, a senior living facility on Broadway. He gets the news to seniors by making announcements over the building's PA system. It's been tough persuading the seniors to stay at home because many define themselves by their routines. Autonomy is something they've worked hard for, and some of them don't have their families around to help, Toy said.

On Tuesday, I reached out to Kristin Fukushima, managing director of the Little Tokyo Community Council. In Little Tokyo, she said, the widespread move to working remotely has eliminated the weekday lunch crowd that many businesses rely on. The council is trying to organize donations and deliveries of food, toilet paper, and other materials to seniors in Little Tokyo Towers, Miyako Gardens, and several other facilities. Other volunteers are translating emergency information into Japanese and Korean and compiling a list of resources for small businesses as well as ways for people to support them. When I see Fukushima and others working around the clock, leading Zoom calls with dozens of volunteers and sending e-mails at 3 a.m., I'm reminded that ethnic communities in Los Angeles have always relied on a human safety net made of people like Fukushima, Toy, and Cheung. That human safety net needs your support more than ever right now.

When this country faces an existential threat, fear looks for a target.

On Wednesday, a few hours after President Trump insisted on labeling the virus a Chinese virus in a news conference, I spoke with Jack Lee, whose son attends the fourth grade at a mostly white elementary school in Orange County.

During a basketball game, two classmates accused his son of having the coronavirus. Lee's son said a curse word in response, and of the three children, he was punished by school authorities most harshly.

Lee was angry. He wrote a long letter to the principal. He made sure to tell his son that it was OK to defend himself. He's never had to talk with his son about race before. His own parents, immigrants from Taiwan, never had to talk to him about it either. But now he's looking for the right words, Lee said.

"I think there are some deeper conversations we're going to need to have," Lee said.

On Thursday, I spoke with Andy Lam, part-owner of Alice's Kitchen, a popular Hong Kong restaurant in Monterey Park. Asian neighborhoods like those in the San Gabriel Valley have been experiencing slowdowns for several weeks already because media reports and public comments about the virus have repeatedly associated the coronavirus with Asian culture, food, and identity.

Now, "closed temporarily" signs are being replaced by "for lease" signs. Lam, who worked for years in the restaurant supply business, said he knew of more than a dozen Chinese restaurants that had already closed. He had to send most of his employees home, and he and two other co-owners of the restaurant are working the kitchen themselves to field the rare take-out order. His friends are asking one another whether they should buy a gun.

The most stressful part is not knowing what the government will do next, Lam said.

"If they order us to shut down, there's nothing we can do," Lam said. "I can't even tell you how long we will last."

At the end of the day, I called my mother, who works at a hospital in Northern California. I asked her to stay home, but her boss told her if she didn't show up, she would lose her job. At work, patients sometimes refuse to be seen by her, because suddenly an Asian woman in a face mask is a threat.

On Friday, I talked to Khinn Muy Ung, 52, who worked as a dealer at Hollywood Park Casino until March 14, when widespread quarantine measures were announced and she lost her job. She's not sure if she'll have work when the restrictions lift.

On top of that, she lives in a building in Chinatown where for the last year landlords have been trying to evict a population of low-income seniors, mostly of Southeast Asian descent.

Volunteers from the Chinatown Community for Equitable Development organized the tenants to protest at the landlord's multimillion-dollar home in Brentwood last October. The landlord sold the property, but the new landlord was no different.

And so in February, as officials announced the first confirmed cases of coronavirus in California, she received another 60-day notice to move out.

Ung said she had no place else to go. Her family lives far away, and she can't afford market rent for a one-bedroom apartment, especially now that she has no money coming in. Her rice costs have doubled since her Chinatown grocery store, Ai Hoa, closed. And she's scared. A few weeks ago, she was jogging in the park and a man followed her, shouting that she was Chinese and blaming her for bringing the virus to America.

"I just pray to God. Just let us live," Ung said. "Let us have peace. I don't understand what's going on."

Ung is a survivor who has dealt with fear and helplessness before, as a young girl in Cambodia during the genocide of the 1970s. She survived the long walk through the countryside to refugee camps in Thailand. She's dodged bullets and land mines and endured beatings and starvation.

But she doesn't know how she'll survive this. A war you can run from, but eviction, layoffs, racism and a lethal new virus?

"It's too much, Frank," Ung said. "It's just too much."

She's crying now, and all of a sudden I'm crying too, stuck here in my apartment, where I've been for two weeks, one self-quarantining man with a keyboard, working on an article that will either add to the noise or be drowned out by it.

I tell her I agree, it is too much, it's not fair. But there's nothing else to say, so I don't say anything, and for a minute, we're just on the phone, crying together.

Frank Shyong, "Coronavirus Devastation Immigrants," reprinted by permission from the Los Angeles Times, March 23, 2020.

ACTIVITY: Analyzing the Rhetorical Situation

1. The COVID-19 pandemic has triggered crises of all kinds. What is the danger of replacing the term "COVID-19" with the "Chinese Virus"?
2. Without overgeneralizing, what audience do you think may be likely to respond favorably to Shyong's evaluation? To Trump's analysis? What audiences may be resistant to either or both of these opinions?
3. What resources does Shyong have as a communicator speaking out on this issue? How does he take advantage of these resources in the way he crafts his statements?
4. What change of attitude or behavior do you think Shyong hoped to accomplish in writing this piece? How does he go about encouraging that change? How might he have reported on public sentiment differently if he wanted to accomplish a different goal?

The Advent Posada Is an Act of Resistance

ARTURO J. BAÑUELAS

A Latino theologian and founder and chair of the HOPE Border Institute, Father Arturo José Bañuelas published this column—a proposal—in the National Catholic Reporter *on December 10, 2019. In it, he relates the nativity story of Jesus's birth in a stable (because there was no room at the inn) to contemporary issues of migration at the border, proposing that we accept migrants in remembrance of Mary, Joseph, and Jesus—and as acts of solidarity with all of humanity. Father Bañuelas is currently the pastor of St. Mark's Parish in the diocese of El Paso, Texas, where he is widely recognized for his work on issues of migration and justice.*

Courtesy of Arturo J. Banuelas

During Advent, all along both sides of the U.S.–Mexico border, families celebrate the popular posadas tradition. For nine evenings, families and friends reenact the search of Joseph and the pregnant Blessed Mother for lodging only to experience rejection. This practice is grounded in a fleeting reference in the Gospel of Luke whereby Mary laid the baby in a manger "because there was no place for them in the inn." (Luke 2:7)

The procession of families and neighbors is led by statues of Joseph and Mary or by youth dressed in costumes as the holy couple followed by the faithful praying the rosary and singing special hymns. They visit three neighborhood homes asking for posada, lodging. The pilgrims are rejected in the first two homes but welcomed in the last home where the fiesta begins and all sing "Jesus is welcomed into our heart."

(CNS photo/Nancy Wiechec)

People from the United States and Mexico take part in a "posada," the commemoration of Mary and Joseph's search for shelter in this Dec. 20, 2015 photo taken in Nogales, Mexico. The annual Nogales event held by the Kino Border Initiative and Dioceses without Borders reflected on the struggles of migrants and migrant families.

Today this posada tradition has special significance for our church because this same pattern of rejection is being lived by the over 55,000 refugees and asylum seekers who are literally knocking at our nation's door. At points of entry like the *Paso del Norte International Bridge* they ask for entrance, but our doors are shut to them. The "remain in Mexico" policy is forcing these vulnerable travelers to wait in dangerous Mexican border cities as their immigration cases are played out, and thousands more wait before they can even file an asylum claim.

These migrants, refugees, and asylum seekers are forced to flee and seek a better life for their families because of violence, hunger, death threats, extreme poverty, and severe climate and natural catastrophes in their countries of origin. Visiting the refugees at the *Paso del Norte International Bridge*, I saw individuals and families living on the streets with plastic makeshift tents as homes. I witnessed children without shoes, a baby with a high fever, and many others sick and suffering from the cold and hunger. One father with his wife and two sons told me that he left his home because thugs put a gun to his head demanding more money than he had. They told him they would return later for more money and if he did not provide it, they would kill his family.

He fled to the United States and was turned back at the border bridge. For three months the family has been waiting in inclement weather to file a claim for asylum. The father told me, "It hurts me to see my family suffer living here on the streets, but I had no choice. We will endure what we have to. God help us!" As a nation, we can surely do better in the way we treat those looking for room at the inn.

The border wall and unjust immigration policies signal, "You are not welcome in the United States, in our country." These racist policies continue to cause suffering and death by targeting our migrant communities. Sadly, xenophobia and hostility to immigrants have always been a defining character of our country, we default to an excuse that there is "no place for them in the inn." For this reason, for us to celebrate the posadas is an act of resistance and protest against racism and xenophobic policies and actions. Posadas call us to practice a profound solidarity that embraces the stranger as brother and sister worthy of being treated with dignity and respect. Posadas can be an example of subverting racism through solidarity, a solidarity experienced in accompanying the vulnerable Holy Family through rejection to welcome.

Solidarity takes us into a deeper place by getting us out of our comfort zones, out of the way we are used to thinking about the poor and marginalized. Solidarity invites us to enter into the lives of those who struggle by making their suffering and pain our own. You suffer therefore I suffer! Real solidarity allows their struggles, their stories, their dreams and their plights to penetrate deeply into our very soul.

In effect our lives are transformed when we recognize that those who are poor, vulnerable, and struggling are our teachers for justice—with a claim on our hearts and resources.

A real encounter of solidarity is mutual, and in this mutuality we become part of each other's lives. We learn from each other, and in the process we both become more fully human, more able to flourish together. These moments of transformation awaken us to each other and mystically open us to the Divine all around us and in us. Such solidarity requires commitments to foster just immigration reform, to be grateful for the gifts immigrants bring to our communities, to confront honestly a racist dark side of our national history. Solidarity lived in compassion manifests when we collectively embrace each other, especially the stranger, with dignity and respect, when we welcome a new moment of incarnate love into our lives.

Posadas in Advent, as an act of resistance, help us to see the world as it is, how it could be, and how it will be. The fiesta that comes at the end of each evening, where the Holy Family and pilgrims find welcome and lodging at last, eschatologically anticipates that time when hate, fear, and racism will be overcome by justice. Each night the posada celebrates a new hope arising in a future filled with God's plans for a reign of peace because there really is a place for all at the inn.

> Posadas in Advent, as an act of resistance, help us to see the world as it is, how it could be and how it will be.

Originally published by National Catholic Reporter. Reprinted with permission.

ACTIVITY: Analyzing the Rhetorical Situation

1. To what rhetorical opportunity is Bañuelas responding? How does he frame the opportunity?

2. Bañuelas expresses his admiration for border initiatives and his disagreement with U.S. immigration policy. What reasons does he provide for his disagreement? What did you learn from his reasoning?

3. How does Bañuelas establish himself as a credible authority on this controversial topic? Does his tone as he responds to other viewpoints affect your reaction to his credibility? What about his status as a priest? What other factors influence his credibility?

4. Who do you think is Bañuelas primary audience? How does he build sympathy for his position with this audience?

5. Imagine that you are a staunch advocate for anti-immigration policy. What parts of Bañuelas's essay would you find most offensive? Most persuasive? Now imagine you are a staunch opponent of such policies. What points persuade you, and where might you challenge his reasoning?

Community Connections

1. Your church, campus, or town undoubtedly has unrest or upheaval of some kind, strong dissatisfaction related to the pandemic response, jobless numbers, racial justice, or immigration. Look through your local newspaper and identify one such incident of unrest. What rhetorical opportunity for change does this incident present? What is one possible fitting response to that opportunity? Be prepared to share your answer with the rest of the class.

2. Regardless of your stance on immigration, what did you learn from these readings that surprised you? What do you understand now that you didn't before? What specific information changed or expanded your thinking? How might you apply your new (or renewed) stance on immigration? Be prepared to share your findings with the rest of the class.

3. Look for stories in the news and evaluate the ways people of different cultures and ethnicities are depicted, using some of the kinds of criteria for evaluating these depictions as you found in some of the essays in this chapter. Be prepared to share your findings with the rest of the class.

28 How Young People Are Changing the Climate Conversation

LEARNING OBJECTIVES

- Summarize the argument of each essay on climate change, identifying the opportunities for change that young people want to address.
- Synthesize information from all the essays to formulate a well-supported stance on a complicated subject.
- Develop the capacity to read long essays and complex infographics closely and critically.
- Apply information from all these essays to various genres.

Perhaps some good things about the 2020 novel coronavirus pandemic are that many people are staying in, slowing down, and reflecting on their place on earth. Whether enforced or voluntary, quarantine is affecting the way some people perceive the outdoors, especially when they realize just how much they took the environment for granted. Perhaps, more than ever, people are determined to get outside, to ride bikes, take walks, and sit on their porches. When they are out now, they talk about appreciating the height of trees, the brilliance of the night sky, the bears and mountain lions loping down their streets, the colors and smells of nature. Photos from around the globe show us clearer waters of Venice's Grand Canal, cleaner air in China, and the lift of pollution in big cities all across the United States.

When marine biologist Rachel Carson published her landmark *Silent Spring* in 1962, she established herself as one of the first (if not the first) in America to argue for the protection of our environment, our climate. That initial book (followed by several more books and many scientific papers) launched the environmental movement in the United States, the first Earth Day in 1970, the creation of the Environmental Protection Agency, and fed directly into what is now referred to as environmental justice. Pollution, ozone depletion, responsible land use, acid rain, and global warming are just a few of the issues propelling the conversations about climate change.

In 2019 Swedish teenager Greta Thunberg (pronounced, *tOOn-bairyeh*) began skipping school on Fridays to stand outside the Parliament building to protest adult irresponsibility and inaction in the face of climate change, specifically that Swedish legislators (much like those all around the globe) were breaking their pledges to the 2015 Paris [Climate] Agreement. She held a sign reading "Skolstrejk for Klimatet" (School Strike for Climate), which soon caught the attention of other young people, who started their own school strikes, #FridaysForFuture. Around the globe, young people, many not old enough to vote, are demonstrating a high level of political and social awareness of—and direct action with regard to—climate change. After all, as they often remark, the older generations have failed them, have stolen their future.

In the following series of essays, young writers enter the climate-change conversation. Together, Thunberg, the National Young Farmers Coalition, the Young Evangelicals for Climate Action, the Youth Climate Movement, and many others comprise an international, youth-driven movement that can be described as The Great Green Hope for our planet. In September 2019, some six million people around the world, representing over 160 countries and all seven continents, participated in the Global Climate Strike that was inspired by Thunberg. The following five essays, all focusing on the ways youth have entered the climate-change conversation, analyze the causes and effects of climate change and propose initiatives for addressing some of these problematic effects. After you read these selections, your instructor may call on you to respond to one of the following opportunities for writing.

1. These essays all challenge current ways of thinking about climate change. Which one issue raised in these essays bothers you the most, invites your rhetorical response to an opportunity for change? In an investigative report, begin by describing the issue at hand, offering a tentative thesis. pages 110–127 (See CHAPTER 7, INVESTIGATIVE REPORTS.) You will want to conduct research— library, online, and possibly in the field (with interviews and your own observations)—in order to establish the necessary facts, details, and direct quotations that help explain the significance of the issue you are investigating. As you develop your thesis (and consider your examples and evidence), take care to acknowledge various perspectives on the issue.

2. How do the theses of the Young Farmers Coalition and the Young Evangelicals for Climate Change align (or not) with yours? Take about

ten minutes to respond to their essays, arriving at your own position on the topic. Be prepared to write a position argument on what you believe should be the relationship between activism and climate change. (See CHAPTER 8, POSITION ARGUMENTS.) As you shape your argument, you will need to describe the problem and how it affects your audience, emphasize pages 128–149 why addressing the problem now is important, and state a thesis. In your position argument, you will outline the major assertions that develop your thesis and support those assertions with specific evidence and examples (facts, figures, quotations, narratives). Even as you acknowledge opposing viewpoints, you will want to reinforce to your audience the benefits of supporting your position.

3. Consider Elaine Kamarck's critical analysis of the resistance to climate change by many who believe that "climate change" is just another term for "weather patterns." Take ten minutes to define and describe problematic aspects related to this issue, explain its significance to you and your audience, and then propose a solution for addressing, supporting, or resolving this resistance. If you decide to develop this draft into a formal proposal, take time to discuss the feasibility of your proposal in terms of time, money, effort, and acceptance as well as address possible objections. (See CHAPTER 9, PROPOSALS.) pages 150–166

Greta Thunberg Wants You—Yes, You—to Join the Climate Strike

LUCY DIAVOLO

Lucy Diavolo is the politics and news editor for Teen Vogue *and covers the climate activist Greta Thunberg in this profile published September 16, 2019. The article helped to give Greta a platform to call for participation in the global climate strike set to begin on September 20.*

I'm on the subway headed to Manhattan to meet Greta Thunberg, the 16-year-old Swedish climate activist who pioneered the climate strike movement, and I'm absolutely kicking myself for forgetting my travel mug. The iced coffee I'm sipping is in a single-use plastic cup—straw and all—and here I am on my way to meet arguably the most visible climate activist in the world.

> "If there is one day you should join, this is the day."

Having completed a transatlantic journey by sailboat, Greta is scheduled to speak at the United Nations General Assembly's Climate Action Summit, another chance she'll have to make her no-nonsense appeal to world leaders about the urgent necessity of international action on the climate crisis. She's famous for being ruthlessly frank with the global elite, so when I meet her in a midtown conference

Per Grunditz/Shutterstock.com

STOCKHOLM, SWEDEN—MARCH 22, 2019: Sixteen-year-old Swedish climate activist Greta Thunberg demonstrating in Stockholm on Fridays. Holding a sign that says "School Strike for Climate."

room on a recent Friday morning, I'm surprised to find a reserved young woman who speaks softly after carefully considering each question I ask.

What's less surprising is the steadfast confidence and grave seriousness that emanates from this teenager who has given voice to an entire generation's existential fear and energized a worldwide movement demanding everything necessary and possible to save our planet.

Asked about how she's liked her visit to the States since her August 28 arrival, she praises the "really nice" people. Other highlights: keeping up her routine of unwinding with long walks by strolling through Central Park and visiting New York's museums, including her (fitting) favorite, the American Museum of Natural History.

But she does have one note about the city that could apply to much of the United States: "You're obsessed with air conditioning."

A Global Sensation Tackling a Global Threat

Greta is shy and serious in person. She considers questions and gives thoughtful answers. I see this during our Friday interview and again on Monday, September 9, when she's on stage with journalist and activist Naomi Klein at an event sponsored by *The Intercept*. The event spotlighted Greta in conversation

with Klein, but also featured Xiuhtezcatl, Vic Barrett, and Xiye Bastida—all accomplished climate activists age 20 or under who each offered a vision of their life in 2029 were the Green New Deal to be enacted.

The line stretches down a city block to get into the auditorium at the New York Society for

Greta Thunberg in New York. Sixteen-year-old activist Greta Thunberg during climate chat with Naomi Klein, sponsored by The Intercept, *September 10, 2019.*

In her introduction ahead of their talk, Klein calls Greta "one of the great truth-tellers of this or any time" and praises her bravery for calling out the world's rich and powerful to their faces at the World Economic Forum in Davos earlier this year. Greta takes the stage to a standing ovation and talks with Klein about the climate strikes, her Asperger's diagnosis, and her boat trip to the States, which she says was lengthy but worth it for the sights of wildlife and the view of the stars she got out on the open ocean.

Ethical Culture. The pew-like seating and giant halo-shaped chandelier overhead lend a vague religious overtone to the evening. While some might think these youthful climate activists are preaching to the choir, at the moment, it feels more like they are speaking gospel.

One on one, Greta comes off as skeptical of the attention she receives. But in front of a full house that prizes activist sensibilities, that skepticism makes her a dynamo. The crowd loves her for laughing off online trolls and for researching absurd conspiracy theories about herself.

Fighting for the Future, Living in the Now

Greta is in a line of work that can be notoriously difficult: Activists often struggle to support themselves in the long term, and the emotional toll of the work can be a serious burden to bear.

She's been open in the past about how she entered activism as she was coming out of a very serious period of depression where she wasn't eating or speaking. Just days before we sat down to chat, she had shared on Instagram how she's been bullied for having Asperger's syndrome, calling out "haters"

> **"I have Asperger's syndrome and that means I'm sometimes a bit different from the norm. And—given the right circumstances—being different is a superpower."**

and writing in a caption, "I have Asperger's syndrome and that means I'm sometimes a bit different from the norm. And—given the right circumstances—being different is a superpower."

Klein asks Greta about this, too—and Greta explains that the way her brain operates can empower her as a climate activist.

"Without [my Asperger's syndrome], I wouldn't have noticed this crisis," Greta says. She tells Klein that after recognizing the climate crisis for what it was, she felt she had no other choice but to take action. She sees that drive, and that of other climate activists she knows on the autism spectrum, as evidence that there's something about the condition that makes for good activists.

"I think it has something to do with we walk the walk and we don't have the distance from what we know and what we say to what we do and how we act," Greta says. "And without my diagnosis, I also wouldn't have been such a nerd, and then I wouldn't have had the time and energy to look through the boring facts and still be interested."

Back in the midtown conference room on Friday, I ask Greta if she views her experience with depression as a potential source of a superpower, too, and she tells me how, even if being different can cause depression, she views it as a strength.

"Depression is something that often people who are different suffer from, either because they work too much or because they are being bullied because they are different or just because they don't feel right in this society—that they feel everything is meaningless," she says. "That is often the people who think a bit outside the box and who can see things from a different, new perspective."

"We need these people, especially now, when we need to change things and we can't see it just from where we are. We need to see it from a bigger perspective and from outside our current systems," she explains. "That's why people who are different are so necessary: because they contribute so much. Therefore, we need to really look after the people who are different and who may not be heard. We need to listen to them and to look after each other."

Climate Change or System Change?

Greta's weekly strikes started outside of her home country's parliament in August 2018. In those early days, it was just her. But she has become a focal point for a youth movement that is taking over the world. Just after our initial interview, Greta joined local climate strikers in New York for the second week in a row.

I ask Greta if she thinks people with economic security in richer countries have any special responsibility to the climate movement, and she tells me she does.

"We have to lead because we have already built infrastructure that other countries need to build, and it takes carbon dioxide to build that infrastructure and to make sure that people in poorer countries can be able to heighten

Just 25 companies have acounted for more than half of global industrial emissions since 1988.

their standard of living," she says. "We have to also give [poorer countries] the opportunity to adapt [to climate crisis], because, otherwise, it doesn't make any sense."

The issue of systemic change is on a lot of climate activists' minds. In 2017, the Carbon Majors Database compiled a list of the largest institutional sources of global greenhouse-gas emissions, finding that just 25 companies have accounted for more than half of global industrial emissions since 1988. Environmental groups have seized on these numbers as evidence of the systemic nature of carbon emissions.

"We young people are building this up," Greta says, making it clear that the strikes are a message to world leaders. "They always say they have listened to us, so this is a chance for them to prove it."

Greta generally operates from a place of granting authority to science. Klein asks about her insistence that she's not prescribing action for political leaders, but just asking them to listen to the science. Greta replies that she vets her speeches with scientists—asking them to check not just for factual accuracy but also for misunderstandings or clarifications. Even if she's taking a year off of school, she's clearly still doing her homework.

Klein is an expert on the climate crisis in her own right. The author of books like *This Changes Everything: Capitalism vs. The Climate* and *On Fire: The (Burning) Case for the Green*

New Deal, she has been a powerful voice connecting our political and economic systems to the climate crisis. She tells me backstage before Monday's event that she believes the climate crisis is one outcome of the capitalist system, prompting me to consider the two side-by-side.

But the most political Greta gets during her conversation with Klein is when she's asked her about concerns within the Democratic Party that a climate response like the Green New Deal is too expensive.

"The money is there," Greta tells her. "If we can save the banks, we can save the world."

The Next Global Climate Strike

Ahead of her speech at the UN Climate Action Summit on September 23, Greta is also trying to get the word out about the next global climate strike, set to begin on September 20, the latest major action in the climate movement's world-saving gambit. She hopes that more people than ever will take the day to strike from work or school.

She tells *Teen Vogue* that whether it's the Swedish government, major corporations, or the United Nations General Assembly, climate strikers are trying to generate political momentum to address the climate crisis—to push governments, corporations, and fellow citizens to do "what is required and what is possible."

"Please think about it from a bigger perspective," she says when I ask if she has advice for those unsure about joining the September 20 strike. "Not just from today but imagine yourself in about 20 or 30 years. How do you want to look back at your life? Do you want to be able to say that you did fight

against it and tried to push for a change early on? Or do you want to say that, 'No, I just went on going like everyone else because it was too uncomfortable.'"

"If you can't be in the strike, then, of course, you don't have to," she continues. "But I think if there is one day you should join, this is the day."

The fact that "perspective" came up twice during our interview doesn't surprise me, nor does it surprise me that Greta talks about the view of the stars from her sailboat or the way she views Asperger's like her superpower. Youth climate activists have a way of giving those of us who might be older and more jaded the perspective to see the potential for a future without crisis, but meeting Greta affirms that this is about more than just hijacking youthful optimism. It is about welcoming the perspective of a generation that is fighting for its own future—for the right to live.

> Youth climate activists [are] about welcoming the perspective of a generation that is fighting for the right to live.

Lucy Diavolo, Teen Vogue © Conde Nast

ACTIVITY: Analyzing the Rhetorical Situation

1. In one sentence, what is Thunberg's main argument (a stated or implied thesis statement)? Write it out. What supporting evidence does she employ to support this thesis statement? Make a list. What details convince you that Thunberg may be right? What additional information would you need to be convinced?

2. In Diavolo's profile of Thunberg, what details are included that enhance (or not) Thunberg's ethos? What evidence does Diavalo include that establishes the logos of Thunberg's argument? What—if anything—is missing from that evidence? What strategies does Diavalo use to develop the pathos of Thunberg's argument? How might you apply these strategies of establishing ethos, logos, and pathos in your own writing, especially in a profile?

3. How did the use of the interview naturally shape the way you read Diavalo's profile? Make a list of the specific ways the author directed you to understand about Thunberg, the movement, and climate change. As you consider those directions, what are your intellectual and emotional responses to them? How did those directions change the way you consider the subject and issues? For what reasons might an author choose to use an interview as the basis of a profile essay?

4. What particular audience does Diavalo address in this essay? How does she reach this audience? What is Diavalo's purpose in addressing this specific audience? How might someone who holds a completely different view respond to this essay?

5. Would you describe this profile essay as providing information, analysis, evaluation, explanation—or what? Using evidence from the text itself, explain what makes it so.

Young Farmers Call for Climate Action

NATIONAL YOUNG FARMERS COALITION

The National Young Farmers Coalition was established in 2010 as an advocacy network dedicated to tackling the obstacles that prevent young people from building careers in agriculture. In September 2019, they published their proposal for taking climate action.

Young Farmers and Ranchers across the Country Are Working to Solve the Climate Crisis. Join Us.

The thousands of young farmers and ranchers in our 45 chapters across the country began careers in agriculture for manifold reasons: to grow healthier food for their communities; to steward the land, water, and natural resources for future generations; to support their families; to honor their ancestors; or out of a love for working outdoors, with livestock, or with their hands. Many of these farmers tell us that despite the long hours, hard physical labor, and low pay, the fulfillment they feel from planting seeds and helping them grow to harvest, or selling the meat and eggs they raised at market, has not diminished since their very first season.

The Call to Farming Is as Diverse as the Individuals in Our Coalition, but the Future of Every Young Farmer in Our Country Is Singularly Challenged by the Climate Crisis.

This year, as thousands of Midwest farms recover from historic floods, farmers along the coasts struggle to rebuild from hurricanes and record-breaking heat waves, and producers throughout the West manage drought and the constant threat of wildfire, the impacts of the climate crisis on U.S. agriculture demand immediate action.

As we come together to address this global emergency, farmers must be centered in these critical conversations. Without rapid and coordinated response, the consequences will be dire: farmers and ranchers will be unable to produce the food, fiber, and fuel we all rely on.

From its inception in 2010, the National Young Farmers Coalition (Young Farmers) has brought farmers together to tackle the obstacles preventing us from building successful careers in agriculture. If we do not take coordinated action now to address the climate crisis, a livable future for beginning farmers and ranchers, and all of us, is gravely at risk.

The Damaging Effects of Climate Change on Agriculture Are Escalating, and the Time to Act Is Now.

Of the 3,500 young farmer respondents to our 2017 National Young Farmer Survey,

66% reported experiencing unpredictable weather patterns, more severe storms, increased pest pressure, increased uncertainty in water supply, and/or increased rate of disease, which they attributed to climate change.

Resultant ecosystem disturbances, crop loss, reduction in cultivated acreage, compromised livestock health and production, and reduced nutritional content of staple crops threaten agricultural productivity and profitability, human health, and the U.S. economy as a whole.

It was noted that 2019 has been the wettest year and July 2019 the hottest month on record for the planet, and extreme weather events are only projected to increase in severity and frequency over the coming decades. These increasingly unpredictable weather patterns are amplifying economic risk for farmers in an industry with already thin margins.

In the almost ten years that I've been farming, the entire growing season is shifting. It's been so much wetter than people are used to. Rain events used to be gentle—long and drizzly—now we see big, windy downpours and much more violent rain and weather events. In 2016, the second half of my season was flooded out. We got 11 inches of rain overnight and the river rose 14 feet.

—Hannah Breckbill, Humble Hands Harvest, Decorah, Iowa

Policymakers, advocates, corporate stakeholders, and all of us who support a brighter future for agriculture must work together to achieve effective climate solutions. Farmers and farm workers don't just need a seat at the table in these

Climate change is not just a future threat—it is here now and disrupting food production across the country and the globe.

discussions—we need comprehensive climate policy that recognizes the people who are putting climate solutions into action on the millions of acres they steward across the country. Farmers stand witness to climate patterns and disruptions and can share unique and valuable insight into the impacts climate change is having on food production, ecology, and rural communities. In short, we need climate policy that acknowledges the exceptional climate leadership capability of our young farmers.

An unpredictable climate future, coupled with the existing high barriers to entry for beginning farmers—including burdensome student loan debt, land access challenges, limited capital, unaffordable health insurance, and lack of skilled labor—will further deter talented young people from launching careers in agriculture unless we take action now.

Climate and Land Access

The U.S. lost nearly 70,000 farms and over 14 million acres of farmland between 2012 and 2017 (USDA, 2017 Census of Agriculture). Finding access to high-quality, affordable farmland is the top challenge for young farmers across the country, and our work to increase affordable and secure land tenure for young farmers is made all the more urgent by the climate crisis.

> Getting young farmers and ranchers on U.S. farmland is a necessary first step in the fight to mitigate climate change.

Increasing the number of young farmers on the land is our best hope for breaking the cycle of farmland loss and unlocking the powerful climate-fighting potential of U.S. soils.

Land use and climate change interact in a series of direct and deleterious cycles. The accelerating trend of development and farmland loss, occurring at a rate of 1.5 million acres per year, reduces the atmospheric carbon sequestration potential of U.S. agricultural soils. In addition to its capacity for carbon sequestration, land is also necessary for maintaining regional food production, food security, water retention, heat absorption, and air quality.

Research from the American Farmland Trust indicates that development occurs disproportionately on soils rated the highest for productivity, versatility, and resiliency—the land best-suited to intensively produce a variety of crops with least environmental impact now comprises less than 17% of the total land area in the continental United States. At the same time that farmland is being lost to development, the impacts of climate change are further degrading the soil on remaining, more marginal lands through processes of erosion, salinization, desertification, and disruption of water cycles.

Taking Farmland Out of Agriculture Denies Us the Opportunity to Unlock the Tremendous Climate Mitigation and Adaptation Potential of U.S. Soils.

Improving soil health through incorporation of perennial crops, conservation tillage, rotational grazing, cover cropping, and boosting soil organic matter is a promising strategy for sequestering carbon, and is only possible if farmland stays in farming and farmers have the security they need to implement these practices.

The National Young Farmers Coalition posts stories of many young farmers on their website. Twenty-six-year-old Andrew Barsness describes organic farming in the National Young Farmer Coalition's Heart and Grain series: Heart and Grain: Andrew Barsness, Hoffman, MN.

Setting Climate Policy that Supports the Next Generation of Farmers and Ranchers

Young farmers and ranchers can have a transformational impact on mitigating climate change through building soil organic matter, reducing synthetic inputs, using more efficient irrigation systems, and other regenerative practices. Farmers need policies and programs that provide financial incentives and make mitigation strategies desirable and practical. Producers who already use these practices should be rewarded for the environmental services they provide.

Above all, farmers need to participate in the research and development of climate policies, and programs need to be adequately funded at the federal, state, and local levels. Farmer participation in the design of these programs paired with adequate funding is the only way to ensure that they will work in practice.

In a series of conversations with farmers, climate experts, agricultural researchers, and policy analysts conducted over the past five months, stakeholders called for specific actions to address the crisis, including:

- Additional funding and capacity for public agriculture and climate research;
- Reforming and increasing funding for existing federal and state conservation programs;
- Expanding extension services and technical assistance to producers on sequestering carbon and adapting to the changing climate;
- Expanding platforms for climate knowledge sharing through climate hubs, extension programs, and land-grant universities;
- Improving and increasing outreach for existing federal and state programs, especially to farmers of color, women, and beginning farmers; and
- Creating green payments to farmers and ranchers for ecosystem services.

As momentum builds for new climate policies and programs in Washington and at the state level, we urge policymakers to pass legislation that includes support for climate adaptation and mitigation in the agricultural sector. Farmers and ranchers should be centered in these policy discussions and given the opportunity to actively shape the climate policies and programs that directly affect them.

Climate Change Is a Social Justice Issue

The wealthiest nations and individuals contribute the vast majority of emissions driving climate change, and it is the most vulnerable communities that are least able to adapt due to limited resources, structural marginalization, and poverty. Crop loss, food shortages, distribution disruption, and eventual increases in food prices and access will impact communities of color and low-income communities first.

Climate change exacerbates food justice issues and inequality.

Many traditional and indigenous farming practices, such as cover cropping, crop rotation, intercropping, agroforestry, organic composting, and integrating crop-animal agriculture, have been "climate-smart" for thousands of years. Some indigenous, black, refugee, and immigrant farmers have voiced that elements of their cultural farming practices are now seen as important tools for mitigating climate change, yet they were not compensated for their knowledge and some were pressured to abandon these practices by farm advisors or indirectly through market pressure to produce higher yields (2019 California Young Farmers Report).

Climate change is largely the result of rampant exploitation of natural resources, which has run parallel to the exploitation of farmworker labor and farming communities throughout American history. This trend continues today through a system of unjust agricultural labor compensation and protections in the United States. Climate change also poses many threats to farmer and farmworker health and labor productivity due to extreme heat exposure, poor air quality, and smoke inhalation and asthma due to increased wildfire activity. The urgency of the climate crisis should be addressed in parallel with the urgency to build equity across the food system. Climate solutions and policies should also revalue and include the concerns of historically underserved, disadvantaged, and exploited communities.

Young Farmers Are Building Stronger, Climate-Resilient Businesses

While the latest IPCC report estimates that food production contributes 37% of total greenhouse gas emissions, there is a long list of time-tested farming and ranching practices that can stem climate change, and meet the three goals of climate-smart agriculture: adaptation, mitigation, and productivity. Though climate solutions differ across regions and on every scale of operation, each farm can take steps toward meeting these goals.

Our farmer leaders are already engaging in federal- and state-level policy advocacy to fight for climate solutions across the country and are using many climate-smart strategies on their farms and ranches. In our 2019 California Young Farmers Report, farmers reported implementing a variety of techniques to build resilience and sequester carbon.

During the 2019 legislative session, our farmer members and New Mexico staff

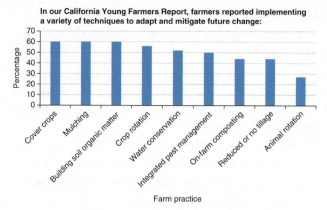

In our California Young Farmers Report, farmers reported implementing a variety of techniques to adapt and mitigate future change:

Farm practice categories (left to right): Cover crops, Mulching, Building soil organic matter, Crop rotation, Water conservation, Integrated pest management, On-farm composting, Reduced or no tillage, Animal rotation

Farm Practices Implemented to Adapt and Mitigate Future Change
Source: 2019 California Young Farmers Report.

joined over fifty partner organizations led by the NM Healthy Soils Working Group to pass the *Healthy Soils Act* (HB 204). This piece of legislation will help promote education and outreach about climate and environmental benefits of improving soil health, as well as statewide implementation of soil health practices such as cover cropping, composting, and low-till methods.

Graham Christensen, a Coalition member in Nebraska, converted his family's fifth-generation corn and soybean operation to no-till. "We as farmers have such a great opportunity to be in a leading role in reducing emissions through good practices," he said, "Trying to improve the productivity and quality of our soil is becoming a much heavier focus."

Many young farmers across the country are employing climate-smart strategies not only out of a sense of environmental urgency, but because they make the most economic sense

for their farm businesses. The increased consumer demand for sustainably grown products, savings on inputs and irrigation achievable with improved soil health, and profits attainable through integration of on-farm renewable energy production are only a few of the many opportunities for boosting farm income.

Investing in America's young farmers is a direct and efficient way to protect the future of agriculture and our environment, to improve our country's climate resilience, generate affordable renewable energy, and to help rural communities benefit from the value of carbon sequestration and other important ecosystem services.

The Young Farmers Coalition sent a package of camera equipment to beginning farmers for its Bootstrap series. Young farmers filmed their farms and told their stories, which were then posted on the Young Farmers Coalition website. This screenshot is from the video done for Clover Mead Farm, a dairy producer in western New York.

We Can't Achieve our Goal of a Bright and Just Future for U.S. Agriculture without Bold, Immediate Action on the Climate Crisis. Our Farms and Futures Depend on it.

The National Young Farmers Coalition supports climate policy change at all levels of government. We are committed to helping our farmers access the programs they need to protect their farms and livelihoods, and to amplifying their voices in advocacy for policies that will protect the future of agriculture from climate change and its devastating impacts.

We hope you will join us.

Reprinted with permission of National Young Farmers Coalition.

ACTIVITY: Analyzing the Rhetorical Situation

1. How do the Young Farmers contribute to the conversation on climate change? What is their (stated or implied) thesis statement? Write it out. What evidence do they use to support that point? Make a list and evaluate the relevance and credibility of that evidence.
2. What rhetorical strategies does the coalition use to establish its ethos, its good will, good sense, good moral character? Make a list and evaluate that evidence according to its effect on you. How effective is this coalition in demonstrating its importance and trustworthiness?
3. Make a list of the strategies you think would be most effective in appealing to their rhetorical audience; then see which set of strategies most resembles the strategies the coalition uses.
4. How does the coalition employ the rhetorical means of development? In what passages does it use which means and to what purpose? How might you use these methods in your own essay?

Generation Climate: Can Young Evangelicals Change the Climate Debate?

MEERA SUBRAMANIAN

Subramanian is an award-winning journalist whose articles on climate change have been featured in Nature, The New York Times, Audubon, USA Today, Smithsonian, The New Yorker, *and* Discover, *among others. She is the president of the Society of Environmental Journalists. This investigative report was published in* Inside Climate News, *a Pulitzer Prize–winning, non-profit, non-partisan news organization dedicated to covering climate change, energy, and the environment.*

For students at this top evangelical college, loving God means protecting creation. That includes dealing with the human sources of climate change.

Diego Hernandez wasn't thinking much about climate change until last summer, when he was traveling with his family along the Gulf

Coast in his home state of Texas, where his ancestors—cowboys and politicians, he said— reach back to the 1600s. His mother suggested they take the "scenic route" for that summer drive, Diego said, his fingers making air-quotes because there was nothing "scenic" about it. All he saw were oil refineries.

"At that moment," said 19-year-old Diego, who considers himself a libertarian, "the switch kind of flipped for me." Why are we putting refineries in this beautiful place? he thought. The impacts from Hurricane Harvey, which had hit Houston the previous August and had affected some of Diego's relatives, were also still lingering in his mind.

"I used to be like, oh, there's oil, go start drilling, you know, because of course it's all about the money, right?" he said, his voice tinged with sarcasm. But after that family outing, he began to ask questions—"What is it doing to our environment? How is it going to affect us in the next 10 to 50 years?"—and since then he's had climate change on his mind.

Diego is a clean-shaven, lifelong Christian wearing a cyan blue button-down and polished cowboy boots, and a sophomore at Wheaton College in Wheaton,

Illinois, which has been called the Harvard of Christian schools. The entrance sign, framed by a glowing bed of zinnias in full bloom, pronounces the school's motto: "For Christ and His Kingdom." But while Diego has all the credentials of a true political conservative— president of Wheaton's Young Americans for Freedom chapter, a cabinet member of the College Republicans—he also finds himself genuinely baffled by the right's stance against acting on climate change.

While many evangelicals are preoccupied with the long-term state of human souls and the protection of the unborn, Diego and the other students I met at Wheaton are also considering other eternal implications and a broader definition of pro-life. They are concerned about the lifespan of climate pollutants that will last in the atmosphere for thousands of years, and about the lives of the poor and weak who are being disproportionately harmed by the effects of those greenhouse gases. While Diego was just shy of eligible voting age in the 2016 presidential election, he's old enough to vote now. He and other young evangelicals thought hard this year about the politicians on offer, the issues they stand for, and who deserved their votes.

> Many evangelicals are preoccupied with the protection of the unborn . . . [; others are] considering eternal implications and a broader definition of pro-life.

What's an Evangelical to Do?

Evangelical Protestants—one in four American adults—are a political powerhouse. They are the single largest religious group in the nation, and they are nearly twice as likely to be Republican as Democrat. And while Baby Boomers are currently the strongest political voting bloc, that's only because the older you are, the more likely you are to vote.

The current crop of younger people— from Gen X to Millennials to the newly minted adults I met at Wheaton—are poised to dominate the eligible-voter body politic. They would definitely tip the voting scales—should they become engaged. There are signs they might be doing just that. From the Parkland school shooting victims to Millennial political candidates, the youth of America are speaking up. And, significantly, they accept the scientific consensus on climate change at a much higher rate than their elders.

This is true even of young evangelicals, as the existence of the Young Evangelicals for Climate Action (YECA) attests. YECA is a ministry of the Evangelical Environmental Network that aims to mobilize students, influence religious leaders, and pressure lawmakers into passing legislation to address climate change. I met Diego at a climate change discussion event on campus that was organized by Chelsey Geisz, a Wheaton junior and a YECA climate leadership fellow.

From Colorado Springs, Colorado, Chelsey, 20, always loved nature, she told me as we sat together in a gazebo in Adams Park, near campus. She'd taken a few classes on sustainability at Wheaton, and last year spent time working at Eighth Day Farm in Holland, Michigan, where Christian volunteers have turned the dirt once trapped below strip mall

pavement into garden plots to grow vegetables for the hungry. These experiences meant she was primed when she heard about YECA.

Though non-partisan, YECA is targeting conservatives, since that's where the facts of climate change have failed to lead to action. According to the organization, they've engaged more than 10,000 young evangelicals so far. Along with Chelsey, there are another half-dozen fellows at other schools across the country, helping to build the grassroots movement. The fellowship includes a summer training session that covers the science of climate change, as well as the socio-cultural and religious aspects of the issue. As a YECA fellow, Chelsey organizes campus events such as the session I attended in September and she serves as Wheaton's executive vice president of campus sustainability, a new position that YECA helped develop.

It can be tough to be an evangelical who cares about climate change, Chelsey said, "because the environmental activists don't trust you and the evangelicals hate you." Or they *could*

Chelsey Geisz, a leader in the Young Evangelicals for Climate Action ministry, uses YouTube to post Chelsey Geisz - Climate Testimony.

hate you; she was quick to point out that the evangelicals she knows personally are generally tolerant of her views. "I'm not encountering anyone at Wheaton, even among my most conservative friends, who disagree with climate change," she told me. She's having some trouble with her father, though, who's troubled by her YECA work. He holds a Harvard law degree, works at a company that invests in resource-rich properties, and associates Chelsey's transformation into a "climate activist" with a liberal agenda he finds suspect. "For a man who has such well-reasoned opinions, I just feel like there's so much emotion for him that it's not about the science at all," she said.

As for liberals themselves, Chelsey said, some of them do treat evangelicals like her with some suspicion. After all, aren't evangelicals the ones who elected anti-environment Trump?

"I think there's some misunderstanding about what our faith compels us to do," she said as the sun set behind her, creating a halo around the edges of her auburn hair.

Praising Natural Systems

Sean Lyon is a recent Wheaton graduate who was also a YECA fellow while he was in school. He feels that he was born to love the natural world; his first word as an infant was "bird," after all, and flying creatures remain a passion he can't quite explain. While in school, he created his own interdisciplinary major of biology and business and spent significant time in Tanzania working with ECHO East Africa, a faith-based sustainable agriculture organization. He still lives in the town of Wheaton, easy commuting distance to Chicago, where he's volunteering at the Field Museum of Natural History.

"If you focus too much on only a personal relationship being the core tenet of your faith, then it means that you're more easily able to marginalize topics like human suffering, which in some cases is spurred by climate change. We are embodied creatures in this planet, so let's live like we are," said Sean Lyon.

Sean, 23, grew up in upstate New York, among "classic North American white evangelicals," where climate was not a concern and politics were conservative. But his love of the natural world shifted his perspective. He saw heaven on earth, and something worth saving, in every wingbeat he witnessed.

"Every ecosystem carries His creativity in it," Sean said, "and every species is a mark of His design." He had a thick brass bangle encircling his wrist, and blue eyes behind clear Lucite-rimmed glasses. Sean drew an analogy to his sister and grandparents, who are all artists. "So how would I treat the art that they created? If I love them, then I'm going to treat their art well. I'm not going to deface it. I'm not going to ignore it. I'm going to really honor it. And so when I see my God as having created everything that I'm interacting with, I want to honor it because that's a way that I can show my love for this Creator."

But God didn't just create singular works, Sean said; he created systems, natural systems that every living being relies on. He hoped that all Christians—no, he corrected himself, all *faiths*—would unite to protect those systems.

"That's my current prayer."

> "Every ecosystem carries His creativity in it, and every species is a mark of His design."

"Structural Sin"

Climate science isn't questioned at Wheaton College the way it often is in the wider evangelical community. The school is a brick-and-mortar rebuttal to the myth that science and religion must be at odds with each other.

When Wheaton students step into their state-of-the-art science building, for instance, they are greeted with signs stating that a "sound Biblical theology gives us a proper basis for scientific inquiry," and a display featuring locally excavated Perry the Mastodon, which carbon dating shows to be more than 13,000 years old.

The school is not alone in intertwining commitments to love God and protect the earth, often referred to as "creation care." The Cape Town Commitment, a global agreement between evangelical leaders from nearly 200 countries, includes acknowledgment of climate change and how it will hurt the world's poor (and it is required reading for Wheaton freshmen). Katharine Hayhoe, an atmospheric scientist at Texas Tech University and an evangelical, has been an outspoken advocate for climate action. And in addition to YECA, there are numerous groups active in this arena, including the Evangelical Climate Initiative, Climate Caretakers, Care of Creation and A Rocha.

In late 2015, the National Association of Evangelicals (NAE)—the biggest umbrella group of evangelicals in the country, representing 43 million Americans—issued a statement accepting climate change, acknowledging the human contribution to it and encouraging action. YECA's advocacy helped bring that statement, called "Loving the Least of These," into being. In it, NAE argues that Christians should be compelled to care about climate change as a matter of social justice, equating those without the resources to adapt to failed farming or dry wells or rising seas as the modern-day equivalents of the widows and orphans of Jesus's day.

When Chelsey reads the Bible, she hears this gospel of social justice, too. "Instead of talking about climate change," she said of her work as a YECA fellow, "I talk about environmental justice. There's definitely a guilty complex, especially among the white evangelical community, about how complicit we've been, and apathetic. People really want to redeem that."

Chelsey's framing reveals that she is steeped in a liberal arts ethos friendly to intersectionality, the idea that humanity's ills, which disproportionately affect the most vulnerable, cannot be conquered until root causes are addressed. This perspective is shaping academic dialogue in both secular and faith-based schools.

But does fighting climate change detract from evangelism? Here there's a rift within the evangelical community. Should the emphasis be on saving souls or saving God's creation? And are the two really at odds?

"That's the Billy Graham evangelicalism," Chelsey said of the personal salvation perspective, referencing Wheaton's most famous alumnus. "It's your faith between you and Jesus." But the problem with that approach, she said, is that it doesn't force Christians to deal with larger systems of injustice. "The evangelical community is really limited when it comes to talking about systemic and structural sin rather than individual sin. Most of us have never heard about systemic racism and climate change in church," she said. Even as evangelical organizations embrace the need for action, the message isn't coming across from the pulpit. "These things never come up because they're apparently not gospel issues," Chelsey said, "But at Wheaton, we think they are."

For Sean, there's not one speck of conflict between his love of God and the gospel and his fierce desire to see action on climate change. They're complementary, he said.

"If you focus too much on only a personal relationship being the core tenet of your faith, then it means that you're more easily able to marginalize topics like human suffering, which in some cases is spurred by climate change," he said. "We are embodied creatures in this planet, so let's live like we are."

> "Instead of talking about climate change, I talk about environmental justice."

Could his concern for the climate be a threat to his faith? I asked him.

"Actually, I see more of a threat in the idea that we can divorce our lives on this earth and the lives of other people and the lives of other creatures from our life of faith," Sean said. Better to revel in God's love. "How much deeper and how much more beautiful is a way of loving Him that involves my whole being and the whole world around me rather than just simply the status of my soul?"

When Pro-Life Means Entire Lives

Abortion was the entry point into American politics for many evangelicals, after the Supreme Court affirmed abortion rights in *Roe v. Wade* in 1973. Before that, evangelicals were generally unconcerned about abortion rights, which had the uncontroversial support of Republicans; they were also generally disengaged from voting. Today, the single-issue anti-abortion preoccupation of many evangelicals, now considered a given by many political leaders, confounds some of the young evangelicals I met at Wheaton.

"If we say we're pro-life, we have to care for people who are experiencing incredible environmental degradation and so directly affected by climate change," Chelsey said. "If we're pro-life, that's a bigger issue to me than abortion."

Sean agreed. "So many people are now saying, okay, if you're going to be pro-life you have to be pro all-of-life, lifelong pro-life, which has primarily come up in the immigration debate. If you're pro-life, how can you be separating children from their parents?"

Diego sees it a little differently. "Abortion is definitely a deal-breaker for me," he said, even though he said he's not generally a one-issue voter. He echoed Sean and Chelsey to some degree, agreeing that "being pro-life doesn't just mean being pro-life to the baby at birth. It also means the life of the mother and the life of the baby after birth." But when he watched the 2016 presidential debates, he found himself agreeing with some of Hillary Clinton's points . . . until he was appalled by what he saw as her "gung-ho" support of abortion rights. He decided he could just not get behind someone with those views.

Young evangelicals wrestle with these difficult choices in the voting booth, confronted with either/or candidates, unsure who will best represent their hopes for life on earth, all life, all of God's creation. Right now, anti-abortion rights Christians typically have only one party to get behind. And it's that party, represented in the White House, that is aggressively rolling back climate protections, from pulling out of the Paris climate accord to promoting coal.

Future Powerhouse at the Polls?

Diego, Chelsey, and Sean are the future. This younger generation has grown up with the realities of climate change and political polarization since they were swinging on monkey bars, and they aren't hesitating to break rank with evangelical Baby Boomers on the issue.

They remain faithful and politically conservative for the most part, but they are more concerned about a climate that they will have to live with much longer than those boomers heading into retirement. The shift aligns with a recent Pew poll that found that among Republicans, young adults were far less likely than their elders to support reliance on fossil fuels.

"Every one of the people who I've talked to who's come to my events and engaged in climate issues from a Christian perspective said, 'My parents don't agree with me,'" Sean told me.

But even with this clear shift toward accepting climate science among young Americans, the quandary for young evangelicals in the voting booth remains.

Sean, who said he couldn't in good conscience vote for either party, opted for Jill Stein in 2016.

Chelsey, as a busy freshman in 2016, followed in her father's footsteps and voted for Trump. Her father had been singularly focused on getting a Republican on the Supreme Court. Now, she hangs her head about the decision.

Diego, about to vote in his first election, grew up in a struggling, hard-working family in San Antonio. His father showed him how to mow lawns when he was six, he said. His mother would pick up her raggedy old Bible and tell Diego, "This is what you should base all of your beliefs and all your values on. It shouldn't be what you hear from someone on TV or C-SPAN or NPR."

Surveys show that the way people view climate change is determined more by political affiliation, along with race and ethnicity, than by religious affiliation. So while 81 percent of white evangelicals voted for Donald Trump, it's important to remember that about a quarter of the country's evangelicals are not white, and it is among minority groups that the evangelical community is growing. And on the issue of climate change, Diego's Latino background makes him part of the American demographic that is most concerned about climate change. He

wonders whether his mother deliberately pushed for that "scenic route" to wake him up a little.

> This younger generation has grown up with the realities of climate change and aren't hesitating to break rank with evangelical Baby Boomers on the issue.

What are the choices for these faithful young? With church membership in decline and the Republican party in flux, how vocal these young people are could shape the future of the climate debate. If the Christian right wants to hold onto the next generation, getting right with the planet might prove as important as getting right with God.

Many concerned about the environment rally for more evangelicals to understand climate change and embrace leadership positions on the issue. "It would be a milestone if you managed to take influential evangelists—preachers—to adopt the idea of global warming, and to preach it," Nobel Prize–winning economist Daniel Kahneman told the host of Hidden Brain, an NPR science show. "That would change things. It's not going to happen by presenting more evidence, that is clear."

And in the book *The Creation: An Appeal to Save Life on Earth*, renowned biologist E.O. Wilson wrote a long letter with the salutation, "Dear Pastor." It is an urgent, heartfelt plea. "We need your help. The Creation—living Nature—is in deep trouble. Scientists estimate that . . . half the species of plants and animals on Earth could be either gone or at least fated for early extinction by the end of the century. A full quarter will drop to this level during the next half century as a result of climate change alone."

These new sermons and stories are unlikely to come from older pastors and preachers, most of whom have become representatives of the Republican Party platform that doesn't want to even acknowledge that climate change is an issue to discuss, let alone embark on the massive undertaking necessary to begin to solve it. But for the young, who will live with the catastrophic predictions that worsen with each new iteration of the UN climate report, there are new stories emerging. They are conversion stories of a new sort, springing from dirt once buried under Midwestern parking lots and held aloft on the wings of Sean's beloved birds. Preachers and politicians seeking to keep the young religious right in their midst may need to leap past the quagmire of a questionable climate change debate and get right to the root of finding solutions for the generations that will be living into the long tomorrow of a warming planet.

Reprinted by permission of Meera Subramanian

ACTIVITY: Analyzing the Rhetorical Situation

1. How do the Young Evangelicals explain the link between their love of God and their climate activism? How exactly might this connection strengthen—or weaken—their argument? How might your answers depend on the original rhetorical audience? The secondary audience? Write out your responses.

2. How does Meera Subramanian summarize her research and series of interviews into a single thesis that defines her entire article? What is that thesis? What evidence does she use to support it? Why might an author use a question as a title?

3. What are some of the rhetorical challenges Subramanian faces in writing an article like this one that links religion with activism? How does she respond to these challenges with supporting evidence? How successful is she?

4. Of the three students interviewed, whose comments do you find most compelling? What is it about that person's comments that you find most compelling?

5. How might a religious person of a different mindset respond to Subramanian's argument—or the arguments of Diego, Chelsey, or Sean? How successful is Subramanian (or any of the three students) in appealing to partisan readers on both sides of the debate? What specific rhetorical strategies does that person use in doing (trying to do) so.

Fires, Droughts, and Hurricanes: What's the Link Between Climate Change and Natural Disasters?

AMINA KHAN

Science writer Amina Khan has written for the Netflix series Bill Nye Saves the World *and has been awarded the prestigious Knight Science Journalism fellowship at MIT. She is currently a staff writer for the* Los Angeles Times *and author of* Adapt, *a book that explores the ways humans can learn from nature to create a better future. On December 5, 2017, the* Los Angeles Times *published her evaluation of various extreme weather patterns.*

One of the most destructive fire seasons in California history keeps getting worse, with three wildfires driven by Santa Ana winds burning brush and homes in the Southland. At the other extreme, four hurricanes—Harvey, Irma, Maria, and Nate—have made landfall in the United States this year, the first time in more than a decade that so many have done so.

Extreme events have been hitting the country from all sides. To what extent does climate change influence them?

Here are a few ways researchers think that climate change's effects could play out.

Wildfires

Ready to Blow

Global warming means less soil moisture on average, which means that stuff burns more easily. (Particularly if you're in a drought-stricken area with a lot of dead, dry trees, for example.)

"Fires tend to be associated with hotter drier weather, everything else being equal," said Benjamin Bond-Lamberty, an ecosystem ecologist with the Joint Global Change Research Institute, a collaboration between the Pacific Northwest National Laboratory and the University of Maryland in College Park. That's assuming, of course, that you have an ignition source and more tinder to burn.

About That Tinder

Climate change may also alter the ecosystems in ways that leave them more vulnerable to wildfire, Bond-Lamberty added. Take the mountain pine beetle. Researchers think the pine beetle used to be held in check in its natural environment thanks to frigid winters—but now, with warmer temperatures, it's been on a rampage, killing trees through the Rocky Mountains into the Pacific Northwest and Canada. That means more dead trees—which means more stuff that's ready to catch fire.

Moving Up the Mountain

As the average global temperature continues to rise, cold-loving trees like pines and spruces may need higher elevations to stay at the cooler temperatures they're adapted to survive in. Deciduous, leafy trees may end up taking their place, and they tend to be less flammable than their coniferous brethren, Benjamin Bond-Lamberty said.

Hurricanes

Sea Level Rise and Storm Surge

As sea levels continue to rise due to global warming, they're increasing the risk of storm surge—the dangerously high floods caused by a storm pushing water onshore. Those floodwaters are responsible for much of the damage left by hurricanes—particularly in highly populated coastal cities.

A 2013 study in PNAS found that the risk of a Hurricane Katrina-level storm surge rose two to seven times for every 1.8-degree Fahrenheit increase in temperature.

Get Ready for Rain

Climate change can influence hurricanes in a number of ways—for example, in the amount of rainfall they drop. As the planet warms, the atmosphere can hold more moisture. So when it rains, it really pours.

"We think that Harvey type of rainfalls will become noticeably more frequent as the century goes on," said Kerry Emanuel, an atmospheric scientist at MIT.

For hurricanes, that can be really dangerous, given the deaths and damage caused by rain and storm-surge flooding, Emanuel said.

"Water is the big killer in hurricanes, not wind," Emanuel said. "Wind gets everyone's attention, but it's water that kills, and it's often water that does most of the damage."

The Heavy Hitters Hit More Often

Some research shows that the number of weaker storms, like Category 1 and Category 2 hurricanes, may go down because of climate change, and so the overall number of such storms might fall. But the strongest storms, Category 3, 4, and 5 storms, will likely become more frequent. And although the Category 1 and 2 storms make up around four-fifths of the storms that occur, it's those rarer Category 3, 4, and 5 storms that do the most damage.

"We do think the incidence of the high-intensity events is going up, and that's sort of what matters for society," Emanuel said. "Those are the destructive ones."

Drought

California is no stranger to drought. But because the multi-year weather cycles known as El Niño and La Niña tend to scramble the overall trend a little, it's a challenge to tease out certain direct connections between droughts and climate change, scientists say. However, there are a few connections researchers can draw.

Drier Ground

Thanks to global warming, which is raising the Earth's temperature, water evaporates out of the soil and into the air, sucking away moisture from plants that rely on it. This potentially helps increase drought conditions, said Lai-yung Ruby Leung, a climate modeler at the Pacific Northwest National Laboratory.

Even if total rainfall stays the same, higher temperatures will probably drive down the average moisture level in the soil, leaving less water available for living things.

Rain-Blocking

On top of that, climate change might mean that subtropical high pressure systems are likely to get stronger and larger. Those systems keep moist air from traveling upward in the atmosphere, where it can condense and eventually fall to the earth as rain or snow. By gaining in size and strength, those systems may become even more effective at blocking precipitation.

"This large-scale feature . . . in the Pacific Ocean is one of the important factors why a lot of climate models, when they project into the future, most of them show drying in the southwestern United States," Leung said.

Final Note

As a rule, climate scientists are generally loathe to say that any particular fire, flood, drought, or hurricane was caused by climate change—but they can point to the general likelihood that such extreme events might occur, or the complex ways in which they're influenced, by climate change.

The bright side of all this extreme weather? The more that extreme events occur, the more that scientists have to study—and the better they will be able to nail those relationships down in the future.

Amina Kahn, "Fires, droughts and hurricanes: What's the link between climate change and natural disasters?" reprinted by permission from the Los Angeles Times, December 5, 2017.

ACTIVITY: Analyzing the Rhetorical Situation

1. To what rhetorical opportunity is Khan responding? What constitutes her rhetorical audience? What can they do to address or resolve that opportunity?
2. What is Khan's thesis? Write it out in one sentence.
3. How does her list of examples (exemplification) enhance or detract from her thesis?
4. How does she employ other rhetorical strategies for development (X-REF) to develop each of her examples? Use textual evidence to support your answer.

The Challenging Politics of Climate Change

ELAINE KAMARCK

Wendy Maeda/The Boston Globe via Getty Images

This report from the founding director of the Center for Effective Public Management at the Brookings Institution, Elaine Kamarck, investigates the politics of climate change. Kamarck's books on public policy include How Change Happens—or Doesn't: The Politics of US Public Policy. *She lectures on public policy at Harvard University and has served in the White House for the Clinton administration.*

We don't really worry about climate change because it's too overwhelming and we're already in too deep. It's like if you owe your bookie $1,000, you're like, "OK, I've got to pay this dude back." But if you owe your bookie $1 million dollars, you're like, "I guess I'm just going to die."

—Colin Jost, *Saturday Night Live* [Colin Jost and Micheal Che's "Weekend Update" on the United Nations October 13, 2018, Climate Report]

The above quote is from a *Saturday Night Live* skit on the weekend following release of a report from the United Nation's Intergovernmental Panel on Climate Change. The report was one of the most dramatic ones yet, predicting that some of the most severe social and economic damage from the rise in global temperatures could come as soon as 2040. And yet, two comedians, Colin Jost and Michael Che, summed up the difficult (and perhaps impossible) politics of the issue in less than three minutes. You don't have to be a climate denier to be, in the end, indifferent to the issue.

As the climate crisis becomes more serious and more obvious, Americans remain resistant to decisive and comprehensive action on climate change. In "The Uninhabitable Earth: Life After Warming," David Wallace-Wells paints a frightening picture of the coming environmental apocalypse. Whole parts of the globe will become too hot for human habitation and those left behind will die of heat. Diseases will increase and mutate. Food shortages will become chronic as we fail to move agriculture from one climate to another. Whole countries like Bangladesh and parts of other countries like Miami will be underwater. Shortages of fresh water will affect humans and agriculture. The oceans will die, the air will get dirtier. "But," as Wallace-Wells argues, "what lies between us and extinction is horrifying enough."[1] That's because, as climate change takes its toll on Earth's physical planet, it will also cause social, economic, and political chaos as refugees flee areas that can no longer sustain them. If this prediction seems a bit extreme, all we have to do is look at recent weather events that keep breaking records to confront the possibility that the threat from climate change may indeed be existential.

Public Opinion on the Climate Crisis

Yet, in spite of the evidence at hand, climate change remains the toughest, most intractable political issue we, as a society, have ever faced. This is not to say that there hasn't been progress. In the United States, the amount of greenhouse gas emissions has held steady since 1990—even though our economy and our population has grown.[2] But globally, greenhouse gases have increased since then, bringing humanity very close to the dangerous levels of global warming that were predicted.[3] As scientific evidence about the causes of climate change has mounted and as a consensus has evolved in the scientific community, the public has remained divided and large, important parts of the political class have been indifferent. For instance, although 2017 was a year of 16 different billion-dollar natural disasters,[4] according to the National Oceanic and Atmospheric Administration, the percentage of voters who were "very concerned" about climate change stayed within the 40% range—where it has been rather stubbornly stuck for the past two years.[5] The

Dramatic and unprecedented natural disasters have had little effect on the public.

following chart shows Gallup public opinion polling for the past two decades.[6] During this period, but especially in the most recent decade, about a third to almost half of the public believes that the seriousness of global warming is generally exaggerated.

Dramatic and unprecedented natural disasters have had little effect on the public. Following blizzards and an unusually frigid winter in 2015, only 37% of Americans said climate change would pose a serious threat to them in their lifetimes.[7] After Hurricane Harvey and Hurricane

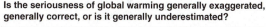

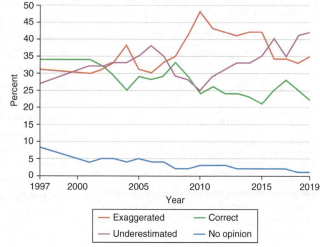

Is the seriousness of global warming generally exaggerated, generally correct, or is it generally underestimated?

Source: Gallup. Note: In 1997, this was asked of a half sample.

Irma in 2017, concern about climate change increased by 7 points among Republicans and 2 points among Democrats.[8] But in the next year, an August 2018 poll taken shortly after the California wildfires showed concern among Republicans down to 44% and up to 79% among Democrats.[9] In a YouGov poll in the summer of 2019—during record heat waves in the United States and Europe—only 42% of the public said that they were very concerned and only 22% of Republicans said that they were "very concerned about climate change."[10]

If natural disasters don't affect attitudes toward climate change, partisanship does. The following chart from Pew Research shows the gulf that exists between Democrats and Republicans on this issue.[11]

Republicans and Democrats are deeply divided on whether climate change should be a top priority

% of U.S. adults who say dealing with global climate change should be a top priority for the president and Congress

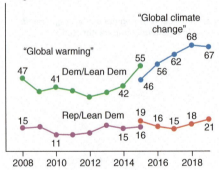

Note: In 2014 and earlier, respondents were asked about dealing with "global warming." In 2015, half the sample each was asked about "global warming" or "global climate change." Source: Survey conducted Jan, 9–14, 2019, and prior surveys.

Source: *Pew Research Center. Aug. 28, 2019. Accessed at:* https://www.pewresearch.org/fact-tank/2019/08/28/u-s-concern-about-climate-change-is-rising-but-mainly-among-democrats/.

The partisan divide began in the late 1990s and has increased over time. In 1997, nearly equal numbers of Democrats and Republicans said that the effects of global warming have already begun. Ten years later, the gap was 34%: 76% of Democrats said the effects had already begun, and only 42% of Republicans agreed.

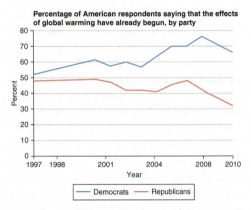

Source: Elke U. Weber and Paul C. Stern, "Public Understanding of Climate Change in the United States," American Psychologist, May–June 2011.

Republican resistance on this issue is one of, but not the only reason why, in the face of mounting evidence, the public remains lukewarm on this existential issue. The dire warnings, the scientific consensus, and the death toll from unprecedented climate events have failed to move the public very much. For two years now, the number of Americans who say they are "very concerned" about climate change fails to reach 50%, as a look at polling from Quinnipiac illustrates.[12]

An even more telling piece of evidence on public indifference to climate change comes from 30 years of open-ended polling conducted by Gallup. Open-ended polling

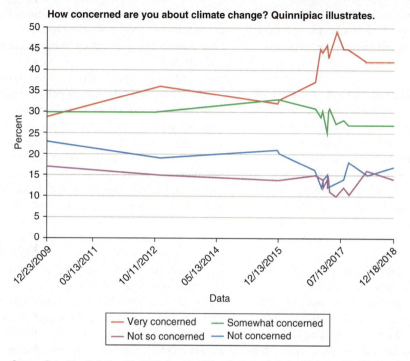

How concerned are you about climate change? Quinnipiac illustrates.

Legend:
— Very concerned   — Somewhat concerned
— Not so concerned — Not concerned

Source: Quinnipiac Poll. Dec. 18, 2018. Accessed https://poll.qu.edu/national/release-detail?ReleaseID=2590.

is especially interesting since it elicits an *unprompted* response from the individual. Between 1989 and 2019, Gallup has asked "What do you think is the most important problem facing this country today?" Jobs, the economy, and health care are often at the top of the list. "Environment/pollution" is not often mentioned. In fact, over a 30-year period, it was mentioned by anywhere from less than 0.5% to 8% of the public. In the most recent 2019 poll (August), "the government/poor leadership" was mentioned by 22% of the public, and "immigration" by 18%. "Environment/pollution/climate change" garnered only 3% of the public. And in some earlier polls, climate change is not even mentioned by a significant portion of the public (although people could be including that within the term environment.)[13]

Why Can't We Get Our Heads Around This?

Given the severity of the climate crisis and the potential for existential damage to the human race and planet, the lack of intensity around the issue is simultaneously incomprehensible and totally understandable. So let's look at the latter. The explanations fall into at least four categories: complexity; jurisdiction and accountability; collective action and trust; and imagination.

Complexity

Complexity is the death knell of many modern public policy problems and solutions. And complexity is inherent in climate change. The causes of global warming are varied, including carbon dioxide, methane, and nitrous oxide. As the climate warms, it affects glaciers, sea levels, water supply, rainfall, evaporation, wind, and a host of other natural phenomena that affect weather patterns. Unlike an earlier generation of environmental problems, it is hard to see the connections between coal plants in one part of the world and hurricanes in another. In contrast, when the water in your river smells and turns a disgusting color and dead fish float on top of it, no sophisticated scientific training is required to understand the link between what's happening in the river and the chemical plant dumping things into it. The first generation of the environmental movement had an easier time making the connection between cause and effect.

Evidence for this comes from approximately three decades of polling on the environment by Gallup. In the following chart, most of the polls took place between 1989 and 2019.[14] Note that, over time, the most worrisome environmental problems are visible pollution problems. Water, soil, and ocean and beach pollution are at the top. These are things average people can see and smell. Global warming or climate change is toward the bottom. These numbers change somewhat over time and understandably so, which is why data is included from 2019 where available. People are more worried about climate change than they used to be. Nonetheless, the complexity of the issue compared to the more straightforward cause-and-effect characteristics of other environmental issues is a major impediment to political action.

Environmental issue	Range of the public who worried about this "a great deal" (from ~1989 to ~2019)	Median percentage	Public who worried about this "a great deal" in 2019
Pollution of drinking water	48% to 72%	57.50%	56%
Pollution of rivers, lakes, and reservoirs	46% to 72%	53%	53%
Contamination of soil and water by toxic waste	44% to 69%	52%	–
Ocean and beach pollution	43% to 60%	52%	–
Loss of natural habitat for wildlife	44% to 58%	51%	–
Air pollution	36% to 63%	45%	43%

(continued)

Environmental issue	Range of the public who worried about this "a great deal" (from ~1989 to ~2019)	Median percentage	Public who worried about this "a great deal" in 2019
Damage to Earth's ozone layer	33% to 51%	43%	–
Loss of tropical rain forests	33% to 51%	40%	39%
Extinction of plant and animal species	31% to 46%	37%	43%
Global warming or climate change	24% to 45%	34%	44%
Urban sprawl and loss of open space	26% to 42%	33%	–
Acid rain	20% to 41%	26.50%	–

Source: Gallup, "Environment." Accessed at: https://news.gallup.com/poll/1615/environment.aspx.

When former Vice President Al Gore was awarded the Nobel Peace Prize in 2007, along with the Intergovernmental Panel on Climate Change, the prize was for "their efforts to build up and disseminate greater knowledge about man-made climate change." Through his books, his famous slide show, and his 2006 movie, "An Inconvenient Truth," Gore made it his mission to explain the scientific processes that make global warming so dangerous. But the inherent complexity of cause and effect in climate change makes it a topic in need of continuous education.

Jurisdiction and Accountability

The second major impediment to political action stems from problems of jurisdiction and accountability. From the beginning, modern government has relied upon the concept of jurisdiction—"territory within which a court or government agency may properly exercise its power."[15] And implicit in the concept of jurisdiction is geography. But two of the stickiest problems of the twenty-first century—climate change and cybersecurity—are challenging because it is so difficult to nail down jurisdiction. When we are able to establish jurisdiction we are able to establish rules, laws, and accountability for adherence to the law—the three bedrock principles of modern democratic governance. In the absence of jurisdiction, everyone is accountable and therefore no one is accountable.

When a cybercrime or cyberattack occurs, we have trouble with jurisdiction. If the perpetrator of a cyberattack on an electrical grid is a Russian living in Tirana, Albania, who routes attacks through France and Canada, who can prosecute the individual? (Assuming, that is, that we can even find the perpetrator.) Similarly, if coal plants in China and cattle ranching in Australia increase their outputs of greenhouse gases in one year and there are droughts in Africa and floods in Europe the next, who is responsible?

We currently attribute greenhouse gas emissions to individual countries under the

United Nations Framework Convention on Climate Change, and we attribute greenhouse gases to their sources within the United States via the Environmental Protection Agency's Greenhouse Gas Reporting Program. But attribution without enforcement mechanisms is only half the battle—if that. Nationally and internationally there is no legal architecture that allows us to reward and/or punish those who decrease or increase their greenhouse gas emissions. Even the Paris Agreement—which President Trump pulled the United States out of—is only a set of pledges from individual countries. Measurement is a first step toward accountability, and measurement needs constant improvement. But measurement in the absence of accountability is meaningless, especially in situations where many people are skeptical of cause and effect.

The Toxic Release Inventory was established by Congress in 1982 as an amendment to the Superfund Bill. Over the years, the steady flow of information about the release of hazardous chemicals into the environment has had many positive effects on regulators, environmentalists, and industrialists.[16] Studies have shown that "facilities reduce emissions by an additional 4.28% on average, and their use of source reduction increases by 3.07% on average when the relative assessed hazard level of a chemical increases compared to when it decreases."[17]

But the Toxic Release Inventory has one advantage that the Greenhouse Gas Reporting Program does not. The effects of dangerous chemicals on a population are generally fairly clear and obvious: dirty water, dirty air, difficulty breathing, unusual rates of cancer, etc. The cause

and effect is often undeniable as the many lawyers who have represented communities and won their cases against large polluters can attest. Greenhouse gas emissions affect people thousands of miles away from their source and make it easier to believe that it wasn't the fossil fuels at all, just the weather pattern or an act of God. Hence, the linkage between jurisdiction and accountability is weak.

Collective Action and Trust

Our increasingly hot summers drive the demand for air conditioning. However, air conditioning adds to the heat outside. Scientists estimate that under a realistic set of circumstances, "waste heat from air conditioners exacerbated the heat island effect, the phenomenon in which densely packed cities experience higher temperatures than similarly situated rural areas."[18] Air conditioning could add as much as 1 degree Celsius (nearly 2 degrees Fahrenheit) to the heat of a city. Which one of us, however, would voluntarily turn off their air conditioning knowing full well that hundreds of thousands of other "free riders" would not?

This is just one simplified version of the collective action problem. People may understand that they should act in a certain way for the greater good, but as individuals, they are loathe to turn off their air conditioning or stop flying places for vacations—knowing that others will not be joining them. This is why government is the most frequent solution to collective action problems. Combating climate change requires collective action on many fronts, and it requires collective action both nationally and internationally. But this is extremely

"It is the lack of trust in government that may be one of the foundational barriers to effective environmental action."

difficult in democracies like the United States, which face strong individualist traditions in the culture along with a lack of trust in government.

In fact, it is the lack of trust in government that may be one of the foundational barriers to effective environmental action. Writing in the journal *Global Environmental Change*, E. Keith Smith and Adam Mayer looked at 35 different countries. They found that a lack of trust in institutions blunts the public's risk perceptions and therefore their willingness to support behaviors or policies to address climate change.[19]

Their findings make intuitive sense especially in the American context. If you are skeptical about government in general, you are skeptical about your government telling you that you need to do something about climate change; you are *even more* skeptical about an international

body like the United Nations telling you that climate change is a very serious problem. Following is a graph showing the moving average over time of Americans who say they can trust the government in Washington to do what is right "just about always" or "most of the time."[20]

Imagination

The final piece to the puzzle of why the political salience of climate change seems so out of step with the physical proof and urgency of the issue may have to do with the realm of imagination. As every journalist knows, it is important to be able to tell a story, and as every teacher knows, we learn best through stories. And novelists and screenwriters are the most effective and powerful storytellers we have in society. And yet, in an intriguing book called *The Great Derangement: Climate Change and the Unthinkable*, the Indian novelist Amitav Ghosh writes

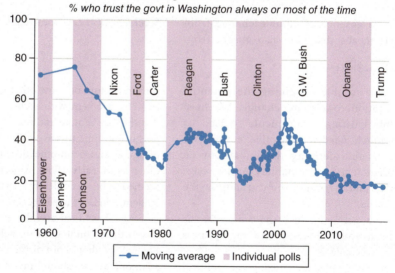

Public trust in government near historic lows.
% who trust the govt in Washington always or most of the time

Source: *Pew Research Center. Aug. 28, 2019. Accessed at:* https://www.pewresearch.org/fact-tank/2019/08/28/u-s-concern-about-climate-change-is-rising-but-mainly-among-democrats/.

that climate change is even more absent in the world of fiction than it is in nonfiction.

To see that this is so, we need only glance through the pages of a few highly regarded literary journals and book reviews, for example, the *London Review of books,* the *New York Review of Books,* the *Los Angeles Review of Books,* the *Literary Journal,* and the *New York Times Review of Books.* When the subject of climate change occurs in these publications, it is almost always in relation to nonfiction; novels and short stories are very rarely to be glimpsed within this horizon. Indeed, it could even be said that fiction that deals with climate change is almost by definition not of the kind that is taken seriously by serious literary journals: the mere mention of the subject is often enough to relegate a novel or short story to the genre of science fiction.[21]

The absence of climate change from novels means that it is also absent from

> A lack of trust in institutions blunts the public's risk perceptions and . . . willingness to support . . . policies to address climate change.

movies and television—the great powerful purveyors of stories in our time. One can't underestimate the power of fiction in shaping society's attitudes. Some older Americans can remember how the 1958 novel *Exodus,* by Leon Uris, and the subsequent 1960 movie by the same name impacted a generation of non-Jewish Americans to be supportive of Israel. Or how the 2000 movie *Erin Brockovich,* based on a true story of a young woman who takes on an energy corporation, helped popularize the environmental justice movement.

Ghosh's contribution to our understanding of this issue is not so much in his sections on politics as it is in his insight that fiction in our age is unable to deal with events that are so improbable and so removed from the agency of the individual that they cannot be written about in any realistic way.

All of which brings us back to our two *Saturday Night Live* comedians.

Conclusion

We have trouble imagining the potential devastation of climate change. We have trouble trusting governments to lead us into much needed collective action. We have trouble defining the links between jurisdiction and accountability. And we have trouble understanding the causality in the first place.

How can we fix this? And can we fix this in time to avoid the most severe consequences of climate change?

Some people, recognizing the political problem, hope for a technological fix such as

carbon capture or some other geoengineering fix. The problem with technological fixes is that they are remote and may very well not be effective in time to stave off massive amounts of social and economic disruption. On the other hand, early-1950s America faced what seemed to be an endlessly heartbreaking polio epidemic; in less than a decade, however, a vaccine was developed and the epidemic ended. Given the technological miracles seen in our lifetime, we should not dismiss a technological solution, and we should invest heavily in one with both public and private dollars.

A second imperative is to increase basic scientific literacy so that the burden of pedagogy does not fall on folks like Al Gore alone. Some of this is already happening with the attention given to STEM [Science, Technology, Engineering, and Math] training in education. But it is clear that climate change is only one of many complex scientific issues that average citizens will be called upon to understand and act on in the future. A renewed focus on scientific literacy may need to be implemented throughout America's schools.

Which brings us to the storytellers. Just as Al Gore won an Emmy for a movie on climate change, the creative elements in our society need to help explain what's at stake. They will find a receptive audience in the younger generation. As evidenced by their activism on this issue—this past week, millions marched in countries around the world to protest inaction around climate change— young people are especially concerned with the environment.[22] The millennial generation is a very large one, and they have so far shown themselves to be civic-minded and environmentally engaged.

A third imperative is to strengthen the link between jurisdiction and accountability. Nationally and internationally, we need to be able to reward and punish private and public

Awareness without the ability to hold corporations, countries, and individuals accountable will not result in major action on environmental issues.

actors for their environmental actions. The condemnation of Brazil's government for deforestation and fires in the Amazon was largely without consequences. Until there are penalties for things like greenhouse gas emissions, they will not be reduced in sufficient amounts.

Because this issue poses the ultimate collective action problem, it requires governmental action, such as treaties, taxes, and regulations, for starters. But very few citizens in our country are going to support governmental action without first trusting government to get it right. We need to restore trust in government. It has been on a steady downward slide since the George W. Bush administration. Unless we restore trust in government, we are not likely to achieve significant collective action.

Of course, all these things must proceed hand in hand. Awareness without the ability to hold corporations, countries, and individuals accountable will not result in major action on environmental issues. But measurement and accountability without an understanding of the connections between a warmer planet and dangerous climate changes will not result in major action either. Above all, we need to restore—through government and other means—our trust in collective action.

Notes

1. David Wallace-Wells. "The Uninhabitable Earth: Life After Warming." Tim Duggan Books, p. 34.

2. "Inventory of U.S. Greenhouse Gas Emissions and Sinks." U.S. Environmental Protection Agency. Accessed at:

https://www.epa.gov/ghgemissions/inventory-us-greenhouse-gas-emissions-and-sinks.

3. "Global Greenhouse Gas Emissions, per Type of Gas and Source, including LULUCF." Netherlands Environmental Assessment Agency. Accessed at: https://www.pbl.nl/en/infographic/global-greenhouse-gas-emissions-per-type-of-gas-and-source-including-lulucf.

4. Adam B. Smith. "2017 U.S. Billion-Dollar Weather and Climate Disasters: A Historic Year in Context." Climate.gov. Accessed at: https://www.climate.gov/news-features/blogs/beyond-data/2017-us-billion-dollar-weather-and-climate-disasters-historic-year#targetText=During%202017%2C%20the%20U.S.%20experienced,crop%20freeze%2C%20drought%20and%20wildfire.

5. "U.S. Voters Say No Wall and Don't Shut Down Government, Quinnipiac University National Poll Finds; Focus On Issues, Not Impeachment, Voters Tell Dems 7-1." Quinnipiac Poll. Dec. 18, 2018. Accessed at: https://poll.qu.edu/national/release-detail?ReleaseID=2590.

6. "Environment." Gallup. Accessed at: https://news.gallup.com/poll/1615/environment.aspx.

7. Lydia Saad. "U.S. Views on Climate Change Stable after Extreme Winter." Gallup. March 25, 2015. Accessed at: https://news.gallup.com/poll/182150/views-climate-change-stable-extreme-winter.aspx.

8. Jacqueline Toth. "As Wildfires Rage, Divide Widens between Democratic, GOP Voters on Climate Change." Morning Consult. Aug. 22, 2018. Accessed at: https://morningconsult.com/2018/08/22/

as-wildfires-rage-divide-widens-between-democratic-gop-voters-climate-change/.

9. Ibid.

10. *The Economist*/YouGov Poll. July 27–30, 2019. Accessed at: https://d25d2506sfb94s.cloudfront.net/cumulus_uploads/document/hash0nbry8/econTabReport.pdf.

11. Brian Kennedy and Meg Hefferon. "U.S. Concern about Climate change Is Rising, but Mainly among Democrats." Pew Research Center. Aug. 28, 2019. Accessed at: https://www.pewresearch.org/fact-tank/2019/08/28/u-s-concern-about-climate-change-is-rising-but-mainly-among-democrats/.

12. "U.S. Voters Say No Wall and Don't Shut Down Government, Quinnipiac University National Poll Finds; Focus on Issues, Not Impeachment, Voters Tell Dems 7-1." Quinnipiac Poll. Dec. 18, 2018. Accessed at: https://poll.qu.edu/national/release-detail?ReleaseID=2590.

13. The Roper Center, Cornell University. Accessed at: https://ropercenter.cornell.edu/CFIDE/cf/action/ipoll/ipollResult.cfm?keyword=most+important+problem&keywordoptions=1&exclude=&excludeoptions=1&topic=Any&organization=Gallup&label=&fromdate=1%2F1%2F1980&todate=12%2F31%2F2019&studyId=&questionViewId=&resultsCurrentPage=1&paging=true&historyID=&keywordDisplay=&queryId=317679189933&sortBy=BEG_DATE_DESC&perPage=20.

14. "Environment." Gallup. Accessed at: https://news.gallup.com/poll/1615/environment.aspx.

15. "Jurisdiction." The Legal Information Institute, Cornell Law School. Accessed at: https://www.law.cornell.edu/wex/jurisdiction.

16. See Chapter 6 in James Hamilton, "Regulation through Revelation: The Origins, Politics and Impact of the Toxic Release Inventory Program" (Cambridge University Press, 2005) for a history of the many impacts the TRI has had.

17. Wayne Fu, Basak Kalkanci, and Ravi Subramanian. "Are Hazardous Substance Rankings Effective? An Empirical Investigation of Information Dissemination about the Relative Hazards of Chemicals and Emissions Reductions." *Manufacturing and Service Operations Management.* May 17, 2018.

18. Sydney Brownstone. "Whoops: Air Conditioning Is Making Cities Hotter, Not Colder." Fast Company. June 11, 2014. Accessed at: https://www.fastcompany.com/3031696/whoops-air-conditioning-is-making-cities-hotter-not-colder.

19. E. Keith Smith and Adam Mayer. "A Social Trap for the Climate? Collective Action, Trust and Climate Change Risk Perception in 35 Countries." *Global Environmental Change,* Volume 49, pp. 140-153. March 2018.

20. "Public Trust in Government: 1958-2019." Pew Research Center. Accessed at: https://www.people-press.org/2019/04/11/public-trust-in-government-1958-2019/.

21. Amitav Ghosh. *The Great Derangement: Climate Change and the Unthinkable,* University of Chicago Press, p. 7.

22. Sandra Laville and Jonathan Watts. "Across the Globe, Millions Join Biggest Climate Protest Ever." *The Guardian.* Sept. 21, 2019. Accessed at: https://www.theguardian.com/environment/2019/sep/21/across-the-globe-millions-join-biggest-climate-protest-ever.

Elaine Kamarck, "The Challenging Politics of Climate Change," Brookings Report, September 23, 2019. Reprinted by permission of Brookings Institution.

ACTIVITY: Analyzing the Rhetorical Situation

1. To what rhetorical opportunity is Elaine Kamarck responding? What situation or situations have created the need for her to write this essay? How fitting is her response to this opportunity?

2. What is the overall effect of the numbers, graphs, and charts that supplement Kamarck's argument? What might her use of such data tell you about her rhetorical audience? How do these data affect her credibility? How do they establish the logos of her essay? What is their overall effect in terms of sparking pathos?

3. What rhetorical strategies does Kamarck use to invite her readers to adopt her point of view? How might you measure the effectiveness of these strategies? How has reading this essay influenced your own view on America's response to the issue of climate change? Write out your answers.

4. Kamarck made some concessions to opposing points of view—for example, by charting the number of Americans who simply do not believe climate change is a

compelling issue for them. How do concessions like these enhance or detract from the nature of her overall argument? How might you use concessions in your essay— and to what end(s)?

5. After reading all or some of these essays, what is your current stance with regard to climate change? Which essays, interviews, or passages of evidence best support your view? To what measure has your view about climate change been strengthened as a result of reading these essays? How and why?

⟫ COMMUNITY CONNECTIONS

1. How do Meera Subramanian's and Elaine Kamarck's essays coincide with or diverge from your own understanding of climate change? Take about ten minutes to write your response. Be prepared to share your response with the rest of the class.

2. Consider your home or college community in terms of climate—or weather. How might you consider the issue of "justice" as a climate-influenced issue? How might location, race, ethnicity, income, and ability, for instance, connect with climate-influenced issues of "justice"? Based on your experience, observations, and reading, analyze the ways climate change is affecting people in your community in unfair, unjust ways (whether to their advantage or disadvantage).

3. Arrange an interview with someone in your community who works in food production, food service, or in the food industry is some way. You might ask to meet with a food science professor on your campus, a civil engineer at a nearby firm, a grocer, restaurant worker, or a farmer. Using the Young Farmers' essay as a guide, make a list of questions that will help you understand the role climate change is playing within this person's field. How does your interviewee perceive these changes? What, if any, actions does this person wish to see in the way climate change is being addressed?

Glossary of Usage

Standardized English is the stylistic option you'll most often choose when working in an academic context. This glossary presents many of those standardized usages and spellings, as well as usages and spellings considered to be conversational (or informal) and even unconventional (or nonstandardized). Using the information in this glossary, you'll be able to make informed decisions about the words you use.

The following labels will help you choose appropriate words for your rhetorical situation.

Conventional Words or phrases listed in dictionaries without special usage labels; generally considered appropriate in academic and professional writing.

Conversational Words or phrases that dictionaries label *informal, slang,* or *colloquial;* although often used in informal speech and writing, not generally appropriate for formal writing assignments.

Unconventional Words or phrases not generally considered appropriate in academic or professional writing and often labeled *nonstandard* in dictionaries; best avoided in formal contexts.

a half a, a half an Unconventional; instead use *half a, half an,* or *a half:* He commutes a half ~~an~~ hour to work.

a lot of A conversational expression for *many, much,* or *a great deal of:* ~~A lot of~~ Many people attended the concert. *A lot* is spelled as two words.

a while, awhile *A while* means "a period of time" and most frequently follows the preposition *after, for,* or *in:* They stopped for a while. *Awhile* means "a short time." It is not used after a preposition: We rested awhile.

accept, except *Accept* is a verb meaning "to receive": He will **accept** the offer. *Except* can be a verb meaning "to exclude": Her criminal record will **except** her from consideration for this job. However, *except* is more commonly used as a preposition meaning "other than": No one knew **except** us. Other forms: *acceptable, acceptance; exception.*

adapt, adopt *Adapt* means "to adjust or change": He will **adapt** to the new climate. *Adopt* means "to take as one's own": The board of directors will **adopt** a new policy. Other forms: *adaptable, adaptation; adoption.*

adverse, averse *Adverse* means "unfavorable": The storm had **adverse** effects on the county's economy. Usually followed by *to, averse* means "reluctant" or "opposed": They are not **averse** to negotiating a compromise. Other forms: *adversity; aversion.*

advice, advise *Advice* is a noun: They asked an expert for **advice**. *Advise* is a verb: He should be able to **advise** us.

affect, effect *Affect* is a verb that means either "to influence" or "to touch the emotions": The threatened strike did not **affect** the company's decision to keep the factory open. The news **affected** us deeply. Psychologists use *affect* as a noun (with the stress on the first syllable) meaning "emotional expression": She noted the patient's lack of **affect**. As a noun, *effect*

587

means "a result": Maren discussed the **effects** of secondhand smoke. When used as a verb, *effect* means "to bring about": They hoped to **effect** real political change. Other forms: *affective; effective.*

agree on, agree to, agree with *Agree on* means "to be in accord with others about something": We **agreed on** the arrangements. *Agree to* means "to accept something" or "to consent to do something": They **agreed to** our terms. They **agreed to** discuss the matter. *Agree with* means "to share an opinion with someone" or "to approve of something": Everyone **agreed with** the chair of the committee. No one **agreed with** my position.

all ready, already *All ready* means "completely prepared": The documents are **all ready** for the meeting. *Already* means "by or before a specified time": We have **already** submitted our final report.

all right Two of the most common meanings of *all right* are "permissible" and "safe": They asked whether it was **all right** to arrive a few minutes late. Everyone in the accident was **all right**. The spelling *alright* is not a generally accepted alternative for *all right,* although it is frequently used in popular writing.

all together, altogether *All together* means "as a group": We sang **all together**. *Altogether* means "wholly, thoroughly": This song is **altogether** too difficult to play.

allude, elude *Allude* means "to refer to indirectly": She **alluded** to the poetry of Elizabeth Bishop. *Elude* means "to evade" or "to escape from": For months, the solution **eluded** the researchers.

allusion, illusion *Allusion* means "a casual or indirect reference": Her **allusion** was to Elizabeth Bishop's poetry. *Illusion* means "a false idea or an unreal image": The magician's trick was based on **illusion**.

among, between According to traditional usage, *among* is used when three or more individuals or entities are discussed: He must choose **among** several good job offers. *Between* is used when referring to only two entities: We studied the differences **between** the two proposals. Current dictionaries also mention the use of *between* to refer to more than two entities when the relationships between these entities are considered distinct: Connections **between** the four coastal communities were restored.

amoral, immoral *Amoral* means "not caring about right or wrong": The prosecutor in the case accused the defendant of **amoral** acts of random violence. *Immoral* means "not moral": Students discussed whether abortion should be considered **immoral**. Other forms: *amorality; immorality.*

amount of, number of Use *amount of* before nouns that cannot be counted: The **amount of** rain that fell last year was insufficient. Use *number of* with nouns that can be counted: The **number of** students attending college has increased. *A number of* means "many" and thus takes a plural verb: **A number of** opportunities **are** listed. *The number of* takes a singular verb: **The number of** opportunities available to students **is** rising.

angry at, angry with *Angry* is commonly followed by either *at* or *with,* although according to traditional usage, *with* should be used when the cause of the anger is a person: She was **angry at** the school for denying her admission. He was **angry with** me because I corrected him in public.

anxious, eager *Anxious,* related to *anxiety,* means "worried" or "nervous": They are **anxious** about the test results. *Eager* means "keenly interested" or "desirous": We were **eager** to find a compromise. Current dictionaries report that *anxious* is often used as a synonym for *eager*, but such usage is still considered conversational.

anymore, any more *Anymore* means "any longer" or "now" and most frequently occurs in questions or negative sentences: We do not carry that product **anymore**. Its use in positive sentences is considered conversational; *now* is generally used instead: All they do ~~anymore~~ now is fight. *Any more* means "additional": Do you need **any more** help?

anyone, any one *Anyone* means "anybody": I did not see **anyone** familiar. *Any one* means "one from a group": **Any one** of them will suffice.

anyplace, everyplace, someplace As synonyms for *anywhere, everywhere,* and *somewhere,* these words are considered informal.

are, our *Are* is a present tense verb: We are happy. *Our* is a possessive pronoun: Our flower bed makes me happy.

as, like According to traditional usage, *as,* not *like,* should begin a clause: Her son talked ~~like~~ as she did. When used as a preposition, *like* can introduce a phrase: He looks **like** his father. That scarf feels **like** silk.

as regards Unconventional. See **regard, regarding, regards.**

assure, ensure, insure *Assure* means "to state with confidence": He **assured** us that the neighborhood was safe. *Ensure* and *insure* can often be interchanged to mean "to make certain," but only *insure* means "to protect against loss": The researcher **ensured** [OR **insured**] the accuracy of the test results. Homeowners **insure** their houses and furnishings.

averse See **adverse, averse.**

awhile See **a while, awhile.**

bad Unconventional as an adverb; use *badly* instead: Some fans behaved ~~bad~~

badly during the game. However, as an adjective, *bad* can be used after sensory or linking verbs (*feel, look, sound, smell,* and *taste*): I felt **bad** that I could not attend her recital.

bear, bare *Bear* is an omnivorous mammal, but can also designate the ability to hold up, support weight, endure, or transmit: The young seem to bear COVID better than the old. *Bare* means naked or exposed: He gave us the bare facts.

being as, being that Unconventional; use *because* instead: ~~Being as~~ Because it was Sunday, many of the stores were closed.

better, had better *Better* is conversational. Use *had better* instead: They ~~better~~ had better buy their tickets tomorrow.

between See **among, between.**

brake, break A *brake* is a device for slowing or stopping. A *break* is a fracture, crack, rupture, or escape.

breath, breathe *Breath* is a noun: I was out of **breath**. *Breathe* is a verb: It was hard to **breathe**.

bunch Conversational to refer to a group: A ~~bunch~~ group of students gathered in front of the student union.

busted Unconventional. Use *broken* instead: The printer was ~~busted~~ broken, so none of us had our papers ready on time.

buy, by To *buy* is to acquire through an exchange of money or the equivalent. *By* is a preposition meaning nearby or close to.

can, may According to traditional definitions, *can* refers to ability, and *may* refers to permission: He **can** read music. You **may** not read the newspaper during class. According to current dictionaries, *can* and *may* are sometimes used interchangeably to denote permission, though *may* is generally preferred in formal contexts.

can't hardly, can't scarcely Both are examples of a double negative, used in some regions of the United States but unconventional. Use *can hardly* or *can scarcely* instead: I ~~can't hardly~~ believe it happened.

capital, capitol, Capitol A *capital* is a governing city; it also means "funds": The **capital** of California is Sacramento. They invested a large amount of **capital** in the organization. As an adjective, *capital* means "chief" or "principal": This year's election is of **capital** importance. It may also refer to the death penalty: In some countries, espionage is a **capital** offence. A *capitol* is a statehouse; the *Capitol* is the U.S. congressional building in Washington, DC.

censor, censure, sensor As a verb, *censor* means "to remove or suppress material that is deemed objectionable or classified": In some countries, the government **censors** the news. As a noun, *censor* refers to a person authorized to remove material considered objectionable or classified: The **censor** cleared the report. The verb *censure* means "to blame or criticize": The committee **censured** her. The noun *censure* is an expression of disapproval or blame: She received a **censure** from the committee. A *sensor* is a device that responds to a stimulus: The motion **sensor** detected an approaching car.

center on, center around *Center around* is conversational. Use *center on* or *revolve around* to mean "focus on" for formal occasions. The critic's comments **centered ~~around~~ on** health care.

cite, sight, site *Cite* means "to mention": She could easily **cite** several examples of altruism. *Sight*, as a verb, means "to see": The crew **sighted** land. As a noun, *sight* refers to the ability to see or to a view: Her **sight** worsened as she aged. We had never seen such a **sight**! *Site*, as a verb, means "to situate": They **sited** their new house near the river. As a noun, *site* means "a location": The **site** for the new library was approved. Other forms: *citation, citing; sighting.*

climactic, climatic *Climactic* refers to a high point (a climax): The film's **climactic** scene riveted the viewers to their seats. *Climatic* refers to the climate: Global warming is creating **climatic** changes.

coarse, course *Coarse* means "rough" or "ill-mannered": Several people objected to his **coarse** language. A *course* is "a route" or "a plan of study": Because of the bad weather, we had to alter our **course**. She must take a **course** in anatomy. *Course* is used in the expression *of course*.

compare to, compare with *Compare to* means "to consider as similar": The film critic **compared** the actor **to** Humphrey Bogart. *Compare with* means "to examine to discover similarities or differences": He **compared** early morning traffic patterns **with** late afternoon ones.

complement, compliment *Complement* means "to balance" or "to complete": Their voices **complement** each other. *Compliment* means "to express praise": After the reading, several people **complimented** the author. Other forms: *complementary* (they have **complementary** personalities); *complimentary* (her remarks were **complimentary**). *Complimentary* may also mean "provided free of charge": I received two **complimentary** books.

compose, comprise *Compose* means "to form by putting together": The panel is **composed** of several experts. *Comprise* means "to consist of": The course package **comprises** a textbook, a workbook, and a CD-ROM.

conscience, conscientious, conscious, consciousness *Conscience* means "a sense of right and wrong": His questionable actions weighed on his **conscience**. *Conscientious* means "careful": She appreciated her **conscientious** research assistant. A *conscientious objector* is a person who refuses to join the military for moral reasons. *Conscious* means "awake": For a few minutes, I wasn't **conscious**. I lost **consciousness** for a few minutes. *Conscious* may also mean "aware": I was **conscious** of the risks involved in starting a new business.

consequently, subsequently *Consequently* means "as a result": They exceeded their budget and **consequently** had little to spend during the holidays. *Subsequently* means "then" or "later": He was arrested and **subsequently** convicted of fraud.

continual, continuous *Continual* means "recurring": **Continual** work stoppages delayed progress. *Continuous* means "uninterrupted": The high-pitched **continuous** noise distracted everyone. Other forms: *continually; continuously.*

convince, persuade *Convince* means "to make someone believe something": She **convinced** us that she was the best candidate for the office. *Persuade* means "to motivate someone to act or change": They **persuaded** me to write a letter to the editor. According to current dictionaries, many speakers and writers now use *convince* as a synonym for *persuade.*

could of See **of.**

council, counsel A *council* is a committee that advises or makes decisions: The library **council** proposed a special program for children. A *counsel* is a legal adviser: The **counsel** said he would appeal the case. *Counsel* also means "advice": They sought her out for her wise **counsel**. As a verb, *counsel* means "to give advice": The adviser **counsels** people considering career changes.

course See **coarse, course.**

criteria, criterion A *criterion* is "a standard": The most important **criterion** for judging the competition was originality. *Criteria* is the plural form of *criterion*: To pass, the students had to satisfy three **criteria** for the assignment.

data, datum *Datum* means "fact"; *data,* the plural form, is used more often: The **data were** difficult to interpret. Some current dictionaries note that *data* is frequently used as a mass entity (like the word *furniture*), appearing with a singular verb.

desert, dessert *Desert,* with the stress on the first syllable, is a noun meaning "a barren land": Cacti grow in the **deserts** of Arizona. As a verb, with the second syllable stressed, *desert* means "to leave": Because of his behavior, his research partners **deserted** him. *Dessert* means "something sweet eaten at the end of a meal": I ordered chocolate ice cream for **dessert**.

device, devise *Device* means "mechanism": The **device** indicates whether a runner has made a false start. *Devise* means "to create": They **devised** a new way of packaging juice.

differ from, differ with *Differ from* means "to be different": His management style **differs from** mine. *Differ with* means "to disagree": We **differed with** each other on just one point.

different from, different than *Different from* is normally used before a noun, a pronoun, a noun phrase, or a noun clause: His technique is **different from** yours. The results were **different from** what we had predicted. *Different than* is used to introduce an adverbial clause, with *than* serving as the conjunction: The style is **different than** it was ten years ago.

discreet, discrete, discretion *Discreet* means "tactful": Because most people are sensitive to this issue, you must be **discreet**. Related to *discreet, discretion* means "caution or self-restraint": Concerned about their privacy, the donors appreciated the fundraiser's **discretion**. *Discrete* means "distinct": The course was presented as three **discrete** units.

disinterested, uninterested *Disinterested* means "neutral": Scientists are expected to be **disinterested**. *Uninterested* means "lacking interest": Knowing nothing about the sport, I was **uninterested** in the score.

distinct, distinctive *Distinct* means "well-defined" or "easily perceived": We noticed a **distinct** change in the weather. *Distinctive* means "characteristic": The **distinctive** odor of chlorine met us in the entryway to the pool.

dyeing, dying *Dyeing*, from *dye*, means "coloring something, usually by soaking it": They are **dyeing** the wool today. *Dying*, from *die*, means "losing life" or "fading": We finished our hike just as the light was **dying**.

eager See **anxious, eager.**

effect See **affect, effect.**

elicit, illicit *Elicit* means "to draw out": Her joke **elicited** an unexpected response from the audience. *Illicit* means "illegal": The police searched for **illicit** drugs.

elude See **allude, elude.**

emigrate from, immigrate to *Emigrate* means "to move from one's own country": His ancestors **emigrated from** Norway. *Immigrate* means "to move to a different country": They **immigrated to** Australia. Other forms: *emigrant; immigrant.*

eminent, imminent *Eminent* means "well-known and respected": An **eminent** scientist from the University of Montana received the award. *Imminent* means "about to happen": As conditions worsened, a strike was **imminent**.

ensure See **assure, ensure, insure.**

especially, specially *Especially* means "remarkably": The summer was **especially** warm. *Especially* also means "particularly": Tourists flock to the island, **especially** during the spring and summer months. *Specially* means "for a particular purpose": The seeds were **specially** selected for this climate.

etc. Abbreviation of *et cetera*, meaning "and others of the same kind" or "and so forth." In academic writing, it is generally used only within parentheses. Avoid using *and etc.*: A noise forecast is based on several factors (time of day noise occurs, frequency of noise, duration of noise, ~~and~~ etc.).

everyday, every day *Everyday* means "routine": They took advantage of **everyday** opportunities. *Every day* means "each day": He practiced **every day**.

everyplace See **anyplace, everyplace, someplace.**

except See **accept, except.**

explicit, implicit *Explicit* means "expressed directly": The **explicit** statement of her expectations left little room for misinterpretation. *Implicit* means "expressed indirectly": Our **implicit** agreement was to remain silent.

farther, further *Farther* usually refers to geographic distance: They drove **farther** than they had planned. *Further* indicates additional effort or time: Tomorrow they will discuss the issue **further**.

fewer, less *Fewer* is used before nouns referring to people or objects that can be counted: **fewer** students, **fewer** printers. *Less* is used before noncount or abstract nouns: **less** water, **less** interest. *Less* *than* may be used with measurements of distance or time: **less than** ten miles, **less than** two years.

first, firstly, second, secondly Although *first* and *second* are generally preferred, current dictionaries state that *firstly* and *secondly* are well-established forms.

foreword, forward A *foreword* is a preface or introduction to a book: In the **foreword**, the author discussed his reasons for writing the book. *Forward* means "in a frontward direction": The crowd lunged **forward**.

former, latter *Former* refers to the first and *latter* refers to the second of two people or items mentioned in the previous sentence: Employees could choose between a state pension plan or a private pension plan. The majority chose the **former**, but a few believed the **latter** would provide them with more retirement income.

further See **farther, further.**

good, well Use *well* instead of *good* to modify a verb. You played ~~good~~ well today. *Good* and *well* can be used interchangeably to mean "in good health": I did not feel **well** [OR **good**] when I woke up.

had better See **better, had better.**

hanged, hung *Hanged* means "executed by hanging": They were **hanged** at dusk. *Hung* means "suspended" or "draped": She **hung** a family photo in her office.

herself, himself, myself, yourself Unconventional when not used as reflexive or intensive pronouns. Jean and ~~myself~~ I prepared the presentation. I **myself** led the discussion.

hopefully Conversational for "I hope": ~~Hopefully,~~ I hope the weather will improve.

hung See **hanged, hung.**

i.e. Abbreviation of *id est,* meaning "that is." In academic writing, it is generally used only within parentheses and is followed by a comma: Everyone donated the same amount (**i.e.,** fifty dollars). Outside of parentheses, use *that is* rather than *i.e.*: The office will be closed for the autumn holidays, **that is**, Labor Day, Columbus Day, Veterans' Day, and Thanksgiving.

illicit See **elicit, illicit.**

illusion See **allusion, illusion.**

immigrate to See **emigrate from, immigrate to.**

imminent See **eminent, imminent.**

immoral See **amoral, immoral.**

impact Considered unconventional in academic writing when used as a verb to mean "to affect": The hurricane will ~~impact~~ affect coastal residents. However, according to current dictionaries, this usage is common in business writing.

implicit See **explicit, implicit.**

imply, infer *Imply* means "to suggest indirectly": I did not mean to **imply** that you were at fault. *Infer* means "to conclude or deduce": Given his participation at the meeting, I **inferred** that he would support the proposal.

in regards to Unconventional. See **regard, regarding, regards.**

ingenious, ingenuous *Ingenious* means "creative": This **ingenious** plan will satisfy everyone. *Ingenuous* means "innocent or naive": No one knew for sure whether she was truly **ingenuous** or just shrewd.

inside of, outside of Delete *of* when unnecessary: They met **outside** ~~of~~ the fortress.

insure See **assure, ensure, insure.**

irregardless A double negative (*ir-* means "not" and *-less* means "not having") that is used in some regions of the United States for *regardless* but is unconventional.

its, it's *Its* indicates possession: The Republican Party concludes **its** convention today. *It's* is a contraction of *it is*: **It's** difficult to predict the outcome. Confusion over *its* and *it's* is responsible for many usage errors.

kind, sort, type Use *this* or *that* to refer to one *kind, sort,* or *type;* avoid using the word *a:* **This kind** [OR **sort** OR **type**] of **a** leader is most effective. Use *these* or *those* to refer to more than one: **These kinds** [OR **sorts** OR **types**] of leaders are most effective.

kind of, sort of Conversational to mean "somewhat": The rock-climbing course was ~~kind of~~ somewhat difficult.

later, latter *Later* means "afterward": The concert ended **later** than we had expected. *Latter* refers to the second of two people or items mentioned in the previous sentence. See also **former, latter**.

lay, lie *Lay* (*laid, laying*) means "to put" or "to place": I will **lay** the book on your desk. *Lie* (*lay, lain, lying*) means "to rest" or "to recline": She **lay** perfectly still, trying to hear what they were saying. *Lay* takes an object (to **lay** something), but *lie* does not. The present tense of *lay* and the past tense of *lie* (which is *lay*) are often confused because they are spelled the same way.

lead, led The noun *lead* is a kind of metal: The gas had **lead** added to it. The verb *lead* means "to show the way" or "to go in front": The director will **lead** the campaign. The past tense of the verb *lead* is *led*: He **led** a discussion on the origins of abstract art.

less, less than See **fewer, less**.

liable *Liable* generally means "likely" but with a negative connotation: If they do not wear the appropriate gear, they are **liable** to harm themselves. Because of her experience, she is ~~liable~~ likely to win easily.

lie See **lay, lie**.

like See **as, like**.

literally Used in conversation for emphasis. In academic writing, *literally* indicates that an expression is not being used figuratively: My friend **literally** took the cake—at least the few pieces that were left after the party.

lose, loose *Lose* means "to misplace" or "to fail to succeed": She hates to **lose** an argument. *Loose* means "unfastened" or "movable": One of the boards had come **loose**.

lots, lots of Conversational for *many* or *much:* ~~Lots of~~ Many fans traveled to see the championship game. You will have ~~lots~~ much to do this year. See also **a lot of**.

may See **can, may**.

may of, might of See **of**.

maybe, may be *Maybe* means "possibly": **Maybe** we will have better luck next year. *May* and *be* are both verbs: I **may be** late.

media, medium *Media,* the plural form of *medium,* should be followed by a plural verb. The **media** ~~is~~ are covering the event. However, current dictionaries note the frequent use of *media* as a collective noun taking a singular verb.

morale, moral *Morale* means "confidence" or "spirits": **Morale** was always high. *Moral* means "ethical": She confronted a **moral** dilemma. *Moral* may also mean "the lesson of a story": The **moral** of the story is live and let live.

myself See **herself, himself, myself, yourself**.

number of See **amount of, number of.**

of Often mistakenly used for the unstressed auxiliary verb *have:* They must ~~of~~ **have** [OR could **have**, might **have**, may **have**, should **have**, would **have**] left early.

OK, O.K., okay All three spellings are acceptable, but usage of any of the forms is considered conversational: The teacher gave her ~~O.K.~~ **permission** to the students. Did the manager ~~okay~~ **agree to** the expense?

one, won *One* designates the singularity of anything. *Won* is the past tense of the verb *win*, which means to achieve victory over others.

outside of See **inside of, outside of.**

passed, past *Passed* is the past tense of the verb *pass:* I **passed** city hall on my way to work. *Past* means "beyond": The band marched **past** the bleachers.

persecute, prosecute *Persecute* means "to harass" or "to oppress": The group had been **persecuted** because of its religious beliefs. *Prosecute* means "to take legal action against": They decided not to **prosecute** because of insufficient evidence. Other forms: *persecution; prosecution.*

perspective, prospective *Perspective* means "point of view": Our **perspectives** on the issue differ. *Prospective* means "potential": **Prospective** graduate students must take an entrance exam.

persuade See **convince, persuade.**

plus *Plus* joins nouns or noun phrases to make a sentence seem like an equation: Supreme talent **plus** rigorous training **makes** this runner hard to beat. Note that a singular form of the verb is required. Avoid using *plus* to join clauses: She takes classes Monday through Friday, ~~plus~~ **and** she works on weekends.

precede, proceed To *precede* is to "go before": A determiner **precedes** a noun. To *proceed* is to "go on": After a layover in Chicago, we will **proceed** to New York. Other forms: *precedence, precedent; procedure, proceedings.*

prejudice, prejudiced *Prejudice* can be a noun or a verb: Because of his **prejudice**, he was unable to make a fair decision. Be aware of your own bias so that you do not **prejudice** others. *Prejudiced* is an adjective: The authorities were racially **prejudiced**.

principal, principle *Principal* is a noun meaning "head" or an adjective meaning "main": The **principal** met the students at the door. The state's **principal** crop is wheat. *Principle* is a noun meaning "standard or belief": The doctrine was derived from three moral **principles**.

proceed See **precede, proceed.**

prosecute See **persecute, prosecute.**

prospective See **perspective, prospective.**

quotation, quote In academic writing, use *quotation*, rather than *quote*, to refer to a copied sentence or passage: Her introduction included a ~~quote~~ **quotation** from *Rebecca*. *Quote* expresses an action: My friend likes to **quote** lines from recent movies.

raise, rise *Raise* (*raised, raising*) means "to cause to increase or move upward": The Federal Reserve Board **raised** interest rates. *Rise* (*rose, risen, rising*) means "to get up" or "to increase": Prices **rose** sharply. *Raise* takes an object (to **raise** something); *rise* does not.

regard, regarding, regards These words are used appropriately in the expressions *with regard to, as regards, in regard to,* and *regarding:* I am writing **with regard to** your purchasing my computer. (*As* *regarding, in regards to,* and *with regards to* are unconventional.)

respectfully, respectively *Respectfully* means "considerately": The scholars **respectfully** disagreed with each other. *Respectively* means "in that order": The diplomat introduced her to the representative, the senator, and the governor, **respectively**.

rise See **raise, rise**.

second, secondly See **first, firstly, second, secondly**.

sensor See **censor, censure, sensor**.

sensual, sensuous *Sensual* refers to physical pleasure, especially sexual pleasure or indulgence of an appetite: The band's lead singer was renowned for his **sensual** movements. *Sensuous* refers to aesthetic pleasure, for example, in response to art: She found the **sensuous** colors of the painting very soothing. Other forms: *sensuality; sensuousness.*

set, sit *Set* means "to place" or "to establish": We **set** the date for the meeting: May 4. *Sit* means "to take a seat": The judges of the competition **sat** on the left side of the stage. *Set* takes an object (to **set** something), but *sit* does not.

should of See **of**.

sight See **cite, sight, site**.

sit See **set, sit**.

site See **cite, sight, site**.

so *So* emphasizes another word that is followed by a *that* clause: We arrived **so** late **that** we could not find a place to stay. Avoid using *so* without a *that* clause; find a more precise modifier instead: She was **so** spectacularly successful.

someplace See **anyplace, everyplace, someplace**.

sometime, sometimes, some time *Sometime* means "at an unspecified time": We will move **sometime** in June. *Sometimes* means "every so often": **Sometimes** the weather changes abruptly. *Some time* means "a short period": After **some time** had passed, they were able to reach a compromise.

sort See **kind, sort, type**.

sort of See **kind of, sort of**.

specially See **especially, specially**.

stationary, stationery *Stationary* means "at a standstill": The planes on the runway were **stationary** for two hours. *Stationery* means "writing paper and envelopes": He objected to the new logo on the **stationery**.

subsequently See **consequently, subsequently**.

than, then *Than* links both parts of a comparison: The game lasted longer **than** we had expected. *Then* means "after that": Read the contract closely; **then** sign it.

that, which *Which* introduces nonessential (nonrestrictive) clauses and is preceded by a comma: The world's tiniest fish, **which** is *Hippocampus denise,* was found in Indonesia. *That* generally introduces essential (restrictive) clauses: He wants to develop a bar code **that** can be used to identify animals. *Which* can be used in an essential clause introduced by a preposition: The legal battle **in which** we find ourselves seems endless.

that, who In essential (restrictive) clauses, *who* is generally used to refer to people: They did not know the protestors **who** [OR **that**] organized the rally.

their, there, they're *Their* is a possessive form: **Their** donation was made anonymously. *There* refers to location: We worked **there** together. *There* can also be used as an expletive: **There** are some unanswered questions. *They're* is a contraction of *they are:* **They're** performing on Wednesday.

~~theirself, theirselves~~ Unconventional for *themselves.* They discussed the topic among ~~theirselves~~ themselves.

then See **than, then.**

there See **their, there, they're.**

they're See **their, there, they're.**

thru Use *through* in academic writing: He lived ~~thru~~ through two world wars.

to, too, two *To* is a preposition, usually signaling a direction: They sent the petition **to** everyone in the neighborhood. *To* is also an infinitive marker: They planned **to** finish their work by Friday. *Too* means "also": She goes to school and works **too.** *Too* also means "excessively": We have made **too** many commitments. *Two* is a number: She moved here **two** months ago.

toward, towards *Toward* is preferred in American English.

type See **kind, sort, type.**

uninterested See **disinterested, uninterested.**

unique *Unique* means "one of a kind" and thus is not preceded by a word such as *most* or *very:* San Francisco is ~~very unique~~. However, according to current dictionaries, *unique* is frequently used to mean "extraordinary."

weather, whether *Weather* refers to the condition of the atmosphere: The **weather** report is usually accurate. *Whether* introduces alternatives: He must decide **whether** to sell now or wait for the market to improve.

well See **good, well.**

whether See **weather, whether.**

which, witch *Which* is a relative pronoun that introduces nonrestrictive elements. A practitioner of sorcery is a *witch.*

which See **that, which.**

who, whom *Who* is the subject or subject complement of a clause: Leon Bates, ~~whom~~ who I believe has great potential, will soon be competing in international events. (*Who* is the subject of *who has great potential.*) *Whom* is used as an object: Anna Holmes, ~~who~~ whom I met at a convention three years ago, has agreed to speak to our study group. (*Whom* is the object of *I met.*) According to current dictionaries, *who* is frequently used in the object position when it does not follow a preposition. See also **that, who.**

whose, who's *Whose* is a possessive form: The procedure was developed by a researcher **whose** mother will benefit from the innovation. *Who's* is the contraction of *who is:* **Who's** responsible for writing the report?

with regards to Unconventional. See **regard, regarding, regards.**

would of See **of.**

your, you're *Your* is a possessive form: **Your** review was chosen for publication. *You're* is the contraction of *you are:* **You're** almost finished.

yourself See **herself, himself, myself, yourself.**

Glossary of Rhetorical Terms

Chapter 1 Understanding the Rhetorical Situation

rhetoric—communication to achieve a specific purpose with a specific audience

rhetorical opportunity—the issue, problem, or situation that motivates the use of language to stimulate change

writer—someone who uses language to bring about change in an audience

message—the main point of information shaped to influence an audience

audience—those who receive and interpret the message of a communication

rhetorical situation—the context that influences effective communication

purpose—in rhetoric, the reason for a communication

rhetorical purpose—the specific change the writer wants to accomplish through the use of language

rhetorical audience—the specific audience most capable of being changed by a message or of bringing about change

stance—the attitude your writing conveys toward your topic, purpose, and audience

genre—a category of writing that has a particular format and features, such as memoir or argument

medium—method of communication: oral, visual, verbal, digital, or print

media (plural of *medium*)—*mass media* is a term used for media like radio, television, and various online forums that reach a broad audience

Chapter 2 Analyzing Rhetorical Choices

problem—in rhetoric, a question for discussion, exploration, and possible solution

problem-solving approach—in rhetoric, an examination of a question on an issue or situation directed at a specific audience

fitting response—a communication whose tone, content, and delivery are carefully constructed to connect to the interests of a specific audience

claim—an assertion that identifies a problem and proposes a solution

thesis statement—a clearly worded statement of your claim that guides the structure of a paper, presentation, or multimedia text

available means of persuasion—include the methods of communication (visual, verbal, digital, print) as well as rhetorical appeals of ethos, logos, and pathos (see pp. 23–24)

rhetorical appeals—the strategies established by ancient Greeks as the foundation for persuasion: ethos (the writer's credibility), logos (the good reasons of the argument), and pathos (the emotional connection with the audience)

ethos—the ethical appeal of the writer's credibility, goodwill, and trustworthiness

common ground—a belief or value shared by the writer and audience that provides the basis for agreement

logos—an appeal to the audience's reason through the logical construction of the argument

evidence—support for your claim that includes testimonials and anecdotes, statistics, facts, and expert opinions

pathos—an authentic emotional connection with the audience

resources (advantages)—in rhetoric, the means needed to effect change in an audience

constraints (limitations)—the obstacles a writer has to overcome to reach and perhaps persuade an audience

Chapter 3 Academic Literacies: Reading Rhetorically

reading process—series of steps, including previewing, skimming, reading, and annotating

Believing and Doubting Game—strategy that includes both reading while believing the writer (and in so doing understanding the writer's message better) and reading while doubting the writer (and in so doing finding the gaps and questions that emerge from the selection)

summary—a type of writing that condenses a selection to its main points

abstracts—brief objective summaries of articles, especially used in writing papers for the social sciences

critical response—a reaction in writing to a text that explains why you agree or disagree with the text

analysis—a breaking down of a text into its constituent parts accompanied by a critical examination of the ways the text responds to the rhetorical situation

synthesis—an examination of how the individual parts of a text or different points of view from different texts fit together and diverge to bring a new perspective to the whole work

synthesis (or critical) question—the question that directs, focuses, and launches your research

Chapter 4 Rhetorical Success in a Digital World

multimedia—images or visuals, text, audio, and video used in combinations in a composition

fonts—styles of print type

serif—fonts with foot-like tips on the ends of letters

sans serif—fonts with no serifs on the ends of the letters

layout—the way words and images are positioned in relation to each other on a page

white space—blank areas around text, graphics, or images

angle of vision—the position of the camera in relation to the image

cropping—the process of editing an image to draw the viewer's attention to the focal point

infographics—images, tables, charts, pie charts, and figures that condense information into a visual presentation

accessibility—in rhetoric, the extent to which a message is designed to be easy to read by those with disabilities that affect seeing, hearing, and manipulating a particular medium

Chapter 5 Memoirs

memoirs—narratives that reflect on personal experience or series of experiences

Chapter 6 Profiles

profile—a portrait in words of a person, place, or event

Chapter 7 Investigative Reports

report—a presentation of objective information on a topic

investigative report—an analysis of the "who, what, where, and why" of a topic

Chapter 8 Position Arguments

position argument—the assertion of a point of view about an issue supported by reasons and evidence

Chapter 9 Proposal

proposal—message that calls for improvement through action

Chapter 10 Evaluations

evaluation—a judgment based on relevant criteria and meant to persuade

Chapter 11 Critical Analyses

critical analysis—a careful examination of the causes or consequences of a situation or phenomenon

Chapter 12 Literary Analyses

literary analysis—an argument for reading a text in a certain way

close reading—an examination of the key characteristics (including style and structure) of a text

fiction—prose stories based on the imagination

poetry—a concentrated language relying on sound and image

drama—a performance where a director and actors interpret a script

interpretive question—a question about the meaning, structure, or significance of a text

reading journal—a record of personal thoughts, ideas, and questions about a text

Chapter 13 From Tentative Idea to Finished Project

listing—jotting down tentative ideas to explore a topic

brainstorming—listing tentative ideas at one sitting

freewriting—writing to explore ideas on a topic without concern for spelling, grammar, style, or who will read it

questioning—structured speculation used to explore a topic in a new way

journalists' questions—Who? What? Where? When? Why? How?

journal—a private record of your understandings and reactions to reading, assignments, class discussion, and lectures

double-entry notebook—a journal with two distinct columns pairing observation and personal response

clustering—a method using arrows, circles, lines, or other visual cues for connecting ideas

outline—a structure that lists the main parts and supporting points of an essay

thesis statement—an explicit claim about your topic, usually in one sentence, that expresses the overarching idea of your paper (a topic and your stance on that topic)

working thesis—a statement that tests a possible framework and controlling idea for your paper

drafting—a process that combines an informal structure with a freewrite

introductions—openings for papers, often including the thesis and establishing credibility on the topic

body—an exploration of a topic that builds a logical structure to support a thesis

conclusion—a final appeal to your audience by making clear how the issue you are exploring affects them

revision—a process of rethinking and rewriting parts of your draft

peer evaluation—a form of collaboration that provides writing advice from fellow students

editing—improving word choice, adding details, and structuring sentences more effectively

proofreading—checking for spelling, typos, grammar, and punctuation errors

Chapter 14 The Power of Paragraphs

topic sentence—a sentence that states the main idea of a paragraph

deductive reasoning—A form of logical reasoning in which a conclusion is formed after relating a specific fact (minor premise) to a generalization

inductive reasoning—The reasoning process that begins with facts or observations and moves to general principles that account for those facts or observations

unified—a paragraph in which every sentence relates to the main idea

coherent—a paragraph in which each sentence follows another in a way that makes the relationship among the ideas logical and clear

chronological order—an arrangement of ideas according to the order in which things happened

spatial order—an orientation that focuses from right to left, near to far, top to bottom

emphatic order—an arrangement of information in order of importance, usually from least to most important

logical order—an orientation that moves from specific to general or from general to specific

Chapter 15 Rhetorical Strategies for Development

narration—a detailed account of events as in a story

characters—people in the story

dialogue—direct speech by the characters in a narration

setting—the time and place of a narration

plot—the sequence of events in a narration

anecdote—a brief story that illustrates a point

point of view—the perspective of the narrator in telling a story

climax—turning point in a narration

flashback—narrative technique that accounts for past events

flash forward—narrative technique that accounts for future events

description—a verbal accounting of physical and mental experiences

sensory details—what we see, hear, smell, touch, or taste

sensibility details—having to do with intellectual, emotional, or physical states

exemplification—the use of examples

definition—a classification that distinguishes, describes, and names something

formal (or sentence) definition—a dictionary or encyclopedia reference that classifies, describes, and names something

extended definition—a classification that provides extended information to describe, distinguish, and name something

historical definition—an overview over a period of time of how a concept or term has been used

negative definition—a classification that distinguishes a concept or term by showing what it is not

stipulative definition—a classification that is specific to a particular context

classification and division—the act of creating categories that distinguish information, objects, or other concepts

comparison and contrast—a description of similarities and differences

basis for comparison—shared characteristics that are used to understand objects, people, and ideas

points of comparison—areas that show how two things are the same and how they are different

cause-and-effect analysis—an explanation for how some things have occurred or a prediction that certain events will lead to specific effects

process analysis—breaking down into a series of steps how something occurs

directive process analysis—a series of steps used to teach an audience how to duplicate the occurrence of something

informative process analysis—a series of steps used to explain how something occurs or has occurred

argument—the presentation of a point of view and logical reasoning in an effort to persuade an audience that something is true or valid

persuasion—the use of emotions as well as logic to move an audience to change their minds or take action

identifiable issue—specific issue related to a problem that can be argued for or against

Chapter 16 Style: An Essential Guide to Effective Sentences

subject—the who or what that carries out the action, experiences something, or is described

predicate—the part of a sentence that expresses what a subject is, does, or experiences

complement—a word or words used to make the meaning of a sentence clear

independent clause—a group of words consisting of a subject + predicate that expresses the main idea of a sentence

dependent clause—a group of words that includes a subject and a predicate and enhances the main idea of the sentence but cannot stand alone without that main idea

sentence fragment—a piece of a sentence that is missing a subject and/or a verb or is a dependent clause

run-on sentence—two sentences or independent clauses run together without punctuation

faulty predication—a sentence error in which the predicate does not logically belong with the given subject

rhetorical question—a question that does not require an answer but is instead used to state an opinion and direct readers to major points.

coordination—the use of grammatically equivalent constructions to link or balance ideas

subordination—the connection of a grammatical structure to another, usually a dependent clause to an independent clause: Even though customers were satisfied with the product, the company wanted to improve it

coordinating conjunction—words used to connect other words, phrases, clauses, or sentences connect of equal grammatical rank (words, such as, *and, but, or, nor, for, so,* and *yet*)

correlative conjunction—Two-part connecting words such as *either/or* and *not only/but also*

subordinating conjunctions—words that specify the relationship between a dependent clause and an independent clause

relative pronouns—words (*who, whom, that, which,* or *whose*) that are used to introduce a clause and that have an antecedent in the main clause

cumulative sentence—a sentence that presents the main idea first, followed by supplementary details and ideas that expand on the main idea.

periodic sentence—a sentence that presents details and ideas first to lead up to the main idea

parallelism—repeated patterns of words or grammatically equivalent forms

abstract noun—nouns that refer to a concept

concrete noun—nouns that refer to something perceivable by the senses

action verbs—verbs that convey action

linking verbs (passive verbs)—verbs that convey states of being and perceptions

active voice—emphasizes the person performing the action

passive voice—emphasizes the recipient of the action

clichés—an expression that has lost its power to interest readers because of overuse

mixed metaphor—a construction that includes parts of two or more unrelated metaphors: Her fiery personality dampened our hopes of a compromise

mixed construction—a confusing sentence that is the result of an unintentional shift from one grammatical pattern to another

inclusive language—writing that shows equal respect for all people, all genders, by using nonsexist and nonracist language

expletive—A word signaling a structural change in a sentence, usually used so that new or important information is given at the end of the sentence

Chapter 17 Strategies for Editing Common Problems

recursive—a process of moving back and forth between global and sentence level drafting and revision

sentence fragment—a piece of a sentence that is missing a subject and/or a verb or is a dependent clause

comma splice—Two sentences that are punctuated as one sentence when they should be punctuated as two sentences (or two independent clauses).

fused sentence—two sentences or independent clauses run together without punctuation

run-on **sentence**—two sentences or independent clauses run together without punctuation

compound subject—two nouns joined by *and*

singular subjects—two nouns linked by *either/or,* or *neither/nor*

antecedent—a word or group of words referred to by a pronoun

collective noun—A noun that refers to a group

modifier—a word or word group that describes, limits, or qualifies another

misplaced modifier—A descriptive or qualifying word or phrase placed in a position that confuses the reader

squinting modifier—a modifier that is unclear because it can refer to words either preceding it or following it

Dangling modifiers—words or phrases that do not clearly modify another word or word group

possessive case—a grammatical construction that indicates ownership and other similar relationships

homophones—words that sound alike but have different meanings

homonyms—words that are spelled alike and sound alike but have different meanings

Chapter 19 Identifying Sources

primary sources—firsthand accounts or original data

secondary sources—sources that interpret or collect firsthand accounts or original data

scholarly books—for a scholarly audience, original research by scholars that includes analysis and interpretation.

popular or trade books—for a general audience, books include information, often about the primary research that has been done by others.

reference books—provide factual information, often including short articles written and reviewed by experts in the field.

periodicals—publications such as magazines and newspapers that are published over a specific period of time (daily, weekly, or monthly)

scholarly journals—publications for a specialized audience that contain original research on academic topics

magazines—periodical publications for the general public, sometimes focused on a particular subject

newspapers—regional, local, or national news publications that also include letters to the editor and editorial opinion pieces

.com—the domain name used on the internet for commercial, for-profit entities

.edu—the domain name used on the internet for a U.S. educational institution

.gov—the domain name used on the internet for U.S. governmental branches or agencies

.org—the domain name used on the internet for nonprofit organizations

government documents—any information printed/published by the local, state, or national government

Social media—Websites and apps that allow users to create and share content, including articles, photographs, and videos, and to network socially.

special collections—library resources on particular topics, people, and places, often including audio-visual and primary sources

interviews—a special type of conversation in which a reporter elicits responses from someone recognized for their status or accomplishments

fieldwork—real-world research that commonly includes observation, interviews, and questionnaires

observation—watching closely what is happening and trying to figure out why

naturalistic study—observation based on direct access to the person or phenomenon being researched

interview questions—questions designed to put your subject at ease and purposefully progress from one subject to another

institutional review boards (IRBs)—committees set up to protect participants' privacy in field research

bibliography—a list of sources used in a research project, including author, title, and other publication data

working bibliography—a preliminary record of source information such as author, title, page numbers, and publication data

Chapter 20 Evaluating Sources

annotated bibliography—list of sources that includes commentary on each source

Chapter 21 Synthesizing Sources: Summary, Paraphrase, and Quotation

plagiarism—the use of others' words and ideas without adequate acknowledgment

function statement—a description of the content of the text and the intention of the author

attributive tags—words that attribute information to a source

paraphrase—a restatement of someone else's ideas in your own words

Chapter 22 Acknowledging Sources in MLA Style

container—the term used in MLA style for the source within which an article or posting is found

Index

ability, in inclusive language, 317
Ablow, Joseph, 356, 357
"Ablow's Objets d'Art," 357–358
abstract noun, 313, 604
abstracts, 41, 600
  in research papers (APA style),
    468, 469
academic literacies, 34–48
academic writing, expectations for,
    230–231
acceptability, of proposal, 162
access date, 449
accessibility, 600
  of multimedia texts, 14, 60–62
accountability, in climate crisis,
    579–580
action verbs, 313, 604
active reading, in rhetorical
    situation, 34, 35, 208
active voice, 313, 604
Addams, Calpernia, 65
ad hominem (logical fallacy), 138, 391
advantages (resources), 31
"Advent Posada Is an Act of
    Resistance, The" (Bañuelas),
    530, 547–550
advertisement/advertising
  rhetorical appeals in, example
    of, 128–129
  in Works Cited list (MLA style),
    436
After Gun Violence (Rood), 268
afterword, in Works Cited list
    (MLA style), 423
age, in inclusive language, 316–317
agriculture, climate change effects
    on, 559–560
"Ain't I a Woman?" (Sojourner
    Truth), 24–26
AJOL (African Journals Online), 430
Alcott, Louisa May, 168–170
Ali, Elama, 515
ambiguous pronoun reference. *See*
    vague pronoun reference
American Heritage Dictionary,
    366–367
American Psychological
    Association (APA), 248
American Psychological Association
    (APA) style, acknowledging
    sources in, 450–475
"Americans Are Closing the Book
    on Reading, Study Finds"
    (Howard), 271

"American Sign Language and the
    Academy" (Brueggemann),
    261
Amethyst Initiative, 27–30, 31
"Am I the only person in the world
    who hates Little Women?"
    (Lothian-McLean), 170–171
ampersand (&), 451
analysis, 13, 600
  analysis and synthesis
    in critical analyses, 193
    in evaluations, 175–176
    in investigative reports, 119
    in literary analyses, 218
    in memoirs, 81
    in position arguments, 138
    in profiles, 99
    in proposals, 156–157
    in reading, 43–48
Anderson, Steven, 350, 351
anecdotes, 24, 602
  in critical analysis, 200–201
  in introductions, 271
  in investigative reports, 132, 133
  in memoirs, 83, 86
  in narrative, 279
  in position arguments, 141
  in profiles, 96, 104, 106, 107
angle of vision, 57, 600
annotated bibliography, 392–394,
    606
annotating, in reading process, 36–37
anonymous authors
  in-text citations for: APA style, 452
  in References list (APA style), 458
  in Works Cited list (MLA style),
    422
antecedent, 332, 605
Antecedents of Man, The (Le Gros
    Clark), 284
anthology, works in
  in-text citation for (MLA style),
    415
  in Works Cited list (MLA style),
    423
"Anti-Homeless Architecture"
    (Drohan), 508, 512–515
AP (Associated Press), 493, 504–505
APA (American Psychological
    Association) style
  for block quotations, 410–411
  for in-text citations, 450–453
  for References list, 454–468
  sample research paper, 468–475

apostrophe, strategies for editing,
    342–345
appeal to tradition (logical fallacy),
    138, 391
argument, as rhetorical strategy,
    292–294, 603. *See also*
    position argument
  persuasion *vs.*, 292
Aristotle, 18, 21
*A Room for Learning: The Making of
    a School in Vermont* (Birdsey),
    266
arrangement
  in multimedia design, 53,
    68–71
  research information and, 388
articles (journal or magazine)
  in References list (APA style),
    460–464
  in Works Cited list (MLA style),
    419–420, 425–428,
    431, 432
art work, in Works Cited list (MLA
    style), 435
Associated Press (AP), 493,
    504–505
assumption, dangers of, 387
asylum seeking, as global
    phenomenon, 528–550
"A Tale of Two Profiles" (Gay),
    187–189
atmosphere, in literary text, 209
attributive tags, 606
  for direct quotations, 409
  when paraphrasing sources, 408
  when summarizing sources, 398
audience, 2, 599. *See also* rhetorical
    audience
  analyzing, 9
  in analyzing assignments, 230
  locating, 355–358
  in memoir, 86
  message and, 7–9
  for multimedia texts, 60–71
  in rhetorical situation, 2
audio recording, evaluating stance
    of, 388–392
audiovisual sources, 373–374
authority, establishing, 21. *See also*
    credibility, establishing
authors
  in-text citations for
    APA style, 452–453
    MLA style, 413–414

critical analyses, (*Continued*)
    guide to writing, 198–201
    key features of, 190
    media critique as, 187–189
    medium of delivery for,
        187, 198
    opportunity for change in,
        identifying, 187, 195
    revision and peer review
        in, 202
critical question, 44, 600
critical reading, in rhetorical
    situation, 35
critical response, 600
    in reading process, 42
cropping, 57, 600
cultural signs, 57
cumulative sentence, 308, 604
currency, of sources, 389

Daily Beast, The, 492
dangling modifiers, 335,
    337, 605
Darkness Visible (Styron),
    281–282
date of publication
    in References list (APA style),
        461, 464
    in Works Cited list (MLA style),
        418, 430
"Dating Sites and Social Media
    Firms Must Do More
    to Protect Users from
    'Catfishing'" (Coffey),
    498–500
Davis, Catherine L., 469–475
deductive reasoning, 259, 602
definition, 602. *See also* extended
    definition; formal definition;
    historical definition;
    negative definition; sentence
    definition; stipulative
    definition
    as rhetorical strategy 282–284
    mismatches in, 300
delivery, Demosthenes on, 67
Delpit, Lisa, 45–46
demo, as presentation element, 71
Demosthenes, 67
dénouement, 208
dependent clause, 603
    in effective sentences, 297
description, 602
    in evaluation, 182
    in investigative report,
        123–124
    in memoir, 85, 87

in position argument, 146
in profiles, 96, 104–106, 107
in proposal, 161
as rhetorical strategy, 266,
    280-281
details, in descriptive writing,
    280
details, necessary but missing, in
    sentence unity, 301
development, rhetorical strategies
    for profiles and, 95
"Devotion" (Haslett), 308
dialect, 32
dialogue, 12, 55, 219, 602
    in literary analysis, 208
    in memoirs, 76, 77, 85–87
    in narrative, 279
    in profiles, 101
Diavolo, Lucy, 553–558
Dickerson, Debra (interview
    subject), 383
dictionaries, in Works Cited list
    (MLA style), 425
Didion, Joan, 309
Digital Object Identifier (DOI),
    417, 418, 429, 430, 465
directive process analysis,
    289, 603
direct quotations
    attributive tags for, 409
    paraphrasing *vs.,* 408
    in profiles, 96
    in summaries, 403
discussion group or forum, in
    References list (APA style),
    466
displacement, as global
    phenomenon, 528–550
documentary films, as audiovisual
    sources, 374
DOI (Digital Object Identifier),
    417, 418, 429, 430
"Do Immigrants 'Steal' Jobs
    from American Workers?"
    (Hoban), 530, 539
"Donuts at Easton's Center Circle:
    Slam Dunk or Cycle of
    Deterioration?" (Walker),
    173–175
double-entry notebook, 235–236,
    387, 601
"Doubts about Doublespeak"
    (Lutz), 398–401
Douglass, Frederick, 39–40, 44
drafting, 601
drafting, in writing process, 228,
    242–244

final draft example, 248–256
first draft example, 243–244
drama, 219, 601
    in-text citation for (MLA style),
        415
    in Works Cited list (MLA style),
        435
dramatic soliloquy, 208
drier ground, 573
Drohan, Freya, 508, 512–515
drought, 573
Dusoulier, Clotilde, 76
Dyson, Michael Eric, 271

editing, 602
    of images, 57
    in writing process, 248
editing, strategies for
    comma splices and fused
        (run-on) sentences,
        326–329
    consistent verb tense, 330–331
    misplaced or dangling
        modifiers, 335–337
    missing comma after an
        introductory element,
        340
    missing comma joining clauses
        with coordinating
        conjunctions, 339–340
    missing comma setting off
        nonessential elements, 341
    parallelism, 337–339
    pronoun agreement, 332–333
    sentence fragments, 323–326
    spelling, 346–347
    subject-verb agreement,
        329–330
    unnecessary commas, 341–342
    unnecessary or missing
        apostrophe, 342–345
    vague pronoun reference,
        333–335
    wrong word, 347–349
edition
    in References list (APA style),
        458, 460
    in Works Cited list (MLA style),
        418
editor
    in Works Cited list (MLA style),
        422–423
editorial
    in References list (APA style),
        463
    in Works Cited list (MLA style),
        428

rhetorical opportunity and, 13
rhetorical situation in, 50–51
multiple works
in-text citation for (MLA style), 414
in Works Cited list (MLA style), 424
multivolume work
in-text citation for (MLA style), 414
in References list (APA style), 459
in Works Cited list (MLA style), 425
Murillo, Nadia, 515
Musicophilia (Sacks), 269
music recording, APA style for, in References list, 467
Musoni, Malcolm-Aime, 509, 524–526
Myspace, 492
"Myth of Multitasking, The" (Rosen), 114–119

narration, as rhetorical strategy, 279–280, 602. *See also* first-person narration
third-person narration
Narrative of the Life of Frederick Douglass, An American Slave (Douglass), 44
narrator, 208, 279
National Association of Evangelicals (NAE), 568
National Newspaper Index, 370
National Oceanic and Atmospheric Administration, 61
National Public Radio website, 372
National Young Farmers Coalition, 552, 558–564
natural disasters, climate change and, 571–573
naturalistic study, 375, 606
natural systems, 567
necessary but missing words, in sentence unity, 302
negative definition, 284, 603
.net (URL suffix), 390
Net Smart: How to Thrive Online (Rheingold), 275–276
newsgroup, in References list (APA style), 466
newspaper articles
in References list (APA style), 463, 465–466
in Works Cited list (MLA style), 427, 428

newspapers, 368, 605
"No-More-Deaths Volunteer Scott Warren Was Acquitted. But Humanitarian Aid Should Never Be Considered a Crime" (Uhlmann), 530, 542–544
nonessential elements, 341
non sequitur (logical fallacy), 138
notebook, double-entry, 235–236
note cards, 388
notes/note taking, 385–386
double-entry notebook and, 235–236
responding to, 387
"Not Seeing the Forest for the Dollar Bills" (Meadows), 273
nouns, 313
NPR (National Public Radio), 372
numbers, volume and issue, in Works Cited list (MLA style), 418
Nunberg, Geoffrey, 130–131

observation, 605
of field research, 375
"Official English Movement, The: Reimagining America" (Nunberg), 131
omniscient narrator, 208
On Fire: The (Burning) Case for the Green New Deal (Klein), 557
"On Keeping a Notebook" (Didion), 309
online book, 431
online databases, in References list (APA style), 465
online publication, in Works Cited list (MLA style), 431–432
online sources, 375
in References list (APA style), 465–466
reliability of, 390–391
in Works Cited list (MLA style), 420, 429–433
Open House: Of Family, Friends, Food, Piano Lessons, and the Search for a Room of My Own (Williams), 272
opportunity
analyzing, 9
in rhetorical situation, 2, 5
opportunity for change, identifying
in critical analyses, 187, 195
in evaluations, 168, 177–178

in investigative reports, 111, 121
in literary analyses, 205, 220–221
in memoirs, 75, 83
in position arguments, 129, 142
in profiles, 92, 101–102
in proposals, 151, 158
oral presentations, 67–71
"Orator in Chief" (Dyson), 271
ordering information, in a summary, 402–403
.org, 605
online sources, 371
URL suffix, 390
organization, of essay, 236–238
organization, patterns of
in paragraphs, 266–268
Other People's Children (Delpit), 45–46
outlining, 237–238, 601
"Out of the Kitchen, Onto the Couch [The Collapse of Home Cooking]" (Pollan), 478, 481–482
oversimplification (logical fallacy), 140, 392

page numbering, of research paper
in APA style, 468
in MLA style, 437
page numbers
in Works Cited list (MLA style), 430
Palmer, Parker, 305
pamphlets, in Works Cited list (MLA style), 436
"Pandemic Shaming: Is It Helping Us Keep Our Distance?" (Tait), 508, 518–523
paragraphs, power of, 257–277
adding essential information, 262
coherent, making, 263–269
conclusion, guiding, 270–276
creating, unity and coherence, 266–268
improving tips for, 264
introduction, guiding, 270–276
main idea, stating, 258–260
main point, developing, 260–262
patterns of organization, 266–268
revising, 276–277
unified, making, 263–269
using details, 261

sea levels, 572
secondary sources, 365, 605
second/subsequent edition, in
    Works Cited list (MLA
    style), 423
Seitz, Anna, 190–193
"Selfies Help Trans and Nonbinary
    People Create Our Own
    Narrative" (Riley R.L.),
    500–504
sensibility details, 602
    in descriptive writing, 280
sensory details, 602
    in evaluation, 182
    genre and, 12
    in memoirs, 77, 83, 87
    in profiles, 96
sentence definition, 283, 603
sentence forms, example for, 297
sentence fragments, 298, 323–326,
    603, 604
    editing fragments, dependent
        clauses, 325
    editing fragments with missing
        subjects and/or verbs, 325
    identifying, 324
sentence-level revision, 323
sentence logic mismatch, in
    sentence unity, 299–300
sentences, attributive tags in,
    positioning of, 409
sentences, effective
    choppiness of, 303
    emphatic repetition, 309
    ordering ideas, 309
    parts of, 296–298
    style guide for, 295–321
    (See also style, guide to
        effective sentences)
    varying sentence openings, 304
serif, 600
serif fonts, 52
setting, 57, 208–209, 219, 279, 602
sexual orientation, in inclusive
    language, 317
Sheffield, Rob, 304–305
short summaries, 405
Shreeve, James, 301
Shyong, Frank, 530, 544–547
Sibo, Alex, 210, 212–217, 222
Silent Spring (Carson, Rachel), 551
simile, 209
Simkanin, Stacy
    research paper in MLA style,
        248–256
    work examples by, 233–238,
        242–244, 247, 248, 256

simple sentence, 297
single work, in Works Cited list
    (MLA style), 423
singular subjects, 329, 604
skimming, in reading process, 36
Skin: A Natural History (Jablonski),
    308
slang in academic writing, 312
Slate Audio Book Club, 222
slide, as presentation element, 71
slippery slope (logical fallacy),
    140, 392
"Smokers Never Win"
    (advertisement), 129
Snapchat, 492
Snowflake: Winter's Secret Beauty,
    The (Libbrecht), 308
social media, 372, 605
    and gender, 491–506
"Social Media and the End of
    Gender" (Blakley), 495–496
social media profiles, 92–95. See
    also profiles
social networking, as medium of
    delivery, 62–63
soils, adaptation potential of, 560
Solnit, Rebecca, 308
Somers-Willett, Susan B.A.,
    206–207
"Sonrisas" (Mora), 210–211
sound, in multimedia design, 55, 57
sound recording, in Works Cited
    list (MLA style), 435
sources for research, 365–375
    books, 365–368
sources, identifying, 363–382
    fieldwork, 375–377
    interview example for, 377–380
    research, 365–375
    working bibliography,
        preparing, 381–382
sources, in research
    acknowledging, 397
    coverage of, 389
    currency of, 389
    evaluating and responding to,
        383–388
    paraphrasing of, 406–408
    quoting, 408–411
    reliability of, 390–391
    summarizing, 397–406
    synthesizing, 395–411
spatial order, 266, 602
speaker, 208
special collections, 373, 605
spell checker, 346–347
spelling, 346–347

spliced or run-on sentence, 326
spliced sentences, 298
square brackets, modifying
    quotations with, 410
squinting modifier, 336, 605
stance, 599. See author's stance
Stars in My Eyes: My Love Affair
    with Books, Movies, and Music
    (Morrell), 272–273
"Star Wars Kid," 198
Star Wars: The Force Awakens, 7, 8
statements, function, 398–402
Statista.com, 92
statistics, 24, 27, 271
    in critical analysis, 200–201
    in investigative report, 124
    in position arguments, 132,
        133, 146
Stepto, Robert, 270
Stevenson, Bryan, 267
sticky notes, 385
stipulative definition, 284, 603
Storming the Gates of Paradise:
    Landscapes for Politics
    (Solnit), 308
storm surge, 572
storytelling
    images for, 56–59
    narration as, 279–280
structured questioning, 233
style, guide to effective sentences,
    295–321
    checklist for, 321
    conciseness, 319–321
    emphasis, 307–311
    essential level of sentence,
        296–298
    parallelism and, 310–311
    precision, 311–319
    sentence unity, 298–302
    using occasional short sentence,
        310
    variety, 302–307
Styron, William, 281–282
subject, 603
    in effective sentences, 296
subject-verb agreement, 298,
    329–330
    examples, 299
subordinating conjunctions, 306, 604
subordination, 306, 604
Subramanian, Meera, 564–571
summaries/summarizing, 602
    clustering and ordering
        information, 402–403
    function statements, 398–402
    one-sentence example, 41